THE FAMILY
IN AMERICA

An Encyclopedia

THE AMERICAN FAMILY

The six titles that make up **The American Family** offer a revitalizing new take on U.S. history, surveying current culture from the perspective of the family and incorporating insights from psychology, sociology, and medicine. Each two-volume, A-to-Z encyclopedia features its own advisory board, editorial slant, and apparatus, including illustrations, bibliography, and index.

Parenthood in America

Edited by Lawrence Balter, New York University

Adolescence in America

Edited by Jacqueline V. Lerner, Boston College,
and Richard M. Lerner, Tufts University;
Jordan W. Finkelstein, Pennsylvania State University,
Advisory Editor

Girlhood in America

Edited by Miriam Forman-Brunell,
University of Missouri, Kansas City

Boyhood in America

Edited by Priscilla Ferguson Clement, Pennsylvania
State University, Delaware County, and Jacqueline S. Reinier,
California State University, Sacramento

Infancy in America

Edited by Alice Sterling Honig, Emerita, Syracuse University;
Hiram E. Fitzgerald, Michigan State University;
and Holly E. Brophy-Herb, Michigan State University

The Family in America

Edited by Joseph M. Hawes, University of Memphis,
and Elizabeth F. Shores, Little Rock, Arkansas

THE FAMILY IN AMERICA

An Encyclopedia

Volume 1
A–G

Joseph M. Hawes
University of Memphis

With the Assistance of
Elizabeth F. Shores
University of Arkansas

Foreword by **Steven Mintz**

A B C ☰ C L I O

Santa Barbara, California
Denver, Colorado
Oxford, England

Library of Congress Cataloging-in-Publication Data
Hawes, Joseph M.
    The family in America : an encyclopedia / Joseph M. Hawes ; foreword
by Steven Mintz.
        p.   cm. — (The American family)
    Includes bibliographical references and index.
    ISBN 1-57607-232-0 (hardcover : alk. paper)
    e-book ISBN 1-57607-703-9
    1. Family—United States—Encyclopedias.   I. Title.   II. Series.
HQ536.H365   2001
306.85'0973'03—dc21

                                                    2002000394

06 05 04 03 02 01   10 9 8 7 6 5 4 3 2 1

This book is also available on the World Wide Web as an e-book. Visit
abc-clio.com for details.

ABC-CLIO, Inc.
130 Cremona Drive, P.O. Box 1911
Santa Barbara, California 93116-1911

This book is printed on acid-free paper ∞.
Manufactured in the United States of America

CONTENTS

A-to-Z List of Entries   *ix*
Contributors and Their Entries   *xiii*
Foreword, Steven Mintz   *xxi*
Preface and Acknowledgments   *xxv*
Introduction   *xxvii*

Volume 1: Entries A-G   *1*
Volume 2: Entries H–W   *505*

Bibliography   *927*
Index   *1019*
About the Editor   *1075*

A-to-Z List of Entries

VOLUME 1, A–G

A

Abortion
AD/HD
Adolescence
Adoptive Parents
Adultery
Affection as a Basis for Marriage
African American Families
After-School Care
Aid to Families with Dependent
    Children
AIDS and the Family
Alcohol and Drug Abuse in Families
Alimony
American Family Association
Anorexia Nervosa
Apprenticeship
Asian American Families

B

Baby Boom
Baby M
Baby Sitting
Banns
Birth Control
Birth Order, Theories of
Blended Families
Breast-Feeding
Bulimia

Burgess, Ernest W.

C

Cambridge Group for History of
    Population and Social Structure
Celibacy
Child Abuse
Child Advocacy
Child Care
Child Custody
Child Development
Child Health Improvement and
    Protection Act of 1968
Child Labor
Child Welfare Policy
Childbirth, Medical Practices of
Children as Parents
Children's Bureau, U.S.
The Children's Defense Fund
Common-Law Marriage
Communes, Families in
The Companionate Family
Complex Marriage
Cooperative Extension Service
Courtship, History of
Cults, Families in

D

Davis, Katharine Bement
Decoration Day
Delinquency

Demography of the Family
Department of Housing and Urban
    Development, U.S.
Disabilities and Family Life
Discipline and Punishment
Divorce, History of
Domestic Violence
Drug and Alcohol Abuse

E

Early Childhood Education
Earned Income Tax Credit
Eating Disorders
Educational Achievement of Parents
Ellis, Havelock
Erikson, Erik
Eugenics and the American Family
Extended Family

F

Family and Film
Family and Medical Leave Act
Family and the Law
Family as a Political Theme
The Family Bed
Family Business
Family Courts
Family Decline in the Twentieth
    Century
Family Medicine
Family Photography
Family Preferences and Immigration
Family Therapy
Family Vacations
Farm Families
Fatherhood
Father's Day
Feminine Mystique
Fertility
First-Cousin Marriage
Freedmen's Families

Freud, Sigmund
Funerals

G

Gender Roles in the American Family
Genealogy
Gerontology
Gifted Children in the Family
Grandparents
The Great Society

VOLUME 2, H–W

H

Hall, G. Stanley
Head Start
Higher Education, Access to
The Hispanic Family
Historiography of the American Family
Home Economics
Home Instruction Program for Preschool
    Youngsters
Home Schooling
Homelessness
Homosexuality and the Family

I

Immigrant Families, Experience of
Immunization
Infant Mortality
Inheritance
Interracial Families

J

Japanese American Families during
    World War II, Internment of

Jewish Families
Juvenile Justice

K

Key, Ellen
Kidnapping
Kinsey, Alfred

L

La Leche League
Latchkey Children
Leisure, Recreation, and Amusements
Literature, Images of Families in
    Children's
Little League
Lynd, Robert and Helen

M

Marriage
Marriage Counseling
Maternal Mortality
Matriarchy
Matrilineal Societies
Medicare and Medicaid
Middle-Class Family
Middletown
Military Families: The Costs of
    Commitment
Miscegenation
Mormon Polygamy
Motherhood
Mother's Day

N

National Congress of Colored Parents
    and Teachers
Neighborhoods

O

The Oneida Community
Orphan Trains
Orphanages

P

Parental Involvement in the Schools
Parenting Education
Parents, Families, and Friends of
    Lesbians and Gays
The Parents' Movement for Special
    Education in the United States
Parent-Teacher Association
Parsons, Talcott
Paternity Suits
Patriarchy
Patrilineal Societies
Pediatrics
The Pill
Planned Parenthood
Polio
Polygamy
Poverty
Premarital Sex
Prenatal Care

R

Race and the Family in American Law
Religion and Family
Remarriage, History of
Reunions, Family
Richards, Ellen Swallow
Roe v. *Wade*

S

Sanger, Margaret
Sex Education
Sexual Revolutions

Shaker Family
Sheppard-Towner Maternity and Infancy
    Act
Single-Parent Families
Smith-Lever Act
Social Security
Society for the Prevention of Cruelty to
    Children
Spock, Dr. Benjamin
Stepparents
Suburbanization
Supplemental Security Income
Syphilis

T

Teenage Pregnancy
Twins

U

Urban Renewal

V

Venereal Disease
Virginity

W

Watson, John B.
Weddings
White House Conferences on Children
Widowhood

CONTRIBUTORS AND THEIR ENTRIES

Lili De Hoyos Anderson
Brigham Young University
Provo, Utah
  Religion and Family

Lori Askeland
Wittenberg University
Springfield, Ohio
  Adultery, Family Therapy, Marriage
    Counseling

Andrea Balis
John Jay College of Criminal Justice
New York, New York
  Immunization, Syphilis

Peter W. Bardaglio
Goucher College
Baltimore, Maryland
  Miscegenation

Elaine S. Barry
Penn State
Uniontown, Pennsylvania
  Anorexia Nervosa, Bulimia, Child
    Development, Infant Mortality

Debra K. Bartelli
University of Tennessee–Memphis
Memphis, Tennessee
  AIDS and the Family, Drug and
    Alcohol Abuse

Barbara Beatty
Wellesley College
Wellesley, Massachusetts
  Early Childhood Education

Rebecca Bell-Metereau
Southwest Texas State University
San Marcos, Texas
  Family and Film

Virginia Bernhard
University of St. Thomas
Houston, Texas
  Father's Day, Mother's Day

Elisabetta Bini
Graduate School of the New School for
  Social Research
New York, New York
  Feminine Mystique

Vangie Novero Blust
Green Mountain College
Poultney, Vermont
  Grandparents

Beverly Greene Bond
University of Memphis
Memphis, Tennessee
  African American Families,
    Freedmen's Families, Interracial
    Families

Heath J. Bowen
Michigan State University
East Lansing, Michigan
  Decoration Day, Family Reunions

Charlotte Brooks
Northwestern University
Evanston, Illinois
  Internment of Japanese American
    Families during World War II

Anne Brophy
Georgia State University
Atlanta, Georgia
  Experience of Immigrant Families

Margaret M. Caffrey
University of Memphis
Memphis, Tennessee
  Complex Marriage, Ellen Key, The
    Pill, Sex Education, Sexual
    Revolutions

Mary I. Campa-Muller
Cornell University
Ithaca, New York
  Ellen Swallow Richards, Smith-Lever
    Act

E. Wayne Carp
Pacific Lutheran University
Tacoma, Washington
  Adoptive Parents

James C. Carper
University of South Carolina
Columbia, South Carolina
  Home Schooling

Peter E. Carr
Independent Scholar
Highland, California
  Teenage Pregnancy

Bret E. Carroll
California State University, Stanislaus
Turlock, California
  Fatherhood

Allan Chavkin
Southwest Texas State University
San Marcos, Texas
  Sigmund Freud

Nancy Feyl Chavkin
Southwest Texas State University
San Marcos, Texas
  Parental Involvement in the Schools

Elizabeth Blair Clark
Harvard University
Cambridge, Massachusetts
  Discipline and Punishment, Domestic
    Violence

Priscilla Ferguson Clement
Penn State Delaware
Media, Pennsylvania
  Poverty

Michael Coulter
Grove City College
Grove City, Pennsylvania
  Earned Income Tax Credit,
    Inheritance, Planned Parenthood

Angela M. Crossman
Institute for the Study of Child
  Development, University of Medicine
  and Dentistry of New Jersey, Robert
  Wood Johnson Medical School
New Brunswick, New Jersey
  Educational Achievement of Parents

Catherine Daligga
University of Michigan
Ann Arbor, Michigan
  Parenting Education

Roger Daniels
University of Cincinnati
Cincinnati, Ohio
    Family Preferences and Immigration

Kathryn M. Daynes
Brigham Young University
Provo, Utah
    Mormon Polygamy, Polygamy

Peter A. de Schweinitz
Fish River Rural Health
Aroostook County, Maine
    Family Medicine

Rebecca de Schweinitz
University of Virginia
Charlottesville, Virginia
    Family Medicine

Crista DeLuzio
Southern Methodist University
Dallas, Texas
    Child Advocacy

Jeffery P. Dennis
Bowdoin College
Brunswick, Maine
    The Hispanic Family

Ellen Donovan
Middle Tennessee State University
Murfreesboro, Tennessee
    Images of Families in Children's
        Literature

Davison M. Douglas
College of William and Mary
Williamsburg, Virginia
    Family and Medical Leave Act

Andrew Doyle
Winthrop University
Rock Hill, South Carolina
    Gender Roles in the American Family

T. D. Eddins
State University of New York at Stony
    Brook
Stony Brook, New York
    Baby M, Virginity

Juliana Elam
Independent Scholar
Memphis, Tennessee
        Celibacy, Families in Communes,
            First-Cousin Marriage

Kristin G. Esterberg
University of Massachusetts–Lowell
Lowell, Massachusetts
    Homosexuality and the Family

Barbara Finkelstein
University of Maryland–College Park
College Park, Maryland
    Child Abuse

Bonnie L. Ford
Emerita, Sacramento City College
Sacramento, California
    History of Courtship, History of
        Divorce, History of Remarriage

Miriam Forman-Brunell
University of Missouri–Kansas City
Kansas City, Missouri
    Baby Sitting

Elizabeth Freeman
University of California, Davis
Davis, California
    Weddings

Rachelle E. Friedman
Fieldston School
The Bronx, New York
    Jewish Families

Milton Gaither
Messiah College
Grantham, Pennsylvania
    Cambridge Group for History of
        Population and Social Structure,
        Historiography of the American
        Family

Mary Elizabeth Glade
St. Cloud State University
St. Cloud, Minnesota
    Funerals, Marriage

Gayle Green
State University of New York at Stony
    Brook
Stony Brook, New York
    Medical Practices of Childbirth,
        Maternal Mortality

Timothy A. Hacsi
Harvard University
Cambridge, Massachusetts
    Aid to Families with Dependent
        Children, Orphanages

JuNelle Harris
Harvard University
Cambridge, Massachusetts
    Child Custody

Leslie Joan Harris
University of Oregon
Eugene, Oregon
    Family Courts, Paternity Suits

Alice Hearst
Smith College
Northampton, Massachusetts
    Family and the Law, Orphan Trains,
        Race and the Family in American
        Law

Linda Heidenreich
Washington State University
Pullman, Washington
    Havelock Ellis, Alfred Kinsey

Robin L. E. Hemenway
University of Minnesota
Minneapolis, Minnesota
    Child Welfare Policy

Janice Hill
York University
Toronto, Ontario, Canada
    Children as Parents

Mabel T. Himel
University of Memphis
Memphis, Tennessee
        After-School Care, AD/HD, Latchkey
            Children

Peter C. Holloran
Worcester State College
Worcester, Massachusetts
    Delinquency

F. Jack Hurley
University of Memphis
Memphis, Tennessee
        Family Photographs, Robert and
            Helen Lynd

Anya Jabour
University of Montana
Missoula, Montana
        Affection as a Basis for Marriage

Lisa M. Jett
University of Memphis
Memphis, Tennessee
    Head Start

Shawn Johansen
Frostburg State University
Frostburg, Maryland
  Middle-Class Family, Premarital Sex

Kathleen W. Jones
Virginia Polytechnic Institute and State
  University
Blacksburg, Virginia
  Motherhood

Nikki Khanna
Emory University
Atlanta, Georgia
  Asian American Families

Connie Ann Kirk
Mansfield University
Mansfield, Pennsylvania
  Homelessness

S. J. Kleinberg
Brunel University
Uxbridge, England
  Widowhood

Christine Kleinegger
New York State Museum
Albany, New York
  The Family Bed, The Oneida
    Community, John B. Watson

Connie L. Lester
Mississippi State University
Mississippi State, Mississippi
  Farm Families

Kriste Lindenmeyer
University of Maryland–Baltimore
  County
Baltimore, Maryland
  Adolescence, U.S. Children's Bureau,
    Sheppard-Towner Maternity and
    Infancy Act, White House
    Conferences on Children

Carol S. Lindquist
State University of New York at Stony
  Brook
Stony Brook, New York
  Access to Higher Education

David I. Macleod
Central Michigan University
Mt. Pleasant, Michigan
  Child Labor

Nancy Farm Männikkö
Independent Scholar
L'Anse, Michigan
  Fertility, Gerontology

William E. Maxwell, Jr.
University of Memphis
Memphis, Tennessee
  Matriarchy, Matrilineal Societies,
    Patriarchy, Patrilineal Societies

Carole McCann
University of Maryland–Baltimore
  County
Baltimore, Maryland
  Margaret Sanger

Richard A. Meckel
Brown University
Providence, Rhode Island
  Pediatrics

Debra Meyers
Northern Kentucky University
Highland Hights, Kentucky
  Single-Parent Families,
    Suburbanization

Sonya Michel
University of Illinois at Chicago
Chicago, Illinois
  Child Care

Traci M. Milam
Independent Scholar
Memphis, Tennessee
   Roe v. Wade, Social Security

Mary C. Miles
Cornell University
Ithaca, New York
   Families in Cults

Joya Misra
University of Massachusetts
Amherst, Massachusetts
   Asian American Families

Caryn E. Neumann
Ohio State University
Columbus, Ohio
   Alimony, Theories of Birth Order,
      Katharine Bement Davis, Little
      League, Talcott Parsons, Polio,
      Venereal Disease

Thomas Newkirk
University of New Hampshire
Durham, New Hampshire
   Baby Boom

J. Wesley Null
Baylor University
Waco, Texas
   G. Stanley Hall

Fran O'Connor
Nassau Community College
Garden City, New York
   Disabilities and Family Life

Dorothy Ogilvy-Lee
Independent Scholar
Arlington, Virginia
   Military Families: The Costs of
      Commitment

Vickie Hankins Peters
University of Memphis
Memphis, Tennessee
   Ernest W. Burgess, Dr. Benjamin
      Spock

Jeanne Phelps
Southwest Missouri State University
Springfield, Missouri
   Twins

Anastasia L. Pratt
University of Michigan
Ann Arbor, Michigan
   Family Vacations

Heather Munro Prescott
Central Connecticut State University
New Britain, Connecticut
   Eating Disorders

David H. Pryce
Independent Scholar
Northport, Alabama
   Military Families: The Costs of
      Commitment

Josephine Pryce
University of Alabama
Tuscaloosa, Alabama
   Military Families: The Costs of
      Commitment

Benjamin G. Rader
University of Nebraska
Lincoln, Nebraska
   Leisure, Recreation, and Amusements

Roblyn Rawlins
The College of New Rochelle
New Rochelle, New York
   Gifted Children in the Family

Brian D. Ray
National Home Education Research
  Institute
Salem, Oregon
  Home Schooling

James W. Reed
Rutgers University
New Brunswick, New Jersey
  Birth Control

Donna Reeves
University of Memphis
Memphis, Tennessee
  Erik Erikson

Theresa Richardson
Ball State University
Muncie, Indiana
  Eugenics and the American Family

Lori E. Rotskoff
Independent Scholar
Larchmont, New York
  Alcohol and Drug Abuse in Families

Diana Selig
Claremont McKenna College
Claremont, California
  The Companionate Family,
    Middletown

Regan Shelton
Virginia Polytechnic University
Blacksburg, Virginia
  Kidnapping

Janann Sherman
University of Memphis
Memphis, Tennessee
  The Great Society, Medicare and
    Medicaid, Social Security

Peggy A. Shifflett
Radford University
Radford, Virginia
  Demography of the Family

Elizabeth Shores
Independent Scholar
Little Rock, Arkansas
  The Parents' Movement for Special
    Education in the United States

Deborah B. Smith
University of Missouri–Kansas City
Kansas City, Missouri
  Home Economics

Rickie Solinger
Independent Scholar
Boulder, Colorado
  Abortion

Edie Sparks
University of the Pacific
Stockton, California
  Family Business

Kathleen Thompson
Independent Scholar
Chicago, Illinois
  The Children's Defense Fund,
    Extended Family

Les Thompson, Jr.
United Methodist Minister, Retired
Yukon, Oklahoma
  Blended Families, Stepparents

Suzanne R. Thurman
University of Alabama at Huntsville
Huntsville, Alabama
  Shaker Family

Jennifer Tilton
University of Michigan
Ann Arbor, Michigan
  Urban Renewal

Sheryl R. Tynes
Trinity University
San Antonio, Texas
  Family as a Political Theme,
    Genealogy

Luise van Keuren
Green Mountain College
Poultney, Vermont
  Banns

Shirley Teresa Wajda
Kent State University
Kent, Ohio
  Apprenticeship

Lynn Y. Weiner
Roosevelt University
Chicago, Illinois
  La Leche League, Parent-Teacher
    Association

Merle H. Weiner
University of Oregon, School of Law
Eugene, Oregon
  Common-law Marriage

David Wolcott
Carnegie Mellon University
Pittsburgh, Pennsylvania
  Juvenile Justice

Jacqueline H. Wolf
Ohio University
Athens, Ohio
  Breast-feeding

Christine Woyshner
Temple University
Philadelphia, Pennsylvania
  National Congress of Colored Parents
    and Teachers

Natasha Zaretsky
Brown University
Providence, Rhode Island
  Family Decline in the Twentieth
    Century

FOREWORD

Each generation writes a history that speaks to its own needs. We live in an era that has witnessed sweeping changes in private life. In the span of little more than a decade beginning in the late 1960s, divorce rates doubled, as did the number of working mothers and single-parent families. Meanwhile, births outside of marriage and the number of couples living together outside of wedlock quadrupled. The rebirth of feminism, the rise of the gay and lesbian rights movement, and the emergence of the pro-life and pro-choice organizations transformed sexuality and gender into hotly contested political issues. It is not surprising that much of the most exciting historical scholarship of our time focuses on family life, gender roles, and sexuality.

Traditionally, history was the story of public life, of politics, diplomacy, and war. But in recent years, historians have shifted attention to life's private side. Scholars have shown that even the most private aspects of our personal lives have a history and that changes in private life are inextricably linked to broader shifts in the values and beliefs of society as a whole. Children's toys, the architecture of our homes, our understanding of the life course, the very meaning and labels we attach to infancy, childhood, and adolescence—all have a fascinating but little-known history.

To recover the history of family life, historians have turned to novel kinds of evidence: census registers, wills, court cases, etiquette manuals, cookbooks, child-rearing tracts, and medical textbooks. They have tested new historical methods, such as quantification, and have broadened the very meaning of history to encompass the fields of demography, folklore, cultural anthropology, and law.

Unfortunately, much of this exciting new scholarship is unknown to the general public. Lacking any historical perspective that goes back further than the 1950s, Americans are particularly prone to romanticizing the past and confusing historical fantasy and reality. Many Americans are convinced that family life is going to hell in a hand basket: that in unprecedented numbers young people are abandoning marriage for less demanding relationships, that deadbeat dads are running away from their paternal responsibilities while too many working mothers are neglecting their children. But knowledge of history reminds us that fears for the family's future are not new and that previous generations of Americans also believed that their families were disintegrating and that parents were growing increasingly irresponsible. Historical perspective is essential if we are to understand precisely what is new and distinctive about contemporary family life and appreciate the genuine improvements as well as the losses that have accompanied familial change.

The Family in America synthesizes a vast range of knowledge and presents it in a succinct, highly readable form. It has a vast topical range, including entries on ethnicity (including African Americans, Asian Americans, and Hispanics), children's health and welfare, family law, government policies affecting families, religion and the family, and rites of passage (ranging from funerals to weddings). Capsule biographies examine the lives and thought of pivotal figures, including Margaret Sanger and Benjamin Spock. For scholars, students, and educated readers alike, the encyclopedia's publication is an important event. It makes a treasure trove of valuable, but previously inaccessible, information readily accessible.

This volume corrects many misleading myths and misconceptions. In the pages that follow, readers will learn that it was not until the 1920s that a majority of American families consisted of a breadwinner-husband, a homemaker-wife, and children attending school. They will also discover that the most rapid increase in unwed pregnancies took place between 1940 and 1958, not in the libertine 1960s, and that the defining characteristics of the 1950s family—a rising birthrate, a stable divorce rate, and declining age of marriage—were historical aberrations, out of line with long-term historical trends. Readers will find that throughout American history, most families have needed more than one breadwinner to support themselves, that a century ago, the United States had the highest divorce rate in the Western world and one child in ten lived in a single-parent home.

One of the most valuable functions that history can serve is to correct myths and misleading generalizations. In recent years, highly romanticized images of the past have contributed to unrealistic expectations about family life. Ahistorical thinking has also led Americans to downplay the gains that have taken place in family well-being, especially the fact that smaller families mean that parents can devote more time and resources to each child. Even worse, a lack of historical perspective has encouraged scapegoating of families that diverge from the dominant norms; and it has blinded Americans to the social, economic, demographic, and ideological pressures that have contributed to familial change—and made transformations in gender roles and family structures irreversible.

In the pages that follow, certain recurrent themes will stand out. One key theme is that over time, virtually every aspect of American family life has undergone far-reaching transformations. The family's roles and functions, organizational structure, demographic characteristics, emotional dynamics, and child-rearing practices have changed profoundly over the past three centuries. So, too, has the American home, its design, furnishings, and technology. Shifts in social values, health, and the nature of the economy have transformed the most intimate aspects of American life. Thus we will see that the so-called traditional family—consisting of the breadwinner-husband, homemaker-mom, and the kids—is less than two centuries old and that our conceptions of childhood as a state of innocence and of adolescence as a period of emotional upheaval are historical constructs that arose at particular moments in the none-too-distant past.

A second major theme that cuts across this volume is the immense variety of American families. Since the seventeenth century, diversity has been a hall-mark of American family life. Family forms, gender roles, courtship patterns, and parenting practices have varied not only according to historical era but also along class, ethnic, regional, and religious lines. The history of the family underscores the extraordinary richness and complexity of the American mosaic.

In American history, no single family type has predominated. In the colonial era, families in New England, the Middle Atlantic colonies, and the Chesapeake region and the southern colonies differed in size, composition, and behavior. In the nineteenth century, the families of the urban middle class differed profoundly from those of rural farmers, enslaved African Americans, western pioneers, and the working class. Indeed, at no time in American history was diversity in family life greater than in the nineteenth century, when families diverged sharply in their gender division of labor, their attitudes toward child labor, their propensity to take in extended kin and boarders, and their styles of child rearing. During the twentieth century, despite concerted efforts by reformers to create greater uniformity especially in the experience of the young, family structure, rituals, and behavior continued to vary, especially along ethnic lines. Contemporary families encompass single- and dual-earner families, empty nests where grown children have left home, single-parent families, blended families formed after divorce, extended and multigenerational families, and gay and lesbian families. Each of these family types finds its place in this encyclopedia.

A third unifying theme is that the family should not be treated simply as a unitary institution. Families consist of a variety of members with distinct roles—

mothers, fathers, sons, daughters—whose meaning has shifted over time. It is a mistake to think that the interests of all of a family's members are identical, and the entries in this volume are especially sensitive to gender differences. This volume's entries reveal fundamental distinctions in the experiences of girls and boys and trace the way that women's and men's domestic roles have been contested and redefined over the past three centuries.

The major events of American history—the Revolution, the Civil War, industrialization, immigration, and world war—have exerted a powerful influence on family life. In recent years, scholars have explored the impact of these seminal events on familial and marital relations, gender roles, and child-rearing practices. By using the family as a lens, they have uncovered the human meaning of the critical events of American history. Recent scholarship has shown, for example, how the Civil War shortened childhood, influenced children's relations with their fathers, and altered children's literature and schoolbooks. Historians and sociologists have also examined the lasting impact of the Great Depression on the values, behavior, and family practices of those who lived through it. Other scholarship has explored the way that families during World War II coped with absent fathers, working mothers, and the rise of a new teenage culture.

This volume does an especially effective job of reminding us of the repeated attempts to construct alternative families that would overcome the flaws of traditional households. Nothing has been more distinctively American than the impulse, as utopian socialist John Humphrey Noyes put it, to extend the intimacy of the family to a wider range of social relationships. From the Shakers onward to the communes of the 1960s and beyond, religious and secular visionaries and reformers have imagined family-like units that would liberate women from patriarchal restrictions and overcome the jealousies and exclusivity that they considered negative features of ordinary family life.

Finally, this volume looks at the historical roots of contemporary social policy debates over abortion, adoption, divorce, domestic violence, teenage pregnancy, and social welfare policy. There is a tendency among many social scientists to think of family history as interesting but largely irrelevant to contemporary policy formation. This volume proves that any hasty dismissal of history's relevance to current policy debates is misguided. The family-related problems that our society confronts are not unprecedented, and many of the solutions we contemplate have been tried before. A knowledge of history allows us to evaluate the effectiveness of a variety of approaches to current social problems.

In the past, scholars tended to think of the history of private life as trivial—as a succession of changing fads and fashions. But, as this volume makes clear, the history of the family is anything but inconsequential. It is the story of how we have tried to raise and educate our children, of how men and women have interacted, of how society has tried to assist the poor.

Over the past three centuries, every aspect of our family lives has undergone profound transformations: not only the family's roles, functions, and composition but also the ways that we celebrate the key events of the life course and relate to loved ones. Thus this volume not only traces the emergence of modern family patterns; it also records fundamental shifts in our emotional sensibilities and values. It is the story of some of the most important developments in history, but transformations that are too often omitted from standard history textbooks: the growth of individualism, the rise of modern notions of privacy, and the gradual development of new notions of women's and children's legal rights.

Steven Mintz

Steven Mintz is John and Rebecca Moores Professor of History at the University of Houston. His books include *Domestic Revolutions: A Social History of American Family Life* (with Susan Kellogg) and *A Prison of Expectations: The Family in Victorian Culture.*

Preface and Acknowledgments

This book is almost entirely the work of the authors of the various entries that follow. They are the experts in the field and to them belongs the credit for having been willing to share their expertise with a larger public by writing for this volume. The editor and the editorial assistant wish to acknowledge the importance of the authors' efforts and to make clear, here at the beginning, that they are those whose work deserves our thanks.

We should also acknowledge the help and encouragement from Karna Hughes of ABC-CLIO, who proved a steadfast friend to the project and a person with many helpful suggestions. It is certainly true that the volume could not have been done without her.

The primary purpose of this volume is to provide essays on major topics relating to the history of the family in the United States. Readers who wish to dig deeper can follow up on a topic by consulting the list of references. We hope our two volumes are both useful and comprehensive. For topics not covered in these volumes, please consult other volumes in the American Family series. Limitations of size and scope and the existence of other volumes in the series have meant that we could not include all possible subjects. Readers should consider the entire American Family series as a single set. We are confident they will not be disappointed.

The family is society's most basic and oldest institution. Because it is so old and so familiar, it has become the object of serious scholarly study only recently. Consequently there are few reference works pertaining specifically and directly to the family in the United States. It is our hope that this volume will be a useful corrective to that lack.

Joseph M. Hawes
Editor
Elizabeth Shores
Assistant Editor

INTRODUCTION

Because of the recent dramatic increase in scholarship about the family in the United States, there is a need for a reference work that will make the principal findings of these scholarly studies available in a convenient, readily accessible format. Thus we provide this volume as an aid to those whose work involves the study of American family history and as an encouragement for further study in the field of the history of American families.

The study of families, in one form or another, is a very old field, but the development of family studies as a professional endeavor is relatively recent. Much of what we now know about families stems from these disciplined efforts. This is not to say that folk wisdom and earlier observations on the nature of families were wrong or incorrect, but rather to say that much of folk wisdom and earlier observations were not collected in any organized or systematic way.

In the late nineteenth and early twentieth centuries the process of disciplined family study began. Unfortunately for the contemporary reader, a number of different disciplines undertook this effort. Anthropologists had begun the effort to trace the relationships between kinship patterns and social structure, and they found, somewhat to their own dismay, that there were many varieties of family structure and lineage and that the variety of family structures was more extensive than previously imagined. Sociologists, close cousins of the anthropologists, looked at human groupings, which in turn led them to the study of families and family structure. Best known of these early students of the family were the sociologists of the Chicago school, including Ernest W. Burgess, W. I. Thomas, and F. Znaniecki. *The Polish Peasant in Europe and America*, a five-volume work by the latter two published between 1918 and 1920, is the classic work of that school.

Most noted of historical works of that period was Arthur W. Calhoun's extensive and formidable *Social History of the American Family*, a multivolume work first published from 1917 to 1919. Psychologists, looking for the roots of human behavior, found that families were a major influence on the development of human personalities, and for psychoanalysts, the family was a cauldron of conflicting drives, desires, feelings, issues, boundaries, and processes. As the newly created social science disciplines developed knowledge about the inner workings of families and about the intricate relationships between family and society, they also learned just how complex and how universal their subject matter was.

Family studies flourished in the early twentieth century and had a decided impact on public policy. Examples of public policies that drew on family studies include the creation of the federal Children's Bureau in 1912 and the donation of substantial sums of money to the study of child development and juvenile delinquency after World War I. The Children's Bureau was the closest thing to a federal family policy agency, and its work over the first half of the twentieth century had a substantial impact on both family policy and families themselves. In particular the Children's Bureau sought to prevent child labor, and it initiated pathbreaking social legislation, the Sheppard-Towner Act, in the 1920s that provided federal money to states to improve prenatal care for pregnant women with the goal of reducing infant mortality. The Sheppard-Towner Act succeeded in its goal, but Congress yielded to the lobbying power of the American Medical Association and canceled the program after less than a decade.

The Great Depression, as devastating as it was for so many American families, saw the passages of pathbreaking social legislation that helped the United States close the gap between it and other advanced industrial countries. And for many Americans the Great Depression brought families closer both physically and psychically. People came home to help out or to join with parents and siblings in an effort to survive. People pooled their resources and joined forces in an effort to survive, and they were willing to support government programs because they believed that government action was appropriate in a time of need.

If the Great Depression brought family members back together (after the dispersals of the 1920s), World War II scattered them back out. Millions of Americans crossed the country to be near husbands in the military or to seek work in expanding defense plants. Vast numbers now left the rural countryside and migrated to the cities. During the 1930s young people had put off marrying because of straitened circumstances, and dating, which had grown rapidly in the 1920s, had declined noticeably. During the war young women followed young men to military encampments, and together they contracted hasty marriages, hoping all would be well once the war was over.

Thus many young men went off to war as newlyweds, and they knew very little about their new brides. The brides were equally uninformed about their new husbands. Given the haste with which these marriages were contracted, it is not surprising that many of them ended in divorce.

During World War II the marriage rate skyrocketed; after the war the divorce rate went up dramatically as well, but both of these trends were overshadowed by the phenomenal growth in the birthrate after the war. The "baby boom," as it was called, was one of the most unusual (and unexpected) events in family and demographic history in all of American history. Not only did returning soldiers, sailors, and airmen have children; they had lots of them. Families with four and five children were common, and the strain on social resources was quite noticeable. Schools had to go on half-day sessions and were still overcrowded. There was a serious housing shortage, which continued in spite of large-scale housing developments such as Levittown outside New York and Philadelphia.

Images in popular media left the impression that the postwar period was a time of joyous domestic tranquillity. Families settled into suburban tract houses nestled behind white picket fences and prepared to live the good life. The prevailing ideology had wives and mothers happily doing housework in high heels (just as June Cleaver did on *Leave It to Beaver*) and readily deferring to their husbands in all matters. The reality was another matter. Historians William Tuttle and Elaine Tyler May have shown convincingly that family life at the end of World War II was anything but blissful (Tuttle 1993; May 1998). Many women—including the mothers of young children—had worked in defense plants during the war, but once the war was over, demand for their services declined as returning soldiers sought jobs. The level of autonomy enjoyed by women during the war contrasted sharply with the restrictions envisioned by the ideology of domesticity after the war.

And all was not tranquil within the families, either. Returning servicemen, especially those who had been in combat or who had been prisoners of war, found that they could not talk about their experiences with civilians. They also found that the families they had left behind no longer worked according to the patriarchal, father-in-charge model they believed they had left behind. (Actually American families had been becoming more democratic since the early nineteenth century, but the power of romantic nostalgia had convinced many former GIs that their own families had been quite Victorian in nature.) One way to cope with this sort of dissonance was to re-create the family structure of the imagined past; this was one of the factors in the baby boom. But a great deal of conflict ensued, and some families came apart in divorce. Not all conflicts led to divorce; many ex-servicemen had serious problems with alcohol abuse during this period and that in turn intensified many family conflicts.

The emergence of clinical expertise on families (not that there were no clinicians dealing with family issues before World War II, but rather that the practice of family therapy became both more common and more widely accepted) coincided with renewed interest in the history of the family or, perhaps it should be noted, in what was believed to be the history of the family. Sociologists who had studied the family believed that it had evolved from an earlier, extended form (best defined as a family with several generations and various other relatives under one roof) to the modern, nuclear form. Some studies have sought to refute this pattern—most notably Peter Laslett's *The World We Have Lost* (1965), which depicted family life in England prior to American colonization as being predominantly nuclear. Historians began to ask different questions from those proposed by earlier students of the family in history. Stimulated in part by the rise of the New Social History—an effort to write history "from the bottom up" and to focus on the lives of nonelite peoples—some historians turned to a study of the family. Among the best of these early family studies was John Demos's *A Little Commonwealth: Family Life in Plymouth Colony* (1970). A model of clarity and precision, Demos's study remains in print. Demos confirmed that early American families were predominantly nuclear but also indicated that many of the households contained a number of people who were not kin to the primary couple. New England families regularly took in servants and placed out excessive children, a practice that puzzled Edmund S. Morgan in his pioneering study, *The Puritan Family* (1944; rev. ed. 1966).

A difficulty with the early studies of the history of the family was that the studies themselves were primarily descriptive, and thus comparisons across place and time were almost impossible to make. More recently some historians have made use of family-cycle and life-course models of family development. A problem in using family-cycle approaches has been that they have relied on the age of the male head of household, which has sometimes distorted other relationships. A modification to this approach is *The Social Organization of Early Industrial Capitalism* (which is a study of family life in Hamilton, Ontario, in the nineteenth century), in which Michael Katz, Michael J. Doucet, and Mark J. Stern used the wife's age as the linchpin of their approach (1982). This tactic solved some of the problems of earlier family-cycle approaches but had difficulties of its own. According to Maris Vinovskis and Laura McCall (1991), all of these models of the family cycle possess limitations for the historian: Many fail to take into account historical contexts, most ignore the experiences of individuals within families, and few are sensitive to the varied social environments of the past. None of these family-cycle models takes into consideration the effects of differences among individuals or families in the timing or sequencing of events. Vinovskis and McCall proposed a modification of the family-cycle approach, which they label the "life-course analysis." This approach focuses on individuals and the transitions in their lives. One of the most notable examples of such an approach is Glen Elder's *Children of the Depression* (1974).

In the meantime a flood of literature on the history of families has emerged since the early 1970s. Some of this literature relies heavily on either family-cycle or life-course theory, but other studies have found ways to solve the problems with older descriptive history, so that these later efforts have been very well received.

It is fair to say that the literature dealing with families and family life has greatly expanded in the recent past. There are a number of reasons for this expansion—the rise of the new social history, a greater interest in the lives of women and (even more recently) the lives of children, together with an increasingly polarized national discourse about the nature of the family and about its history.

Works of synthesis in American family history are still relatively rare, but among those that reflect the more recent scholarship is Carl Degler's *At Odds: Women and the Family in America from the Revolution to the Present* (1980), which argued that women cannot be both independent and family oriented at the same time. A most impressive effort that dealt with English families is Lawrence Stone's *The Family, Sex and Marriage in England 1500–1800* (1977). Stephanie Coontz's *The Social Origins of Private Life: A History of American Families 1600–1900* (1988) dealt primarily with the colonial period and the nineteenth century. Her later and better-known work, *The Way We Never Were: American Families and the Nostalgia Trap* (1992), focused on families since the nineteenth century and especially on twentieth-century misconceptions about nineteenth-century family history. The most comprehensive of the new works of synthesis is *Domestic Revolutions: A Social History of American Family Life* by Steven Mintz and Susan Kellogg (1988). It remains the standard work on American family history. Also broad in scope (but nearly as detailed) is Robert Wells's *Uncle Sam's Family: Issues in and Perspectives on American Demographic History* (1985). Impressive and important though limited in scope is Mary Ryan's *Cradle of the Middle Class: The Family in Oneida County, New York, 1790–1865* (1981).

Thus *The Family in America* rests on the shoulders of others who have pioneered in the work of the history of the family in the United States, and it is the work of the experts who have written the entries that follow. It is our hope that this work will fill a wide gap and thereby bring the rich and diverse field of American family history within the reach of many users who would otherwise have great difficulty in identifying and accessing this great body of knowledge.

References

Calhoun, Arthur W. 1917–1919. *Social History of the American Family.* Cleveland: Arthur H. Clark.

Coontz, Stephanie. 1988. *The Social Origins of Private Life: A History of American Families 1600–1900.* New York: Verso.

Coontz, Stephanie. 1992. *The Way We Never Were: American Families and the Nostalgia Trap.* New York: Basic Books.

Degler, Carl. 1980. *At Odds: Women and the Family in America from the Revolution to the Present.* New York: Oxford University Press.

Demos, John. 1970. *A Little Commonwealth: Family Life in Plymouth Colony.* New York: Oxford University Press.

Elder, Glen. 1974. *Children of the Depression.* Chicago: University of Chicago Press.

Hawes, Joseph M., and Elizabeth I. Nybakken, eds. 1991. *American Families: A Research Guide and Historical Handbook.* Westport, CT: Greenwood Press.

Hawes, Joseph M., and Elizabeth Nybakken, eds. 2001. *Family and Society in American History.* Urbana: University of Illinois Press.

Katz, Michael, Michael J. Doucet, and Mark J. Stern. 1982. *The Social Organization of Early Industrial Capitalism.* Cambridge: Harvard University Press.

Laslett, Peter. 1965. *The World We Have Lost.* London: Methuen.

May, Elaine Tyler. 1988. *Homeward Bound: American Families in the Cold War Era.* New York: Basic Books.

Mintz, Steven, and Susan Kellogg. 1988. *Domestic Revolutions: A Social History of American Family Life.* New York: Free Press.

Morgan, Edmund S. 1966. *The Puritan Family.* New York: Harper and Row.

Ryan, Mary. 1981. *Cradle of the Middle Class: The Family in Oneida County, New York, 1790–1865.* New York: Cambridge University Press.

Stone, Lawrence. 1977. *The Family, Sex and Marriage in England 1500–1800.* New York: Harper and Row.

Thomas, William I., and Floria F. Znaniecki. 1918–1920. *The Polish Peasant in Europe and America.* 5 vols. Chicago: University of Chicago Press.

Tuttle, William M. 1993. *Daddy's Gone to War: The Second World War in the Lives of America's Children.* New York: Oxford University Press.

Vinovskis, Maris A., and Laura McCall. 1991. "Changing Approaches to the Study of Family Life." In *American Families: A Research Guide and Historical Handbook,* edited by Joseph M. Hawes and Elizabeth I. Nybakken, 15–32. Westport, CT: Greenwood Press.

Wells, Robert. 1985. *Uncle Sam's Family: Issues in and Perspectives on American Demographic History.* Albany: State University of New York Press.

A

Abortion

Abortion refers to the purposeful termination of a pregnancy. Since the Supreme Court's legalization of abortion in 1973 (*Roe* v. *Wade*), the term has been used generally to refer to the termination of a pregnancy that a woman determines she is unable to manage.

The history of abortion in the United States has two main aspects. The first deals with the experiences over time of millions of girls and women who have sought and received abortions during the two eras when the procedure was legal (the eighteenth century to the mid-nineteenth century and 1973 to the present) and during the criminal era (mid-nineteenth century to 1973). The second aspect involves the legislative, medical, judicial, religious, political, and popular responses to abortion that have constrained or enabled access to abortion services in both the legal and criminal eras. These two aspects are, of course, intertwined, but it is important to underscore the fact that across the history of the United States, females have gotten abortions in very large numbers, no matter what the legal status and public attitudes toward the procedure were at any given time. For example, during the 1950s, when abortion was illegal, public health experts estimated that as many as one million criminal abortions were per-

formed each year in this country (Fischer 1951, 242–249).

In the first decades of nationhood, the legal status of the procedure was governed by British common law that viewed abortion before quickening as a legal act. (*Quickening* referred to the sensation of fetal movement felt and reported by the pregnant woman herself.) After quickening, destruction of the fetus without cause was considered a crime.

Many women in the early national period were aware of and employed herbal and other remedies that caused abortion, sometimes with the assistance of midwives or physicians who consented to remove "menstrual blockages." Enslaved African American women used abortion to resist coerced reproduction and slavery itself, employing the knowledge of African-based midwifery culture and folk medicine.

Connecticut was the first state to criminalize abortion, in 1821. This and other early state antiabortion laws were not essentially responses to popular objections to abortion per se. Rather, the statutes appear to have been most concerned with protecting women from dangerous substances and techniques associated with pregnancy termination; thus, Connecticut's antiabortion statute, first and foremost, was enacted to protect the lives of women. In addition, these laws were

A dispute between anti- and pro-abortion activists in Boston, 1985. (Bettmann/Corbis)

expressions of an innovative collaboration between legislators and physicians, who, in the 1820s and the following decades, faced competition from midwives and other "irregular" practitioners in the area of obstetrics. Medical doctors worked with lawmakers to pass laws against abortion in order to consolidate the authority of university-trained medical doctors ("regulars") in the area of obstetrics and to secure their pregnant and parturient client base.

Over the course of the nineteenth century, as women's lives were shaped by urbanization, industrialization, and the experiences of migration and immigration, abortion became more common and more visible. By midcentury, observers estimated that 20–25 percent of all pregnancies ended in abortion. The combined growth of urban newspapers and advertising enabled broad dissemination of information about abortion providers and abortifacients.

Most famously, Mme. Restell, the "female physician," prominently advertised her abortion practice and abortifacients in urban newspapers for thirty-five years (Mohr 1978, 48–52). In these ads, Restell explained the efficacy of her preparations, "now acknowledged by the medical fraternity to be the only safe, mild, and efficient remedy to be depended upon in long-standing cases of suppression, irregularity or stoppage of those functions of nature, the neglect of which is the source of such deplorable defects on the female frame, dizziness in the head, disturbed sleep, sallow complexion, and the innumerable frightful effects that sooner or later terminate in incurable consumption." In a nod to prevailing propriety and standards of decency, the abortionist advertised her pills and powders to "married ladies" and aimed to preserve "many an affectionate wife and fond mother from an early and premature grave." Young white women beginning to enter the workforce and married women concerned about adjusting family size to urbanizing settings took advantage of this information.

Leaders of the emergent women's rights movement in the nineteenth century publicly expressed negative views of abortion, especially their belief that the practice was degrading to women. Abortion, they believed, became necessary when men ignored women's health concerns and their sensibilities and refused to curb male lust. The elimination of abortion, feminists argued, would follow the elevation of women's status. Once women were educated and enfranchised, then they could resist men's sexual imprecations. The need for abortion would then wither away. In the meantime, feminists promoted the goal of controlled conception (through "voluntary motherhood," or sexual abstinence). Many white, native-born women considered these feminist ideas, weighed the exigencies of their lives, noticed the new visibility of abortion, then sought out practitioners such as Mme. Restell who would help them resist traditional reproductive experiences, including serial episodes of childbearing.

Having worked successfully with a number of state legislatures to enact antiabortion laws, medical doctors intensified their campaign after the founding of the American Medical Association in 1847. Dr. Horatio Robinson Storer was a leader in these efforts, which yielded anti-abortion statutes in every state by the end of the nineteenth century. The new laws were a triumph for physicians, now fully invested with scientific authority; midwives and "irregular" doctors were excluded as legitimate abortion practitioners, and the women-centered "quickening" doctrine was abandoned. The new laws had sharply moral content; for example, they deepened the stigma attached to abortion by associating it with "obscenity." In addition, the laws reflected a triumph for sexual conservatism and medical doctors' determination to block middle-class women from employing abortion as a tool for resisting traditional roles and facilitating new ones. Finally, the successful antiabortion campaign expressed middle-class doctors' and lawmakers' class and racial commitment to bolstering procreation among white Protestant women whose birthrates were falling at that time in relation to the birthrates of poorer women, immigrants, and women of color.

Despite the criminalization of abortion, however, many women of every class and race, married and unmarried, continued to use abortion to limit their childbearing. Given women's determination, the new laws could not stop abortion, but as political scientist Rosalind Petchesky has written, they "revealed it, regulated it, certified it as a legitimate domain of public intervention and control" (Petchesky 1990, 73).

In the early twentieth century, women found midwives, physicians, and various kinds of lay practitioners to perform illegal abortions. Increasingly, cities and towns were home to abortion providers who had full-time abortion practices, worked semi-openly, and were highly proficient because they performed so many abortion procedures, day in and day out, for years. Trial records and other sources indicate that these practitioners probably rarely caused complications or deaths, which were much more likely the result of self-induced abortions and abortions performed by the relatively small number of untrained lay practitioners who understood that the combination of antiabortion statutes and women's desperation created a lucrative opportunity.

Periodically, in that era, journalists and police forces, often in league with politicians and medical doctors, orchestrated local exposés of abortion practices. Typically, the exposés targeted and tainted midwives—who chiefly served immigrant women and women of color—but not physicians. Female lay practitioners were generally easier to indict and convict than medical doctors, since the public, including jurors, assessed the women as untrained, unskilled, and unprotected. Antiabortion campaigns combined a mix of agendas, all of which were incorporated into antiabortion rhetoric. The campaigners championed medical prerogatives, demanded female sexual purity and conformity, opposed women's rights, and enforced eugenic and demographic goals.

Many contemporary observers and historians have noted that these campaigns did not halt the practice of abortion, nor did they stir public indifference to the crime of abortion, although the salacious content of raids and trials did engage the newspaper-buying public. Nevertheless, the campaigns were effective in promoting the agendas noted above and especially effective in warning all women of the dangers that could beset any woman who tried with abortion to control her own fertility.

Interestingly, during the Great Depression of the 1930s, a massive number of women who could not afford babies obtained abortions, but the number of exposés and prosecutions of abortion providers declined. Leslie Reagan has pointed out that in this era, doctors spent more time debating which conditions warranted therapeutic abortions than they spent collaborating with police and politicians to stamp out abortion (Reagan 1997, 143–147).

In the 1930s, abortion was, in fact, a very lucrative business. Abortion syndicates and solo practices flourished in every region of the country since the demand was so high and so many practitioners performed abortions then unimpeded by the law. In an era before penicillin and antibiotics, however, abortions—like other invasive surgeries—remained dangerous for women who found professionals, and also, especially, for poor women and women without information or other resources who resorted to self-induced abortions. One study in the early 1930s showed that 76 percent of these involved complications (Stix 1935).

The World War II and postwar eras marked a change in the response to abortion. After some years of unofficial tolerance, in which most law enforcement entities employed the principle of "no death, no prosecution," politicians and police forces around the country once again engaged in exposés, arrests, and trials, this time more frequently than ever before, even in cases where there was no evidence of abortion-related damage or death. In many cities, postwar crackdowns, with their sensationalized media coverage of police raids and trials, transformed abortion from an everyday, if semisecret, occurrence into a crime. Often, scandal-tainted mayors and police forces were looking for opportunities to demonstrate that municipal governance and law enforcement were not ineffectual or corrupt, as charged. Abortion prosecutions became opportunities for these officials to look like hardworking, antivice agents. In Los Angeles, San Francisco, Cincinnati, St. Louis, Trenton, and other cities, even though there was no expressed antiabortion agenda, women practitioners and their clients became attractive targets because of the political opportunity they presented and because they had almost no recourse to credible defense. In the largest sense, the abortion trials became arenas to address the culturally crucial questions: Who is a "real" woman, and who is not? By defining abortion practitioners and their clients as perverse and unwomanly as they occupied the witness stand, the qualities of "real womanhood" were reaffirmed.

Historians have argued that this postwar crackdown was similar to, or a feature of, the postwar anti-Communist fervor. It aimed to eradicate "the enemy within," to demonstrate that the United States was a vigilant, virtuous country, and to enforce a conforming, conservative code of female sexual behavior, just as the seeds of "the sexual revolution" and the Women's Liberation movement were beginning to sprout.

At the same time, medical doctors began to construct hospital abortion boards charged with implementing group decision making regarding which women applying to the boards to end their pregnancies would be granted permission, based on which physical symptoms were legitimate contraindications to continued pregnancy. On the one hand, these committees were antithetical to the interests of women. They reinforced medical authority and forged a protective, fraternal relationship between doctors and a legal system that acknowl-

edged only board-sanctioned abortions as legitimate. (In one large midwestern hospital in this era, 75 percent of the abortions performed there were accompanied by sterilization; other hospitals pursued similar policies [Russell 1953].) Boards also significantly reduced the number of in-hospital abortions. This, coupled with the effects of the antiabortion crackdown, deepened the desperation of many women dealing with pregnancies they could not manage. Many women without the resources to leave the country to obtain an abortion or to pay a private physician in the United States willing to perform an illegal procedure—or to meet the requirement of abortion boards that every request had to be accompanied by letters from two physicians—resorted to dangerous self-abortion. Not surprisingly, that era saw a rise in abortion complications and deaths, disproportionately borne by poor women and women of color.

On the other hand, abortion boards gave some women the opportunity to express their determination to end their pregnancies and the means to obtain abortions, an experience that prefigured women's behavior after legalization. In that era, women seeking abortions, together with psychiatrists, constructed the "psychiatric indication" for abortion, which forced some women to define themselves as suicide-prone or unfit to be a mother in order to get board permission, but gave many women grounds upon which to negotiate for permission.

The development of imaging technology in this era allowed doctors to construct the fetus as a "little person." In fact, many physicians and others began now to describe pregnancy first as a process of fulfillment and realization for the fetus and to refer to the pregnant woman's body in terms that suggested a safe reproductive container. As doctors adopted and promoted these ideas—in the context of postwar confusion about women's roles—the number and the rate of therapeutic abortions performed in U.S. hospitals plummeted.

Beyond the hospital walls, by the 1960s, many observers acknowledged that antiabortion statutes could not be enforced. Moreover, the conditions of women's lives were changing in ways that intensified their need for fertility control, including access to safe and legal abortion. For example, female labor force participation and college attendance rates were increasing; age at first marriage was rising. Many liberal physicians, clergy, academics, and others, recognizing the inevitability of abortion, began to advocate abortion reform.

In addition, politicians concerned about welfare expenditures and "ghetto unrest" and population controllers worried about the "population bomb" spoke out in favor of abortion reform. The American Law Institute published guidelines for reform in 1960, and the American Medical Association endorsed reform in 1967, a year in which one study showed 87 percent of physicians favoring liberalization ("Abortion and the Law" 1967, 25). The National Association for the Repeal of Abortion Laws was formed in 1969.

Some leading African American activists in the late 1960s and early 1970s opposed abortion reform, associating abortion with other white-sponsored attempts to limit or otherwise control the fertility of African American women. Over time, as African American women used abortion in their own interests, this outspoken opposition abated.

Also during the late 1960s and early 1970, small groups around the country

began to claim publicly that abortion was a woman's right and to fight for the repeal of antiabortion statutes. They also began to educate women about their bodies and abortion (Pat Maginnis's Society for Humane Abortion in California), to teach women how to perform "menstrual extraction" (Carol Downer and Lorraine Rothman's project in Los Angeles), to contract with doctors to provide illegal abortions and later to perform abortions on their own (JANE, an underground feminist abortion service in Chicago), and to refer large numbers of women to willing practitioners (the national clergy abortion referral service). Meanwhile, some "doctors of conscience" around the country performed abortions and referred patients to others because they were convinced that women should have access to this service.

In the mid- to late 1960s, national feminist leaders and grassroots feminist organizations were focusing on abortion as a key to women's liberation and racial justice. Through the Young Lords, the Black Panthers, the National Welfare Rights Organization, and other organizations, some women of color spoke out about reproductive rights. In the late 1960s, Frances Beal of the Black Women's Liberation Committee of the Student Nonviolent Coordinating Committee asserted, "Black women have the right and responsibility to determine when it is in the interest of the struggle to have children or not to have them and this right must not be relinquished" (Beal 1973, 393). The Redstockings, a feminist group in New York City, held the country's first "speak-out" on abortion in 1969, during which women publicly described their experiences in obtaining illegal abortions. In the late 1960s and early 1970s, several state legislatures, including those of New York, Colorado, and North Carolina, liberalized their abortion statutes.

These developments—demographic trends, the rise of the population control movement, the emergence of feminism and grassroots support of abortion reform, the persistence of abortion, the actions of a few state legislatures, and the climate of the era that supported "rights" claims—pushed the medical and legal communities to support formal legalization. *Roe* v. *Wade*, the 1973 Supreme Court decision legalizing abortion, was, in part, a pragmatic response to this complex range of developments.

The *Roe* v. *Wade* decision was based on four constitutional principles: (1) Women have a fundamental, constitutional right to reproductive autonomy and privacy, and government restrictions to that right must be subjected to "strict scrutiny." (2) The government must remain neutral regarding a woman's decision whether or not to have an abortion. (3) In the period before "viability" (the point at which a fetus is sufficiently developed so as to be able to live outside of the woman's womb), the government may restrict abortion only in the interests of protecting the woman's health. (4) After "viability," the government may prohibit abortion, but laws must make exceptions that permit abortion when necessary to protect a woman's health or life. *Roe* established a "trimester" concept of pregnancy: During the first third of the pregnancy, women have an unimpeded right to abortion; during the following two trimesters, an increasing schedule of restrictions applies.

Ironically, the feminist claim for reproductive rights was transformed, in the process of legalization, to a weaker, consumerist "choice" claim. The language of

the Supreme Court's majority in the *Roe* v. *Wade* opinion, as expressed by Justice Harry Blackmun, referred to abortion as "this choice" a number of times. In addition, the abortion rights movement's determination to develop a respectable, nonconfrontational single-issue set of institutionalized tactics to secure the *Roe* decision after 1973 encouraged many proponents of legal abortion to adopt the term *choice* in place of *rights.* These proponents also built a tightly framed association between "choice" and "abortion," thus cropping the bigger picture that "reproductive rights" envisioned.

The dissenters in the *Roe* decision, Justices Byron White and William Rehnquist, defined "the power of choice" represented by abortion as based on a woman's "convenience," "whim," "caprice"; on women's being willing to "exterminate" their pregnancies "for no reason at all" or because of their "dislike of children." These negative characterizations of women who would exercise their right to determine whether and when to become mothers reflected and stimulated the rise of the organized antiabortion movement immediately following the Supreme Court's decision.

The years since legalization have been marked by millions of women obtaining safe abortions. These years have also been marked by a rise in female labor force participation and wages, changes in family composition, and other economic and cultural shifts that sparked the rise of the New Right and the antiabortion movement. Using demonstrations, clinic blockades, myriad legislative strategies, judicial appointments and legal challenges, and violent tactics such as clinic bombings and even murder, various segments of the antiabortion movement have significantly reshaped the abortion arena.

The 1976 Hyde Amendment that denies Medicaid funding for abortion was Congress's first successful attempt to limit access to abortion. In June 1977, Rep. Henry Hyde of Illinois explained, "I certainly would like to prevent, if I could legally, anybody having an abortion, a rich woman, a middle-class woman, or a poor woman. Unfortunately, the only vehicle available is the HEW Medicaid bill" (*Congressional Record* 1977, 19698–19715). In 1980, when the Supreme Court, in *Harris v. McRae* (448 U.S. 316), decided that the Hyde Amendment was constitutional, even when poor women were denied public funding for medically indicated abortion, Justice Potter Stewart wrote for the majority that the government is not responsible for a person's poverty or for alleviating it. The government's responsibilities, Stewart wrote, must be narrowly drawn: "[A]lthough government may not place obstacles in the path of a woman's exercise of her freedom of choice, it need not remove those not of its own creation: Indigency falls in the latter category." Following the Hyde Amendment, similar limitations on federal spending—covering federal workers, military personnel, women on reservations, and inmates, among others—were enacted in the following years.

In the decades since legalization, access to abortion services has also been reduced as a result of dozens of initiatives in state legislatures, many of which have become law. These have included such things as requirements that married women involve their husbands in their abortion decision, waiting periods and various nonhealth-based counseling requirements, parental notification rules, restrictions on abortion coverage in state Medicaid programs and state employee health plans, bans on the performance of abortions in public hospitals, bans on particular types of procedures, and regulations on abortion providers' practices that are not placed on the practices of other physician-specialists but that can make abortion prohibitively expensive and drive providers out of practice. In 2000, forty-three antiabortion measures were adopted by legislatures around the country. Between 1994 and 2000, 262 such measures were implemented by the states ("Laws and Regulations Affecting Medical Abortion" 2001).

Proponents of restricting or ending abortion rights argue that mandatory waiting periods, to take one commonly legislated state regulation, work in the interests of women who may be confused or uncertain about their decision to terminate a pregnancy. Abortion rights proponents argue in response that women already carefully consider their options and that waiting periods force them to lose more work time, pay more money, travel twice as far, and wait as long as ten days or two weeks to undergo the procedure, since there are few practitioners in most areas and those may only work in a given clinic one or two days a week.

The successes of the antiabortion movement have constrained the abortion access of poor women and young women most sharply. Middle-class women are still probably more likely to access abortion services relatively unimpeded, although abortion rights proponents have been pushed into a defensive mode. Studies of the experiences of abortion-seeking girls and women have shown that women who got abortions in the illegal period suffered a sense of fear and stigma for having to go outside of the law or having to appear before committees of physicians, seeking permission to control their own bodies. In the period immediately following *Roe*, when abortion was still, to some extent, associated with the rights claim of the movement for legalization, few women reported feeling shame. But in the wake of anti-abortion–rights activism and legislation, many women, once again, report feeling fear and shame when they seek abortion services, particularly when doing so has entailed negotiating phalanxes of protesters and heavily guarded facilities.

Since *Roe* v. *Wade*, the U.S. Supreme Court has considered a number of abortion cases; over this period, a diminishing majority has sustained legal abortion. In the important 1992 case, *Planned Parenthood* v. *Casey*, the majority replaced the "strict scrutiny" standard with an "undue burden" standard; that is, a law could not impose an "undue burden" in the path of a woman seeking a previability abortion. Under this new standard, the Court upheld Pennsylvania's mandatory delay/informed consent law but struck down the husband notice requirement. Most striking, the Court reaffirmed *Roe*'s "core holding" that states may not ban abortions or interfere with any woman's ultimate decision to terminate a pregnancy.

Since the *Casey* decision, the Court's most important ruling came in 2000 when, in *Stenberg* v. *Carhart*, a bare five-person majority struck down a Nebraska ban on so-called partial-birth abortion, as a violation of *Roe* v. *Wade*, finding the ban to be so broad and vague that constitutionally protected abortion procedures performed before viability could be prohibited. Also, the majority determined that the Nebraska ban failed to include an exception to preserve the health of the woman.

At the beginning of the twenty-first century, abortion is still legal, but access to services is more limited than in the 1970s. Nevertheless, 43 percent of American women will have at least one abortion in their lives, and each year in the United States more than one million abortions are performed (Mueller and Dudley 1997).

Abortion practitioners are working under deeply harassing, sometimes life-threatening circumstances. Since the anti-abortion–rights movement became a force after 1973, seven abortion providers and clinic staff have been murdered, and hundreds of clinics have been damaged or destroyed. Not surprisingly, many physicians are reluctant to perform abortions in this climate. Fifty-seven percent of current practitioners are over fifty years old. And 86 percent of the counties in the United States lack an abortion provider (Mueller and Dudley 1997).

At the beginning of the twenty-first century, a pill facilitating medical (rather than surgical) abortion, RU-486, was approved by the Food and Drug Administration. This pill can be taken within forty-nine days of the beginning of a woman's last menstrual period to terminate an early pregnancy. Many doctors and public health officials believe that its availability creates a strong new option for women and a health advantage because public health experts agree that an earlier abortion is a safer abortion. Similarly, those who support women's reproductive autonomy champion the new availability of the "morning after pill"—which can be taken within three days of sexual intercourse to prevent ovulation or block implantation of a fertilized egg. Experts estimate that the use of this method could prevent 1.7 million unplanned pregnancies and 800,000 abortions annually (Trussell, Ellertson, and Stuart 1996). Opponents of these pills consider them abortifacients, and many are engaged in efforts to make sure that abortion restrictions apply to these methods.

Although many politicians, jurists, and ordinary Americans oppose women's reproductive autonomy and aim to overturn *Roe* v. *Wade* in the twenty-first century, a national poll on religious attitudes conducted in January 2000 by Celinda Lake of Lake, Snell, Perry and Associates showed that 80 percent of Americans believe "a person must follow her own faith, personal beliefs, and conscience in considering whether or not to terminate a pregnancy." Apparently, abortion will continue to be a flashpoint in the United States for those with opposing views about the status of women in society and about definitions of life.

—*Rickie Solinger*

See also Birth Control; *Roe* v. *Wade*; Sanger, Margaret; Teenage Pregnancy

References and Further Reading

"Abortion and the Law." 1967. *Journal of the American Medical Association* (January 16): 25.

Beal, Frances M. 1973. "Double Jeopardy: To Be Black and Female." In *Sisterhood Is Powerful*, edited by Robin Morgan, 387–398. New York: Random House.

Brodie, Janet Farrell. 1994. *Contraception and Abortion in Nineteenth-Century America*. Ithaca, NY: Cornell University Press.

Congressional Record. 1977. Vol. 123, pt. 16: 19698–19715.

Fischer, Russell. 1951. "Criminal Abortion." *Journal of Criminal Law and Criminology* 42 (July-August): 242–249.

Fried, Marlene Gerber. 1990. *From Abortion to Reproductive Freedom: Transforming a Movement*. Boston: South End Press.

Garrow, David. 1994. *Liberty and Sexuality: The Right to Privacy and the Making of* Roe v. Wade. New York: Macmillan.

Joffe, Carole. 1995. *Doctors of Conscience: The Struggle to Provide Abortion before and after* Roe v. Wade. Boston: Beacon Press.

Kaplan, Laura. 1995. *The Story of Jane: The Legendary Underground Feminist Abortion Service*. New York: Pantheon.

"Laws and Regulations Affecting Medical Abortion." Center for Reproductive Law and Policy. www.crlp.org/proabortion. html (cited 29 October 2001).

Mohr, James C. 1978. *Abortion in America: The Origins and Evolution of National Policy*. New York: Oxford University Press.

Mueller, Stephanie, and Susan Dudley. "Access to Abortion." http://www. prochoice.org/Facts/Factsheet/F85.htm (cited 1997).

Petchesky, Rosalind Pollack. 1990. *Abortion and Women's Choice: The State, Sexuality, and Reproductive Freedom*. Boston: Northeastern University.

Reagan, Leslie J. 1997. *When Abortion Was a Crime: Women, Medicine, and the Law in the United States, 1967–1973*. Berkeley: University of California Press.

Roberts, Dorothy. 1997. *Killing the Black Body: Race, Reproduction, and the Meaning of Liberty*. New York: Pantheon.

Russell, Keith P. 1953. Changing Indications for Therapeutic Abortion: Twenty Years Experience at Los Angeles County Hospital." *Journal of the American Medical Association* (January 10).

Solinger, Rickie. 1994. *The Abortionist: A Woman against the Law*. New York: The Free Press.

Solinger, Rickie. 2001. *Beggars and Choosers: How the Politics of Choice Shapes Adoption, Abortion, and Welfare in the United States*. New York: Hill and Wang.

Solinger, Rickie, ed. 1998. *Abortion Wars: A Half-Century of Struggle, 1950–2000*. Berkeley: University of California Press.

Stiegine. 1935. "A Study of Pregnancy Wastage." *Milbank Memorial Fund Quarterly* 13: 347–365.

Trussell, James, Charlotte Ellertson, and Felicia Stuart. 1996. "The Effectiveness of the Yuzpe Regimen of Emergency Contraception." *Family Planning Perspectives* 28(2): 58–64, 87.

AD/HD

Attention deficit hyperactive disorder (AD/HD) is the term identified in 1987 by the American Psychology Association to describe a neurobehavioral disorder characterized by developmentally inappropriate attention skills, impulsivity, and hyperactivity. It affects an estimated 3 to 5 percent of the child population (Children and Adults with Attention-Deficit/Hyperactive Disorders 2001, 1). Diagnosis is based on symptoms that appear before age seven and that occur for at least six months, and on the history of the child's behavior from information taken by parents, teachers, and physicians. Symptoms range from mild to severe in three subtypes and are often accompanied by other antisocial behav-

iors or learning disorders. Interventions include stimulant medication therapy, instructional and behavior modification, and education of school staff and families. Although no cure exists, early identification and intervention are shown to improve development.

The behaviors have been around for centuries. Bad parenting was suspected as the cause during the early nineteenth century. From 1890 to 1950, minimal brain damage (MBD) was cited as the cause because of characteristics in common with those of children with brain damage from encephalitis. During the 1950s and 1960s, brain mechanisms, genetics, and environmental conditions were suspected, as shown in the names *hyperkinetic* and *hyperactive child syndromes*.

A hyperactive student in a first-grade classroom. (Elizabeth Crews)

In the 1970s, increased public interest and research efforts helped to eliminate several suspected causes, such as food additives and allergies. Education opportunities changed owing to such federal laws as the Individuals with Disabilities Education Act (IDEA) and Section 504 of the Rehabilitation Act of 1973. These laws provided funds and special services while requiring the least restricted environments. For decades, AD/HD was considered a childhood condition. It was accepted that children outgrew these behaviors, yet adults faced similar difficulties in their jobs and personal lives. They began seeking diagnosis and intervention; they are now protected in employment and public accommodations under the Disability Act of 1990.

—*Mabel T. Himel*

See also Disabilities and Family Life

References and Further Reading
American Psychiatric Association. 1994. *Diagnostic and Statistical Manual of Mental Disorders.* 4th ed. Washington, DC: American Psychiatric Association.
Barkley, Russell. 1998. *Attention Deficit Hyperactivity Disorders: A Handbook for Diagnosis and Treatment.* New York: Guilford Press.
Children and Adults with Attention-Deficit/Hyperactive Disorders. "CHADD Facts: The Disability Named AD/HD." http://www.chadd.org/facts/addfacts01.htm (cited 4 January 2001).
Lerner, Janet, Barbara Lowenthal, and Sue Lerner. 1995. *Attention Deficit Disorders: Assessment and Teaching.* New York: Brooks/Cole.

Adolescence

Like childhood and family, adolescence is a socially constructed concept more than it is a period of life or status determined by biology. For most of U.S. history, the term *adolescence* was synonymous with *youth,* referring to the years roughly from age eleven to twenty-five or, in other words, from the period of childhood dependency until an individual became a participant in the adult economy. In 1904, G. Stanley Hall spelled out the psychological and physiological perimeters for a modern definition of adolescence in his seminal three-volume work, *Adolescence: Its Psychology and Its Relations to Physiology, Anthropology, Sociology, Sex, Crime, Religion and Education.* Hall's conceptualization emphasized the teen years as a period of awkwardness, confusion, vulnerability, dramatic physical change, and eccentricities. He believed that a troubled adolescence was physically and psychologically unavoidable. In 1928, Margaret Mead tried to discredit Hall's conclusions in her book *Coming of Age in Samoa* by arguing instead that culture determined the perimeters of adolescent experience. Nonetheless, Hall's interpretation, built on a middle-class family model formed during the mid-nineteenth century, has dominated social and academic notions about adolescence throughout the twentieth century and beyond.

More than half of the nation's population was sixteen years of age or younger at the time of the American Revolution (U.S. Bureau of the Census 1976, 9, 13). Life expectancy was short (about forty), and many parents did not live to see their children reach the teen years. Few young people attended school; instead, they worked alongside adults. Precocious youths such as Thomas Jefferson were encouraged, not condemned as acting inappropriately for their age. Social definitions of childhood, youth, and adulthood were fluid. Work and physical capacity were the primary factors distinguishing childhood, youth, and adulthood.

Although few males in their teens had sufficient incomes to start families of their own, apprenticeships that separated male adolescents from their parents were common. Benjamin Franklin's experience was somewhat typical of many urban adolescent males. Born on 17 January 1706, the fifteenth child and tenth son of a Boston soap and candle maker, Franklin began working at age ten for his father and was apprenticed at age twelve to his older brother James, a local printer. Franklin worked in his brother's shop for five years but complained of physical and mental abuse. In 1723, at the age of seventeen, he ran away to Philadelphia. From there Franklin traveled to London and two years later returned to Philadelphia to open his own printing shop. Like most young men of his generation, Franklin was married and a father by age twenty-four. Rural males usually remained at home until at least their midteens to work on the family farm. Some, however, set off for the frontier or the nation's growing cities in order to gain economic and social independence from their parents.

Most females of Franklin's generation waited until they married to leave their parents' homes, but marriage during the teen years was common. Few respectable jobs were open to females of any age, and single women were generally viewed with suspicion. Besides, an economy based on household production and the lack of reliable birth control resulted in large families in which mothers depended on older daughters to care for younger siblings. By their mid- to late teens, many young women were anxious to care for their own children and chose to marry.

Most eighteenth-century females were either pregnant or nursing during their childbearing years. Physical growth was

A portrait of Private Joph White, a drummer boy in the Civil War, Virginia Regiment. (Library of Congress)

stunted by an inadequate diet and childhood illnesses. Although menstruation began for many at age thirteen, most females did not experience menarche until age sixteen or seventeen, therefore delaying the primary reason for marriage until the mid- to late teens. The younger a woman married, however, the more children she was likely to have during her lifetime. In 1800, the average female in the United States gave birth seven times (U.S. Bureau of the Census 1976, 49). The ability to have children marked a girl's entry into adulthood. There were some differences in age-at-first-marriage patterns based on region, class, and ethnic background. For example, Scots-Irish Americans tended to marry at much younger ages than those of English Puritan descent. But in general, regardless of age, females were considered the social, legal, and economic dependents of men. Few parents thought about a discrete period of adolescence for their daughters during the seventeenth, eighteenth, and early nineteenth centuries.

Blacks who lived as slaves were also considered to be in a permanent state of dependency. Slaves were most often called "boy" or "girl" no matter what their age. The ability to bear children marked the move to adulthood for black girls, and the physical capacity to do adult labor signaled that boys were no longer children. Enslaved youngsters had a shortened childhood and no adolescence. Free blacks generally labored at the bottom of the economic ladder in the United States and were also pushed into adult roles very early in life.

As Alexis de Tocqueville observed in 1835, there was no adolescence for most youth in the early United States (de Tocqueville 2000, 253, 258–259). American ideas about adolescence began to shift at about the same time de Tocqueville made his observation, however. By the mid-nineteenth century, the beginnings of an industrial economy contributed to the growth of an urban middle class. These couples had fewer children than parents in the past. In addition, urban middle-class parents focused more attention on their offspring and formed the basis of the shift to a consumer-based economy less dependent on household and agricultural production. This situation made urban middle-class families less reliant on the labor of children and adolescents for survival. Such parents believed that childhood and adolescence were special periods of life with specific needs and limited responsibilities. Education beyond the rudimentary skills of reading and writing became increasingly

important as white-collar employment rose in urban centers. By the mid-nineteenth century, the term *adolescence* generally referred to this urban middle-class model.

In 1821, the nation's first high school opened in Boston, Massachusetts. Usually called academies, early high schools such as the one in Boston were private, often residential, and segregated by sex. Urban middle-class parents viewed sending a son or daughter to an academy as a way to maintain or even improve a family's status. Sons were trained for employment and girls were schooled in the domestic skills necessary for running a "proper" Victorian household.

Horace Mann's common school movement stimulated the development of public high schools by the 1860s. Unlike the private academies, these institutions were open to both boys and girls, and students lived with their parents. Some nineteenth-century adults worried about adolescent males and females attending high school classes together, but most communities could not afford to fund sex-segregated secondary schools. By the late nineteenth century most urban middle-class parents wanted to send their adolescent children to high school. There was little distinction between college and high school curricula, but high schools were a more practical and less costly alternative to college for most urban middle-class families. High schools prepared sons for white-collar positions in business or, for a few, college and then professional careers in law or medicine. Middle-class daughters who graduated from high school could also consider college or easily move into teaching positions for a few years before marrying in their twenties. More than any other single development, the creation of high schools helped to redefine adolescence as a period of life in which "school" was the only acceptable full-time job.

Nevertheless, most parents could not afford to send their children to high school, and many adolescents as well as adults believed that going to high school was an impractical luxury. In 1900, only 6.3 percent of seventeen-year-olds in the United States were in high school. By 1920, attendance had increased to 16.3 percent of that age cohort, but few remained in school long enough to earn a degree. The numbers almost doubled during the 1920s but still included fewer than half of U.S. adolescents. High school attendance was even lower for black Americans, who were segregated into separate and inferior schools in the South by law and in the North and West by social practice (U.S. Bureau of the Census 1976, 370, 379). Farm families had always depended on the labor of maturing children. By the mid- to late nineteenth century, urban working-class parents were also looking to wage-earning adolescents in the nation's expanding industrial economy to contribute to family income.

When twelve-year-old Andrew Carnegie immigrated with his parents to the United States from Scotland in 1835, he got a job as a bobbin-boy in a Pittsburgh textile mill. Ironically, this was the same kind of steam-powered factory that had made his father's skills as a weaver obsolete in Scotland. The ambitious young Carnegie also took night classes where he learned Morse code. This knowledge led to a better job with the Western Union Telegraph Company and then, when he was only eighteen, to a position as personal assistant to the Pennsylvania Railroad's western division chief, Thomas Scott. Still a teen, Carnegie was a seasoned businessman with little formal education but possess-

ing desirable technical and business management skills.

The American Civil War served as a further spark to industrial expansion, bringing even more teens into the wage labor force. It also created a larger propertyless class, driving more Americans of all ages into wage work. In addition, many adolescent males served in the military for the Union or the Confederacy during the war. Preteen drummer boys and soldiers in their early to mid-teens were common sights on Civil War battlefields. Adolescents also worked in a variety of support roles. Susie King Taylor, born a slave in Georgia in 1848, became a refugee at age fourteen. She married a black Union soldier and worked throughout the war as an unpaid and untrained nurse for the 33rd U.S. Colored Troops, Late 1st South Carolina Volunteers. Taylor later published a book about her experiences during and immediately after the war (Taylor 1988). Her adolescent viewpoint is one of the few accounts of the conflict written by a black "woman" and clearly shows how the war disrupted the lives of adolescents as well as adults.

The war also led to the deaths of many male breadwinners, especially in the South. Textile manufacturers and other industrialists established mills in southern states after the war because of the large pool of widows and orphans willing to work as low-wage laborers. In addition, the southern economy was so devastated that many parents depended on the meager wages earned in the new factories by their adolescent and even younger children. Persistent poverty in the former Confederate states continued this trend well into the twentieth century.

Nineteenth-century literature reflected the varied circumstances of adolescents.

Jo March in Louisa May Alcott's 1868–1869 *Little Women* and Huck in Twain's 1844 *The Adventures of Huckleberry Finn* are two of the century's most memorable literary characters. Horatio Alger Jr. wrote about working-class adolescence in his popular dime novels, such as the 1868 *Ragged Dick; or, Street Life in New York with the Bootblacks* and his 1887 *The Cash Boy.* Although the books by Alcott, Twain, and Alger tell very different tales, they share a theme: warning adults and young people about precocious behavior by those in their teens. Although the middle-class model was not accessible to the majority of American families, by 1900 child welfare advocates, social reformers, educators, psychologists, and physicians increasingly promoted the urban middle-class definition of adolescence for *all* American young people.

Reformers began to demanded enforcement of compulsory school attendance laws and reforms in child labor practices. Massachusetts and Connecticut had passed the country's first child labor laws in 1842 (limiting the workday to ten hours for children under twelve years of age and twelve hours for those under fourteen). But in an era without birth certificates and lackluster government enforcement, parents, employers, and young people easily circumvented compulsory school attendance and child labor laws. The percentage of young people ten through fifteen years of age working for wages actually increased from 1870 to 1910 (13.2 percent to 18.4 percent respectively) (U.S. Bureau of Labor Statistics 1910–1913). Working in the nation's factories and mines and on its streets, adolescent wageworkers were a visible part of American life. In 1906 a dedicated group of reformers, troubled by

what they viewed as the physical and emotional exploitation of children in an increasingly modern nation, organized the National Child Labor Committee (NCLC). The group called for the end of all child labor for those under fourteen years of age and demanded the regulation of child labor for anyone less than seventeen. Over the next decade the NCLC waged a nationwide propaganda campaign utilizing photographs taken by Lewis Hine and grounded in the middle-class ideal for adolescence and childhood. Congress responded in 1916 by passing the Keating-Owen Act. This law, scheduled to go into effect on 1 September 1917, prohibited the interstate or export shipment of materials produced in mines or quarries that employed young people under sixteen years of age and of products manufactured in facilities employing anyone under fourteen or where adolescents between the ages of fourteen and sixteen inclusive worked more than eight hours a day, six days a week, or at night (before 6:00 A.M. or after 7:00 P.M.).

The idea of restricting the work of children and adolescents was not popular with everyone, however. On 11 August 1917, Roland H. Dagenhart filed suit in a North Carolina district court that would prevent the Charlotte district attorney, William C. Hammer, from enforcing the new law on 1 September. Dagenhart argued that the law violated the constitutional rights of his two sons, Ruben (age fourteen) and John (age twelve). A North Carolina judge ruled in favor of Dagenhart. The state then appealed to the U.S. Supreme Court, which, in a five-to-four decision released on 3 June 1918, held the Keating-Owen Act unconstitutional. Although the opinion in *Hammer* v. *Dagenhart* overturned the first national child labor law, the Court unanimously agreed that child labor was an evil that needed to end in the best interest of the general public welfare. In response, Congress passed a proposed constitutional amendment in 1924 prohibiting child labor and regulating the employment of adolescents. The necessary number of states never ratified the amendment, however. States passed their own regulations, but the 1930 census reported that 2,145,919 boys and girls from ten through sixteen years of age were "gainfully employed." Only 28.8 percent of seventeen-year-olds had graduated from high school (U.S. Bureau of the Census 1976, 379).

The onset of the Great Depression finally led to progress by the child labor reform movement and a parallel growth in high school attendance. The New Deal included the first national restrictions on the employment of young people sixteen and under. In addition, Congress passed the National Labor Standards Act in 1937 prohibiting wage labor for anyone under fourteen and limiting work hours and types of employment for those sixteen and seventeen. Rules set under the law remain the basic standards for adolescent employment. The severely constricted pool of jobs for adults during the Great Depression led to the passage of the nation's first permanent child labor restrictions, and for the first time a majority of American adolescents attended high school. In 1940, 49 percent of seventeen-year-olds had graduated from high school (U.S. Bureau of the Census 1976, 379).

Keeping young people in school and out of the workplace had been a major goal of child welfare reformers since the Progressive Era. Working adolescents were generally not in school, the only acceptable "job" for young people in the middle-class ideal. Schools became a means for Americanizing young people as a new wave of immigrants from southern and eastern Europe coupled with a rising tide of southern blacks migrating to northern cities in the late nineteenth and early twentieth century. Stories about youth gangs and promiscuous girls, especially from immigrant or black families, had been a consistent part of U.S. popular culture throughout the nation's history. Turn-of-the-century reformers, however, stirred new fears about unacceptable social behavior perpetuated by adolescents who labored instead of attending school. Child welfare advocates called for the creation of a separate court system to deal with children and adolescents. Illinois created the first state-mandated juvenile court system in 1899. By 1920, forty-five states had established juvenile courts, and the three remaining states (Connecticut, Maine, and Wyoming) passed special laws for dealing with juveniles. Fourteen states limited the jurisdiction of juvenile courts to juveniles under age sixteen, thirteen states set the limit at seventeen years of age, and in seventeen states the limit was eighteen for girls and twenty for boys. Maryland established the limit at eighteen for girls and twenty for boys. California used twenty-one for both sexes. State lawmakers were motivated by sympathies distinct to children and youth, but many also feared the growing influence of a burgeoning youth culture in the United States that seemed to be out of control. Juvenile courts could ignore legal procedures guaranteed to adults, and reform schools became the primary "treatment" for juvenile offenders (Breckinridge and Jeter 1918, 15–16).

States also passed laws prohibiting individuals under twenty-one from purchasing tobacco products or liquor. The invigorated Prohibition movement, led by the Women's Christian Temperance Union (WCTU) and the Anti-Saloon League, argued that the very existence of alcohol threatened the nation's young people and their families. Many adults worried that gambling, violence, promiscuity, and other "adult" temptations were threatening the nation's youth and, therefore, the very future of the United States. Keeping such vices out of the hands of adults, advocates argued, would also prevent adolescents from being corrupted.

The WCTU's purity crusade beginning in 1889 is symbolic of the new attention centered on protecting adolescence. The WCTU called for states to raise their minimum age in sexual consent laws. During the 1880s, most states set the minimum age at ten or twelve based on precedents established in English common law since 1576 (in Delaware the minimum was seven). The WCTU demanded reforms that would establish the minimum age of consent at sixteen or eighteen. This meant that any male having sex with a female younger than sixteen or eighteen could be charged and convicted of rape, even if the girl had consented to intercourse. The WCTU's campaign was so successful that by 1920 every state but Georgia (where the law changed from twelve to fourteen) had raised its minimum age of consent to sixteen or eighteen (Odem 1995, 14–15). WCTU advocates argued that the change was a step toward moral purity and evidence of society's acceptance of superior female virtue.

In a similar vein, reformers focused attention on the nation's laws for minimum age at marriage. The Russell Sage Foundation's Mary Richmond and Fred S. Hall argued that rising divorce and desertion rates could be curbed if young people were prohibited from marrying before reaching "full maturity." In 1925, the allowable age at marriage was twelve (or as low as seven by judicial order) for females in fourteen states. Eight states set the minimum at fifteen; seventeen states at sixteen years of age, and one at eighteen (Richmond and Hall 1925, 20, 49). Richmond and Hall's anti–child marriage campaign encouraged legislatures to raise their minimums. Nonetheless, the transition was much slower than the establishment of juvenile courts or the adoption of antivice laws and did not receive universal acceptance of age eighteen until the 1980s.

In 1900, fewer than 1 percent of males and 11 percent of females fourteen through nineteen years of age had ever been married. Despite the anti–child marriage campaign's efforts, over the next six decades this proportion increased four times for boys and rose slightly for girls. The median age at first marriage in 1900 was 25.9 for males and 21.9 for females. By 1950 the median age was down to 22.8 for males and 20.3 for females (U.S. Bureau of the Census 1976, 20). These idealized "family values" decades of the 1940s, 1950s, and 1960s included the twentieth century's lowest age-at-marriage rates and highest teen birthrates (79.5, 91, 69.7). In 1960, nearly one-third of females in the United States had their first child before reaching age twenty (U.S. Bureau of the Census 1976, 52). There was little public excitement about this trend because most pregnant adolescent females married before giving birth. But this behavior illustrates a resistance by young people to legal efforts attempting to curb sexual behavior and marriage.

Another aspect of this resistance to adult control was the development of a powerful youth culture that offered greater autonomy from adults. In the first decades of the twentieth century, anxious mothers and fathers worried that frequenting commercial dance halls and going to amusement parks, movie theaters, and other "modern" attractions ruined the morals of adolescents, especially daughters. Public dance halls where couples could do the grizzly bear, the bunny hug, and the kangaroo dip grew in popularity after 1900. Parental supervision weakened as young people rejected chaperoned courtships, common in the nineteenth century, in favor of "going out" and "dating." Working-class youth led these cultural changes as they increasingly took advantage of opportunities for wage work in the nation's expanding cities. Middle-class parents tried to prevent their children from listening to ragtime music or frequenting dance halls and amusement parks by creating organized sports and after-school clubs in high schools. The establishment of the Boy Scouts and Girl Scouts as well as the Young Men's Christian Association (YMCA) and Young Women's Christian Association (YWCA) was also designed to control adolescent behavior. Nonetheless, young people inside and outside high schools found the new youth culture contagious. By the 1920s, spending time at amusement parks, dancing in public spaces, and going to movies were universal experiences for adolescents of virtually all socioeconomic classes and ethnic groups. Blacks were often discriminated against in such public facilities. A segregated youth culture developed in black communities. In fact, the jazz and dance culture of urban black neighborhoods such as Harlem fueled modern youth culture across racial and ethnic lines. Prostitution declined as expressions of female sexuality became more accepted among young people. Jazz music and petting, in which adolescents and young adults engaged in all forms of sexual intimacy except intercourse, defined youth culture of the 1920s.

The Great Depression hindered the purchasing power of adolescents, therefore somewhat limiting youths' opportunities to participate in a separate consumer culture. In addition, the New Deal only marginally spoke to the needs of adolescents. The Civilian Conservation Corps was open only to males aged seventeen through twenty-three. The largest New Deal program for young people, the National Youth Administration, did provide part-time jobs for high school– and college-age youth, but that program was not established until 1935. Some young people wandered the country looking for work, but adult fears about adolescent hobos were more myth than reality. Instead, the lack of jobs for young people meant that a majority of adolescents attended the nation's high schools for the first time in U.S. history.

Movies serve as a window to changing adult perceptions about adolescence. As young people became a smaller proportion of the population, filmmakers and reformers paid more attention to them. Individuals under nineteen years of age constituted less than 45 percent of the total U.S. population by 1900, and the percentage continued to decline throughout most of the twentieth century until young people were less than 20 percent of the total in 1999 ("Statistical Abstract of the United States, Population" 2001). By the 1920s, a growing number of filmmakers were fascinated with youth culture, which seemed to set the tone for "modern" life. The flapper—a young woman who refused to wear a corset, bobbed her hair, smoked cigarettes, drank illegal alcohol, dated men, and flaunted her sexuality in short dresses—was featured in many popular films. Legendary director D. W. Griffith warned of the temptations of urban life, especially for young women, in his classic movie *Way Down East* (1921), starring the waiflike Lillian Gish. Unlike Griffith, however, most filmmakers tantalized film audiences with the excitement of youth culture. A sampling of 1920s film titles shows this trend: *The Flame of Youth* (1920), *Reckless Youth* (1922), *Youth Must Have Love* (1923), and *Passionate Youth* (1925). Although most characters were not strictly adolescents, the films suggested that modernity and youth were synonymous.

During the 1930s, the depiction of adolescence in film and other forms of popular culture was more innocent and age specific in films. For example, the characters portrayed by Mickey Rooney and Judy Garland were the complete opposite of 1920s "flaming youth." They lived with their parents and followed the rules. In reality, adolescents were demanding more democratic treatment from their parents and teachers during the 1930s. Girls who wanted to date and boys who smoked and drank in public were an expression of adolescent independence that must have been difficult for many parents to understand.

The economic prosperity spurred by World War II renewed public concerns about unacceptable adolescent behavior. The 1942 zoot suit riots in Los Angeles, in which sailors and soldiers attacked Mexican American adolescents wrongly accused of being draft dodgers and drug dealers, ironically underscored for many adults what they perceived as rising delinquency among young people. A 1960s report by the U.S. Children's Bureau declared that such perceptions

were false (Bradbury 1960), but during the 1940s and 1950s adults became increasingly concerned with juvenile delinquency. Sen. Estes Kefauver of Tennessee oversaw congressional subcommittee hearings during the mid-1950s examining the threat and causes of juvenile delinquency. The Kefauver subcommittee heard testimony linking comic books, movies, and television with antisocial behavior among adolescents.

Most teens, however, were not juvenile delinquents, but the teen years were increasingly viewed as a time of life vulnerable to antisocial and dangerous behavior. A 1941 article in *Popular Science Magazine* used the word *teenager* in print for the first time. Although some adolescents left school for full-time jobs, most teens worked only part-time while remaining in school. This prosperity and age segregation gave birth to the modern "teenager." The military draft included a deferment for all males attending high school through age nineteen, but many younger men joined up anyway, lying about their age. As a result, the military unintentionally universalized American youth culture in ways inconceivable before wartime mobilization. Although strictly controlled by the military, teen sailors, soldiers, and marines when off duty were exposed to temptations generally limited to adults before the war. The opening of jobs to teens on the home front also created greater financial and social independence for adolescents. Parents worked long hours, and overcrowding in high schools left many young people with little adult supervision. Although it is difficult to document, sexual activity among teenagers likely increased during the war. United Service Organizations (USO) canteens attracted adolescent girls who were encouraged to "do their part" for the war

Seventeen-year-old girls hanging out in a bedroom and reading magazines. (Elizabeth Crews)

effort by providing "company" for home-sick soldiers. Radio, popularized during the 1930s, had already made stars of swing bandleaders and singers who served as the background music to the war years. The jitterbug and swing music fostered very physical and sexually expressive dances.

Somewhat ironically, the war further commercialized youth culture and accel-erated the path to adulthood for many adolescents at the same time that society created an ambiguous status for teen-agers. By the 1950s, the term *teenager* symbolized rock 'n' roll and rebellion. When eighteen-year-old Elvis Presley recorded his first record in 1953, he spoke the language of young Americans. In

1948, the majority of seventeen-year-olds graduated from high school for the first time in U.S. history (52.9 percent) (U.S. Bureau of the Census 1976, 379). The bat-tle to get into public high schools became the primary symbol of the postwar civil rights movement. Adolescents and col-lege-age youth were the foot soldiers in this battle for racial equality. In addition, during the 1960s and early 1970s, the first adolescents of the baby boom gener-ation became some of the most vocal supporters and protesters of U.S. involve-ment in the Vietnam War. The military draft collected the nation's youngest age cohort ever sent to war. Despite this col-lection of evidence that seems to suggest a popular perception of maturity among adolescents, Holden Caulfield, the main character in J. D. Salinger's 1951 classic novel *Catcher in the Rye*, was the confused and angst-ridden adolescent defined by G. Stanley Hall in 1904 that continues to shape popular attitudes about the teen years.

In the late twentieth century the most serious threats to adolescents became accidents and violence. Automobiles are the single greatest hazard, but obtaining a driver's license remains a modern rite of passage. Homicide is the second leading cause of death for fifteen- to twenty-four-year-olds. Despite popular perceptions to the contrary, most young crime victims die in their homes or on the streets, not in school. Only twenty-six youngsters were killed at school in 1999, and that number includes the sixteen teenagers murdered by their classmates at Colorado's Columbine High School. The most likely child murder victim is black, urban, between twelve and twenty years of age, and male—not white, middle-class, and suburban as media attention suggests (U.S. Public Health Service 2000, chap. 2).

Americans remain ambivalent about adolescence. Many adults expect little from teenagers. They believe adolescence to be a time of raging hormones and emotional immaturity that necessitates adult control. On the other hand, advertisers appeal to teenage sexuality and young people's desire to be treated as adults. And young people do have money to spend. Many earn it themselves and are not direct contributors to their family's basic income. Although federal laws have generally eliminated the worst offenses of child labor, more adolescents work for wages in the United States than in any other industrialized nation. And technologically skilled adolescents and youth drive the new economy. Twenty-year-old

Bill Gates began Microsoft with his twenty-two-year-old childhood friend, Paul Allen, in 1975.

Adults criticize contemporary teenagers for trying to grow up too fast. They complain that many are "having too much sex," whereas in reality the 1970s, 1980s, and 1990s constituted the century's lowest teen pregnancy rates (53.0, 59.9, 57.0 births per 1,000 females aged fifteen through nineteen) (Luker 1996, 196). As acquired immunodeficiency syndrome (AIDS) has become a bigger threat to teens than adolescent pregnancy, it appears that most teens have changed their sexual behavior in response. The U.S. Supreme Court declared the right of school administrators to censor student speech and newspapers in *Bethel School District No. 403* v. *Fraser* (1986) and *Hazelwood School District* v. *Kuhlmeir* (1988). Many Americans are calling for violent teenagers to be tried as adults, even though they believe their own children should enjoy an extended adolescence through the college years.

As in the past, teenagers are continuing to define their own place in society as adults struggle with the slippery definition of adolescence. Volunteer rates among young people are the highest of any age cohort. Longer life expectancy and the economics of modern life have created new age stratifications that continue to adjust to a changing world. Adolescence is not a strictly defined period of life that fits a universal prescription in the past or the future.

—*Kriste Lindenmeyer*

See also Apprenticeship; Delinquency; Discipline and Punishment; Family Courts; Hall, G. Stanley; Juvenile Justice; Teenage Pregnancy

References and Further Reading

Bradbury, Dorothy E. 1960. *The Children's Bureau and Juvenile Delinquency: A Chronology of What the Bureau Is Doing and Has Done in This Field.* Washington, DC: Government Printing Office.

Breckinridge, Sophonisba P., and Helen R. Jeter. 1918. *A Summary of Juvenile-Court Legislation in the United States.* U.S. Children's Bureau Publication 70. Washington, DC: Government Printing Office.

Bremner, Robert H., ed. 1970. *Children and Youth in America: A Documentary History.* Cambridge: Harvard University Press.

de Tocqueville, Alexis. 2000. *Democracy in America.* New York: J. and H. G. Langley, 1840. Reprint, Indianapolis, IN: Hacket Publishing.

Gilbert, James B. 1986. *Cycles of Outrage: America's Reaction to Juvenile Delinquency of the 1950s.* New York: Oxford University Press.

Graff, Harvey T., ed. 1987. *Growing Up in America: Historical Perspectives.* Detroit: Wayne State University Press.

Hall, Granville Stanley. 1904. *Adolescence: Its Psychology and Its Relations to Physiology, Anthropology, Sociology, Sex, Crime, Religion, and Education.* 3 vols. New York: D. Appleton and Company.

Hine, Thomas. 1999. *The Rise and Fall of the American Teenager.* New York: Avon Books.

Kett, Joseph F. 1977. *Rites of Passage: Adolescence in America, 1790 to the Present.* New York: Basic Books.

Lindenmeyer, Kriste. 1997. *"A Right to Childhood": The U.S. Children's Bureau and Child Welfare, 1912–1946.* Urbana: University of Illinois Press.

Luker, Kristin. 1996. *Dubious Conceptions: The Politics of Teenage Pregnancy.* Cambridge: Harvard University Press.

Mead, Margaret. 1928. *Coming of Age in Samoa.* New York: William Morrow.

Newberger, Julee. "Teens Say Sex Can Wait. Connect for Kids." The Benton Foundation. http://www.connectforkids.org/newsletter-url1571/newsletter-url.htm (cited 10 July 2000).

Odem, Mary E. 1995. *Delinquent Daughters: Protecting and Policing Adolescent Female Sexuality in the United States, 1885–1920.* Chapel Hill: University of North Carolina Press.

Palladino, Grace. 1996. *Teenagers: An American History.* New York: Basic Books.

Peiss, Kathy Lee. 1986. *Cheap Amusements: Working Women and Leisure in New York City, 1880 to 1920.* Philadelphia: Temple University Press.

Richmond, Mary E., and Fred S. Hall. 1925. *Child Marriages.* New York: Russell Sage Foundation, 1925.

"Statistical Abstract of the United States, Population." U.S. Bureau of the Census. http://www.census.gov/prod/www/statistical-abstract-us.html (cited 5 October 2001).

Taylor, Susie King. 1988. "Reminiscences of My Life in Camp with the 33rd United States Colored Troops Late 1st S.C. Volunteers." In *A Black Woman's Civil War Memoirs,* edited by Patricia W. Romero. New York: Marcus Wiener. (Originally privately published, 1902.)

U.S. Bureau of the Census. 1976. *Historical Statistics of the United States, Colonial Times to 1970.* Bicentennial ed., pt. 1. Washington, DC: Government Printing Office.

U.S. Bureau of Labor Statistics. 1910–1913. *An Investigation of Women and Child Wage-Earners in the United States.* 19 vols. Washington, DC: Government Printing Office.

U.S. Public Health Service. 2000. *Youth Violence: A Report of the Surgeon General.* Washington, DC: Government Printing Office. (Also online at http://www.surgeongeneral.gov/library/youthviolence/order.htm.)

Adoptive Parents

People who legally adopt are adoptive parents. During the first three centuries of American history (1607–1907), adoptive families were rare. The first adoption law came into existence only in the mid-nineteenth century (1851), and adoptive families became a public phenomenon only during the Progressive Era (1900–1917). Prospective adoptive couples were reluctant to adopt for a host of reasons, including the nation's cultural bias favoring blood kinship and the social and medical stigma against children born of unwed mothers. A revolution began in the world of adoption, however, as a product of the Great Depression, World War II, and changes in sexual mores. Consequently, as a result of the baby boom of the 1950s, there was a spectacular growth in the number of adoptive families and more acceptance of adoption by American society, though it still is viewed as an inferior type of kinship relation. During the past fifty years, adoptive families have lived through the increasing trend away from strict "matching" criteria, the increasing inclusion of children deemed "adoptable," the emergence of protest movements against sealed adoption records, the growth of state and federal child-centered laws governing adoption, and the standardization and professionalization of adoption practices. More recently, the number of traditional adoptive parents has begun to shrink. At the same time, the Internet has played an important role in facilitating adoptions between childless couples and orphans, though abuses abound. According to incomplete and partial estimates in 1992, there were a total of 126,951 domestic adoptions, of which approximately 63,475 (50 percent) were nonrelative adoptions (Flango and Flango 1995, 1027).

Although colonial Americans derived their culture and laws from England, they departed from English practices in the area of adoption. English common law did not recognize adoption. English legal opposition to adoption stemmed from a desire to protect the property rights of blood relatives in cases of inheritance, a moral repugnance of illegitimacy, and the availability of other quasi-adoptive devices such as apprenticeship

and voluntary transfers. Consequently, it was not until 1926 that England enacted its first adoption statute. In contrast, what is noteworthy about the history of adoption in the United States is that at its inception, colonial Americans were less preoccupied with the primacy of biological kinship, practicing adoption on a limited scale and frequently "placing out" children as apprentices in what today we would call foster care. The fluid boundaries between consanguine and nonconsanguine families in colonial America led in some cases to the informal adoption of children, particularly in Puritan Massachusetts and Dutch New York.

Adoptive families increased in the second half of the nineteenth century under the impulse of the "orphan train" movement, a movement of home placement for urban poverty-stricken children begun by New York's Children's Aid Society (CAS). The group was founded in 1853 by the Reverend Charles Loring Brace, a transplanted New Englander and graduate of Yale Divinity School. In the following forty years, the CAS placed out 84,000 eastern children on orphan trains in the "western" states of Michigan, Ohio, Indiana, Iowa, Missouri, and Kansas. Middle-class farm families adopted some of these older children, roughly ten to thirteen years of age, though exactly how many is unknown.

The large-scale placing-out movement inaugurated by the widely imitated CAS had enormous consequences for the history of adoption and adoptive families. In fact, the origins of the first adoption laws in the United States can be partly traced to the increase in the number of middle-class farmers who wished to legalize the addition of a child to the family. In 1851, Massachusetts legislators passed an Act to Provide for the Adoption of Children. It is commonly considered the first modern adoption law. It codified earlier state court decisions that had transformed the law of custody to reflect Americans' new conceptions of childhood and parenthood, which emphasized the needs of children and the contractual and egalitarian nature of spouses' rights of guardianship.

The Massachusetts statute differed from all earlier statutes in its emphasis upon the welfare of the child by making the adopted person the prime beneficiary of the proceeding. Moreover, the evaluation of the parental qualifications of the adopters was introduced. The Massachusetts Adoption Act, as it was commonly called, was the first statute to establish the principle of judicial supervision of adoptions. The law required the judge, before issuing the decree, to ascertain that the adoptive parents were of sufficient ability to bring up the child and furnish suitable nurture and education and also required that the magistrate be satisfied that the adoption was "fit and proper." The concern for the child's welfare drew upon the "best interests of the child" doctrine, which had been evolving slowly in custody cases since the early 1800s and which would be the cornerstone of modern adoption law. In the next quarter of a century, as the Massachusetts Adoption Act came to be regarded as a model statute, twenty-five states enacted similar laws.

During the early twentieth century, in the Progressive Era (1900–1917), social workers initiated a child welfare reform movement that culminated with the growth of sectarian child welfare institutions, professionalization of social workers, standardization of adoption procedures, and an expanded state role in regulating adoptions. The implementa-

tion of this movement's goals—keeping families of origin together, ensuring biological parents' consent to the severing of kinship ties, thoroughly investigating adoptive parents and homes before placement, protecting the privacy of children born out of wedlock, and preventing third-party or independent adoptions, the practice by which doctors and lawyers placed children for adoption—became the raison d'être of professional social workers.

Child welfare reformers were successful in many respects. In the early twentieth century, these reformers began to lobby state legislatures to enact these goals into law. With respect to adoption, one of the most important legislative results of Progressive reformers was the Children's Code of Minnesota, enacted in 1917, which became the model for state laws in the next two decades. The Children's Code of Minnesota was the first state law that required an investigation to determine whether a proposed adoptive home was suitable for a child. It became the responsibility of the state's Board of Control to examine the adoption petition and advise the court in writing on every adoption case. The statute also provided for a six-month probationary period of residence by the child in the home of the adopting parents. Moreover, it ordered that adoption records be closed to inspection by the public but not to those directly involved in the adoption, namely the adoption triad: adopted persons, adoptive parents, and birth parents. This point needs to be underscored because it is commonly believed that throughout the history of U.S. adoption, state laws denied triad members access to their adoption records. Child welfare reformers hailed Minnesota's Children's Code as a model law.

Parents at the adoption proceedings for a nine-month-old adopted daughter. (Elizabeth Crews)

Child welfare advocates were also successful in lobbying many states for the removal of the word *illegitimate* from birth certificates and "inventing" the amended birth certificate to shield children from public opprobrium of their adoption. Although adoption workers instructed adoptive parents to tell their children they were adopted, an overwhelming majority never did. They lived in fear that their children, when they grew up, would request their birth certificates that would reveal that they were illegitimate, and hence adopted. In 1933, two enterprising registrars of vital statistics, Henry B. Hemenway and Sheldon L. Howard, proposed that when the name of the adopted child was changed, the clerk

of the court would forward the adoption decree to the state registrar of vital statistics, who would then make "a new record of the birth in the new name, and with the name or names of the adopting parent or parents" (Howard and Hemenway 1931, 646). Both the amended and original birth certificates, like other adoption records, were to be sealed from the public, but not from members of the adoption triad and the courts.

But adoption as a social institution did not grow. Acting as a counterweight to the reform of adoption practices was Americans' cultural definition of kinship, based on blood, which stigmatized adoption as socially unacceptable. Social workers had to overcome widespread popular prejudice toward adoption, in order to convince would-be adopters that taking a child into the home was not abnormal. During the late nineteenth and early twentieth centuries, a broad segment of the public in the United States believed that adoption was an "unnatural" action that created ersatz or second-rate families. The very language underscored the inferior nature of adoption: In popular discourse, adoptive parents were always juxtaposed with "natural" or "normal" ones. Discriminatory laws reinforced the notion that the adoptive relationship was inherently flawed. Jurists regularly ruled in inheritance cases, for example, that adoption violated the legal principle of consanguinity or blood ties. In practice, this meant that adopted children did not have the same inheritance rights as birth children. In other cases dealing with disputed custody rights of adopted children, both courts and legislatures favored natural parents' appeals to restore their children to them. Medical science contributed to popular cultural prejudices coupling adoption with the stigma of illegitimacy. After 1910 the rise of the eugenics movement and psychometric testing led adopted children to be linked to inherited mental defects, particularly criminality and feeblemindedness. These cultural and medical stigmatic aspects of adoption made many potential adopters extremely wary.

In addition to these zeitgeist worries, would-be adoptive parents also expressed practical worries about assuming the parental role. They had nightmares that the biological parents would show up on their doorstep. Adoption agencies required that prospective adoptive couples take children on a six-month to a year trial basis. Returns were common during the trial period. To some adoptive couples, "family" meant responsibilities and emotions and not a legal piece of paper; they were also reluctant to pay the high costs of making the adoption legal.

Based on the adoption case records of the Children's Home Society of Washington (CHSW) from 1896 to 1973 and on other sources, some generalizations can be made about adoptive parents' gender, age, social status, and income. The majority of adoptive parents were married couples aged twenty-five to thirty-five (Adamec and Pierce 2000, 20). Recent research, however, has revealed that during the first quarter of the twentieth century, it was not uncommon for single women to also be adoptive parents (Berebitsky 2000, chap. 4). Of the adoptive parents, some 80 percent of fathers worked at high-prestige jobs such as professionals or managers, foreman/skilled craftsmen, or proprietors of their own businesses. Before World War II, these CHSW adoptive parents had extremely high incomes, ranging from $9,000 to above $21,000, when the median income of 29 million American families in the 1930s was $1,160, supporting the public's contemporary perception that adoption was only for socially prominent, wealthy individuals (U.S. Bureau of the Census 1975; 275; Colby 1941, 40). CHSW's adoptive parents' high level of home ownership, averaging 80 percent, added to this perception. By the mid-1930s, social workers were actively denying the relationship and assuring the public that one need not be a millionaire to adopt a child. After World War II, CHSW's tendency of placing children with wealthy adoptive parents underwent significant change. A decided trend toward choosing middle-class families continued and increased until by the 1970s, instead of favoring the rich, the CHSW increasingly placed a majority of the children with middle-class adoptive parents with incomes below or slightly above the median of white, American families (Carp and Leon-Guerrero forthcoming).

Before World War II, the overwhelming majority of adoptive parents wanted to adopt a child for a variety of sentimental reasons, including a desire for companionship, wanting to start a family, a willingness to adopt (in contrast to indenture), their love of children, and a wish to act altruistically. They also had a decided preference in the child they wanted to adopt: girls. Researchers have speculated about why adoptive parents preferred girls. Proposed reasons include the belief that they were easier to raise than boys and the ultimate decision-making power of adoptive mothers who wanted girls for companionship.

Before 1930, adoptive parents preferred older children to infants. Some 19 percent of CHSW prospective adoptive parents preferred infants, 41 percent desired "older" children one to three years old, and 50 percent preferred a child over three years of age (Carp and Leon-Guerrero forthcoming). Adoption expert Sophie Van Senden Theis undertook a pioneering study in 1922. Examining 910 children placed in adoptive homes by the State Charities Aid Association of New York, she found that only 12 percent of the children were infants, that is, under one year old, and 30 percent were under three years of age. Thus, slightly more than 70 percent of the children placed by the SCAA were over three years old (Theis 1924, 13). Similarly, a study of 852 children adopted in Massachusetts between 1922 and 1925 revealed that 19 percent were under the age of one year (Parker 1927, 12–13).

The initial sign that the old order was changing was the decline during the 1920s and 1930s of the eugenic stigma surrounding adopted children, as studies demonstrated the successful social adjustment of adoptions, medical experts repudiated eugenic "science," and adoption agencies and the popular media assured adoptive parents that the "danger" of adoption had been largely obviated by scientific advance. The second sign that adoption practices were changing was the incremental practice after World War II by social workers and state bureaucrats to shroud adoption in secrecy. They acted for many reasons, including a desire to defend the adoptive process, protect the privacy of unwed mothers, increase their influence and power, and bolster social work professionalism by treating clients with psychoanalytic theory. The result was that after World War II, secrecy became pervasive, preventing those directly involved in adoption from gaining access to family information about their own lives.

Demographic changes after 1940, as adopted children's numbers and availability increased, accelerated the change in adoption practices. In addition to the continued high numbers of homes broken by death, divorce, and desertion, there occurred a veritable demographic explosion in the number of children born out of wedlock. With social bonds loosened by wartime, illegitimacy rates, especially among nonwhites, began to soar and continued their upward flight for the next forty years.

Prospective adoptive couples began to change their preferences from "older" child to infants and this "demand" by childless couples for newborns during the cold war was an additional factor leading to radical changes in traditional adoption practices. The baby boom, beginning in the mid-1940s and reaching its peak in the late 1950s, with its dramatic rise in marriages and births, was largely responsible for the increased demand for children to adopt and resulted in adoption agencies' being inundated with requests for children. Parenthood during the cold war became a patriotic necessity. The media romanticized babies, glorified motherhood, and identified fatherhood with masculinity and good citizenship. Uncomfortable at being childless and the subject of public opprobrium, an unprecedented number of childless couples sought to adopt as one solution to their shame of infertility.

Wartime prosperity, a postwar pronatalist climate of opinion, and medical advances in infertility diagnosis combined to produce a remarkable increase in the number of applications by childless couples to adopt a child. Between 1937 and 1945, adoptions had increased threefold, from 16,000 or 17,000 to 50,000 annually; a decade later the number of adoptions had nearly doubled again to 93,000 and by 1965 had climbed to 142,000, of which a third to a half were adoptions by relatives (Theis 1937, 23; Smith 1947, 24). In less than thirty years, the number of adoptive families had grown nearly ninefold. Overwhelmed with the number of applications and constricted by inflexible rules, adoption agencies aroused in childless couples much ill-will and resentment.

Meanwhile a revolution was occurring in adoption agency policies, which would have far-reaching effects on adoptive families. The causes were close to hand: They ranged from the pressure from would-be adoptive parents to alter their policies, to a deeply felt humanitarianism (spawned by a revulsion of atrocities

of World War II and Allied propaganda espousing the cause of democracy), to a response to demographic shifts in population and a consequent liberalization of race relations as over one million African Americans moved out of the South to northern and western cities.

Whatever the reason, nowhere were these changes more noticeable than in agencies' policies and practices toward the "adoptable" child, with the result of diversifying adoptive families. Before World War II, social workers refused to accept children with physical and mental handicaps in the belief that adoptive parents desired only "perfect" children. In the postwar era, social workers began to abandon the idea of the unadoptable child and broadened the definition of adoptability to include any child who needed a family and could develop within it and for whom a family could be found that would accept the child with his or her physical or mental capacities. With the enlarged definition of adoptability, social workers for the first time initiated serious efforts to place disabled, minority, older, and foreign-born children in adoptive homes. They discovered there were would-be adoptive couples in abundance eager to adopt the "unadoptable" child.

With the Child Welfare League of America (CWLA) taking the lead, minorities, especially dependent African American children, also soon felt the effects of the profession's expanded definition of *adoptable*. The war years represented a turning point in opening up the child welfare system in the United States to the idea of placing black children for adoption. Progress was slow. But years before *Brown* v. *Board of Education* (1954), and more than a decade before the civil rights movement, many of the nation's adoption agencies began placing an increasing number of African American children for adoption.

The end of World War II also witnessed the first phase of an upsurge of intercountry adoptions. In the immediate period after World War II, between 1946 and 1953, U.S. citizens and organizations such as International Social Services, American Branch, brought to the United States for adoption 5,814 foreign-born orphans and abandoned children, many from war-torn Greece, Germany, and Japan. Between the end of the Korean War in 1953 and 1962, the second phase of intercountry adoptions began, a period that ended only recently. In this period, for the first time in history, relatively large numbers of American couples adopted children who were racially and culturally different from themselves. Almost one-third of the 15,000 children adopted during this period and 65 percent of the additional 32,000 foreign-born children adopted by U.S. citizens in the following decade (1966–1976) came from Asia, primarily the Republic of Korea. Consequently, Korean children became the largest group of foreign adoptees within the United States and this nation the leading receiver of foreign children in the world (Altstein and Simon 1990, 3).

From the 1970s to the 1990s, adoptive families became even more diverse as a result of unanticipated racial, sexual, constitutional, and demographic changes in U.S. society. One trend that continued with renewed energy was the placement of special-needs children, especially African Americans, in adoptive homes. In 1967, the CWLA created the Adoption Resource Exchange of North America, an independent, national clearinghouse for hard-to-place children, which helped agencies find homes for almost 200 "spe-

cial-needs" or physically, emotionally, or mentally disabled children annually. By 1969, public and private adoption agencies' concerted efforts to find homes for minority children resulted in more than 19,000 children being placed. Eight percent or 14,000 of the 171,000 children adopted that year were African American (Carp 1998).

It was during this period that transracial families became prominent. The social work profession responded in a number of ways to increase special-needs adoption. In their vigorous recruitment efforts, agencies were surprised to discover that occasionally a white family would request a black infant for adoption or, when approached by caseworkers, agree to adopt a black baby. By 1965, transracial adoption had become the "little revolution," as agencies all over the nation increasingly placed black babies with white families. Four years later, the CWLA revised its *Standards* to reflect the new practice, unequivocally supporting it. In 1971, transracial adoptions reached their peak when 468 agencies reported 2,574 such placements (Carp 1998). The next year, the National Association of Black Social Workers, influenced by the Black Power movement with its emphasis on racial separatism, revolutionary violence, and black nationalism, denounced transracial adoption as cultural genocide. The organization was remarkably effective. Within three years, transracial adoptions had practically ceased in the United States, as child welfare workers preferred to keep African American children in foster care rather than place them with a white family, even though repeated studies demonstrated that transracial adoptions were successful. Concern over social workers' discriminatory practices prompted Congress to enact the Howard M. Metzenbaum Multiethnic Placement Act of 1994, which prohibited adoption agencies from denying any person the opportunity of becoming an adoptive parent based solely on the person's race, color, or national origin.

Social workers also failed to foresee in the 1970s the radical decline in the availability of white, out-of-wedlock infants for adoption, which resulted in some of the most important changes in adoption policy. A number of factors were responsible, including the 1960s sexual revolution, the Supreme Court's legalization of abortion in *Roe* v. *Wade* (1973), and unwed mothers' decisions not to relinquish their babies for adoption. As a result of these profound cultural, social, legal, and demographic changes in U.S. society, there was a substantial decline in the number of adoptions and adoptive families. Nonrelative adoptions in the United States fell from a record high of 89,200 in 1970 to 47,700 in 1975 and then rose slightly to 50,720 in 1982. They remained at about this level for the rest of the decade (Carp 1998). By 1975, adoption agencies across the nation began to stop taking applications from couples for healthy, white infants. Social workers often informed prospective adoptive parents that they would likely wait three to five years for such a child.

A second consequence of the 1970s demographic decline was again to diversify adoptive families and redefine the population of adoptable children, one that was more inclusive and less concerned with "matching" the physical, mental, racial, and religious characteristics of adopted children with adoptive parents. Increasingly, the population of adoptable children was composed of older children, members of minority groups, and special-needs children. In the 1990s, drug-exposed infants, children with acquired immunodeficiency syndrome (AIDS), and infants born human immunodeficiency virus (HIV) positive were added to the special-needs category. As social work agencies were unable to find adoptive homes or unable to free these children, numbering 100,000, legally for adoption, they became fixtures in foster care, where they were shunted from one caretaker to another (see the U.S. Children's Bureau web site at http://calib.com/naic/pubs/s foster.htm). This situation prompted Congress to pass the Adoption Assistance and Child Welfare Act of 1980, one of the first federal laws ever to address the problems of adopted children. "Permanency planning," as Congress's landmark legislation was soon referred to, had as its goal placing children in permanent homes, either by returning them to their family of origin or placing them in an adoptive home. Consequently, there has been an increasing number of older child and special-needs adoption since the 1980s.

As a result of the dearth of white, American-born infants and the rise of the adoption rights movement in the 1970s and 1980s, there was an increase in intercountry adoptions. These adoptions shifted from Korea in the 1950s to Latin America in the 1970s and 1980s and most recently to Russia and China. Intercountry adoptions now constitute a small but significant number of adoptions in the United States, numbering 18,234 or 14 percent of all adoptive placements (see the U.S. Department of State web site at http://travel.state.gov/orphan_numbers.html). Although such adoptions are popular among private agencies and prospective adoptive parents, numerous critics denounce them for failing to protect the rights of birth parents, encouraging trafficking of children for financial gain, and cultural genocide. Critics' objections were met in April 2000 with the signing by the United States of the Hague Convention, which regulates intercountry adoption by placing adoption agencies under the scrutiny of the international community.

Another outcome for adoptive families of the decline in healthy, white, out-of-wedlock infants and the movement to open adoption records was open adoption, a major and controversial innovation in adoption practice. In an effort to encourage birth mothers to relinquish their babies for adoption, caseworkers began experimenting with allowing birth mothers to make the decision about who would parent their children. The result was open adoption, in which the identities of birth and adoptive parents were exchanged and ongoing contact between the parties was encouraged. By the mid-1980s, open adoption had evolved into a continuum of interactions between birth mothers and adoptive parents ranging from simply an annual update on the child's welfare to having both parties actively engaged in raising the child. Open adoption has become increasing popular, commanding center stage in adoption practice. Between 1990 and 2000, a majority of adoption agencies in the United States had moved toward fully disclosed open adoptions.

Not surprisingly, the social revolution of the past thirty years has resulted in the decline of the traditional adoptive family. Thirty percent of adoptive parents are single mothers, and gay couples are increasingly winning the legal right to become adoptive parents (Stolley 1993, 37; Markey 1998, 721–722). And as an outgrowth of in vitro fertilization technology, researchers have developed "embryo adoption," in which an infertile couple can adopt a donated frozen embryo, bringing into question the very meaning of the institution of adoption. Such an embryo, created by combining a nongenetically related woman's egg and a man's sperm, is implanted into the uterus of the adopting mother who wants and is able to experience childbirth. Embryo adoption obviates the need for legal adoption because many state laws maintain that a woman who gives birth to a child is the biological parent. Adoptive families are also being formed on the Internet where dozens of web sites exist to help childless couples find orphans. All of these trends are likely to continue.

—*E. Wayne Carp*

See also Interracial Families; Orphan Trains

References and Further Reading
Adamec, Christine, and William L. Pierce. 2000. *Encyclopedia of Adoption.* 2d ed. New York: Facts on File.
Altstein, Howard, and Rita James Simon. 1990. "Introduction." In *Intercountry Adoption: A Multinational Perspective,* edited by Howard Altstein and Rita James Simon, xvi–xviii. New York: Praeger.
Berebitsky, Julie. 2000. *Like Our Very Own: Adoption and the Changing Culture of Motherhood, 1851–1950.* Lawrence: University Press of Kansas.
Carp, E. Wayne. 1998. *Family Matters: Secrecy and Adoption in the History of Adoption.* Cambridge: Harvard University Press.
Carp, E. Wayne, and Anna Leon-Guerrero. Forthcoming. "When in Doubt Count: World War II as a Watershed in the History of Adoption." In *Historical Perspectives on American Adoption,* edited by E. Wayne Carp. Ann Arbor: University of Michigan Press.
Colby, Mary Ruth. 1941. *Problems and Procedures in Adoption.* Children's Bureau Publication 262. Washington, DC: Government Printing Office.
Flango, Victor Eugene, and Carol R. Flango. 1995. "How Many Children

Were Adopted in 1992." *Child Welfare* 74 (Sept.-Oct.): 1018–1032.

Grotevant, Harold D., and Ruth G. McRoy. 1998. *Openness in Adoption: Exploring Family Connections.* Thousand Oaks, CA: Sage Publications.

Hollinger, Joan H., et al., eds. 1989. *Adoption in Law and Practice.* 2 vols. New York: Mathew Bender.

Howard, Sheldon L., and Henry B. Hemenway. 1931. "Birth Records of Illegitimates and of Adopted Children." *American Journal of Public Health* 21 (June): 643–647.

Markey, Karen. 1998. "An Overview of the Legal Challenges Faced by Gay and Lesbian Parents: How Courts Treat the Growing Number of Gay Families." *New York Law School Journal of Human Rights* 14 (Spring): 721–755.

Parker, Ida R. 1927. *"Fit and Proper"? A Study of Legal Adoption in Massachusetts.* Boston: Church Home Society for the Care of the Protestant Church.

Smith, I. Evelyn. 1947. "Adoption." In *Social Work Year Book 9*, 22–27. New York: Russell Sage Foundation.

Stolley, Kathy S. 1993. "Statistics on Adoption in the United States." *The Future of Children* 19, no. 1 (Spring): 26–42.

Theis, Sophie Van Senden. 1924. *How Foster Children Turn Out.* New York: State Charities Association.

Theis, Sophie Van Senden. 1937. "Adoption." In *Social Work Year Book 4*, 23–25. New York: Russell Sage Foundation.

U.S. Bureau of the Census. 1975. *Historical Statistics of the United States, Colonial Times to 1970.* Bicentennial ed., part I. Washington, DC: Government Printing Office.

Zainaldin, Jamil S. 1979. "The Emergence of a Modern American Family Law: Child Custody, Adoption and the Courts." *Northwestern University School of Law* 73 (February): 1038–1089.

Adultery

Traditionally and legally, adultery signifies consensual sexual intercourse between a married person and someone other than that person's lawful spouse.

Divorce laws in most of the United States were initially framed primarily in terms of the common-law tradition inherited from England, where ecclesiastical courts could grant permission to divorce only on the basis of adultery or abandonment. Criminal conversation, moreover, was the name eventually given in the Anglo-American legal tradition to civil suits that involved husbands' seeking financial compensation from wives' lovers for purported damages—alienation of affections, and so on—caused by adulterous relationships. Adultery, in fact, remains a crime in most states in the early twenty-first century, although the no-fault divorce system of the post–World War II era has made such laws largely irrelevant. Yet, despite radical changes resulting from the "sexual revolution" and the movement for women's rights, concerns about extramarital relationships did not disappear during the post–World War II period. Computer-based systems of telecommunication, particularly the Internet, together with the increased visibility of nonheterosexual relationships—as well as the high publicity surrounding the adultery-related impeachment proceedings of Pres. William Clinton—raised new debates in the United States about what kinds of behavior "count" as infidelity, along with questions about the very nature and meaning of marriage itself.

In many English colonies, religious precepts attempting to confine sexual activity to the marriage bed combined with more earthly concerns, such as inheritance rights and the need to maintain clear patrilinear lines of descent, to make adultery a serious offense. Such was especially true of those colonial settlements in which the family, and not the individual, was viewed as the basic element of a patriarchal social structure. Adultery

An illustration from Nathaniel Hawthorne's The Scarlet Letter, *showing Hester Prynne carrying her baby. (Bettmann/Corbis)*

was, in fact, a capital crime in colonies founded by Puritan sects, although apparently very few persons were ever executed. In each of the three recorded cases in which the death penalty was invoked, however, the "guilty party" was a woman. Given the patriarchal nature of most European cultures, married women were punished more severely and more frequently for any breach of marital fidelity than men were—both within the legal system and in many social and religious networks. As *The Scarlet Letter*, Nathaniel Hawthorne's famous novel of adultery, demonstrates, punishment in Puritan New England often involved some kind of public shaming rather than death—for example, whippings, brandings, or being forced, like Hester Prynne, to wear a letter A (or AD) on one's garments or to stand in the marketplace wearing a white sheet and confessing one's sins. Men were more likely than women to pay a fine rather than endure public punishment when convicted, having greater access both to money and cultural power.

Even in Puritan New England, however, marital norms were being established in a multicultural context. Puritan authorities expressed dismay not only at European settlers such as Thomas Merton, who attempted to establish at Merry Mount a community with more liberal rules for sexual behavior, but also at the practices of Native American tribes, which to the eyes of the Puritans seemed to condone various forms of adulterous behavior—including polygamy and unstigmatized separation and remarriage. Many scholars have noted, however, that in encountering this new but already populated continent, European settlers—whether English, French, or Spanish—may have exaggerated the differences between their own "civilized" marital norms and those of the "savage" native populations in order to justify their own colonization efforts.

Even among only the English colonies, moreover, differing socioeconomic conditions and settlement patterns dictated differing sexual attitudes and practices. The colonies of the Virginia and Chesapeake regions were initially settled not by family groups sharing a common religious vision, but by large numbers of unmarried men, many of whom were young, indentured servants, living on plantations and farms that were much more widely dispersed than those in the northern colonies. High mortality rates, a shortage of women, and the late marriages resulting from indentureship contracts all combined to create a much less stable Euro-

pean population for a longer period than in the North. Consequently, marriage was also a much less stable, enforceable institution in those white communities throughout the seventeenth century. Adultery was regarded as a crime, but the southern laws were less extensive, and, perhaps more important, the widely scattered and usually nonrelated European settlers were also both less able and less motivated to monitor the sexual activities of their neighbors. With clergy in short supply in many rural areas, people were more likely to form heterosexual unions without official legal marriage. The shortage of women, meanwhile, meant not only that women could easily find mates but also that their sexual crimes were almost certain to be less severely punished than in the North, which may have made engaging in adulterous behavior a fairly reasonable option—especially for those who found themselves in unsatisfactory marriages.

Slavery's increasing presence in the South further complicated the European tradition of enforcing monogamous marriage as the one acceptable site for sexual relations. Many African societies practiced polygamy, and some were more accepting of serial monogamy. Slavery, of course, ripped persons from their families and cultures, and once in the United States, African slaves faced not only the specific horrors of chattel slavery but also the same problematic conditions faced by Europeans: isolation, high mortality rates, a low ratio of black women to black men, and, therefore, late marital unions and low birthrates. Given the early shortage of white women and the increasing reliance on slavery for cheap labor instead of indentured servitude, some southern white males not surprisingly took African American women as mistresses or even formed marriages with them.

The law did not initially prohibit interracial marriage. As slavery became entrenched in the South, however, not only were interracial unions forbidden, but enslaved persons were also denied all rights to legal matrimony. In fact, after most southern colonies followed the precedent-setting 1662 Virginia law that determined that the child of one enslaved and one free adult should "follow the condition of the mother," there was a positive premium placed on interracial adultery for white, slave-owning men. Mary Boykin Chesnutt, an advocate of slavery from the planter class, rued the presence of the children resulting from these relationships in her Civil War diary: "Like the patriarchs of old our men live all in one house with their wives and their concubines, and the mulattoes one sees in every family exactly resemble the white children . . ." (Morris 1996, 24). It was this very sort of racial mixing and "immorality" that northern white abolitionists highlighted to help make the case against slavery prior to the Civil War. Such tactics, however, also often played into racialized sexual stereotypes that continued to serve to define white people, especially white women, as more "pure," more "civilized"—that is, less adulterous and less "adulterated"—than persons of other races. It is important to note, however, that despite differing traditions regarding "sexual purity" and serious impediments to the legal union of African American men and women, enslaved people typically formed strong kinship networks. These networks honored and supported long-term, exclusive, consensual unions, which not uncommonly lasted twenty years or more, even though they had no legal standing and

could be broken up at any time by a slaveholder's financial decisions, death, or whims.

During the eighteenth century, middle-class European settlers increasingly celebrated and affirmed ideals associated with what has come to be called a "companionate marriage," a union based on mutual love and affection as opposed to familial connections and financial concerns. During the revolutionary era, Americans were actively exploring the nature of all social contracts and the extent to which a people have the right to break free from what they view as an oppressive, "paternalistic" government. Thus, it is perhaps not surprising that after the Revolutionary War, a marital paradigm was frequently asserted to describe the union among the states—a metaphor that would become haunted by the threat of divorce during the Civil War. Many scholars have since argued that the founding, individualistic rhetoric of the United States created a climate in which the automatic authority granted to the patriarchal structure of traditional families was weakened. Many states created fairly liberal divorce laws, expanding the potential grounds of divorce well beyond traditional ones of adultery and abandonment. A consensus seemed to be developing in the middle classes that any marriage that did not promote both individual happiness and the good of society could be ended. Furthermore, many persons in the expanding, mobile young republic chose to live in "adulterous" states, as a significant portion of the population engaged in both "self-divorce" (by consensual separation or desertion) and informal (or common-law) marriage—and remarriage—although bigamy remained a criminal act. Many communities, particularly those of the working classes and on the frontier, accepted these unions without stigma, so long as basic levels of propriety were maintained.

By the mid-nineteenth century, however, most married American adults seemingly retained their belief in the goodness of monogamy—regardless of how strictly they may have actually practiced it—and certainly most still frowned upon open adultery, especially for women. Indeed, women's financial and social vulnerability, particularly after any sex-related scandal, allowed them, in some states, to achieve divorce on the grounds of a *false* charge of adultery. In addition, however, numerous small but highly visible minority groups actively pursued utopian living experiments, some of which were purposely adulterous by traditional standards. Intentional communities, including groups as diverse as the completely celibate Shakers and the "complex marriage" participants of the Oneida community in New York, can be viewed as a logical expression of the questioning of all social contracts that was suggested in the Declaration of Independence and other revolutionary documents. They were often, thus, centered on a radical questioning of familial bonds, marriage in particular, and all the traditional proscriptions created by this singular legal relationship. The Nashoba Community in Tennessee was probably the most radical of all such attempted utopias, in that it not only advocated sexual relations between any of its male and female members based on unconstrained free choice—regardless of marital status—but it was also interracial by the design of its founder, a Scots immigrant named Frances Wright. An independently wealthy woman, Wright believed that only amalgamation could possibly resolve racial divide in the United States.

Although Wright publicly advocated "free love," anyone who recommended even small changes to single, lifelong, monogamous marriage was liable to be labeled a "free lover." A widely misunderstood movement, both then and now, it did not mean that free love advocates necessarily sought free sexual relations with a large number of partners. Most of them, in fact, believed in various forms of sexual purity, which they viewed as deeply connected to spirituality. All believed, however, that love—given freely and without the interference or enforcement of legal matrimony—ought to be the basis for all sexual relations. Instead of viewing monogamous marriage as an almost sacred state, then, and adultery as the highest sin against it, "free love" partisans often viewed matrimony as a license for untrammeled masculine lust, subjecting the wife to a form of sexual slavery and creating an unhealthy atmosphere for children.

After the Civil War, as the frontier began to close, marriage in many ways reasserted itself in the form of stricter rules against experimental living arrangements, most notoriously represented by the battle against the Mormon polygamy, which was also widely equated with sexual despotism—specifically with that imagined to occur in the harems of Eastern, non-Christian, nonwhite cultures. At the same time, numerous highly publicized adultery cases made the headlines of major papers for weeks or even months at a time, especially a criminal conversation charge raised against Henry Ward Beecher in 1874. When statistics demonstrated in 1889 that the United States had the highest divorce rate in the world, moreover, many states severely restricted their divorce laws. Increasingly states sought once again to identify which party was at "fault" and on what grounds; South Carolina, in fact, completely prohibited the dissolution of marriage, and New York reduced the acceptable grounds of divorce to include only one: adultery.

Moving back onto this familiar ground for divorce proceedings did not succeed, however, in reducing the rate of divorce in the decades that followed. Many couples seeking to divorce would simply tell the "legal fiction" necessary to achieve their goal, and others would temporarily move to a more liberal divorce state, desert their spouse completely, or even openly commit adultery to break an undesired marital bond. By the twentieth century, as sexuality was increasingly detached from purely reproductive ends and tied to the pursuit of personal happiness, terms such as *marital infidelity* and *extramarital affair* began to take the place of the term *adultery*, which began to have more strictly religious connotations. The long separations of spouses during World War II nevertheless raised widespread fears of wartime infidelity— both at home and abroad—with a few widely publicized cases of wives having taken up with new mates in the absence of their soldier-husbands, not surprisingly serving as a kind of scapegoat for postwar anxieties about reshaping the U.S. social world for peacetime.

Although the postwar reassertion of the "traditional" family created both marriage and baby booms, those were echoed by a loud divorce boom. The sexual revolution and the feminist movement that followed in the 1960s and 1970s combined to liberalize divorce laws and, further, to introduce such concepts as "swinging," "key parties," and "open marriage." Indeed, in almost a mockery of the religious underpinnings of adultery, journalist Gay Talese entitled his best-selling report on Sandstone, an upper-class sexual retreat in California, *Thy Neighbor's Wife* (1980). Yet, even as the gay rights movement also began to question the status of marriage as a strictly heterosexual privilege, groups such as the Christian Coalition built upon the work of the Moral Majority in the 1970s to call for a return to "traditional family values," seeking to bring back fault-based divorce and to restigmatize all forms of nonmarital sexuality, including adultery. With the Defense of Marriage Act of 1996 and various highly publicized cases of marital infidelity— including those of several presidents— both marriage and adultery remained, at the beginning of the twenty-first century, highly symbolic institutions for many Americans, serving as flashpoints for conflicting views of both individual freedom and the very nature of the social order.

—Lori Askeland

See also Divorce, History of; Mormon Polygamy; The Oneida Community; Shaker Family

References and Further Reading
Cott, Nancy F. 2000. *Public Vows: A History of Marriage and the Nation.* Cambridge: Harvard University Press.
D'Emilio, John, and Estelle B. Freedman. 1988. *Intimate Matters: A History of Sexuality in America.* New York: Harper and Row.
Grossberg, Michael. 1985. *Governing the Family: Law and the Family in Nineteenth-Century America.* Chapel Hill: University of North Carolina Press.
Korobkin, Laura Hanft. 1998. *Criminal Conversations: Sentimentality and Nineteenth-Century Legal Stories of Adultery.* New York: Columbia University Press.
May, Elaine Tyler. 1980. *Great Expectations: Marriage and Divorce in*

Post-Victorian America. Chicago: University of Chicago Press.

Mintz, Steven, and Susan Kellogg. 1988. *Domestic Revolutions: A Social History of Family Life.* New York: The Free Press.

Morris, Thomas D. 1996. *Southern Slavery and the Law, 1619–1860.* Chapel Hill: University of North Carolina Press.

Affection as a Basis for Marriage

The idea of marriage as an affectionate partnership affected middle- and upper-class men and women on both sides of the Atlantic beginning in the seventeenth century. Ideally, companionate marriage permitted individual choice in marriage based on personal affection and sexual attraction and encouraged loving, rather than authoritarian, relationships between husbands and wives.

Although Americans valued affection as a basis for marriage from the earliest days of settlement, colonial Americans, wary of unrestrained emotions, attempted to regulate their emotions and to achieve a family life characterized by tranquillity and harmony rather than by passion and desire. Moreover, colonial Americans, viewing the family as "a little commonwealth," organized family life along the hierarchical principles of patriarchy—a pattern in which the relationship of husband to wife reflected that between king and subject (Demos 1970).

The ideal of affectionate relationships became more pronounced in the revolutionary era, when "the American revolution against patriarchal authority" encouraged couples to view intimate relationships, like citizenship, as a matter of individual choice (Fliegelman 1982). For increasing numbers of Americans, "the pursuit of happiness" included the quest for a mutually fulfilling relationship of love and respect (Lewis 1983).

Courtship patterns in the United States in the eighteenth and nineteenth centuries reflected this new ideal. Abandoning such traditions as chaperonage and marrying daughters off in birth order, increasing numbers of Americans granted young men and women a degree of freedom from parental direction and supervision in order to enable them to evaluate their chances for happiness with potential mates. Although parents, relatives, neighbors, and advice-book authors all urged young lovers to marry within their own race, class, and religion, romantic love was becoming the most important factor in courtship as well as in marriage.

For those for whom marital bliss proved to be only an illusion, divorce increasingly was an option. Divorce decrees reflected the increasingly popular belief that affection was a necessary ingredient in a marriage. Between the American Revolution and the Civil War, states passed new divorce laws that extended the grounds for divorce from adultery, desertion, and cruelty to permit the dissolution of unions marred by neglect, jealousy, and simple unkindness.

Notwithstanding the glorification of marriage in the nineteenth-century United States, a growing proportion of the population was single, either as the result of divorce or as the result of avoiding marriage in the first place. For increasing numbers of Americans, singlehood appeared a desirable alternative to marriage without love; for women in antebellum America, the "cult of single blessedness" sanctioned the choice to delay marriage or evade it entirely (Chambers-Schiller 1984, 10).

The shift "from patriarchy to companionship" was neither swift nor complete

Young married couple expecting their first child. (Elizabeth Crews)

(Griswold 1982, 1). Well into the nineteenth century, couples struggled with the contradictions of companionship, finding that their commitment to conjugal mutuality conflicted with their belief in male authority. For many couples—particularly, although not exclusively, in the slaveholding South—the persistence of "domestic patriarchy" undermined the ideal of companionship (Kulikoff 1986, 165).

The conflict between affection and authority that was so evident in the lives of nineteenth-century couples such as Virginians Elizabeth and William Wirt (Jabour 1998) continued to hinder couples' quest for marital happiness in the twentieth century. As the century progressed, guidebooks and marriage experts laid ever-greater emphasis on the importance of both sexual and emotional satisfaction in marriage even as rising birthrates pitted reproductive and romantic imperatives against each other. In the years following World War II, in particular, the postwar generation, anxious about the cold war, turned to home and family as secure anchors in an insecure world.

Despite—or, perhaps, because of—the tremendous significance with which modern American culture imbued marriage, twentieth-century couples often experienced difficulty in achieving either personal fulfillment or the much-vaunted togetherness idealized by the baby boom generation. In surveys conducted at mid-century, husbands and wives revealed dramatically different perceptions of their relationships, with husbands recording satisfaction with their marriages and wives exposing deep dissatisfaction (May 1988, 193). Although husbands valued the security they found in marriage, wives complained that their husbands were cold and distant, failing to give their mates the assurance of affection that the companionate ideal had promised.

In the closing decades of the twentieth century, as in the mid-nineteenth century, rising divorce rates testified both to the high standards that Americans held for marital satisfaction and to their willingness to end relationships that did not provide them with the affection and happiness that they expected from marriage.

—*Anya Jabour*

See also The Companionate Family; Courtship, History of; Divorce, History of; Extended Family; Family Decline in the Twentieth Century; Gender Roles in the American Family; Marriage; Sanger, Margaret

References and Further Reading

Bleser, Carol, ed. 1991. *In Joy and in Sorrow: Women, Family, and Marriage in the Victorian South, 1830–1900*. New York: Oxford University Press.

Chambers-Schiller, Lee Virginia. 1984. *Liberty a Better Husband: Single Women in America: The Generations of 1780–1840*. New Haven: Yale University Press.

Demos, John. 1970. *A Little Commonwealth: Family Life in Plymouth Colony*. New York: Oxford University Press.

Fliegelman, Jay. 1982. *Prodigals and Pilgrims: The American Revolution against Patriarchal Authority*. Cambridge: Cambridge University Press.

Griswold, Robert L. 1982. *Family and Divorce in California, 1850–1890: Victorian Illusions and Everyday Realities*. Albany: State University of New York Press.

Jabour, Anya. 1998. *Marriage in the Early Republic: Elizabeth and William Wirt and the Companionate Ideal*. Baltimore: Johns Hopkins University Press.

Kulikoff, Allan. 1986. *Tobacco and Slaves: The Development of Southern Cultures in the Chesapeake, 1680–1800*. Chapel Hill: University of North Carolina Press.

Lewis, Jan. 1983. *The Pursuit of Happiness: Family and Values in Jefferson's Virginia*. New York: Cambridge University Press.

Lystra, Karen. 1989. *Searching the Heart: Women, Men, and Romantic Love in Nineteenth-Century America*. New York: Oxford University Press.

May, Elaine Tyler. 1988. *Homeward Bound: American Families in the Cold War Era*. New York: Basic Books.

Riley, Glenda. 1991. *Divorce: An American Tradition*. New York: Oxford University Press.

Rothman, Ellen K. 1984. *Hands and Hearts: A History of Courtship in America*. New York: Basic Books.

Spurlock, John C., and Cynthia A. Magistro. 1998. *New and Improved: The Transformation of American Women's Emotional Culture*. New York: New York University Press.

Stone, Lawrence. 1977. *The Family, Sex and Marriage in England, 1500–1800*. London: Weidenfeld and Nicolson.

Weiss, Jessica. 2000. *To Have and to Hold: Marriage, the Baby Boom and Social Change*. Chicago: University of Chicago Press.

African American Families

African American families are Americans of African descent linked in intimate associations by bonds of ancestry, marriage, informal or formal adoption, or mutual consent. African American families are characterized by diversity in family structure and social class. While fulfilling their traditional functions of procreation and socialization, these families have served as buffers against widespread racism and oppression. Some critics, assuming that there is a homogenous culture in the United States, have argued that African American families are pathological, deviant, and dysfunctional. When considered in its own right, however, African American family life reflects ongoing and successful adaptation to social, political, and economic conditions in American society. Responses to slavery, emancipation, segregation, disfranchisement, migration, and the transition from rural agricultural to urban industrial lifestyles argue for the uniqueness and resiliency of these families.

African American families trace their origin to individuals who migrated from West and Central Africa to the Americas as a result of the Atlantic slave trade. From the sixteenth to the nineteenth centuries, from 9 to 12 million men, women, and children were transported to the Western Hemisphere. About one-third perished in the Atlantic crossing. African laborers supplemented and eventually replaced Native American and European contract workers in the mines and on farms and plantations throughout

An African American family at the Hermitage, a plantation in Savannah, Georgia. (Library of Congress)

the Western Hemisphere. Millions of African families and communities were disrupted in the warfare that generated this labor force.

European and African cultural concerns and labor needs meant that two-thirds of Africans transported to the Western Hemisphere were men. This gender disparity had an impact on family structure in Africa as well as on family formation in the New World. In Africa, the presence of large numbers of unprotected enslaved women in African communities resulted in changes in the institution of marriage and a decline in the status of women. In the Americas, the first generation of Africans had difficulty establishing families and maintaining African traditions of family life. Colonial masters in the Caribbean and South America depended on the continual migration of Africans to maintain their labor force. But in North America slave populations increased naturally with the establishment of stable family life by the early 1700s.

Africans in North America adapted their African customs and values to New World settings. Family was the basis of social, economic, and political life in

African societies. Lineage was traced matrilineally or patrilineally, and families included all living descendants of the same ancestor. Matrilineal descent guaranteed women influential positions in some societies. Queen mothers determined political succession and managed the affairs of their towns. Women also exercised complementary social, political, and economic authority in African families and communities. A husband was expected to guarantee his wife's good treatment and pay compensation for taking her away from her family. Polygyny was not universally practiced but where it did exist, women shared household and conjugal duties, and child rearing was the responsibility of a broad extended network of kin. Kin networks sometimes extended across villages to form clans that claimed common ancestry.

The extent to which African constructions of family survived the transatlantic slave trade and American slavery has been debated by numerous scholars. Some argue that there is no reliable evidence that African culture had any influence on the development of the African American family, since African American slaves retained only vague memories of the traditions of their African parents, had little opportunity to re-create African family life, and were subjected to influences that tended to destroy the cultural context of African traditions. Other scholars suggest, however, that African American slaves retained memories of African constructions of family and that these memories shaped African American family life. Factors such as time, location, the organization of plantation labor, and the demographics of the internal and import slave trade, as well as colonial and state slave codes, affected the extent to which Africans and African Americans

were able to create and sustain families and the degree to which they were able to perpetuate African traditions.

African-born slaves understood "family" in the African context in which marriage united lineages and fertility was prized. The first generations of African slaves in most of the mainland British colonies were often scattered over frontier agricultural communities or in urban households, where they worked and lived alongside Native American and European indentured laborers. They had few opportunities to form families based solely on African traditions. In the Carolina colonies, however, where planters brought larger numbers of African slaves from the West Indies to more secluded lowland and island plantations, Africans and African Americans had more opportunities to form families and to perpetuate African constructions of family life. Permanent, chattel slavery was recognized in mainland colonial laws by the end of the seventeenth century. Black children inherited their status as slaves or free persons from their mothers. Black family life was framed by the slave codes of individual colonies and the economic fortunes and personal discretion of slaveholders. Yet within these parameters, Africans and African Americans adapted African family traditions to hereditary, racialized slavery.

The creation and perpetuation of slave families benefited both owners and slaves. Family units were at the core of a slave's personal life. Family life provided slaves with a supportive environment for dealing with oppression, a basis for community development, and an opportunity for creating African American culture. Enslaved men and women alone, or with the input of their owners, chose spouses from their own plantation community or among slaves on neighboring farms or plantations. Marriage ceremonies ranged from informal rites performed by older slave men or women to services performed by white ministers in the presence of slave owners, their families, and the slave community. "Jumping the broom" together symbolized the union of enslaved men or women; but it also reflected the informality of slave marriages. Although many slaves, especially on large plantations in the Deep South, lived in two-partner households, slave marriages had no legal standing and could be dissolved at the discretion of the master. Allowing slaves to establish families strengthened the plantation regime by promoting the growth of the slave population and restraining opposition to the owner's authority. Separation from family members was a slave's worst fear.

In the early nineteenth century many slave families were disrupted by the expansion of cotton cultivation. Families created by "abroad" marriages (in which the husband and wife lived in different places) were divided when individual owners moved west. Other families were separated when slave owners in the Old South sold surplus laborers to planters in developing agricultural regions west of the Appalachian Mountains. "Slave breeding" existed in some places, with owners forcing women into sexual relationships to produce children for sale in the profitable internal trade. "Dr. Ware had a fine man he bred his colored house women to," one slave woman interviewed in the 1930s remembered. "He was hostler, looked after the stock and got wood. The women hated him, and the men of the place done as well. They hated him too" (Rawick 1972, 119).

Family life on some Deep South plantations was relatively stable throughout the nineteenth century. Many slaves lived in two-parent families surrounded by real and fictive kin. African American families on large plantations were housed in single or double cabins arranged along a street near the master's house or in "quarters" some distance from the main house. On smaller farms, families lived with their owners or in cabins close to the owner's house. Husbands and wives contributed emotionally and materially to the well-being of their families, but their roles varied from place to place. Fertility rates were higher among second- and third-generation African American women than they had been for the African women, but infant and maternal mortality rates were high. Poor nutrition, overwork, and inadequate child care accounted for many deaths. Mothers often took nursing babies to the field while older children were left in the slave quarters in the care of elderly women or slave children who were not old enough to do fieldwork.

Childhood was short for slave children. Children began doing minor chores around the plantation house or in the quarters when they were ten or twelve years old. They entered the plantation workforce as quarter- or half-hands in their early teens and as full hands by their late teens. Entry into the plantation workforce separated a child from parental protection and authority. Although children were socialized to servitude, parents tried to maintain influence in their children's lives or to shield them from abuse. Many children, however, could not escape personal attacks from their owners, nor could they avoid seeing their parents whipped or humiliated.

Free African Americans presented another view of black family life in the antebellum period. By 1860, there were nearly half a million nonslave African

Americans almost evenly divided between the northern and southern states. The free black population was a product of natural increase as well as manumission, escape, and self-purchase. Free blacks had a major impact on the development of African American culture, communities, and politics. Although free blacks could legally marry and own property, most southern states restricted their movements and associations. Some free blacks owned slaves. But most of these slaves were family and friends who had been purchased with the goal of either manumitting them or allowing them to live as free persons. Many free blacks remained in the South because of these family connections. Some were still married to slaves, others had children, parents, or siblings who remained in bondage.

Free black families adopted middle-class, white American definitions of gender roles in which men were protectors and providers for their families and communities and women were guardians of the household. Although most lived in double-headed families, the number of female-headed households increased over time. Free black women who remained single controlled their own wages, property, and families. Since free black women in urban communities were generally confined to low-paying jobs as household or domestic servants, however, their poverty made family life precarious. Women who could not support their families risked losing their children to forced indentures or apprenticeships.

The Civil War brought dramatic changes for African American families, particularly southern slave families. Individually and with friends and kin, thousands of enslaved men, women, and children ran away from their owners and made their way to the sanctuary of Union lines. Thousands of fugitive slaves were housed in hastily constructed "contraband" camps near Union army camps. Union military officials, however, had a greater need for able-bodied black men to serve as laborers and soldiers than for the women and children who accompanied them to the camps.

African Americans were encouraged to legitimize relationships they had established in plantation marriage ceremonies. Freedmen were recruited into the Union army, and women who were not legally married were excluded from the contraband camps. Women who had no means of support were encouraged to sign labor contracts for themselves and their children and sent back to rural farms and plantations. Some women, however, found jobs as cooks, washerwomen, nurses, and domestic servants and remained in urban communities in the South.

African American families were the basis of institution-building in the post–Civil War South. Schools, churches, and other community organizations were the centers of black family life. Political activity was also rooted in family life. Black women and children accompanied their husbands and fathers to political rallies and participated in Fourth of July parades and celebrations. Black leaders such as Frederick Douglass, Frances Ellen Watkins Harper, and Sojourner Truth supported suffrage but were divided over whether black male suffrage should be sacrificed when proposals for the Fifteenth Amendment excluded women. Douglass saw the vote in terms of the protections it would bring to all African Americans. Truth, however, was concerned that black male suffrage might lead to black women's exchanging white masters for black masters. Yet Harper felt that when black men exercised suffrage rights, they did so not as individual owners of a ballot but as agents of their families.

In the aftermath of emancipation, African American families were transformed from female-centered structures existing within white patriarchal households to double-parent nuclear families led by black men. Single-parent households composed of nonrelatives were rare, particularly in rural areas. African American nuclear families in rural areas, however, often functioned within broad kinship networks. In times of crisis these extended families housed relatives or friends, provided emotional and financial assistance, or adopted the children of deceased or lost relatives. Black men asserted control in their families by demanding respect for the women in their families and removing women from the direct control of white overseers and landowners, protesting the unfair application of state apprenticeship laws, and negotiating labor agreements as heads of their family units. Although many black women supported male authority as protectors and providers, they rejected the assertion of male hegemony through physical abuse and neglect of themselves and their children and adultery.

African American families were also affected by changes in southern labor systems after the emancipation. Most black farmers were unable to realize their goal of acquiring land in the post–Civil War South. Instead, they turned to sharecropping as an alternative to wage labor. Sharecropping enabled rural families to work together on sections of farmland for a share of the profits. Many hoped that they might eventually accumulate enough money to purchase their own farms. Sharecropping arrangements also recognized the authority of black men to make

economic decisions for their families. Fathers negotiated contracts that obligated the entire family to labor for a particular landowner. The sharecropper family provided the labor, and the landowner provided the land, seed, equipment, and fertilizer as well as food, housing, and supplies. The landowner sold the crop and retained his or her share of the profit, usually one-half to two-thirds, plus whatever costs were advanced for seed, equipment, and other supplies. The rest was given to the sharecropper. Sharecroppers had little control over the prices landowners charged for the seed, equipment, food, and other supplies they provided, nor were most sharecroppers involved in the sale of the crop. Many families were trapped in endless cycles of indebtedness and rural poverty.

In some African American families, black women withdrew from the rural labor force to concentrate on household and child-care responsibilities. But black women who did not do fieldwork were ridiculed as lazy. White landowners tried to coerce African American families to put all able-bodied members into fieldwork. In reality, most farm women did fieldwork, but at the discretion of their own families, not the demands of white landowners. Some women also did paid domestic labor in white households. African American children in sharecropping families remained an important part of the family labor force.

The African American population shifted dramatically in the late nineteenth and early twentieth centuries from predominantly rural and southern to increasingly urban and national. The "great exodus" of the late 1870s and later migrations in the 1890s drew African Americans to states and territories in the Midwest and Far West. By 1910 blacks made up about 5–10 percent of populations in some midwestern cities (Hine et al. 2000, 382) and about 33 percent of some southern urban populations (Trotter 2001, 307). Although some African Americans were able to find industrial jobs during this period, most were confined to the domestic and service occupations of their parents and grandparents.

The Great Migration of the twentieth century drew even larger numbers of African American families to cities outside the South. Poverty and low wages, discrimination and racial violence, and the expansion of northern industry were motivations for this migration. Southern blacks were also encouraged to leave by friends and relatives, by African American newspapers, and by recognition of their political and civil rights and the prospect of better education for their children. The Great Migration began about 1915 and continued until the end of World War II. About 700,000 to 1 million African Americans left the South for northern and western cities during World War I; another 800,000 to 1 million migrated during the 1920s, nearly 400,000 in the 1930s, and about 1.5 million in each decade of the 1940s and 1950s. By 1960 5 million African Americans had abandoned the South for the North, Midwest, or Far West (Palmer 1998, 157).

Leaving the South was a family decision, since it required emotional and material support, often meant periods of long separation, and could possibly result in the eventual migration of other family members. Most migrants were poor or working-class people who had few resources and depended on family and kin already relocated to help find them housing and jobs in the cities. Men usually worked their way north, stopping in various towns and cities along the way,

then sent for their families to join them. Women made a single trip, sometimes accompanied by a relative or with kin or friends waiting to receive them.

Migration altered the structure of African American families and the configuration of black households. Most households had been male-headed and based on kinship and marital ties. Urban households, however, were more likely than rural households to include friends and boarders. Households headed by women were likely to be the result of death, divorce, or desertion. Many migrants created surrogate families to cushion their adjustment to urban life. Boarders, employers, coworkers, church or club members, and neighbors acted as unofficial parents or godparents, siblings, aunts, or uncles. For some urban black migrants, surrogate family members provided the emotional and economic support important to large extended families in rural communities. Urban black families also included younger or older female relatives who came to assist with child care or young children who were also sent north to be educated. Although children's labor was important to the economic well-being of migrant families, African American parents frequently took extra jobs so that their children could stay in school.

Many migrants maintained ties to family in the South by sending their children for summer visits, making trips home, or bringing family members for visits. These visits were particularly important for women who left children with relatives when they came north. In her study of the gender implications of migration in the Midwest, Darlene Clark Hine found that absentee mothering made adjustment to urban life a long, drawn-out, and often incomplete process (Hine

1991). Women who left children in the South maintained emotional ties to their families through correspondence and frequent visits. Despite the pressures of migration and adjustment to new urban lifestyles, however, most migrant families were intact, two-parent households.

African American families suffered more in the economic upheaval of the 1920s and 1930s and received less from government programs than did other American families. Rural black laborers suffered from declining incomes and from landowners who cut back on supplies to sharecroppers. African American landowners were hurt by declining prices, and many lost their farms because of their insolvency. The unemployment rate for blacks was roughly twice that for whites. Urban black workers were often unable to find employment or had to take jobs at reduced wages. They were the first fired when factories and businesses experienced economic downturns. The jobless rate for African American men in urban areas ranged from 40 percent in Chicago to 60 percent in Detroit. In southern cities, economic conditions were even more dire, with 80 percent of black workers in Norfolk, Virginia, seeking welfare in the mid-1930s (Hine et al. 2000, 420).

Many African Americans continued to depend on kinship- and community-based institutions for help during the Depression. African American women "creatively manipulated" family resources, took in boarders, and cared for each other's children or for the sick and elderly. Families living in tenements shared bathroom facilities and household utensils, bartered or exchanged goods and services, or held rent parties. In rural areas, African American families kept gardens, canned fruits and vegetables, fished, or hunted to supplement families' food supplies.

In the 1930s, Pres. Franklin Roosevelt's New Deal programs provided relief to some African American families. African American efforts at receiving relief were frequently unsuccessful or inadequate, however, since federal relief programs were grounded in the customary and legal segregation of the period. Only about 5 percent of slots in the Civilian Conservation Corps (CCC) went to African American men and boys in the first year of its operation, but those who enlisted sent money home to help support their families (Hine et al. 2000, 427). As director of the National Youth Administration (NYA) Division of Negro Affairs, educator Mary McLeod Bethune also promoted educational programs and organized two conferences to examine the problems of African American youth. Although New Deal programs such as the Farm Credit Administration (FCA) and the Federal Housing Administration (FHA) helped some African American families hold on to family farms or get mortgages for new homes, programs such as the Agricultural Adjustment Act (AAA), the National Recovery Administration (NRA), and the Social Security Act (SSA) maintained the economic and social status quo. White landowners pocketed AAA payments intended to help all farm families and evicted sharecropping families. The SSA excluded domestic and agricultural workers, the labor categories in which a disproportionate number of African Americans were concentrated. Businesses that worked out codes of fair business practice under the NRA paid black workers lower wages or, in occupations in which blacks predominated, shifted to white workers when forced to negotiate wage increases.

African American families were affected by the widespread social, political, and economic changes in society in the United States from the 1940s through the 1960s. African American families benefited from widespread employment of men and women during World War II. U.S. industries relaxed their resistance to black workers, and 600,000 black women shifted from domestic to industrial labor. Nearly a million black men entered the military service during the war. The war also spurred more migrations, and by 1950 only 68 percent of African Americans remained in the South (Hine et al. 2000, 482). The dismantling of Jim Crow segregation and elimination of restrictions on black voters in the South brought more blacks into the American mainstream. But African American families have experienced a dramatic deterioration since the 1960s. Until the 1960s, 75 percent of black families were double-headed; however, there has been a sharp rise in female-headed households since 1970 (Billingsley 1992, 36). Continuing discrimination in employment, abusive family environments, and crime are among a myriad of causes of this shift in family structure. Daniel Patrick Moynihan described this trend in his 1965 study, *The Negro Family: The Case for National Action* (Moynihan 1965). Drawing on the earlier work of sociologist E. Franklin Frazier (Frazier 1966), Moynihan suggested that African American families were vulnerable because of past discrimination and exploitation, the strain of urbanization, and persistent unemployment. These forces weakened the role of black males and led to a disproportionate number of dysfunctional female-headed households. Critics of the Moynihan report countered that there had been a preference for two-parent families among African Americans throughout much of their history and that

An African American family at the beach. (RNT Productions/Corbis)

African American family structure (including female-headed households) reflected functional adaptation to racism and discrimination. Historians such as Herbert Gutman, Deborah Gray White, and John Blassingame countered charges that female-headed households were dysfunctional with evidence that Frazier and Moynihan may have underestimated the prevalence of two-parent families in the past.

In the last two decades of the twentieth century, scholars and politicians continued to describe a crisis among African American families as the number of female-headed households grew. By the early 1980s, 40 percent of black families with related children under eighteen were headed by women (St. Jean and Feagin 1998). Fifty percent of black children lived in female-headed households (Hine et al. 2000, 566). The number of African American families in poverty increased in the 1970s, declined slightly by the mid-1980s, but rose again by 1990. By 1993, one-third of African Americans were poor, and nearly half of all poor black persons were children under eight years of age (U.S. Bureau of the Census, "The Black Population," 2001). In the 1980s, these statistics lent support to the myth of single-parent American families as consisting of black teenage unwed mothers and their households living on welfare payments.

By the end of the twentieth century, many scholars and politicians were convinced that there was an African American family crisis consisting of a cluster of conditions including poverty, domestic violence, homelessness, criminal behavior, suicide, homicide, physical and mental illness, sexually transmitted diseases and acquired immunodeficiency syndrome (AIDS), unemployment, working mothers, marital conflicts, stress, divorce, single parenthood, teenage pregnancy, and substance abuse. Although none of these conditions is exclusive to African American families, all are more common and debilitating among African American families than among others. Suggestions for dealing with this crisis ranged from restructuring the federal welfare system with the Personal Responsibility Act of 1996 to providing community support for single mothers and female-headed households to appreciating the diversity in African American family structure.

—*Beverly Greene Bond*

See also Courtship, History of; Extended Family

References and Further Reading
Allen, Walter R., and Angela D. James. 1998. "Comparative Perspectives on Black Family Life: Uncommon Explorations of a Common Subject." *Journal of Comparative Family Studies* 29(1): 1–12.
Anderson, Karen. 1991. "African American Families." In *American Families: A Research Guide and Historical Handbook,* edited by Joseph M. Hawes and Elizabeth I. Nybakken, 259–290. New York: Greenwood Press.
Billingsley, Andrew. 1992. *Climbing Jacob's Ladder: The Enduring Legacy of African American Families.* New York: Simon and Schuster.
Blassingame, John W. 1972. *The Slave Community: Plantation Life in the Antebellum South.* New York: Oxford University Press.
Franklin, John Hope. 1980. *From Slavery to Freedom: A History of Negro Americans.* New York: Alfred A. Knopf.
Frazier, E. Franklin. 1966. *The Negro Family in the United States.* Chicago: University of Chicago Press.
Gutman, Herbert G. 1976. *The Black Family in Slavery and Freedom, 1750–1925.* New York: Vintage Books.
Hine, Darlene Clark. 1991. "Black Migration to the Urban Midwest: The Gender Dimension, 1915–1945." In *The Great Migration in Historical Perspective: New Dimensions of Race, Class, and Gender,* edited by Joe William Trotter, 127–146. Bloomington: Indiana University Press.
Hine, Darlene Clark, et al. 2000. *The African-American Odyssey.* Upper Saddle River, NJ: Prentice Hall.
Mann, Susan A. 1989. "Slavery, Sharecropping, and Sexual Inequality." *Signs* 14 (Summer): 774–798.
Moynihan, Daniel Patrick. 1965. *The Negro Family: The Case for National Action.* Washington, DC: Government Printing Office.
Palmer, Colin A. 1998. *Passageways: An Interpretive History of Black America.* Vol. 2. Fort Worth, TX: Harcourt Brace College Publishers.
Phillips, Kimberley L. "'But It Is a Fine Place to Make Money': Migration and

African-American Families in Cleveland, 1915–1929." *Journal of Social History* 30(2): 393–415.

Rawick, George, ed. 1972. *The American Slave: A Composite Autobiography.* Vol. 2, pt. 1: *Arkansas Narratives.* Westport, CT: Greenwood Press.

Schiele, Jerome H. 1998. "The Personal Responsibility Act of 1996: The Bitter and the Sweet for African American Families." *Families in Society: The Journal of Contemporary Human Services* 79(4): 424–413.

St. Jean, Yanick, and Joe R. Feagin. 1998. "The Family Costs of White Racism: The Case of African American Families." *Journal of Comparative Family Studies* 29(1): 297.

Trotter, Joe William, Jr. 2001. *The African American Experience.* Vol. 2. Boston: Houghton Mifflin Company.

U.S. Bureau of the Census. "The Black Population." http://www.census.gov/ population (cited 7 January 2001).

U.S. Bureau of the Census. "Households and Families. http://www.census.gov/ population (cited 7 January 2001).

White, Deborah Gray. 1985. *Ar'n't I a Woman: Female Slaves in the Plantation South.* New York: W. W. Norton.

After-School Care

After-school care is child care provided for elementary- and middle school–aged children before and after normal school hours until working parents can pick them up. The need for quality before- and after-school programs changed as the United States moved from an agricultural to an industrial to a technological society and as women with young children joined the labor force. Seventy-eight percent of mothers of school-age children were employed in 1999 (U.S. Bureau of Labor Statistics 2000). Other factors related to the increased need for after-school care are high mobility rates that take families away from their extended families, increased numbers of single-parent families, and greater opportunities for females in once male-dominated careers. Increased emphasis on quality care has been a direct result of concern for "latchkey children"; their academic, social, and safety issues; and the bombardment of violent media and technical images. Programs vary considerably from individual care in homes and small group care by relatives, friends, and agencies to large group programs in schools and community agencies. Local, state, and federal moneys are being targeted toward improving and expanding existing facilities, increasing new facilities, offering effective facilities to all children, and expanding half-day to full-day or part-year to full-year care. Suggestions for effective programs include a homelike atmosphere, opportunities for privacy to complete homework, assistance with homework or self-help skill development, nutritious meals and snacks, and considerable physical activity. Children's advocates continue to press for increased funding, increased hours of availability, and certified/trained personnel.

The care of the nation's youth has changed since the days when the United States was a rural society in which large, extended families were the majority. Older siblings or assigned family members cared for very young children while other family members worked in the home or on the farm. As children entered schools, they worked alongside family members after the school day and during summer months until they were ready to take on full responsibilities. In cities, children began working at very young ages as they ran errands, sold newspapers, polished shoes, or delivered messages and were supervised fairly closely by their employers (Nasaw 1985). Older preteens and teens were supervised closely in apprenticeships. As the nation became more industrial, workers of all ages were exposed to long work hours and unhealthy work conditions in factories, mills, and sweatshops. As child labor and compulsory education laws were passed to protect children from unhealthy work conditions and to ensure an educated citizenry, they also removed children from the workforce and increased their years of childhood. This occurred simultaneously as mothers of young children entered into the workforce during the world wars and have remained in increasing numbers since then. Changing family structures, including the growth of single-parent families and high numbers of children in poverty, also contribute to current, critical needs for before- and after-school care.

Reviews of research show concerns related to unsupervised children between the hours of 3:00 and 7:00 P.M.: increased rates of juvenile violence, home injuries and injury-related deaths, and incidences of substance abuse. Unsupervised children are also reported to experience higher rates of truancy, mental depression, and poorer academic performance (Children's Defense Fund 2001, 47). Many school systems and private agencies have taken on the responsibilities of after-school care to better meet the educational needs of their children.

The best programs offering after-school care meet three developmental needs of the whole child: academic, recreational, and cultural. Academic services are needed for children to boost lagging reading and comprehension scores or math and science computational skills. Regular school-day teachers are encouraged to work as program staff and provide homework assistance, organize activities related to promoting basic skills mastery, and assess student progress. One-on-one tutoring is often used to enhance group activities. School programs utilize existing facilities and reduce travel time. Some tutoring occurs in individual homes or in community agencies.

Ample opportunities for physical activities for youth beyond the school physical program, such as sports, team games, and individual skills, help to meet recreational needs. These programs can provide children with opportunities to develop skills they choose while also helping them learn good sportsmanship, coping strategies, and problem solving. Examples of such programs are Boys' and Girls' Clubs, the Young Men's Christian Association (YMCA), and the Young Women's Christian Association (YWCA).

Cultural aspects are developed to help youth cultivate important skills not addressed by the school curriculum and can help develop self-confidence and social skills. Hobbies such as sewing or fishing can be enhanced. Lessons in social skills or self-help skills can also enhance emerging self-esteem. Museums, zoos, and art councils often provide cultural activities during after-school hours, on weekends, and during summer breaks. Learning a second language, playing a musical instrument, or cooking foods from various world regions are examples of cultural activities beyond the school day.

Programs are being developed from a variety of models emerging from particular identified needs. Five general categories can be used to review these types of programs: (1) Language arts programs focus on increasing students' literacy and language skills. Parent components encourage families to read and visit libraries together and parents to help

A teacher plays with K–3 kids in an after-school program in San Francisco, California. (Elizabeth Crews)

children with their homework. (2) Study skills programs are designed for at-risk students to enhance study and comprehension skills that hamper their academic achievement. Teachers provide strategies for organizing and retaining information taught in the classroom and preparing for tests. (3) Some programs address specific areas such as science or computer technology and are categorized as academic subject types. Some are developed as enrichment programs by for-profit organizations, such as chess clubs or dance groups. (4) Tutoring programs are developed to meet individual learning needs in language arts or other subject areas. Tutors help students to improve their reading and comprehen-

sion abilities while reviewing classroom assignments. (5) The fifth type includes community-created or community-based programs. These are often developed within the community to meet local needs. Some branches are subgroups of national programs, such as scouting. They are more likely to emphasize recreational, social, or cultural activities, although they may be housed in schools.

Local efforts stem from faith-based organizations, parks and recreational departments, libraries, schools, and community organizations. City and county efforts have focused on creating networks of family care providers, increasing families' access to accredited providers, expanding part-day to full-day and part-year to full-year programs, improving facilities, and ensuring that opportunities are available to all children who need them. Businesses and community agencies are taking giant steps in supporting children's organizations through donations, grants, and partnerships. For example, the United Auto Workers (UAW), Ford Motor Company, and Visteon Corporation developed the Family Service and Learning Center program. This union-management partnership supports working families, individuals, retirees, and the communities. This program is intergenerational and includes high-quality child-care services, before- and after-school preteen and teen programs, adult and family education classes, and volunteer support networks.

Community learning centers are public schools that extend the school day to include nontraditional hours and summers. With school doors kept open, students, parents, and the community are offered access to valuable educational resources. These can be safe havens for children, where learning takes place in buildings removed from the violence, drugs, and lack of supervision many children are facing at home alone. The benefits of using public schools as community learning centers are numerous. Relatively low-cost, accessible locations reduce transportation problems for parents. These ongoing programs provide children with long-term mentoring experiences and provide community members with opportunities to be actively involved while close to home.

Many schools are touting high achievement and improved attitudes through a combination of community services provided in before- and after-school care services. One such example is in Yulee, Florida, where the Reading Renaissance Program is used to promote reading not only during the day but also in three popular after-school and community programs (Rouse and Banegas-Pena 2001, 6–7). A tutoring program through the local Boys' and Girls' Club is held at the middle school. Night Owl, a two-hour Monday night program, provides a time for parents and their children to visit the school's computer lab to read and take quizzes together. A community outreach program on Saturday mornings provides tutoring sessions at local community centers and churches. The program started with one community center in 1998 and opened a fourth in 2001. The principal cites motivated students, improved parent-teacher relations, and a unified campus as benefits of the partnership.

Interest in the quality of before- and after-school programs has increased. Parents are recognizing that their children need a safe place to spend nonschool time and an organized program for both reinforcing the school curriculum and cultivating strengths and talents not developed in school. In urban and low-income areas, after-school programs are essential to counteract the effects of limited opportunities and resources. Although numbers of programs are increasing, estimates for the year 2002 show that only about 25 percent of the demand for school-age children will be met (National Institute on Out-of-School Time 2000).

The Afterschool Alliance is an emerging alliance of public, private, and nonprofit groups committed to raising awareness and expanded resources for after-school programs. Initiated and currently coordinated by the Charles Stewart Mott Foundation, the alliance grew out of a partnership between the foundation and the U.S. Department of Education. Initial partners are the Charles

Stewart Mott Foundation, the U.S. Department of Education, J.C. Penney, the Advertising Council, the Entertainment Industry Foundation, the Creative Artists Agency Foundation, and *People* magazine. The combination of retail and industry is an example of networking to support school and community development.

Current research findings support effective after-school programs. Specific outcomes are difficult to identify, however. Few evaluations have been conducted based on low-income populations, and many studies are limited in scope because families that volunteer with children in after-school care may be different from those that do not have children in after-school care. Another obstacle is that children from one after-school program may not attend the same school. Schwartz (2001) identified several characteristics of a successful program: well-trained staff and volunteers, a solid structure related to clear program goals and procedures, ongoing assessment, inclusion of families in program planning, and an active advisory board.

Children's advocates support new funding to improve and expand child-care facilities to ensure that children are in healthy, safe, and appropriate environments; that programs meet the needs of working parents; and that child-care providers and teachers are adequately trained and fully certified.

—Mabel T. Himel

References and Further Reading
"Afterschool Alert: Poll Report." AfterSchool Alliance. http://www.afterschoolalliance.org/about2.html (cited 25 May 2001).
Bronfenbrenner, Urie. 1986. "Alienation and the Four Worlds of Childhood." *Phi Delta Kappan* 67(6): 430, 432–436.
Children's Defense Fund. 2001. *The State of America's Children Yearbook, 2000.* Washington, DC: Children's Defense Fund.
Elder, Glen H., Jr., John Modell, and Ross D. Parke, eds. 1993. *Children in Time and Place: Developmental and Historical Insights.* New York: Cambridge University Press.
Nasaw, David. 1985. *Children of the City at Work and at Play.* New York: Oxford University Press.
National Center for Education Statistics. 1997. *The Condition of Education 1997* (NCES 97-388). Washington, DC: U.S. Department of Education.
National Institute on Out-of-School Time. 2000. *Fact Sheet on School-Age Children's Out-of-School Time.* Wellesley, MA: Center for Research on Women at Wellesley College.
Rouse, Phyllis, and Anna Lisa Banegas-Pena. 2001. "Two Principals Describe How They Use Renaissance to Promote Reading Outside the Classroom: Outreach Programs Unite the Community." *School Improvement Report* 1(6): 6–7. Madison, WI: Renaissance Learning.
"Safe and Smart: Making the After-School Hours Work for Kids." U.S. Department of Education. http://www.ed.gov/pubs/safeandsmart (cited 25 May 2001).
Schwartz, Wendy. "Urban After-School Programs: Evaluations and Recommendations." ERIC Clearinghouse on Urban Education Digest, no. 140. http://eric-web.tc.columbia.edu/digests/dig140.html (cited 25 May 2001).
Snyder, Howard, and Melissa Sickmund. 1999. *Juvenile Offenders and Victims: 1999 National Report.* Washington, DC: U.S. Department of Justice, Office of Juvenile Justice and Delinquency Programs.
U.S. Bureau of Labor Statistics. 2000. *Employment Characteristics of Families.* Washington, DC: Government Printing Office.
U.S. Department of Education. 2000. *21st Century Community Learning Centers: Providing Quality Afterschool Learning Opportunities for America's Families.* Washington, DC: U.S. Department of Education.
Vandell, Deborah, and James Posner. 1994. *Low-income Children's After-school*

Care: Are There Beneficial Effects of After-school Programs? Child Development 65(2): 440–456.

Aid to Families with Dependent Children

How (and whether) to help people living in poverty was an enduring question for local, state, and federal governments across the twentieth century; for two-thirds of the century, Aid to Dependent Children (ADC)/Aid to Families with Dependent Children (AFDC) was the answer. In the United States, providing welfare to the poor has always been done in a limited fashion. Doing so shifted from being the responsibility of local governments to that of state governments and then became a combined federal-state responsibility, between 1900 and the 1930s. From the 1930s to the early 1990s, welfare was provided to a growing number of the poor, though usually in small or moderate amounts. In the 1990s responsibility for providing for the poor was largely relegated back to the states, with some federal involvement. Nineteenth-century debates over which groups of people deserved help (the "deserving" or "worthy" poor) and which did not (the "undeserving" or "unworthy" poor) continued in the twentieth century and helped shape policy right to the end of the century. From the 1910s to the 1940s, widows with children were held up as the most deserving example of needy people, and the image of such widows helped lead to the federal government's commitment to providing welfare during the New Deal of the 1930s. In the latter decades of the century, the image of unmarried teenage mothers living on welfare was used as the most glaring example of people who did not deserve help and helped lead to restrictions on welfare and eventually its end as a federally guaranteed program in the 1990s.

In colonial America, relief for the poor was closely modeled on English methods, as embodied in the Elizabethan poor laws. Towns often gave small amounts of aid to poor families but did so less readily for individuals, unless they were orphaned children or elderly. This aid came in different forms, including cash, food, and firewood to help families get through the winter. Providing these sorts of assistance was known as "outdoor relief" in contrast to "indoor relief," which meant placing families or individuals into institutions such as poorhouses. Outdoor relief was less stigmatizing than indoor relief and helped families to maintain themselves in their own homes. It was also less expensive; more people could be helped through outdoor relief than through indoor relief in institutions for the same amount of money. Outdoor relief remained the most common way of helping people living in severe poverty for several decades after the American Revolution, into the early decades of the nineteenth century.

The number of people requesting aid grew in the decades before and after 1800 in the United States (and in England), in part owing to the increasing size of the nation's urban centers. As a result, taxes to support the poor also increased, as did complaints about those rising taxes. By the early 1800s, distinctions were regularly being made between the "worthy poor" who deserved aid from the community and the "unworthy poor" or "paupers" who did not. A widow with children would be seen as worthy of help, since she was not presumed to have done anything immoral that created her situation. A healthy adult man would be seen as a pauper who should not be helped, since he was assumed to be capable of working but unwilling to do so.

The question for many became, how do you aid the "worthy" poor while discouraging the "unworthy" poor? In practice, this often meant policies designed to make relief stigmatizing or otherwise unappealing, so that only those who were truly desperate would seek help. Critics of aid to the poor developed and advocated poorhouses, which were extremely unattractive places to live, in part to cut down on the number of applicants for aid. They assumed that the poor chose not to work and were undeserving of aid and that if the only aid available were in unattractive, restrictive institutions, people would not seek help. In a number of places this harsh view of the poor succeeded in ending outdoor relief, but the practice of providing some aid to the poor in their own homes persisted across the nation throughout the nineteenth century (Katz 1986; Katz 1989).

More benevolent views toward at least some people living in poverty developed in the early twentieth century, during the Progressive Era. The idea that single mothers were a growing societal problem developed between 1890 and 1910, but with a far different perspective than it would develop in the latter third of the twentieth century. Much of the discussion in the early 1900s focused on the desertion of families by fathers and husbands; along with this went attempts to assign the blame for that desertion to fathers, mothers, environmental factors such as unemployment, or some combination of these issues. In the 1910s the discussion of single-motherhood as a social issue shifted to focus on the group that actually did make up the majority of single-mother households at the time: widows. This change in

emphasis occurred because, as Linda Gordon states, "welfare reformers redrew the image of the single mother, from deserted wives to widows, for reasons of welfare-state-building strategies" (Gordon 1994, 27). Widows were seen as more "worthy" of aid than deserted wives or pretty much anyone else except possibly orphans, and so advocates of providing state government relief to single-mother households focused on widows (Gordon 1994).

That aid came in the form of state programs know as mothers' pensions or widows' pensions. The 1909 White House Conference on the Care of Dependent Children had called for private, charitable subsidies to allow poor mothers to keep their children with them at home, instead of having to place them in orphan asylums, as many poor women had had to do. In short order the idea of using public money for such subsidies was being advocated by a number of social reformers, though not without resistance; the idea was a call, in effect, for a return to outdoor relief. Once the movement for mothers' pensions took hold, it spread with amazing speed. Twenty states adopted programs between 1911 and 1913, and by 1920 another twenty had joined them. Many of these programs provided limited funds, served a small number of people, or both, but they represented a fundamental change in the treatment of one impoverished group, women with children in single-parent households (Skocpol 1992; Gordon 1994).

When the stock market crashed in 1929, setting off the longest and deepest economic depression in the history of the United States, it also set the stage for mothers' pensions to become a federal program. The shift took time. After Franklin D. Roosevelt's election in late 1932, the new president took immediate action to provide more extensive relief to the unemployed and poor through the programs of the first New Deal of 1933. It was the second New Deal two years later, however, that institutionalized relief for families with one parent. The Social Security Act of 1935 has remained the central piece of legislation related to poverty in the United States ever since and one of the most important pieces of social legislation of any kind. It created a number of programs, two of the most important being Social Security and unemployment insurance. Three of the act's other programs were designed to provide relief to specific needy groups: the elderly, the blind, and children in low-income families with one parent. The last of these programs, known as Aid to Dependent Children, is the program that was known as "welfare" in the public mind throughout the remainder of the twentieth century.

ADC was a joint federal-state program. The federal government implemented some standards and left others up to states to decide, including the amount of aid provided to families under ADC and who would be eligible for aid. As a result, more conservative states, including most southern states, could choose to provide very small amounts of aid, whereas more liberal states might decide to provide more adequate relief. States could also shape eligibility policy to keep their relief rolls small and to try to keep certain kinds of people (such as specific racial groups or mothers who had never married) from receiving aid as easily as others. The financial cost was also divided between federal and state government, with the latter supplying two-thirds of the money supplied to families.

One of the results of the creation of these three relief programs was that peo-ple who did not fit within them, including families with two parents and healthy, nonelderly adults, were left to the mercies of local welfare programs, which generally provided very little aid even to those people they did consider eligible for aid. It should be noted that no one, including Roosevelt, expected ADC to become an especially large program. Most mothers' and widows' pension state programs in the 1920s had remained limited in scope, and few observers expected ADC to be very different.

Throughout the 1950s ADC continued to vary dramatically from state to state, both in how much aid was provided to families and in what people, and how many people, were allowed to receive relief at all. Southern relief rates were especially meager. In many places, the rights of people seeking aid were regularly, and blatantly, denied; this was particularly true for African Americans.

Between 1945 and 1960, the number of people receiving ADC rose from 700,000 to 3 million. The average amount of relief stipends also increased by 77 percent in purchasing power adjusted for inflation. In multiple ways, then, the program was becoming both larger and more generous (Patterson 2000, 85–86). There was little controversy surrounding the growth of ADC in the 1950s. In the early 1960s ADC was still seen by most politicians as a desirable program. In 1962 the program was renamed Aid to Families with Dependent Children, reflecting the simple fact that it helped parents as well as children. That same year, the federal government decided to encourage states to provide services in addition to cash to AFDC recipients. The federal government offered 75 percent of the funding for services provided by local welfare offices. One of the goals of this service provision was to keep the welfare rolls from continuing their rapid growth, but instead the number of people enrolled in the program continued to grow. There were multiple reasons for this, none of which were really addressed by the provision of social services. Perhaps the most important were the large migration of African Americans to northern cities, the lack of day care for working-class and poor parents (especially single parents), and the lack of jobs for unskilled workers, particularly women.

Welfare caseloads continued to grow across the 1960s, for those reasons and more. The civil rights movement also served to encourage various groups to more aggressively seek their legal, political, and social rights. The best-known example was the feminist movement, but in the late 1960s and early 1970s there was also a small welfare rights movement. Additionally, by the late 1960s, becoming an AFDC recipient also meant access to other highly desirable services, most notably Medicaid and food stamps.

Criticisms of welfare recipients grew during the 1960s, also for a variety of reasons. The growing number of people on welfare, and the increasingly assertive nature of welfare advocates, played a role. Changing views toward the proper role of women probably played a larger role. The number of women, including women with children (whether those women were married or not), going into the workforce had grown during the 1950s and continued to do so in the 1960s. The idea that women who did not have small children at home could, and even should, work became much more widely accepted in the late 1960s than it had been before; as a result, women on AFDC, who by definition were not working,

came under increasing attack. Halting attempts were made to encourage AFDC mothers to work, including provisions that women who did not have a child under age six should work. An incentive provision was introduced in 1967 that allowed women to retain part of their earnings from a job while receiving AFDC benefits.

A number of important programs were created in the 1960s to aid the poor, as Pres. Lyndon B. Johnson introduced his War on Poverty. In 1965, both Medicare and Medicaid were created as amendments to the Social Security Act. Medicare got the most attention, providing, as it did, health insurance for many of the elderly. Like Social Security, Medicare was a social insurance program that was managed by the federal government and involved payments by its recipients; it was, in other words, a subsidy that people were viewed as earning. Medicaid was similar to AFDC, with the federal government paying part of the cost and leaving the rest of the cost, and the actual administration of the program, to the states; it was a public assistance program. Because its recipients were poor people who were not seen as contributing to the program, Medicaid, like AFDC, was prone to stigmatizing its recipients and open to political attack.

In states such as California and New York, Medicaid was initially open to a much wider array of working-class people than simply the poor who qualified for AFDC. During the mid-1960s, some states' Medicaid populations grew rapidly; and in response, by 1970 the federal government had limited the program to people earning 133 percent of each state's standard for AFDC eligibility. In other words, it came to serve people who qualified for AFDC (whether they enrolled in the program or not) and those with incomes low enough to be in danger of qualifying for welfare, but Medicaid did not provide health care to the working-class as a whole.

Another crucial program for the poor, food stamps, was created in 1964, after attempts to provide food to the poor more directly proved unwieldy. AFDC recipients were automatically eligible, but local welfare departments could allow other families in as well. At first the program was voluntary; state and local entities could decide not to provide it. Later federal amendments strengthened and regularized the program and made it mandatory. The food stamps program was far less controversial than AFDC or Medicaid and provided a crucial supplement to typically small AFDC checks.

By the time Richard Nixon became president in 1969, virtually everyone was unhappy with AFDC as it existed, though their unhappiness sprang from very different reasons. Liberals were upset that welfare paid only tiny amounts in most states, that eligibility was tightly limited, and that it focused on single-parent homes, leaving out poor two-parent families. Conservatives were upset that the provision of government subsidies allowed people to stay on the welfare rolls who could have and, in their view, should have been working. They were also unhappy that work incentives that had been added in 1967 allowed many working mothers to receive AFDC who should not, they believed, be able to do so. Nixon proposed replacing AFDC with a Family Assistance Plan (FAP) that would provide federal assistance to all families falling below a certain income level. It was, in effect, a national guaranteed income. But the disagreements

between liberals and conservatives in Washington and elsewhere over welfare doomed FAP over the next several years. Questions of who deserved help, how much help, and what level of government should provide that help would continue to make changes in welfare extremely difficult to accomplish across the 1970s and 1980s.

Nixon's main mark on welfare may have been his expansion and renovation of the food stamp program, which became available to millions of working-class families with low incomes. Other changes in provision for poor groups occurred in the mid-1970s. In 1974 two of the three relief programs created in 1935, aid for the elderly and for the blind, were both placed into the social insurance system within the Supplemental Security Income program. As a result, only AFDC remained as a highly visible "welfare" program, and only AFDC recipients were seen by many as including large numbers of "unworthy" poor. In a very real sense, the elderly poor and blind were finally deemed part of the "worthy" poor, whereas impoverished single-parent households were not (Gordon 1994).

Ronald Reagan's election to the presidency in 1980 and a new, harsher attack on welfare, and more specifically AFDC, went hand in hand. As historian Michael B. Katz writes, "a war on welfare accompanied the conservative revival of the early 1980s" (1989, 137). The economy had been weak since the mid-1970s, and numerous social programs were under siege at the local, state, and federal levels. In the meantime welfare rolls had continued to grow, and the public image of a typical "welfare mother" had become that of a teenage, unmarried African American woman who had more than one child and who stayed on welfare for year after year. (The truth was quite different, as most women on welfare were white, and most welfare recipients had either one or two children and left welfare within a year or two of enrolling in the program.) The most damaging attack on welfare was the widespread belief that the program's existence encouraged single women to have children, since they knew they would be supported by the government (Katz 1989).

In the first years of Reagan's presidency, a number of social programs were either reduced or eliminated. AFDC, somewhat surprisingly, was weakened but maintained. In the mid-1980s the most notable change in welfare was that many states were experimenting with "workfare" programs that required AFDC recipients to undertake job training and search for work. Studies showed that the programs had a small positive impact on earnings and slightly reduced welfare dependency. Despite the limited research in support of this approach, it was appealing to conservatives and likewise hard for most liberals to challenge. It was therefore not surprising that work incentives were a central part of the Family Support Act of 1988, which was seen at the time, probably without merit, as the most significant reform in welfare policy since the creation of ADC in 1935. AFDC recipients were expected to go through job training and to try to find work; if they failed to do so, they would lose their benefits (though their children would not lose theirs). The act also included provisions seeking to have fathers of children in the program identified so that child support could be actively sought out.

When Bill Clinton became president in 1993, one of the promises from his campaign was that he would "end welfare as we know it." The years before and after his inauguration were a time of experiments by states in various kinds of welfare reform, and it was widely recognized that the federal government would change AFDC before too long. The change came in 1996, when Clinton signed welfare reform into law. Unlike most previous changes, which added to or modified the program in one or two ways, the 1996 reform was far-reaching. More effectively than the Family Support Act of 1988, it required welfare recipients to undergo job training and seek out work. It put time limits on how long recipients could receive aid, both in one stretch and over the course of their lifetime. It returned a great deal of authority over their programs to state governments and made it difficult for legal immigrants to enroll. In sum, it *did* end welfare as Americans had come to know it over the previous six decades, ending the entitlement of the poor to receive government aid. The change was extremely popular with the American public (Katz 2001).

The image of who actually received welfare had shifted gradually but powerfully over sixty years, as had the reality of who made up welfare rolls (though the image in the 1990s was less accurate than it had been in the 1930s). So had the job market and assumptions about the proper place of women. AFDC was replaced by Temporary Assistance for Needy Families (TANF). In the late 1990s there was growing disparity between how different states' TANF programs worked. The federal effort from the 1930s to the 1960s to ensure certain standards for welfare programs across the nation had largely given way to a desire to encourage experimentation by states. One constant remained: the tensions stemming from trying to develop a program that would help those seen as deserving, while restricting those seen as undeserving, in a world in which agreement about who was worthy and who was not was impossible to reach.

—*Timothy A. Hacsi*

See also White House Conferences on Children

References and Further Reading
Berkowitz, Edward D. 1991. *America's Welfare State: From Roosevelt to Reagan.* Baltimore: Johns Hopkins University Press.
Gordon, Linda. 1994. *Pitied but Not Entitled: Single Mothers and the History of Welfare, 1890–1935.* New York: The Free Press.
Jansson, Bruce S. 1988. *The Reluctant Welfare State: A History of American Social Welfare Policies.* Belmont, CA: Wadsworth Publishing.
Katz, Michael B. 1986. *In the Shadow of the Poorhouse: A Social History of Welfare in America.* New York: Basic Books.
Katz, Michael B. 1989. *The Undeserving Poor: From the War on Poverty to the War on Welfare.* New York: Pantheon Books.
Katz, Michael B. 2001. *The Price of Citizenship: Redefining the American Welfare State.* New York: Metropolitan Books.
O'Connor, Alice. 2001. *Poverty Knowledge: Social Science, Social Policy, and the Poor in 20th-Century U.S. History.* Princeton, NJ: Princeton University Press.
Patterson, James T. 2000. *America's Struggle against Poverty in the Twentieth Century.* Cambridge: Harvard University Press.
Skocpol, Theda. 1992. *Protecting Soldiers and Mothers: The Political Origins of Social Policy in the United States.* Cambridge: Belknap Press of Harvard University Press.
Trattner, Walter I. 1999. *From Poor Law to Welfare State: A History of Social Welfare in America.* 6th ed. New York: The Free Press.

AIDS and the Family

AIDS is the acronym for acquired immune deficiency syndrome, a clinical diagnosis made up of one or many defined symptoms or illnesses. AIDS is caused by the virus known as the human immunodeficiency virus (HIV). First diagnosed in 1981 in a small population of homosexual men, AIDS has spread beyond its original risk group to include heterosexual males and females, hemophiliacs, intravenous drug users, and perinatally exposed infants. HIV infection is spread by exchange of infected blood or blood products, by sexual intercourse, and by an infected mother to a fetus through the placental wall or through breast-feeding. Although HIV has been recovered in the saliva of infected persons, in amounts lower than in the blood, studies have shown that no infections have resulted after skin or mucous-membrane exposure to the infected saliva. There is no evidence to indicate that insects or casual human contact can transmit the virus. There is currently no cure for AIDS and no vaccine to prevent its spread.

Epidemiology

AIDS was first identified in 1981 among homosexual men and intravenous drug users in New York and California. Shortly after its detection in the United States, evidence of AIDS grew among heterosexual men, women, and children in sub-Saharan Africa. AIDS is now recognized as a worldwide epidemic, affecting virtually every nation. By 1999 an estimated 33.6 million adults and 1.2 million children worldwide were living with HIV infection or AIDS. The World Health Organization (WHO) estimates that from 1981 to the end of 1999, about 16.3 million people died as a result of HIV infection. More than 3.6 million of those who died were children under the age of fifteen (World Health Organization 2000).

In 1999, the last year for which complete reporting exists, an estimated 320,282 people were living with AIDS in the United States, and another 111,129 people were reported to be living with HIV, not AIDS (Centers for Disease Control and Prevention 2000a). The number of AIDS cases represents an 84 percent increase in people living with the disease between 1993 and 1999. Much of the increase is due to improvements in therapeutic regimens that have resulted in reduced mortality and increased longevity. In the United States in 1999, 16,273 people died of AIDS compared to 45,381 reported AIDS-related deaths in 1993. The decline in mortality has not been uniform across population groups, however. The number of deaths due to AIDS among U.S. men declined 68 percent between 1993 and 1999; during the same time, deaths declined only 36 percent among women. Similarly, during this seven-year span, the number of AIDS deaths among whites declined by 78 percent, whereas the decline among people of color was only 52 percent (World Health Organization 2000).

Women and HIV/AIDS
Women, particularly women of color, increasingly bear a disproportionate share of the AIDS burden in the United States. The proportion of women with HIV infection has increased steadily since 1985, when women represented only 7 percent of reported cases. By 1999, women represented 23 percent of AIDS cases and 32 percent of the HIV cases reported. Among women, blacks and Hispanics account for 77 percent of cases of HIV infection even though together they represent less than 25 percent of all U.S. women (Centers for Disease Control and Prevention 2000a).

In the United States, most women who now have AIDS became infected with HIV by injecting illegal drugs. But the rate of infection through heterosexual transmission has been rising dramatically and has surpassed injecting drug use as the leading transmission route since 1995 (Centers for Disease Control and Prevention 2000a). The Centers for Disease Control and Prevention (CDC) reports that, because many women in the United States are unaware they are at risk for HIV infection, those who are HIV-infected often remain undiagnosed until the onset of AIDS or until one of their infected children becomes ill.

Women with HIV/AIDS face greater social, emotional, and financial burdens than infected males. Their dual roles as patient and caregiver, lower socioeconomic status, and lack of connection to information and resources as compared to males represent formidable barriers to coping with a diagnosis of HIV/AIDS. Most HIV-infected women are living in poverty and have limited access to health care. Lack of access delays diagnosis, a circumstance that in turn affects survival. Compared to men, poor women with HIV are diagnosed with HIV later, have more advanced illness when they enter care, and, if they are a member of a minority group, are less likely to receive medications. Limited access to care and late diagnoses in women have contributed to reports that women's survival time is shorter than men's. If a woman is diagnosed at the same point in the disease as a man, however, her survival is, on the average, the same.

Mother-to-child transmission of HIV occurs at one of three stages: during pregnancy, during birth, or after delivery through breast-feeding. Such transmissions account for 90 percent of all cases of AIDS in children. In many developing nations, particularly in sub-Saharan Africa, the rate of transmission from infected mothers to newborns can be as high as 60 percent. In the United States, the rate of transmission ranges between 3 percent and 25 percent (Connor, Sperling, Gelber, Kiselev et al. 1994). The scientific advances that in recent years have dramatically reduced the rate of HIV transmission from mother to child led to the enactment of legislation in many states mandating the offering of HIV screening to all pregnant women as a means of preventing new cases of HIV in newborns. Although it is controversial, some states have mandated testing of all pregnant women and newborns. Concerns about civil liberties and intrusion of the state have launched a national debate on the merits and the ethics of legislatively mandating testing for HIV infection. With the exception of accused rapists in some states, U.S. citizens cannot be tested for HIV unless they have first provided informed consent to be tested (AIDS Alliance for Children, Youth and Families 2000). Proponents of mandatory testing of pregnant women argue that the benefits of early intervention outweigh any potential negative consequences. Opponents, on the other hand, argue that pregnancy should not invalidate a woman's legal and ethical right to medical autonomy and informed decision making. Calling for universal HIV counseling and voluntary HIV testing, the latter group claims that when offered the choice, most women voluntarily agree to testing and that mandatory testing may prevent some women from seeking prenatal care.

HIV/AIDS in Children

The first four cases of AIDS in children were reported by the CDC in December 1982 (Centers for Disease Control and Prevention 1982). Within ten years, 4,249 cases of AIDS had been reported in children under thirteen years of age. New approaches to treatment have dramatically reduced the incidence of HIV and AIDS in children in recent years. In the United States in 1999 there were only 263 reported cases of pediatric AIDS. This represents only 28 percent of the 947 cases that were reported in 1992. Most of this decline is due to the success in decreasing transmission from mother to child (Centers for Disease Control and Prevention 1993).

HIV infection in children generally progresses more rapidly than in adults, most likely because of undeveloped immune systems in children. The disease is particularly aggressive in infants. Until recent therapeutic advances, more than half of the infants born with an HIV infection died before age two. Once a child is infected, the child's immune system cannot prevent the virus from multiplying quickly in the blood, which speeds the progression of the disease. In contrast, when adults become infected with HIV, their immune system generally fights the infection. Therefore, HIV levels in adults remain lower for an extended period, delaying the progression of the disease. Children infected with or affected by HIV face many formidable challenges. Children with HIV infection often require a multidisciplinary care team that includes developmental, medical, social, and psychological specialists. Children develop many of the opportunistic infections that befall adults but also exhibit symptoms not observed in older patients. Among infants and children, HIV infection produces wasting syndrome and slows growth (generally referred to as failure to thrive). HIV typically infects a child's brain early in the course of the disease, impairing intellectual development and coordination skills. Although HIV can infect the brains of adults, it usually does so toward the later stages of the disease and produces different symptoms. Children also show a susceptibility to more bacterial and viral infections than adults. More than 20 percent of HIV-infected children develop serious, recurring bacterial infections, including meningitis and pneumonia (Pizzo and Wilfert 1998). Many struggle in school owing to learning disabilities including memory, attention, and motor skills deficits. In addition to dealing with the potentially debilitating physical effects of HIV disease, infected children often face multiple challenges including social isolation, rejection, denial, and loss of one or both parents.

HIV/AIDS in Adolescents

The number of HIV-infected adolescents is rapidly increasing. Twenty percent of the people in the United States with HIV (not AIDS) are aged thirteen to twenty-four years. The risk taking and experimentation common to adolescents place them at particular risk for HIV and other sexually transmitted diseases. The majority of infected teens have acquired HIV through high-risk sexual and drug use behaviors. Unprotected sexual intercourse is the most common route of transmission, especially for young women. The 1999 Youth Risk Behavior Surveillance study revealed that nearly half of high school students were or had been sexually active and that 42 percent of sexually

active students had not used a condom at last sexual intercourse. By twelfth grade, 65 percent of U.S. teens are sexually active, and one in five has had four or more sexual partners. The abuse of alcohol and other drugs also contributes to increased risk of HIV infection in youth (Centers for Disease Control and Prevention 2000b).

Most infected young people are unaware that they carry HIV. Those who do learn that they are HIV-positive may not have access to or know where to get adequate care. Compared to adults and children, adolescents and young adults are less likely to have health insurance, which further reduces the chances that they will seek care.

Impact on Families

Trend data reported by the CDC indicate a steady rate of HIV incidence in U.S. women of childbearing age. Each year in the United States, approximately 6,000 to 7,000 HIV-infected women give birth. And, according to the CDC, approximately 2,741 women of childbearing age (eighteen to forty-five) die of HIV/AIDS-related causes each year. It has been estimated that approximately 75 percent of HIV-positive women have children (Centers for Disease Control and Prevention 2000a).

The shifting demographics of the AIDS epidemic in the United States are having a dramatic effect on families. Often referred to as a multigenerational family disease, AIDS either directly or indirectly affects children, parents, grandparents, and extended family members. In addition to the physical sequelae associated with HIV infection, the illness brings with it a host of social, emotional, and economic burdens that often create nearly insurmountable barriers to appropriate care. Because of the disease's prevalence among gay men and drug users, tremendous social stigma continues to accompany a diagnosis of AIDS. Denial, fear of disclosure, and failure to seek care are common responses within families affected by HIV/AIDS. Unfortunately, these responses can have seriously negative consequences for the whole family. Adults and adolescents infected with the virus may attempt to hide their illness from other family members. Secrecy and denial often create barriers to care seeking or adherence to medical regimens. Lack of or inadequate treatment leads to disease progression. Infected parents may become too ill to care for their children, thus requiring unprepared grandparents or other extended family members to step in.

Researchers have identified an array of psychosocial stressors of women and family members coping with HIV/AIDS: adjustment to the diagnosis, dealing with how the infection was contracted, fears of contagion, dealing with altered familial roles and responsibilities, preparing for the loss of ill family members, and planning for the future. In addition, although normal circumstances associated with parenting can be difficult, HIV-positive mothers are often dealing with extremely stressful situations, including their own longevity, custody planning, and, in some cases, the health of an infected child. In addition, women who lack necessary social support from family and friends, either owing to fear of disclosure or lack of information and understanding, carry an enormous burden and are often plagued by depression, anxiety, and guilt.

For both infected and uninfected children of parents with HIV, the illness and loss of parents and siblings are the most devastating. In 1994, an estimated 7,300 children and adolescents were orphaned by HIV/AIDS. Projections in the early 1990s were that by the end of the century, there would be more than 80,000 children in the United States orphaned by the disease. Owing to declining death rates and slowed disease progression, the actual number of orphans in this country is probably much lower (Levine and Stein 1994). In the developing world, however, the picture is much bleaker. According to UNAIDS figures, by 1997 approximately 8.2 million children under fifteen years had lost their mothers or both parents to AIDS. More than 95 percent of these children live in sub-Saharan Africa, and one-third are younger than five years of age (UNAIDS 1998).

Societal Response to HIV/AIDS

In the United States, since the beginning of the AIDS epidemic in 1981, grassroots organizations have been created to meet the medical, economic, and emotional needs of people with AIDS. Literally thousands of nonprofit organizations have been formed to provide medical, educational, emotional, logistical, and advocacy services for people with AIDS.

In addition, the U.S. government has dedicated billions of dollars to help people cope with HIV disease and to assist research efforts aimed at finding a cure. In 1990 the Americans with Disabilities Act (ADA) was passed, protecting people with disabling diseases, including AIDS, from discrimination in activities such as applying for jobs or buying a house. The 1990 Ryan White Comprehensive AIDS Resources Emergency (CARE) Act was reauthorized in 1996 and again in 2000. This program provides medical and dental care, counseling, transportation, and home and hospice care for low-income or uninsured people living with AIDS. The AIDS Drug Assistance Program (ADAP) is funded in large part by this act and administered by all fifty states. It pays for costly AIDS medications for people who do not have private insurance and who are not poor enough to be eligible for Medicaid.

—*Debra K. Bartelli*

See also Homosexuality and the Family

References and Further Reading
Adnopoz, Jean A., and Steven J. Berkowitz, eds. 2000. *Child and Adolescent Psychiatric Clinics of North America. Children and Adolescents Affected by HIV/AIDS: A Mental Health Challenge.* Philadelphia: W. B. Saunders Company.

AIDS Alliance for Children, Youth and Families. 2000. *Understanding the Debate: Pregnant Women and HIV Counseling and Testing.* Washington, DC: AIDS Alliance for Children, Youth and Families.

Boyd-Franklin, Nancy, Gloria L. Steiner, and Mary Boland, eds. 1995. *Children, Families, and HIV/AIDS.* New York: The Guilford Press.

Centers for Disease Control and Prevention. 1982. "Unexplained Immunodeficiency and Opportunistic Infections in Infants—New York, New Jersey, California." *Morbidity and Mortality Report* 31(40): 663–667.

Centers for Disease Control and Prevention. 1993. *HIV/AIDS Surveillance Report: US AIDS Cases through December 1992.* Atlanta, GA: Centers for Disease Control and Prevention.

Centers for Disease Control and Prevention. 2000a. *U.S. HIV and AIDS Cases Reported through December 1999.* Year-end ed., vol. 11, no. 2. Atlanta, GA: Centers for Disease Control and Prevention.

Centers for Disease Control and Prevention. 2000b. "Youth Risk Behavior Surveillance—United States, 1999." *Morbidity and Mortality Report* 49(SS-5).

Cohen, Felissa L., and Jerry D. Durham, eds. 1993. *Women, Children, and HIV/AIDS.* New York: Springer Publishing.

Connor, Edward M., Rhoda Sperling, Richard S. Gelber, Pavel Kiselev et al. 1994. "Reduction of Maternal Infant Transmission of Human Immuno Deficiency Virus Type I with Zidovudine Treatment." *New England Journal of Medicine* 331: 1173–1180.

Levine, Carol, and Gary L. Stein. 1994. *Orphans of the HIV Epidemic: Unmet Needs in Six U.S. Cities.* New York: The Orphan Project.

National Pediatric and Family HIV Resource Center. 2000. *Making the Invisible Visible: Services for Families Living with HIV Infection and Their Affected Children.* Newark: University of Medicine and Dentistry of New Jersey.

Pizzo, Philip A., and Catherine Wilfert, eds. 1998. *Pediatric AIDS: The Challenge of HIV Infection in Infants, Children, and Adolescents.* 3d ed. Baltimore: Williams and Wilkins.

The Source. 2000. "Legal Permanency Planning for HIV-Affected Families: The Need to Plan, Current Legal Options, and Future Direction." *Newsletter of the National Abandoned Infant Resource Center* 19(2).

UNAIDS. 1998. *AIDS Epidemic Update.* Joint United Nations Programme on HIV/AIDS. New York: United Nations.

World Health Organization. 2000. *WHO Report on Global Surveillance of Epidemic-prone Infectious Diseases.* Geneva, Switzerland: World Health Organization.

Alcohol and Drug Abuse in Families

Over the course of American history, citizens have faced problems caused by the abuse of drugs and alcoholic beverages. From the colonial era to the present, the habitual use of intoxicating substances has had a major impact on people's roles and responsibilities in family life. Popular and medical attitudes toward drug abuse and excessive drinking have changed significantly over time. So too have forms of treatment and therapy. But although abusive consumption has occurred as long as Americans have had access to drugs and alcohol, the notion of addiction or alcoholism as a "family disease" is a relatively modern invention—one that took root in the mid-twentieth century, especially during the post–World War II decades. The history of drug and alcohol treatment is closely connected to broader social, cultural, and political developments as well as to shifts in normative roles for men, women, and youth in society in the United States.

The first American to label chronic inebriety a disease was the eighteenth-century physician Benjamin Rush. In 1784, Rush published a thirty-six-page tract entitled *An Enquiry into the Effects of Spirituous Liquors upon the Human Body, and Their Influence upon the Happiness of Society*. His famous description of the common drunkard paired physical symptoms of intemperance (such as hand tremors, jaundice, and inflamed eyes) with corresponding moral vices (such as idleness, lying, and stealing). Rush believed that drunkards became progressively addicted to alcohol over time, and he recognized that the tendency toward intoxication was transmitted intergenerationally within families. In 1810, he proposed the creation of a Sober House where drunkards could be rehabilitated upon evidence of intoxication, unemployment, and ill treatment of family members.

Rush's concern about indulgence in alcohol in the United States was well founded. Indeed, the period from the 1790s through the early 1830s was among the eras of heaviest drinking in the nation's history. In 1792, the annual per capita rate of pure alcohol consumption was 2.5 gallons, a figure that climbed to 7.1 gallons per person by 1830

(Lender and Martin 1987). The greater availability of distilled spirits, especially whiskey, contributed to this national "drinking spree." Many drinkers were single men who organized their work lives and leisure time around the company of other men. Unfettered by obligations to family or community in an era of rapid industrialization, they moved to the growing cities of the North and Midwest or out west to the expanding frontier. Countless numbers of men, many of them immigrants, gathered in village taverns and town saloons in search of alcohol, companionship, and a good time. Uprooted men, or "drifters," were especially prone to unrestrained drinking, gambling, fighting, and other forms of debauchery. Eventually, many bachelors married and settled down—but they did not always curb their drinking habits. The problems associated with alcohol abuse were not confined to saloons but permeated homes and communities throughout the nation.

By the 1840s, the U.S. temperance movement was ripe for expansion. That decade witnessed the creation of a new temperance organization, the Washingtonian Society, that urged drinkers to take a pledge of abstinence and reform other drunkards in their midst. In addition, special meetings were organized by the Martha Washington Society, which gave special support to female drunkards and the family members of male inebriates. Founded in New York in 1841, these groups gave food, clothing, and shelter to reformed drunkards; some even helped them find new jobs and resume their financial obligations. Encouraging women to banish alcohol from their homes, at parades the Martha Washington societies waved flags proclaiming "Total abstinence or no husband!" The Washingtonians promoted the use of sober alternatives to the saloon, including county fairs, parades, concerts, balls, picnics, and reading rooms. Although the Washingtonian movement was short-lived, dying out within a decade of its founding, it set the stage for future cycles of temperance reform.

By the late nineteenth century, another reform organization took the lead in campaigning against alcohol abuse. The Women's Christian Temperance Union (WCTU), headed by the tireless crusader Frances Willard, aimed to destroy saloons and the liquor manufacturers who supplied them. Members of the WCTU believed that alcohol turned respectable men into drunken brutes who wasted their money, lost their jobs, and attacked or deserted their wives and children. The accepted standard for middle-class families during the nineteenth century required men to provide for the family's financial support while women performed domestic tasks such as cleaning, cooking, and caring for children. If a family strayed far from this ideal, a woman's security could be severely threatened. A drunken husband endangered the entire family; abandonment, child abuse, and financial ruin were just some of the potential disasters women and children faced. Thus, the WCTU adopted the motto "home protection" in its symbolic and literal crusade against Demon Rum. Mothers frequently brought young children to antiliquor demonstrations, carrying banners that read "Outlaw the Saloon and Save the Boy." The WCTU also crusaded against narcotics, prostitution, and tobacco as "social evils" that poisoned family life.

While the WCTU was busy lobbying politicians to render the sale of booze illegal, physicians and other medical practitioners opened special hospitals, known as inebriate asylums, to cure drunkards and drug abusers of their dangerous habits. Financed by state funds as well as private money, many asylums treated opium and cocaine addicts as well as alcoholics. Patients in these hospitals came from all walks of life. The inebriate hospital in Massachusetts, for example, admitted patients who worked at occupations ranging from shoemakers, bartenders, and carpenters to doctors, engineers, and journalists. Treatment methods varied from asylum to asylum—and depending upon the severity of their condition, patients remained confined for a time ranging from several months to several years. Isolation from the stresses and temptations of daily life was viewed as the first step on the road to sobriety. For recovering drunkards with wives and children, such isolation continued to put a strain on family life. Wives and mothers of patients often took up temporary residence near the inebriate hospital in order to provide support to their spouses or sons. Some physicians, however, were wary of familial involvement and believed that women unwittingly enabled men to continue drinking. In some cases, addicts made a full recovery and reintegrated themselves into successful family life. Other patients made repeated visits to asylums, unable to stop drinking or using drugs on a permanent basis.

Although the majority of patients in treatment hospitals were men, women also abused drugs and alcohol during the nineteenth century. Although alcoholism or addiction certainly threatened a man's reputation as an upstanding citizen, women drunkards and addicts were doubly stigmatized by their behavior. Because women were heralded as the pure, virtuous sex, they had farther to fall on the moral escalator when they degraded themselves with addictive substances. Because the saloon was generally a masculine social sphere, women often drank in private settings, especially the home. Many female alcoholics became addicted to "patent medicines"—composed largely of alcohol—prescribed to cure a variety of minor aches and pains. Although male drunkards were chastised for failing as husbands and fathers, drunkenness in women aroused even more concern for children's welfare, because mothers were the primary caretakers of youth.

Women of all social classes were vulnerable to addictive behavior. Poor and working-class women often succumbed to distilled liquor, whereas the consumption of champagne in upper-class society prompted some affluent women to abuse the festive beverage. A large percentage of opiate addicts in the nineteenth century were wealthy, educated women who hid their drug addiction behind a veil of other socially acceptable ailments. Women faced special obstacles in getting help for their addiction-related problems. Even asylums that catered to women kept separate living quarters and entrances to protect their patients' secrecy. Others maintained a male-only environment. One physician even justified gender exclusion by claiming that women could smuggle liquor into the hospital in the folds of their petticoats and dresses! Thus, although some women benefited from treatment, others continued to harm themselves—and their families—in part owing to gender stereotypes and barriers.

While credentialed healers worked to develop legitimate therapies for alcoholics and drug addicts, phony "quack doctors" concocted pills and potions promising "miracle cures" for inebriates. For over a century, alcoholics and addicts and their loved ones have responded to false promises of quick remedies purveyed by unethical salesmen. Some advertisements and mail-order catalogs targeted wives and family members of alcoholics, claiming that drunkards could be cured without their cooperation or knowledge of treatment. Such ads instructed wives secretly to add drops to their husbands' drinks—in order to magically cure them of their affliction. In reality, such potions induced vomiting but failed to offer a lasting cure. Other fraudulent cures contained quantities of the drugs they were alleged to cure. Patent medicines often contained large doses of alcohol and sometimes also included opium, morphine, or cocaine. Before 1906, when the federal government passed the Pure Food and Drug Act requiring medicines to be sold with accurate labels, unscrupulous healers could peddle these products without disclosing their true contents. The 1906 act did help to reduce the number of fraudulent medicines sold in the United States, but even today Americans must remain skeptical of drugs, gimmicks, or "quick-fix" programs that promise easy solutions to complex addiction problems.

As the nineteenth century gave way to the twentieth, the temperance movement successfully campaigned for its ultimate achievement: enacting a federal statute outlawing the sale of alcoholic beverages. In 1919, the nation passed the Eighteenth Amendment to the Constitution, the beginning of the Prohibition era in the United States. It is difficult for historians to know for sure, however, the extent to which Prohibition actually prohibited Americans from drinking to excess. Evidence suggests that drinking declined among the poor and the working class. Contraband and stockpiled booze was available during the 1920s, but high prices made it more accessible to Americans who had the money, and often the social connections, to obtain it. In general, medical evidence reveals that Prohibition probably helped to reduce mortality from alcoholism and cirrhosis of the liver. Furthermore, economic data suggest that the broad ranks of working-class and middle-class families spent considerably less money on alcohol—and used that extra income to buy domestic appliances, conveniences, and necessities to enhance home life. Some families funneled previous drink expenditures into savings accounts, an added bonus for parents and children alike. It can also be assumed that, like most other Americans, women as a group drank less during Prohibition. One group that may have increased its consumption is youth, especially young men and women of the more affluent social classes. As immortalized in the classic stories and novels of F. Scott Fitzgerald, upscale youth often drank at fashionable private clubs, parties, and speakeasies—sometimes to excess.

But to those drinkers who did not curtail their consumption during the 1920s, Prohibition was not particularly kind. Not only did pubs and taverns close their doors when alcohol was rendered illegal, so too did the majority of treatment hospitals and clinics. Although excessive drinking had always had a moral stigma attached to it, inebriety was not considered a criminal act during the nineteenth century. But after the Eighteenth Amendment was passed, the public assumed—at least outwardly—that the problems of chronic drinkers would vanish with the saloon. Since drinking had become a criminal matter, Americans were less likely to support a humane therapeutic environment that would treat (rather than punish) inebriates. Therefore, even though a large number of families benefited from Prohibition, those families that did include alcoholics tended to suffer from a scarcity of treatment options.

Morphine addicts also suffered from the fact that more doctors were refusing to help manage the withdrawal process by prescribing calculated amounts of addictive substances. After several Supreme Court cases in the 1910s cracked down on physicians who aided addicts in this manner, nearly all of the nation's "morphine maintenance clinics" shut down in the face of government and community pressure. Sarah Graham-Mulhall, author of *Opium: The Demon Flower* (1926), is quoted as saying that "addicts are not only turned away from hospitals, but they are shunned by civic and philanthropic organizations. Every one is afraid of them; no one cares what becomes of them" (White 1998, 114–115). In addition, there was a significant demographic change with respect to drug addicts in U.S. cities. Compared to earlier reports that most narcotic addicts were affluent middle-aged women, by 1920 most drug addicts in New York City were young males. A third of the addicts treated at the New York City Narcotics Clinic in 1919 were under twenty years of age—a new trend that raised concerns about the health and behavior of urban youth (White 1998). Many of those addicts were viewed as social misfits and "underworld types" who banded together in groups on the margins of dance halls, pool rooms, and other places of commercialized amusement. For well over a century, Americans had evinced concern for children raised by addicted parents. But by the 1920s, it was clear that parents, too, needed to worry about the drinking and drug use of the younger generation.

The repeal of Prohibition in 1933 marked a watershed in the history of drugs and alcohol. Repeal not only marked a fundamental shift in moral and cultural values but also opened up new possibilities for the treatment of substance abuse. Of paramount importance was the founding of Alcoholics Anonymous (AA) in 1935—a not-for-profit fellowship of men and women who meet together on an egalitarian basis to overcome their common affliction. Founded by two men in Akron, Ohio, AA is commonly known as a "self-help" organization—a therapeutic community run not by doctors or other medical experts, but collectively by alcoholics themselves. The foundation of AA is the Twelve Steps: guidelines for spiritual commitment and interpersonal behavior that form the heart of the program's philosophy. Although the fellowship originated during the Great Depression, it gained a nationwide reputation during the 1940s, when mass-circulation magazines and newspapers began to publicize the new program. In 1957, there were approximately 200,000 members of AA across the United States. Since that time, AA has become the largest and most influential addiction treatment program in the world. The fellowship's main publication, the Big Book—also known as the "bible" of AA—has become the most widely read book on alcoholism in twentieth-century U.S. history, selling over 10 million copies by 1999 (Makela et al. 1996; Makela 1957).

Alcoholics Anonymous has been intimately connected with families and family life since its founding. The two founders of AA—Bill Wilson of New York City and Dr. Robert Smith of Akron, Ohio—were both middle-aged, white, Protestant, married men when they joined together in search of sobriety. From the beginning, their wives—Lois Wilson and Anne Smith—were involved in their husbands' treatment rituals and eventually worked to establish an auxiliary fellowship for wives and other family members of alcoholics. During the 1940s, the majority of AA members were men (a fact that did not begin to change significantly until at least the 1970s). From the outset, the wives of AA members began to meet informally to discuss their own situations and the problems of living with alcoholic husbands. In 1952, Lois Wilson officially founded the Al-Anon Family Groups (also known as Al-Anon) to serve the needs of spouses, parents, and children affected by a loved one's alcoholism. (Anne Smith died in 1949, so she did not live to see the expansion of Al-Anon on a national level.) To some extent, AA and Al-Anon mirrored the Washingtonian and Martha Washington movements that had flourished a century earlier. But in terms of longevity and cultural influence, they have far surpassed their predecessors.

The spouses of alcoholics in the 1940s and 1950s shared many experiences with their nineteenth-century counterparts. In both eras, heavy drinkers frequently failed to manage their domestic responsibilities, were prone to job-related problems and unemployment, and often lapsed into emotionally neglectful or physically abusive behavior. But by the post–World War II era, the fellowships of AA and Al-Anon—along with a range of medical and psychological experts—treated families of alcoholics in very different ways. Despite Benjamin Rush's early diagnoses of inebriety, prior to the mid-twentieth century, alcohol abuse was generally regarded as a moral problem. But after World War II, experts engendered a new conception of "the alcoholic family" to go along with the modern view of alcoholism as an illness. In the minds of temperance reformers, the "drunkard's wife" was a helpless victim of circumstance. But for twentieth-century experts, both drinkers and their nondrinking spouses played a formidable role in creating a dysfunctional family in which both marital partners deviated from normative gender roles. Psychiatrists and social workers counseled wives of alcoholic men and believed that they were active participants in the "marital misery" they suffered. Whereas the WCTU believed that a man's drinking posed a threat to *all* women and children in society, postwar experts assumed that alcohol abuse was problematic only in particular households. Rather than try to stop all people from drinking, they urged individual women to scrutinize and improve their emotional reactions to their husbands' drinking.

Some psychiatrists and social workers, incorporating Freudian theories into their analyses, even criticized women for selecting alcoholic husbands in the first place. In their view, such women subconsciously wanted to marry ineffectual, passive men whose drinking would allow their wives to become the dominant member of the family. Such women became overbearing spouses and mothers, treating their husbands and children like helpless dependents. Other experts, however, viewed both wives and husbands of alcoholics more sympathetically. Certainly, the founders of Al-Anon aimed to help—and not to blame— women who were trapped in an alcoholic marriage. But they shared with other experts the notion that the spouses of abusive drinkers could play a significant role in perpetuating, or stopping, a loved one's drinking. In their view, a man or woman seeking to achieve sobriety needed the emotional and spiritual support of a spouse who would help him or her through the difficult recovery process. During the 1950s, few experts or AA members advised women to divorce their husbands, even in cases of adultery or mildly abusive behavior. Indeed, society at large cast a disapproving eye toward divorce in the 1950s—so alcoholism experts were in lockstep with the general culture in this regard. With few exceptions, families were urged to stay together no matter what the cost during the mid-twentieth century. For those couples who were able to maintain sobriety and a more harmonious marriage, this trend had a positive effect. But for those who continued to experience unhappiness, antidivorce sentiment worsened domestic discontent.

Of course, alcohol was not the only substance to be abused during the 1950s. Although many people drank in order to relieve stress and anxiety, others turned to doctors and psychiatrists to prescribe mind-altering drugs. Indeed, during the late 1950s and 1960s, drugs called the minor tranquilizers were commonly discussed in the media and used by millions of Americans. These tranquilizers, which included brand names such as Valium and Miltown, were often called "happy pills" or "mother's little helpers" in the popular press. Drug companies claimed that tranquilizers were not habit forming, and doctors prescribed them to millions of Americans—especially women— in an effort to improve their lives. Advertisements for these drugs told physicians that tranquilizers would relieve their patients' "emotional and muscular tension," making it easier for people "to lead a normal family life"

A ten-year-old watches disapprovingly as her parents smoke and drink. (Elizabeth Crews)

(Smith 1985, 66–82). Although some people no doubt were helped by the limited use of such drugs, many others developed addictions and learned the hard way that the stresses and problems of daily life cannot simply be swallowed away with a pill.

During the 1960s, many Americans continued to drink alcohol and use prescription drugs—but with the dawn of the "counterculture," illegal drugs gained a larger following and caused a great deal of social concern. Against a backdrop of vehement social protest and outrage against the Vietnam War, many college-age youth became "hippies," participating in a subculture in which illicit and

experimental drugs played a prominent role. In particular, the use of marijuana increased rapidly, spreading from communities of Mexican farm laborers and African American city dwellers to the broader ranks of the white working and middle classes. Used and praised by rock musicians, marijuana became popular among millions of youth who were not part of the counterculture per se. Hallucinogenic drugs, including lysergic acid diethylamide (LSD), also gained a following during the 1960s and 1970s. Indeed, by the late 1970s, when the tail end of the baby boom generation became high school seniors, about 40 percent of them affirmed that they "regularly" smoked marijuana—a statistic that clearly points to a sea change in the values and behavior of American youth (White 1998). For many, experimental drug use was "just a phase," associated with a broader cultural rebellion against the political establishment and the adult generation. But for others, casual drug use could develop into a powerful addiction.

This generation of drug users, embarking on young adulthood by the 1980s, helped fuel a great expansion of the drug treatment industry. Although AA and Al-Anon remain voluntary nonprofit organizations, their Twelve-Step programs have been adopted by treatment centers, counselors, and other segments of the addiction-treatment industry in order to produce profits as well as sober patients. The number of private addiction communities—often known simply as "rehab"—have mushroomed. In the short span of time from 1979 to 1982, the number of hospital-based and independent addiction treatment units increased by almost 50 percent. To some observers, addiction treatment even qualified as a kind of fad. No less a prominent citizen than the wife of a former president, Betty Ford, became associated with a line of treatment centers, which served over 33,300 people by the mid-1980s (White 1998).

During this period, the term *codependency* was coined, becoming a major buzzword in popular culture in the United States. The contemporary idea of codependency emerged out of therapists' growing emphasis on the ways in which family members—and the family as a dynamic system—adjusted to the deteriorating role performance of an addicted family member. Al-Anon planted the seeds of the notion that well-intended relatives could inadvertently help, or "enable," alcoholics to sustain their

compulsive drinking. During the 1980s, many experts extended this concept to suggest that family members were themselves afflicted with a disease—the "disease" of codependency. Further attention was also paid to the idea that parental alcoholism afflicted emotional damage upon children. In 1957, Al-Anon added a new branch of support groups explicitly designed for the teenaged children of alcoholics. Alateen is based on the premise that young people growing up in an alcoholic home face special problems that can best be overcome by interacting with youth facing similar challenges. During the 1980s, other specialty groups were formed for the "adult children" of alcoholics. Codependency experts argued that childhood trauma altered one's passage into adulthood, producing a lifetime of psychological turmoil and self-destructive behavior. According to some critics, this branch of addiction treatment takes the focus away from actual drug and alcohol abuse and traps people into an infantilizing model of emotional development. At the same time, however, teenagers with substance-abuse problems have received increasingly sophisticated treatment since the 1980s. Some recent trends in the treatment of adolescents include better educational and recreational services, more family involvement and family therapy, and a greater understanding of the importance of peer networks and social support in treatment.

—*Lori E. Rotskoff*

See also Divorce, History of; Drug and Alcohol Abuse

References and Further Reading
Epstein, Barbara L. 1981. *The Politics of Domesticity: Women, Evangelism, and Temperance in Nineteenth-Century*

America. Middletown, CT: Wesleyan University Press.

Farber, David. 1994. *The Age of Great Dreams: America in the 1960s.* New York: Hill and Wang.

Graham-Mulhall, Sarah. 1926. *Opium: The Demon Flower.* New York: Harold Vinal.

Kurtz, Ernest. 1979. *Not God: A History of Alcoholics Anonymous.* Center City, MN: Hazelden.

Lender, Mark Edward, and James Kirby Martin. 1987. *Drinking in America: A History.* New York: The Free Press.

Makela, Klaus. 1957. *Alcoholics Anonymous Comes of Age.* New York: Harper Brothers.

Makela, Klaus, et al. 1996. *Alcoholics Anonymous as a Mutual-Help Movement: A Study in Eight Societies.* Madison: University of Wisconsin Press.

Rapping, Elayne. 1996. *The Culture of Recovery: Making Sense of the Self-Help Movement in Women's Lives.* Boston: Beacon Press.

Rotskoff, Lori E. Forthcoming. *Sober Husbands and Supportive Wives: Men, Women, and Alcohol in Post-war America.* Chapel Hill: University of North Carolina Press.

Smith, Mickey C. 1985. *Small Comfort: A History of the Minor Tranquilizers.* New York: Praeger.

White, William L. 1998. *Slaying the Dragon: The History of Addiction Treatment and Recovery in America.* Bloomington, IL: Chestnut Health Systems.

Alimony

Alimony is monetary support given by one spouse, generally the husband, to maintain the other partner following a divorce. In legal thought, the marital tie that obliges a husband to provide for his wife is not severed by a divorce decree. An alimony award orders periodic payments, the amounts of which are determined according to the needs of the wife and the ability of the husband to pay. Until the liberalization of divorce laws, only very serious and aggravated types of marital transgressions entitled a wife to a divorce. As the injured party, a woman received sympathy from the courts, and her application for a large amount of permanent alimony would be granted. In the minds of some judges, the notion of punishment, depending on the degree of the husband's moral delinquency, played a part in determining alimony. A woman might be awarded as much as half of the combined income of the spouses, and often she received about a third of their joint income.

As societal changes in the 1970s resulted in more women entering the workforce, alimony awards changed to reflect a wife's ability to support herself. Husbands also began to receive alimony. The majority of alimony awards at the opening of the twenty-first century are designed to provide the injured spouse with enough time to make a transition to a new life but prevent an able-bodied spouse from living off the labors of the former partner. These awards are given irrespective of the obligor's ability to pay more support and irrespective of the standard of living established during the marriage.

For women who entered marriage with the expectation of spending the rest of their lives as homemakers or women who focused on child care instead of a career, the virtual elimination of long-term support has often caused grievous harm. Unable to match the income of a partner who has spent his life on a career track and frequently faced with the demands of raising children, these women experience a significant drop in their standard of living. Where the financial situation of both the parties is approximately equal, no alimony is ordered. The majority of marriages end without a grant of alimony. If a large imbalance in the financial circumstances of the spouses exists, courts have held that this disparity outweighs the importance of the recipient's ability to be self-supporting. The recipient is entitled to maintain the marital standard of living.

—*Caryn E. Neumann*

See also Divorce, History of

References and Further Reading
Katz, Sanford N., and Monroe L. Inker. 1979. *Fathers, Husbands and Lovers: Legal Rights and Responsibilities.* Chicago: American Bar Association
Mason, Mary Ann. 1988. *The Equality Trap.* New York: Simon and Schuster.
Peterson, Richard R. 1989. *Women, Work, and Divorce.* Albany: State University of New York Press.

American Family Association

The American Family Association (AFA) was founded by Donald Wildmon, a Methodist minister, in 1977. In its early years, the organization was called the National Federation for Decency and focused its efforts on removing programs it considered antifamily from television. Rooted in Christian fundamentalism, this included all programs that contained nonprocreative sex or that featured non-traditional families. Its first boycott, held in 1978, was of Sears Roebuck for its sponsorship of the television programs *Three's Company*, *Charlie's Angels*, and *All in the Family*. In recent years the AFA has become more directly involved in politics. In the 1990s it headed the drive to restrict federal funding of art that could be categorized "obscene," and it joined the Christian Coalition in promoting anti–gay and lesbian rights legislation. It publishes a monthly journal listing objectionable television programs as well as products to boycott and is an advocate of home schooling. The organization is an example of the resurgence of grassroots, Religious Right organizations in the late twentieth century.

Throughout its history, the AFA has been consistent in condemning television programs it considers antifamily. Perhaps its most famous struggle in this field was in the 1990s, when it called for its members to boycott *NYPD Blue*. Also well publicized was its boycott of Disney, which it called because it felt the values represented in recent Disney films had become antifamily and because Disney hosted "gay and lesbian days" at Disney World. The AFA has had a significant income ($6 million in 1993; Berlet 1995), so it has also had the resources to influence politics at the local, state, and national levels. Consequently it has challenged local legislation and school board decisions, at times appealing all the way to the U.S. Supreme Court. Its headquarters is in Tupelo, Mississippi.

—*Linda Heidenreich*

References and Further Reading
Adams, William E. 1994. "Pre-Election Anti-Gay Ballot Initiative Challenges: Issues of Electoral Fairness, Majoritarian Tyranny, and Direct Democracy." *Ohio State Law Journal* 55: 583–647.
Berlet, Chip. 1995. *Eyes Right: Challenging the Right Wing Backlash.* Boston: South End Press.
Diamont, Sara. 1998. *Not by Politics Alone: The Enduring Influence of the Christian Right.* New York: Guilford Press.
Frum, David. 1994. *Dead Right.* New York: HarperCollins.
Strossen, Nadine. 1998. "Lisa Herdahl and Religious Liberty." *Cleveland State Law Review* 49: 289–304.
Terl, Allan H. 2000. "An Essay on the History of Lesbian and Gay Rights in Florida." *Nova Law Review* 24: 793–853.

Anorexia Nervosa

Anorexia nervosa is an eating disorder characterized by the loss of excessive amounts of weight (15 percent or more of body weight). It is a serious psychological disorder that is extremely difficult to treat. People who suffer from anorexia are generally female (95 percent) and are usually adolescents or young adults (Santrock 1999, 531). It is estimated that up to 1 percent of adolescent females suffer from the disorder (American Psychiatric Association 1994, 543). In the past, anorexia was a disorder for middle-class white girls, but recent research indicates that the disorder is now more equally distributed across racial and socioeconomic classes. Because of the growing popularity of the topic in the mass media in the last few decades of the twentieth century and the influential role of the cultural desire for thinness, anorexia is often thought to be a new disorder. "Starvation sickness" has been recognized for centuries, however, and has always primarily affected females. The newest thing about the disorder is our cultural understanding of its cause and import. In past centuries, women starved themselves to be more "spiritual" and closer to God, and the starvation only became a problem when the victim was close to death.

Characteristics

In current times, as a precursor to their extreme loss of weight, anorexics have a constant preoccupation with food and dieting. Although they often refuse to eat, or eat very little, anorexics generally like being around, preparing, and even talking about food. Exercise often becomes an obsession as the anorexic struggles to lose weight, resulting in hyperactivity. If the desired weight loss is achieved, an even more extreme goal is often set in order to become as thin as possible. Despite the success of the dieting and despite the weight loss being reflected in the measurements of the scale, however, anorexia is also characterized by a disturbed body image. That is, the anorexic fails to see herself in a positive light and continues to be unhappy with her body even after weight loss. It would appear that anorexics are unable to see themselves as they really are—they are unable to respond appropriately to their own visual image in the mirror (Rice 1999, 119). Often, even after being hospitalized for their condition, anorexics continue to report "feeling fat."

Associated Conditions

The most common age of onset is during adolescence, when normal physiological changes occur as the body enters puberty. For females, this means a layer of body fat that is deposited especially around the hips and breasts in preparation for reproductive maturity. In order for a female to experience menarche (first menstruation), her body fat must be at least 17 percent. Anorexics who lose massive amounts of weight and accompanying body fat eventually stop menstruating. In addition to this, anorexics experience many other symptoms, some more serious than others (Rice 1999, 118). Along with appearing extremely thin and emaciated, anorexics feel cold much of the time. Often a fine layer of body hair grows over the body as it struggles to maintain body heat for the anorexic, because hypothermia is a problem. Dehydration is also a problem, resulting in constipation, changes in metabolism, and electrolyte imbalances. Abdominal distress and kidney malfunctions may also occur. Heart problems include slow heartbeat, low blood pressure, and cardiac arrest (often ending in death). Up to 10 percent of anorexics die from medical conditions related to malnutrition resulting from starvation (Rice 1999, 118). Psychological problems are also commonly associated with anorexia. Depression, moodiness, and helplessness may occur along with diminished interest in sex (American Psychiatric Association 1994, 541). Loneliness is a commonly experienced emotion, especially with insecurity and isolation. Low self-esteem is synonymous with anorexia, as are high levels of anxiety. Malnutrition also results in brain abnormalities and impaired mental functions, adding to the serious nature of the illness.

Causes of Anorexia

Anorexia tends to run in families, and this statistical fact contributes to the problem of trying to determine its cause. Currently, there are at least four different theories about what causes anorexia (Rice 1999, 120). One of these, possibly the most popular theory today, is a social theory that attributes anorexia to the cultural importance placed on thinness and attractiveness. Perceived societal pressures to be thin and to conform to cultural definitions of beauty may drive some young women to develop an eating disorder. Although anorexics tend to have negative attitudes about physical attractiveness, their desire to be thin still threatens their health.

Sexual identity issues lie at the core of another theory about the cause of anorexia. The disorder normally first appears during puberty, when the adolescent is also grappling with sexual identity conflicts. As anxiety develops regarding the physiological changes of puberty, the adolescent is forced to confront her own sexual identification. It may be that adolescents who are not yet ready to accept

their feminine sexual identities may somehow seek to "repress" their physical development, therefore halting puberty. Dieting and exercise ensure a thin, masculine appearance, and even menstruation stops and body fat falls far below normal levels. At the same time, the adolescent's body image becomes greatly distorted, exaggerating any remaining vestiges of pubertal development.

Family systems theory offers another possible explanation for anorexia. It has long been known that people with eating disorders, especially anorexia, have negative relationships with their parents. Often the parents appear to be overcontrolling, rigid, and extremely strict. Self-initiated starvation, a preoccupation with food, and obsessive exercising may all be attempts by the anorexic to maintain some sense of control, at least regarding her own body. Since anorexics often have perfectionistic personality characteristics, this attempt at control through extreme self-denial makes sense. There is an alternative explanation for this correlation, however. In fact, it is impossible to know whether negative relationships with parents appear before the onset of the disorder or after its onset, as parents fear for their children's health and attempt to take steps to handle the situation by assuming more control and more rigid behavior and expectations.

Biological theories point toward a possible genetic component, as well as physiological or neurochemical disturbances. Specifically, disturbances to the hypothalamus in the brain may result in anorexic behavior, and so may excesses in the brain neurotransmitter serotonin. Starvation may serve as a mechanism to reduce the amount of serotonin present in the brain, which also reduces anxiety. As levels of serotonin decrease, the sensitivity of serotonin receptors in the brain increases to make up for the smaller amount of the available neurotransmitter. Thus, a vicious cycle is created whereby functionally there is still too much serotonin in the brain and starvation decreases that amount, increasing receptor sensitivity, and so on.

Anorexia has proven to be an extremely difficult psychological disorder to treat (American Psychiatric Association 1994, 543). Each of the theories mentioned above has a corresponding course of treatment, but so far the most effective treatments are behavioral approaches. At least in the short term, rewarding hospitalized anorexics by allowing them to leave the room or to spend time socializing after they have eaten has been successful in accomplishing weight gain. Long-term psychological therapy is usually necessary in order to prevent relapse and to establish acceptable levels of self-esteem and self-confidence for normal functioning.

—Elaine S. Barry

See also Bulimia; Eating Disorders

References and Further Reading
American Psychiatric Association. 1994. The Diagnostic and Statistical Manual of Mental Disorders. 4th ed. Washington, DC: American Psychiatric Association.
Rice, F. Philip. 1999. The Adolescent: Development, Relationships, and Culture. Boston: Allyn and Bacon.
Santrock, John J. 1999. Adolescence: An Introduction. Dubuque, IA: Brown and Benchmark.

Apprenticeship

Apprenticeship, historically, was a form of servitude in which an individual, usually a young boy, was bound by legal contract or by informal agreement to an employer ("master") who in turn was bound for a specified number of years to instruct the youth in the skills of a given trade, craft, or profession. An examination of apprenticeship in the British North American colonies and later the United States intersects the private history of the family, the history of work and labor amid the rise of capitalism, and the larger evolution of American individualism. Bound most often by legal contract, young boys in the seventeenth, eighteenth, and early nineteenth centuries entered into households of kin or of strangers as they learned the skills peculiar to a craft or trade. By the eve of the American Civil War, however, industrialization and its massive reformation of U.S. society and culture had eclipsed the custom of apprenticeship. Indeed, the story of the young American apprentice who overcomes cruel masters to achieve success, replicating the American revolutionary rhetoric of the patriots severing ties with a heartless, all-powerful monarch, became popular only after the turn of the nineteenth century when apprenticeship itself was on the wane.

The British colonists in the New World brought with them a system of apprenticeship well devised for the English economy and social structure. Dating back to the Middle Ages, apprenticeship had become by the seventeenth century a traditional practice with which to secure the training of the males of "middling sort" families. In 1563, the English Statute of Artificers required parents to "bind" their sons in a trade or in agriculture and forbade the practice of a trade or craft without the completion of an apprenticeship. Exempt from this law were families whose wealth or connections allowed them to provide business

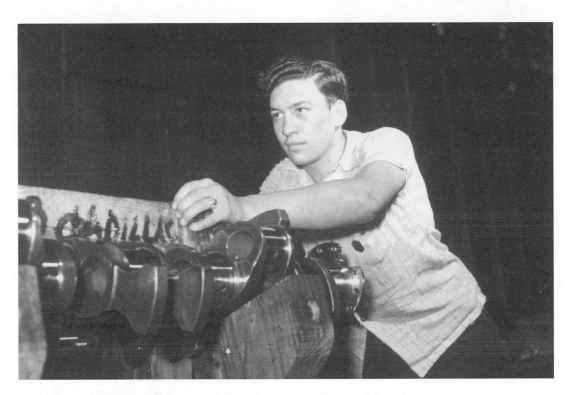

An apprentice at the Allison Motor Plant, Detroit, Michigan, 1942. (Library of Congress)

or professional training for their sons. By the seventeenth century, the problem of the "strolling poor" was to be resolved by the 1601 Poor Law, which allowed the state to intervene in family life. For those families unwilling or unable to apprentice their offspring, local authorities were empowered to expropriate parental authority and bind children. The typical apprenticeship lasted seven years; on the average, young males completing their terms ranged in age from twenty-one to twenty-four.

The craft guild system in England enforced these laws as well as other customs regarding apprenticeship. Composed of masters and journeymen (those men who had completed their apprenticeships but had not yet the resources with which to maintain their own shops or trades), these guilds controlled membership to ensure high wages, regulated training, and maintained quality control over work. Membership in a guild required that the journeyman exhibit knowledge of his craft through the completion of a masterpiece.

In the American colonies, however, the requirements of labor differed, and guild governance was difficult, if not impossible, to maintain. In a primarily agricultural economy, guilds were unnecessary, and the power of law was greatly curtailed by the lack of a full-fledged legal system. Too, resources for craft production—both labor and materials—were scarce and often an ocean's distance away. As a result, a "master" might not have been sanctioned by the pertinent guild or even adequately trained in the craft he advertised. He could legally bind as many apprentices as he liked and offer expert or little or no training at all to his charges. No guild oversight or sanctions meant that training was unregulated and the quality of craftsmanship was varied and more often poor. Those apprentices nearing the end of their servitude were not required to create masterpieces, and as journeymen could join no guild that would protect their livelihood. The guild system was rendered obsolete, especially in New England, where agrarian livelihoods mandated a different labor system. Farmers tended to teach themselves a skilled craft to augment income and fill long winter hours. Farmers trained their own sons and took in apprentices from the local area. Barter in goods was often the medium of exchange, and this local economy of labor and goods created a family-based system of training. Girls were exempt from apprenticeship, although records showed that women learned crafts from family members, usually a father or husband, or were indentured to "huswifery," likely a form of legal guardianship for indigent girls. The plantation economy of the southern colonies (and later states) greatly diminished the need for apprentices as laborers. Slave artisans, bound for life, created the goods needed for their master's gain.

In the British colonies of North America, apprenticeship became a matter of agreements, whether as legal contracts or as informal verbal arrangements between parents and masters. Apprenticeship was a form of indentured servitude and was legally recognized in a specific document. Indentures were more or less standardized in form: A master agreed to shelter, feed, clothe, and care for his young charge as well as teach him the "art and mystery" of the specific craft or trade. Some indentures included specific provisions for public education specific to the craft or trade. In turn, the apprentice agreed to abide by the master's rules, to forgo marriage and immoral and illegal activities, and to protect the sanctity of the master's business as well as the master's household. The agreement—written, signed, and witnessed in duplicate on a single sheet of paper—was torn with an indented edge, the two halves retained by the contracting parties. The indented edges offered proof of the authenticity of the contract if ever legally contested. Once the apprenticeship was completed, the two duplicates were cancelled and often destroyed. Thus this form of evidence of the extent of the apprentice system in the colonial period is historically incomplete, for only in eastern seaports were these agreements registered through any public agency, in a move to prevent runaway apprentices from passing as journeymen.

The American Revolution not only severed the political ties in the guise of the father-son relationship encoded in the political government of monarch and people but also disrupted the already tenuous tradition of apprenticeship. Economic fluctuations caused by postwar depression, the War of 1812, and a series of boom-and-bust cycles of the early nineteenth century greatly diminished apprenticeship. The rise of mechanization, the factory system, and the lure of cash wages—the market revolution—proved at one and the same time too irresistible to youths wishing freedom and too overwhelming for masters to ignore. The traditional master-apprentice relationship collapsed under the weight of the predations of the new economy. The rise of print, for example, allowed more young men to learn the "art and mystery" of various artisan skills and cultures through reading, rather than practice. Industrialization replaced certain craft traditions, such as shoemaking. And the second Great Awakening brought evangelical reform to the household. Willfulness and authoritarianism in a master/father/husband were considered detrimental to the development of personal responsibility in other household members, and apprentices were no exception. The costs of republicanism and of religious beliefs were "insubordinate" apprentices who no longer deferred to their masters' control.

In turn, an "apprentice culture" was formed in the first half of the nineteenth century, a response both to economic dislocations and to the ferment of reform characteristic of the era. As Americans' concepts of childhood changed, so did their attitudes toward apprenticeship as an institution. Educational reformers counseled kindness and not violence (physical or otherwise), and after 1820 the nation's public school system offered youth an alternative to a tradition in which obeisance to authority was mandated. Moreover, educators encouraged students to go beyond the memorization of the "wisdom of the ages" offered in previous generations by teachers and masters alike. Apprentices themselves improved their collective lot, creating "apprentices' libraries" (especially in the years of economic depression) to which under- or unemployed young males could apply themselves in learning new technologies and business strategies. Other impoverished youths banded together as gangs (often called "street Arabs" by critics), seeking in their numbers protection and survival on the dark streets of rapidly growing cities. Clearly the rise in indigency marked the in-

eluctable decline in the traditional apprenticeship system. Mid-nineteenth-century reformers worked to place these young boys with farmers, at houses of refuge, or in reform schools.

After the panic of 1837, the ability of apprentices to rise to the ranks of journeymen and masters fell precipitously, as they were unable to compete with large-scale mechanization and the flourishing of the factory system. No longer a temporary member of a master's family, the apprentice sought out peers to form anew a culture based on personal autonomy. Little wonder, then, that that quintessential rags-to-riches story of Benjamin Franklin's rise from abused apprentice to self-realized man of enlightenment and wealth became so popular a book in this era. Franklin's *Autobiography* (1987), along with the myriad of advice books dedicated to American youth published in the years before the Civil War, documents many historical shifts in the history of family: from deference to reciprocity, from tradition to innovation, from collectivism to individualism.

—*Shirley Teresa Wajda*

References and Further Reading
Clark, Christopher, and Donald M. Scott. 1988. "The Diary of an Apprentice Cabinetmaker: Edward Jenner Carpenter's 'Journal,' 1844–45." *Proceedings of the American Antiquarian Society* (October): 303–394.
Darton, William. 1823. *Little Jack of All Trades, or Mechanical Arts Described in Prose and Verse, Suited to the Capacities of Children, with Engraved Representations of the Different Trades.* London: Harvey and Darton.
Franklin, Benjamin. 1987. *Benjamin Franklin: Writings.* Ed. J. A. Leo Lemay. New York: Library of America.
Quimby, Ian M. G. 1963. "Apprenticeship in Colonial Philadelphia." M.A. thesis, University of Delaware.

Rorabaugh, W. J. 1986. *The Craft Apprentice: From Franklin to the Machine Age in America.* New York: Oxford University Press.

Asian American Families

Like families of Native Americans and Latino/as, Asian American families are characterized by considerable diversity. Although they may be viewed by outsiders as homogenous, Asian Americans encompass a multitude of ethnic groups originating in over two dozen nations, with extremely diverse cultures, languages, immigration histories, religious practices, and physical features. Differences in social class and time of immigration may further subdivide ethnic

A Chinese woman carries her child down a street in Chinatown, San Francisco. Photo by Arnold Genthe 1900–1910. (Library of Congress)

groups. Family structures among these groups reflect these divergences.

Research on Asian American families has been fairly limited, owing in part to their historically small population (approximately 3 percent of the U.S. population in 1990 [U.S. Bureau of the Census 1990]); in addition, most Asian Americans are clustered in a few regions of the United States. These two factors combine to make Asian Americans relatively invisible to the general public. An additional factor contributing to the lack of attention to Asian American families is the perception that Asian Americans are one of the more "successful" minority groups in the United States. Media and scholars have pointed to cultural and family values to explain their successes, but at the same time little systematic attention has been given to Asian American families. The primary reason there has been little research on Asian American families, however, is that it is difficult to generalize about such a diverse population. Asian American families have failed to show any one consistent pattern throughout their history in the United States. Family structure has been shaped by each group's unique history in the United States, varying immigration experiences, individual cultures, and social class. No one model can accurately describe the Asian American family, and stereotypes may mask great differences between groups.

Common generalizations made about Asian American families are that they are stable, highly disciplined and successful, and patriarchal. Although these trends may be true for some Asian American families, there is considerable diversity found among Asian ethnic groups, social classes, and generations.

First, family stability is evident through relatively high marriage rates and low

FIGURE 1   Percent Ever Married by Asian Ethnic Group and Age, 1990

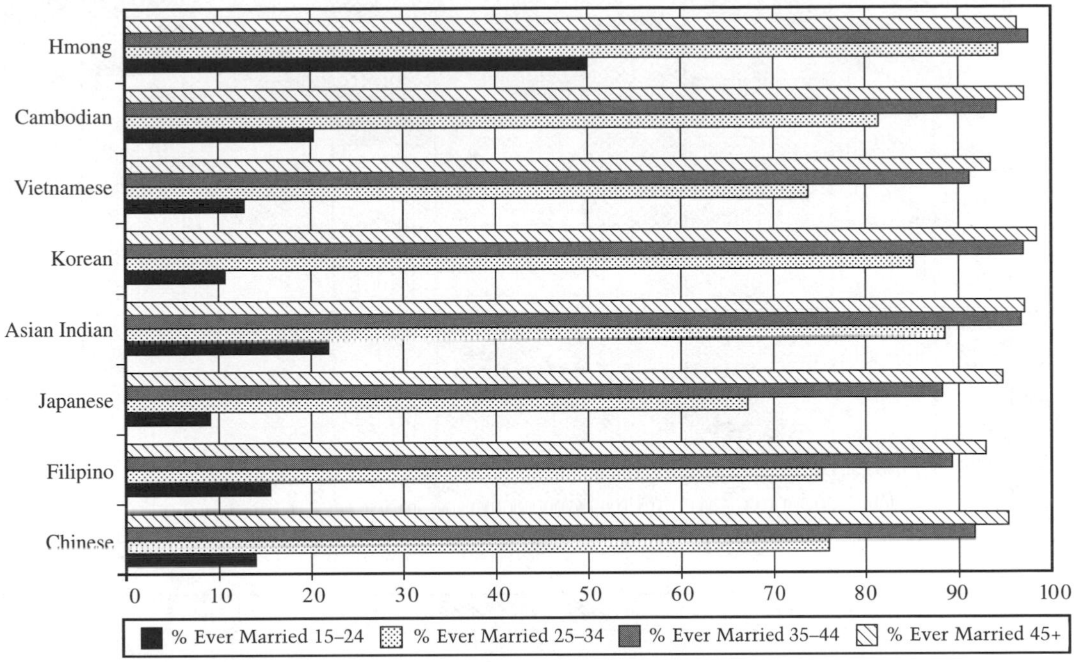

Source: U.S. Bureau of the Census. 1990. *Census of the Population and Housing.* Subject Summary Tape File 5. Washington, DC: Bureau of the Census.

divorce rates among Asian Americans. Figure 1 illustrates marriage patterns by age for a number of Asian American groups in the United States. Norms for marriage are clearly strong for all groups, but there is significant variation among groups. Although marriage is delayed for certain groups, notably Japanese Americans, other groups, such as the Hmong and Indian Americans, are much more likely to marry fairly early. Further, the divorce rate among Asian Americans is at 3.7 percent, well below the national average of 8.3 percent. There is also considerable variation, however. Japanese Americans, one of the immigrant Asian groups who have been in the United

States the longest, have the highest divorce rate of all Asian American groups at 5.4 percent. At the other extreme are Asian Indians, who have the lowest divorce rate among Asian Americans at 2.1 percent (U.S. Bureau of the Census 1990; Fong 1998, 200).

Second, Asian American families have been characterized as having strong family ties. They are often stereotyped as maintaining a solid nuclear family unit, as well as a close extended family. Figure 2 describes family structure for families with children under eighteen in 1998 in the United States. These figures suggest that Asian American families are fairly similar in pattern to white families;

FIGURE 2   Family Structure for Families with Children, 1998

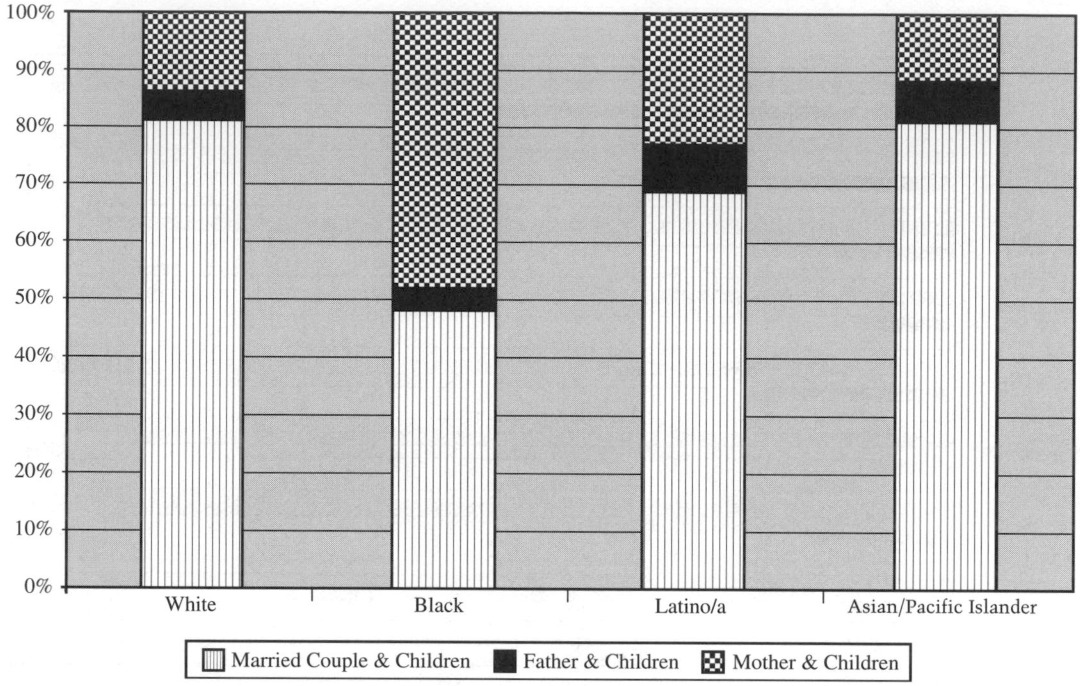

Source: U.S. Bureau of the Census. 1990. *Census of the Population and Housing.* Subject Summary Tape File 5. Washington, DC: Bureau of the Census.

indeed, Asian American children are slightly more likely to live in two-parent families than are children in white families. Only 12 percent of Asian American households with children under eighteen are headed by women, compared to 14 percent for whites, 47 percent for African Americans, and 23 percent for Latinos. This suggests that Asian American children are more likely to grow up in two-parent households. Looking more closely at these statistics, however, we can see that there are important differences between groups. As Figure 3 shows very clearly, even though rates of single-parent households in the United States are low in general, rates of single-parent households are relatively high for some groups, challenging overgeneralizations about the strength of Asian families (U.S. Bureau of the Census 1999, 62; U.S. Bureau of the Census 1990).

Third, Asian American families have been characterized by strong discipline and hard work, traits said to be rooted in Asian culture and the family. Researchers point to extraordinary achievements by Asian Americans in education, income, and occupational attainment as compared to white Americans and other minority groups. Asian Americans may rank close to whites and higher than most ethnic groups in levels of education, family income, and occupational prestige. Severe

FIGURE 3   Family Structure by Ethnic Group, 1990

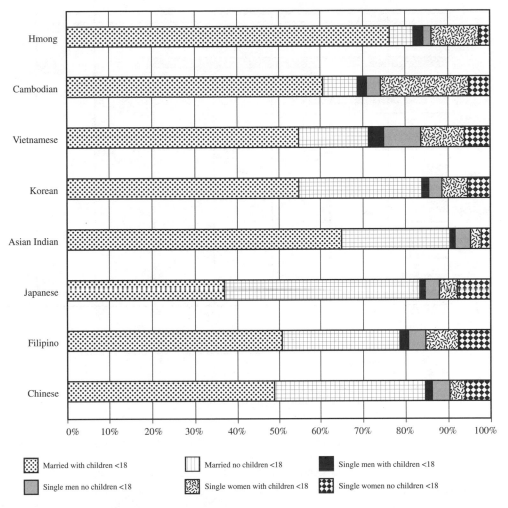

Married with children <18

Married no children <18

Single men with children <18

Single men no children <18

Single women with children <18

Single women no children <18

Source: U.S. Bureau of the Census. 1990. *Census of the Population and Housing.* Subject Summary Tape File 5. Washington, DC: Bureau of the Census.

differences, however, exist among Asian ethnic groups, creating great divisions and economic stratification within the Asian American community. For example, certain groups, notably Southeast Asian refugees, show high school completion rates below 50 percent (Kitano and Daniels 1995, 18). Similarly, although some Asian American families have been financially successful, this success often is related to the higher number of family members who earn and contribute income to the family. Many other families are disadvantaged financially. It is critical to recognize the reality of economic polarization within the Asian American community and to address the needs of the variety of Asian American families.

Figure 4 illustrates some of these trends. In 1990, 14 percent of Asian

FIGURE 4   Poverty Rates and Public Assistance Receipt by Group, 1990

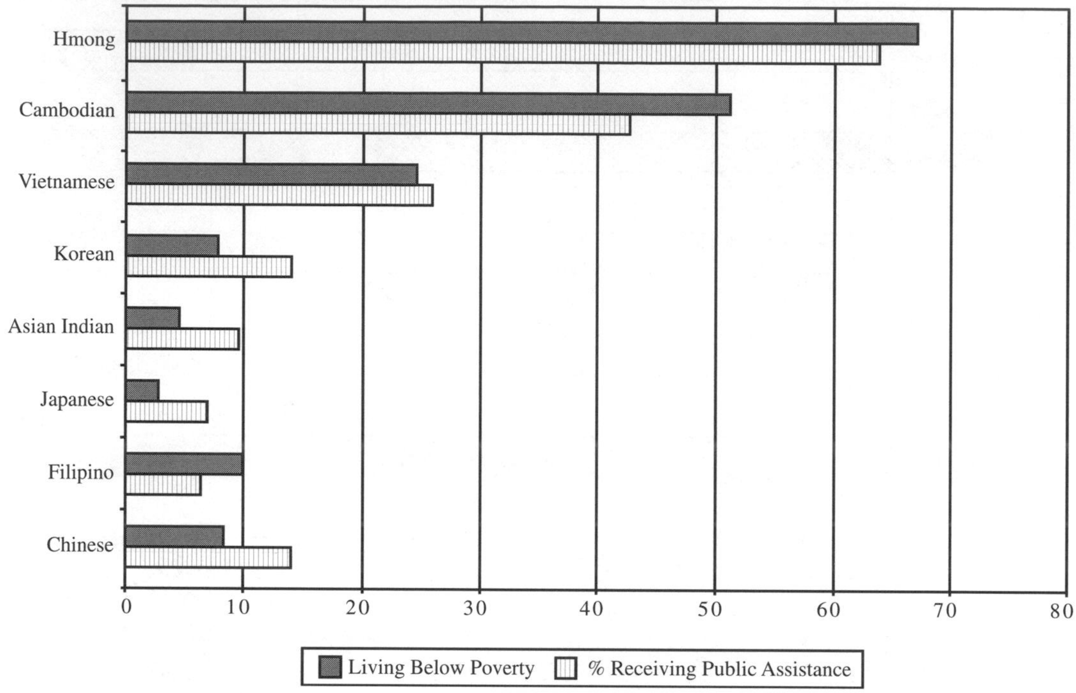

Source: U.S. Bureau of the Census. 1990. *Census of the Population and Housing.* Subject Summary Tape File 5. Washington, DC: Bureau of the Census.

American families in the United States were classified as living in poverty, well above the average for non-Hispanic whites (8 percent) (U.S. Bureau of the Census 1990; Kitano and Daniels 1995). Within Asian American families, there are particularly high levels of poverty for Hmong, Cambodians, and the Vietnamese; these families are also more likely to rely on public assistance. Stereotypes about Asian American families being affluent may have important political and policy ramifications, in particular limiting government support for poor Asian American families.

Finally, Asian American families have been described as patriarchal. Families have been characterized as dominated by husbands and fathers, with preference given to boy children, rather than girls. Women are seen as submissive and subservient to the men in their families. Yet gender relations vary substantially for Asian American families by area of origin, class level, generation, and level of assimilation. Changes in women's status are continually evolving. It is important to note, however, that domestic abuse continues to be a serious problem in many Asian American communities. This may be particularly salient for newly arrived immigrant families, in which women may be culturally isolated, cut off from family and friends in their home country, and dependent upon their husbands. Although reliable statistics on domestic violence among Asian American families are not available, there has been a remarkable increase in recognition of this problem, including a number of organizations that provide support, information, and legal aid for battered Asian and Asian American women and their children.

In short, Asian Americans and Asian American families are extremely diverse. Generalizations and stereotypes tend to mask the huge differences among Asian ethnic groups. We now highlight four distinct Asian American ethnic groups that represent the largest segments of the Asian population in the United States: Chinese American, Japanese American, Filipino American, and Indian American families.

Chinese American Families
Chinese American families have been labeled with several "typical" characteristics such as family stability, close ties, economic self-sufficiency, conservatism, and female subordination. These features, however, are mere generalizations of a group that is marked by considerable diversity and heterogeneity. Reflecting the diversity found among Asian Americans, Chinese American families are composed of various social classes and subgroups as well as variations in family structure depending upon the historical period and period of immigration.

Chinese Americans were the first group of Asian Americans to enter the United States, and as of 1990, they made up the largest portion of Asian Americans in the nation (one-fifth of the total Asian American population). They first arrived as a source of cheap labor in U.S. mining, agriculture, and railroad construction. Only prime-age male workers were allowed

entry, creating a Chinese community that was composed almost entirely of men. For instance, in 1890, there were 2,678 men for each 100 women (Kivisto 1995). This early gender imbalance created a bachelor society, and as a consequence, families had difficulty in developing as a part of the ethnic community. The few women were either wives or concubines of the wealthier Chinese merchants or severely exploited prostitutes held in California brothels. Antimiscegenation laws, by preventing Chinese men from marrying outside their race, further hindered any family development (Fong and Shinagawa 2000; Kitano and Daniels 1995; Kivisto 1995; Marger 1994; Taylor 1994).

Despite obstacles to family formation, the United States began to see a growth in Chinese American families in urban Chinatowns beginning in the 1920s and 1930s, owing to changes in immigration laws. These families were first formed by former laborers who had accumulated enough capital to start small businesses and who were then able to save money and send for their wives back in China. These families have been characterized as the small producer family, in which husband, wife, and children engaged in a family business, oftentimes in a laundry or restaurant. Husband and wife were mutually interdependent and in need of each other for economic survival, which led to a relatively egalitarian relationship that differed from the patriarchal relationships found in China. The absence of in-laws further freed wives of additional subordination. Although records show low divorce rates, relationships were not always harmonious. For most women, there was no alternative and no place for divorced women in the community. Further, the traditional dependency of children on parents was reversed, as children

A Japanese American family playing pickup sticks. (Elizabeth Crews)

learning English became cultural mediators and translators for their parents.

After the passage of the Immigration Act of 1965, which lifted restriction on Asian American immigration, the Chinese American community grew in size and diversity. Previous immigrants had come from the same few villages; they spoke the same language and dialect and shared the same culture. They settled in urban Chinatowns and formed tightly knit communities. Chinese immigrants after 1965, however, came from more diverse backgrounds. Many were highly educated, were from urban backgrounds, and moved into white neighborhoods and suburbs instead of inner-city enclaves. These professional dual-breadwinner families also showed a trend toward assimilation as their children attended public schools, spoke English at home, and spent considerable time with their school peers. Countering this trend, however, was a group of working-class immigrants who also immigrated after the 1965 Immigration Acts. These families first entered Chinatowns, and both husbands and wives worked long hours in less professional positions. For these families, ties between generations decreased as children spent more time unsupervised. The absence of the traditional close-knit family has been blamed for the rise in youth rebellion, delinquency, and gang violence in Chinatowns in the 1960s and 1970s.

By 1990, immigration had normalized the gender ratio in Chinese American communities, which have become almost completely balanced. Women continue to play a central economic role in the family, as reflected by the high rates of labor force participation, a characteristic shared with black women. Owing to immigration laws and sponsorship, in which families host newly arrived family members, households are still likely to include extended family members. Divorce is less common among Chinese Americans than the general population, partly as a result of social and economic barriers. A final characteristic of the Chinese American families is that an increased rate of marriage to non-Chinese is likely to transform the Chinese American community and family. Chinese American women, those with high socioeconomic backgrounds, and American-born Chinese have all been shown to be the most likely to marry non-Chinese mates.

Japanese American Families
The first wave of Japanese immigrants was composed of male laborers who migrated to Hawaii and the mainland in the late 1800s. Like early Chinese Americans, the Japanese American community faced a gender imbalance, as men far outnumbered women. Thus the Japanese family was a rarity. This changed with the gentleman's agreement in 1908 in which Japan agreed to stop issuing passports to male laborers, and the United States simultaneously agreed to prevent their entry. Instead of curbing Japanese immigration as first intended, the practice merely shifted immigration to Japanese women. The ratio of men to women was 25:1 in 1900 but shifted to 2:1 in the years following the gentleman's agree-

ment (Kitano and Daniels 1995; Marger 1994; Mindel and Habenstein 1981; Taylor 1994).

The first Japanese American families, called the Issei or first generation, were strongly shaped by the cultural traditions back in Japan and were marked by hierarchy and collectivity. They retained the hierarchical Japanese family system, in which lines of authority were heavily drawn by age and gender. Women were subservient to men, and fathers had complete authority over their children in all respects, including their future occupation and mate. Family cohesion was held intact through rigid rules rather than emotional affections and also through feelings of obligation and responsibility. Alcohol abuse, domestic violence, and long hours working in the family business were common problems.

Following the bombing of Pearl Harbor in Hawaii during World War II, more than 100,000 Japanese Americans on the West Coast were forced from their homes and imprisoned in relocation camps. The upheaval of the internment radically altered the organization of Japanese American families, as the economic and social basis of Issei authority was taken away. After the war, resettlement allowed the Nisei, or second generation, to live and work independently of their parents for the first time. Nisei families showed the effects of assimilation. The Nisei were more likely to choose their own mates, and relationships between husbands and wives were relatively more egalitarian than those of the previous generation, although there remained a significant division of labor within the family.

Today, the third generation (the Sansei), who are now of middle age, and the fourth generation (the Yonsei), who are now school-aged, show even greater equality within the family. Work is equally important, and occupation is a critical portion of identity for both men and women. Labor force participation of Japanese women continues to outrank that of most other groups in U.S. society. Thus, there is less dependence in marriage for women, which may explain why there is a higher percentage of divorce among Japanese Americans as compared to other Asian American groups (Fong 1998).

Fertility among Japanese Americans is well below that of earlier generations and lower than that of other Asian Americans, white Americans, African Americans, and Hispanics. Fertility rates first dropped in internment camps as lack of privacy prevented conjugal relations, and rates have steadily declined ever since. Combined with low rates of Japanese immigration, this decline in fertility rates has raised questions of the sustainability of the Japanese American community, which is aging rapidly. Since the 1965 Immigration Reform Act, Japanese have made up only about 3 percent of all Asian immigrants. Further, trends toward intermarriage have raised additional questions about a possible erosion of the ethnic community. Records show that only about 5 percent of the Issei intermarried, as compared to 15 percent of the Nisei and 50 percent of the Sansei (Taylor 1994). Researchers estimate that Japanese Americans are currently marrying non-Japanese at rates of 50 to 60 percent, giving this group the largest rate of exogamy of any ethnic group in the United States (Taylor 1994). This raises questions about how Japanese American families will be defined in the future (Kitano and Daniels 1995; Mindel and Habenstein 1981; Taylor 1994).

Filipino American Families
The first of three significant waves of Filipino immigration began in the early 1900s as several thousand Filipino students, many of whom were sponsored by the U.S. government, entered the United States. The second wave of Filipino immigration came in the 1920s and 1930s. Unlike earlier Filipinos who were drawn by educational opportunities, this group of Filipinos, who came with few occupational skills and little education, was attracted by economic motives. They worked in agriculture, menial service jobs, and the Alaskan fish canneries. Like the Chinese and Japanese who came before them, the Filipino population was primarily composed of men. In 1930, 94 percent of Filipinos on the mainland were men. Filipino men were more likely than Chinese and Japanese men to enter intimate relationships with white women. As compared to the Japanese, the Filipino community had fewer cultural norms that impeded forming relationships with whites, in part owing to years of colonization (Kitano and Daniels 1995; Kivisto 1995; Marger 1994).

At first, existing antimiscegenation laws that prevented Chinese and Japanese men from intermarrying did not apply to Filipino men, since Filipinos were not considered of the Mongoloid race. By 1946, an estimated 50 percent of the children of Filipino immigrants were offspring of biracial unions (Takaki 1998). Although Filipino-white couples formed small communities in some cities, they also faced tremendous prejudice and discrimination. The composition and definition of Filipino families differed considerably from the Philippines to the United States (Kitano and Daniels 1995; Kivisto 1995; Takaki 1998).

The third wave of Filipino immigrants came after the 1965 Immigration Act lifted nationality quotas on the number of people entering the United States. This change transformed the size and composition of the Filipino American population. From 1960 to 1990, the population increased eightfold, and the Philippines became the second major provider of immigrants to the United States (after Mexico) (Kivisto 1995). In addition, unlike the less skilled and less educated group that had come before, two-thirds of this wave of Filipinos came from professional classes. Driven by economic motivations, they are considered part of the "brain drain" from Third World nations (Kivisto 1995).

Despite the fact that most are highly educated professionals, Filipino Americans have faced considerable downward mobility after immigration. Many have been forced into unskilled and semi-skilled occupations while obtaining licenses and credentials to resume their previous positions. As a result, they remain in subordinate positions as compared to other Asian Americans and white Americans. Culture shock, unemployment, and licensing remain problems for Filipino American families. The median income for Filipino American families is well below that of other Asian American groups and falls midway between that of whites, on the one hand, and Hispanics and African Americans, on the other hand (Kitano and Daniels 1995). High rates of employment for women, however, have aided in lowering the poverty rate below that of many minority groups as well as white Americans. Further, high rates of women's employment outside the home have increased women's status within the family.

Filipino Americans resemble other Asian American groups in that they have strong nuclear families. Their divorce rate is approximately half that of white Americans and similar to most other Asian ethnic groups. The percentage of children under the age of eighteen years, living in two-parent households, is comparable to most other Asian American families at 83.6 percent. This rate is slightly lower than those of Japanese and Korean Americans, as well as whites, but remains higher than most other racial and ethnic groups, indicating strong nuclear families (Fong 1998).

Like Japanese Americans, Filipino Americans also show high rates of intermarriage. In Los Angeles County alone, Filipinos had an almost 41 percent rate of marriage to non-Filipinos in 1989 (Kitano and Daniels 1995). Filipino women, in a trend similar to that of Japanese Americans, were more likely to marry non-Filipinos than were men. Another phenomenon on the rise is that of mail order brides from Asia, and in particular, the Philippines. Some Asian and women's groups have criticized this practice for dehumanizing women into subservience and exploitation.

Indian American Families

Indian Americans are the fastest growing Asian American group. Just as it is difficult to generalize all Asian American families, it is extremely difficult to lump together all Indian Americans owing to their unparalleled diversity. Indians are the most diverse ethnic group originating from any one nation. People differ by language, religion, caste, and provincialism as well as by food, dress, lifestyle, religious festivities, and overall culture. This makes it difficult to generalize about Indian American families.

The Indian presence in the United States is relatively new as compared to other Asian American groups. Even though there are records of Indians in California in the late 1800s, they were small in number. That group was composed primarily of Indian men from the state of Punjab who entered California for agricultural, lumbering, and railroad jobs. Since the Indian American population was male dominated, fewer than 2.5 percent of marriages were with Indian women before 1946. Approximately 80 percent of marriages were between Indian American men and Mexican American women from migratory worker families. Filipino Americans are the only other Asian American group to show such high rates of intermarriage during this time (Kitano and Daniels 1995; Marger 1994; Takaki 1998; Taylor 1994).

Before 1965, quota restrictions allowed only about 100 Indians to enter each year. It was only after the Immigration Act of 1965 that Indians for the first time began to enter the country in large numbers. Indian American families have been strongly shaped by Indian culture and social class, but they also show signs of assimilation to American culture. Indians in India oftentimes live in joint family households, meaning that married couples live with their unmarried children as well as the families of their married sons. Thus a household may contain three or more generations living under one roof. In the United States, however, a large number of Indian Americans are middle-class professionals or business entrepreneurs, and their families are beginning to reflect the middle-class structure of the United States. More often families are nuclear, including two parents and two to three children.

Like traditional Chinese and Japanese families, Indian families stress interdependence and group solidarity over individual interest. Roles are determined in part by age and gender. Women are subservient to men, and children are submissive to their parents. Indian American women, however, are increasingly entering the labor force; many are highly trained professionals, participating in the workforce as doctors, scientists, and engineers. As a result, a major shift in household roles has begun, and researchers have pointed to husbands' taking on larger shares of household chores. The primary responsibility of child care and household tasks remains with the wife, however. Although an emphasis remains on patriarchal families, research shows that this is steadily changing.

The divorce rate among Indian Americans is the lowest of all Asian American groups (Fong 1998). It is difficult to assess family stability, however, since divorce is strongly stigmatized in the Indian community. Single parenthood is, as a result, rare. Both low divorce rates and taboos against parenthood without marriage contribute to this trend.

In India, children are submissive to parents and elderly and remain relatively obedient to their parents even in adulthood. Deference to parents is evident in the parents' power to choose their child's mate in a system of "arranged marriage" that is still fairly common in India. An estimated 95 to 99 percent of the married population in India have had their marriages arranged by their families, although the level of this arrangement varies significantly by class and caste (Gupta 1996). For many middle- and upper-class families, "arranged marriage" refers to matchmaking, in which either the prospective bride or groom can reject a potential match. In the United States, Indian American children still show deference to their parents, but the close parental control and hierarchical communication often create conflict between generations. Young Indian American children are oftentimes affected by the conflicting desires to please their family and to have freedom and independence. This is further evident in the declining rates of arranged marriage among Indian Americans. Researchers predict that rates of arranged marriage will continue to decrease with each generation and with subsequent assimilation.

—*Nikki Khanna and Joya Misra*

See also African American Families; The Hispanic Family; Immigrant Families, Experience of; Interracial Families; Japanese American Families during World War II, Internment of; Race and the Family in American Law

References and Further Reading

DeGenova, Mary Kay. 1997. *Families in Cultural Context.* Mountain View, CA: Mayfield Publishing.

Espiritu, Yen Le. 1992. *Asian American Panethnicity.* Philadelphia: Temple University Press.

Fong, Timothy P. 1998. *The Contemporary Asian American Experience.* Upper Saddle River, NJ: Prentice Hall.

Fong, Timothy P., and Larry H. Shinagawa. 2000. *Asian Americans: Experiences and Perspectives.* Upper Saddle River, NJ: Prentice Hall.

Gupta, Rashmi. 1996. "The Elder Caregiver Burden in South Asian Families in the United States: A Causal Analysis." Ph.D. thesis, University of Texas at Arlington.

Kitano, Harry H. L., and Roger Daniels. 1995. *Asian Americans: Emerging Minorities.* Englewood Cliffs, NJ: Prentice Hall.

Kivisto, Peter. 1995. *Americans All.* Belmont, CA: Wadsworth Publishing.

Marger, Martin N. 1994. *Race and Ethnic Relations: American and Global Perspectives.* Belmont, CA: Wadsworth Publishing.

Mindel, Charles H., and Robert W. Habenstein. 1981. *Ethnic Families in America.* New York: Elsevier North Holland.

O'Hare, William P., and Judy C. Felt. 1991. *Asian Americans: America's Fastest Growing Minority Group.* Population Reference Bureau.

Palumbo-Liu, David. 1999. *Asian American Historical Crossings of a Racial Frontier.* Stanford, CA: Stanford University Press.

Takaki, Ronald. 1998. *Strangers from a Different Shore: A History of Asian Americans.* Boston: Little, Brown.

Taylor, Ronald L. 1994. *Minority Families in the United States.* Englewood Cliffs, NJ: Prentice Hall.

U.S. Bureau of the Census. 1990. *Census of Population and Housing.* Subject Summary Tape File 5: The Asian and Pacific Islander Population in the United States (machine-readable data file). Washington, DC: Bureau of the Census.

U.S. Bureau of the Census. 1999. *Statistical Abstract of the United States.* Washington, DC: Bureau of the Census.

B

Baby Boom

The term *baby boom* first appeared in *Life* magazine in 1941 to describe the demographic advantage, in the form of a higher birthrate, that the United States held over Germany. The more common usage, however, refers to the post–World War II period, 1946–1964, when servicemen returned home and the birthrate increased. The term refers to this demographic change and to the social and economic consequences of a disproportionately large generation, for example the effects on such programs as Social Security. The term also refers to a set of generational traits that boomers supposedly hold in common; it encompassed attitudes toward sex, marriage, work, and the central event of their time—the Vietnam War.

In the popular imagination, this post–World War II period is seen as a time of unprecedented childbearing, a radical shift from earlier periods. Statistics on birthrates only partially support this picture. After the war the birthrate peaked in 1955 at about 25 births/thousand, up from 20.4 in 1945 when U.S. troop commitment was at its highest. It was a significant increase but not a radical shift. In fact, the birthrate was actually higher between 1910 and 1920, reaching the highest level in the century in 1910 at 30.1 (U.S. Bureau of the Census 2001). Put another way, even during the times of most extensive World War II deployment, the birthrate was actually 33 percent *higher* than it was at the end of the millennium. The boom was caused not so much by a spike in birthrates as by the steady decline that followed (U.S. Bureau of the Census 2000). The relatively high birthrate after World War II was only part of the reason for the demographic shift; the infant death rate declined dramatically from 1915 to 1955. Of the babies born in 1915, one in ten would not live out the first year. By 1955, this figure had been reduced to one in forty. This generation was the first real beneficiary of a variety of antibiotic drugs, most notably penicillin, that could defeat infant killers such as pneumonia. Vaccines for whooping cough, diphtheria, and tetanus became a regular feature of health care, often required for admittance to school. In 1955, lines of children stood outside schools and public buildings, awaiting their polio shot, as Jonas Salk conquered that feared disease. Also, the children of the baby boom generation, unlike their parents, were almost universally born in hospitals where sterilization procedures prevented infection.

Paradoxically the drug with the most pervasive effect was not one that cured disease; it was one that regulated pregnancy. Without this protection, sexual activity always carried the danger of an

Soldiers carrying bodies to helicopters during the Vietnam War, 1968. (Bettmann/Corbis)

unwanted pregnancy, and churches strongly warned against premarital sex that undercut the sanctity of marriage. But in the 1950s, scientists began developing a safe, effective form of oral contraception, which was successfully tested in the early 1960s. Then in two pivotal Supreme Court cases, "the pill" was permitted to be sold to married couples (in 1964) and to unmarried women (in 1972). The pill's easy availability removed the fear of unwanted pregnancies, and it allowed women to manage the timing of childbirth, creating the preconditions for their reentry into the job market. Although their mothers had the limited choices of teacher, nurse, and secretary, the women of the boomer generation systematically dismantled the barriers that kept them out of traditionally male professions, paving the way for *their* daughters to achieve virtual parity in law school admissions and to approach parity in admissions to medical school.

The sheer size of the baby boom generation has implications ranging from the number of Golden Oldies radio stations to the impending obligations it will place on following generations. Programs such as Social Security and Medicare work on a pay-as-you-go system, with current workers paying the benefits of retirees. As the boom generation retires, a severe burden will be placed on their children, and by some estimates Social Security funds will be depleted by the 2030s, unless politically painful tax increases or benefits reductions are enacted. Medicare is in more immediate trouble. Fortunately, the birthrates among immigrant populations, particularly Hispanics, will help alleviate this situation. By contrast, the birthrate in Russia is so low (about one child per couple)—so far below the level needed to maintain population—that Russian boomers are doomed to severe poverty (Feshback 2001).

All generations contain the full range of character types, and even to speak of distinct generations obscures deep continuities. But each is also shaped by its own shared history. Rarely has the generational conflict been as sharp as that which took place between the baby boomers and their parents. Social commentators in the 1950s observed—and criticized—the extent to which this older generation, particularly the men, submerged their identities in institutions and groups. They were belongers, what William H. Whyte called "organization men" (Whyte 1956). David Riesman coined the term *other-directed* to describe a prevalent personality type that defined itself in terms of others' perceptions (Riesman 1950). This group felt little tension between business interests and their own life goals, agreeing with Charles Wilson, an Eisenhower cabinet secretary, who proclaimed that "what was good for our country was good for General Motors and vice versa. The difference doesn't exist" (*Bartlett's Familiar Quotations* 2000).

The older generation had a residual trust in political leadership that had, after all, guided the successful prosecution of the war that established the global preeminence of the United States. It was a generation that had little reason to question the moral rightness of America's foreign policy in its ongoing epic battle with communism. Whyte and Riesman stressed the need for a new individualism that would break away from the "social ethic" that was so focused on belonging. But they could hardly have predicted the vehemence of the generational conflict and the intense preoccupation with self-fulfillment that would characterize the revolt.

During the 1960s, this revolt was celebrated in the long-running Broadway show *Hair* (long hair being the quintessential sign of rebellion), in the revival of classics from the 1950s (most notably Joseph Heller's *Catch-22*, Jack Kerouac's *On the Road*, and J. D. Salinger's *Catcher in the Rye*), in the extravagant sexuality of the Rolling Stones' music, and most indelibly in the 1968 film *The Graduate*. That film, in which Benjamin Braddock returns from college to his home in affluent southern California, opens with an excruciating graduation party, at which one of the guests, an old family friend, takes Ben aside to say "just one word" that will help him decide his future. He makes sure Ben is listening, then unleashes his secret: "plastics." It was the laugh line for a generation. Plastics are nonnatural products, they are mass-produced, they are completely malleable, and they form facsimiles of something *real*. Ben wanted something "different."

The Vietnam War set the boomer generation against political leaders, against parents, and tragically against itself. The leaders who committed the United States to fight were "the best and the brightest"; they had been educated at elite schools, and many of them, including John Kennedy himself, had been tested in World War II. Steeped in a cold war mentality, they could only see Vietnam as part of the epic struggle with communism and failed to recognize the nationalist roots of the struggle. They overestimated the efficacy of U.S. firepower and

Dustin Hoffmann in The Graduate. *(Kobal Collection/Embassy)*

high-level bombing; they underestimated the difficulty of fighting guerilla warfare where the enemy looked no different from the ally; they failed to appreciate the power of television to bring the war into the living rooms of Americans—and the effect it might have; and ultimately they failed to understand the country's unwillingness to support a war that had no end in sight (despite regular claims that one more escalation would turn the tide).

Unlike World War II, in which all social classes served, the war in Vietnam was fought disproportionately by the poor, the black, and the less educated. Although the actual number of serious war protesters was relatively small, middle-class college students became adept at exploiting the complex system of deferments and exemptions. It was often fairly easy to find a sympathetic physician who would document "severe asthma" and make an old football injury appear particularly disabling. Bill Clinton relied on his uncle to get him into Reserve Officers Training Corps, effectively eliminating the possibility of actual combat. George W. Bush Jr. used his powerful family connections to gain a posting in the Air National Guard, and his vice president, Dick Cheney, avoided service with an educational deferment by attending, sporadically, a Wyoming community college. One would have to go back to the Civil War, when the wealthy could actually buy a replacement, to find a system so easily manipulated by those with connections. This unwillingness to serve deprived political leaders from the boomer generation of one standard test of manhood and set them in marked contrast to their parents' generation, described in one best-selling tribute as the "greatest generation" (Brokaw 1998).

Some of the "radical" ideas of the 1960s and early 1970s were absorbed into the mainstream. The first Earth Day in 1970 was viewed as a fringe cause, led by wild-eyed, impractical environmentalists. Yet over the next three decades, the protection of the environment became coded into law; wetlands were protected and air quality standards were set. Boomers were also strikingly more tolerant of racial and sexual diversity than their parents. They were far more accepting of interracial dating and marriage than their parents. In the 1960s it was a breakthrough for Ella Fitzgerald to sing with Frank Sinatra, but in the 1980s Stevie Wonder and Paul McCartney's "Ebony and Ivory" was safely mainstream. The most dramatic evidence of sexual tolerance came at the end of President Clinton's second term when his approval rating remained stubbornly high despite graphic evidence of his affair with intern Monica Lewinsky—much to the consternation of the House Republicans who sought to impeach him.

In the 1970s and later, the stigma of divorce also lessened. Divorce laws eased so that marriages could be dissolved without complex legal findings of fault. And as women began to work, they were no longer totally dependent on the male "breadwinner" and could leave unhappy, abusive, or simply unsatisfying marriages, though often at the cost of a severe drop in the standard of living. In all, the divorce rate doubled from 1950 to 1980, leveling off after that point. In 1990, only 55 percent of marriages involved an undivorced bride *and* groom. A large number of children are now raised in one-parent families (usually by the mother) or in the "blended family" that forms with remarriage. At the time of these changes, it was often assumed that children could adapt to divorce and that separations were preferable to the turmoil of living with quarreling parents. Subsequent research, summarized by Barbara Dafoe Whitehead in *The Divorce Culture* (1996), demonstrates that divorce is often more devastating to children than previously thought. On any number of measures, including performance in school, children of divorced parents do poorly. Even in remarriages, stepparents rarely make the same commitment to the children of their spouse, and too frequently child abuse comes at the hands of stepparents (Whitehead 1996).

Robert Putnam's masterful study, *Bowling Alone: The Collapse and Revival of American Community*, might be viewed as the great report card for the boomer generation (Putnam 2000). Written exactly fifty years after Riesman's *The Lonely Crowd* (and obviously echoing the title), Putnam documents the loss of what he calls "social capital"—the benefits that accrue when people actively participate in social groups. These benefits are numerous—goodwill, fellowship, a sense of safety, happiness, even good health. Putnam argues compellingly that it was the parents of the boomers who gained social capital by voluntary participation in a variety of groups; they bowled in leagues, whereas their children and grandchildren were more likely to "bowl alone." They voted in huge percentages. They turned out for Parent-Teacher Association meetings. Where Riesman and Whyte criticized the conformity of the "belongers," Putnam reverses the argument. Social capital, he claims, strengthens us and makes us better and more expansive (Putnam 2000). His book, celebrating the communal spirit of the men and women who emerged from World War II to raise families, can only be sobering reading for a generation that took such special pleasure in mocking its elders.

—*Thomas Newkirk*

See also Birth Control; Divorce, History of; Infant Mortality

References and Further Reading
Bartlett's Familiar Quotations. http:71www.bartleby.com (cited 2000).
Brokaw, Tom. 1998. *The Greatest Generation.* New York: Random House.
Leinberger, Paul, and Bruce Tucker. 1991. *The New Individualists: The Generation after* The Organization Man. New York: HarperCollins.
Lyons, Paul. 1994. *Class of '66: Living in Suburban Middle America.* Philadelphia: Temple University Press.
Putnam, Robert D. 2000. *Bowling Alone: The Collapse and Revival of American Community.* New York: Simon and Schuster.
Riesman, David. 1950. *The Lonely Crowd: A Study of the Changing American Character.* New Haven: Yale University Press.
Russell, Cheryl. 1993. *The Master Trend: How the Baby Boom Generation Is Remaking America.* New York: Plenum Press.
U.S. Bureau of the Census. 1980. *Statistical Abstract of the United States 1980.* Washington, DC: Department of Commerce.
U.S. Bureau of the Census. 2000. *Statistical Abstract of the United States 2000.* Washington, DC: Department of Commerce.
U.S. Bureau of the Census. "BabyBoomerData." http://www.census.gov/population/www/socdemo/age.htm#bb (cited 10 December 2001).
Whitehead, Barbara Dafoe. 1996. *The Divorce Culture.* New York: Alfred A. Knopf.
Whyte, William H., Jr. 1956. *The Organization Man.* New York: Simon and Schuster.

Baby M

The case of Baby M was the first time that a widely followed trial dealt with the issues of surrogate motherhood and the broader ethical concerns involving reproductive technology in general.

William Stern and Mary Beth Whitehead entered into a surrogacy contract in 1985. According to the contract, Elizabeth, Stern's wife, was unable to carry a child without undue risk of bodily harm because of her multiple sclerosis. But the Sterns still wanted a child. Whitehead was willing to supply that child as the mother, by donating an ovum and carrying the baby to term, with William Stern as the father. Stern agreed to pay Whitehead $10,000 upon delivery of the child.

The surrogacy contract outlined that through artificial insemination using Stern's sperm, Whitehead would become pregnant, carry the child to term, bear it, and give it to the Sterns. After the delivery, she would also do whatever was necessary to terminate her maternal rights so that Elizabeth Stern could subsequently adopt the child. Elizabeth Stern was not a party in the surrogacy contract. Whitehead pledged to do all actions required to invalidate her parental rights. The contract further gave Elizabeth Stern sole custody of the child in the situation of William Stern's death, even though she was not a party to the surrogacy agreement.

Problems arose when Mary Beth Whitehead declined to relinquish her parental rights. When ordered to turn the child over to the Sterns by the courts, Whitehead fled the state of New Jersey with the baby. After several months of hiding, Whitehead was found, and the child was placed in the temporary custody of the Sterns.

The case was brought before the New Jersey Supreme Court. In 1988, the New Jersey Supreme Court held (in *In the Matter of Baby M* [537d. 2d. 1227 NJ 1988]) that although surrogacy agreements in general are not valid, it was in the best interests of the child for Baby M to be placed with the Sterns.

—*T. D. Eddins*

References and Further Reading

Allen, Anita. 1996. "The Socio-Economic Struggle for Equality: The Black Surrogate Mother." In *Applications of Feminist Legal Theory to Women's Lives: Sex, Violence, Work, and Reproduction*, edited by Kelly D. Weisberg, 1117–1125. Philadelphia: Temple University Press.

Andrews, Lori B. 1996. "Surrogate Motherhood: The Challenge for Feminists." In *Applications of Feminist Legal Theory to Women's Lives: Sex, Violence, Work, and Reproduction*, edited by Kelly D. Weisberg, 1092–1104. Philadelphia: Temple University Press.

Corea, Gena. 1996. "Junk Liberty." In *Applications of Feminist Legal Theory to Women's Lives: Sex, Violence, Work, and Reproduction*, edited by Kelly D. Weisberg, 1112–1116. Philadelphia: Temple University Press.

Posner, Richard A. 1996. "The Ethics and Economics of Enforcing Contracts of Surrogate Motherhood." In *Applications of Feminist Legal Theory to Women's Lives: Sex, Violence, Work, and Reproduction*, edited by Kelly D. Weisberg, 1105–1111. Philadelphia: Temple University Press.

Radin, Margaret Jane. 1996. "Market-Inalienability." In *Applications of Feminist Legal Theory to Women's Lives: Sex, Violence, Work, and Reproduction*, edited by Kelly D. Weisberg, 1126–1148. Philadelphia: Temple University Press.

Tong, Rosemarie. 1995. "Feminist Perspectives and Gestational Motherhood: The Need for a Unified Legal Focus." In *Reproduction, Ethics, and the Law: Feminist Perspectives*, edited by Joan Callahan, 55–79. Bloomington: Indiana University Press.

Weisberg, D. Kelly, ed. 1996. *Applications of Feminist Legal Theory to Women's Lives: Sex, Violence, Work, and Reproduction*. Philadelphia: Temple University Press.

Winkler, Norma Juliet. 1986. "Society's Response to the New Reproductive Technologies: The Feminist Perspective." *Southern California Law Review* 59: 1043–1057.

Baby Sitting

Before World War II, "minding the children" was an ungendered activity provided by family, friends, and neighbors, the young as well as the old; women, men; girls along with boys across race, class, and ethnic lines. World War II increased the demand for baby sitters, however, as women of all ages (many of whom were mothers) left home for the workplace. Many teenage girls also found wage work at plants and places that offered them more money and greater opportunities than did baby sitting. Others joined the corps of elementary school children who baby sat long hours for low wages. Expected to "keep house" as well as provide child care, however, high school girls organized baby-sitter unions in 1947 in an effort to improve working

An in-home baby sitter entertaining her two-year-old charge. (Elizabeth Crews)

izration, expanding consumer culture, changing leisure patterns, and rising affluence further contributed to a surging demand for baby sitters. The bobbysoxer, shaped by traditional gender roles that limited employment options for girls but influenced by a commercial youth culture that stimulated consumer desire, assumed the new social role of baby sitter. But as the sitters were surprisingly more interested in earning money than learning maternal skills, many of them frustrated their employers by indulging their interests and exploiting available resources (for example, the telephone, the television, the hi-fi, and the fridge). "Good sitters" were hard to come by: *Baby sitter*, a recently coined term, was as unlikely to be included in the dictionaries of the period as baby sitters were to be found in most postwar suburban communities where young couples and little babies predominated.

Baby sitting became uniquely complex among the many service industries that ministered to the needs of families in the United States. Youthful adults still typically receive low pay to care for parents' emotionally priceless children. Although most of the time there is calm and consensus, conflict has been known to arise among employers, baby sitters, and the children in their care. Baby sitters feel as if they are occasionally on the front lines where the children they care for are more like the enemy. Hired to serve in loco parentis, baby sitters occasionally become the brunt of "bratters" who contest the authority of parental surrogates. This undervalued, feminized field is characterized by such labor abuses as last-minute calls, last-minute cancellations, bounced checks, late returns home, drunk drivers, and sexual harassment. Parents' broad expectations of

conditions and standardize wages. In suburban communities in the Northeast and Midwest, sitters issued "codes" and "manifestoes" that have become the basis of the job's informal rules and regulations (for example, leaving emergency numbers for the sitter).

Influenced by the ideology of domestic containment in the postwar period, women discouraged from taking fulltime jobs were encouraged to find fulfillment in family life instead. But suburban housewives' desperation for a "night off" from relentless routines of child care and housekeeping and their isolation from relatives' traditional caregiving were factors that contributed to the growth of baby sitting. The baby boom, suburban-

baby sitters often encompass an underlying distrust that has been widely reflected and reinforced in the popular culture since the 1960s. In numerous popular and made-for-television movies, destructive baby sitters generate disorder by threatening the safety of children, the stability of family life, and the fidelity of marriages. Although some real baby sitters have been charged with child abuse, many more have been suspected of misdeeds and wrongdoing.

Since the 1950s, parents' fears, personnel problems, labor costs, and chronic baby-sitter shortages (due to demographic dips and greater employment opportunities for teens) have led employers to seek alternate child-care providers. In popular magazines, educational journals, and etiquette manuals, experts have promoted boy sitters welcomed by parents frustrated with teenage girls' lack of professionalism. Although most boys in the 1950s delivered newspapers, mowed lawns, and did odd jobs, some enrolled in courses offered by local nursing associations where they practiced baby sitting on life-sized dolls. By 1957, *Life* magazine would report that nearly one-quarter of all boys—said to possess such androgynous qualities as "gentle determination"—worked as baby sitters. An early 1960s rock 'n' roll hit, "Baby Sittin' Boogie," even celebrated the bonding between a teenage boy and a toddler. Whether represented as boys or as male animals at the top of the food chain (for example, *Carl the Dog*), fictionalized boy baby sitters have been consistently commended for the brains and brawn they use to transform troublesome kids into tractable ones.

Though experts had warned postwar parents not to hire a baby sitter who was "younger than her midteens," the use of preadolescent girls as baby sitters has become more prevalent since the mid-1980s. Often certified as "safe sitters," preadolescent girls have been idealized in late-twentieth-century fiction. For example, the Baby-Sitters Club book series draws upon a "girl power" ethos characterized by (1) a privileging of female friendships; (2) a lack of structural inequalities based on race, class, and gender; (3) a belief that determination, ambition, individual achievement, competence, and hard work (such as baby sitting) enable girls to realize their dreams; (4) freedom from obstacles (for example, gender inequality) that hindered their mothers' generation; (5) girls' economic role in the consumer market; and (6) empowerment through pleasure, style, fashion (makeup), and attitude.

Parents have also explored other alternatives to female adolescent baby sitters. Mature women (often employed by agencies) have been frequently stereotyped in the popular culture as masculine, demanding, rigid, and old-fashioned. Few turn out to be as lovable as the movie character Mrs. Doubtfire, who is not really a woman after all but is instead a devoted father in masquerade. Formalizing the good "old-fashioned good-neighbor swap," baby-sitter cooperatives were launched by many suburban parents (especially mothers) who believed that parents made the best baby sitters of all. By the mid-1970s, however, spiraling divorce rates, rising female employment, and high rates of mobility led to the collapse of most. Recent trends indicate that all of the many unresolved problems associated with baby sitting are leading contemporary middle-class parents to adopt working-class strategies: reliance on friends and family and combining child care with recreation.

—*Miriam Forman-Brunell*

References and Further Reading
Forman-Brunell, Miriam. 1998. "From Truculent to Tractable: Conflict, Culture, and the Gendering of Baby Sitting, 1947–1960." In *Delinquents and Debutantes: Twentieth-Century American Girls' Culture*, edited by Sherrie A. Inness, 61–82. New York: New York University Press.

Forman-Brunell, Miriam. 2001. "Monsters, Maternity, and Murder: Legends in Babysitting Horror." In *Sugar, Spice, and Everything Nice: Contemporary Cinemas of Girlhood*, edited by Frances Gateward and Murray Pomerance. Detroit, MI: Wayne State University Press.

Forman-Brunell, Miriam. Forthcoming. *Get a Sitter?: Fears and Fantasies about Baby Sitters*. New York: Routledge.

Margolin, Leslie. 1992. "Deviance on Record: Techniques for Labeling Child Abusers in Official Documents." *Social Problems* 39, no. 1 (February).

Neus, Margaret Marie. 1990. "The Insider's Guide to Babysitting: Anecdotes and Advice from Babysitters for Babysitters." M.A. thesis, Emerson College.

Banns

The word *banns* simply means *proclamation* but has come to refer specifically to a series of public notices given to announce the intent of a couple to marry. Such notice provides an opportunity for anyone to come forward who knows of any obstacle (possibly of various kinds) to the planned marriage. Banns are asked, proclaimed, posted, or published, and those lodging an objection to the marriage are said to forbid the banns. Of ancient roots well established by the medieval period, the proclamation of banns was customary in the religious faiths of many Europeans who settled in America. In England, the custom of proclaiming the banns was sanctioned by the Synod of Westminster in 1200 and the Lateran Council of 1215, and successive editions of the Book of Common Prayer, from the sixteenth century on, outline the required procedures.

Practice in the United States has varied over time. Usually the banns were to be read aloud (in some cases posted) by a clergyman (sometimes a layperson) for three successive Sundays or other prescribed days. Civil officials were sometimes authorized to announce or post banns in town halls or courthouses. Civil involvement reflects, in part, the fact that some American cultural communities regarded marriage as a civil practice, not a religious one. As a rule, banns were to be read in the parish of both partners (or in the nearest existing congregation) or more widely broadcast, if thought necessary. If the wedding did not follow promptly, the banns had to be asked again. They might be waived in extraordinary instances, such as wartime or at a deathbed.

Those aware of an "impediment" to a marriage were obliged to come forward and, in some cases, could be penalized for objecting falsely. Impediments could make a marriage unlawful or invalid. Common impediments included an underage bride or groom, lack of parental consent, unlawful closeness in relatedness (consanguinity), having taken holy orders prohibiting marriage, abduction or coercion, difference in religion, an unbaptized bride or groom, an already existing marriage, and other previous obligations.

In colonial America the asking of banns was widely required. The first statute regulating marriage, in the Plymouth colony in 1636, required the banns to be read three times or, where no congregation was established, posted for fifteen days. Quaker couples in Pennsylvania and North Carolina were permitted to announce their own banns in the meetinghouse for successive weeks (Howard 1904, 3:250–251). There were strict penalties for failing to publish the banns properly. In seventeenth-century Rhode Island, the marriage was made invalid, and the groom and all his "accessories" each had to pay the "parents of the Maid" a fine of five pounds (Howard 1904, 3:148). A minister in Virginia in that period who married a couple without proper license or proclamation of the banns had to pay a fine of 10,000 pounds of tobacco, a large penalty at that time (Howard 1904, 3:229).

The publishing of banns has been part of a historic social scrutiny of marriage in the United States. Traditionally, marriage has involved considerable arrangement, including the influence and consent of parents and family, a negotiated dowry, a written contract, and civil licensing. From our earliest history there has been an aversion to secret marriages, a means of undermining this social surveillance. In some places they were illegal. The pronouncing of banns was discontinued by some religious sects in the nineteenth and twentieth centuries, however. The custom has been retained in some religious faiths and made optional in others. It has been widely replaced by marriage license requirements, a practice that actually goes back to fourteenth-century Europe (Cross and Livingston 1997, 1031). Today in the United States licenses are uniformly required, involving a declaration that no legal impediment exists to the marriage. Required counseling or instruction within a religious community, church membership, and civil laws requiring health tests or other documentation are all means of carrying forth the purpose of the proclamation of banns, namely, to ensure a wholesome and secure basis for marriage and family.

—*Luise van Keuren*

See also Courtship, History of

References and Further Reading
Cripps, H. W. 1937. *A Practical Treatise on the Law Relating to the Church and Clergy.* London: Sweet and Maxwell.
Cross, F. L., and E. A. Livingston. 1997. *Oxford Dictionary of the Christian Church.* New York: Oxford University Press.
Howard, George Eliot. 1904. *A History of Matrimonial Institutions, Chiefly in England and the United States.* 3 vols. Chicago: University of Chicago Press.
Panati, Charles. 1996. *Sacred Origins of Profound Things.* New York: Penguin.
Roberts, J. B 1931. *Banns of Marriage: An Historical Synopsis and Commentary.* Catholic University of America Law Studies, no. 64. Washington, DC: Catholic University Press.
Smith, P. M. 1969. "I Publish the Banns of Marriage. . . ." *Modern Churchman* n.s. 12: 299–308.

Birth Control

Birth control, the prevention of pregnancy, is practiced by individuals who wish to separate sexual intercourse from procreation in order to have fewer children or to avoid having children altogether. The term is sometimes used as a synonym for *family planning* and *population control*, but the latter term is usually associated with public policies that encourage lower fertility, whereas birth control and family limitation are more often associated with decisions to avoid pregnancy made by individuals in their self-interest. Although efforts to prevent conception were ancient and widespread, no social movements to justify or promote birth control emerged until the nineteenth century. Before then, individuals pursued their self-interests through such practices as periodically abstaining from sexual intercourse, using coitus interruptus, placing objects in the vagina to create a barrier between sperm and uterus, or inducing abortion through drugs or mechanical means, but they did so in flagrant violation of official standards of sexual conduct.

Beginning in the late eighteenth century, apparently in response to changes in family roles associated with economic development, significant numbers of married couples began to self-consciously limit their fertility through abstinence from sexual intercourse, contraception, and induced abortion. By the early nineteenth century, marriage manuals advocating contraceptive practice found a mass market, and thereafter organized groups advocated birth control. Some birth-control advocates emphasized the need to relieve women from the burdens of excessive childbearing; others argued that the practice would strengthen marriage by improving erotic bonds among husbands and wives. In the late nineteenth and early twentieth centuries some birth-control advocates warned that population was growing faster than food supplies. Some wanted to limit the birthrates of such stigmatized groups as the poor, the foreign-born, and racial minorities.

By the mid-twentieth century, advances in public health had led to rapid world population growth. Social scientists and environmental activists claimed that population control was essential to avoid ecological degradation of the earth. New contraceptive devices such as the anovulant pill and intrauterine devices (IUDs) were developed; federal courts established the right of individuals to have access to contraceptives, and the federal government included contraceptives in the medical services mandated in its welfare programs. The increasing strength of the women's rights movement in the 1960s coincided with an apparent consensus that birth control was both an individual right and an important public policy, but in the early 1970s changes in state abortion laws and the U.S. Supreme Court's decision in *Roe v. Wade* (1973), which established the right to "abortion on demand" during the first trimester of pregnancy, aroused widespread opposition among religious fundamentalists and social conservatives. Republican president Richard Nixon made abortion a partisan issue during the 1972 presidential campaign by courting antiabortionists as part of his strategy to win urban ethnic voters away from the Democrats. Subsequent Republican presidents used executive prerogatives to limit congressional spending on birth-control services, and Democrats made access to all forms of birth control a party issue. Birth control remained both a widespread practice and a source of intense public policy controversy at the turn of the twenty-first century.

The Founding Fathers of the United States followed Benjamin Franklin in celebrating population growth among the white British colonists of North America. Franklin noted in 1751 that the colonial population was doubling every twenty-five years and argued that this vigorous growth would force the mother country to treat the colonists with more respect. After the first U.S. census in 1790, Secretary of State Thomas Jefferson was disappointed that fewer than 4 million had been counted and feared that this figure would provide ammunition for European critics of the United States.

While the population did grow rapidly in the nineteenth century owing to both natural increase and mass migration from Europe, concerns were often expressed over both the rates of growth and the sources of growth. American nativists complained that native-born white women were having fewer children and that immigrants, whom they perceived as inferior to native stock, were displacing English-speaking Protestants. In fact, native-born Americans would be world leaders in the "demographic transition" from high birthrates to low birthrates that is associated with economic development. Some social groups, such as Pennsylvania Quakers, had begun to limit marital fertility by the late eighteenth century and set a pattern that would soon become a general trend. The average native-born white woman bore seven or eight children in the late eighteenth century, but by the middle of the nineteenth century she was the mother of five; by the early twentieth century, the mother of three; and by the middle of the Great Depression of the 1930s, the mother of two. One of the remarkable aspects of the U.S. demographic transition is that there were no sustained declines in infant mortality before 1900. Several generations of American women had fewer children than their mothers despite high infant mortality and vigorous attempts by social leaders to encourage higher fertility (Reed 1983, 3–4).

We now understand the fertility decline as a response to a changing social environment. As the home ceased to be a unit of production and as the manufacture of clothing and other goods moved to factories, children no longer provided necessary labor in the family economies of the emerging middle and white-collar classes. Rather, they became expensive investments requiring education, capital, and an abundance of "Christian nurture" from mothers who measured respectability by being able to stay home and efficiently manage the income won by their husbands in a separate, public sphere of work. Marriage manuals, some containing instructions for contraception, were prominent among the self-help books that became a staple of U.S. culture after 1830. Romantic love became the rationale for marriage, and religious leaders such as Brooklyn's Henry Ward Beecher gave new prominence to the erotic bonds between husbands and wives. Thus, socially ambitious married couples bore the burden of reconciling sexual passion with a manageable number of children.

Contemporaries advanced many theories to account for the increasing prevalence of the small family. Some argued that changes in biological capacity were responsible; others blamed the hedonism of young adults who sought to maximize their pleasures by avoiding social duties. Francis A. Walker, an economist and director of the ninth census (1870), argued that the native born were being "shocked" into infertility by exposure to and competition with the foreign-born, but he did not explain whether the nativist revulsion worked through biological or psychological changes. No voices were raised in favor of a stable or declining population. Population growth was viewed as an important index of social health.

Historians now agree that the primary means of accomplishing the fertility decline were restrictive practices—contraception, abortion, and abstention from coitus—rather than biological changes or shifts in the percentage of individuals who married or their age at marriage. These efforts by individuals to control their fertility for personal reasons inspired the first self-conscious attempts to suppress birth control. Between 1840 and 1870, leaders of the medical profession such as Harvard medical school professor Horatio Storer organized successful campaigns to criminalize abortion through new state laws. The culmination of the campaigns against abortion in state legislatures coincided with the passage of the Comstock Act (1873), a strengthened national obscenity law in which no distinctions were made among smut, abortifacients, and contraceptives—all were prohibited. As a result, explicit discussions of contraception were omitted from post-1873 editions of marriage manuals in which the subject had been given space.

Anthony Comstock was a lobbyist for the New York Society for the Suppression of Vice. Twentieth-century accounts of his activities sometimes mocked his concerns by portraying him as an idiosyncratic fanatic whose success depended on congressional desire to divert attention from the political scandals of the Grant presidency. Comstock's concerns were shared, however, by the prominent New York businessmen who paid his salary, the eminent physicians who campaigned for criminalization of abortion, and political leaders at all levels of government. By attempting to suppress contraception and abortion, these social leaders were responding to social changes that they thought threatened Christian values and the stability of the middle-class family. Despite their efforts, birthrates continued to decline. Married couples reconciled the conflict between their personal needs and social values by practicing contraception, seeking abortions, or cultivating the ethos of sexual repression that would later be mocked as "Victorian prudery."

In 1901 sociologist Edward A. Ross coined the phrase "race suicide," and Pres. Theodore Roosevelt declared that the future of the United States as a world power was being undermined by the pursuit of the soft life as exemplified by barren marriages. Exhortations to reproduce had limited effect, however, in the booming consumer economy of the early twentieth century.

The emergence around 1915 of a movement to legitimate contraceptive practice was a logical, if not inevitable, response to a major tension in the personal lives of many Americans. Margaret Sanger won her place as the charismatic leader of the birth-control movement in the United States through her ability to develop a compelling rationale for the acceptance of contraception as an alternative to the appalling number of women who died from septic abortion. Drawing upon her experience as a visiting nurse in the tenements of New York's Lower East Side, Sanger claimed that the death of one of her clients from a self-induced abortion led her to focus all her energy on the single cause of reproductive autonomy for women. In the story of Sadie Sachs, a truck driver's wife who was scornfully refused contraceptive advice by a doctor and instructed instead to have her husband sleep on the roof, Sanger found a compelling myth that conveyed her outrage at the suppression of knowledge that women needed, whether their primary concern was the economic survival of their families or the desire for greater personal freedom.

As a radical activist in the socialist and labor movements, Sanger was well acquainted with anarchist Emma Goldman's efforts through speeches and pamphlets to spread birth control as part of her larger program of human liberation. Frustrated by the condescending attitudes toward women's issues displayed by some of her radical colleagues, as well as by censorship of her newspaper articles on women's sexual health, Sanger became convinced that women needed a distinctive voice representing them as an interest group in the struggle for social justice, and she argued that sexual reform was the paramount issue for women, a cause that had to precede the struggle for higher wages and control of the workplace. Sanger's first task in the fight to win reproductive autonomy for her sex was to winnow through the vast array of birth-control methods in order to identify a safe, effective, female-controlled contraceptive. She hoped to mobilize a mass demand for legalization of birth control through publication, beginning in March 1914, of her militantly feminist journal, *The Woman Rebel*, where the term *birth control* was coined in the June 1914 issue. The post office declared the journal obscene even though it gave no specific contraceptive advice. After being indicted for violation of the postal code, Sanger departed for Europe in October 1914. Left behind were her instructions for mass distribution of her how-to-do-it pamphlet *Family Limitation*, which provided the most detailed and informed discussion of contraceptive technique available in English.

During a year of exile in Europe, Sanger became an intimate friend of Havelock Ellis, author of *Studies in the Psychology of Sex* (1897–1910). Influenced by Ellis and other British intellectuals, she began to develop a more cautious propaganda that exploited the rhetoric of social science and sought to win social elites to the cause of sexual liberation. In the Netherlands Sanger found contraceptive advice centers staffed by midwives and attended classes in the fitting of the spring-loaded vaginal diaphragm, which became the primary method she recommended. Sanger returned to the United States and in October 1916 opened a women's clinic in the Brownsville section of Brooklyn, where 464 mothers got contraceptive advice during the ten days before a police raid closed the center (Chesler 1992, 150). Her trial and brief imprisonment made Sanger a national figure, and in appealing her case, she won a clarification of the New York law that forbade distribution of birth-control information. Judge Frederick Crane ruled that the 1873 statute under which Sanger had been arrested was reasonable because it allowed doctors to prescribe condoms for venereal disease. In rejecting Sanger's claim that the law was unconstitutional because it forced women to risk death in pregnancy against their will, Crane established the right of doctors to provide women with contraceptive advice for "the cure and prevention of disease," thus widening the venereal disease clause to include women.

Sanger interpreted the Crane decision as a mandate for doctor-staffed birth-control clinics. Although she continued to send revised editions of *Family Limitation* to those who asked for it, she adopted the strategy of lobbying for "doctors only" bills that removed legal prohibitions on medical advice. This pragmatic concession was bitterly opposed by Mary Ware Dennett, Sanger's chief rival for leadership of the birth-control movement in the 1920s, but Sanger's willingness to cultivate support among doctors was part of her shift in strategy as a reformer. Gradually she broke her ties with old comrades, played down her radical past, stressed eugenic arguments for birth control that were in vogue among academics, and found financial angels among socialites and philanthropists. Such support allowed her in 1921 to organize the American Birth Control League.

By 1923 Sanger had developed the network of support that allowed her to open the Birth Control Clinical Research Bureau in New York City and to keep it open despite a 1929 police raid. The first doctor-staffed birth-control clinic in the United States, the clinic provided case histories that demonstrated the safety and effectiveness of contraceptive practice. Irresponsible claims by social conservatives that diaphragms caused cancer and madness, and did not work anyway, were refuted. The clinic also served as a teaching facility where hundreds of physicians received instruction in contraceptive technique at a time when it was not a part of the medical school curriculum. Finally, the clinic was a model for the nationwide network of over 300 birth-control clinics established by Sanger and her supporters by 1938 (Reed 1983, 116–128). Staffed mainly by women doctors and supported by women volunteers, these clinics provided access to reliable contraceptive advice and were responsible for important improvements in the effectiveness of contraceptive practice.

During the 1930s, Sanger organized a major lobbying campaign to remove contraception from the federal Comstock Act. The effort failed because the ideal of reproductive autonomy for women was literally a joke among male legislators at a time when the birthrate had fallen below the level needed to maintain the existing population. Pres. Franklin Roosevelt's New Deal political coalition depended heavily on the votes of urban ethnics, who were often Roman Catholics and shared Anthony Comstock's view that efforts to separate sex from procreation

violated natural law. Sanger was able to win a major revision in federal law, however, by opportunistic use of the courts, a public forum in which the political power of Roman Catholics was minimized and success depended on finding a judge who recognized that the social mores of Americans had fundamentally changed since the late nineteenth century. In the early 1930s Sanger's National Committee on Federal Legislation for Birth Control was participating in multiple courts actions challenging bans on contraceptives. When a shipment of Japanese pessaries intended for Dr. Hannah Stone, the medical director of the Birth Control Clinical Research Bureau, was confiscated, federal judge August Hand ruled in *United States* v. *One Package* (1936) that the clinical data on the effectiveness of contraceptive practice made available since the passage of the Comstock Act mandated recognition of the right of physicians to receive contraceptive materials. This legal victory set the stage for a 1937 resolution by the American Medical Association that recognized contraception as an ethical medical service.

Robert L. Dickinson, a gynecologist who had retired from private medical practice in 1920 to devote himself to full-time medical sex research, was the key figure in the campaign to win the American Medical Association endorsement. Dickinson spoke for a significant minority of physicians and social workers who were not feminists but believed that the legal and social taboos on contraception had a destructive impact on families. They shared Sanger's concern over the harm done by illegal abortions and argued that unwanted or ill-timed pregnancies damaged women and their families. In 1923 Dickinson organized the Committee on Maternal Health ("National" was added to the title in 1930) to promote medical sex education and research. The committee sponsored a series of monographs, such as Dickinson's 1931 *Control of Conception,* his 1931 *One Thousand Marriages* (written with Lura Beam), and his 1933 *Atlas of Human Sex Anatomy,* which served as handbooks for doctors interested in sexual counseling and as justification for shifts in medical opinion.

By the late 1930s Dickinson's protégé, Dr. Clarence J. Gamble, an heir to the Ivory Soap fortune, became the most energetic birth-control advocate associated with the committee. Gamble publicized the scandalous practices in the commercial manufacture and marketing of contraceptives, with the result that the Food and Drug Administration began to test condoms and to confiscate defective articles, the American Medical Association began to issue reports that defined standards for contraception products, and efforts were made to suppress ineffective feminine hygiene douches that were marketed as contraceptives. In contrast to Sanger, who wanted to liberate women from unwanted pregnancies, or the majority of pro–birth control physicians, who hoped to strengthen family life through better marital sex, Gamble's principal concern was differential fertility among classes and the high cost of social programs for the poor. Gamble initiated a series of experiments in the mass delivery of contraceptives. In Logan County, West Virginia, for example, door-to-door distribution of free lactic acid jelly between 1936 and 1939 led to dramatic declines in birthrates among the poor women who were willing to try the method. In Logan County, as elsewhere, Gamble's efforts ran into problems of cost and the reluctance of public officials to devote scarce resources to contraception.

On the eve of World War II, the limits of the birth-control movement seemed to have been realized. A majority of Americans practiced some form of fertility control, but there was widespread concern about the low birthrate and little support for public subsidy of services. In 1942 the national organization substituted "family planning" for "birth control" in its title as part of an effort to avoid the feminist stigma that a public relations adviser perceived in Sanger, who at the age of sixty-three had lost control of the organization and had retired to Arizona. After World War II, however, influential social scientists such as Frank Notestein of Princeton University's Center for Population Research provided a new rationale for birth control by drawing attention to rapid population growth in the Third World and arguing that the United States risked losing the cold war because economic development compatible with capitalism might be impossible if means were not found to curb birthrates. The discovery of "the population explosion" turned birth control from a private vice practiced by self-interested individuals to a public virtue needed to save the earth from ecological catastrophe.

John D. Rockefeller III became the leader of the revived movement to promote fertility control by founding the Population Council in 1952. As the eldest of John D. Rockefeller Jr.'s five sons, he had been reared to follow his father as a professional philanthropist. As a Princeton undergraduate he developed a strong interest in population issues, and in 1928 his father had him appointed to the board of directors of the Bureau of Social Hygiene, the means through which the Rockefellers invested money in social science research and action programs in criminology, sex education, and birth control. When the bureau was terminated in 1934, Rockefeller informed his father that he would maintain a strong interest in birth control. He traveled extensively in Asia, became convinced that the future would be shaped by events in the non-Western world, and was concerned by the lack of appreciation in the United States for non-Western cultures. When he failed to convince the directors of the Rockefeller Foundation that his interests warranted major new initiatives, he used his own resources to found the Population Council (1952) as well as the Council on Economic and Cultural Affairs to promote increased food production in Asia.

The Population Council subsidized the development of academic demographic research in the United States and foreign universities and by the late 1950s was providing technical assistance to India and Pakistan for family planning programs. Concerned over the failure rates of the conventional barrier contraceptives, the council invested in the clinical testing, improvement, and statistical evaluation of IUDs, which had been shunned before the development of antibiotics because of their association with pelvic infection. Through council sponsorship, redesigned plastic IUDs became a mainstay of Asian population control programs in the 1960s. A second major advance in contraceptive technology came with the marketing of an oral contraceptive by J. D. Searle and Company in 1960. "The pill" depended on recent advances in steroid chemistry that provided orally active, and inexpensive, synthetic hormones, but Margaret Sanger ensured that these new drugs would be exploited for birth control by recruiting Gregory Pincus of the Worcester Foundation for Experimental Biology for the work. She introduced him to a feminist colleague, Katharine Dexter McCormick, who provided the funds Pincus needed to realize their dream of a female-controlled method that was divorced from sexual intercourse. These new methods brought contraceptive research from "messy gadgets" notoriety into mainstream biomedical science, and in 1963 Roman Catholic gynecologist John Rock, who had led the clinical trials of the first oral contraceptive, proclaimed in *The Time Has Come* that contraception was, thanks to the pill, now compatible with natural law theology. Rock's optimism seemed to be justified when Pope Paul VI disclosed the creation of a special commission on population and the family in June 1964. The papal encyclical *Humanae Vitae* (July 1968) disappointed liberals by confirming traditional teachings that prohibited artificial contraception, but by then a majority of married Catholics had concluded that the church's position was wrong.

A series of federal court decisions and new welfare policies reflected the changed status of birth control in public opinion. In 1965 the U.S. Supreme Court, in *Griswold* v. *Connecticut*, struck down an "uncommonly silly law" that prohibited contraceptive practice (Garrow 1994, 255). The court continued to expand the rights of individuals to defy outdated restrictions in *Eisenstadt* v. *Baird* (1972), which established the right of the unmarried to contraceptives. As Pres. Lyndon Johnson's War on Poverty emerged from Congress in 1964, a number of planned parenthood groups successfully applied to the Office of Economic Opportunity for funds, and the Social Security Amendments of 1967 specified that at least 6 percent of expanding maternal and child health care funds be spent on family planning services. The Foreign Assistance Act of the same year provided aid for international programs, and contraceptives were removed from the list of materials that could not be purchased with Agency for International Development funds. A political consensus seemed to favor birth control as a private practice and a part of welfare policy. Arguments for coercive population control programs at home and abroad gained attention through the efforts of Dixie Cup tycoon Hugh Moore, who founded the Population Crisis Committee and spent lavishly on full-page newspaper advertisements warning of the ticking "population bomb" that, Moore claimed, threatened world order.

The election of Republican president Richard Nixon in 1968 marked growing resistance to the rapid social changes associated with the expansion of the welfare state and civil rights movements for African Americans, women, and homosexuals. In 1970 Nixon signalized his perception that birth control was a mainstream policy by appointing John D. Rockefeller III as chairman of the Commission on Population Growth and the American Future, but in 1972, as Nixon prepared to stand for reelection, he repudiated the commission's recommendations on sex education and abortion law reform because they had become intensely controversial. By the late 1960s, feminists and population control advocates were successfully challenging state laws that limited access to abortion. In 1973 the U.S. Supreme Court attempted to forge a new consensus in *Roe* v. *Wade,* which recognized the right of abortion on demand during the first trimester of pregnancy. The Court's decision simply added fuel to an escalating firestorm of controversy as Roman Catholic leaders found common cause with Protestant fundamentalists and social conservative critics of the welfare state in a Right-to-Life and Family

Values movement. That movement fed upon the insecurities generated by a declining standard of living for U.S. workers and by the broad changes in the economy that led a majority of married women into wage labor outside the home. From the left, groups such as the Committee to End Sterilization Abuse (founded in 1974) charged that minority women were being coerced by government maternal health programs that they viewed as genocidal (Shapiro 1985, passim). Revelations that disproportionate numbers of Hispanic and black women were sterilized in government programs that lacked adequate ethical guidelines supported complaints by such organizations as the National Women's Health Movement and the International Women's Health Coalition that the health-care establishment in the United States had gone radically wrong in its high-tech, top-down, paternalistic approach to reproductive health issues (Gordon 1990, 436–446; Dixon-Mueller 1993, 47–53).

At the 1974 United Nations World Population Conference, held in Bucharest, Hungary, John D. Rockefeller III recognized the criticisms of conventional family planning programs that had been mounted by feminists, and the Population Council was reorganized to emphasize holistic approaches to women's health issues. New ethical guidelines were developed for federally sponsored maternal health programs as well, but deep social divisions remained between pro-choice and pro-life advocates, with the Democratic Party embracing the former and the Republican Party embracing the latter. Despite numerous challenges in state and federal courts and legislatures, *Roe* v. *Wade* remained the law of the land. In the late 1990s federal and state expenditures for subsidized family planning, including contraception, sterilization, and therapeutic abortion, exceeded $700 million annually. The birthrate among the native-born was below the level needed to maintain the population, which continued to grow because of liberal immigration laws and mass immigration to the United States (Critchlow 1999, 1, 226, 230–231).

—*James W. Reed*

See also Ellis, Havelock; Fertility; Sanger, Margaret; Teenage Pregnancy

References and Further Reading
Brodie, Janet Farrell. 1994. *Contraception and Abortion in 19th-Century America.* Ithaca: Cornell University Press.

Chesler, Ellen. 1992. *Woman of Valor: Margaret Sanger and the Birth Control Movement in America.* New York: Simon and Schuster.

Critchlow, Donald T. 1999. *Intended Consequences: Birth Control, Abortion, and the Federal Government in Modern America.* New York: Oxford University Press.

Critchlow, Donald T., ed. 1996. *The Politics of Abortion and Birth Control in Historical Perspective.* University Park: Pennsylvania State University Press.

Dixon-Mueller, Ruth. 1993. *Population Policy and Women's Rights: Transforming Reproductive Choice.* Westport, CT: Praeger.

Garrow, David J. 1994. *Liberty and Sexuality: The Right to Privacy and the Making of* Roe v. Wade. New York: Macmillan.

Gordon, Linda. 1990. *Woman's Body, Woman's Right: A Social History of Birth Control in America.* Revised and updated. New York: Grossman, 1976. Reprint, New York: Penguin Books.

Grant, Nicole J. 1992. *The Selling of Contraception: The Dalkon Shield Case, Sexuality, and Women's Autonomy.* Columbus: Ohio State University Press.

Marks, Lara V. 2001. *Sexual Chemistry: A History of the Contraceptive Pill.* New Haven: Yale University Press.

McCann, Carole R. 1994. *Birth Control Politics in the United States, 1916–1945.* Ithaca: Cornell University Press.

McLaren, Angus. 1990. *A History of Contraception: From Antiquity to the Present Day.* Cambridge, MA: Blackwell.

Mohr, James C. 1988. *Abortion in America: The Origins and Evolution of National Policy, 1800–1900.* New York: Oxford University Press.

Reagan, Leslie J. 1997. *When Abortion Was a Crime: Women, Medicine, and Law in the United States, 1867–1973.* Berkeley: University of California Press.

Reed, James. 1983. *The Birth Control Movement and American Society: From Private Vice to Public Virtue.* New York: Basic Books, 1978 (as *From Private Vice to Public Virtue: The Birth Control Movement and American Society since 1830*). Reprint, Princeton, NJ: Princeton University Press.

Shapiro, Thomas M. 1985. *Population Control Politics: Women, Sterilization, and Reproductive Choice.* Philadelphia: Temple University Press.

Tone, Andrea. 2001. *Devices and Desires: A History of Contraceptives in America.* New York: Hill and Wang.

Ward, Martha C. 1986. *Poor Women, Powerful Men: America's Great Experiment in Family Planning.* Boulder, CO: Westview Press.

Watkins, Elizabeth S. 1998. *On the Pill: A Social History of Oral Contraceptives, 1950–1970.* Baltimore: Johns Hopkins University Press.

Birth Order, Theories of

Every aspect of how a person chooses a job and a mate, relates to coworkers, and relates to family members is determined by that individual's placement in his or her birth family. As each child enters a family, the roles and expectations for children within that family change. These differences, as Sigmund Freud was the first psychotherapist to note, mean that each child is treated in a different way and each will establish a distinct

An early-twentieth-century family portrait with several children of different ages. (Library of Congress)

identity by using different behaviors to get approval and attention. All other things being equal, birth order traits develop on the basis of five circumstances of birth: the order of birth, the sex of the child, the number of years between the births of siblings, the sex of siblings, and the birth order of the parents.

The first child in a family usually identifies with the values of the parents and works at becoming what they want. Guardians of the status quo, eldest children do not like change. Since parents emphasize achievement with a firstborn, these children tend to be tenser, more serious, more reserved, and less playful than others. An eldest brother of brothers may find it difficult to work with women, while an eldest sister of brothers

may be quite comfortable exercising authority over male employees.

The next child, unable to compete with the eldest, often gets recognition by becoming a rogue, the very opposite of the firstborn. Although these children benefit from the more relaxed atmosphere that accompanies later births in families, middle children are soon displaced by the new baby. As adults, they are sensitive to being left out or slighted. Middle children are less pressured by the parents to succeed and show fewer tendencies to take initiative or think independently. Adept at dealing with all kinds of people, they are skilled negotiators.

Youngest children often remain dependent on others and are more likely than their siblings to be undisciplined in their personal lives. The youngest tend to procrastinate continually, to be risk takers, and to be happiest in jobs that involve social interaction. With no experience caring for others, youngest children tend to be neglectful parents.

Only children show some of the characteristics of oldest children yet are likely to remain childlike into adulthood. They have a higher self-esteem than the eldest ones, with less need to control others. Since they did not have to negotiate with siblings, only children do not understand the necessity of sharing control. Very comfortable living alone and lacking experience with children, only children are the least likely birth order to enjoy marriage and the most likely to remain childless. Only children have trouble adjusting to the different personalities of too many peers at the same time and generally prefer occupations that allow them to work alone.

—*Caryn E. Neumann*

References and Further Reading
Freud, Sigmund. 1965. *Introductory Lectures on Psychoanalysis.* New York: W.W. Norton, 1929. Reprint, New York: W.W. Norton.
Richardson, Ronald W., and Lois A. Richardson. 1990. *Birth Order and You.* North Vancouver, BC: Self Counsel Press.
Toman, Walter. 1976. *Family Constellation: Its Effects on Personality and Social Behavior.* 3d ed. New York: Springer.

Blended Families

Blended families are the most common family configuration in the United States today (Rosenberg 1990). In 1987, there were 4.3 million blended families, or stepfamilies, in this country. About 8.7 million children under eighteen, one out of five minors, was a stepchild (Rosenberg 1990). The academic literature on steprelations—with all of their ins and outs, trials, and compromises—has largely come into being since the 1970s, its birth coinciding generally with the emergence of divorce as the cause of more marriage breakups than the death of a spouse. In fact, one-third of all marriages in 1988 were remarriages for one or both partners (Coates 1996).

Historically, there have been blended families virtually as long as there have been families. In Europe and the Americas, most were the result of remarriage after the death of a spouse, as divorce was unacceptable to the church and, therefore, to lawmakers. There was no divorce or legal separation in the American colonies. Indeed, until midway through the nineteenth century, relatively few divorces were granted in the United States. The grounds of those that were granted were desertion, adultery, and cruelty. A century later, the situation was considerably different. By 1950, more than half the divorces in this country were granted on grounds of cruelty, often mental cruelty, a term that was liberally interpreted. Two decades later, no-fault divorces became legal, and the rise in blended families began. In a majority of cases now, a remarriage usually includes the complexity of relationships with former spouses and their extended families.

A blended family is a family that consists of parts of two other families, joined by the decision of two adults. The new family can include the children of the husband and the wife, ex-spouses, two pairs of biological grandparents, two sets of stepgrandparents, and children in the custody of the ex-spouse. Unless the stepparent adopts the stepchild, there is no legal relationship between the stepparent and the stepchild. This fact may cause embarrassment. In an extreme situation it might even contribute to the death of a child. A stepparent may be confronted with the refusal by a school, hospital, or some other group to accept the stepparent as one with sufficient authority to sign papers allowing emergency treatment, as in the case of accident or illness. Blended families face problems and difficult situations not only because those are inherent to the complexities of steprelationships but also because some subsystems want to deny the problems exist.

Although society's attitudes regarding divorce and remarriage have become more accepting, there are still vestiges of the Cinderella myth of the wicked stepmother and the unwanted child. Some childhood stories tell of the adult female in conflict with children. Stories of the wicked stepmother, jealous siblings, and the unwanted stepchild have been found in Chinese literature as early as A.D. 850. Similar stories in over 500 versions have appeared all over Europe (Smith 1999). The term *stepchild* has long indicated something secondhand or unwanted. Wicked stepfathers are rare in children's literature but abundant in adult literature, and if one can accept the evidence in the press, wicked stepfathers in real life are plentiful. In fact, psychologists Martin Daly and Margo Wilson argue that having a stepparent is the greatest risk factor for severe child abuse (Daly and Wilson 1999). Recent work by counselors and family theorists, however, has begun to address this and many of the problems the blended family may face.

Because there was little written about stepfamilies when the numbers began to multiply in the 1970s, people began to write about their own lives as stepfamilies. Possibly the first material available was in syndicated newspaper columns such as "Ann Landers" and "Dear Abby." Some of those who wrote were counselors, psychologists, and social scientists, many of whom probably began with their personal stories and added masked stories of their patients. Soon, some churches became involved, creating "blending ceremonies" that acknowledged the complex emotional situation faced by both adults and children. Legally, however, the status of the blended family has not changed.

Much of the literature on blended families is anecdotal and is both strikingly alike and strikingly varied: alike as the families present common categories of experiences and varied because no two stepfamilies are identical. An exhaustive list of specific problems faced would be prohibitive, but citing just a few will point to the variety of these problems.

Is the couple subsystem to be the primary subsystem in considering how any problem is to be dealt with?

How will the couple acquire the time and the privacy necessary for the development of the trust, intimacy, and strength needed in their relationship?

How will the couple handle the bond between the child and the biological parent, especially if the child and parent were part of or all of a single-parent family for quite a while?

How will two sets of children with different backgrounds be disciplined?

How will the couple handle the child's fear of losing another parent, this one to the new stepparent?

What will happen if love between stepparent and stepchild fails to develop?

As counselors and clergy help blended families address these issues, society will need to address legal questions. The welfare of children in these families may depend on legislative attention to questions of the rights of nonadopting stepparents and other complexities of new forms of kinship.

—*Les Thompson Jr.*

See also Adoptive Parents; Divorce, History of; Remarriage, History of; Stepparents

References and Further Readings
Bloomfield, Harold H., with Robert B. Kory. 1994. *Making Peace in Your Stepfamily: Surviving as Parents and Stepparents.* New York: Hyperion, 1993. Reprint, New York: Hyperion.
Bray, James H., and John Kelly. 1998. *Stepfamilies: Love, Marriage, and Parenting in the First Decade.* New York: Broadway Books.
Coates, Joseph F. 1996. "What's Ahead for Families: Five Major Forces of Change." *The Futurist* 30 (September): 1–5.
Craven, Linda. 1982. *Stepfamilies: New Patterns of Harmony.* New York: Messner.
Daly, Martin, and Margo Wilson. 1999. *The Truth of Cinderella: A Darwinian View of Parental Love.* London: Weidenfeld and Nicolson, 1998. Reprint, New Haven: Yale University Press.
Felker, Evelyn H. 1981. *Raising Other People's Kids: Successful Child Rearing in the Restructured Family.* Grand Rapids, MI: Wm. B. Erdmans.
Johnson, Colleen. 1988. *Ex Familia: Grandparents, Parents and Children Adjust to Divorce.* New Brunswick, NJ: Rutgers University Press.
Keshet, Jamie Kelet. 1987. *Love and Power in the Stepfamily.* New York: McGraw-Hill.
Lofas, Jeannette, and Dawn B. Sova. 1985. *Stepparenting: Everything You Need to Know to Make It Work.* Kensington, NY: Kensington.
Rosenberg, Maxine B. 1990. *Talking about Stepfamilies.* New York: Bradbury Press.
Smith, William Carlton. 1999. London: Weidenfeld and Nicolson, 1998. Reprint, Chicago: University of Chicago Press.
Sobol, Harriet. 1988. *My Other Mother— My Other Father.* New York: Macmillan.

Breast-Feeding

Before pure food laws, the universal pasteurization of milk, and the ability to keep milk cold in the home, whether or not a mother breast-fed her infant was the most important factor in determining an infant's survival. The connection between infant death and artificial feeding became especially obvious in the late nineteenth century as infant feeding practices changed and women began to wean babies earlier, exposing them to the spoiled and adulterated cows' milk common to late-nineteenth-century cities. Infant deaths from diarrhea soared. Consequent crusades to clean up cows' milk eventually eradicated diarrhea as a primary cause of infant mortality. By the 1920s, pasteurization and refrigeration had eliminated the most egregious problems associated with the use of cows' milk as a food for human infants, and artificial feeding had become the predominant practice. Today, although breast-feeding is no longer the vital determinant of infant morbidity and mortality that it was before the 1920s, whether or not a baby is breast-fed continues to impact children's short- and long-term health.

During the colonial era, American mothers breast-fed their infants through their babies' second summer and, as often as not, beyond. This "second summer" custom was telling because most infant deaths occurred during the summer when food spoiled quickly. Deaths were especially common during that second summer when babies began to eat food other than their mother's milk. By the last quarter of the nineteenth century this venerable custom had largely vanished. Although the majority of mothers still breast-fed their babies for a time immediately after birth, urban women often weaned their babies at or well before three months of age and/or supplemented their breast milk with cows' milk and worse. The results were catastrophic. In the 1890s, as urban public health departments compiled infant mortality statistics for the first time, an alarming 13 to 30 percent of babies in the United States were dying before their first birthday, and more than half the dead succumbed to diarrhea. In Chicago, the Department of Health estimated in 1910 that fifteen artificially fed babies died for every one breast-fed baby. "Obviously," observed one doctor at the nation's first annual conference on the cause and prevention of infant mortality in 1909, "nature's normal nutriment does not predispose to death" (Wile 1909, 140).

Raw cows' milk, the primary substitute for human milk during that era, was commonly spoiled, dirty, and adulterated, hence the enormous death rate among infants from diarrhea. Stored in uncovered eight-gallon vats, cows' milk traveled in unrefrigerated railroad cars for up to three days as it made its way from rural dairy farmer to urban consumer. To hide a number of defects, the farmers, shippers, and merchants who handled milk adulterated it as a matter of course. Dairy farmers, for example, often added chalk to whiten dirty milk. Merchants added aniline dye to make skimmed milk look rich with cream. Formaldehyde was a common milk preservative. Everyone (including consumers) used a "milk expander," composed of soda, ammonia, salt, and water, to stretch this expensive commodity.

As infant feeding patterns changed and fewer mothers breast-fed for prolonged

The Chicago Department of Health hung this poster in every Chicago neighborhood beginning in the summer of 1911. The poster appeared in eight different languages. Health departments throughout the country also used this illustration in their breast-feeding and pure milk campaigns, although the wording accompanying the illustration differed from city to city. (Reprinted from Bulletin Chicago School of Sanitary Instruction, *June 3, 1911.)*

periods, if at all, public health departments throughout the country attacked infants' consequent deaths from diarrhea in two ways. Between roughly 1890 and 1930, municipalities fought to have milk bottled, sealed, and pasteurized; to have milk shipped in refrigerated railroad cars; and to have cows tested for bovine tuberculosis. Simultaneously, and equally important in the eyes of the medical community, health authorities promoted breast-feeding as a way to keep babies healthy. Fresh and pure cows' milk, physicians advised, might be a second-best alternative to human milk, but as one physician lectured mothers in a popular women's magazine in 1909, "I say 'best,' but in this connection the word is almost meaningless, for the difference between mother's milk and cows' milk is abysmal. The first is at once a perfect food and an efficient medicine, while the second is a very unsatisfactory food and no medicine at all" (Hirshberg 1909, 262).

In keeping with the nature of the emergency, the public pleas urging mothers to breast-feed were dramatic. One Civic Federation of Chicago poster explaining that "Mother's Milk Is Best of All" was headlined "Don't Kill Your Baby." A 1911 Chicago Department of Health broadside pleaded, "To Lessen Baby Deaths Let Us Have More Mother-Fed Babies. You Can't improve on God's plan. For Your Baby's Sake—Nurse It!" Women learned from newsletters that before birth a baby needs mothers' blood, "after birth it needs her milk." The Chicago Health Department's booklet, "Our Babies," distributed to all mothers of newborns beginning in 1916, called human milk "the Child's Life Insurance" and admonished women that "no mother who has only a spark of mother love in her heart would deprive a child of its natural nourishment either on purpose or selfishly" (Chicago Department of Health 1916, 123).

Chicago was by no means alone in its efforts. Every major U.S. city orchestrated simultaneous crusades in the early twentieth century to clean up its cows' milk supply and urge mothers to breast-feed. Minneapolis, thanks in large part to Julius Parker Sedgwick, chief of the Department of Pediatrics at the University of Minnesota, conducted the most extensive and successful early-twentieth-century breast-feeding campaign of any U.S. city. Sedgwick, a longtime breast-feeding advocate, deemed human milk so vital to infant health that he pleaded in 1912 for breast-feeding to be made the cornerstone of national plans to lower infant mortality. In 1919 Sedgwick set up the Breastfeeding Investigation Bureau, whose workers followed all Minneapolis babies for nine months after birth to urge infants' mothers to breast-feed and to assist mothers with any problems they encountered while breast-feeding. The campaign was an unqualified success. More than 96 percent of babies born in Minneapolis during the first five months of 1919 were still breast-feeding at the end of their second month, and more than 72 percent were still breast-feeding at the end of their ninth month. Infant mortality in Minneapolis declined almost 20 percent, from eighty deaths per thousand live births in 1918 to sixty-five in 1919 (Wolf 1999a).

The success in Minneapolis, however, was isolated, and most cities' infant mortality rates did not take a marked downturn until the cows' milk supply was safe. In Chicago, for example, infant deaths from diarrhea went from 59 percent of the 5,735 infant deaths (out of 38,764 births) in 1897 to only 13 percent of the 3,103 infant deaths (out of 58,083 births) in 1930. This decline occurred slowly and only after the passage of laws in Chicago that required that milk be sealed (in 1904), bottled (in 1912), pasteurized (in 1916), and kept cold during shipping (in 1920) and that dairy farmers test dairy cattle for bovine tuberculosis (in 1926) (Wolf 1999a).

With the relative safety of cows' milk ensured by the 1930s in most communities, the dangers of artificial feeding became less obvious. Younger pediatricians, who had never seen a baby die from consuming artificial food and only rarely saw one sicken, were largely indifferent to whether or not mothers breast-fed. As one pediatrician assured women, "There is nothing mysterious or sacred about breast milk. It is just a food" ("Are Infant Feeding Methods Changing?" 1931, 583). By the 1940s, infant mortality from diarrhea was so low that most in the medical and lay communities believed that the pasteurization, bottling, and sealing of milk had taken care of any health threat to babies posed by their consumption of bovine, rather than human, milk.

A mother breast-feeding her baby, 1905. (Library of Congress)

This new attitude toward mothers' milk coincided with a dramatic rise in hospital births. Hospital births went from virtually zero in 1900 to almost 50 percent in 1938 to 95 percent in 1955. In hospitals, where women customarily remained for ten to fourteen days even after normal vaginal births, rigid feeding schedules and the routine separation of mothers from their babies virtually guaranteed that any mother wanting to breast-feed would fail. Immediately after a birth, nurses now hustled babies off to hospital nurseries. As long as mothers remained hospitalized, they rarely saw their infants more than five times in twenty-four hours and never saw them at night. Nurses commonly bottle-fed even breast-fed infants. Artificial food thus received medical sanction while mothers' milk supplies languished.

The lengthy hospitalization of women after giving birth also provided condensed milk and infant formula companies the ideal opportunity to indoctrinate new mothers. Company salesmen provided hospitals and postpartum women with free condensed milk, formula, and assorted gifts. Gifts included booklets suggesting what to name infants, name cards for babies' cribs, and diaper bags all emblazoned with company logos. Although the early weaning of babies from the breast had been common even at the end of the nineteenth century, by the 1930s and 1940s, in addition to the prevalent practices of early weaning and early mixed feeding, most women never even initiated breast-feeding.

When health-reform activists in the women's movement launched the "natural childbirth" movement, breast-feeding rates began to rise in the early 1970s. Feminists argued that unmedicated birth and breast-feeding would return practices to women that doctors had medicalized unnecessarily. The activities of La Leche League, a voluntary organization that originated in a Chicago suburb in 1956, also contributed to the rise in popularity of breast-feeding. From an initial meeting of twelve women in 1956, La Leche League breast-feeding support groups grew to 43 in 1961, 430 in 1966, 1,260 in 1971, and 3,000 in 1976. The organization reached an even wider audience via its book, *The Womanly Art of Breastfeeding*, first published in 1958. A second revised edition of the book in 1963 sold 1,172,200 copies (Weiner 1994, 1359; Wolf 2001, 197).

Breast-feeding rates increased in the United States from 22 percent of newborns in 1972 to a high of 62 percent in 1982. Between 1982 and the present, rates have hovered between 52 and 58 percent. These latter statistics are deceptively high, however, for they represent only the percentage of mothers who leave the hospital breast-feeding and include newborns fed human milk supplemented with artificial food. Prolonged breast-feeding rates remain very low; only 18.9 percent of babies are still nursing at six months and only 5.6 percent continue to nurse until their first birthday. Exclusive breast-feeding rates are lower still (Wolf 2001).

In December 1997, in an effort to increase breast-feeding rates, the American Academy of Pediatrics (AAP) issued new breast-feeding guidelines. Harking back to traditional breast-feeding practices in the United States, the AAP urged mothers to breast-feed their babies exclusively for six months, to continue breast-feeding until a baby was at least a year old, and to breast-feed thereafter for as long as a mother and infant desired. Although the connection between low breast-feeding rates and ill health is not as immediate and obvious as it was in the late nineteenth century, the AAP advised that low breast-feeding rates continue to impact public health in the United States.

Research now suggests that breast-feeding decreases the incidence and severity of diarrhea, ear infections, respiratory infections, and bacterial meningitis in infants and children and offers possible long-term protection against insulin-dependent diabetes, lymphoma, leukemia, Crohn's disease, ulcerative colitis, and a host of allergic diseases (American Academy of Pediatrics 1997).

—*Jacqueline H. Wolf*

See also Infant Mortality; La Leche League

References and Further Reading

American Academy of Pediatrics. 1997. "Breastfeeding and the Use of Human Milk." *Pediatrics* 100 (December): 1035–1039.

Apple, Rima D. 1987. *Mothers and Medicine: A Social History of Infant Feeding 1890–1950.* Madison: University of Wisconsin Press.

Apple, Rima D. 1994. "The Medicalization of Infant Feeding in the United States and New Zealand: Two Countries, One Experience." *Journal of Human Lactation* 10: 31–37.

"Are Infant Feeding Methods Changing?" 1931. *Public Health Nursing* 23: 581–585.

Chicago Department of Health. Division of Child Hygiene. 1916. *Our Babies.* Chicago: Department of Health.

Golden, Janet. 1996. *A Social History of Wet Nursing in America: From Breast to Bottle.* New York: Cambridge University Press.

Hirshberg, Leonard Keene. 1909. "What You Ought to Know about Your Baby." *The Delineator* 73 (February): 262.

Levenstein, Harvey. 1983. "'Best for Babies' or 'Preventable Infanticide'? The Controversy over Artificial Feeding of Infants in America, 1880–1920." *The Journal of American History* 70: 75–94.

Meckel, Richard A. 1990. *Save the Babies: American Public Health Reform and the Prevention of Infant Mortality, 1850–1929.* Baltimore: Johns Hopkins University Press.

Salmon, Marylynn. 1994. "The Cultural Significance of Breastfeeding and Infant

Care in Early Modern England and America." *Journal of Social History* 28 (Winter): 247–269.

Treckel, Paula A. 1989. "Breastfeeding and Maternal Sexuality in Colonial America." *Journal of Interdisciplinary History* 20 (Summer): 25–51.

Weiner, Lynn Y. 1994. "Reconstructing Motherhood: The La Leche League in Postwar America." *The Journal of American History* 80: 1357–1381.

Wile, Ira S. 1909. "Educational Responsibilities of a Milk Depot." *Prevention of Infant Mortality: Being the Papers and Discussions of a Conference Held at New Haven, Connecticut*, 139–153. Easton, PA: American Academy of Medicine.

Wolf, Jacqueline H. 1998. "'Don't Kill Your Baby': Feeding Infants in Chicago, 1903–1924." *Journal of the History of Medicine and Allied Sciences* 53: 219–253.

Wolf, Jacqueline H. 1999a. "'Let Us Have More Mother-Fed Babies': Early Twentieth-Century Breastfeeding Campaigns in Chicago and Minneapolis." *Journal of Human Lactation* 15: 1–5.

Wolf, Jaqueline H. 1999b. "'Mercenary Hirelings' or 'A Great Blessing'?: Doctors' and Mothers' Conflicted Perceptions of Wet Nurses and the Ramifications for Infant Feeding in Chicago, 1871–1961." *Journal of Social History* 33: 97–120.

Wolf, Jacqueline H. 2001. *Don't Kill Your Baby: Public Health and the Decline of Breastfeeding in the 19th and 20th Centuries*. Columbus: Ohio State University Press.

Bulimia

Bulimia is an eating disorder characterized by periodic bouts of binge eating followed by episodes of purging. When it was first identified as a disorder in 1979, bulimia was diagnosed as a subtype of the eating disorder anorexia nervosa. It has since been given its own designation as a separate eating disorder (American Psychiatric Association 1994, 545), in recognition of the fact that, unlike anorexia, binge eating occurs in both obese individuals and those of normal weight. Despite the fact that bulimia has only been recognized as a disorder in the last few decades, bingeing and purging behavior has been around at least since the time of Christ, when the ancient Romans were doing it in specially built vomitoriums.

Bulimia is two to three times more common than anorexia, and as is the case with most eating disorders, most people who suffer from bulimia are females. Adolescent and young adult women suffer from the disorder with ten times the frequency of males. Some estimates predict that up to 10 percent of females will be bulimic at some point in their lives, and even more will demonstrate some type of binge-purge behavior (Rice 1999).

Bingeing episodes are events in which very high amounts of high-calorie food are consumed very rapidly, within a short time frame. Between 1,000 and 10,000 calories may be consumed in a single binge. Since bulimics often want to look thin and have a slender idealized body image, they must then purge their system of the unwanted calories. One research study found that almost two hours per day on average were spent in binge eating. These episodes may be very short or long and may occur many times per day. Purging typically takes the form of induced vomiting but may also include the use of laxatives, diuretics, enemas, or amphetamines. Compulsive exercising or fasting may also be used to counteract the huge intake of calories (Rice 1999, 119). Despite their desire for thinness, and their purging behavior, bulimics seldom lose weight. For this reason bulimics are usually able to hide their disorder more successfully and longer than people with anorexia, in whom the extreme weight loss eventually becomes obvious.

Causes of bulimia are still under investigation, but there are several strong possibilities. Cultural ideals of thinness create unrealistic expectations and low self-esteem. A negative body image, especially in young women who may feel societal pressure to be thin, can result. Food and its consumption may also act as substitutes for love, affection, and attention for the bulimic, beginning a cycle of intake to satisfy those needs and expulsion to maintain some control over weight. There is also a possible biochemical explanation in that bulimics have been found to have low levels of the brain neurotransmitter serotonin. Intake of massive amounts of food may serve as an attempt to increase these levels of serotonin.

Although bulimia is hard to treat, treatments are usually more effective than treatments for anorexia, and even without treatment bulimic symptoms often disappear by the age of forty. Few bulimics die from the disorder, but the cost of bulimia can nonetheless be high. Extensive tooth decay (from throwing up stomach acid), stomach problems, skin lesions, and even loss of hair can result from various purging methods. Psychologically, low self-esteem, depression, shame, and guilt are common correlates of bulimia.

—Elaine S. Barry

See also Anorexia Nervosa; Eating Disorders

References and Further Reading
American Psychiatric Association. 1994. *The Diagnostic and Statistical Manual of Mental Disorders*. 4th ed. Washington, DC: American Psychiatric Association.
Rice, F. Philip. 1999. *The Adolescent: Development, Relationships, and Culture*. Boston: Allyn and Bacon.

Burgess, Ernest W.

Ernest Watson Burgess (1886–1966) established new fields of study in community and family sociology during his fifty-year tenure at the University of Chicago. One of the first graduate students trained in the Chicago school of sociology, Burgess expanded the field from a concentration on institutions to consideration of individuals and interpersonal relationships. Although he began his career in the study of race relations, urban studies, and juvenile crime, his foremost concern became family dynamics. Using the city of Chicago as a laboratory, he and his graduate students conducted unprecedented empirical research into individual and collective social problems. One of his contributions was the construction of variables that could predict the behavior of particular persons in given situations, a model that he successfully applied to paroled prisoners and engaged couples. Burgess initiated research projects in family relationships, marriage, juvenile delinquency, and aging—studies that were the foundations of such subdisciplines as criminology and gerontology. His influence extended far beyond the University of Chicago through his textbooks, public service, and distinguished graduate students.

Born in Tilbury, Ontario, on 16 May 1886, Burgess emigrated with his parents to Michigan in 1889. After graduating from Oklahoma's Kingfisher College in 1908, he entered graduate school at the University of Chicago. Burgess taught in Kansas and Ohio before returning to Chicago in 1916. In 1921, Burgess and his mentor, Robert E. Park, collaborated on the classic textbook, *Introduction to the Science of Sociology* (Park and Burgess 1921). Burgess published other groundbreaking works on juvenile delinquency, urban sociology, marital and family relations, and the role of the aged. During his distinguished public service career he served on national councils and conferences investigating child health, retirement, public education, and family problems stemming from the Depression and World War II. His research in the USSR on the effect of communism on the traditional family structure inspired a charge of disloyalty by a congressional committee, but further investigation cleared him. Never married, Burgess remained active in research and writing until his death in 1966.

—*Vickie Hankins Peters*

References and Further Reading

Bogue, Donald J., ed. 1974. *The Basic Writings of Ernest W. Burgess.* Chicago: Community and Family Center, University of Chicago.

Burgess, Ernest W. 1916. *The Function of Socialization in Social Evolution.* Chicago: University of Chicago Press.

Burgess, Ernest W., ed. 1960. *Aging in Western Societies.* Chicago: University of Chicago Press.

Burgess, Ernest W., ed. 1961. *Retirement Villages.* Ann Arbor: University of Michigan, Department of Gerontology.

Burgess, E. W., and J. C. Baumgartner. 1942. *The American Family: The Problems of Family Relations Facing American Youth.* Washington, DC: National Council for the Social Studies.

Burgess, Ernest W., and Herbert Blumer, eds. 1935. *Human Problems of Social Planning.* Chicago: H. G. Adair Printing.

Burgess, E. W., and Donald J. Bogue, eds. 1964. *Contributions to Urban Sociology.* Chicago: University of Chicago Press.

Burgess, Ernest W., and Leonard S. Cottrell Jr. 1939. *Predicting Success or Failure in Marriage.* New York: Prentice Hall.

Burgess, E. W., and Morris Fishbein, eds. 1947. *Successful Marriage: An Authoritative Guide to Problems Related to Marriage from the Beginning of Sexual Attraction to Matrimony and the Successful Rearing of a Family.* Garden City, NY: Doubleday.

Burgess, E. W., and Harvey J. Locke. 1945. *The Family: From Institution to Companionship.* New York: American Book.

Burgess, E. W., and Paul Wallin. 1953. *Engagement and Marriage.* Philadelphia: J. B. Lippincott.

Burgess, E. W., et al. 1951. *The American Veteran Back Home.* New York: Longmans, Green.

Cottrell, Leonard S., Jr., Albert Hunter, and James F. Short, eds. 1973. *Ernest W. Burgess on Community, Family, and Delinquency.* Chicago: University of Chicago Press.

Park, Robert E., and Ernest W. Burgess. 1921. *Introduction to the Science of Sociology.* Chicago: University of Chicago Press.

Park, Robert E., Ernest W. Burgess, and Roderick D. McKenzie. 1926. *The City.* Chicago: University of Chicago Press.

C

Cambridge Group for History of Population and Social Structure

Established in 1964, the Cambridge Group for History of Population and Social Structure has revolutionized the methodology and content of family history. Through the painstaking compilation of enormous databases culled largely from parish registers, the Cambridge Group established a method for reconstructing the history of families from the preindustrial world to today that has been followed by historians operating in continental Europe, the Americas, and Asia. On the basis of this evidence, prior claims concerning the postindustrial origins of the nuclear family and the gradual increase in age of marriage have been displaced. Most scholars now believe the nuclear family to have existed in England especially and western Europe more generally well before the industrial age, and we better appreciate the historic connections among economic prosperity, age of marriage, and birthrate.

Prior to the 1950s, work in the history of the family had been largely conjectural, based on scant evidence culled from literary sources. But in the 1950s and 1960s a combination of factors conspired to change this. On the one hand, new computer technologies, though primitive by today's standards, for the first time made it possible to create and manipulate large databases of names, dates, places, and other variables. On the other hand, at the same time the academic world was beginning to revolt against an exclusive focus on elites and to seek out new paths to the creation of a history of the common people. In 1964 British historians Peter Laslett and E. A. Wrigley, encouraged by the progress made by French historians seeking to reconstruct population demographics from parish records, created the Cambridge Group for History of Population and Social Structure. The founders realized that it would require the coordinated effort of several hundred scholars and volunteers to collate the data residing in the basements and attics of thousands of English parishes and so established the organization to promote large-scale collaboration. Historians working with the Cambridge Group databases have been able to reconstitute the life cycles of generations of English people by connecting—via computer—birth, marriage, and death records. The conclusions drawn from these data have revolutionized the way we understand the preindustrial family.

It was long held that the Industrial Revolution created the nuclear family by shattering the cottage industry and the extended kinship networks it had fostered. Furthermore, it was believed that the Industrial Revolution led women to marry later and have fewer children. But the records of England's parishes reveal quite another story. It turns out that the nuclear family was in fact the norm in England from the reign of Queen Elizabeth on and that women often married late and had few children, especially during periods of economic hard times. When food was scarce, so were marriage and illegitimate births, but when times improved, the marriage age dropped and fertility rates, both legitimate and illegitimate, rose. The western European tendency to connect marriage rate not to female biology but to economic prosperity was an important factor that led to the creation of surplus wealth, a necessary precursor to the manufacture on a large scale of durable goods. The nuclear family turns out to have helped cause the Industrial Revolution.

The Cambridge Group's findings have not gone unchallenged. It has been charged that their methods fail to appreciate the extent to which nonrelatives such as servants and apprentices lived in premodern households, that households themselves had a life cycle that would vary from nuclear to extended depending on the stage, and above all, that whatever English data may show, we must not be too quick to overgeneralize about other parts of the world.

—*Milton Gaither*

References and Further Reading
Laslett, Peter, and Richard Wall, eds. 1972. *Household and Family in Past Time.* Cambridge: Cambridge University Press.
Levine, David. 1998. "Sampling History: The English Population." *Journal of Interdisciplinary History* 28(4): 605–632.
Wrigley, E. A. 1998. "Small-Scale but Not Parochial: The Work of the Cambridge Group for the History of Population and Social Structure." *Family and Community History* 1 (November): 27–36.

Celibacy

Although the term *celibacy* in its original usage meant the condition of being unmarried, over time its definition has become more inclusive; to be celibate or to be chaste means the same by modern standards. Because celibacy can define a characteristic of married and unmarried lifestyles in the United States today, its role in the changing face of the American family must be acknowledged.

Whether the term is used to designate one's unmarried status, virginal condition, or abstinence from sexual intercourse, its application with some form of religious or spiritual focus is more commonly recognized. A vow of celibacy, required by the Roman Catholic Church of its clerical civil servants since the twelfth century, allows those who accept this "gift from God" to better serve the church and its practitioners. The initial logic held that the sole purpose for sexual intercourse was procreation, and procreation occurred, or at least should occur, only within the married state. Those who did not marry, the celibate, therefore refrained from any sexual relationships. The church imposed celibacy as a mandatory requirement. Increasingly, however, celibacy by choice has become the rally point for change.

Additionally, the church instructed its lay followers to abstain from marital sexual activity during a woman's fertile time if, as a couple, they chose not to have children. Institutionally imposed celibacy fails to fit with modern Catholics' lifestyles, particularly in the United States. The Roman Catholic Church faces several dilemmas today because of its stance on mandatory celibacy: fewer priests and nuns to administer to a growing body of practitioners, increased criticism for media highlights of child molestation, and what appears to some to be a critical problem—the inability to attract heterosexuals to increasingly homosexual religious communities. Ironically, the hierarchy in the United States, with Rome's blessing, has allowed a small percentage of married priests to not only stay married but to work in parishes. According to Thomas Fox, exceptions for married ministers or priests from other faiths who have converted to Catholicism have been allowed because of the critical shortage within the U.S. priesthood (Fox 1995).

Other religions, or more appropriately religious movements, in U.S. history have imposed mandatory celibacy on their members. Some utopian or socialist communities in the nineteenth century, such as the Shakers and the Rappites, imposed celibacy. Other communes, such as the Amana colonies and the Oneida experiment, allowed marriage but with restrictions; those denied marriage or, in the case of the Oneida Community, those not chosen to procreate, would be expected to abstain from sexual relationships. Limited celibacy for members of these communities and for others throughout U.S. history did occur; lifelong adherence was not expected.

Self-restraint and *voluntary motherhood* are among some of the terms employed to designate limited periods of celibacy. Eighteenth- and nineteenth-century medical practitioners recommended that a man should abstain from sexual relations with his wife throughout the time she nursed their newborn; these practitioners believed that intercourse had a negative effect on the milk. Such physical stimulation could make the milk go bad. During the pre-reservation period, Cheyenne fathers could voluntarily practice celibacy for a limited time under a "dedication vow." Like those who vow to remain celibate to focus on a higher calling, a Cheyenne father abstained from sex to focus and to dedicate his life, for a chosen period of years, to his child's upbringing. Voluntary motherhood, practiced by several suffragists, mandated that women abstain from sexual relations with their husbands as a means of contraception.

Voluntary celibacy is a term that has received increasing use and attention over the past couple of decades in the United States. Voluntary celibates are men or women who have decided to give up sexual relationships, though not their sexuality, for a designated period of time or indefinitely. They choose to be without a sexual partner for positive reasons: higher life goals, self-awareness, revitalization, creativity, emotional health, or as an alternative way to love, to name a few. Additionally, for partners to live together in an asexual arrangement has become commonplace in today's world despite the ease of divorce. "Companionship and convenience" rather than "passionate, romantic love" appear to be the basis of a growing number of what psychologist Joanna Gutmann described as "asexual couplings" in her article, "The Girls of Gen X," in the January 1998 *American Enterprise.* At the same time, an increasing number of women are choosing not to marry or remarry. Calling themselves "leather spinsters," these "happily unmarried" women have a large following, as exemplified by their publishing company, newsletter with 300,000 subscribers, and web site.

Involuntary celibacy also has attracted the attention of the media and scholars recently. Using the term *incel* for lack of a better word to refer to themselves, involuntary celibates find themselves both inside and outside of marriage. Involuntary celibacy within marriage, or a sexually inactive marriage, occurs when one partner but not both makes the decision to end sexual relations and, at the same time, decides not to end the marriage. This could occur for a number of reasons: health issues, emotional turmoil, or lack of interest, for example. Unfortunately, according to Prof. Denise A. Donnelly, attempts to understand the magnitude of involuntary celibacy within marriage remain difficult because people tend to underreport such nonactivity and the stigma attached to a sexually inactive marriage remains strong (Donnelly 1993). Professor Donnelly and her colleague, Elisabeth O. Burgess, both at Georgia State University, have been funded to conduct further studies on involuntary celibacy during the 2001–2002 academic year.

Involuntary celibacy outside marriage also occurs for various reasons. Divorce or death of one's partner may force an individual into involuntary celibacy. In our youth-oriented culture, women, more so than men, often find themselves in this position in the later years of their lives. Anyone who has not dated in a long time, or has never dated, could classify himself or herself as an involuntary celibate if attempts to form sexual relationships have failed. Health or emotional issues could lead someone into a condition of involuntary celibacy if such conditions are beyond the individual's control. Involuntary celibacy for the layperson in many ways parallels mandatory celibacy for the clergy; both affect the future of American families.

—*Kay J. Blalock*

See also Birth Control, Theories of; Courtship, History of; The Oneida Community; Shaker Family; Virginity

References and Further Reading
Abbott, Elizabeth. 2001. *A History of Celibacy*. New York: Da Capo Press.
Berry, Jason. 1992. *Lead Us Not into Temptation: Catholic Priests and the Sexual Abuse of Children*. New York: Doubleday.
Brown, Gabrielle. 1980. *The New Celibacy*. New York: McGraw Hill.
Davis, Elizabeth. 1995. *Women, Sex, and Desire: Understanding Your Sexuality at Every Stage of Life*. Alameda, CA: Hunter House.
Donnelly, Denise A. 1993. "Sexually Inactive Marriages." *Journal of Sex Research* 30(2): 171–179.
English, Regena. 1998. *Leather Spinsters and Their Degrees of Asexuality*. Houston: St. Mary's Publishing.
Fox, Thomas C. 1995. *Sexuality and Catholicism*. New York: George Braziller.
Golden, Janet. 1997. "The New Motherhood and the New View of Wet Nurses, 1780–1865." In *Mothers and Motherhood: Readings in American History*, edited by Rima D. Apple and Janet Golden, 72–89. Columbus: Ohio State University Press.
Williams, Donna Marie, Becky Cabaza, and Dawn Daniels, eds. 1999. *Sensual Celibacy*. New York: Simon and Schuster.
Wolter, Dwight Lee. 1992. *Sex and Celibacy: Establishing Balance in Intimate Relationships through Temporary Sexual Abstinence*. Minneapolis: Fairview Press.

Child Abuse

Abuse against children and youth is nothing new in human history. Indeed, infanticide, child beating, economic exploitation, neglect, abandonment, prostitution, child barter, "baby farming," and enslavement are all time-honored traditions in human history in the lives of families and for boys and girls alike. What is less time honored is a vision of children as vulnerable and in need of protection, of families as protective enclaves and tutorial institutions, of government agencies as guarantors of children's well-being, of workplaces as potentially exploitive sites, of relatives and neighborhoods as sources of danger, of schools as appropriate sites of socialization for the young, of systematic punishment as the just due of perpetrators of child abuse, or of boys and men as distinct classes of perpetrators and victims. Historically viewed, child abuse, as we know it today, has been an important feature of family life for centuries, most especially during the period prior to the seventeenth century, when families functioned less as educative institutions and agencies of moral nurture than institutions through which name and property were transmitted (Aries 1962; deMause 1974). Discovered only over time, child abuse gradually has become a specific object of public concern, social condemnation, therapeutic intervention, and political organization. This entry focuses specifically on family-related features of child abuse as they have evolved over time in the United States.

The concept of child abuse, like the concept of childhood vulnerability and protective families, is a relatively recent historical discovery. The appearance of the concept of child maltreatment in the middle decades of the seventeenth century reflected a growing awareness of children as an endangered species in need of restraint and of mothers as gentle governors. A vision of child maltreatment has inspired serial generations of social reformers to generate policies designed to exorcise violence, sexual assault, and physical brutality from the arsenal of permissible actions taken by parents and other family members against children, by teenage boys against boys, and by boys against girls. Ironically, the discovery of abuse proceeded simultaneously with the discovery of families as educative institutions and parents as inadequate, neglectful, malicious, and/or unfit for the tasks of child rearing. The discovery of abuse has led reformers to establish principles of custody and oversight designed to protect children from maltreatment through policy initiatives that disengage children from families labeled as unfit. What follows is a minihistory of the discovery of child abuse in the United States, the evolution of approaches to prevention and punishment, and the conditions that sustain child abuse as a cultural practice—most especially as such abuse is revealed with regard to the cultural practices of families.

The attempt to exorcise violence from the lives of young people is reflected in a series of social discoveries that, over the course of time, have unpeeled an array of once-invisible forms of assault against children. There was the discovery among seventeenth-century theologians of the need for systematic education, calibrated age-appropriate discipline for young men, and restraints on sexual expression and physical violence and on the responsibilities of mothers to cultivate restraint (Beales 1979; Greven 1990; Hiner 1979). The following poem, written by Anne Bradstreet, an eighteenth-century New England poet and mother, reveals the emergence of a new view of mothers as moral persuaders:

She was well versed in Domastick cares
Did prudently Order her house Affaires
The Education of her Children young,
She knew full well, did unto her belong:
And o how Loveingly with awefull heed,
She did her Children, and her Maidens
  Breed.

*That with a look, a nod, in silence
  Beckt,
She could command Obedience, due
  Respect.*
                    (Beales 1979, 11)

Later there was the discovery of child-hood innocence among Romantic poets and transcendental philosophers who, in the early decades of the nineteenth century, projected childhood as a divine rather than a corrupt condition. They called, among other things, for a physical and moral liberation of children's minds and bodies and a modicum of self-discipline and self-government from its children. Samuel Coleridge articulated this new sentiment:

> In the Education of children, love is first to be instilled, and out of love obedience is to be educed. The impulse and power should be given to the intellect and the end of a moral being exhibited.
> My experience tells me that little is taught or communicated by contest or dispute, but everything by sympathy and love. Collision elicits truth only from the hardest heads. (Plotz 1979, 71)

There was the discovery by moral reformers of the early nineteenth century of street children and beggars as a class of people in need of protection and benevolent "moral" tutors and of child neglect as a deplorable and even dangerous social condition, most especially when family indifference endangered boys and girls, left them on their own, or rendered them vulnerable to bullying and sexual exploitation. Commenting on parental involvement in the exploitation of children and

youth, a nineteenth-century Boston newspaper observed:

> [T]he factory girl who goes young to the mill, and children who grow up in the towns where factories are located, must always be sufferers. The cupidity of parents induces them to place their offspring in one establishment as soon as possible [Emphasis in original]. . . . Here . . . is a source from which an ignorant, unhealthy, and permanently unhappy manufacturing population is raised, to swell the numbers of our degraded, enslaved, citizens of the country. (Bremner 1970–1974, 1:622).

There was the discovery of child labor as a form of exploitation and a symptom of family failure. There was the invention of moral persuasion as a more humanitarian approach than physical coercion or corporal punishment in the regulation of otherwise ungovernable children (deMause 1974; Trennert 1989).

In the late nineteenth century and the early decades of the twentieth century, parental inadequacy was revealed with the discovery of adolescence as a vulnerable and bombastic period of youth development, juvenile delinquency as a specialized category of curable criminality, boys as potential perpetrators as well as victims in need simultaneously of protection and regulation, and battered children as a special class of children in need of shelter (Schlossman 1977; Kett 1977; Jenkins 1998; Finkelstein 2000). It was during that same time period that cruelty to children emerged as a specialized concern of advocacy groups, a rationale for the investigation of families, a focus for public consciousness raising (Finkelstein 1985; Gordon 1988; Hiner 1979). The fol-

A barefoot shoeshine boy, Columbus, Georgia 1940. (Library of Congress)

lowing kind of published incident called attention to the realities of parent-perpetrated child abuse:

> An eleven-year-old boy . . . was beaten to death by his step-father in February, 1888. The boy's mother died in June, 1887. . . . A witness . . . [testified that he] heard sounds of a whipping and plaintive cries of "papa" at eleven o'clock at night, and then a heavy fall as of a body hurled on the floor. At seven in the morning the beating was renewed . . . [after which the father] bade the boy to "get his Bible and read the Commandments." In the afternoon he was dead. . . . The post-mortem examination found the body covered with new scars from the knees to the neck. . . . Thirty six of these had been made with one instrument, the iron buckle of a strap. . . . [The father] was . . . sentenced to imprisonment for life. (Hiner 1979, 238)

Over the course of the twentieth century, attempts to expand concepts of abuse and root out violence against children took new forms as scholars, theologians, journalists, and educators discovered and revealed the existence of long traditions of labor exploitation, child beating, incest, and sexual abuse in families across the social spectrum and across centuries (Finkelstein 2000; Gordon 1988;

Jenkins 1998). Among these reformers were some who devoted themselves to the study of boys; they redefined concepts of manhood in the late nineteenth and early twentieth centuries and elevated combativeness, aggression, and physical prowess as important norms and standards of masculinity. This group of reformers, while deploring violence against women, nonetheless took patterns of assault by men on boys and boys on boys as natural consequences of their manliness (Connell 1995; Kimmel 1995; Rotundo, 1993). Recently, with the public acknowledgment of date rape, child pornography, prostitution, and pedophilia and with the discovery of homophobia, new as well as once-invisible and silenced realities have become visible (Books 1998; Polakow 2001). The emergence of statistics documenting the existence of forced sex and incest practiced, in preponderant numbers, by fathers against daughters has become a matter of public concern (Polakow 2001). Through the efforts of contemporary child advocates, the omnipresence of institutional punishments such as physical beatings, sexual violence, the harsh treatment of incarcerated juveniles, and the emergence of youth-perpetrated violence in schools has claimed the attention of the public, as have statistics documenting the existence of forced sex and incest practiced in preponderant numbers by men against girls within households.

The discovery of different forms of child abuse is not the only effect of an evolving perspective that children and youth are vulnerable and in need of protection. The identification and punishment of perpetrators constitute another. In an ironic turn of fate, the discovery of parents, clergy, and lay church workers as perpetrators has proceeded simultane-ously with a concern for the regulation and protection of young people (Greven 1990; Trennert 1989; Polakow 2001). The mistreatment of apprentices in the seventeenth and eighteenth centuries not only led to the discovery of boys as an ungovernable class of potentially disruptive citizens but also revealed the existence of abusive masters who, acting in loco parentis, had failed to carry out the moral and educational obligations of their contracts. The perceived neglect of certain classes of urban children in the nineteenth century led to their removal from families to orphanages and "baby farms," where yet a different class of perpetrators was created—the keepers of the asylum (Crenson 1998). Typically the keepers were young men and women who had no particular preparation, were relatively unsupervised, and received almost unlimited authority to do as they would in the name of moral guidance. The participation of wage-earning girls in households, cotton factories, and piecework mills and of boys in coal mines, cigar shops, and whiskey-bottling works over the course of the nineteenth and early twentieth centuries inspired the discovery of labor exploitation as a form of child abuse, factory owners as potential perpetrators, inhumane conditions as seedbeds of criminal behavior, and factories as sites of sexual harassment. The passage of compulsory education laws requiring children to spend long periods of time in school had a potential to transform teachers into potential perpetrators and, with the passage of stringent reporting laws, into victim identifiers as well. With the rise of psychological, medical, and social expertise, dysfunctional families came clearly into view (Garbarino 1997; Gordon 1988; Jenkins 1998). More recently, the emergence of an unrestrained press has also revealed the existence of abuse practiced by youths on youths in the form of gun assaults, gay bashing, date rape, and so on (Polakow 2001). The emergence of laws prohibiting sexual harassment and assigning punishments to perpetrators constitutes a new discovery that has both reflected and revealed the widespread practice of abuse in churches, households, and neighborhoods.

The discovery of different forms of child abuse and the identification and punishment of fathers and mothers, men and boys, as both perpetrators and victims are not the only effects of an evolving perspective that children and youth are vulnerable and in need of protection. Efforts to transform the status of children and root out abuse are also visible in the emergence of child advocacy as an approach to social action and a strategy for political and organizational development as well. From the latter decades of the nineteenth century to the latter half of the twentieth century, many changes took place that reflect continuing efforts to define abuse, identify violence, and protect children from the more draconian expressions of violence in previously unregulated and/or invisible social spaces. Among these changes were the emergence of the Children's Aid Society and religiously based protectories in the latter decades of the nineteenth century; the emergence of the National Federation of Day Nurseries and the Children's Bureau during the Progressive Era; the emergence of child-focused physicians and psychologists in the early twentieth century; the founding of the Boy Scouts of America, the Young Men's Christian Association, the Girl Scouts of America, and an array of other regulatory settings for boys and girls; and the creation of the UN Declaration of Human Rights at midcentury and of institutions such as the United Nations Children's Fund and the Children's Defense Fund in the latter half of the twentieth century. Among the more important agendas that have emerged recently are those centering on the identification and financial accountability of fathers as well as mothers and on the assignment of responsibility and a measure of blame to boys and young men.

The attempt to exorcise violence from the lives of children has found expression in a gradual, if limited, involvement of local government agencies in the business of child protection over the course of two centuries. There is a corpus of law creating alternative institutions for the rearing of children considered to be victims of abandonment, neglect, malnutrition, battering, and sexual abuse. Orphanages came and went in the nineteenth century to be replaced by substitute families outside of cities and ultimately by a limited welfare system (Crenson 1998). There were specialized public institutions to serve and regulate the lives of previously unsupervised and/or abused young people: juvenile reformatories in the early twentieth century, foster-care systems, and child abuse prevention centers, among others, at century's end (Finkelstein 1985; Hawes and Hiner 1985; Polakow 2001).

An evolving corpus of law has established specialized public agencies for the protection of the young—children's aid societies in the nineteenth century, societies for the prevention of cruelty to children in the latter decades of the nineteenth and early decades of the twentieth centuries, child protective services, family court, a National Center for Missing and Exploited Children, and child abuse hotlines in the latter decades of the twentieth century (Jenkins 1998). More

An abused toddler sucking her thumb on a staircase. (Hannah Gal/Corbis)

recently, centers for the identification of recalcitrant fathers and mothers have emerged.

The discovery of widespread domestic violence, incest, and assault has given new urgency to the need for publicly supported shelters, foster families, faith-based interventions, and new therapeutic approaches. Excesses of violence have also constituted the rediscovery of young men as perpetrators within households and on the streets. There are legal traditions regulating the conditions of child labor, and laws in more than thirty states limit, if they do not prohibit, the use of corporal punishment in families and public schools. There are laws limiting the power of patriarchal authority within

families, defining children's rights, and assessing penalties for spousal and child abuse. There are chinks in the armor of a traditional legal assumption that concepts of family reconciliation are necessarily in the best interests of children. What is more, new legal standards are expanding the effective definition of child abuse to go beyond battery and sexual assault to include protection from violent, traumatizing environments. These new legal standards might threaten custody for those parents who fail to protect their children from witnessing violence and abuse in the household.

It is clear that traditions of violence persisted in the United States of the 1990s, notwithstanding many factors arguing against such traditions: a historically evolving concept of childhood and child abuse; the gradual discovery of child innocence, child neglect, child rights, baby battery, sexual assault, excessive corporal punishment, child abuse, and incest as social conditions in need of remediation; a 200-year history of child advocacy; the expansion of government in the business of child protection and the involvement of physicians and teachers in its identification; the emergence of institutional mechanisms for the reporting of abuse; and the presence of thousands of people who, over the course of two centuries, have condemned violence in all of its forms. Sixteen million children and teens lived in poverty in the 1990s. Some 350,000 young are confirmed victims of violent and sexual abuse inflicted by caretakers (mostly parents) every year. Given such conditions, teenage violence is not surprising; it is just like the adult violence from which it stems (Books 1998, 192).

Abuse against children is still visible in the informal spaces of children's lives in neighborhoods, streets, playgrounds, and schools; in the grounded routines of legally constituted educational institutions; in the deep structures of gender, class, and race relations in the United States; in the protected domestic enclaves of hundreds of thousands of families and religious institutions; as well as in publicly and privately constituted institutions for adjudicated young people. It is hidden behind the structured silences that result from the array of incest taboos that serve to shield as well as to condemn assaults against young children, male and female. Teenage boys have emerged as a newly discovered class who are being redefined as criminals rather than adolescents or delinquents, subjected to mandatory "zero tolerance," incarcerated at increasing rates, bound over as adults at age thirteen, subjected to capital punishment, and otherwise penalized as adults might be for violence perpetrated against other children as well as adults.

The persistence of child abuse in the United States is a subject that has claimed the attention of an array of scholars, educators, policymakers, and child workers who, as they seek to discover its various manifestations, also seek to understand the social, economic, political, and cultural bedrock that sustains or protects the practices of abuse against children. There is work that explains the persistence of child abuse as a reflection of historic definitions of manliness that elevate the status of combative behavior, physical aggression, toughness, and domination as idealized states (Connell 1995; Kimmel 1995; Rotundo 1993). There is work that explains abuse against children—both inside and outside families and schools—as a natural condition in a society that protects gun ownership; rationalizes the use of force to settle dis-

putes; makes heroes of gun-toting, physically dominating bullies and overbearing fathers; and otherwise tolerates or even celebrates public expressions of violence (Garbarino 1997; Polakow 2001). There is work that explains the persistence of child abuse as a reflection of historic commitments to political practices that protect family privacy and church autonomy and limit the capacity of government to regulate child rearing and/or to provide blankets of protection for children who are outside the reach of public authorities. These could include children under five years of age; children who attend relatively unregulated child-care centers in households, neighborhoods, and churches; children who are homeless; children with working parents; young people who inhabit the streets and malls during out-of-school hours; boys who participate in the aggressive world of contact sports and locker room brawls; gay boys who are victimized by parents and peers; and girls who are preyed upon by men and boys within their households as objects of domestic violence, incest, and date rape (Finkelstein 2000; Polakow 2001). There is work that explains the persistence of violence against children as a reflection of economic commitments that privilege wage labor, limit support for the care of dependents, impose contradictory demands and pressures on already overburdened families, limit the quality and quantity of support they can expect, structure frustration, and otherwise do little to prevent outbreaks of violence (Gordon 1988). There is work that explains the persistence of child abuse as a reflection of powerful religious beliefs that support the use of corporal punishment as a legitimate instrument of moral education (Greven 1990). Finally, there is developing work that explains the persistence of child abuse as an outcome of social and legal policies that identify and punish perpetrators and extirpate battered children from abusive family situations but fail to attend systematically to the improvement of children's environments. The good news is that child abuse has been discovered and condemned. The bad news is that the cultural, political, economic, or social wherewithal to prevent it or to root it out is not as yet fully conceived.

—*Barbara Finkelstein*

See also Apprenticeship; Child Advocacy; Child Care; Children's Bureau, U.S.; Delinquency; Divorce, History of; Domestic Violence; Orphanages

References and Further Reading

Aries, Philippe. 1962. *Centuries of Childhood: A Social History of Family Life.* Trans. R. Baldick. New York: Knopf.

Beales, Ross W. 1979. "Anne Bradstreet and Her Children." In *Regulated Children/Liberated Children: Education in Psychohistorical Perspective,* edited by Barbara Finkelstein, 11. New York: The Psychohistory Press.

Books, Sue, ed. 1998. *Invisible Children in the Society and Its Schools.* Mahwah, NJ: Erlbaum.

Bremner, Robert H. 1970–1974. *Children and Youth in America: A Documentary History.* Vol. 1: *1600–1865;* Vol. 2: *1866–1932;* Vol. 3: *1933–1973.* Cambridge: Harvard University Press.

Connell, R. W. 1995. *Masculinities.* Berkeley: University of California Press.

Crenson, Matthew A. 1998. *Building the Invisible Orphanage: A Prehistory of the American Welfare System.* Cambridge: Harvard University Press.

deMause, Lloyd, ed. 1974. "The Evolution of Childhood." *History of Childhood Quarterly* 1: 503–575.

Fass, Paula. S., and Mary Ann Mason, eds. 2000. *Childhood in America.* New York: New York University Press.

Finkelstein, Barbara. 1985. "Uncle Sam and the Children: A History of Government Involvement in Child Rearing." In *Growing Up in America: Children in Historical Perspective,* edited by J. M. Hawes and N. R. Hiner, 155–265. Westport, CT: Greenwood Press.

Finkelstein, Barbara. 2000. "A Crucible of Contradictions: Historical Roots of Violence against Children in the United States." *History of Education Quarterly* 40(1): 1–22.

Garbarino, James J. 1997. "The Role of Economic Deprivation in the Social Context of Child Maltreatment." In *The Battered Child,* edited by M. E. Helfer, R. S. Kemp, and R. Krugman, 5th ed., 49–61. Chicago: University of Chicago Press.

Gordon, Linda. 1988. *Heroes of Their Own Lives: The Politics and History of Family Violence, Boston, 1880–1960.* New York: Viking Books.

Greven, Phillip. 1990. *Spare the Child: The Religious Roots of Punishment and the Psychological Impact of Physical Abuse.* New York: Vintage.

Hawes, Joseph M., and N. Ray Hiner, eds. 1985. *American Childhood: A Research Guide and Historical Handbook.* Westport, CT: Greenwood Press.

Hiner, N. Ray. 1979. "Children's Rights, Corporal Punishment, and Child Abuse: Changing American Attitudes, 1870–1920." *Bulletin of the Menninger Clinic* 43(3): 233–248.

Jenkins, Philip. 1998. *Moral Panic: Changing Concepts of the Child Molester in Modern America.* New Haven: Yale University Press.

Kett, Joseph J. 1977. *Rites of Passage: Adolescence in America, 1790–1970.* New York: Basic Books.

Kimmel, Michael. 1995. *Manhood in America: A Cultural History.* New York: The Free Press.

Males, M. A. 1996. *The Scapegoat Generation: America's War on Adolescents.* Monroe, ME: Common Courage Press.

Nightingale, C. H. 1993. *On the Edge: A History of Poor Black Children and Their American Dreams.* New York: Basic Books.

Plotz, Judith. 1979. "The Perpetual Messiah: Romanticism, Childhood, and the Paradoxes of Human Development, New York." In *Regulated Children/ Liberated Children: Education in*

Psychohistorical Perspective, edited by Barbara Finkelstein, 63–96. New York: The Psychohistory Press.

Polakow, Valerie, ed. 2001. *The Public Assault on America's Children: Poverty, Violence, and Juvenile Injustice.* New York: Teachers College Press.

Rotundo, E. Anthony. 1993. *American Manhood: Transformations in Masculinity from the Revolution to the Modern Era.* New York: Basic Books.

Schlossman, Steven L. 1977. *Love and the American Delinquent: The Theory and Practice of "Progressive" Juvenile Justice, 1825–1920.* Chicago: University of Chicago Press.

Trennert, Robert A. 1989. "Corporal Punishment and the Politics of Indian Reform." *History of Education Quarterly* 29(4): 595–619.

Child Advocacy

Child advocacy is social action that seeks to enhance the status of children and balance the complementary and competing interests of the family, the child, and the state. By law and custom, as well as by virtue of their developmental immaturity, children are dependent on adults, who may be unwilling or unable to act in their best interest. Child advocates recognize this and work to guarantee children rights and protection through the mobilization of the political and legislative processes. Child advocacy comprises three categories of rights. Protective rights safeguard children against various forms of harm, including physical and sexual abuse, abandonment and neglect, and exploitation as workers. Provision rights ensure that children are granted some basic level of economic and social security. Finally, participation rights recognize that children possess civil and political liberties as individual citizens in a democracy (Edmonds and Fernekes 1996, 2). Agitation for children's rights began in the seventeenth century and has

continued to the present. Numerous conflicts have shaped this history: among the relative importance of the three categories of rights themselves, between state and parental power, between individual rights and family claims to privacy and integrity, between child welfare standards and the constraints of poverty, and among competing class, ethnic, and racial conceptions of respectable child rearing. Children have both gained and lost as a result of adult efforts to advocate on their behalf. Although commitments to children's rights have expanded over time, it remains for contemporary child advocates to discern whether these commitments truly serve children's best interests and if so, to make sure that they come to be realized in children's lives in tangible and meaningful ways.

The initial expression of the idea that children have a right to be protected and provided for was inaugurated through the laws and customs of the seventeenth and eighteenth centuries. Throughout the British colonies, the hierarchical household was the basic unit of social organization, responsible for both the socialization of its members and economic production. Fathers presided at the head of the household, and all members were expected to relate to one another according to the principles of mutual obligation. Subordinate members were to keep in their place and defer to those above them in the family hierarchy, and those with superior status had a duty to support and care for their dependents. Even as this scheme granted free fathers almost absolute control over the members of their households, it also recognized some provision and protective rights for children. Under English common law and various colonial statutes, parents were held responsible for educating and maintaining their natural, legitimate children and providing them with a start in life. Parents who failed to meet their obligations to educate and provide for their children were subject to fines, imprisonment, and loss of custody.

In the New England colonies, children were entitled to some rights of protection as well as provision. The Body of Liberties, a code of laws adopted by Massachusetts in 1641 and modified in 1646, made children's cursing and striking of their parents a capital crime. At the same time, the code also allowed children to act against their parents in self-defense and required parents to bring their "stubborn" children before the court, rather than mete out indiscriminate punishment on their own. Similar laws were passed in Connecticut in 1650, Rhode Island in 1668, and New Hampshire in 1679. Although no child was ever put to death under these laws, they underscored the importance of children's obedience to parental authority and the state's interest in preserving parental power. They also recognized, however, that the state had a role to play in limiting the worst excesses of that power, and as such the laws comprise the first legal protections of children in the Western world.

Claims by colonial governments to the right to intervene in family life were derived from the doctrine of parens patriae, which declared the state to be the ultimate parent of every child. In that period, the primary interest of the state was not in the nurturing of children but in ensuring the productivity of children as current and future workers, preserving the male-dominated family, and maintaining social order. There was no explicit commitment to children's rights or an organized child advocacy movement in the colonial period. Nevertheless, by the

end of the eighteenth century, the principles had been established that children were entitled to material support and education and had a right to be free from excessive physical punishment by parents and guardians.

The nineteenth century saw the founding of the first organizations and institutions dedicated to the improvement of children's lives. Additionally, custody law established the "best interests of the child" standard (Mason 1994, 61), which some child-saving reformers adopted as a guiding principle of their work. During this period, as children became the objects of heightened social concern in the face of the changes wrought by a newly industrializing, urbanizing, and democratizing society, the state expanded its role as parens patriae and increasingly supplemented the family's responsibilities for child welfare. These developments were accompanied by changing, and often conflicting, notions of children and childhood. In the early nineteenth century, the Puritan belief in infant depravity gave way to rational and romantic conceptions of children. Children were now seen both as imperfect creatures in need of regulation, but capable of moral improvement, and as precious repositories of promise in need of solicitude and protection. The weakening of forces of external authority in the democratic republic and the exigencies of the market economy meant that above all, children had to develop self-reliance and self-control. Otherwise, they threatened to endanger the stability and advancement of the democratic and capitalist social order. The key in cultivating such qualities was in striking the correct balance between love and discipline in rearing the child. In the nineteenth century, this was a responsibility that fell to mothers in the private home and, increasingly, to those public and private institutions created by child-saving reformers devoted to the child's interests.

Four institutions and organizations established in the nineteenth century laid important foundations for further social action on behalf of children: the common school, the house of refuge, the practice of placing out, and the Society for the Prevention of Cruelty to Children. The most significant of these was the common school, which intended to provide children from all classes with the moral instruction and practical knowledge they needed to become upstanding citizens, responsible family members, and capable workers. Although the common schools of the nineteenth century fell far short of meeting the needs of all children and were compromised by gender, racial, ethnic, and class inequalities, they nonetheless advanced the notion that children had a right to a universal and free public education, for their own sake as well as that of society. For those children whose home and schooling so failed to inculcate correct moral values that they acted out in criminal or inappropriate ways, privately funded houses of refuge and public reformatories were created. The first house of refuge was founded in New York City in 1825, followed by similar institutions in Boston and Philadelphia. In 1847, Massachusetts incorporated the first state-supported institution for juvenile delinquents. Houses of refuge and reform schools attempted to rehabilitate juvenile offenders through a program of strict discipline, education, and work. These reformatories claimed broad jurisdiction over family and children's lives by confining not only juvenile criminals but also vagrant, idle, disobedient, and neglected children.

Treated as a special class in need of improvement and protection, children were also hereby denied the constitutional safeguards afforded adults. Some children may have benefited from such institutional efforts on their behalf, but this came at the price of far-reaching state control over their behavior and family life.

In the 1840s and 1850s, reformers arrived at a new remedy for dealing with the delinquent, poor, and neglected children who were corrupting and being corrupted by the streets of U.S. cities. In 1853, Charles Loring Brace founded the New York Children's Aid Society (CAS), which pioneered in the placing out of needy urban children to rural farm families who would provide their charges with work and an education. Profoundly distrustful of the capacity of poor and working-class parents to care for their children, the CAS sent both orphans and nonorphans to what it perceived to be homes more conducive to healthy upbringing. Like the houses of refuge and reform schools, the CAS extended the notion of children's rights by suggesting that children had interests apart from those of their families, including a right to be raised in an environment encouraging of their growth. But it also limited those rights by curbing children's autonomy and relying on poverty as a justification for removing children from their homes.

The New York Society for the Prevention of Cruelty to Children (SPCC), founded by upper-class child savers in New York in 1875, was similarly influenced by class bias. The first organizations to convey an explicit doctrine of children's rights, SPCCs around the country claimed for children the right to be free from excessive physical abuse (without eschewing corporal punishment altogether) as well as from neglect and the dangers of harmful employment. Abuse and neglect that were the result of poverty did not, however, prevent children from being removed from their parents. Thus, the SPCCs, like the CAS, bolstered child protection along with standards of child rearing often impossible for poor and working-class parents to meet.

Building on the institutional and organizational developments of the nineteenth century, the Progressive Era (1890–1920) became a "great watershed" for child advocacy (Hawes 1991, 26). In this age of optimistic reform, the romantic view of the child was supplemented by a scientific view, proffered by child "experts" in the newly forming professions of psychology, psychiatry, education, and social work. The creation of a vast body of knowledge about childhood in the behavioral sciences gave rise to the advocacy for a new set of emotional and psychological rights for children, including the right to mental health, personal fulfillment, and the realization of one's full potential. The rise of the social sciences and the professions that attended them also led, however, to increased incursions into family life by the state and justified the narrowing of children's rights before the law. This tension was most pronounced in the greatest achievement of child advocates of the Progressive Era, the creation of the juvenile court in Chicago in 1899. Like the earlier reformatories, the juvenile court broadly construed the delinquent child to include those who were criminal, disorderly, idle, and neglected. Armed with scientific knowledge about the "best interests of the child," the court pledged to approach youthful transgressions with compassion and to put the needs of the child first. In doing so, it frequently ignored parental interests and denied children the procedural rights of due process essential for the attainment of justice.

The early decades of the twentieth century also witnessed the first federal government commitments to children's protective and provision rights. In 1909, the White House held its inaugural Conference on the Care of Dependent Children, asserting that the federal government had a role to play in the shaping of public opinion and public policy concerning the needs of children. The U.S. Children's Bureau, located in the Department of Labor and Commerce, was created in 1912 with the purpose of gathering and disseminating information about all aspects of child welfare and children's rights. The work of the Children's Bureau, along with the National Child Labor Committee, one of the first national child advocacy organizations, led to the passage of the first permanent federal law regulating child labor in 1938. Another milestone was the Social Security Act of 1935, which included several provisions aimed at improving child welfare. As the first federal aid program for children, Social Security recognized the need for dependent children to be supported in their homes. The policy tied that aid to the "suitability" of the mother, however, thereby perpetuating the contingent nature of the government's responsibility to children's rights and protection. During World War II, Congress passed two laws intended to further the war effort that had the effect of promoting child welfare. Both the Lanham Act, which made federal funds available for day care, and the Emergency Maternity Infant Care Program, which provided maternity care for wives of enlisted men, held the promise of a greater federal commitment to children's rights, but both lasted only for the duration of the war.

Throughout the first half of the twentieth century, a coalition of child advocates was forming, composed of parents, educators, social workers, juvenile court staff, academics, medical professionals, lawyers, and government administrators. By the 1960s, influenced by the social activism and liberation orientation of these years, the groups had coalesced into a full-blown child advocacy movement. Child advocates of this period built on earlier efforts to protect children from harm and provide for their welfare. At the same time, they criticized the existing child welfare system's reliance on the "best interests of the child" standard, its use of state power to limit children's autonomy and intrude in family life, and its tendency to punish families for their poverty. Thus, the identification of "battered child syndrome" by the medical profession in 1961 led to the passage of state and federal laws to combat child abuse as well as to more judicious consideration of parental rights and greater attempts to distinguish between gross abuse and neglect brought on by poverty. Likewise, the Supreme Court decision in the *In re Gault* case of 1967, along with reforms on the state level, established a higher standard of due process for delinquents brought before the juvenile court. *Gault* raised questions about the doctrine of parens patriae and has been followed by a growing body of case law that seeks to guarantee that a child be treated fairly by its "ultimate parent" in the juvenile justice, educational, and child welfare systems.

Within the contemporary child advocacy movement, a decided tension exists between those advocates oriented toward child welfare, which encompasses both protective and provision rights, and those advocates oriented toward children's liberation. Emerging in the 1970s, child liberationists argue that children have been oppressed by the history of child-saving efforts and now should be granted all of the rights that adults possess, including the rights to vote, to work, and to choose one's guardians. Child welfare advocates are not opposed to a greater degree of autonomy for children, but they do reject the erasure of difference between children and adults that a liberation orientation implies. The Children's Defense Fund (CDF), which since its founding in 1973 has become the nation's leading child advocacy organization, thus continues to press for policies and programs that serve children's special interests and needs. Directed by Marian Wright Edelman, the CDF heads up numerous initiatives to ensure that children are guaranteed their rights to health, safety, economic security, equal educational opportunity, and fair treatment before the law.

—*Crista DeLuzio*

See also Children's Bureau, U.S.; The Children's Defense Fund; Family Courts; Juvenile Justice; Society for the Prevention of Cruelty to Children; White House Conferences on Children

References and Further Reading
Edmonds, Beverly C., and William R. Fernekes. 1996. *Children's Rights: A Reference Handbook*. Santa Barbara: ABC-CLIO.
Eldeman, Marian Wright. 1989. *Families in Peril: An Agenda for Social Change*. Cambridge: Harvard University Press.
Eldeman, Marian Wright. 2000. *The State of America's Children, Yearbook 2000: A Report from the Children's Defense Fund*. Boston: Beacon Press.
Gordon, Linda. 1988. *Heroes of Their Own Lives: The Politics and History of Family Violence, Boston 1880–1960*. New York: Viking Press.
Gordon, Linda, ed. 1990. *Women, the State, and Welfare*. Madison: University of Wisconsin Press.

Hawes, Joseph M. 1991. *The Children's Rights Movement: A History of Advocacy and Protection.* Boston: Twayne Publishers.

Lindenmeyer, Kriste. 1997. *A Right to Childhood: The U.S. Children's Bureau and Child Welfare, 1912–1946.* Champaign: University of Illinois Press.

Mason, Mary Ann. 1994. *From Father's Property to Children's Rights: The History of Child Custody in the United States.* New York: Columbia University Press.

Pleck, Elizabeth. 1987. *Domestic Tyranny: The Making of American Social Policy against Family Violence from Colonial Times to the Present.* New York: Oxford University Press.

Van Bueren, Geraldine. 1995. *The International Law on the Rights of the Child.* Dordrecht, the Netherlands: Martinus Nijhoff.

Child Care

The term *child care* refers to the regular care of children provided by persons other than their parents, usually while parents are pursuing education, training, or paid employment outside the home. In the United States today, child-care provision is divided into two distinct sectors, public and private. In both sectors, several different types of services may be available, ranging from in-home care to child-care centers, but the methods of payment differ. In the private sector, middle- and upper-income parents choose and pay for services directly, whereas in the public sector, poor and low-income parents must find child-care centers or family day-care providers that will accept state-issued vouchers to be reimbursed at fixed rates, or they may, in some instances, receive state reimbursement for individual arrangements with kith or kin. Although it appears that the private sector is wholly self-supporting, in fact it, too, is subsidized indirectly by the federal government through various income tax provisions and incentives to employers who establish child-care services.

The division between public and private provisions is the outcome of the erratic history of child care in the United States. Over the centuries, child care has taken many forms, including in-home care by other relatives, domestic servants, and babysitters; care in institutions variously named crèches, day nurseries, day-care centers, and child-care centers; and care in institutions designed for other purposes, including summer camps, preschools and nursery schools, and even orphanages. Because of the enduring value placed on "mother care" within the culture of the United States, child care has come under frequent criticism, and efforts to gain support for public services have met with strong opposition. The federal government offered inconsistent support for child care briefly during the New Deal and World War II and has offered it more extensively since the 1960s, as part of its efforts to reform public welfare policy.

Formal child care was rarely needed in the preindustrial societies of North America; both Native Americans and European Americans were able to combine child rearing with other domestic and productive tasks. In these hunting-and-gathering or agrarian economies, adults placed their offspring nearby while they worked, using various devices, including cradleboards and standing stools, to keep very young children out of harm's way. Most care was provided within the household, though during busy seasons, colonial New Englanders might send slightly older children to inexpensive, loosely organized "dame schools" for supervision and rudimentary education. In general, child care was

A nursery school for migrant children conducted by teachers trained by the WPA, 1939. (Library of Congress)

not seen as the exclusive task of mothers but was shared with fathers, older siblings, servants, and neighbors.

These arrangements became strained as market-based demands sped up the pace of production and factories drew workers out of homes and fields, making it difficult for household members to combine produc-

tive and reproductive tasks. At the same time, late colonial and early Republican ideologies, both patriotic and religious, defined a more distinctively gendered division of labor within families by enshrining motherhood and emphasizing fathers' breadwinning responsibilities. Although the value of women's productive labor declined, their child-rearing and home-making roles expanded and gained new stature. But the realities of life in industrializing America—illness, poverty, unemployment, desertion, early death—often prevented parents from fulfilling these ideals. Women left to maintain households on their own struggled to get by on paltry wages and whatever their children could earn on the streets. Torn between serving as both caretakers and breadwinners, many ended up entering a workhouse or almshouse and giving their children up for indenture.

It was within this context that the first formal child care in the United States developed. In 1793, a group of female Quaker philanthropists in Philadelphia, moved by the plight of dozens of women who had become widowed as the result of a yellow fever epidemic, decided to circumvent the inexorable course of family breakup by providing mothers with a means of supporting themselves and keeping their children with them. The House of Industry set up by the Female Society for the Relief and Employment of the Poor allowed the majority of women to work at spinning and weaving while their children were supervised in a separate nursery by some of the older widows. This not only provided the mothers with a small income but also kept the children off the streets; at the same time, it gave philanthropists an opportunity to inculcate the children with the "habits and virtues" of an industrious life.

Other female philanthropists in Philadelphia as well as in cities across the United States soon followed the Quaker women's lead, but few, if any, of the "day nurseries" they set up seem to have included workrooms. Services were, for the most part, "custodial"; that is, children were fed, clothed, and kept safe, but their routines were highly regimented, and little attention was paid to education. By the 1870s, dozens of day nurseries were in operation, but their capacity was still far too small to accommodate the needs of the thousands of mothers thrown into the workforce by the vicissitudes of the economy and then the Civil War and its aftermath. Despite the persistence of maternal employment among poor and working-class families, middle-class child-care philanthropists continued to present their services not as something mothers might turn to on a regular basis, but as something to be used only when they were in distress. Moreover, many mothers were put off by the moralistic tone that characterized the nurseries.

Some parents were able to find a more hospitable form of child care in one of the many infant schools that were started in cities and villages along the eastern seaboard from the mid-1820s to the late 1840s. Inspired by several British models, including one established by the utopian industrialist Robert Owen in New Lanark, Scotland, the founders of these schools emphasized education as well as supervision and claimed that even very young children could benefit from attendance. Aware that employment was common among the mothers of the lower classes and that older children were often kept out of school to care for younger siblings, these founders sought to enroll all children on a regular basis, not only when their families were deemed to be in crisis. This, unfortunately, led to the decline of such schools, for middle-class parents, imbued with the ideal of mother care, began to fear that their own influence would be supplanted by that of the schools and withdrew their support. After about two decades, the infant school movement died out.

Another form of child care could be found in the antebellum South, where slaveholding planters regularly assigned slaves who were either too old or too young for heavy labor to care for very young slave children while their mothers worked at other tasks. On larger plantations, a "nuss house" might hold up to 100 African American children. This system was, of course, devised wholly to benefit the planters; it allowed them to maximize both the productive and reproductive labor of their female slaves while minimizing the need for family ties among the slaves themselves and also controlling the socialization of their children. Ironically, although female slaves were denied the right to nurture their own offspring, they were frequently pressed into service as "mammies" or even wet nurses to slaveholders' children.

After emancipation, African American women continued to work outside the home in greater numbers than white women, often as domestic servants and caretakers of white children. African American women's organizations such as the National Association of Colored responded to the ongoing need for child care by founding a number of day nurseries, particularly in the urban South. The Neighborhood Union in Atlanta, for example, founded five free kindergartens between 1905 and 1908. Unlike their white counterparts, black child-care philanthropists regarded maternal employment as a normal (if less than desirable) part of family life and thus sought to create long-term, rather than temporary, services. Instead of the wealthy funding child care for the poor, support was spread widely across African American communities.

Throughout the nineteenth century, lone mothers (and sometimes fathers) of all races who were compelled to work but had no alternative form of care sent their children to orphanages for various lengths of time in order to avoid indenture. These parents had no intention of surrendering the children for adoption; indeed, they often paid for the children's room and board. By the second half of the century, the placement of "half-orphans" in asylums became so widespread that some critics accused parents of shirking their responsibilities.

Most orphanages refused to admit infants, creating a dilemma for mothers of newborns who needed to support themselves. To accommodate this group, in 1854, female philanthropists in New York City founded the New York Nursery and Child's Hospital, and in 1873, Philadelphia women followed suit with the Philadelphia Home for Infants. Such institutions offered two options: Mothers could place their children in the nursery and hire themselves out as wet nurses or remain in the hospital and receive room and board while nursing another infant in addition to their own. Unfortunately, the mortality rate in these nurseries was very high, owing to the lack of biomedical remedies and the severe impact of infectious contagion among infants whose resistance was lowered by what later physicians would diagnose as "hospitalism" or "failure to thrive" under institutional conditions.

Throughout this period, parents who had to work outside the home also turned to older siblings and other relatives or neighbors for informal care. Reformers deplored situations in which children were either left alone or in the care of "little mothers"—sisters only slightly older than their charges—but they reserved their severest criticism for "baby farms," the term they used for informal caretaking arrangements in poor urban neighborhoods. Although scurrilous newspaper reports and investigations accused these "shady" and "notorious" operations of trafficking infants or allowing them to perish through starvation or neglect, later studies suggest that most such caretakers acted responsibly and provided affordable services to low-income mothers who felt more comfortable leaving their children in a familiar environment (often with coethnics, an important consideration for minorities and immigrants), rather than in the sterile, rigid surroundings of a charitable day nursery.

At the end of the nineteenth century, then, child care in the United States had come to consist of a range of formal and informal provisions that were generally associated with the poor, minorities, and immigrants and stigmatized as charitable and custodial. This pattern of practices and institutions provided a weak foundation for building twentieth-century social services. As women's reform efforts picked up steam during the Progressive Era, however, child care became a target for reform and modernization. To draw attention to the need for child care and demonstrate "approved methods of rearing children from infancy on" (*The Children's Building of the World's Columbian Exposition* 1893, 23) a group of prominent New York philanthropists led by Josephine Jewell Dodge set up a Model Day Nursery in the Children's Building at the 1893 World's Columbian Exposition in Chicago and then went on to found the National Federation of Day Nurseries (NFDN), the first nationwide organization devoted to this issue, in 1898.

The philosophy of the NFDN was somewhat self-contradictory. Bent upon bringing day nurseries "up-to-date" by incorporating the methods of the emerging fields of social work and early childhood education, its leaders nevertheless clung to nineteenth-century attitudes toward maternal employment; that is, they continued to regard it as an emergency stopgap, not part of normal family life. In keeping with this philosophy, nurseries subjected applicants to strict scrutiny and expelled children once their families were no longer in dire need, regardless of the educational benefits they might be enjoying. As a result of such practices, day nurseries came to be seen as backward and were pushed to the margins of progressive social services.

In the meantime, reformers began to formulate another solution to the dilemma of poor mothers who were compelled to work outside the home: mothers' or widows' pensions. In the view of prominent Progressives such as Jane Addams, day nurseries only added to poor women's difficulties by encouraging them to take arduous, low-paid jobs while their children suffered from inadequate attention and care. Thus she and her Hull House colleagues, including Julia Lathrop, who would go on to become the first chief of the U.S. Children's Bureau (CB) when it was founded in 1912, called for a policy that would support mothers so they could stay at home with their children. Unlike child care, the idea of mothers' pensions quickly gained popular support because it did nothing to challenge conventional gender roles. Indeed, some reformers argued that mothers, like soldiers, were performing a "service to the nation" and therefore deserved public support when they lacked a male breadwinner. Pensions "spread like wildfire" as several large national organizations, including the General Federation of Women's Clubs and the National Congress of Mothers, mounted a highly successful, state-by-state legislative campaign. By 1930, nearly every state in the union had passed some form of mothers' or widows' pension law, making this the "policy of choice" for addressing the needs of low-income mothers and pushing child care further into the shadows of private philanthropy.

Despite the rhetoric, however, mothers' pensions could not fully address the problems of poor and low-income mothers, and many had no alternative but to go out to work. In most states, funding for pensions was inadequate, and many mothers found themselves ineligible because of highly restrictive criteria or stringent, biased administrative practices. African American women in particular were frequently denied benefits, in the North as well as the South, on the grounds that they, unlike white women, were accustomed to working for wages and thus should not be encouraged to stay at home to rear their children. Because pension coverage was sporadic and scattered, maternal employment not only persisted but increased, adding to the demand for child care. Philanthropists were hard put to meet this growing need using private funding alone. With mothers' pensions monopolizing the social policy agenda, however, they had no prospect of winning public funding for day nurseries.

This pattern continued into the 1920s, as the U.S. Children's Bureau conducted a series of studies of maternal and child labor in agriculture and industries across the country. Although investigators found many instances of injuries, illness, and even fatalities resulting from situations in which infants and toddlers were either left alone or brought into hazardous workplaces, the CB refused to advocate for federal support for child care

but instead worked to strengthen mothers' pensions so more mothers could stay at home. CB officials were influenced, in part, by the thinking of experts such as Dr. Douglas Thom, an advocate of child guidance who argued that "worn and wearied" wage-earning mothers who had no time for their children's welfare stifled their development (Thom 1924, 15). At the same time, the reputation of day nurseries continued to slide as efforts to upgrade their educational component flagged owing to lack of funds, and nursery schools, the darlings of Progressive early childhood educators, began to capture the middle-class imagination.

The Depression and then World War II had a mixed impact on the fortunes of child care. On the eve of the Great Depression, fewer than 300 nursery schools were in operation, compared to 800 day nurseries, but as unemployment rose, day nursery enrollments fell sharply and charitable donations also declined, forcing 200 day nurseries to close down between 1931 and 1940. Meanwhile, at the urging of prominent early childhood educators, the Works Progress Administration (WPA), a key New Deal agency, established a program of Emergency Nursery Schools (ENS). Primarily intended to offer employment opportunities to unemployed teachers, they were also seen as a means of compensating for the "physical and mental handicaps" caused by the economic downturn (Hopkins 1933, 155). Nearly 3,000 schools, enrolling more than 64,000 children, were started between 1933 and 1934; over the next year, these were consolidated into 1,900 schools with a capacity for approximately 75,000 students. In addition to forty-three states, the program covered the District of Columbia, Puerto Rico, and the Virgin Islands. Unlike the earlier nursery schools, which were largely private, charged fees, and served a middle-class clientele, these free, government-sponsored schools were open to children of all classes.

Designed as schools, not child care, the ENS were only open for part of the day, and their enrollments were supposedly restricted to the children of the unemployed. They did, however, become a form of de facto child care for parents employed on various WPA work-relief projects. Unlike the situation in the day nurseries, the educational component of the ENS was well developed because of early childhood educators' strong interest in the program. Organizations such as the National Association for Nursery Education, which was eager to promulgate the ideas of progressive pedagogy, even sent in their own staff members to supervise teaching training and oversee curriculum. The educators were frustrated, however, by inadequate facilities and equipment and by difficulties in convincing teachers with conventional classroom experience to adopt a less structured approach to working with young children. By the late 1930s, the ENS also began to suffer from high staff turnover as teachers left to take up better-paying jobs in defense plants. Between 1936 and 1942, nearly 1,000 schools were forced to close down.

Although the approach of World War II reduced the unemployment crisis in the United States, it created a social crisis as millions of women, including many mothers, sought employment in war-related industries. Despite a critical labor shortage, the federal government was at first reluctant to recruit mothers of small children, claiming that "mothers who remain at home are performing an essential patriotic service" ("Program for the Care of Children of Working Mothers"

1941, 31). Gaining support from social workers, who opposed maternal employment on psychological grounds, government officials dallied in responding to the unprecedented need for child care. In 1941 Congress passed the Lanham Act, which was intended to create community facilities in "war-impact areas," but it was not until 1943 that this was interpreted as authorizing support for child care. In the meantime, Congress allocated $6 million to convert the remaining ENS into child-care facilities. The organization of new services bogged down in interagency competition at the federal level and the considerable red tape involved when local communities applied for federal funding. According to the government's own guidelines, one child-care slot was required for every ten female defense workers; however, when the female labor force peaked at 19 million in 1944, only 3,000 child-care centers were operating, with a capacity for 130,000—far short of the 2 million that were theoretically needed.

Public opinion was slow to accept the dual ideas of maternal employment and child care. Although the popular media frequently reported on the spread of "latchkey children" and instances of sleeping children found locked in cars in company parking lots while their mothers worked the night shift, such stories served to castigate "selfish" wage-earning mothers, not point up the need for child care. At the same time, children's experts warned parents that children in group care might suffer the effects of "maternal deprivation" (Wolf 1942, 96) and urged them to maintain tranquil home environments to protect their children from the war's upheaval. What child care there was did little to dispel public concerns; hastily organized and often poorly staffed, most centers fell far short of the high standards early childhood educators had sought to establish for the ENS. One exception was the Child Service Centers set up by the Kaiser Company at its shipyards in Portland, Oregon. Architect-designed and scaled to children's needs, they offered twenty-four-hour care (to accommodate night-shift workers), a highly trained staff, a curriculum planned by leading early childhood experts, and even a cooked-food service for weary parents picking up their children after an arduous shift.

Despite its inadequacies, federally sponsored New Deal and wartime child care marked an important step in U.S. social provision. Congress, however, was wary of creating permanent services and repeatedly emphasized that public support would be provided "for the duration only." Soon after VJ Day, Lanham Act funding was cut off, forcing most of the child-care centers to shut down within a year or two. But the need for child care persisted as maternal employment, after an initial dip due to postwar layoffs, actually began to rise. Across the country, national organizations such as the Child Welfare League of America, along with numerous local groups, demonstrated and lobbied for continuing public support. These groups failed to persuade Congress to pass the 1946 Maternal and Child Welfare Act, which would have continued federal funding for child care, but they did win public child-care provisions in New York City, Philadelphia, Washington, D.C., and the state of California. During the Korean War, Congress approved a public child-care program but then refused to appropriate funds for it. Finally, in 1954, Congress found an approach to child care it could live with: the child-care tax deduction. This per-

mitted low- to moderate-income families (couples could earn up to $4,500 per year) to deduct up to $600 for child care from their income taxes, provided the services were needed "to permit the taxpayer to hold gainful employment."

The tax deduction offered some financial relief to certain groups of parents, but reformers were not satisfied, for such a measure failed to address basic issues such as the supply, distribution, affordability, and quality of child care. Building on the experience they had gained in lobbying for postwar provisions, in 1958 activists formed a national organization devoted exclusively to child care, the Inter-City Committee for Day Care of Children (ICC; later to become the National Committee on the Day Care of Children). The organization was led by Elinor Guggenheimer, a longtime New York City child-care activist; Sadie Ginsberg, a leader of the Child Study Association of America; Cornelia Goldsmith, a New York City official who had helped establish a licensing system for child care in that city; and Winifred Moore, a child-care specialist who had worked in both government and the private sector. Unlike its predecessor, the National Federation of Day Nurseries (which had been absorbed by the Child Welfare League of America in 1942), the ICC believed that private charity could not support child care on its own; instead, the new organization sought to work closely with government agencies such as the CB and the Women's Bureau (WB) to gain federal support.

The ICC experimented with a number of different rationales for child care, generally preferring to avoid references to maternal employment in favor of stressing the need to "safeguard children's welfare" (Inter-City Council for the Day Care of Children RG 86, 1–2). In 1958 and

Caregivers feeding lunch to children in an infant day-care center. (Elizabeth Crews)

1959, the ICC helped mobilize grassroots support for several child-care bills introduced into Congress by Sen. Jacob Javits (R–New York), but to no avail. They did succeed in convincing the CB and WB to cosponsor a National Conference on the Day Care of Children in Washington, D.C., in November 1960. At that conference, several government officials pointed to the growing demand for labor and what now appeared to be an irreversible trend toward maternal employment, but many attendees continued to express ambivalence about placing young children in group care. Guggenheimer, however, noted that mothers would work "whether good care is available or not. It is the child," she emphasized, "that suffers when the care is poor" (Hoffman 1961, 6). Guggenheimer did not call directly for government support for child care, but she made it clear that private and voluntary agencies could no longer shoulder the burden. The CB and WB, under the direction of chiefs appointed by Pres. Dwight D. Eisenhower, were reluctant to take the lead on this issue, but President-elect John F. Kennedy, in a message to the conference, expressed his awareness of the problem, stating, "I believe we must take further steps to encourage day care programs that will protect our children and provide them with a basis for a full life in later years . . ." (13–14).

Kennedy's message, along with subsequent statements, implied that his administration sought a broad-based approach to child care. In a widely circulated report, the President's Commission on the Status of Women acknowledged that maternal employment was becoming the norm and pointed out that child care could not only help women who decided to work outside the home but could also be a developmental boon to children and help advance social and racial integration. But the Kennedy administration could not muster sufficient political support to push through a universal child-care policy. Instead, in two welfare reform bills passed in 1962 and 1965, Congress linked federal support for child care to policies designed to encourage poor and low-income women to enter training programs or take employment outside the home. The goal was to reduce the number of Americans receiving "welfare" (Aid to Families with Dependent Children, or AFDC) or prevent women from becoming recipients in the first place.

For the next three decades, direct federal support for child care was limited to such "targeted" policies. At the same time, however, the federal government offered several types of indirect support to middle- and upper-class families in the form of incentives for employer-sponsored child care and several different types of income tax plans. In the 1980s, under the Reagan administration, federal funding for low-income child care was dramatically reduced, whereas expenditures for child care benefiting middle- and high-income families nearly doubled. Such measures stimulated the growth of voluntary and for-profit child care, much of which was beyond the reach of low-income families. This group received some help from the Child Care and Development Block Grant (CCDBG), passed in 1990, which allocated $825 million to individual states.

The Personal Responsibility and Work Opportunity Act of 1996 replaced AFDC with time-limited public assistance coupled with stringent employment mandates. Acknowledging the need for expanded child care to support this welfare-to-work plan, Congress combined CCDBG, along with several smaller programs, into a single block grant—the Child Care and Development Fund. Though more public funds for child care became available than ever before, problems of supply and quality continue to limit access to child care for welfare recipients who are now compelled to take employment and moderate-income families who must cope with ever-rising costs for child care. For all families, the quality of child care is compromised by the high rate of turnover in the field, in itself the result of low pay and poor benefits.

Because of its long history and current structure, the child-care system in the United States is divided along class lines, making it difficult for parents to unite and lobby for improved services and increased public funding for child care for all children. When it comes to public provisions for children and families, the United States compares poorly with other advanced industrial societies, such as France, Sweden, and Denmark, which not only offer free or subsidized care to children over three but also provide paid maternity or parental leave. Unlike the United States, these countries use child care not as a lever of harsh mandatory employment policy but as a means of helping parents reconcile the demands of work and family life.

—*Sonya Michel*

See also After-School Care; Aid to Families with Dependent Children; Child Welfare Policy; Children's Bureau, U.S.; Latchkey Children; Orphanages

References and Further Reading
Berry, Mary Frances. 1993. *The Politics of Parenthood: Child Care, Women's Rights, and the Myth of the Good Mother.* New York: Viking.
The Children's Building of the World's Columbian Exposition. 1893. Chicago: N.p.
Goodwin, Joanne L. 1997. *Gender and the Politics of Welfare Reform: Mothers' Pensions in Chicago, 1911–1929.* Chicago: University of Chicago Press.
Hoffman, Gertrude I., comp. 1961. *Day Care Services: Form and Substance.* U.S. Children's Bureau Publication no. 193. Washington, DC: Government Printing Office.
Hopkins, Harry L. 1933. "Announcement of Emergency Nursery Schools." *Childhood Education* 10, no. 3 (December): 150–155.
Inter-City Council for the Day Care of Children. "Recommendations for Programs" (30 April 1959). RG 86. National Archives.
Levy, Denise Urias, and Sonya Michel. 2002. "More Can Be Less: Child Care and Welfare Reform in the United States." In *Child Care at the Crossroads: Gender and Welfare State Restructuring,* edited by Rianne Mahon and Sonya Michel, 211–235. New York: Routledge.
Michel, Sonya. 1999. *Children's Interests/Mothers' Rights: The Shaping of America's Child Care Policy.* New Haven: Yale University Press.
"Program for the Care of Children of Working Mothers." 1941. *The Child* 6, no. 2 (August): 31–35.
Rose, Elizabeth. 1998. *A Mother's Job: The History of Day Care, 1890–1960.* New York: Oxford University Press.
Thom, D. A. 1924. *Habit Clinics for the Child of Preschool Age: Their Organization and Practical Value.* U.S. Children's Bureau Publication no. 135. Washington, DC: Government Printing Office.
Wolf, Anna W. M. 1942. *Our Children Face War.* Boston: Houghton Mifflin.

Child Custody

Child custody has historically referred to the right and responsibility of a parent or someone acting in a parental capacity to control and support a dependent child. Laws and social norms governing custody of children have undergone great change over the course of American history. For the purpose of this entry, these changes have been synthesized into three broad historical periods distinguished by shifts in dominant attitudes toward custodial rights: first, the privileging of the rights of male household heads to custody of biological children and other dependents (spanning from approximately the 1600s to 1800); second, increased emphasis on children's interests and a tendency toward maternal preference based upon women's perceived importance as primary caretakers of children (1800 through the 1900s); and third, continued heed to children's interests accompanied by a turn toward recognition of the state's custodial role on the one hand, and parental equity on the other (1900 to the present).

In recent decades, developments including rising rates of out-of-wedlock pregnancy and adoption, greater attention to child abuse, and the advent of new reproductive technologies have made the issue of child custody more problematic. Although children's interests continue to be recognized as the most important determinant of custody decisions, many have argued that courts have not gone far enough in legally protecting these interests. Following is a brief treatment of each of the three periods identified above, with a concluding section devoted to the most recent developments in child custody. It is necessary to note an important limitation of any work claiming treatment of legal change in the United States: namely, that even though general patterns may be discerned, laws developed unevenly in different states, though these disparities have lessened over time. Where possible, discussion of general trends in custody law will be supported by important developments in specific states as well as crucial exceptions in other states.

Though many modern Americans associate the question of custody of children primarily with parental disputes in cases of divorce, historically custody has been more broadly concerned with the prerogative of male household heads to control the lives, labor, and education not only of their biological children but also of wards, servants, slaves, and apprentices. Laws and social norms governing custody of children in colonial America reflected broader cultural conceptions of the household, which was considered to include servants and other dependents as well as nuclear family members; of women, who were unequal in relation to men; and of children and childhood, which were viewed with little of the sentimentality that would develop over the course of the nineteenth century.

Male prerogative was recognized in British common law, which also prohibited divorce on the grounds that it disrupted familial, and hence male-dominated, social order. With few exceptions—particularly the Puritan-founded colonies in Massachusetts and Connecticut—divorce was not readily available in the American colonies before the American Revolution and formation of the new republic. Many states allowed divorce only by passage of a private act before state legislative bodies, and South Carolina, for example, did not grant a right to divorce until the latter half of the nineteenth century. Parental disputes over the custody of children were correspond-

ingly rare, and even in states with more liberal divorce law, little documentary evidence of custody decisions exists.

In Connecticut, for instance, few seventeenth- and eighteenth-century divorce records contain provisions for custody of children. Explicit instructions were probably offered only in cases in which one or the other parent was considered morally unworthy of guardianship—and here, women appear to have been favored in custody decisions, even if found to be the guilty party in a divorce. Because many divorce cases also involved desertion, it is probable that the deserting partner had, in essence, already forfeited custody rights to his or her spouse (Dayton 1995).

Other states, which more closely heeded the strictures of British common law, upheld paternal rights in contested custody cases even when the father was found guilty of adultery or desertion. Some women were probably dissuaded from pursuing divorce at all, fearing that they would lose custody of their children. Paternal prerogative was also important in the case of widowhood—men, in their wills, could assign custody of their surviving children as well as their estate to either their wives or a male guardian. Frequently, separate provisions were made for custody of estate and custody of persons, with the former going to a male executor and the latter going to the wife of the deceased. If custody provisions were not made in a will, the court might appoint a male guardian at its discretion. When a widow remarried—as was common given high male mortality rates, especially in the Chesapeake area—her new husband would usually assume custodial rights of her children residing in his household.

An important variation on the prevalent presumption of male legal rights to custody of children occurred in cases of illegitimacy. Better-off women would often deliver an illegitimate child in their family's household, which assumed responsibility for the child's upkeep. Though a woman could sue the biological father for the support of a child, he could not generally claim custodial rights because the children were not under his household. Bastard children were often removed from poor women, however, by local poor officials concerned about the cost to the community of supporting them; such children were placed in other homes as servants or apprentices. Under British common law, illegitimate children were considered *filius nullius*—the children and heirs of no one—though states such as Virginia and Rhode Island later came to offer more expanded inheritance rights to bastards (Wells 1980).

Colonial masters had custody and control over servants, indentured servants, apprentices, and slaves residing in their households; masters' legal rights and responsibilities in relation to these dependents were likened to those a father possessed over his own children. Courts might rule on custody disputes involving children and their masters in cases involving allegations of gross abuse by masters, instances of runaway children, and disagreements between a child's parents and his or her master over the conditions of servitude, indenture, or apprenticeship. The latter example, however, involved only parents who had voluntarily arranged servitude or apprenticeship for their children; both indentured servants and slaves forfeited rights to their children to their masters. Over the course of the seventeenth century, slavery—considered to be a lifetime condition—increasingly came to be considered a heritable condition for black children based

upon the status of their mother, and both black and white indentured servants were punished for illegitimacy by the sentencing of their children to long periods of labor (usually twenty-four to thirty years). This practice was justified as both punishment and provision for out-of-wedlock births by indentured and slave women. Eventually, bastardy laws came to disproportionately affect black women and, a number of scholars have argued, helped to define slavery as a heritable condition based upon skin color (Brown 1996).

Although the break from British patriarchal governmental authority brought about by the American Revolution did little to disrupt patriarchal control over women, children, and other dependents within the political sphere, republican ideology contributed to the growth of a new model of domestic relations. Women were granted greater civic importance as the instructors of future citizens of the new republic and as guardians of its virtue (Kerber 1976). Correspondingly, great emphasis was placed on the significance of proper child rearing, and children took a place at the center of the companionate republican family, based upon separate spheres and reciprocal obligation (Grossberg 1985). These developments helped to set the stage for the major changes in child custody practice that would occur over the course of the nineteenth century.

In the early nineteenth century, the loosening of the United States' ties to Britain also led to a loosening of the strictures of common law; the development of a distinct American legal tradition had several important consequences with regard to the question of custody law. First, as divorce became more readily available in most states, divorce-related custody disputes gained new attention—though a large portion of early divorce cases involved childless couples (Basch 1999). Second, early feminists contesting the principle of coverture—the legal unity of a woman with her husband under British common law—demanded equal rights for women to own property; gain guardianship of their children in the case of divorce, separation, or a husband's death; and vote in elections. Finally, the emergence of what Michael Grossberg has termed a "judicial patriarchy" in the United States led to a greater weighting of children's interests; the popular connection of women to children and the home, sometimes referred to as domestic ideology, led judges to rule that by nature and nurture mothers could better meet children's needs than could fathers (Grossberg 1985, 290–296). Increasingly, concern about children's interests trumped older concerns about patriarchal order as even women who were considered to be the guilty party in divorce—for reason of adultery, for instance—but who still qualified as parents were awarded custody of their children.

Beginning at the turn of the nineteenth century, U.S. courts presiding over custody disputes in cases of desertion, divorce, or death increasingly favored women as guardians, weakening the male prerogative codified in common law. These decisions were usually justified by reference to the "best interests of the child"; women were especially likely to win custody of young children based upon a doctrine of "tender ties" linking mothers to their care. Although early decisions in favor of mothers, such as *Nickols* v. *Giles* in Connecticut (1796) and *Prather* v. *Prather* (1809) in South Carolina, represented judicial innovation, over time they won the support of more and more state judges (Grossberg 1985). Especially after passage of laws—beginning in Pennsylva-

nia in 1816—removing divorce from the domain of the legislature and placing it under that of the bench, judges practiced greater discretion in fitting their decisions to the needs of individual cases. Several states also passed legislation allowing women who were separated from their husbands to file writs of habeus corpus, allowing the court to decide on placement of children even when divorce had not occurred.

The decision in favor of the mother in the high-profile 1840 d'Hauteville custody case—tried in Pennsylvania though it involved Ellen Sears d'Hauteville, daughter of a Boston manufacturer, and the Baron d'Hauteville, a Swiss aristocrat—further advanced the notion that women's role as caretakers of children should be legally protected. Ellen Sears d'Hauteville's lawyer, John Cadwalader, relied not only on popular notions of motherhood—"everyone knows that a father is unfit to take care of an infant"—but also on recent scientific research on child development he had obtained from the National Academy of Natural Sciences. Although the Pennsylvania court found Cadwalader's arguments compelling enough to award Ellen Sears d'Hauteville custody of young Frederick d'Hauteville, others disagreed with the ruling on the grounds that as a married woman, she did not possess the independent legal status necessary to be appointed independent guardian of a child (Grossberg 1985; Grossberg 1996).

Early American feminists recognized women's lack of independent legal identity as a primary source of their debased status in society at large and linked the issues of married women's property rights, mothers' custody of children, and female enfranchisement. Feminist reformers were fond of pointing out that not only were married women denied guardianship of their children, their legal status was little better than that of children. The campaign for passage of an expansive married women's property act in New York in 1848 helped to give birth to the modern women's movement in the United States; greater property rights for women, feminists recognized, helped to strengthen their case for guardianship and maintenance of children as well as their demands for increased civic participation (Basch 1982). The Declaration of Sentiments drafted by women's rights activists, including Elizabeth Cady Stanton and Lucretia Mott, and read at the 1848 Women's Rights Convention in Seneca Falls, New York, decried women's lack of custody rights alongside their lack of control over property and access to the vote: "He [man] has so framed the laws of divorce, as to what shall be the proper causes of divorce; in case of separation, to whom the guardianship of the children shall be given; as to be wholly regardless of the happiness of women—the law, in all cases, going upon a false supposition of the supremacy of man, and giving all power into his hands" (Stanton 1998, 2035–2037). Although judges increasingly favored women in custody cases in the courts, feminist reformers continued to face considerable difficulty through the nineteenth century in securing legislation mandating equitable parental rights to the guardianship of children.

Judicial practice, rather than legislation, proved to be definitive in changing custody provisions, though passage of married women's property acts—by extending to women greater access to independent legal standing and financial means to maintain their children—helped put mothers on firmer ground before the court. Maternal fitness, how-

ever, remained a predominant concern of the court; women were usually granted custody not on the basis of legal parental equity but instead based upon their importance to children as maternal nurturers. Divorce increased dramatically in the final decades of the nineteenth century, and where guardianship of children was contested, custody was overwhelmingly awarded to the wife despite many judges' reticence to disrupt paternal authority (U.S. Bureau of the Census 1909). Though a man's chances of winning custody were even lower if it was decided that he was the guilty party in a divorce, a woman's presumed maternal attributes might lead a judge to overlook her moral transgressions—particularly adultery—when granting guardianship. Despite emphasis on children's welfare, it is uncertain how frequently children's opinion regarding their custody arrangements was actually solicited.

Several other, related developments in family law during the nineteenth century also had an impact on custody decisions. In each case, concern for children's best interests motivated shifts in prior legal practice. First, the Massachusetts legislature moved, in 1851, to pass the earliest law in the United States providing for the legal adoption of children. By allowing for the transference of parental rights based upon both the parental qualifications of the adopters and the welfare of the child in question, this legislation struck a blow at the nearly absolute patriarchal rights assumed under common law. In addition, it set a precedent for increased intervention into domestic relations by the state. Second, the extension of inheritance rights and legal acceptance to illegitimate children in many states arose at least in part from an interest in the needs of these children and again weakened the commitment to patriarchal family structure enshrined in common law. Mothers' rights to custody of illegitimate children not recognized by their father's family were also legally strengthened in the early decades of the nineteenth century. Finally, both increased attention to children's welfare and the particular economic conditions of nineteenth-century America led to a decline in the family-based apprenticeships that had been a major source for custody disputes in earlier centuries. The prolonging of childhood, greater availability of public education, and emergence of factory labor—which displaced much skilled trade work—all contributed to this decline. When disputes did arise, judges were far more willing than they had been in previous centuries to weigh children's interests over those of their masters.

As in the colonial era, a double standard existed for black children and their families. Following the signing of the Emancipation Proclamation in 1861, the status of children of former slaves was temporarily uncertain. Since most slave unions were not legally recognized, these children technically fell under custody laws concerning illegitimacy and were considered members of their mothers' families. Not until nearly a decade after the end of the Civil War did all former slave states recognize the validity of slave marriages and the legitimacy of their offspring. In the interim, many of these states passed laws allowing former slave children to be placed in involuntary indentures, ostensibly as a provision for their support.

The doctrine of children's best interests led to increasing outside intervention in the home during the late nineteenth and early twentieth centuries. The cause of child welfare was embraced by many "child-saving" Progressive reformers, who were committed to improving the moral state as well as physical condition of children. Some believed both private charities and the state had a role to play, though many were split on this question. As was the case with removal of illegitimate children from homes by poor officials in colonial America for placement in involuntary indentures, turn-of-the-century efforts to promote child welfare disproportionately affected poor children and their families and persons of color. Efforts were no longer directed only at alleviating the financial burden posed to the community by these children, though; indeed, reformers questioned the fitness of parents who held their children out of school to work for wages.

Some reformers believed negligent or abusive parents should be relieved of custodial rights to their children by either state or private agencies; others stressed that the family should be maintained at all costs—even in cases of abuse or destitution. The former type of reformers relied on the "placing out" of children—modeled after earlier apprenticeship agreements—as well as on orphan asylums; although it was hoped that these children would eventually be adopted, this was seldom the case. The latter category of reformers relied upon home visits, parental education, and payment of benefits by both private and state agencies to help improve the situation of children within home environments. A particularly striking instance of this strategy is the policy of payment of maternal benefits adopted by nearly all states in the years prior to World War I. These "mothers' pensions" were intended to help women of good character—primarily widows and divorced women rather than mothers of children born out of wedlock—provide for their children while staying at home. One historian has described mothers' aid as "a kind of child custody reform for the poor" because it allowed poor women to escape abusive marriages without losing their children (Gordon 1994, 39). At the same time that states began to provide maternal benefits, many toughened up laws mandating support by fathers of children of divorced, deserted, and unmarried women; though women continued to be granted custody of children in most cases, fathers were increasingly expected to pay for their upkeep.

Significant growth in divorce rates beginning at the end of the nineteenth century and continuing through the twentieth also led to increased state mediation of familial disputes, where judges had enjoyed considerable discretion in deciding the outcomes of divorce proceedings and custody disputes in the nineteenth century. In the twentieth century, however, legislatures began to take steps to regularize procedure. By the mid-1930s, most state legislatures had finally passed laws granting women equal rights to men in custody disputes and formally overturning the male prerogative protected in common law. Although feminists had attempted to pass such laws since the mid-nineteenth century, it was claims by social reformers and experts on behalf of children's welfare that finally brought about legal change.

The development of no-fault divorces, in which marriage failure—as opposed to adultery, cruelty, desertion, and other acts formerly described as "marital offenses"—is adequate grounds for divorce, is another important example of state legislative action. The adoption of no-fault divorce by each of the fifty states between 1969 and 1985 helped to remove much of the stigma previously attached to divorce. As no-fault divorce became more widely accepted, parental disputes over the custody of children became more prevalent. Women continued to enjoy preference in many custody decisions through the 1980s and, given an increase in their numbers in the workplace as well as expanded civic rights, became better able to support children. Still, even as states also toughened enforcement of provisions for child support, financial issues remained a barrier to many divorced women's ability to raise their children alone.

Since 1970, many states have taken steps to promote gender neutrality in custody decisions. In 1972, the California legislature, for instance, revised portions of the Family Law Act of 1969, omitting references to preference for maternal custody and reiterating a doctrine of the best interests of the child. More and more, groups advocating "fathers' rights" have also demanded that judges move away from maternal preference in custody decisions. Increasingly, divorces result in joint custody arrangements allowing both parents access to children; some arrangements differentiate between physical and legal custody of children by allowing one parent primary day-to-day care of a child while affirming the legal custodial rights of both parents. These arrangements have become particularly popular in cases of private ordering, where divorcing parents negotiate financial and custodial conditions outside of court, and a judge intervenes only to resolve issues that cannot be privately worked out. Though provision for joint custody arrangements may facilitate resolution of divorce proceedings between parents, social scientists have been divided as to their effects on children.

Over the course of the twentieth century, expert opinion on child welfare has emerged as an important determinant in custody decisions. Just as John Cadwalader used early research in child development to support Ellen Sears d'Hauteville's custody claims during the mid-nineteenth century, twentieth-century divorcing parents have turned to expert witnesses—usually psychologists or psychiatrists—to alternately question the fitness of the other parent or to demonstrate their own capacity to meet the child's needs. Social scientists and legal authorities have also taken their views on issues related to child custody to the broader court of public opinion, arguing the benefits and disadvantages to arrangements ranging from single-parent custody and joint custody to gender-based custody and custody by nonbiological parents. Other commentators—including journalists, politicians, and religious leaders—speak not only of children's welfare but of the broader social good when discussing factors related to custody, including—in addition to divorce—higher rates of out-of-wedlock births, growing acceptance of same-sex unions, greater viability of reproductive technologies including surrogate mothering, and increased incidence of adoption. This discussion reflects the historical relation of custody to broader cultural change in the law, the family, gender norms, the role of the state, and scientific opinion. It remains to be seen to what extent children's voices, largely silent despite two centuries of attention to children's welfare, will be heard in this discussion in the future.

—*JuNelle Harris*

See also Adoptive Parents; Apprenticeship; Blended Families; Divorce, History of; Inheritance; Orphanages; Stepparents

References and Further Reading

Basch, Norma. 1982. *In the Eyes of the Law: Women, Marriage, and Property in Nineteenth-Century New York*. Ithaca: Cornell University Press.

Basch, Norma. 1999. *Framing American Divorce: From the Revolutionary Generation to the Victorians*. Berkeley: University of California Press.

Brown, Kathleen. 1996. *Good Wives, Nasty Wenches, and Anxious Patriarchs: Gender, Race, and Power in Colonial Virginia*. Chapel Hill: University of North Carolina Press.

Bruch, Carol. 1988. "And How Are the Children? The Effects of Ideology and Mediation on Child Custody Law and Children's Well-being in the United States." *International Journal of Law and the Family* 2: 116–121.

Chambers, David. 1990. "Stepparents, Biologic Parents, and the Law's Perception of 'Family' after Divorce." In *Divorce Reform at the Crossroads*, edited by Stephen Sugarman and Herma Hill Kay, 102–129. New Haven: Yale University Press.

Chused, Richard. 1994. *Private Acts in Public Places: A Social History of Divorce in the Formative Era of American Family Law*. Philadelphia: University of Pennsylvania Press.

Dayton, Cornelia. 1995. *Women before the Bar: Gender, Law, and Society in Connecticut, 1639–1789*. Chapel Hill: University of North Carolina Press.

Goldstein, Joseph, Anna Freud, and Albert J. Solnit. 1973. *Beyond the Best Interests of the Child*. New York: The Free Press.

Grossberg, Michael. 1985. *Governing the Hearth: Law and Family in Nineteenth-Century America*. Chapel Hill: University of North Carolina Press.

Grossberg, Michael. 1996. *Judgment for Solomon: The D'Hauteville Case and Legal Experience in Antebellum America*. New York: Cambridge University Press.

Hartog, Hendrik. 2000. *Man and Wife in America: A History*. Cambridge: Harvard University Press.

Kerber, Linda. 1976. "The Republican Mother: Women and the Enlightenment—An American Perspective." *American Quarterly* 28: 187–205.

Maccoby, Eleanor E., and Robert H. Mnookin, with Charlene E. Depner and

H. Elizabeth Peters. 1992. *Dividing the Child: Social and Legal Dilemmas of Custody*. Cambridge: Harvard University Press.

Mason, Mary Ann. 1994. *From Father's Property to Children's Rights: The History of Child Custody in the United States*. New York: Columbia University Press.

Stanton, Elizabeth Cady. 1998. "Declaration of Sentiments." In *The Heath Anthology of American Literature*, edited by Paul Lanter et al., 2035–2037. Boston: Houghton Mifflin.

Thompson, Ross A. 1987. "Fathers and the Child's 'Best Interests': Judicial Decision Making in Custody Disputes." In *The Father's Role: Applied Perspectives*, edited by Michael F. Lamb, 61–102. New York: John Wiley.

Tiffin, Susan. 1982. *In Whose Best Interests? Child Welfare Reform in the Progressive Era*. Westport, CT: Greenwood Press.

Trattner, Walter I. 1974. *From Poor Law to Welfare State: A History of Social Welfare in America*. New York: The Free Press.

U.S. Bureau of the Census. 1909. *Special Reports: Marriage and Divorce. 1867–1906, Part 1*. Washington, DC: Government Printing Office.

Weitzman, Lenore. 1985. *The Divorce Revolution: The Unexpected Social and Economic Consequences for Women and Children*. New York: The Free Press.

Wells, Robert. 1980. "Illegitimacy and Bridal Pregnancy in Colonial America." In *Bastardy and Its Comparative History*, edited by Peter Laslett, Karla Oosterveen, and Richard M. Smith. Cambridge: Harvard University Press.

Zainaldin, Jamil S. 1979. "The Emergence of a Modern American Family Law: Child Custody, Adoption, and the Courts, 1796–1851." *Northwestern University Law Review* 73: 1038–1089.

Child Development

Child development is defined as the study of children and their development, from the prenatal period through adolescence. Topics of study include physical development, cognitive development, and socioemotional development, and the goals of child development are generally to describe, explain, and predict children's development in each of these three areas. Promoting "optimal" development based on the goals just stated and in the context of children's physical, cognitive, and socioemotional development is an additional purpose of studying child development.

History and Background

Ancient Views. Early attempts to investigate child development chiefly focused on description. For example, in the fourth century B.C., Aristotle defined three stages of human development, ending in the ability to choose self-determination (Santrock 1999, 9). According to Aristotle, infancy was characterized by the mastery of spoken language, ending around age seven years; boyhood described the years between seven and puberty; and the years from puberty until age twenty-one comprised young manhood (Papalia, Olds, and Feldman 1999). The idea that children develop into adults through a series of predictable stages has been a popular and useful one, as will be shown later in this entry. In addition to the ancient Greeks and Romans, the Bible has even made mention of the special nature of children (15).

Preindustrial Views. In the eighteenth and nineteenth centuries, "diary studies" of infant development became popular, especially following Charles Darwin's publication of his journal regarding his own son's sensory, cognitive, and emotional development during his first year (Papalia, Olds, and Feldman 1999, 16). Like the much earlier interest in child development, these journals contained descriptions of child activities and development without explanation.

Modern Views. The official beginning of the modern, scientific era of child development can be traced to U.S. psychologist G. Stanley Hall in the late nineteenth century. The modern era focuses on prediction and explanation in addition to the description of child behavior. In 1891 Hall began his famous "child study movement" (White 1992, 28) and ushered in an unprecedented scientific interest in children that continues today in such fields as psychology, education, human development, family studies, health and human services, social work, and others. Hall primarily used questionnaires directed toward teachers that inquired about children's habits, curiosity, personality traits, and behavior. The aim was to discover the contents of children's minds, and this method of study has been hailed as the first "normal science of child development" (White 1992, 32). This body of work focused primarily on school-age children and adolescents, serving as a precursor to Hall's famous two-volume series, *Adolescence,* in 1904 (Hall 1904). James Mark Baldwin, a U.S. contemporary of Hall, also had a profound influence on the early modern era of studying child development. He is noted for writing *Mental Development in the Child and the Race* in 1895 and emphasizing the importance of social development, especially in infants (Baldwin 1895; Cairns 1992, 18). Thus, a scientific interest in children from infancy through adolescence was already well in place by the turn of the twentieth century.

Key Issues in Child Development
Improving scientific methods of child study and the availability of more complex statistical analyses resulted in the ability to ask more and more sophisticated and philosophical questions regarding the development of children. Today, the scientific study of child development centers around several key issues. They include the following, which will be discussed in turn: active versus passive development, quantitative versus qualitative development, and the role of nature versus nurture in development. In addition to these definitional issues, there have been several different types of theories representing ways of describing, predicting, and explaining child development, each with a unique focus. Among these are the biological view, the psychoanalytic view, the learning view, the cognitive view, and the contextual view. Each of these approaches, complete with representative theories and their role in understanding physical, cognitive, and emotional development, will also be discussed in turn.

Active versus Passive Development. One of the first issues that any theory of child development must tackle is the fundamental nature of children's growth and development—that is, is the child an active participant in his or her own development? Or is the child merely a passive creature acted upon by external forces? Through time both of these views have shared time in the spotlight, and the active versus the passive nature of children is still being argued today. With the advent of machine technology and advances in sciences such as physics, the passive view has gained proponents. In this view, the child is seen as a passive organism, driven by external forces that drive development in a predictable way, according to known scientific (physical, biological, psychological, and so on) laws.

Thus, the child is a product of known (or knowable) events, circumstances, and/or experiences. The best-known proponent of this view was British philosopher John Locke, who held that young children entered the world tabula rasa, as blank slates, ready and waiting for the world to write experiences upon them.

The active view of child development is modeled not on machines, but on living systems. The goals and motivations of the living child actively direct the child in certain directions and not others, and each child is seen as constructing his or her own development. Thus, the child's understanding of the world around him or her is based on his or her own activity within that environment, and even the same experience by two different children can be "constructed" or understood in two different ways. French philosopher Jean Jacques Rousseau exemplified this view with his understanding of children as "noble savages," who were born with positive tendencies and who would develop accordingly if society provided a minimum standard.

Quantitative versus Qualitative Development. Another important issue in the field of child development is that of whether development proceeds in a qualitative fashion or in a quantitative fashion. For most people who study child development, this is the question about stages. Are there distinct, recognizable stages that proceed in a known, predictable manner? Or is development really a matter of continuous and gradual accumulation of knowledge? Qualitative, stage theorists posit that development proceeds through periodic changes in structure or organization. That is, development occurs through changes in kind or type in the phenomenon of interest.

New abilities, new ways of thinking, and new patterns of behavior emerge in a new stage owing to reorganization of existing elements. Each stage, though it builds on the previous stage and prepares for the next stage, is qualitatively different from both. The classic example in physical science is the development of a frog from a tadpole and an egg. Each stage in the frog's life cycle is qualitatively different from the others. With regard to human children and their development, this view often focuses on the appearance of new physical or mental abilities (as in the ability to think in symbols or to use logic).

Quantitative development, on the other hand, focuses on the amount of knowledge or information that a child has. Older children have more knowledge and experience than younger children, enabling them to think differently about cognitive or social issues. Thus, from a quantitative viewpoint, it is not a distinct new stage that directs thinking for children of different ages, but simply the accumulation of more information, experience, and knowledge in more structured and complex ways by older children, separating them from younger children. For quantitative theorists, this change is often gradual and occurs in small increments (Miller 1993, 21).

Nature versus Nurture. Finally, the nature versus nurture argument is definitely the oldest argument in psychology, having its foundations in ancient philosophical arguments regarding the relative importance of heredity and environment. Nature refers to natural abilities, genetics, heredity, and biology, whereas nurture refers to experience, learning, environment, and culture. Proponents of one side have historically undervalued the arguments favoring the opposing view.

With increasing understanding of biology and genetics as well as culture, this argument has recently changed from an either/or argument to a "how much of which" argument that still rages today. Thus, virtually all current thinking in the field of child development acknowledges interactions between nature and nurture, resulting in specific child behavior. The relatively new field of behavioral genetics (BG) has evolved to provide answers to this question. In BG, both the genetic and environmental factors, as well as their interactions, are examined through careful methodological processes. Conclusions are then drawn regarding the relative contributions of nature and nurture for psychological traits and behavior.

Biological Views of Child Development. Biological views generally emphasize nature, a passive child, and qualitative or quantitative development. In addition, they usually focus on physical development or even cognitive development while largely ignoring socioemotional development.

Arnold Gesell. One of Hall's students, Arnold Gesell, became another pioneer in the field of child development. Gesell began studying children early in the twentieth century and like Hall, subscribed to a maturational (biological) view of children's development. Because he felt that mental development was continuous with and driven by the same processes that produced physical development, he argued that understanding the patterns of physical development is necessary in order to understand the patterns of mental development (Thelen and Adolph 1992, 369). To that end, he spent much of his professional career cataloging infant and child behavior. The result of this

work was his comprehensive description of child developmental norms, including linguistic, social, sensory, and perceptual abilities. Gesell distributed these norms to clinicians for the purposes of diagnosing abnormal deviations in development. For Gesell, the process of development (physical or mental) was driven by the unfolding of genetic structures, so what mattered most in development was the maturation of these biological processes. Thus, developmental norms could be used to assess children's development in order to guide the environment to provide for optimal growth by gearing the environment toward the growth potential of each child. In addition to his contributions to descriptions and explanations of child behavior, Gesell pioneered many methods of studying children that are still used today. He used both cross-sectional (many different groups at one time point) and longitudinal (one group followed over many time points) designs, as well as intake interviews, behavioral observations, the use of photography, and true experiments.

Myrtle McGraw. Publishing heavily during the first part of the twentieth century, Myrtle McGraw also emphasized neurological growth relative to child development. Unlike Gesell, however, McGraw was interested not in establishing developmental norms but in establishing the developmental sequence through which children passed when developing a new skill. She was also very interested in the extent to which early training would modify or influence later development of a skill (Bergenn, Dalton, and Lipsitt 1992, 382). The other basic difference between McGraw and Gesell concerns their assumptions regarding the role of neural development. Gesell felt that neural development allowed for subsequent motor and mental development, whereas McGraw felt that neural development proceeded alongside motor and mental development. That is, neural development allows for new and different patterns of activity, which in turn influence future neural development.

McGraw is also well known for her work on "critical periods" or windows of opportunity for learning new skills. Although her work is often interpreted to indicate that biological maturation is more important than training, her actual conclusions were much more complex. In line with her findings regarding neural development described above, McGraw's research supported the notion that when neurological development indicated readiness, experience would enhance further neural development in line with the environment, optimizing developmental processes (Bergenn, Dalton, and Lipsitt 1992, 385).

Psychoanalytic Views of Child Development. Psychoanalytic views generally emphasize nature, an active child, and qualitative development. In addition, they usually focus on socioemotional development and exclude physical or cognitive development.

Sigmund Freud. A discussion of Sigmund Freud's controversial theory of psychosexual development in children can be found in every textbook of child development. It is important to note, however, that large-scale studies attempting to establish relationships between children's personality and parental child-rearing practices based on Freudian theory have not been successful (Maccoby 1992, 1008). Nevertheless, popular interest in Freud's ideas continues to be prevalent

and certainly informs the arts, literature, and in some ways even current developmental theories. For example, his emphasis on the importance of early experience continues to be debated today and is currently represented in various forms of developmental theory.

One of Freud's most important ideas was that of the human as pleasure seeker. He felt that children constantly sought gratification through sexually related urges that manifested themselves in varying parts of the body over time. According to Freud's psychosexual view, children go through five consecutive stages of development, each focusing on conflicts between the child's inborn biological desires and the regulations imposed by society. Each stage is characterized by the child's seeking gratification through a different part of the body. If the child is inhibited in his or her gratification, or if the child is allowed to obtain too much gratification, then the child may become "fixated." A fixation means that the child's adult personality will be marked in somewhat predictable ways by his or her experience in that stage.

Erik Erikson. A former student of Freud, Erik Erikson's psychosocial view of human development has been much more widely accepted than Freud's psychosexual view. Like Freud, Erikson believed that development occurred in distinct, ordered stages, each resulting in the resolution of a crisis. Unlike Freud, however, Erikson's stages are centered not around sexual urges and desires but around major personality issues. Importantly, Erikson's theory is a life-span theory, in which five of his eight stages occur from birth until young adulthood, and the remaining three stages occur from adulthood until death. As the human struggles with the crisis of each stage, his or her personality and virtue are shaped by the success of the outcome.

Erikson's first five stages, those that concern child development, are the following: (1) Trust versus mistrust, ages birth to eighteen months, centers around the infant's developing hope that the world is a good place and that his or her needs will be met. (2) Autonomy versus shame and doubt, ages eighteen months to three years, is the stage in which the child develops his or her will, after balancing independence with insecurity. (3) Children from three to six years are in Erikson's third stage, initiative versus guilt. Children develop purpose as they experience new things if they are not overburdened by guilt. (4) Stage four is industry versus inferiority, in which children from about six years until puberty learn and practice the skills and tools of the culture. (5) In stage five, adolescents face the crisis of identity versus identity confusion and must discover a sense of self without becoming confused about their multiple and changing roles in society.

Learning Views. Learning views generally emphasize nurture, a passive child, and quantitative change. In addition, they generally focus on the development of patterns of behavior, which are more closely associated with socioemotional development than with physical or cognitive development.

Behaviorism. The name *behaviorism* stems from its emphasis on objectively observable behavior, rather than on invisible (internal) mental processes, as a topic of study. It has also been called "stimulus-response psychology" since it focused on understanding the relationship between environmental stimuli and the behavioral responses they produce. One particularly important area of behaviorism was a type of learning called operant conditioning. This type of learning is usually defined as behavior that is shaped by its consequences. That is, getting reinforced for something makes it more likely that the behavior will recur, whereas a punishment lessens the chance that it will recur. Psychologist B. F. Skinner is best known for his work on understanding conditioning in terms of reinforcements or punishments. Reinforcement always makes it more likely that the behavior will be repeated; but how it does so depends on which type of reinforcement it is. Positive reinforcement is giving a reward for the behavior, making it more likely to occur again. Negative reinforcement is removing something aversive (still, a type of "reward") for the behavior, again making the response more likely to be repeated. Punishment, on the other hand, always reduces the likelihood that the behavior will occur. The application of something aversive and the removal of something pleasant are both types of punishments.

This type of learning has been used by Skinner and others to try to understand child development. The principles of behaviorism can explain some aspects of children's behavior quite well. As a general theory of child development, however, behaviorism fails to explain fundamentally important phenomena such as the emergence of new skills, new ways of thinking, and other cognitive activities such as the development of language.

Social Learning. Social learning theories posit that children learn by observing models and imitating their behavior. A model is anyone that the child is

Third graders working together with flash cards. (Elizabeth Crews)

observing, and the model may or may not be aware of this observation. Psychologist Albert Bandura is the most well-known social learning theorist, and his studies of the importance of modeling are groundbreaking. One of his most famous studies (Bandura, Ross, and Ross 1963) demonstrated that children watching aggressive models on film subsequently acted more aggressively. The question of how viewing aggression on television or film affects children's aggressive behavior has been a point of concern since that time. Recently, in the summer of 2000, four important groups interested in matters concerning public health issued a joint statement finally concluding through hundreds of research studies what Bandura had suspected forty years previously—that "viewing entertainment violence can lead to increases in aggressive attitudes, values and behaviors, particularly in children" (American Academy of Pediatrics 2001). The four groups who issued the statement are the American Psychological Association, the American Medical Association, the American Academy of Pediatrics, and the American Academy of Child and Adolescent Psychiatry. The American Academy of Family Physicians and the American Psychiatric Association also signed the statement. Despite such a united front presented by groups with normally very different points of focus, virtually no changes have occurred in the entertainment industry to protect children from viewing violent and aggressive programming.

In addition to aggressive behavior, social learning theory explains how children can learn proactive behaviors, problem-solving skills, interpersonal skills, emotions, and gender-appropriate behaviors. Even cognitive skills such as reading can be modeled, making it more likely that the child will spend time reading.

Cognitive Views. Cognitive views generally emphasize nature and nurture, an active child, and quantitative or qualitative development. In addition, they usually focus on cognitive development to the exclusion of physical or socioemotional development.

Jean Piaget. Jean Piaget is perhaps the best-known researcher in child development. Understanding children's thinking, thought Piaget, was the key to understanding children's behavior in any context. This was possible, he felt, because the child's thinking reflected the way in which the child understood the world and his or her surrounding environment. Piaget's theory is a theory of the "whole" child. In other words, according to Piaget, there are certain key principles that guide development, and patterns can be discovered in each stage of children's development that demonstrate those principles. Some of his most important principles of development include schemes, assimilation, accommodation, and equilibrium. Development produces increasingly complex knowledge structures. Part of these knowledge structures are referred to as schemes—mental representations used to make sense of the world. Another way of describing schemes is as organized patterns of behavior that the child uses in order to explore, perceive, and understand the world. For example, newborns will suck on new objects because they apply a "sucking scheme" to understand the new object. This is also an example of assimilation—understanding the world through an already-existing scheme. For example, recognizing that a German shepherd is a dog indicates that the animal fits the "dog scheme." If a pony is mistakenly called a dog (also assimilation), however, the child must change the "dog scheme" to add a "pony scheme" to incorporate the new information, a process referred to as accommodation. Thus, through assimilation and accommodation an interactive balancing act develops that expands the child's knowledge structures. A stable balance between these two activities is referred to as equilibrium and is the point at which children can learn new information. Through these and other principles of development, Piaget proposed a series of four stages through which children moved as they had more experience with the world and developed a more complex system of knowledge (Piaget 1959, 194). Eventually, these processes in development culminate in the ability to think logically, to think abstractly, to deal with hypothetical situations, and to use a systematic approach to problem solving.

Information Processing. The information-processing approach is often referred to as the "cognitive" approach. Unlike Piaget's theory of the "whole child," the information-processing approach parses out the developing aspects of children and investigates them individually. For example, language development is usually studied separately from memory development, which is usually studied separately from the development of perception, problem solving, decision making, and so on. The cognitive view acknowledges that developing systems can interact and influence each other, but research methods favored by this approach demand this type of reductionism. Additionally, most cognitive models of development do not theorize the existence of stages but instead focus more on the continuity of development, represented by quantitative change. Perceptual and memory development are core to cognitive developmental views because other cognitive abilities (such as language, problem solving, and so on) can often be understood in reference to the perceptual and memory models.

Information-processing models of child development often take the analogy of the computer, since the child's developing cognitive processes resemble those of a computer in some ways. For example, computers take in information, process it, change it or translate it in order to be understood, store it, retrieve information, and sometimes even "lose" information. Children also do all these things. By understanding the steps that are involved in processing information and how those steps change with development, cognitive researchers attempt to understand children's thinking and intelligence (Kail 1990, 4–5).

Contextual Views. Contextual views generally emphasize nurture, an active child, and quantitative development. In addition, they focus on socioemotional development and cognitive development, but not physical development.

The best single example of this is the theory of Lev Vygotsky, a Russian psychologist in the 1930s whose work did not become known in the United States until the 1960s and 1970s. He was a contemporary of Piaget, however, with whose work he was very familiar. Like Piaget, Vygotsky was interested in general principles of children's development, and he also felt that the reason why a child gave a certain response was more important than the response itself. Unlike Piaget, who held a very individualistic view of children in their development, Vygotsky held a very social view. In fact, Vygotsky felt that the child and his or her development could only be studied in the context of those around the child, especially adults. He emphasized the importance of context because the same developmental process could lead to different outcomes, depending on the surrounding environment and its impact.

The term *zone of proximal development* (ZPD) is the term most closely associated with Vygotsky and his ideas. By this he meant that there is a theoretical zone around each child's current level of development wherein optimal learning can occur (Rieber and Carton 1987, 209). It appears just before the child can accomplish some task on his or her own and includes the time frame in which the child can successfully negotiate the task with some adult guidance. The adult guidance that is given during the ZPD is termed "scaffolding." Thus, as children's skills and abilities develop, the adult provides less and less scaffolding, until the child can handle the task independently.

One other aspect of development that was critical for Vygotsky had to do with the role of conflicts and their resolutions. As children develop, their established ways of dealing with the world no longer work, so they must devise new methods. It is important for children to resolve these conflicts according to their physical and psychological knowledge so that their understanding of the world extends their mental development.

Future of Child Development
Today is the most exciting time to be in the field of child development, as new research continually produces a better understanding of children and their development. Work continues in the tradition of each of the views described above and shows every sign of pushing the envelope of our knowledge as far as possible in the coming decades.

—*Elaine S. Barry*

See also Discipline and Punishment; Freud, Sigmund; Hall, G. Stanley; Spock, Dr. Benjamin; Twins

References and Further Reading
American Academy of Pediatrics. "Policy Statement: Children, Adolescents, and Television." www.aap.org/policy/re0043.html (cited 29 October 2001).
Baldwin, James M. 1895. *Mental Development in the Child and the Race: Methods and Processes.* New York: Macmillan.
Bandura, Albert, Dorothea Ross, and Sheila A. Ross. 1963. "Vicarious Reinforcement and Imitative Learning." *Journal of Abnormal and Social Psychology* 67: 601–607.
Bergenn, Victor W., Thomas C. Dalton, and Lewis P. Lipsitt. 1992. "Myrtle B. McGraw: A Growth Scientist." *Developmental Psychology* 28: 381–395.
Cairns, Robert B. 1992. "The Making of a Developmental Science: The Contributions and Intellectual Heritage of James Mark Baldwin." *Developmental Psychology* 28: 17–24.
Hall, G. Stanley. 1904. *Adolescence: Its Psychology and Its Relations to Physiology, Anthropology, Sociology, Sex, Crime, Religion, and Education.* 2 vols. New York: Appleton-Century-Crofts.
Kail, Robert. 1990. *The Development of Memory in Children.* New York: W. H. Freeman and Company.
Maccoby, Eleanor E. 1992. "The Role of Parents in the Socialization of Children: An Historical Review." *Developmental Psychology* 28: 1006–1017.
Miller, Patricia H. 1993. *Theories of Developmental Psychology.* New York: W. H. Freeman and Company.
Papalia, Diane E., Sally W. Olds, and Ruth D. Feldman. 1999. *A Child's World: Infancy through Adolescence.* St. Louis: McGraw Hill.
Piaget, Jean. 1959. *Judgment and Reasoning in the Child.* Totowa, NJ: Littlefield, Adams and Company.
Rieber, Robert W., and Aaron S. Carton. 1987. *The Collected Works of L. S. Vygotsky.* Vol. 1: *Problems of General Psychology.* New York: Plenum Press.
Santrock, John J. 1999. *Adolescence: An Introduction.* Dubuque, IA: Brown and Benchmark.
Thelen, Esther, and Karen E. Adolph. 1992. "Arnold Gesell: The Paradox of Nature and Nurture." *Developmental Psychology* 28: 368–380.
White, Sheldon H. 1992. "G. Stanley Hall: From Philosophy to Developmental Psychology." *Developmental Psychology* 28: 25–34.

Child Health Improvement and Protection Act of 1968

Proposed by Pres. Lyndon B. Johnson both in 1968 and in 1969, the Child Health Improvement and Protection Act would have provided access to health services for low-income mothers from prenatal care through a child's first year. As part of Johnson's War on Poverty, the proposal aimed to lower the nation's birth defect and mortality rate by improving medical care to pregnant women who fell below the poverty line. Although his proposal failed, it was representative of social service legislation introduced and passed throughout the 1960s, which strove to eliminate poverty from the United States and establish what President Johnson called the Great Society. A number of new health and social welfare programs under his administration did improve the quality of health care for low-income pregnant women. According to Irwin Unger, in 1963 only 53 percent of low-income women saw doctors for prenatal care. Following the implementation of War on Poverty programs, in 1970, that figure increased to 71 percent (Unger 1996, 362).

Through Johnson's War on Poverty, he sought to provide all families with access to basic resources such as food, education, and medical care. Although the Child Health Improvement and Protection Act did not pass under his administration, similar legislation passed both during his administration and immediately following it. The Child Health Act of 1967 provided limited grants for projects related to maternity and infant care, and in 1969, under the Social Security Act, Congress allotted funds for states to aid pregnant women and infants. Under the Social Security Act, however, funding was only available to states on a matching basis. With Johnson's departure from office and a downturn in the nation's economy, some of his social programs were cut back. Many of the War on Poverty's programs to aid low-income families, such as Head Start, however, have continued into the twenty-first century.

—Linda Heidenreich

Sources and Further Reading
Bremner, Robert H. 1974. *Children and Youth in America: A Documentary History*. Vol. 3: *1933–1973*. Cambridge: Harvard University Press.
Cuciti, Peggy L., and Marshall Kaplan, eds. 1986. *The Great Society and Its Legacy: Twenty Years of U.S. Social Policy*. Durham, NC: Duke University Press.
National Archives and Records Administration. "Lyndon Baines Johnson Library and Museum." http://www.lbjib.utexas.edu (cited 14 August 2001).
Unger, Irwin. 1996. *The Best of Intentions: The Triumphs and Failures of the Great Society under Kennedy, Johnson, and Nixon*. New York: Doubleday.

Child Labor

Child labor has generally signified work considered excessive or otherwise harmful to youthful workers. Twentieth-century reformers sought to include more kinds of work within this definition and to raise the age for classifying young people as children. Even by the 1990s, however, no single definition prevailed in U.S. law, belief, or practice. Traditionally considered a legitimate contribution to the family economy, by the mid-nineteenth century child labor conflicted with the emerging middle-class ideal of a sheltered childhood. By the early 1900s a reform movement directed mainly against manufacturing and other nonfarm paid labor by children under age fourteen began to win modest successes in state legislation. But it failed to secure enduring federal regulation of child labor until the 1938 Fair Labor Standards Act (FLSA), itself a limited measure. Meanwhile child labor to earn money for the family declined for reasons more economic and cultural than legal. Part-time work by high school students financing their own spending mushroomed around the 1950s, and policymakers' concern began to shift toward finding jobs for minority youths. Oppressive child labor continued, however, among migrant farmworkers and elsewhere. Reformers of the 1990s sought stronger regulation, but U.S. policy remained more accepting of child labor than prevailing opinion in international agencies and other developed countries.

Traditionally households produced most of what people consumed, and children contributed. In the eighteenth and early nineteenth centuries, when almost all Americans worked on farms and plantations, children started young. Daniel Drake, a Kentucky boy of the 1790s, "was about six when he began fetching the cow from the woods, grinding corn until his knuckles bled, and riding and guiding the horse while his father plowed" (Reinier 1996, 127). Since rural school terms were short and attendance irregular, the spread of public schooling across the North by the 1850s only marginally reduced farm children's workloads. From ages seven to twelve, boys and girls did similar chores. Then boys specialized in field labor while girls toiled around the house and barn, garden and chicken coop. During labor crises, all might work in the fields. Historians have debated just how early slave children began heavy work. The former slave who recalled chores "soon's us could toddle" may have overstated, but "slave children customarily started to work year-round between the ages of six and ten" (King 1995, 23; Clement 1997, 126). "Many [perhaps most]" did "work that was coerced, drudging, and constant long before puberty," possibly on short rations (Alston 1992, 227). Because their owners invested little in them, slave children brought their masters wealth. For free parents the costs of rearing children and giving them a start in life typically outweighed the value of their work or wages (Craig 1993, 90–92; Macleod 1998, 12). But children's labor much reduced their cost, making large nineteenth-century families relatively affordable.

Alexander Hamilton's 1791 "Report on Manufactures" proposed that children would be "rendered . . . more early useful, by manufacturing establishments" (Goldin and Sokoloff 1982, 767). In 1820 children up to age seventeen comprised 23 percent of workers in northeastern manufacturing (748–749). By mechanizing or at least subdividing and routinizing tasks, manufacturers could replace highly paid craftsmen with unskilled children. Whether nineteenth-century children's families benefited is uncertain, since industries such as textiles that employed extensive child labor commonly offset children's earnings with low adult wages (Parsons and Goldin 1989, 655).

Although most Americans continued to believe that children should make themselves useful, among parents of the urban middle class a rival view of child labor as exploitive took hold in the nineteenth century. These parents advocated a sheltered childhood, centered on schooling and play and devoted to the child's personal development. By the 1850s most kept sons and daughters at home and often in school well into their teens. Advocates of child labor restriction would argue by 1900 that "if children were useful and produced money, they were not being properly loved" (Zelizer 1985, 72).

Such ideals bypassed the countryside. Yet in 1900 half of all American children lived on farms; in 1920, 36 percent still did (Macleod 1998, 101). Children of the impoverished South labored especially hard. "In lowland North Carolina in the 1910s, two-thirds of white and three-quarters of black farm children ages five to fifteen did field work in addition to chores. . . . No child was exempt; a mother explained that 'when she puts one at it, [she] puts them all at it'" (70). A midwestern girl also recorded extensive duties: "filling the woodbox, sweeping the steps, watering the calves, bringing home the livestock, chopping the kindling, shelling corn for the chickens, pulling vegetables for the pigs, filling the fuel basket with chips, picking up and sorting fruit, . . . collecting the eggs, . . . weeding the cornrows" (Babener 1992, 313). These were merely chores—never counted as child labor—and yet failure to complete them with a "cheerful spirit" brought punishment (314). Interviews with former farm children reveal satisfaction at having done one's duty but less often pride in building skills: "As we got older, each time the shovel got a little bigger, and the pitchfork got a little bigger, because we lived on the farm" (Macleod 1998, 104). Judged by its potential effects on children's development and by the level of coercion, this was child labor. And children's farmwork was more than tedious; it overstrained and endangered them. Small boys handled skittish horses and plowed with the handles above their ears. Girls toiled at laundry and made soap using corrosive lye. A day could well include "fourteen hours or so of hard work" (West 1996, 34–35). A typical rural twelve-year-old of 1900 spent at least twice as many hours a year on farmwork as at school (Macleod 1998, 106). Yet idealization of children's farmwork as something between outdoor play and healthful character building (plus the political power of farmers) shielded it from regulation or even criticism.

Many factors spurred reformers' concern about child labor in the years around 1900. The first U.S. census to tabulate working children reported 765,000 ages ten through fifteen in 1870; the 1900 total grew by almost a million (Macleod 1998, 110). Employment of children surged in southern textile mills, from 9,000 in 1890 to 25,000 in 1900, almost half under age twelve (107). Age-graded urban schools competed for children's time and fostered the belief that those under fourteen (the age for completing eight grades) should attend full-time. Meanwhile, journalists such as Jacob Riis heightened middle-class alarm about mass immigration and urban poverty.

The reformers' concern was highly selective, as unpaid labor for parents went uncounted and reformers long ignored agriculture. Leading objects of sympathy were workers in the South's whites-only textile mills who stood for long hours in humid, lint-filled air, the girls checking for broken threads and the boys replacing empty bobbins. Meanwhile black children toiled unnoticed in cotton fields and white families' kitchens. By 1910 or so, the dangers of mining inspired relatively effective state bans on underground work by children, but aboveground "breaker boys" were hunched over, black with dust, picking unwanted slate from rivers of coal. Northern industries furnished grim accounts of boys toiling all night in the inferno of Pennsylvania's glass factories and girl painters in unventilated lofts inhaling varnish and naphtha. Heavy equipment maimed, crushed, or electrocuted fatigued and heedless children. The dangers to store clerks were less apparent, but reformers charged that long hours and low pay left young workers exhausted, undernourished, and prey to sexual harassment and that elevators contributed their share of grisly accidents. Working at home at low piece rates, unknown numbers of children supplemented their families' incomes by rolling cigars, stitching clothes, and stringing, pasting, or packaging small items. Although usually safe and less likely than factory work to preclude schooling, paid home work inspired reformers to heated denunciations of money-hungry mothers and shiftless fathers. Children who scavenged and traded on city streets also vexed reformers, who disliked such freedom and access to cash. Investigators depicted newsboys, most only eleven to fourteen years old, "pitching pennies, trading dirty stories, . . . and stuffing themselves with 'trash'" (Nasaw 1985, 70). Still, by the early 1900s most lived at home, sold only before or after school, and contributed much of their earnings to family expenses.

Far more at risk were rural child laborers. Initially, however, only the plight of migrant families working in the quasi-industrial setting of fruit, vegetable, and seafood canneries drew sustained attention. Children began as helpers (off the payroll and thus unrecorded) as young as seven or eight. By the 1910s, the new sugar beet industry hired entire migrant families for seasons lasting into November. "In Colorado in 1920, three-fifths of eight-year-olds in families under contract and almost all those over age 10 worked at least the seasonal peaks, averaging 9 to 13 hours daily" (Macleod 1998, 106). Children topped the beets with sharp knives, then wrenched them from the ground, handling twelve to fifteen tons a day (Trattner 1970, 151). Increasing numbers of studies in the later 1910s and the 1920s exposed the labor and lost schooling of farm children. But concern still centered on paid work, and the famed reform photographer Lewis Hine pictured only white cotton pickers. The chair of the National Child Labor Committee (NCLC) declared in 1938 that "no person in his right senses" would consider work on a family farm "child labor" (West 1996, 121).

Child labor outside agriculture had no icon to match the family farm, but it drew support from reverence for industrious-

ness and family duty and from simple need. The political power of newspaper publishers, the myth of newsboys as budding businessmen, and the street traders' own evasive skills all prevented effective regulation. Textile mill operators and the National Association of Manufacturers strongly defended child labor. Although many working children attributed their employment to poverty and family misfortune, many also claimed a sense of accomplishment missing at school: "You never understands what they tells you in school, and you can learn right off to do things in a factory," explained a Chicago boy (Macleod 1996, 111). Like farmers, many other parents—especially recent immigrants—saw children's work as a debt owed by dutiful offspring. And yet some workingmen's groups asserted as early as the 1880s that children should not work younger than fourteen or fifteen. Parental defensiveness was inevitable as long as reformers, hemmed in by minuscule governmental spending on social needs, proposed to ban child labor without furnishing any substitute income. Advocates of prohibitory legislation dealt "more with symptoms than with causes," argued Elliott West. "The basic problem was grinding poverty and the low pay of adult breadwinners" (West 1996, 71).

Nascent concern spurred state legislation, but its limitations reflected continuing disagreement concerning child labor. By 1889 Colorado and New York had banned manufacturing employment under age fourteen (Bremner et al. 1971, 667). Twenty-eight states had passed child labor laws by 1900, but these typically regulated only manufacturing and mining, usually set minimum ages only at ten or twelve and maximum hours at ten or more, often permitted exemptions for claims of family need, and almost never funded effective enforcement (Trattner 1970, 41).

The movement for legislation gained momentum with formation of the National Child Labor Committee in 1904. The NCLC initially sought state laws directed against mines, mills, and factory-like canneries. Thirty-five states had reached or closely approached NCLC standards by 1914: a minimum age of fourteen for manufacturing employment and sixteen for mining, an eight-hour day and no night work for those fourteen and fifteen, and documentary proof of age to curb cheating (Bremner et al. 1971, 603). But southern states resisted; elsewhere enforcement was spotty and evasion common.

Turning to Congress, the NCLC secured the Keating-Owen Act of 1916, which imposed a thirty-day delay on interstate shipment of products from factories that hired children under age fourteen or worked fourteen- or fifteen-year-olds after seven P.M. or longer than eight hours six days a week. The federal Children's Bureau briefly enforced the act, but southern manufacturers sponsored a father's suit charging that his boys would lose their occupation and he would lose their income. In *Hammer* v. *Dagenhart* (1918), the U.S. Supreme Court quashed the Keating-Owen Act as an unconstitutional extension of congressional power to regulate interstate commerce. A 1919 congressional attempt to achieve the same ends by taxing products of child labor met Supreme Court rejection in *Bailey* v. *Drexel* (1922).

Congress responded in 1924 by passing a proposed constitutional amendment giving itself "power to limit, regulate, and prohibit the labor of persons under eighteen years of age" (Trattner 1970, 168). Although supporters insisted that Con-

gress would not ban child labor wholesale, organized manufacturers, farmers, and most Roman Catholics opposed the amendment as dangerously broad, socialistic, harmful to agriculture, and inimical to parents' rights. Massachusetts voters defeated the amendment nearly three to one in a referendum; elsewhere most state legislatures rejected it (176–178); and the amendment never approached ratification by the necessary thirty-six states.

Despite legislative setbacks, the percentage of American children performing serious labor probably declined from 1870 onward. The extent, timing, and causes of the decline remain uncertain, however. The Census Bureau's reporting on child labor has been fragmentary and unreliable. Published figures on "children 10 to 15 years old" (that is, between their tenth and sixteenth birthdays) "engaged in all occupations" showed a gradual rise to a plateau around 1900. The 1870 census reported 764,965 (13.2 percent of all children ten through fifteen). The total rose to 1,118,356 (16.8 percent) in 1880, 1,503,771 (18.1 percent) in 1890, and 1,750,178 (18.2 percent) in 1900. The 1910 census initially reported an increase to 1,990,225 (18.4 percent); but the Census Bureau subsequently reestimated this downward, indicating a decline to 1,621,726 (15.0 percent). Then the 1920 census reported a startling drop to 1,060,858 working children (8.5 percent), but this time the bureau reestimated upward to 1,416,684 (11.3 percent), slowing the apparent decline. The 1930 census recorded another sharp drop to 667,118 or 4.7 percent (Edwards 1943, 97). The 1940 census failed to collect data on children working under age fourteen, preventing comparison with earlier information (Bremner 1974, 359). From 1940 onward, the Census Bureau conducted a monthly

Current Population Survey for the Bureau of Labor Statistics (BLS) but continued to enumerate only workers fourteen and older and in 1967 switched to reporting only those sixteen and older (U.S. Bureau of the Census 1975, 121–122). Frustrated investigators in 1998 reported "little information" about workers under age fifteen and urged that the BLS and the decennial census collect data (National Research Council 1998, 7). During the second half of the twentieth century, child labor opponents made do with ad hoc estimates of the numbers of children working at early ages. In 2001 web sites offering detailed statistics on children typically ignored child labor.

Even when the Census Bureau reported the employment of children from age ten upward, the results were marred by pervasive undercounting. The 1880 census should have showed 22.5 percent of children ten to fifteen gainfully employed, instead of 16.8 percent (Carter and Sutch 1996, 7). The census particularly underreported children's work in farm households. Enumeration ignored children under age ten and all who attended school, even though most spent far more time at farmwork.

Setting the 1900 and 1910 census dates for April, when intensive work was just beginning in the cotton South and well before the summer peak in the North, guaranteed that enumerators would fail to count many children about to embark on months of hard work. Instructions not to count "children working for their parents at chores, errands, or general housework" invited enumerators to dismiss girls' efforts as "housework" and boys' as "chores" (Macleod 1998, 110). For 1920 the bureau moved the date to 1 January, the nadir of farmwork (110). Elliott West found similar failings in the 1930 census,

concluding that "the percentage of American youngsters engaged in 'child labor' . . . was . . . perhaps even double or triple the five percent reported" (West 1996, 126). Hard, sustained work by children was much more widespread than the census recognized, although such labor gradually decreased as it grew less common in cities and as the number of farm children declined.

Historians seeking to explain reductions in child labor have offered a multitude of interrelated explanations. These include technological changes that reduced demand for young workers; restrictive legislation; rising incomes that made child labor less vital to the family economy; demand for more educated workers that fostered extended schooling; falling birthrates that made prolonged dependency in childhood more affordable; and changing values within families, ethnic subcultures, and the shared national culture.

Of these possibilities, technological changes furnish the best stories: In the early 1900s cash registers and pneumatic tubes displaced the boys and girls who formerly ran around department stores with customers' change and packages. Telephones displaced messenger boys. Machine-made cigarettes replaced the cheap hand-rolled cigars formerly produced by children. Once canneries invested in expensive equipment, child labor became uneconomical: "A child occupies . . . as much space as a woman and accomplishes much less per hour" (Brown et al. 1992, 752). Similarly, mechanical cotton pickers and herbicides drove young African American workers from the South's cotton fields in the 1950s. But no single-industry explanation accounts for all child labor. And new technologies and forms of business could also spawn new jobs: The telephone led grocers to hire boys to deliver phoned-in orders and the later spread of supermarkets after World War II furnished employment to young people stocking shelves and ringing up purchases.

Other explanations, though plausible, are hard to prove. Economists have found that passage of state child labor laws had no statistically significant effect on the numbers of children working (Moehling 1999, 72–95). But enforcement varied widely and was typically weak—adequately enforced laws might have worked. Furthermore, states were most likely to pass strong laws when child labor was already declining. A study of child workers in Pennsylvania silk mills between 1899 and 1919 found no impact of rising incomes (Holleran 1996, 86), but such a narrow test cannot refute the plausible assumption that long-term growth in incomes nationwide reduced pressures on parents to send children out to earn money. Impressionistic evidence suggests that steadily falling birthrates between 1800 and the 1930s permitted parents in each successive generation to invest more in each child's education (Macleod 1998, 12–13). A parallel cultural argument holds that a shift in values rejected the propriety of expecting children to be economically useful, treasuring them instead as emotionally precious and thus "priceless" (Zelizer 1985, 56–72). On the other hand, belief persisted that work on a family farm benefited children and that newspaper carriers were learning responsibility and enterprise.

No single explanation of decline or persistence will serve. Rising incomes and smaller families made sheltered childhoods feasible, even as the ideal of childhoods devoted to play and schooling probably combined with child labor laws

and technologically induced job losses to inspire couples to limit their fertility. Conversely, newspaper publishers who had no technological substitute for child carriers used the newsboy myth to secure legal exemptions that permitted delivery to continue.

Despite Depression-era pressures to reserve employment for men, many children of the 1930s contributed to their families' subsistence. Support for federal legislation against child labor revived, and in 1938 Congress passed the Fair Labor Standards Act, which both instituted the first federal minimum wage and became the basis of federal child labor law for the rest of the century. It imposed a thirty-day delay on interstate shipment of goods produced by children under age sixteen in manufacturing and eighteen in dangerous occupations such as mining. Outside of manufacturing, fourteen- and fifteen-year-olds employed in nonfarm jobs could work no more than three hours per day and eighteen per week during the school year and eight hours a day, forty a week at other times. In 1941 the Supreme Court unanimously upheld the law. Initially, however, it affected fewer than 6 percent of all working children (Trattner 1970, 204–207).

Amendments in 1949 changed the thirty-day delay to direct prohibition, greatly expanded the range of businesses covered by federal law, and somewhat strengthened regulation of agricultural child labor. The amendments also exempted newspaper delivery from minimum wage and child labor laws (Bremner 1974, 347–348). Hence a 1970 study found that carriers in Salt Lake City earned about half the federal minimum wage (Whisnant 1972, 299). In 1998 FLSA age and hours limits for nonfarm workers remained as in 1938, including permis-

An African American boy shines a man's shoes on the sidewalk in New York City, c. 1955. (Hulton/Archive)

sion for those aged sixteen or seventeen to "perform any nonhazardous job for unlimited hours" (National Research Council 1998, 166).

Agricultural interests had preserved even more permissive laws for farming. Children working on their parents' farms were entirely exempt from limits on age, hours, or hazardous activities. Those six-teen and older could "perform any job, hazardous or not, for unlimited hours." Children of fourteen and fifteen could work any hours at any nonhazardous job except when local schools were in ses-sion; those twelve and thirteen could do so with parental permission or on the same farm as their parents (in other words, hire on as a family for migrant labor). Children under age twelve could do so on farms employing fewer than 500 "man days" of labor per quarter—a limit that some employers met by hiring families but listing only heads of households on their payrolls (National Research Council 1998, 158, 152).

State laws and other federal regulations offered little further protection. In 1955 only twenty-five states set sixteen as the minimum age for factory work (Trattner 1970, 223). In 2000, when asked the youngest age at which their state's children could legally perform paid agricultural labor, just eight state labor departments answered age fourteen; thirteen said age twelve; two said ten; one said nine; fifteen reported there was no minimum age; and the rest did not reply (Child Labor Coalition 2001). The Occupational Safety and Health Administration (OSHA) waited until 1987 before promulgating rules requiring toilets and drinking and washing water in the fields. Except regarding radiation, OSHA issued no separate rules for children, most OSHA standards did not apply to agriculture, and Congress banned enforcement of OSHA regulations on farms with fewer than eleven workers (National Research Council 1998, 159, 173–174).

Some of the lack of concern reflected important shifts in the nature of child labor. World War II drew children into service industries and gave their work legitimacy: A twelve-year-old who set bowling pins until midnight was bolstering war workers' morale. Amid wartime prosperity, young workers probably kept more of their earnings for personal use. If so, they foreshadowed a momentous shift: During the 1950s increasing numbers of children fifteen and older began part-time work—not as earlier generations did in industry, street trades, and

agriculture but in service and retail businesses: stocking shelves, pumping gas, cooking, and waiting on diners. Previously much of children's pay had helped "meet their family's needs. Now, however, teenage workers were keeping their earnings almost completely for themselves" (West 1996, 217). By the 1980s, 80 percent of students worked during the school year at some point in their high school career. Ironically, these jobs went disproportionately to the prosperous. Minority and poor teenagers were less likely to find jobs and, if they did, more likely to work in hazardous occupations (National Research Council 1998, 35, 49–50).

As these patterns took shape, writers in the 1950s began to advocate relaxing child labor laws to cure youthful unemployment and juvenile delinquency. Amid 1960s worries about alienated young people and joblessness among inner-city youth, work became a prescription for responsibility and social integration. In 1974 the Panel on Youth of the President's Science Advisory Committee proposed getting youths at work sooner with school-to-work programs and a lower minimum wage for ages fourteen to eighteen (Coleman et al. 1974, 147–168). In 1990, when raising the minimum wage, Congress "created a 'subminimum' wage for teenagers after business groups warned that the higher minimum would devastate industries like restaurants. But . . . only 2 percent of employers used the teen wage. When it expired, no one noticed" (Solomon 1993, 45).

By then teenagers were twice as likely to work as in 1950 (Waldman and Springen 1992, 80). Entire businesses depended on young workers and teenage consumers. In an antiregulatory climate, little support for strengthening child labor laws existed outside the circles of child-welfare activists. Debate in the early 1990s pitted business advocates of teaching the young good work habits against educators who warned that work interfered with schooling and would undercut U.S. competitiveness in a high-tech global economy, an argument that was weakened by the strong economy of the late 1990s. Despite mixed research results, experts concluded that work (nobody called it child labor) up to somewhere between ten and twenty hours per week benefited teenagers but that longer hours fostered low grades, quarrels with parents, and substance abuse (National Research Council 1998, 113–140).

Medically oriented researchers nevertheless expressed renewed concern for children's health and safety. Young workers were injured at higher rates than adults. Between 1992 and 1995 at least seventy workers per year under age eighteen died of work-related causes. Agriculture accounted for about 40 percent; half of those agricultural deaths occurred on family farms (National Research Council 1998, 70–82). Meanwhile longer-term threats to adolescents from chemical exposures and ergonomic stresses remained unstudied.

Blatantly oppressive and dangerous forms of child labor had not disappeared, although the children involved were outnumbered by those from more prosperous households holding part-time retail and service jobs. With governments providing little effective regulation or even gathering statistics and some of the activity illegal, most knowledge of oppressive child labor depended on reporters and private agencies working against hostile employers. In 1970 an American Friends Service Committee task force estimated that one-quarter of farm wageworkers were under age sixteen, about 800,000 children (Taylor 1973, 5). Farmers responded angrily that "work is the greatest thing in the world for children, especially work on the farm . . . six years is none too soon to start work on the farm" (18).

For their part, farm laborers were desperately poor and avoided employers who refused to employ ten-year-olds. Pesticide poisoning was common from wind drift and work on sprayed crops (39). Deaths of child farmworkers were only occasional—128 confirmed cases over a span of sixteen years in California—but in 1969, blood tests of farmworker children found that almost half in a small sample had pesticide residues (43).

A Human Rights Watch investigation centered on Arizona and published in 2000 found similar problems. An average annual income of less than $7,500 for adult farmworkers in 1999 pressured children to work. Despite enhanced concern about pesticides since 1970, Environmental Protection Agency (EPA) standards assumed adult body size, and harmful exposure remained commonplace. Piece rates rewarded speed, but cramped, repetitive motions hurt young bodies. At least one-third of juvenile workers earned below the minimum wage. Workdays began between 4:00 and 7:00 A.M. and commonly lasted through dangerous midday heat (Human Rights Watch 2000, 5, 16–30, 37–47).

In smaller numbers, urban sweatshops—particularly in the garment industry—continued to employ children as young as nine or ten in the 1990s. Like migrant farmworkers, many of whom were Hispanic or Haitian immigrants, underage sweatshop workers were most often children of Chinese or Hispanic immigrants. Much as they had in canneries and textile mills of the early 1900s, children accompanied their mothers for lack of child care, volunteered or were pressured into helping, and soon worked on or off the payroll. Those who attended school could still work six or seven hours afterward (Lii 1995, 16).

Weak enforcement shielded employers. A 1992 *New York Times* article reported that "at least 4 million children ages 14 to 18 are legally employed. But an estimated 2 million other children work illegally, either because businesses or family members pay them in cash to avoid taxes and minimum wages, or, more ominously, because they work too many hours, late hours, at hazardous jobs, or are under 14 and thus too young to be working at all except on farms" (Kolata 1992, 1). That year OSHA had 2,000 inspectors for the entire country, and the Labor Department's Wage and Hour Division had about 1,000 to investigate both illegal child labor and all adult offenses. In contrast, the Fish and Wildlife Service had 12,000 inspectors (18). In 1993 only three states employed fifty or more officers to enforce adult and child labor laws combined (National Research Council 1998, 181). Federal wage and hour inspectors concentrated on population centers and seldom reached the distant fields. In 1990, sweeps directed at child labor found 27,634 illegal workers in 9,542 inspections. More typical enforcement in 1997 discovered 5,270 young people working in violation of child labor laws (180–181). But even these modest numbers dwarfed the total of 104 minors working illegally in agriculture whom wage and hour inspectors identified in 1998—perhaps one in every thousand such illegal child laborers. And farm employers often shifted liability to their labor contractors (Human Rights Watch 2000, 61–65).

In contrast to relatively permissive U.S. policies, governments of other developed countries, nongovernmental organizations, and international agencies have expressed more blanket opposition to child labor. American concerns have centered on jobs for low-income teenagers, health and safety issues, and the impact of work on schooling, whereas internationally "it is the legitimacy of child labor itself that is debated" (National Research Council 1998, 26–27). The 1973 International Labor Organization (ILO) convention on child labor—unratified by the United States—declares as its objective "'the effective abolition of child labour.' . . . The only exceptions envisioned for developed countries are employment in conjunction with vocational education programs and 'light work' that impinges minimally on youngsters' physical, social, and educational development" (26–27). This document and the 1990 United Nations Convention on the Rights of the Child define children as all those under age eighteen (Human Rights Watch 2000, 10). In 1999 the ILO adopted a convention, Elimination of the Worst Forms of Child Labour, that was somewhat closer to American views; it focused on slavery, military conscription, prostitution, drug trafficking, and other "work likely to harm the health, safety or morals of children" (90). Even so, Human Rights Watch charged that U.S. failure to protect young farmworkers would lead the United States "toward noncompliance" (4).

In the 1990s, proposals to bring U.S. regulations closer to international standards merged with calls to eliminate distinctions based on the context in which child labor occurred. Thus a committee sponsored by the National Research Council defined child labor in 1998 as "activities that contribute to the production of a marketable product, good, or service, whether that activity is done for pay or not. This definition of work includes tasks performed in family businesses and on family farms, even when those enterprises are not covered under current U.S. child labor laws" (National Research Council 1998, 20). The committee recommended that Congress authorize the Labor Department to limit hours worked by sixteen- and seventeen-year-olds during the school year, update prohibitions regarding dangerous occupations, eliminate farm nonfarm distinctions governing hours and hazards, prohibit dangerous activities even when children work for a parent, and consider applying OSHA regulation to all farms (11–14). In 2000 Human Rights Watch proposed similar changes, including state and federal bans on most farm employment under age fourteen, broadened safety and health authority for OSHA and the EPA, and much stronger enforcement. Yet even Human Rights Watch flinched at extending the age limit to children working on a parent's farm (Human Rights Watch 2000, 6–9).

—David I. Macleod

See also Adolescence; Apprenticeship; Farm Families

References and Further Reading
Alston, Lester. 1992. "Children as Chattel." In *Small Worlds: Children and Adolescents in America, 1850–1950*, edited by Elliott West and Paula Petrick, 208–231. Lawrence: University Press of Kansas.
Babener, Liahna. 1992. "Bitter Nostalgia: Recollections of Childhood on the Midwestern Frontier." In *Small Worlds: Children and Adolescents in America, 1850–1950*, edited by Elliott West and Paula Petrick, 302–320. Lawrence: University Press of Kansas.
Bremner, Robert H. 1974. *Children and Youth in America: A Documentary History*. Vol. 3: *1933–1973*. Cambridge: Harvard University Press.
Bremner, Robert H., et al. 1971. *Children and Youth in America: A Documentary History*. Vol. 2: *1866–1932*. Cambridge: Harvard University Press.
Brown, Martin, et al. 1992. "The Decline of Child Labor in the U.S. Fruit and Vegetable Canning Industry: Law or Economics?" *Business History Review* 66: 723–770.
Carter, Susan B., and Richard Sutch. 1996. "Fixing the Facts: Editing of the 1880 U.S. Census of Occupations." *Historical Methods* 29(1): 5–24.
Child Labor Coalition. "2000 State Child Labor Survey." http://www. stopchildlabor.org/pressroom/ statesurvres.html (cited 29 April 2001).
Clement, Priscilla Ferguson. 1997. *Growing Pains: Children in the Industrial Age, 1850–1890*. New York: Twayne Publishers.
Coleman, James S., et al. 1974. *Youth: Transition to Adulthood*. Chicago: University of Chicago Press.
Craig, Lee A. 1993. *To Sow One Acre More: Childbearing and Farm Productivity in the Antebellum North*. Baltimore: Johns Hopkins University Press.
Edwards, Alba M. 1943. *Comparative Occupation Statistics for the United States, 1870 to 1940*. Washington, DC: Government Printing Office.
Goldin, Claudia, and Kenneth Sokoloff. 1982. "Women, Children, and Industrialization in the Early Republic." *Journal of Economic History* 42: 741–774.
Holleran, Philip M. 1996. "Explaining the Decline of Child Labor in Pennsylvania Silk Mills, 1899–1919." *Pennsylvania History* 63(1): 78–95.
Human Rights Watch. 2000. *Fingers to the Bone: United States Failure to Protect Child Farmworkers*. New York: Human Rights Watch.
King, Wilma. 1995. *Stolen Childhood: Slave Youth in Nineteenth-Century America*. Bloomington: Indiana University Press.
Kolata, Gina. 1992. "More Children Are Employed, Often Perilously." *New York Times*, 21 June, 1, 18.

Lii, Jane H. 1995. "Week in Sweatshop Reveals Grim Conspiracy of the Poor." *New York Times*, 21 March, 1, 16.

Macleod, David I. 1998. *The Age of the Child: Children in America, 1890–1920.* New York: Twayne Publishers.

Moehling, Carolyn M. 1999. "State Child Labor Laws and the Decline of Child Labor." *Explorations in Economic History* 36: 72–106.

Nasaw, David. 1985. *Children of the City: At Work and at Play.* Garden City, NY: Anchor/Doubleday.

National Research Council. Commission on Behavioral and Social Sciences and Education. Committee on the Health and Safety Implications of Child Labor. 1998. *Protecting Youth at Work: Health, Safety, and Development of Working Children and Adolescents in the United States.* Washington, DC: National Academy Press.

Parsons, Donald G., and Claudia Goldin. 1989. "Parental Altruism and Self-Interest: Child Labor among Late Nineteenth-Century American Families." *Economic Inquiry* 37: 637–659.

Reinier, Jacqueline S. 1996. *From Virtue to Character: American Childhood, 1775–1850.* New York: Twayne Publishers.

Solomon, Jolie. 1993. "Too Soon to Panic." *Newsweek*, 30 August, 44–45.

Taylor, Ronald B. 1973. *Sweatshops in the Sun: Child Labor on the Farm.* Boston: Beacon Press.

Trattner, Walter I. 1970. *Crusade for the Children: A History of the National Child Labor Committee and Child Labor Reform in America.* Chicago: Quadrangle Books.

U.S. Bureau of the Census. 1975. *Historical Statistics of the United States, Colonial Times to 1970.* Washington, DC: Government Printing Office.

Waldman, Steven, and Karen Springen. 1992. "Too Old Too Fast?" *Newsweek*, 16 November, 80–88.

West, Elliott. 1996. *Growing Up in Twentieth-Century America: A History and Reference Guide.* Westport, CT: Greenwood Press.

Whisnant, David E. 1972. "Selling the Gospel News, or: The Strange Career of Jimmy Brown the Newsboy." *Journal of Social History* 5: 269–309.

Zelizer, Viviana A. 1985. *Pricing the Priceless Child: The Changing Social Value of Children.* New York: Basic Books.

Child Welfare Policy

Child welfare policy in the United States has meant the ongoing social and political response to issues surrounding the care, protection, education, physical and mental health, and general well-being of children. Since the colonial era, local, state, and federal policies have been enacted to safeguard the interests of America's children. Child welfare policies have covered a wide range: statutes granting funding and licenses for orphan asylums and reform schools; regulatory policies for foster care and adoption programs; legislation allowing for the prosecution of neglectful or abusive parents; the treatment, rehabilitation, or punishment of juvenile delinquents; the establishment of family and children's courts; funding for education; economic and medical aid for low-income children; federal guidelines and funding for child care; and protective legislation restricting the content of popular media.

In colonial America, family and child welfare policy was defined by a balance between private and public responsibility for children (Wall 1990, 61). Drawing from legislation such as the English Poor Law Act of 1601, which mandated paternal support of children, laws such as the Massachusetts Act of 1642 gave poor-relief officials the power to remove children whose parents could not or would not support them (Sidel 1992, 78; Mason 1994, 10). Colonial officials also sought to control and punish children who engaged in socially disruptive behavior. Stubborn Child laws in Connecticut, Rhode Island,

Shipped to federal boarding schools in the East, far away from their families and tribes, Native American children were forced to shed their cultural dress, language, and religion. Pictured here is classroom instruction in art, United States Indian School, Carlisle, Pennsylvania, c. 1901–1903. (Library of Congress)

and Massachusetts, for example, ordered punishment (including in some cases death sentences for children over sixteen) for children found guilty of disobeying or disrespecting their parents (Mason 1994, 11; Pleck 1987, 25–26).

Both the family and the community were responsible for dependent children. If relatives could not care for them, neglected or orphaned children were bound out through orphan courts to private families, who, in exchange for labor, would be responsible for the child's care (Wall 1990, 92). In 1672 Virginia passed an Act for Suppressing of Vagabonds and Disposing

of Poor Children to Trades, giving courts the power to apprentice poor children; by 1692 every colony had adopted similar legislation (Mason 1994, 10; Wall 1990, 105–106).

Enslaved African American children, as property, were subject by law to the authority of their masters rather than parents and as such could be sold, traded, and whipped or even killed. In 1662 Virginia enacted a statute stating that the free or enslaved status of black children was to be determined by the status of the mother (King 1995, 6). Other policies affecting African American children, even offspring of free blacks, included laws prohibiting marriage and baptism (Mintz and Kellogg 1988, 32–33).

By the time of the American Revolution, child welfare policy began to reflect the growing conviction that, as future citizens of the new republic, children should be instilled from an early age with the rigorous moral training and education necessary for independent citizenship (Mintz and Kellogg 1988, 47). Laws establishing public schools were passed in several states by the 1780s, and by 1785 the young federal government had issued a land ordinance reserving space for public schools in every township (Hawes and Hiner 1985, 620).

The 1830s witnessed a growing faith in the power of the institution as a method of caring for and educating neglected, orphaned, or delinquent children. Child-specific asylums such as orphanages, houses of refuge, juvenile asylums, state schools for the blind, and state reform schools were intended to provide care for children away from the immoral and degrading influence of almshouses, prisons, and other adult institutions (Tiffin 1982, 63–64; Sidel 1992, 79–80). Although African American children were largely excluded from most orphanages, asylums such as the Colored Orphan Asylum in New York were established by members of the Society of Friends in the 1820s and 1830s (Billingsley and Giovannoni 1972, 27–28).

Not all child welfare reformers shared the zeal for institutions. Championing family rather than institutional life, reformers such as Charles Loring Brace advocated placing dependent children with private families in exchange for the child's contribution to the household. Brace founded the Children's Aid Society in 1853, and his orphan trains shipped thousands of primarily immigrant children from urban areas to be adopted by rural western families in the late 1800s. Between 1854 and 1874, 20,000 "orphans" (many had living parents) were adopted through Brace's program (Carp 1998, 9).

A rationale of child welfare was sometimes used to justify removing immigrant, Native American, and African American children from their families. In the wake of federal policies pushing American Indian tribes onto reservations, Native American children were rounded up in large numbers and shipped off to boarding schools in eastern states. The Indian boarding schools were intended not only to educate but also to convert the children to Christianity and teach them to shed their native dress, language, and behavior (Adams 1995). In the months immediately following the end of the Civil War, former slave owners used apprenticeship laws throughout the South to indenture hundreds of African American children. Using old support laws that gave courts the right to remove children from parents deemed unable to support them, former slave owners claimed that recently freed African Americans were too poor to provide for their families (King 1995, 151–155).

Beginning in the 1860s, newly formed state boards of charities sought to regulate private child welfare organizations, using a national conference forum to report on policies and procedures for treatment, funding, and licensing and administration guidelines in use by city and state social service and charitable organizations across the country (Katz 1996, 89). By the 1870s organized philanthropists and child welfare reformers had embarked upon a national child-saving movement. Part of the period of reform known as the Progressive Era, the child-saving movement was marked by the professionalization of the social work field; the growing influence and legitimacy of developmental psychology, pediatrics, and scientific approaches to child rearing; and growing concerns about rising urban poverty, urbanization, immigration, and crime (Tiffin 1982; Ashby 1984).

Child abuse became a major child policy issue in this period, when it was "discovered" in 1874 (Gordon 1988, 27). The sensational rescue of a young girl named Mary Ellen Wilson from her abusive foster mother led to the formation of the New York Society for the Prevention of Cruelty to Children (SPCC), followed quickly by the establishment of state SPCCs nationwide. The SPCCs were authorized by city and state statutes to investigate reports of child cruelty and neglect and, if necessary, to remove children from their parents or guardians. The SPCCs also sought to "protect" exploited children in the theater and street trades, lobbying, for example, for passage of the federal Padrone Act in 1874, which outlawed the indenture of Italian children to organ grinders and beggars (Gordon 1988, 27–58). Concerns about cruelty to children and their exposure to immoral influences also prompted major state legislation such as New York's 1875 Children's Act, which authorized removal of children from almshouses, gave commitment power to poor-relief officials and orphanage superintendents, and prosecuted neglectful parents (Katz 1996, 108).

Removing children from parents or guardians deemed guilty of abuse, neglect, or exploitation, however, posed the financial and logistical problem of how to care for them. Although asylums continued to play a major role in public child care, by the time of the first White House Confer-ence on Children in 1909, policy had begun to reflect the growing conviction that families, not institutions, were the best place for children. Moreover, reformers and policymakers had begun to worry that overzealous child savers removed children from their parents too readily, and the White House conference recommended that "poor but worthy" parents should be allowed to keep their children (Mason 1994, 91; Tiffin 1982, 110–135). As a result, both paid foster care and adoption placements increased. Many adoption or foster care practices were unregulated, however, and reformers fought for state legislation, such as the 1917 Children's Code of Minnesota, requiring licensing and regulation of placement agencies and investigations of potential families (Carp 1998, 21). Despite shifts toward family care, however, institutions, rather than private homes, continued to play a dominant role in the care of dependent children until the 1920s (Tiffin 1982, 97, 105).

Upon the recommendation of the 1909 conference, the U.S. Children's Bureau was established in 1912 to serve as a national center for information and policy recommendations about child health, education, and other welfare issues (Lindenmeyer 1997, 18–24). The Children's Bureau, in cooperation with other organizations such as the National Congress of Mothers, advocated policies that would aid deserted or widowed mothers (Lindenmeyer 1997, 153–154). First enacted in 1911 with Illinois's Fund to Parents Act, mothers' or widows' pensions were intended to help "worthy" mothers keep their families together. By 1921, forty states had enacted similar legislation (Goodwin 1997, 3). Day-care services for working mothers were also provided in some cities. Organizations such as the National Federation of Day Nurseries, founded in 1898, campaigned in cities such as New York and Chicago for local and state regulation of day nurseries (Michel 1999, 56–57).

Concerns about poor mothers and children reflected a growing awareness of children's health and safety issues. Inspired by exposés of the lives of the urban poor by journalists such as Jacob Riis, reformers conducted investigations of housing for the poor and lobbied for tenement housing reform, better sanitation and public health awareness, parenting education for mothers, and funding for the construction of urban playground areas (Tiffin 1982; Ladd-Taylor 1994). Child health reformers were also instrumental in passage of the first major federal legislation for maternal and child health in 1921, the Sheppard-Towner Act (Ladd-Taylor 1994). Concern about child health played a role in the Progressive Era campaign against child labor. By 1904 a National Child Labor Committee had been established to address child labor conditions and to lobby for restrictions. Opposition to restricting child labor—on the part of factory owners, poor parents for whom a child's income could be indispensable, and those who felt such legislation undermined parental autonomy— was so strong, however, that federal child labor policies did not take hold until the Great Depression (Zelizer 1985, 56–72).

Reformers used education as a weapon in the fight against child labor, lobbying for the passage of such laws as the 1903 New York City law prohibiting children under fourteen from working during school hours. By 1918 mandatory school attendance laws existed nationwide (Katz 1996, 134–135). African American children, however, dealt with racist policies that hampered equal access to education,

such as the "separate but equal" Jim Crow laws upheld by the 1896 Supreme Court decision in *Plessy* v. *Ferguson.*

By the 1910s, several states had established domestic relations and juvenile courts to address issues relating specifically to children and families, including divorce, custody issues, child abuse, and delinquency (Pleck 1987, 136). In 1899 Illinois had enacted its Juvenile Court Act, establishing the first juvenile court in the country. As juvenile delinquency policies began to focus on the causes of delinquency and psychological evaluation of youthful criminals, several states funded organizations for research into the causes and treatment of juvenile crime (Hawes and Hiner 1985, 429–430).

By the time the White House sponsored a Conference on Child Welfare Standards in 1919, the child-saving movement had spawned dozens of public and private national child welfare organizations, as well as a myriad of municipal, state, and federal policies designed to protect children in (or from) the family, the orphanage, the school, the prison, the court, and the workplace. By 1929, almost every state had passed regulatory policies for child-helping institutions and agencies (Tiffin 1982; Hawes and Hiner 1985).

After the stock market crash of October 1929 and the onset of the Great Depression, thousands of children and their families found themselves in dire poverty, suffering from hunger, malnutrition, and lack of access to proper health care, housing, and sanitation (Mintz and Kellogg 1988, 133–149). As unemployment reached 23.6 percent by 1932, municipal, state, and federal provisions for services to children became ever more important (Mintz and Kellogg 1988, 134). The White House sponsored several major conferences in the early 1930s to address issues confronting women and children, including the White House Conference on Child Health and Protection and the Conference on Children in 1930 and the 1933 Conference on the Emergency Needs of Women (Gordon 1994).

In 1933, Pres. Franklin D. Roosevelt passed his first round of New Deal policies, intended to provide jobs and relief for the families of millions of low-income Americans. Some New Deal legislation worked to prohibit child labor and to reserve scarce jobs for adult men with families, such as the 1933 National Recovery Act (NRA) codes banning labor by children under sixteen (Zelizer 1985, 65). Other policies sought to provide jobs and activities for adolescents, such as the Civilian Conservation Corps and the National Youth Administration. The National Youth Administration's Division of Negro Affairs had an especially important impact on black youth, owing primarily to the efforts of director Mary MacLeod Bethune (Katz 1996, 252; Hawes and Hiner 1985).

Although many child welfare measures instigated in the 1930s were stopgap emergency programs, the 1935 Social Security Act had a dramatic impact on the shape of twentieth-century child welfare (Ashby 1984; Mintz and Kellogg 1988, 148). The Social Security Act set up Aid to Dependent Children (later Aid to Families with Dependent Children [AFDC]), which provided monthly stipends to families with children. Other New Deal family policies provided assistance for children in the form of health-care, education, and day-care provisions (Gordon 1994). Although New Deal family welfare policies were ostensibly intended for all Americans, local and state eligibility guidelines often served to discriminate against blacks and other minorities.

During World War II, the dramatic national increase in the number of working mothers led to important policy shifts in the arena of day care. Women's work was now seen as a matter of national defense, necessary for wartime production, and as a result federal funding for day care increased significantly. The White House sponsored a Conference on Day Care of Children of Working Mothers in 1941, and in 1942 Congress passed the Community Facilities Act, or Lanham Act, giving federal assistance to establish day-care facilities across the United States (Michel 1999, 118–149).

In the postwar era, a strong economy, the federal bureaucratization of many family and child services, a rising birthrate, and an increased national emphasis on the importance of children resulted in a range of improved child welfare services. Despite the popular vision of this period as a time of affluence and domestic harmony, however, policy reflected public anxieties about child health, poverty, child abuse and child neglect, the care of dependent children, and juvenile delinquency (Hawes and Hiner 1985; Mintz and Kellogg 1988, 177–201).

Abused and neglected children received renewed attention in the 1950s and 1960s with the "rediscovery" of child abuse and the federal government's acknowledgment of child abuse and neglect as a national welfare policy. By the 1960s, child psychologists, social workers, and policymakers were using the term *battered child syndrome* to describe the cycle of child abuse and were pushing for increased funding for reporting, investigation, and treatment. By 1967, every state had passed child abuse reporting legislation (Pleck 1987, 165–173).

Although child abuse and neglect were very real problems in the postwar United

States, children of poor minorities were especially vulnerable to investigation and removal from their homes. In 1958, the Bureau of Indian Affairs, in cooperation with the Child Welfare League, began the Indian Adoption Project. A 1971–1972 congressional investigation determined that in those years in Minnesota alone, almost 25 percent of Native children under one year of age were placed for adoption and that 90 percent of all adoptions of Native American children were into white homes (Monsivais 1997, 6).

Another area of concern was the rise in single motherhood in the United States. Convinced that unwed mothers were responsible for the increase in the number of welfare recipients, some states enacted "suitable home" policies to deny welfare benefits to children born to unmarried mothers. By 1960, twenty-three states had passed such disqualifying legislation (Solinger 1992, 58). Adoption services for the children of minority women, particularly teen mothers, were also scarce. Only 9 percent of adoptions in 1958, for example, were for nonwhite infants (Solinger 1992, 57–58). Black activists in the 1940s and 1950s lobbied for improved adoption services for black children, organized projects such as ADOPT-A-CHILD and the national project on Foster Care and Adoptions for Negro Children, and promoted the establishment of black infant adoption units (Billingsley and Giovannoni 1972, 139–174; Solinger 1992, 198).

Although policies protecting juvenile rights and streamlining parole and probation guidelines emerged in this period, other policies reflected the growing alarm about violent juvenile crime (Pleck 1987, 127). In 1961, Congress passed the Juvenile Delinquency and Youth Offenses

Act, submitted by Pres. John F. Kennedy, in an effort to address youth violence, drug use, and gang activity. Preventative policies were also enacted, including employment, recreational, and education programs for youth such as the Neighborhood Youth Corps and the college prep program Upward Bound. In 1974 the Juvenile Justice and Delinquency Prevention Act was to again address problems in the juvenile justice system (Katz 1996, 281).

In the 1960s and 1970s a War on Poverty resulted in new family welfare legislation, including a series of public welfare and Social Security amendments, designed to confront poverty issues. Economic downturn and a rising divorce rate had resulted in a vast increase in the number of women and children who lived in poverty and received federal aid (Coontz 1992, 79–82). Between 1960 and 1974, the number of people on public assistance rose from 7.1 million to 14.4 million (Katz 1996, 270, 271–275). Project Head Start, part of the Economic Opportunity Act, which was established in 1964 to give needy or disadvantaged children a boost in the education system, also provided for medical and social services (Sidel 1992, 121). Public welfare and Social Security amendments also increased funding for aid and loosened eligibility requirements for federal services. The amendments created programs such as the Work Incentive Now (WIN) program, designed to help single mothers become financially independent by providing funds for job training and day care (Sidel 1992, 121; Katz 1996, 270–272, 281). In 1975 AFDC requirements mandated that states locate and demand support from noncustodial fathers, or "deadbeat dads," of children receiving aid. In part to facilitate this process, Congress passed the Uniform Parentage Act to help state welfare agencies determine parentage (Mason 1994, 148).

Social programs for expansion of health services to children in the 1960s and 1970s included federally funded neighborhood health centers, Social Security programs for prevention of developmental disabilities, and the 1967 Child Health Act. Medicaid and Medicare provisions also significantly expanded health-care services to poor children, especially in the areas of prenatal and infant care (Katz 1996, 272). In 1974, the Special Supplemental Nutrition Program for Women, Infants, and Children (WIC) began under the U.S. Department of Agriculture, providing health services and food assistance to young low-income children (Owen and Owen 1997, 777).

In 1974 policymakers passed the Child Abuse Prevention and Treatment Act, which provided states with financial incentives for child abuse prevention programs. The act was renewed in 1978 with a more comprehensive definition of child abuse, now including "new" offenses toward children such as abduction, sexual abuse and exploitation, and moral endangerment (Pleck 1987, 176–177).

At this time Native American groups began to work to halt the removal and adoption of children away from the tribal community, pushing for state licensing of Native foster homes and assistance for the development of tribal on-reservation family and child services. In 1978 Congress passed the Indian Child Welfare Act, which sought to protect the rights of Native parents and children and provide funding for the development and improvement of tribal family services (Monsivais 1997).

Since the 1980s, child welfare has been marked by a variety of policy reforms that reflect public alarm about both "old" and

A single mother on the Child Assistance Program (an alternative to welfare) talks to her daughter. (David H. Wells/Corbis)

"new" child welfare issues. Long-standing concerns over such arenas as poverty, hunger, infant malnutrition, child abuse and neglect, juvenile crime, and education have taken new legislative turns to address contemporary issues. At the same time, the public's definition of what constitutes a danger to children's welfare has expanded. Gang violence, drug use, gun control, sexual abuse, abduction, school violence, violence and popular culture, and Internet "obscenity" are just a few of the "modern" issues confronting America's children (Gustavsson and Segal 1994; Coontz 1992).

In the 1980s and 1990s, in response to widespread public outrage about the welfare system, policymakers enacted a series of reform measures in an attempt to reduce the number of women and children receiving federal aid. Presidents Ronald Reagan and George Bush approved cutbacks to many welfare-associated programs, such as food stamps and Title XX of the Social Security Act (Sidel 1992, 127). In 1988 the Family Support Act sought to reduce welfare rolls by providing work and education incentives, day care, and more vigorous prosecution of noncustodial fathers (Sidel 1992, 213–214; Katz 1996, 307–308).

In the 1990s, welfare reform was again on the agenda as Pres. William Clinton, promising to "fix" the welfare system, oversaw the 1996 welfare reform legislation known as the Personal Responsibility and Work Opportunity Reconciliation Act. The 1996 legislation discontinued AFDC and other, older family assistance programs, replacing them with Temporary Assistance for Needy Families (TANF). TANF makes states responsible for their own welfare programs but requires them to develop work incentive programs and, most important, instill time limits on how long aid can be received. Although such policies have been targeted primarily to parents, critics charge that welfare reform will dramatically increase the number of children living in poverty.

Critics also charge that welfare "reform" policies treat minority women and children unfairly and have targeted controversial state welfare policies, such as birth-control and marriage incentive programs, that promise welfare benefits to women who agree to be implanted with a contraceptive device or get married. The massive influx of immigrants into the United States has also contributed to debates about who should have access to public aid and public resources. Under fire have been state policies such as California's ultimately unsuccessful Proposition 187, which in 1994 sought to deny immigrant children medical care and public education. The 1996 Personal Responsibility Act also restricted eligibility for immigrant families, making it more difficult for immigrant families to obtain welfare benefits for their children.

In 1980 the Adoption Assistance and Child Welfare Act was passed to help reduce foster care "drift" (extended foster care stays for children), expedite adoption proceedings for children whose parents' custodial rights had been terminated, and generally reduce child welfare service agencies' reliance on foster care (Sheldon 1997, 74). Targeting particular children who were in foster care "limbo," the act provided incentives to states to either reunify parents and children with the help of counseling and aid or to proceed with the termination of parental rights to free children for permanent adoption. Although recent tragedies involving the deaths of children returned to abusive parents have led to the loosening of standards for terminating parental rights in several states, adoptions have not kept pace with parental rights termination, dramatically increasing the number of children in state care (Sheldon 1997). Recent legislation, such as the 1997 Adoption and Safe Families Act, has continued the trend toward child removal from families, rather than reunification. New approaches to foster and adoptive care in the late twentieth century, however, also focused on such alternatives to traditional placement strategies as open adoption and kinship foster care.

Child welfare legislation seeking to protect the unborn child, runaway or thrown-away children, and abducted or exploited children has also increased in recent years. Heightened public awareness of abducted and runaway children, for instance, led to the passage of laws such as the 1980 Federal Parental Kidnapping Prevention Act and the 1984 Missing Children's Assistance Act in

1984. Child abductions have also prompted renewed public alarm about the sexual abuse and exploitation of children not only by sexual predators but by child pornography and prostitution rings as well. Policymakers have lobbied for harsher punishments, including the death penalty, for abductors and child murderers, as well as sex offender notification laws that require state criminal justice systems to notify the public when a convicted sex offender will be released (Fass 1997).

Late-twentieth-century children's health issues focused on infant health, safety issues, increased access to medical care for low-income children, drug and tobacco use, and sexually transmitted diseases such as human immunodeficiency virus (HIV). Key protection policies have included the imposition of federal safety standards on toy manufacturers and automakers, seatbelt laws, and federal and state funding for antismoking and drug prevention programs in the schools, such as the federally funded Drug Abuse Resistance Education (DARE) program (Gustavsson and Segal 1994).

The rise of gang-related crime and tragedies such as the 1998 massacre at Columbine High School in Jefferson County, Colorado, has prompted national discussion about violence in schools, on the streets, and within popular culture (Gustavsson and Segal 1994). Recent years have seen an increase in antigang policies, antiguns laws for youth such as the Youth Gun Crime Enforcement Act of 1999, harsher penalties for juveniles convicted of violent crimes, and policies holding parents liable for juvenile crime. Policies such as the 1996 Child Pornography Prevention Act and the 1998 Child Online Protection Act have also targeted violence, pornography, and other "adult"

content in music, television, film, and on the Internet, requiring warning labels on adult materials and tightening age restrictions and rating guidelines (Doherty 1999).

—Robin L. E. Hemenway

See also Adoptive Parents; Aid to Families with Dependent Children; Child Abuse; Child Labor; Children's Bureau, U.S.; Child Care; Family Courts; Head Start; Juvenile Justice; Orphan Trains; Orphanages; Sheppard-Towner Maternity and Infancy Act; White House Conferences on Children

References and Further Reading
Adams, David. 1995. *Education for Extinction: American Indians and the Boarding School Experience, 1875–1928.* Lawrence: University Press of Kansas.
Ashby, LeRoy. 1984. *Saving the Waifs: Reformers and Dependent Children, 1890–1917.* Philadelphia: Temple University Press.
Billingsley, Andrew, and Jeanne M. Giovannoni. 1972. *Children of the Storm: Black Children and American Child Welfare.* New York: Harcourt Brace Jovanovich.
Carp, Wayne. 1998. *Family Matters: Secrecy and Disclosure in the History of Adoption.* Cambridge: Harvard University Press.
Clapp, Elizabeth J. 1998. *Mothers of All Children: Women Reformers and the Rise of Juvenile Courts in Progressive Era America.* University Park: Pennsylvania State University Press.
Coontz, Stephanie. 1992. *The Way We Never Were: American Families and the Nostalgia Trap.* New York: Basic Books.
Costin, Lela B., Howard Jacob Karger, and David Stoesz. 1996. *The Politics of Child Abuse in America.* New York: Oxford University Press.
Doherty, Kelly M. 1999. "Www. obscenity.com: An Analysis of Obscenity and Indecency Regulation on the Internet." *Akron Law Review* 32: 259–299.
Fanshel, David. 1972. *Far from the Reservation: The Transracial Adoption of American Indian Children.* NJ: Scarecrow Press.

Fass, Paula. 1997. *Kidnapped: Child Abduction in America.* Cambridge: Harvard University Press.

Goodwin, Joanne L. 1997. *Gender and the Politics of Welfare Reform: Mother's Pensions in Chicago, 1911–1929.* Chicago: University of Chicago Press.

Gordon, Linda. 1988. *Heroes of Their Own Lives: The Politics and History of Family Violence.* New York: Penguin Books.

Gordon, Linda. 1994. *Pitied but Not Entitled: Single Mothers and the History of Welfare.* Cambridge: Harvard University Press.

Gustavsson, Nora S., and Elizabeth A. Segal. 1994. *Critical Issues in Child Welfare.* Thousand Oaks, CA: Sage Publications.

Hawes, Joseph M., and N. Ray Hiner. 1985. *American Childhood: A Research Guide and Historical Handbook.* Westport, CT: Greenwood Press.

Hondagneu-Sotelo, Pierrette. 1995. "Women and Children First: New Directions in Anti-Immigrant Politics." *Socialist Review* 25(1): 169–190.

Jacobs, Francine H., and Margery W. Davies, eds. 1994. *More Than Kissing Babies: Current Child and Family Policy in the United States.* Westport, CT: Auburn House.

Katz, Michael B. 1996. *In the Shadow of the Poorhouse: A Social History of Welfare in America.* New York: Basic Books.

King, Wilma. 1995. *Stolen Childhood: Slave Youth in Nineteenth-Century America.* Bloomington: Indiana University Press.

Ladd-Taylor, Molly. 1994. *Mother-Work: Women, Child Welfare, and the State, 1890–1930.* Urbana: University of Illinois Press.

Lindenmeyer, Kriste. 1997. *"A Right to Childhood": The U.S. Children's Bureau and Child Welfare, 1912–1946.* Urbana: University of Illinois Press.

Mason, Mary Ann. 1994. *From Father's Property to Children's Rights: The History of Child Custody in the United States.* New York: Columbia University Press.

Mason, Mary Ann, and Eileen Gambrill, eds. 1994. *Debating Children's Lives: Current Controversies on Children and Adolescents.* Thousand Oaks, CA: Sage Publications.

Michel, Sonya. 1999. *Children's Interests, Mother's Rights: The Shaping of America's Child Care Policy.* New Haven: Yale University Press.

Mintz, Steven, and Susan Kellogg. 1988. *Domestic Revolutions: A Social History of American Family Life.* New York: The Free Press.

Monsivais, Jose. 1997. "A Glimmer of Hope: A Proposal to Keep the Indian Child Welfare Act of 1978 Intact." *American Indian Law Review* 22: 1–36.

Owen, Anita L., and George M. Owen. 1997. "Twenty Years of WIC: A Review of Some Effects of the Program." *Journal of the American Dietetic Association* 97(7): 777–782.

Pleck, Elizabeth. 1987. *Domestic Tyranny: The Making of American Social Policy against Family Violence from Colonial Times to the Present.* New York: Oxford University Press.

Rose, Elizabeth. 1999. *A Mother's Job: The History of Day Care, 1890–1960.* New York: Oxford University Press.

Sheldon, Jill. 1997. "50,000 Children Are Waiting: Permanency, Planning and Termination of Parental Rights under the Adoption Assistance and Child Welfare Act of 1980." *Boston Third World Law Journal* 17 (Winter): 73–100.

Sidel, Ruth. 1992. *Women and Children Last: The Plight of Poor Women in Affluent America.* New York: Penguin Books.

Skocpol, Theda. 1992. *Protecting Soldiers and Mothers: The Political Origins of Social Policy in the United States.* Cambridge: Belknap Harvard Press.

Solinger, Ricki. 1992. *Wake Up Little Susie: Single Pregnancy and Race before Roe v. Wade.* New York: Routledge.

Tiffin, Susan. 1982. *In Whose Best Interests: Child Welfare Reform in the Progressive Era.* Westport, CT: Greenwood Press.

Usher, Charles L., Karen A. Randolph, and Harlene C. Gogan. 1999. "Placement Patterns in Foster Care." *Social Service Review* 73(1): 22–23.

Wall, Helena. 1990. *Fierce Communion: Family and Community in Early America.* Cambridge: Harvard University Press.

Zelizer, Viviana. 1985. *Pricing the Priceless Child: The Changing Social Value of Children.* Princeton, NJ: Princeton University Press.

Childbirth, Medical Practices of

The medical practices of childbirth are the methods used historically and currently by the medical profession to intervene in the birth process. Childbirth has changed over time, ranging from the practices before 1760, when most women gave birth attended by female friends, family, or a midwife; to the practices of the end of the eighteenth century, when doctors began to supplant the place of midwives and began to use medical technology to aid the birth process; to the current practices at the beginning of the twenty-first century, which utilize medical technology but also allow for women to have greater control over the birth process. The early medical practices of childbirth were often quite dangerous. Sterile practices were not followed, bloodletting was frequently practiced, doctors were often lacking in practical training, and unregulated use of opiates was common. Childbirth under the influence of these opiates was given the name twilight sleep, as women were placed under the anesthetic and the doctor delivered the child with the woman completely unconscious and nonparticipatory in the birth process.

As medicine evolved, births began to take place primarily in hospitals, and the medical practices began to reflect the increasingly accurate medical knowledge available to the profession. As opiates were found to be unsafe, other anesthetics came to take their place, including drugs that allowed women to be conscious during delivery. Cesarean section, a surgical procedure that delivers the child by making an incision in the woman's abdomen and through her uterus to allow the fetus to be delivered without having to pass through the cervix and vagina, has existed through-out nearly all of human history. C-sections, as they are commonly called, began to be performed regularly by the medical profession in the twentieth century and were used increasingly from the 1940s on. The epidural, a nonnarcotic and presumably safe method by which doctors can control the pain of labor and delivery while protecting both the child and mother from any effects of a drug that would be introduced into the bloodstream, was introduced in the 1940s. It was also at that time that fathers began to be allowed into the delivery rooms, whereas previously all persons except for the mother and hospital personnel were excluded on medical grounds.

During the late 1960s and continuing to the current day, the women's movement has encouraged women to take a more active part in the labor and delivery process. There has been a renewed interest in home birthing as well as midwife-assisted birth. For women who still choose the hospital-delivery route, doctors have allowed women more choice in making decisions about the birth process, including the choice of whether or not to use drugs or have an epidural.

Childbirth began to be medicalized during the early twentieth century in the United States. At that time, the medical profession was attempting to establish itself as an authority with a legitimate purpose. In order to become more legitimate, the American Medical Association undertook a campaign to discredit and delegitimatize midwifery, painting midwives as incompetent and unscientific. As this was the beginning of the American movement toward science and discovery, people were quick to seize on the scientific and advanced way of giving birth, and the public began to embrace medicalized childbirth as a better and safer way to give birth. As these were the early days of medicine, however, and the profession was unaware of medical facts that had not yet been discovered, such as germ theory, there was an extremely high mortality rate for women who were attended by a physician during the birth process. Nonsterile practices were routinely followed, such as the breaking of the bag of waters with an unwashed fingernail. As was customary during this time, bloodletting was common, with doctors and patients alike believing in its healing effects. Anesthetics, from opium to laudanum to ether, became increasingly popular during the late nineteenth century but were often given in improper doses, resulting in accidental overdoses and illness. Also, the use of forceps delivery was a popular, yet potentially dangerous, procedure, as many doctors were untrained in the use of forceps. These forceps deliveries resulted in deaths as well as injuries to countless mothers and children. In addition, many, if not most, doctors were quite ignorant of women's anatomy, as the Victorian morals of the day prevented the male doctors (all doctors at this time were male) from viewing the genitalia of women. Most doctors performed examinations without looking at a woman's vagina, and most women would have been quite upset if their doctor had violated the moral code of the day. Physicians were trained on mannequins, never attending a live birth until they were faced with one in their practice.

Germ theory was not introduced until late in the nineteenth century, and until then physicians did not sterilize instruments or wash their hands; as a result, many women became infected. "Childbirth fever," or puerperal fever, was a common cause of death for women of childbearing age until the 1920s. Doctors unknowingly infected women as well as babies. It is important to note that prior to the 1920s, however, not all women made use of the services of the medical profession. Doctor's services were utilized mainly by the wealthy, as doctors' fees were often too high for most women to afford. The bulk of women in the United States still utilized the services of a midwife, unless something went quite wrong and a doctor needed to be called in; for example, if a fetus died and needed to be removed. The physician-attended birth was a luxury that people desired, even if most were unable to afford it. The physician-attended birth held the promise of a pain-free and presumably safer delivery for the women of the time.

By the turn of the twentieth century, approximately half of the nation's births were attended by a physician, but nearly all births took place in the home (Wertz and Wertz 1979). As the public's perception of hospitals began to change, shifting from the hospital as a place for the poor to die to a place for people to be cured, hospital births became more common. After the 1920s, partly driven by and partly driving the move to the hospital, new medical technologies began to develop. Scopolamine, a new anesthetic that needed to be given in a hospital setting, was becoming popular. Also, the use of labor-inducing drugs became more commonplace. It was this move from the home to the hospital and the technologies that went with it that shifted control of labor and delivery from the woman to the doctor. Now, not only did the doctor have the tools to control the childbirth process, but the entire event took place in an unfamiliar, medicalized location.

During the 1930s it began to become clear that the medicalized process of childbirth might not have been as advantageous as it was perceived to be. Even with all of the advances in medical technology and knowledge, maternal and child death rates remained relatively stable. This was attributed to the high level of often unnecessary interventions that characterized the hospital birth. In the 1940s, after the discovery of germ theory and the introduction of sulfa drugs and, later, penicillin, rates of infection and of maternal and child death decreased significantly. It was during this period that childbirth came under the control of the doctor, rather than the patient. By 1955, 99 percent of births in the United States occurred in a hospital, a figure that has remained steady to this day (Wertz and Wertz 1979). Anesthetics had progressed at this point, making their use less risky to the health of the mother and the child. Many women were "put under" and rendered unconscious during labor and birth. No alternative methods were widely used to control pain in a more natural fashion. Fathers were also excluded from the birth process, being relegated to the waiting rooms of hospitals. Even the teaching of obstetrics in medical schools stressed the lack of control that mothers had over labor and delivery, claiming that contractions were involuntary and that it was up to the physician to bring the child out.

In the 1950s, the epidural came into use to ease the pain of childbirth. This procedure blocks nerve activity from the lower back down, allowing women to feel less pain during labor and delivery. Epidurals carry less risk for mother and child but effectively paralyze the woman, rendering her unable to walk around. The epidural must be administered in the hospital setting by an anesthesiologist, further necessitating a hospital visit. Near this time, the episiotomy began to

be a relatively common practice during vaginal delivery. The episiotomy is a cut that is made in the perineum area to create more room to allow the baby to exit the mother's body. The procedure is quite painful, especially as it heals, and like the epidural, necessitates a hospital delivery. Recently, there has been debate regarding the necessity of these episiotomies, which like the forceps delivery before them may be a case of medicine performing a procedure because it *can* be done, not necessarily because it *must* be done.

In the late 1960s, however, medical doctors began to discuss alternatives to many common medical practices of childbirth. Dr. Fernand Lamaze and others became part of the growing natural birth movement, which was a logical outgrowth of the women's movement as well as of the growing awareness of natural alternatives in the 1960s. The Lamaze method of childbirth stresses the mother's control over the delivery process, as well as controlling her pain through breathing exercises and different positions rather than through the use of medications. The Lamaze method encourages women to use breathing techniques to distract them from the pain. This method is a step to increase women's control over their labor and delivery, to take the power out of the hands of doctors and put it into the women's hands. Also, there is renewed interest in fathers in this method; fathers are often the coaches for their wives and are encouraged to be part of the birth process, rather than nonparticipants.

Currently, there is growing awareness within the obstetrical community that birth is a natural process, rather than an illness that needs to be treated with medical intervention. Birth is becoming less medicalized and more of the family experience that it once was. There has

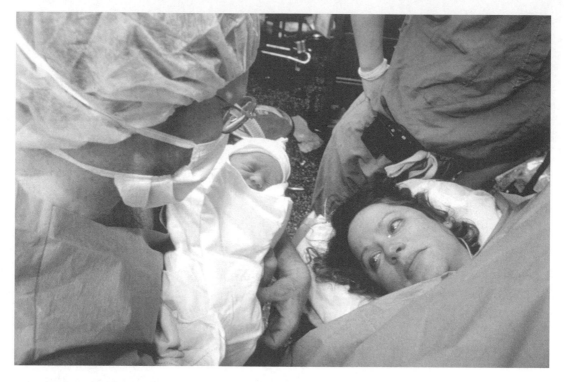

A mother being shown her newborn infant. (Annie Griffiths Belt/Corbis)

recently even been an increase in interest in midwifery as well as home births. But even within the confines of the hospital, women are exerting more control over their childbirth experiences. In hospitals, there has been a movement toward labor/delivery rooms that have a home-like atmosphere and allow a woman to remain in the same space for the duration of her stay in the hospital. This is in contrast to the earlier method, which involved three rooms during a stay: a labor room, where the prebirth labor took place; then a move to a delivery room, which is similar to an operating room; and then a move to a recovery room, where the mother would stay, separated from her infant, until she went home. Now, mothers are encouraged to keep their newborns in the same room with them. During the birth process itself, women are encouraged to stick to their birth plan, a set of ideas and decisions made by the mother (and partner), in consultation with their physician, as to how they would like to see the birth proceed. It is here that women can express their preferences regarding whether they would like to have pain medication or whether they choose to have a "natural" birth; if they approve of the doctor's administering labor-inducing hormones, such as pitocin, which increase the frequency and intensity of the contractions; if they would agree to having an episiotomy; under what conditions, if any, the mother would agree to a cesarean section; and how to proceed if the baby is presented in a breech position. Compared to even the 1970s, this level of control over the birth process is staggering. But as in the past, not all women have equal access to this type of control or information. Studies have shown that the level of control that women have over the process of childbirth, as well as the quality of care received while in the hospital, varies greatly by race and socioeconomic status. Poorer women and minority women have lower levels of control over the birth process and receive a lower standard of care.

The current medical practices of childbirth extend past the hospital environment. Childbirth has changed dramatically since the 1960s, particularly with respect to older and higher-risk pregnant women. The medical practices available to women who earlier would not have been able to give birth have increased dramatically. Procedures such as IVF (in vitro fertilization), GIFT (gamete intrafallopian transfer), the use of donor eggs, and fertility medications have allowed older women, infertile women (or men), and lesbians to experience pregnancy and childbirth. Along with these technologies, however, have come increased risks during delivery. Many fertility medications, along with the IVF and GIFT procedures, carry with them an increased risk of multiple births. In fact, it has been estimated that the rate of multiple births has increased from 1 in 100 to 2 in 100 in a single generation (Hildt and Mireth 1998). Multiple births are risky for both mother and babies, with a higher risk of preterm labor and low-birth-weight babies. Also, women carrying multiples are at higher risk of certain pregnancy complications, including hypertension, anemia, and abruptio placenta. Older mothers are more likely to miscarry, have a child with a genetic abnormality, or go into preterm labor.

There has been a dramatic increase in the rate of cesarean sections, which can at least in part be attributed to the increase in high-risk deliveries. Generally, C-sections are performed when a labor would be a danger to the mother's health or when a fetus's distress signals to the doctors that labor would endanger the child's health. Recently there has been much discussion over the necessity of many of the C-sections performed today in the United States. The rate of C-sections has increased dramatically in recent times, and some people attribute some of the increase to obstetricians' fear of being sued if they do not perform a C-section. Cesarean section rates in the United States are significantly higher than rates in Great Britain, for example.

Cesarean sections are under debate because they involve a longer recovery time, both in the hospital and at home; are much more painful to recover from; and prevent women from being able to experience labor and a vaginal delivery, something that many women eagerly anticipate. Also, cesarean sections carry with them more danger of death and complication; however, part of that risk may be due to the serious nature of the problem that gave rise to the C-section in the first place and not to the procedure itself. But many women greet the news that they require a C-section with trepidation and disappointment. The surgical procedure itself is very disconnecting. A woman is taken to an operating room, where she receives either general anesthetic or an epidural (depending on how emergent the situation is), if she has not already done so. Her husband or partner must wait outside until the doctors are ready to begin the procedure. Generally, only one person is allowed to be there to support the woman, and if the procedure is performed in an emergency, there may not be time for anyone to be there for the woman. A sterile drape is placed in front of the woman, so that she cannot see the procedure; however, this also prevents her from being able to view the actual birth. The woman is removed from the birth process, and the doctors bring the child into the world, which many women find upsetting after nine months of looking forward to delivering their child.

Beyond those births where there are complications and increased risks, there is a multitude of medical procedures surrounding childbirth. Upon admission, the woman is first examined to determine what stage of labor she is in. If the doctor decides that the woman is in very early (or latent) labor and will not deliver anytime soon, the doctor can decide to send the woman home until the early stage of labor is over. If the decision is made for the woman to remain in the hospital, she will most likely undergo a few procedures immediately following her admission. Blood and urine samples would be taken, and in many cases, an enema will be given and the pubic area will be shaved. The necessity of both of the latter procedures is under discussion in the medical community. Neither is clearly justified by medical necessity; in fact, shaving may actually pose more of a risk for infection. Both procedures are generally performed as a matter of routine, as is the administration of an IV. Many women find the procedures degrading and unpleasant. Given that most practitioners have no reason to perform these procedures except for their own convenience, one must question why they are performed. As has been the case

historically, some of the reason is thought to lie in the medicalization of childbirth: performing a medical routine on each patient rather than treating each patient based on her individual needs. In some hospitals, the woman may have her food and fluid intake restricted during the labor. This is done partly so that the stomach is empty in case a cesarean would need to be performed.

Most women undergo some type of fetal monitoring. Three types of monitoring exist. The first is external fetal monitoring, which involves the use of two devices that are strapped to the abdomen, one to monitor the fetus's heartbeat and one to monitor the strength and duration of the contractions. The second type is stethoscope monitoring, in which the nurse or doctor monitors the fetal heartbeat through the use of a stethoscope. In internal monitoring, the third type, an electrode is attached to the fetus's scalp through the cervix. Monitoring is used in order to know if the fetus is experiencing any distress. It is during this early phase of labor that pitocin is administered if the physician decides that labor is not progressing quickly enough. If the woman does not experience stronger and more regular contractions, or if she is not dilating (less than three centimeters of dilation after twenty hours of labor), then the physician may decide either to administer pitocin to increase the intensity and regularity of the contractions, which results in an increase in the amount of dilation, or to proceed to a cesarean section.

At the end of early labor (when the cervix has dilated, or opened, at least three centimeters), the mother begins to move into active labor. It is at this time— at the beginning of the second phase of labor—that most women are admitted to the hospital. Contractions begin to become stronger and to come more often. It is during this phase of labor that the physician will rupture the bag of waters artificially if it has not already ruptured. This procedure usually helps speed up the pace of the labor. If very slow progress (less than 1 to 1.5 centimeters per hour) or no progress is being made, however, then pitocin may be administered. In about half of these cases of stalled labor, a cesarean is performed, owing to a presumed disproportion between the baby's head and the mother's pelvis.

Advanced active labor, or transition, as it is commonly referred to, is marked by the final three centimeters of dilation of the cervix. This is usually very fast, with most women moving through this phase in fifteen minutes to one hour. If the birth will take place in a delivery room, rather than a birthing room, then the woman will usually be moved to the delivery room during this phase. During this phase an epidural and/or pain medication will usually not be administered (unless the decision is made to perform a C-section), as they are thought to interfere too greatly with the mother's ability to push or, in the case of the epidural, would not take effect quickly enough. Up until this point, pain medication or an epidural will be offered to the mother.

After the transitional phase is over, the woman moves to the second stage of childbirth: pushing and delivery. This second stage is when the woman pushes the baby through the birth canal. This stage generally lasts between a half-hour and an hour but can range from ten minutes to upward of four hours. It is now that the physician is called for the actual delivery; until this point, he or she would have come into the room for occasional checkups on the mother's progress. In a normal delivery, the woman will push with

nearly every contraction and will move the baby down the birth canal. If labor stalls during this stage, a forceps delivery may occur, depending on both how far the baby has descended into the birth canal and how experienced the physician is with a forceps delivery. If a forceps delivery is called for, the forceps will be placed around the baby's head and the child will gently be pulled down the birth canal. If the baby has made significant progress down the birth canal, a vacuum extraction may be used to ease the baby out the rest of the way. But in a normal progression, once the head becomes visible, delivery generally is imminent.

It is at this point that the need for an episiotomy may occur. The episiotomy is a procedure in which the doctor makes an incision into the perineal area in order to allow the head more room to exit. The procedure is defended in that it is thought to reduce the tearing and stretching of the mother's vaginal area. In some cases, this is a valid claim. An episiotomy is much easier to repair than a jagged tear in the vaginal wall and is less painful. Some physicians perform an episiotomy as a matter of routine, however. Some advocates of natural childbirth claim that massaging the perineal area prevents tearing, creates more elasticity, cuts down on abnormal stretching, and eliminates the need for an episiotomy. An episiotomy is undoubtedly painful; one must question its use in cases where it may not be needed. When the baby's head crowns, the doctor will apply counterpressure to the head, easing it out slowly. He or she may direct the mother's pushing, telling her how much to push and when or when not to push. After the head is delivered, the shoulders will be eased out, one by one. The rest of the baby will then be slid out. The doctor, or the father/partner, will then clamp and cut the umbilical cord. The child will either be placed on the mother's abdomen or taken to be examined. After the baby has been delivered, the placenta, or afterbirth, will be delivered and then any tears or the episiotomy will be repaired.

In the case of a breech presentation, the birth process may proceed very differently. A breech presentation occurs when the head of the fetus is not pointed down into the birth canal. There are many types of breech presentation, from footling (with one leg pointing down) to complete breech (baby's bottom down, legs crossed) to frank presentation (bottom down, legs folded straight up). Labor is allowed to proceed in some cases, although some physicians elect to perform a cesarean as soon as labor begins. If the doctor does not elect for a cesarean at this point, labor will be allowed to proceed as long as it proceeds at a normal pace. If labor stalls, however, most physicians will elect to perform a cesarean. If labor does continue, and depending on the exact nature of the breech presentation, then a vaginal delivery can be performed. Usually an episiotomy must be performed, and in most cases, the head and shoulders of the baby are delivered with the use of forceps. The danger in attempting to vaginally deliver a breech baby is that if the head or shoulders are larger than the mother's pelvis, the head or shoulder could become stuck in the birth canal, creating a potentially life-threatening situation. If that were to occur, an emergency C-section would be performed, and the baby would have to be pushed back up through the birth canal and pulled out of the uterus, potentially depriving it of oxygen.

—*Gayle Green*

References and Further Reading

Banks, Amanda C. 1999. *Birth Chairs, Midwives and Medicine.* Jackson: University of Mississippi Press.

Devries, Raymond, ed. 2000. *Birth by Design: Pregnancy, Maternity Care and Midwifery in North America and Europe.* New York: Routledge.

Edwards, M. 1984. *Reclaiming Birth: History and Heroines of American Childbirth Reform.* Trumansburg, NY: The Crossing Press.

Eisenberg, A., H. E. Murkoff, and S. E. Hathaway. 2002. *What to Expect When You're Expecting.* New York: Workman Publishing.

Hildt, Elisabeth, and Dietmar Mireth, eds. 1998. *In Vitro Fertilization in the 1990s: Towards a Medical, Social, and Ethical Evaluation.* Brookfield, CT: Ashgate.

Leavitt, J. W. 1985."Science Enters the Birthing Room: Obstetrics in America since the 18th Century." In *Sickness and Health in America*, edited by J. W. Leavitt and R. L. Numbers, 115–135. Madison: University of Wisconsin Press.

Scholten, Catherine M. 1985. *Childbearing in American Society, 1650–1850.* New York: New York University Press.

Wertz, Richard W., and Dorothy C. Wertz. 1979. *Lying In: A History of Childbirth in America.* New York: Schocken Books.

Children as Parents

Children serve as parents in situations in which individuals under the age of eighteen act as the primary caretakers of children they have or have not birthed. Acknowledging the social, and especially biological, parenthood of those under the age of consent challenges traditional views that regard parenting and the sexual activity that predated it as adult undertakings. In contemporary American society, views about the appropriate age of parenthood are influenced by moral codes that link marriage and sex to child rearing.

Recent statistics generated for the U.S. Department of Health and Human Services indicated two trends in teenage births. First, there was an overall decline in births to teenage females of all ethnic origins. Births per 1,000 teenage women dropped from 62.1 in 1991 to 51.1 in 1998. An especially dramatic decline was reported among blacks. The rate of 85.3 births per 1,000 teenage women was the lowest in the past forty years. The highest rate of teen births was reported among Hispanic women, despite a reported decline to 93.7 in 1998 from 106.7 per 1,000 in 1991. The birthrate for white teens in 1998 remained almost half the rate for black teens. It was recorded at 45.4 births per 1,000 white teenage women. The Asian/Pacific Islander teen birthrate remained substantially lower than other ethnic groups, declining to 23.1 births per 1,000 teen women in 1998 (Child Trends Incorporated 1999, 388–391).

The second trend noted a positive correlation between teen birthrates and age. As age increased, so did the birthrate among teens. The highest rate of 82 per 1,000 teens was recorded for women aged 18 or 19 in 1998. The lowest rate of 1 per 1,000 teens aged 10 to 14 was recorded during that same year (Child Trends Incorporated 1999, 388–391).

Despite statistics indicating a recent overall decline in teen births, social fears about births to teenagers, especially to young women of black and Hispanic origin, continue to grow. This is partly due to the perceived relationship between early-aged parenting and other "social ills" such as sexual promiscuity, teenage pregnancy, single motherhood, absent fathers, hasty marriages, and high divorce rates. Without social support networks to help them meet their familial obligations, teenage parents achieve lower levels of education and experience lim-

ited employment opportunities. This accounts for the higher rates of poverty associated with early parenting, and especially with single teenage mothering (Coontz 1992). Today, early-aged parenting is often conflated with single motherhood. This reflects the reality that many young women raise their children without the steady involvement of the child's father.

Contemporary social fears about teenage parenting are rooted in historical perceptions that associate early-aged parenting with "delinquency" and poverty. In the past, higher rates of childbirth among teens from working-class, black, Hispanic, and certain immigrant populations fueled widespread perceptions that teen births were a manifestation of class and race. This view was reified in late-nineteenth-century scientific and moral frameworks. Within the popular scientific theory of recapitulation, for example, G. Stanley Hall claimed that the early sexual maturity of particular racial groups indicated their proximity to earlier stages of human evolution. According to Hall, black and Hispanic children developed secondary sex characteristics such as breasts or facial hair long before white children, whose racial superiority was illustrated by their delayed maturation (Hall 1904). Interestingly, the clothing trends of upper-class children tended to downplay emergent sex characteristics and to present white children as less sexually mature than their nonwhite peers (Kline 1998, 103–104).

The tendency to see less fertile white children as more highly evolved grew out of earlier theories put forth by "racial scientists" such as Louis Agassiz in the 1850s. Following the logic of Malthusian demographics that stated that the most fecund members of a species will eventually constitute the bulk of the population,

Agassiz claimed that lower rates of fertility among whites meant that the United States would eventually be overrun by inferior races who reproduced more quickly. He believed that the overall quality of America's population would degrade, since more highly evolved whites would eventually reproduce with members of less evolved racial groups. These partnerships would produce inferior children. Ramifications of the miscegenation of America's population were seen as profound. Without its more highly evolved white race, the United States would suffer severe political, economic, and national degradation (Gould 1991, 46–50).

Similarly, contemporary attitudes toward early-aged parenting are linked to late-nineteenth and early-twentieth-century moralities that regarded young parents, and especially single mothers, as both sexually irresponsible and morally unfit. Religious morals dictated sexual abstinence prior to marriage and "sex-for-procreation" only among married couples. Premarital and "recreational" sex was associated with moral inferiority and social degradation. It was expected that any unplanned pregnancy would result in marriage of the sexual partners, to avoid scandal and damage to the reputation of the woman, who would be labeled a "fallen woman." Premarital sex and any resulting "illegitimate" births were associated with numerous other "immoral" behaviors, such as alcoholism, gambling, and infidelity, that were frequently attributed to working-class and immigrant populations (Valverde 1991; Little 1998).

Exploring the history of our contemporary views of early-aged parenting highlights certain problems associated with how we think of children and parents. In the minds of most Americans, childhood and parenthood are mutually exclusive social categories; that is, children should not be parents, and parents should not act like children. This has not always been the case, however. Regarding early-aged parenting as inappropriate, undesirable, and nonnormative is a relatively new association that has emerged alongside of other changing views of childhood (Bernardes 1997, 168).

Philippe Aries related changing views of childhood, and the appropriateness of certain behaviors, to an overall process of liberalization in the West. He claimed that during the last 200 years, our collective perceptions of childhood have increasingly acknowledged the "special status" of childhood, in which the individuality of each child is honored and the expression of their free will is encouraged. Sentimentalization occurred, so that children are now regarded as love objects and no longer as the property of their parents. Childhood is depicted as a time of playful indulgence and sexual innocence, a natural stage of physical development through which children are expected to progress in order to reach healthy maturity. Aries maintained that liberal politics called upon all capable adults to fulfill their social parenting role and provide children with the nurture, guidance, and education required to reach healthy maturity (Aries 1962). In defining childhood as a time to be parented, and adulthood as a time to parent, this liberal perspective provides the basis of our contemporary tendency to see childhood and adulthood as mutually exclusive.

The reality of teen parenting, however, challenges the categorical construction of childhood as distinct from adulthood and as a time that precludes parenting. Teen birthrates challenge liberal views that depict childhood as a time of sexual innocence. Fertility rates challenge views that children's bodies are too immature to conceive and give birth. When young people reproduce, the classical distinction between childhood and adulthood is blurred (Postman 1994). Toward the end of the nineteenth century, adolescence emerged as a modern social category that described this in-between stage of human development, where youngsters were physically mature enough to procreate but too emotionally childlike to be regarded as adults capable of social parenting (Jenks 1996).

Freudian psychoanalytic theory emerged in the early 1900s to challenge the common liberal perspective that depicted childhood as sexless and children's sexual behavior as unnatural and deviant. In his theory of infantile sexuality, Freud claimed that the sucking behavior of all infants was innately sexual. In this first stage of development, known as the oral stage, infants satisfied their sexual desire to suck at the breast of their mothers. Eventually, toddlers moved to the anal stage of development, where sexual desire was fulfilled by mastery over their bowels. Young children could exercise independence by withholding or releasing their feces. In the phallic stage, boys under the age of six discovered the sexual pleasure of their penis while girls learned to envy the pleasurable possibilities presented by the penis. After age six, children entered a period of latency, during which sexual urges were repressed and sexual behaviors were punished (Cleverley and Phillips 1986, 54–79). Freud's theory of infantile sexuality challenged popular views that a young person's sexual desire "emerged ready-made" at puberty and placed children's sexual development within the greater continuum of their maturation process. In so doing, Freud's

approach questioned the liberal notion of sexual innocence as a key distinction between childhood and adulthood.

Today, the blurring between childhood and adulthood is increasingly apparent in contemporary U.S. society. Despite the foundational tendency to regard childhood as a time of sexual innocence, children of all ethnic origins are increasingly sexualized. In particular, the advertising and entertainment industries have contributed to the "disappearance of childhood," as models become younger and the sexual lives of movie stars increasingly public. Neil Postman documented the disappearance of children's culture where children's clothing resembles adult fashions, and children no longer spend their leisure time playing childhood games (Postman 1994). As the boundaries between childhood and adulthood become less distinct, and American society becomes more comfortable with expressions of young people's sexuality, it is possible that early-aged childbirth and parenting will become increasingly more accepted.

—Janice Hill

See also Freud, Sigmund; Gender Roles in the American Family; Hall, G. Stanley; Poverty; Premarital Sex; Sexual Revolutions; Single-Parent Families; Teenage Pregnancy

References and Further Reading
Aries, Philippe. 1962. *Centuries of Childhood*. London: Cape Press.
Bernardes, Jon. 1997. *Family Studies: An Introduction*. New York: Routledge Press.
Child Trends Incorporated. 1999. *Trends in the Well-Being of America's Children and Youth*. Washington, DC: Office of the Assistant Secretary for Planning and Evaluation, U.S. Department of Health and Human Services.
Cleverley, John, and D. C. Phillips. 1986. *Visions of Childhood: Influential*

Models from Locke to Spock. New York: Teachers College Press.

Coontz, Stephanie. 1992. *The Way We Never Were: American Families and the Nostalgia Trap*. New York: Basic Books.

Cunningham, Hugh. 1991. *The Children of the Poor: Representations of Childhood since the Seventeenth Century*. Oxford: Blackwell Press.

Gould, Stephen Jay. 1991 *Bully for Brontosaurus: Reflections on Natural History*. New York: Norton.

Hall, G. Stanley. 1904. *Adolescence*. New York: D. Appleton.

Jenks, Chris. 1996. *Childhood*. New York: Routledge Press.

Kline, Stephen. 1998. "The Making of Children's Culture." In *The Children's Culture Reader*, edited by Henry Jenkins, 95–109. New York: New York University Press.

Little, Margaret. 1998. *"No Car, No Radio, No Liquor Permit": The Moral Regulation of Single Mothers in Ontario, 1920–1997*. Oxford: Oxford University Press.

Postman, Neil. 1994. *The Disappearance of Childhood*. New York: Vintage Books.

Stanton, W. 1960. *The Leopard's Spots: Scientific Attitudes towards Race in America 1815–1859*. Chicago: University of Chicago Press.

Valverde, Mariana. 1991. *The Age of Light, Soap, and Water: Moral Reform in English Canada, 1885–1925*. Toronto: McClelland and Stewart.

Zelizer, Viviana. 1994. *Pricing the Priceless Child: The Changing Social Value of Children*. Princeton, NJ: Princeton University Press.

Children's Bureau, U.S.

The U.S. Children's Bureau was the first national agency in the world established solely to investigate and report on the needs of children and youth. Pres. William Howard Taft signed legislation establishing the U.S. Children's Bureau (*U.S. Statutes at Large* 1912, 79) within the Department of Commerce and Labor on 8 April 1912. This significant act mandated that the new agency "investigate and report . . . upon all matters pertaining to the welfare of children and child life among all classes of our people" (79). The creation of the U.S. Children's Bureau marked the permanent entrance of the national government into the broad arena of social welfare.

Progressive reformers Florence Kelley and Lillian D. Wald are most often given the credit for originating the idea for a federal children's bureau. In a series of lectures given from 1900 to 1903 and later published in her 1905 book, *Some Ethical Gains through Legislation*, Kelley argued that "a right to childhood . . . must be guarded in order to guard the Republic" (Kelley 1969, 127). She asserted that a federal commission on children would best help to secure the right to childhood for every child in the United States. Lillian Wald remembered that Kelley also discussed the idea one morning over breakfast. Why settle for only a commission, Wald complained to her friend; "if the Government can have a department to look after the Nation's farm crops, why can't it have a bureau to look after the Nation's child crop?" (Bradbury 1956, 1).

Although the solution seemed logical to Kelley and Wald, the new idea, like many others, took years before the Children's Bureau became a reality. Supported by a growing army of child welfare activists, such as the National Child Labor Committee (NCLC), and women's groups such as the General Federation of Women's Clubs and the National Congress of Mothers, the children's bureau idea got a boost when those attending the 1909 White House Conference on Dependent Children endorsed the plan. Still, it took another three years for the proposal to gain sufficient attention in Congress.

Enacted during 1912, an election year often identified as the high point of Progressive reform, the Senate passed the Children's Bureau bill by a vote of 54–20 and the House 177–17.

Despite its apparent popularity, the U.S. Children's Bureau faced some strong criticism. Opponents felt that the agency's mandate overstepped the federal government's role by creeping too far into state jurisdiction and, possibly, family and private life. Support for the bureau from the NCLC meant that manufacturing and other corporate interests opposed to child labor regulation also looked at the Children's Bureau with suspicion. The hierarchy of the Roman Catholic Church feared that any government agency focused on children had the potential to interfere with parochial education. Some critics contended that the Children's Bureau duplicated work already under the jurisdiction of other federal agencies (primarily the U.S. Public Health Service [PHS] and the Bureau of Education). Julia C. Lathrop, who led the bureau during its first years of work (1912–1921), was the first woman to serve as chief of a federal agency. Under her leadership the U.S. Children's Bureau sought to thwart such opposition and laid the groundwork for twentieth-century child welfare policy. Sensitive to critics, Lathrop and her staff promoted the same middle-class family ideal (a father as the sole breadwinner, a mother who worked full-time as a housewife and mother, and children who attended school and labored only at household chores) embraced by social conservatives. Lathrop also tried to keep the bureau out of partisan politics. The third strategy was to strictly hold to a philosophy claiming that only a single agency could best meet the needs of the "whole child."

Lathrop picked the least controversial aspect of child welfare as the bureau's first project: infant mortality. With a staff of only fifteen and a tiny budget of $25,640, the U.S. Children's Bureau established a plan of action relying on data collected by other federal agencies as well as an army of female volunteers. In its first published report, in 1913, the bureau estimated that the annual infant mortality rate of 132 deaths per 1,000 live births placed the United States behind New Zealand (83), Norway (94), Ireland (99), Sweden (104), Australia (108), Bulgaria (120), and Scotland (123).

In order to discover why so many babies died in the United States, beginning in 1913 the U.S. Children's Bureau undertook a comprehensive study of infant mortality in a single community, Johnstown, Pennsylvania. The Johnstown study, the first scientific investigation of infant mortality in the United States, found that poor sanitation, lack of good medical care, and poverty were major factors contributing to the deaths of babies. In addition, lamenting the lack of good statistical information on infant mortality, the Children's Bureau undertook a campaign to better educate mothers, improve public sanitation, and require birth certificates in all the states.

Largely as a result of this early work, in 1921 Congress passed the Sheppard-Towner Maternity and Infancy Act. Over the next eight years this significant legislation provided federal matching funds to states for programs designed to reduce the nation's high infant and maternal mortality rates. The Children's Bureau approved all state-administered programs and provided publications and advisory staff to the participating states. Although limited to education, diagnosis, and investigation, by 1926 the Sheppard-Towner Act spurred strong opposition from the American Medical Association (AMA). The AMA labeled Sheppard-Towner "socialized medicine" and criticized the program because it was administered by the Children's Bureau and not the PHS. The majority of the Children's Bureau's staff were trained female social workers, although two medical doctors, Grace L. Meigs (1915) and Dorothy Reed Mendenhall (1917), had also joined the agency. Congress, sensitive to AMA pressure and the more conservative political climate of the 1920s, ended funding for Sheppard-Towner in 1929. Despite Sheppard-Towner's demise, the Children's Bureau had drawn new public attention to issues surrounding children's health. The popularity of the agency's educational pamphlets, "Infant Care" and "Prenatal Care," and the thousands of letters the bureau received each year showed that women were hungry for information about prenatal and maternal care and about children's general health care. In 1935, Children's Bureau representatives Grace Abbott, Katharine F. Lenroot, and Martha May Eliot, M.D., wrote the child welfare sections of the Social Security Act. They included federal funding for maternal and infant care for poor mothers and children in Title V. During World War II, Title V programs were expanded to provide prenatal, maternal, and infant care for the wives and newborns of enlisted servicemen. Although it was only a wartime measure designed to enhance morale in the military, one of every seven babies born in the United States from 1942 through 1946 benefited from the Emergency Maternity and Infant Care program, and infant mortality rates in the United States declined to 33 per 1,000 live births (U.S. Bureau of the Census 1976, 57).

After launching the agency's initial work in infant mortality, Julia Lathrop also decided to combat a more controversial subject, child labor. The U.S. Census Bureau had reported in 1910 that 1,990,225 children under fourteen years of age (18.4 percent of the total cohort) worked for pay. The number was probably much higher, since this count did not include those under ten years of age and most of those who performed piecework at home, were illegally employed, or worked as "independent merchants." From 1915 through 1935 the bureau and its supporters continued their crusade to end the worst abuses of child labor. But these efforts failed to result in a permanent federal law regulating the labor of those under eighteen. High adult unemployment during the Great Depression led to the first permanent restrictions on child labor. These were included in the 1938 Fair Labor Standards Act; they specifically prohibited the employment of young people under fourteen years of age and restricted the paid labor of those fourteen to eighteen. The tightest restrictions were on fourteen- through fifteen-year-olds, but even those sixteen and seventeen were not permitted to work past 10:00 P.M. on school nights, in certain industries, or in specified jobs. The U.S. Children's Bureau was given responsibility for administering the law.

Juvenile courts were another area on which Lathrop and her staff focused attention during the Children's Bureau's early years. In July 1899, Cook County, Illinois, had established what is generally recognized as the first full-fledged juvenile court system in the world. The Children's Bureau pointed to the Illinois law as something other states should imitate. By 1920, forty-five of the then-existing forty-eight states had enacted some form of juvenile court. The Children's Bureau praised this expansion, drew up standards, and gathered information on juvenile courts. Most states removed the death penalty for those under eighteen, and by the 1940s juvenile courts became family courts mandated to oversee the rights of children brought before the state judicial system for any reason.

Destitute, orphaned, abandoned, homeless, or abused children were among those who often appeared before the nation's juvenile courts. The 1909 White House conference had called attention to these children with special needs. During its early years the bureau agreed with the White House meeting's conclusion that part of a right to childhood was a "normal homelife." Therefore, the agency advocated foster homes over institutional care and promoted the expansion of state and local mothers' pension programs. The Children's Bureau recognized illegitimacy as a social problem and condemned discrimination against unwed mothers. Also written by Abbott, Lenroot, and Eliot, the 1935 Social Security Act's Aid to Dependent Children (ADC) Program (renamed Aid to Families with Dependent Children—AFDC) and Title VII (which provided federal funds for handicapped children) addressed some of the needs of special-needs children. But this victory also foreshadowed the demise of the agency. The administration of ADC was given to the newly established Social Security Board, therefore undermining the Children's Bureau "whole child" philosophy.

The U.S. Children's Bureau and its supporters were never able to fully convince policymakers that its "whole child" philosophy was the best means to protect the right to childhood. Political opposition continued to plague the bureau despite the agency's widespread popularity with the public. The most aggressive criticism continued to come from the PHS. In 1946, Pres. Harry S. Truman reorganized the federal government along functional rather than constituency lines. The Children's Bureau lost most of its regulatory authority to larger agencies and became a small office limited to investigation and reporting within the newly created Federal Security Administration. For its supporters, the removal of "U.S." in the agency's name symbolized its "dismemberment."

The history of the U.S. Children's Bureau mirrors much of the history of childhood in the twentieth-century United States. The agency's establishment in 1912 marked a significant change in notions about the federal government's role in protecting children as a resource for the nation's future. Childhood had been sentimentalized and children gained new significance in the Progressive Era. Professionals connected to the Children's Bureau were responsible for the most significant federal legislation regarding children passed during the twentieth century: the Sheppard-Towner Maternity and Infancy Act, the child welfare sections of the Social Security Act, the regulation of child labor under the 1938 Fair Labor Standards Act, and the standardization of state juvenile court procedures. The agency's staff also underscored the important role women have played in writing U.S. social welfare policy for children and their families. Following Julia C. Lathrop, the U.S. Children's Bureau was headed by Grace Abbott (1921–1934), Katharine F. Lenroot (1934–1951), Martha May Eliot (1951–1956), and Katherine B. Oettinger (1956–1969). The bureau was transferred to the new Office of Child Development in the Department of Health, Education, and

Welfare upon Oettinger's retirement in 1969. Associate chief Frederick C. Green served as acting chief until 1972, when Pres. Richard M. Nixon appointed the first male to head the agency, Edward F. Zigler. Zigler was also the first African American to head the Children's Bureau. Since 1972 the Children's Bureau has continued its minor role as an agency investigating and reporting on the state of children in the United States. It is now only a shadow of its former self, but during its early years the U.S. Children's Bureau established the legislative agenda for the nation's youngest citizens and their families.

—*Kriste Lindenmeyer*

See also Aid to Families with Dependent Children; Child Health Improvement and Protection Act of 1968; Child Labor; Family Courts; Juvenile Justice; Sheppard-Towner Maternity and Infancy Act; Spock, Dr. Benjamin; White House Conferences on Children

References and Further Reading

Bradbury, Dorothy E. 1956. *Four Decades of Action for Children: A Short History of the Children's Bureau.* U.S. Children's Bureau Publication no. 358. Washington, DC: Government Printing Office.

Goodwin, Joanne L. 1997. *Gender and the Politics of Welfare Reform: Mothers' Pensions in Chicago, 1911–1929.* Chicago: University of Chicago Press.

Kelley, Florence. 1969. *Some Ethical Gains through Legislation.* New York: Macmillan, 1905. Reprint, New York: Arno Press.

Ladd-Taylor, Molly. 1986. *Raising Baby the Government Way: Mothers' Letters to the Children's Bureau, 1915–1932.* New Brunswick, NJ: Rutgers University Press.

Ladd-Taylor, Molly. 1994. *Mother-Work: Women, Child Welfare, and the State, 1890–1930.* Urbana: University of Illinois Press.

Lemons, J. Stanley. 1973. *The Woman Citizen: Social Feminism in the 1920s.* Urbana: University of Illinois Press.

Lindenmeyer, Kriste. 1997. *"A Right to Childhood": The U.S. Children's Bureau and Child Welfare, 1912–1946.* Urbana: University of Illinois Press.

Meckel, Richard. 1989. *Save the Babies: American Public Health Reform and the Prevention of Infant Mortality, 1850–1929.* Baltimore: Johns Hopkins University Press, 1989.

Michel, Sonya. 1999. *Children's Interests/Mothers' Rights: The Shaping of America's Child Care Policy.* New Haven: Yale University Press.

Muncy, Robyn. 1991. *Creating a Female Dominion in American Reform, 1890–1935.* New York: Oxford University Press.

Trattner, Walter I. 1970. *Crusade for Children: A History of the National Child Labor Committee and Child Labor Reform in America.* Chicago: Quadrangle Books.

U.S. Statutes at Large. 1912. Vol. 79, p. 79.

The Children's Defense Fund

The Children's Defense Fund (CDF) is the leading advocacy organization for children in the United States. It is also the sponsoring organization for the Black Community Crusade for Children. The organization says that its mission is "to leave no child behind" and to "ensure that every child has a Healthy Start, a Head Start, a Fair Start, a Safe Start, and a Moral Start in life." A not-for-profit organization, it receives no government funding, in part because it carries on lobbying activities.

"I find it amazing," says the organization's founder, Marian Wright Edelman, "that in the wealthiest nation in history, we let—seemingly without shame—our children be the poorest of its citizens. That in a nation that leads the world in military technology, we let a child be killed by guns every hour and a half. And that in a nation that pretends to be for family values, we would rather spend $20,000 to imprison a child than spend the $3,500 a year to give that child a

Head Start" (Hiraoka 1996, 7). The passionate commitment Edelman expresses in this quotation from an interview in *NEA Today* in March 1996 comes from a background of involvement in activism. Marian Wright was born on 6 June 1939 in Bennettsville, South Carolina. Her parents, Arthur Jerome Wright and Maggie Leola Bowen Wright, instilled in their five children the belief that serving their community was one of life's highest duties. Marian went to Marlboro Training High School and then on to Spelman College in Atlanta, Georgia. The traveling overseas that she did while still a student changed Edelman's perspective on the world. "After a year's freedom as a person," she said, "I wasn't prepared to go back to a segregated existence" (Guy-Sheftall 1992, 310).

By her senior year, Wright was back in the United States. It was 1960, and civil rights demonstrations were beginning all over the South. When she participated in a sit-in in Atlanta, she was among fourteen students who were arrested. Soon she had decided to forgo graduate studies in Russian and become a lawyer. She graduated as valedictorian from Spelman and entered Yale University Law School as a John Hay Whitney Fellow. Her civil rights activities continued. She went to Mississippi to work on voter registration in 1963 and, after graduation, returned as one of the first two National Association for the Advancement of Colored People (NAACP) Legal Defense and Education interns. She opened a law office, became the first black woman to pass the bar in Mississippi, got demonstrating students out of jail, and was put in jail herself. She also became involved in several school desegregation cases and served on the board of the Child Development Group of Mississippi, which represented one of the largest Head Start programs in the country.

In 1968, Wright went to Washington, D.C., on a Field Foundation grant and started the Washington Research Project. Her goal was to find out how new and existing laws could be made to work for the poor. Shortly after Robert Kennedy was shot, Wright married Peter Edelman, who had been a legislative assistant to Kennedy. She and Edelman had met in Mississippi. Although she moved with her husband to Boston in 1971 and became director of the Harvard University Center for Law and Education, Marian Wright Edelman regularly flew back to Washington so that she could remain at the helm of the Washington Research Project, which developed into the Children's Defense Fund.

Founded in 1973, the CDF quickly became the nation's most effective advocate for children, and Edelman, as its dedicated director, became known as "the children's crusader." The CDF owes much of its success to Edelman's abilities as a lobbyist and her skill at communicating. Her books include *Children out of School in America* (1974), *Portrait of Inequality: Black and White Children in America* (1980), and the best-selling *The Measure of Our Success: A Letter to My Children and Yours* (1992).

Edelman's 1996 confrontation with the Democratic administration exemplifies the work of the CDF. The organization opposed Republican plans to end "welfare as we know it." Pres. Bill Clinton, whose wife once worked for the CDF and who had been Edelman's ally in past battles, looked ready to compromise with Republicans in the Senate. Edelman and the CDF called for a Stand for Children rally at Washington's Lincoln Memorial on 1 June, in an attempt to influence

Clinton to stand by his principles and veto welfare reform. She wrote an open letter that included the sentence, "For me, this is a defining moral litmus test for your presidency" (*People Weekly* 1996, 78). *People* magazine commented on the situation:

> Ultimately the President failed Edelman's test, signing a bill on Aug. 22 that will cut $54 billion from food-stamp and other welfare programs over the next six years. "It was an attempt to tear down the effort to make the American dream real for every child," says Edelman, who has spent 23 years battling for increased spending on needy families. In September her husband of 28 years, Georgetown University law professor Peter Edelman, 58, quit his high-ranking Health and Human Services job in protest. (*People Weekly* 1996, 78)

The many activities of the CDF are carried out by a staff of about 150 people, with a budget of about $13 million a year.

Children's Defense Fund
Action Council
The CDF Action Council, according to the organization's web site (www.childrensdefense.org), "provides a strong, effective voice for all the children of America who cannot vote, lobby, or speak for themselves." The organization does a considerable amount of research concerning the situation of children in the United States and disseminates that research widely in an attempt to educate the public. Indeed, a very large proportion of newspaper and periodical articles about the problems of children base their conclusions on research reports from the CDF. Researchers, as well as legal consul-

tants, also work with legislators to help draft bills changing policies and practices that result in neglect or maltreatment of children. Another major focus of the CDF is the monitoring of federal agencies that work with children and families. The CDF staff investigates complaints and explores problems with the services that government agencies are responsible for providing to children and adolescents.

Child Watch Visitation Programs
The CDF operates extensively in the area of community organizing, working with state and local groups to address issues of child welfare, child health, adolescent pregnancy protection, child care and development, family income, family services, prevention of violence against and by children, and child mental health.

The CDF works with coalitions of local organizations to operate Child Watch Visitation Programs. Community leaders—including businesspeople, philanthropists, and political figures—are invited to participate in an experience of learning and consciousness raising. The four major components of any visitation program are on-site visits to programs serving children and families, briefings by public policy experts and others, written information, and what the CDF calls "experiential activities." This final component is designed to give the participants a sense of the lives of children in need of help. In Hartford, Connecticut, for examples, participants were asked to play a game to see how well they could work within a family budget based on a monthly welfare check. Religious leaders in Fort Worth, Texas, were asked to take their Child Watch tour on empty stomachs. In Williamson, West Virginia, participants listened for eight minutes to a tape of a six-year-old screaming to a 911 operator for help as the child's mother was beaten by a boyfriend.

In the past decade, Child Watch Visitation Programs have been carried out in more than 200 communities. Each program makes participants familiar with the kinds of problems that exist in that particular community and then presents some of the actions that are being taken to address those problems. The goal is to increase understanding, garner supports, and inspire further action.

Beat the Odds
The Beat the Odds celebrations were created to honor young people who have succeeded despite terrible odds. Celebrations are organized locally by community organizations and leaders, with the help of an organizing manual published by the CDF.

In addition to the programs for children in general, the CDF focuses special attention on African American children. "At the CDF," said Edelman in a *Psychology Today* interview, "we've always asked two questions: How does policy, or its absence, affect all children, and how does it affect the kids at the bottom? I recognized in the beginning that children as a group tended to be voiceless and uncared for, and certain kids have the shortest end of that stick" ("Mother Marian" 1993, 26).

Black Community Crusade for Children
Coordinated nationally by the CDF, the Black Community Crusade for Children (BCCC) is, according to the CDF's web site (www.childrensdefense.org), "a massive effort to mobilize the African American community on behalf of Black children and families who now face the worst crisis since slavery."

Freedom Schools
Freedom Schools were first established in 1964, during what was called Freedom Summer. In 1962 local civil rights groups in Mississippi joined with the Student Nonviolent Coordinating Committee (SNCC), the Committee on Racial Equality (CORE), the NAACP, and the Southern Christian Leadership Conference (SCLC) to form an umbrella group called the Council of Federated Organizations (COFO). COFO then launched an all-out effort to get out the black vote in Mississippi. By the summer of 1964, the goals of COFO had expanded and become clearly defined. Bob Moses stated them clearly when he went to Stanford University to recruit students to go to Mississippi to help in the effort. The goals of Freedom Summer were as follows:

> to expand black voter registration in the state; to organize a legally constituted "Freedom Democratic Party" that would challenge the whites-only Mississippi Democratic party; to establish "freedom schools" to teach reading and math to black children in a state where there was no mandatory attendance law and black children more often worked in the fields than went to school; and finally, to open community centers where indigent blacks could obtain legal and medical assistance. (Williams 1987, 239)

Although Mississippi lawmakers immediately made it illegal to operate a school without a permit from the county government, thus outlawing the proposed freedom schools, the work went on. Even after three civil rights workers disappeared, the freedom schools were set up in communities around the state. In the end, not only children but also African Americans of all ages who had been denied an education attended the schools to learn academic subjects as well as black history. Teaching in them was punishable by six months in prison, but volunteers were undeterred by the possibility of imprisonment.

Today, Freedom Schools organized and supported by the CDF provide summer options for children in places where none exist and help to strengthen the involvement of the community in the year-round achievement of black children. According to the CDF's web site (www.childrensdefense.org), Freedom Schools "serve children ages 5 to 18 for six to eight weeks and integrate reading, conflict resolution, and social action in an activity-based curriculum that promotes social, cultural, and historical awareness." The staffs of Freedom Schools consist, for the most part, of college-aged young adults who are part of the Student Leadership Network for Children.

The Student Leadership Network for Children

One of the activities of the BCCC is the Student Leadership Network for Children (SLNC). The goal of the SLNC is to develop a new generation of leaders to work for child advocacy and social change. Its members range in age from eighteen to thirty and may be trained at the Ella Baker Child Policy Institute, another arm of the BCCC. Some of the members work as mentors and as coordinators of Freedom Schools. Others work as volunteers with organizations in their communities that serve the needs of children. The CDF also informs SLNC members of important legislation in order that they can effectively support or oppose such legislation.

Ella Baker Child Policy Training Institute

The Ella Baker Child Policy Training Institute operates development training sessions for members of the SLNC at the former Alex Haley Farm in Clinton, Tennessee. It provides intensive workshops, carried out over two to three days, teaching skills needed for operating Freedom Schools and for working in community services for children. Juvenile and family court judges, as well as education and community leaders, serve as facilitators and trainers. Among those who have taught at the institute are Harvard African American studies professor Cornel West, Yale child studies professor James Comer, and former civil rights activist and mayor of Mayersville, Mississippi, Unita Blackwell.

—*Kathleen Thompson*

References and Further Reading
Davis, Marianna W. 1982. *Contributions of Black Women to America.* Columbia, SC: Kenday Press.
Guy-Sheftall, Beverly. 1992. "Marion Wright Edelman." In *Notable Black American Women,* edited by Jessie Carney Smith. Detroit: Gale Research.
Hine, Darlene Clark, Elsa Barkley-Brown, and Rosalyn Terborg-Penn, eds. 1992. *Black Women in America: An Historical Encyclopedia.* Brooklyn: Carlson Publishing.
Hine, Darlene Clark, and Kathleen Thompson. 1998. *A Shining Thread of Hope: The History of Black Women in America.* New York: Broadway Books.
Hiraoka, Leona. 1996. "More Than a Prayer." *NEA Today* 14, no. 7 (March): 7.
Low, W. Augustus, and Virgil A. Clift, eds. 1981. *Encyclopedia of Black America.* New York: McGraw-Hill.
"Mother Marian." 1993. *Psychology Today* 26, no. 4 (July-August): 26.
People Weekly. 1996. V. 46, no. 27 (December 30): 78.

Williams, Juan. 1987. *Eyes on the Prize: America's Civil Rights Years, 1954–1965.* New York: Viking.

Common-Law Marriage

Common-law marriage is marriage that does not comply with the formal statutory requirements for marriage but that is still approved by the state. The rights and duties of the parties to a common-law marriage are the same as if they were married formally. The parties may only dissolve the marriage by divorce or annulment. The requirements for a valid common-law marriage are determined by state law, and these requirements vary by state. A couple is typically considered to have a common-law marriage when they agree to be presently married, hold themselves out as married, and cohabit. Courts sometimes infer the agreement to be married from the holding out and cohabitation. A common-law marriage is invalid if either party lacks the capacity to enter the marital relationship on account of, for example, the party's age, marital status, or gender. As Homer Clark described the situation: "In most instances . . . people drift into common law marriage either because one of the parties persuaded the other that they could really be married in this fashion, or because the customs of their social class sanction this kind of union" (Clark 1988, 59–60). Contemporary proponents of common-law marriage say that the institution honors people's expectations and reduces illegitimacy.

Common-law marriage has its origins in canon law. The Catholic Church encouraged marriages with religious ceremonies, but as early as A.D. 1145 also tolerated informal marriages. (Morland 1946, 42). "Due partly, doubtless, to the Roman tradition, partly to anxiety to keep people out of meretricious relations and to make children legitimate, and doubtless partly to the fear of driving men out of or not retaining them in the church, it recognized many clandestine unions as valid, though irregular, and presumed everything in favor of the validity thereof" (50). In 1563 at the Council of Trent, the church, asserting its political power in response to the Protestant Reformation, outlawed informal marriages in an attempt to eliminate clandestine marriages (Dillon 1942, 35; Weyrauch 1979, 424–425).

Common-law marriage existed in England and could be established either by mutual assent to marry as manifested in words of the present tense (*sponsalia per verba de praesenti*) or by an agreement to marry in the future, followed by consummation of the marriage (*sponsalia per verba de futuro cum copula*) (Pollock and Maitland 1911, 368). The ecclesiastical courts applied Roman canon law and recognized common-law marriage (Dillon 1942, 2–4). After the Act of Supremacy of 1534 and Henry VIII's break with the Roman Catholic Church, England no longer recognized canon law (Setaro, 348). Ecclesiastical jurisdiction in family law matters continued, however, until the Matrimonial Causes Act of 1857 (An Act to Amend the Law Relating to Divorce and Matrimonial Causes in England, 1857, 20 & 21, Vict. ch. 85, cl. 2). Consequently, common-law marriages continued, even after the Council of Trent, as England was not bound by the council's acts. Although these marriages were valid, they were not equivalent to marriage with the requisite formalities. For example, the wife could not claim dower (Pollock and Maitland 1911, 374–375). Lord Hardwicke's Act, passed in 1753, required "solemnization in facie ecclesiae" (An Act for the Better Preventing of Clandestine Marriage, 1753, 26 Geo. 2 ch. 33). The act was meant to end secret "fleet" marriages among young people performed by unscrupulous clergy (Stone 1977, 33). The act required, among other things, publication of the banns, solemnization by clergy, and maintenance of parish marriage registers (Stein 1969, 274–275).

Common-law marriage received a mixed response in the pre-revolutionary United States. Some colonies rejected it. For example, as early as 1639, the Puritans in the Colony of New Plymouth passed laws requiring marriage formalities (Koegel 1922, 58–59), and in 1801 the Massachusetts courts affirmed that common-law marriages could not exist. (Mangue v. Mangue [1 Mass. 240]). Yet by the late 1800s, common-law marriage was firmly entrenched in U.S. law. Between 1860 and 1895, for example, courts in Alabama, Ohio, Arkansas, Illinois, Iowa, Minnesota, Wisconsin, Indiana, Kansas, Nebraska, and Colorado allowed these marriages. In 1877, the U.S. Supreme Court gave its approval to the institution, stating that "there can be no doubt" that a common-law marriage is a marriage, "in view of the adjudications made in this country, from its earliest settlement to the present day." The Court explained that marriage statutes did not invalidate informal marriages "unless they contain[ed] express words of nullity" (Meister v. Moore [96 U.S. 76]). Although the majority of states accepted common-law marriage by the turn of the nineteenth century (Bowman 1996, 722), courts in Maryland, West Virginia, and Washington rejected such marriages during that period.

One scholar has concluded that "there can be no single explanation for the adoption of common law marriage in some states and its prohibition in others" (Bowman 1996, 731). The institution arguably was particularly suited to the frontier, where great distances and difficult travel made formal marriage difficult (McChesney v. Johnson [79 S.W. 2d 658 (Tex. Civ. App. 1934)]). Some states may have embraced common-law marriage as a way to recognize the customary informal marriages that were common among the indigenous people in the jurisdiction (727, 730–731).

The legal divide can be explained, in part, by each jurisdiction's understanding of English common law. Those jurisdictions that accepted the practice typically believed that English common law recognized common-law marriage, whereas courts that believed otherwise often refused to adopt it (Denison v. Denison [35 Md. 361 (1872)]). Most notably, the Supreme Court of New York found in 1809 that English common law required no formal ceremony, and the court upheld the validity of common-law marriage. This case, Fenton v. Reed (4 Johns. 52 [N.Y. Sup. Ct. 1809]), allegedly authored by Chancellor Kent, became well known when it was cited by him in Kent's Commentaries, an influential treatise (Stein 1969, 279). Commentators subsequently questioned the accuracy of the Fenton court's characterization of English common law (Friedman 1985, 202–203; Koegel 1922, 79–81; Stein 1969, 278–279). Scholars also questioned the accuracy of the Fenton court's holding since the court failed to discuss an act passed by the Colonial Assembly of New York that required formalities (Morland 1946, 53–54). Certainly English common law was far from clear, and the English House of Lords itself held, in a divided and much criticized opinion in 1843, that the common law of England did not permit common law marriage (*Reg.* v. *Millis* [8 Eng. Rep. 844]).

Despite some strong supporters in this country, such as Joel Bishop in his 1891 *New Commentaries on Marriage and Divorce* (Bishop 1891, §389), the institution of common-law marriage became suspect. By the mid- to late 1800s, the public, academics, and legislators were growing increasingly skeptical of the institution. By the early twentieth century it "met almost universal public condemnation" (Grossberg 1985, 101). The American Bar Association and the Commission on Uniform State Laws were opposed to it (Koegel 1922, 10). Arguments about immorality were buttressed by claims that states should collect vital statistics on marriage, that states should use marriage to promote goals such as health screening for venereal disease or eugenics, that states should minimize the legal uncertainty surrounding the question of marriage validity, that fraudulent claims were possible, and that the frontier was closing (Stein 1969, 297; Bowman 1996, 750). There were also fears that secret marriages "might lead to disputes over property rights, to public scandal, and to the perils of bigamy" (Friedman 1985, 204). In the post–Civil War period after African Americans gained the right to marry, "the desire to discourage [miscegenation] contributed to the disapproval of common law marriage" (Bowman 1996, 739). More states enacted laws requiring a marriage license and formal solemnization of the marriage. Yet, Michael Grossberg has explained, "judges preserved much of their discretion by retaining the axiom that marital regulations without explicit language making them compulsory were only directory" (Grossberg 1985, 95). Simply, despite the public outrage, "common law marriage remained a legal option in most jurisdictions" (Grossberg 1985, 101), although some state courts abolished common-law marriage during that period (Bowman 1996, 732).

Hostility to common-law marriage continued into the mid-twentieth century (Stein 1969, 290–292). The criticisms of the institution remained largely the same, although a new concern about administrability arose with the advent of government benefit programs such as workers' compensation and Social Security benefits (Bowman 1996, 746). By 1946 there were only eighteen states that permitted common-law marriage (Morland 1946, 34). In 2001, the number had fallen to ten (Alabama, Colorado, Iowa, Kansas, Montana, Pennsylvania, Rhode Island, South Carolina, Texas, and Utah), plus the District of Columbia.

Today states that do not permit common-law marriage nonetheless recognize it under the doctrine of *lex loci celebrationis:* A marriage valid where entered is valid everywhere unless recognition of the marriage would be contrary to strong public policy. In addition, where common-law marriage is not permitted, courts may obtain similar results through legal presumptions about the existence and validity of marriage (Weyrauch 1979, 426–427; Stein 1969, 281–287). Courts also have acknowledged doctrinal alternatives to recognize the parties' expectations, including express, implied, and quasi-contract claims; estoppel claims; putative spouse notions; and unjust enrichment arguments. Also, some statutes define family relations functionally; for instance, they use terms such as *dependent* instead of *wife* to afford benefits to de facto spouses.

One state, Utah, adopted a statutory form of common-law marriage in 1987 (Recognition of Common Law Marriages Act, Act of 25 February 1987, ch. 246, § 2, 1987 Utah Laws 1217 [codified at Utah Code Ann. § 30–1–4.5 (2000)]). The state permits common-law marriage if, within one year following the termination of the relationship, a court or administrative order is entered certifying that such a relationship existed. Utah's law was enacted to limit a family's eligibility for governmental benefits, particularly Aid to Families with Dependent Children (Crabtree 1988, 280–281).

Commentators disagree about whether these alternatives are an improvement over common-law marriage, and in fact, some well-respected scholars call for the retention or reintroduction of common-law marriage (Bowman 1996; Clark 1988; Crawley 1998–1999). Bowman, for example, claimed that the decrease in common-law marriage had had a disparate negative impact on women who were unable to obtain the benefits of marriage, for example both governmental benefits and divorce remedies (Bowman 1996, 754–759).

—Merle H. Weiner

See also Divorce, History of; Marriage

References and Further Reading
Bishop, Joel. 1891. *New Commentaries on Marriage, Divorce, and Separation.* Vol. 1. Chicago: T. H. Flood.
Bowman, Cynthia G. 1996. "A Feminist Proposal to Bring Back Common Law Marriage." *Oregon Law Review* 75: 709–780.
Clark, Homer H., Jr. 1988. *The Law of Domestic Relations in the United States.* 2d ed. St. Paul, MN: West Publishing.
Crabtree, David F. 1988. "Recent Developments in Utah Law: Recognition of Common-Law Marriages." *Utah Law Review* 149: 273–284.
Crawley, Hon. John B. 1998–1999. "Is the Honeymoon over for Common Law Marriage: A Consideration of the Common Law Marriage Doctrine." *Cumberland Law Review* 29: 399–426.
Dillon, Robert E. 1942. *Common Law Marriage.* Washington, DC: The Catholic University of America Press.
Dubler, Ariela R. 1998. "Governing through Contract: Common Law Marriage in the Nineteenth Century." *Yale Law Journal* 107: 1885–1920.
Friedman, Lawrence M. 1985. *A History of American Law.* 2d ed. New York: Simon and Schuster.
Grossberg, Michael. 1985. *Governing the Hearth, Law and the Family in Nineteenth-Century America.* Chapel Hill: University of North Carolina Press.
Kent, James. 1827. *Commentaries on American Law.* Vol. 2. New York: O. Halsted.
Koegel, Otto E. 1922. *Common Law Marriage and Its Development in the United States.* Washington, DC: John Byrne and Company.
Morland, John W., ed. 1946. *Keezer on the Law of Marriage and Divorce.* 3d ed. Indianapolis, IN: Bobbs-Merrill.
Pollock, Frederick, and Frederic W. Maitland. 1911. *The History of English Law before the Time of Edward I.* 2d ed. Vol. 2. London: Cambridge University Press.
Setaro, Franklin C. "A History of Ecclesiastical Law (Part II)." *Boston University Law Review* 18: 342–399.
Stein, Stuart J. 1969. "Common Law Marriage: Its History and Certain Contemporary Problems." *Journal of Family Law* 9: 271–299.
Stone, Lawrence. 1977. *The Family, Sex and Marriage in England 1500–1800.* New York: Harper and Row.
Weyrauch, Walter O. 1979. "Metamorphoses of Marriage." *Family Law Quarterly* 19: 415–440.

Communes, Families in

According to one of the most comprehensive studies on American communes, the United States has the distinction of being "the only place where voluntary communes have existed continuously" since the early 1700s (Oved 1993, xiii–xiv). Observers and researchers, early and contemporary, tend to agree that the traditional family structure—father, mother, child or children—hinders the success of any commune. In the United States today, changing conditions have resulted in a constant redefinition of the American family. Redefining the American family has been the aspiration of communes since their inception.

The commune's purpose, if religious in nature, necessitated changes to traditional values. Religious convictions rather than communal living resulted in abolition of the traditional family structure. Celibacy became the goal of members joining most spiritual communes. The eighteenth-century Ephrata commune, or cloister, in Lancaster County, Pennsylvania, considered celibacy an asset, though that commune allowed marriage. Approximately one hundred men, women, and children contributed to its nearly half-century success. Little is written about its concept of family.

Better known are the Shakers, who established several communes during the eighteenth and early nineteenth centuries. Each family of approximately sixty members shared work, resources, and food. A male and female elder served as father and mother of each self-supporting family, supervising the family's buildings and land. More than one family could live in a Shaker community. For example, a community with three families contained approximately 180 people.

Minimal contact, however, existed between men and women. Shaker communes insisted on adherence to celibate and separate living; those who joined as families were expected to abide. Parents gave up their children, who would be henceforth supervised by elders; boys lived apart from girls, just as men lived apart from women. Husbands and wives committed themselves to separation. The communal home comprised separate living spaces; even though occasional activities allowed intermingling, physical contact was forbidden. The commune's inability to survive by natural increase necessitated the adoption, into the Shaker family, of orphans or children whose parents could not afford to adequately provide for them. Educational activities for children focused on integrating them into the communal family. As might be expected, the Shaker proclivity for celibacy attracted few young members. One by one the Shaker communes died out. In 1981, ten members of the last surviving Shaker family could be found living in Maine.

A community of German immigrants established itself in Pennsylvania in the early nineteenth century under the direction of George Rapp. They called themselves the Harmony Society and like the Shakers eventually adopted celibacy. Unlike the Shakers, married men and women did not separate, or divorce, but continued to live together under the same roof as brother and sister, proving possible the seemingly contradictory term *married celibacy*.

Apparently in several nineteenth-century religious or socialist communes, children were separated from their parents. Such was the case at Oneida, though male continence within a "complex marriage," rather than celibacy, defined the family structure. The commune's founder, John Humphrey Noyes, deliberately limited procreation for a twenty-year period beginning in 1848. Noyes believed in selective breeding,

Members of a commune pose for a portrait. (Bettmann/Corbis)

condemning traditional marriage as a haphazard means for producing quality children. Believing that monogamous marriages left too much to chance, he proposed something more scientific. Selected couples lived together for a time before and after the birth of a child. Until babies reached nine months of age, their mothers cared for them day and night. From nine months to eighteen months of age, mothers cared for their children only at night. Once children reached eighteenth months of age, they were placed in the collective nursery and cared for by male and female nurses during infancy.

Though children, once they outgrew the infant section and were placed in the children's department, could visit their parents twice weekly, neither parents nor children dared show any sign of affection for which they would be publicly criticized. Bred children, or "stirps" as they were called, received their education and socialized with other children in the commune.

When the Oneida commune incorporated after legal troubles in the late nineteenth century, the system of complex marriages was abandoned, and thirty-seven legal, traditional marriages were formed. Children were allowed to remain in the community until the age of sixteen, at which time they were given $200 to begin a life outside the commune.

The Amana Colonies of the late nineteenth century proved an exception to the disintegration of the traditional family. Families shared homes, and married couples could belong but never attain the highest order. At Amana, the education of children was a priority. Students in the commune's school received a diverse education beginning at age six and continuing for another seven years. Music, Bible study, and the sect's Inspirationist doctrine combined with traditional subjects such as mathematics and reading. Additionally, within the Amana communal family, practical work applied even to the young; male and female students could be found knitting scarves and gloves as well as other articles. By the 1930s, the Amana family had opted to incorporate.

Another sect settled its communal family at Point Loma in southern California in 1897. Adherents of theosophy, they hoped to establish a commune that revolved around a boarding school for children. New members, mainly artists and educators, applied for admission to the community and paid a hefty application fee of $500. Their children and others in residence received academic and vocational training. Some as young as two years of age could be found in mathematics and spelling classes. Children, separated from their parents, lived in small cottages, dormitory-style, raised by educators who directed all their activities. The community's goal was that upon graduation, these initiates would go out into the world and establish other communes.

A decline in membership during the 1920s and the Great Depression that followed brought an end to the Point Loma commune. Other communes had begun to break apart near the end of the nineteenth century, as members died or quit. Some, such as Amana and Oneida, survived by incorporating. Apparently most children raised in these communes left once they reached adulthood.

Over thirty years would pass before the United States experienced another commune boom. One unique community, a response to the Depression, had its beginnings during the 1940s. With their founder Clarence Jordan, six families formed an "integrated Christian community" in Sumter County in southern Georgia. An interracial community, Koinonia Farm's purpose was to provide a place for displaced rural families. Depending on cash crops and a few small industries, communitarians worked as paired partners, and individual families received a salary based on need.

Families owned their single-family dwellings, but the land was considered everyone's property. A communal dining room existed into the 1970s, and members of the community ranging in age from twenty to seventy, not counting the children, could be found there. Because of trouble with the Ku Klux Klan during the 1950s, the black families left. Legal problems continued when the local school board refused entry of Koinonia children to the county schools. Koinonia has survived despite these difficulties. By 1969 the commune had incorporated; Koinonia Farms became Koinonia Partners. From 1969 to 1992 the partnership built 194 homes, of which 61 can be found on the original "farm" land. The building of no-interest-mortgage homes led to the founding of Habitat for Humanity International. Mortgage payments collected from the homes built by the Koinonia Partners go into the Fund for Humanity, which supports the Habitat organization. Ministries extend from what remains of the original communal organization. The Koinonia Partners do not share a common "purse," but their nonprofit incorporation holds to the values of the original founder (Koinonia Partners 2001).

A new communitarian movement resulted from the difficulties that accompanied the 1960s. The counterculture produced a number of dropouts who formed the hip, or hippie, communes of the decade. Living the alternative lifestyle became the rage, particularly for disenchanted, college-aged, white, middle-class youth. Several of the communes that opened or came into being during the late 1960s fit the stereotype—nudism, promiscuity, drugs, poor sanitary conditions, and few if any rules. The children born on these communes belonged to all, though they often recognized their biological parents as such. The hip communes were "notoriously unstable" and survived less than two years, if that long, according to Ron Roberts (Roberts 1971, 68).

Exceptions did exist. The anarchist commune Tolstoy Farm in Davenport, Washington, proved "atypical." According to Roberts, Tolstoy families had their own homes and money. The co-op school offered Tolstoy children an opportunity to study anything that interested them. Another anarchist commune, Drop City, in southeast Colorado, was composed mainly of former University of Colorado students; it proved to be long-lasting, compared to most. Based on Buckminster Fuller's geodesic dome design, Drop City's structures, called "zomes," gave a new look to the commune scene. Unlike in the average hip commune, modern conveniences were part of the communal package there. In the children's room, a television provided cartoon entertainment for youngsters. A communal kitchen and dining room provided opportunities for the members of the commune, who often lived in separate zomes, to join together as one family.

The members of Reba Place believed in redefining family. Unlike the rural communes of the 1960s, this urban Chicago commune, established by Mennonite idealists, hoped to offer its community of families support that the typical nuclear family often could not or did not provide. Members contributed to a common treasury that provided a living allowance and support for other necessities for all family members. Though monogamy and traditional values formed the core perspective toward sex, members believed their communal family provided "more emotional security than the isolated family," wrote Roberts (1971, 68).

The design for a modern utopian commune appeared before the 1960s when psychologist B. F. Skinner published *Walden Two.* Skinner's theories became a real experiment by 1970 with the establishment of Twin Oaks in Virginia, a commune that survives today. Operating much like the Israeli kibbutzim, there are no gender-specific tasks, and as in Skinner's model, children are managed rather than raised, or disciplined, by their biological parents. In fact, the members of Twin Oaks intend to evolve beyond the biological family as a social institution. At least that was the plan in the 1970s. Child managers tend to ignore rather than condemn disruptive behavior. Praise or some other form of reward can be expected by children who behave correctly.

After thirty years, Twin Oaks remains committed to communal living. Its bylaws state as much and indicate that members "share all income and expenses, rear their children communally, and are collectively responsible for all the needs of the Community's members and children. . . ." Whether they have been able to dispense with the traditional family structure, as expected in the 1970s, is uncertain. Seven miles away, another commune has appeared. Started in 1993,

Acorn members pursue cooperative endeavors with the older commune. They describe themselves as a multicultural community "building a close-knit extended family." A statement entitled "children in our community" can be found at their web site (www.ic.org/acorn). Child care is considered "parent-centered and integrated into the daily life of the community . . . keeping firmly in mind the importance of balancing the needs of the child and family with the needs of the community" (Twin Oaks 2001).

Several other new communes were established during the 1990s. Others have survived since their beginnings in the 1970s. The Federation of Egalitarian Communities (FEC) provides a directory that lists member communities. It also has a web site: www.thefec.org. Most communes today actively seek new members, though the drop-in style of the 1960s is discouraged or prohibited. The literature suggests that the biological family has not disappeared. Though children are welcomed, cherished, and more often than not communally raised, parental responsibility is expected. Some communities share child care; others do not specifically support or design a communal program for the care of their children. The communities listed with the FEC all appear to offer some kind of community philosophy on children and families. Like the communes of earlier times, they fully recognize that the fate of the community can rest with the children. Unlike communes of earlier times, however, current communities seem to recognize the continued appeal of the traditional family structure, and instead of attempting to abolish it, they hope to strengthen it.

The communal way of life remains attractive, and Sandhill Farm and Dancing Rabbit in northeastern Missouri, Beacon Hill and Jolly Ranchers in the heart of Seattle, and East Wind in Missouri's Ozark Hills, to name a few, offer an alternative.

—*Kay J. Blalock*

See also Celibacy; Complex Marriage; Extended Family; Family Decline in the Twentieth Century; The Oneida Community; Shaker Family

References and Further Reading
Fogarty, Robert S. 1990. *All Things New: American Communes and Utopian Movements, 1860–1914.* Chicago: University of Chicago Press.
Hedgepeth, William. 1970. *The Alternative: Communal Life in New America.* New York: Macmillan.
Koinonia Partners. www.koinoniapartners.org (cited 22 October 2001).
Oved, Yaacov. 1993. *Two Hundred Years of American Communes.* New Brunswick, NJ: Transaction Publishers.
Roberts, Ron E. 1971. *The New Communes.* Englewood Cliffs: Prentice Hall.
Streissguth, Thomas. 1999. *Utopian Visionaries.* Minneapolis: The Oliver Press.
Twin Oaks. www.twinoaks.org (cited 22 October 2001).
Whitworth, John McKelvie. 1975. *God's Blueprints: A Sociological Study of Three Utopian Sects.* London: Routledge and Kegan Paul.

The Companionate Family

The ideal of the companionate family—also known as the "affectionate family"—emerged in response to the social transformations of the early twentieth century. In the 1920s, a spate of books and articles attempted to redefine the nature of marriage and child rearing in an industrialized world. This literature, written by an influential group of psychologists, physicians, educators, and reformers, popularized a new conception of family relationships for a middle-class audience. These experts advanced the notion of the "modern" family bound together by ties of companionship, mutual affection, and personal fulfillment.

The new family ideology reflected changes in family structure and women's lives. The 1920s saw rising divorce rates, declining birthrates, greater female participation in education and the labor force, and new notions of female sexuality. As women delayed child rearing, family size decreased, especially among the urban middle class. Family function shifted as well. By the first decades of the twentieth century, the family had lost many of its traditional responsibilities as outside institutions took over earlier economic, social, and educational roles. The family's chief economic role shifted from production to consumption. Industrialization and urbanization brought production outside the home and diminished patriarchal authority.

Anxiety over these changes brought a reevaluation of marriage, child rearing, and sexual mores. Many Americans worried that the family was disintegrating. Although conservatives responded with a call to return to Victorian standards, other observers rejected old family patterns as hierarchical and unemotional, inappropriate to industrial society. They criticized the patriarchal authority and sexual repression they saw in earlier generations. Rather than reinstating the Victorian family, with its emphasis on duty, morality, and sacrifice, they attempted to update marriage and the family for modern conditions.

The companionate family offered a new kind of middle-class family ideal. The modern family, in this revision, now extended beyond the traditional focus on economic security, procreation, and religious training. It assumed new responsibility for the emotional and psychological well-being of its members in a number of ways. Family life would be based on mutual affection and compatibility. It would meet the needs of each of its members and foster personal satisfaction. Spouses were now idealized as friends and lovers, united in marriage by romance, sexual satisfaction, and emotional fulfillment. Advocates of this ideology favored easier divorce, legalization of birth control, and sex education to prepare young people for marriage. They argued that sexual attraction and adjustment were an important component of marriage and that suppressing sexual desire was unhealthy.

Relations between parents and children also took on a more democratic cast. Child rearing assumed a central role in the companionate family. Children and parents would relate as "pals," with intimacy and affection. Young people would enjoy more freedom from parental control and greater interaction with their peers. Parents would receive training and advice from experts in child development. This "child-centered" family would promote the self-expression, personality development, and individual potential of each child.

This model was largely directed toward middle-class Americans. Its ideals were difficult to reach for poor and working-class families, rural families, or immigrants and minority groups. These groups often faced varying social and economic conditions and drew on different cultural patterns regarding family function and behavior.

The ideal of the companionate family had mixed implications for women. It offered new recognition of female sexuality and emphasized the importance of sexual satisfaction for both partners. Rather than confining women to an exclusively maternal role, it depicted women as sexual beings with rights to sexual fulfillment. At the same time, however, the promise of partnership was limited to the realm of sexuality and marriage. The companionate family promoted greater emotional satisfaction for wives but did not imply greater equality for women in public life. The sexual division of labor remained, and even within the democratized family, women were still expected to carry the burden of household duties. The companionate family model also had the effect of reinforcing heterosexual norms and stigmatizing same-sex relationships. Its celebration of the egalitarian potential of marriage made suspect women who remained unmarried or childless. It channeled female sexuality toward men and marriage as the path to personal fulfillment.

The ideal of the companionate family helped shape important social and cultural developments in twentieth-century America. It brought higher expectations for marriage and family life. Its implications included pressure for freer access to birth control and divorce, the rise of sex education and marriage counseling, the emergence of the parent education movement, and the focus on the family as a site of consumption rather than production. Although postponed by the exigencies of Depression and war, the ideal of the companionate family reappeared in the postwar years.

—*Diana Selig*

See also Affection as a Basis for Marriage; Family Decline in the Twentieth Century; Gender Roles in the American Family; Marriage; Middle-Class Family; Parenting Education; Sexual Revolutions

References and Further Reading
Cott, Nancy. 1987. *The Grounding of Modern Feminism.* New Haven: Yale University Press.
Fass, Paula. 1977. *The Damned and the Beautiful: American Youth in the 1920's.* New York: Oxford University Press.
Mintz, Steven, and Susan Kellogg. 1988. *Domestic Revolutions: A Social History of American Family Life.* New York: The Free Press.

Complex Marriage

Complex marriage was an experiment with marriage and family life developed and practiced at the utopian community of Oneida in upper New York State from 1848 to 1879 under the leadership of John Humphrey Noyes.

In complex marriage all adults saw themselves as married to every other adult in the community. They took this belief from the idea in Matthew 22: 23–30 that in heaven there would be neither marriage nor giving in marriage, bolstered by other passages from the New Testament, which Noyes interpreted to mean that in heaven all would be married to each other. They believed they were forerunners of this perfected state on earth, modeling the future in the present.

Although everyone was married to everyone else, this was not a community that even considered homosexuality a possibility or approved of sexual license between men and women. Members who wished to sleep with one another generally asked an older person to act as intermediary. Members were free to decline to sleep with each other without embarrassment. Men and women were encouraged to seek those more spiritually advanced than themselves as bed partners, as sex was seen as one more path toward God. Noyes himself had the final power to

Oneida Community of Free-Lovers in the library at night, c. 1855. (Bettmann/Corbis)

decide if people should sleep together and to decide if this would be a step in their spiritual advancement. The development of an exclusive relationship between a man and a woman was condemned by the community.

Noyes believed there were two branches of sexual relations—the *amative*, or social union of companions, and the *propagative*, to beget children. He saw the amative as the higher form, in which men and women reflected God's love on each other and together grew toward the divine. Influenced by seeing his wife go through five pregnancies in the first six years of their marriage and producing one living child, Noyes developed a method of intercourse that he called "male continence," which was practiced within the community to pro-

duce the amative form of sexual relations. This was sexual intercourse that stopped short of male orgasm. This was not coitus interruptus, but a form of male self-control in which sexual union, carried on in moderation, took place without ejaculation, according to Noyes. This acted as a form of birth control in which men took responsibility rather than women and kept the community birthrate low from its beginnings until 1869, when the community decided to allow more propagative sex.

From 1869 to the end of the community in 1879, members practiced their own eugenic program to breed superior children, which they called *stirpiculture*, a word Noyes coined from the Latin word *stirpes*, meaning root, stock, or strain. The community set up first an informal, then a formal, committee to decide who could have children. Couples desiring to be parents applied to the committee, and at times, the committee suggested the pairing up of certain spiritually advanced men and women, to which both had to give free consent. In reality, John Humphrey Noyes had the final say.

The community held all its property in common, giving up the idea of private property. Since the community saw itself as one large family, all children were seen as the children of everyone in the community. Children stayed with mothers while nursing, then began day care in the Children's House, returning to the mothers at night. From about the age of three a child went to live full-time in the Children's House. Birth parents were freely allowed to see their children, but an exclusive relationship was disapproved by the community and all who wished to do so participated in the children's lives. Noyes believed motherhood was not women's primary role and that they had the right and duty to develop as individuals before God. Women and some men served as caretakers and teachers for short terms and in rotation. Those with special aptitude and desire to work with children became long-term caretakers. Children stayed in the Children's House until about the age of twelve, when they joined the adult community.

In contrast to mainstream society in the United States, women in the community cut their hair to shoulder length or shorter and wore the bloomer costume, a blouse and short skirt over pants, which made activity easier. In fact, they claimed to have invented this way of dress. An ideal of the community was the equality of women with men. Women were encouraged to try activities outside their sphere, some learning to play base-

ball and become outdoor workers and managers, although the majority of women remained primarily in domestic occupations. Complex marriage itself was seen as a way to free women from their role in traditional marriage as the property of a man and to give them equal choice with men in sexual relations and in choosing to have children.

In 1879, as a result of outside pressure, a split in the community, and the flight of John Humphrey Noyes to Canada to avoid possible legal prosecution, the community formally gave up the idea of complex marriage, returning to traditional paired marriage relations. On 1 January 1881, the community itself dissolved and reformed as a joint-stock company, giving shares to former members. The Oneida silverware that is sold to the present time became the staple product of the company.

There have been other utopian communities in the United States that believed in and practiced group marriage, particularly in the 1960s and 1970s: places such as Harrad West of Berkeley, California; the Cro Research Organization of Oregon, known as Crow; and the Family, near Taos, New Mexico. But none of them reached the level of structure in relationships that bound together the nineteenth-century members of Oneida.

—*Margaret M. Caffrey*

See also The Oneida Community

References and Further Reading
Carden, Maren Lockwood. 1998. *Oneida: Utopian Community to Modern Corporation.* Syracuse, NY: Syracuse University Press, 1969. Reprint, Syracuse, NY: Syracuse University Press.
Fairfield, Richard. 1972. *Communes, U.S.A.: A Personal Tour.* Baltimore, MD: Penguin Books.

Herrick, Tirzah Miller. 2000. *Desire and Duty at Oneida: Tirzah Miller's Intimate Memoir.* Edited by Robert S. Fogarty. Bloomington: Indiana University Press.

Klaw, Spencer. 1994. *Without Sin: The Life and Death of the Oneida Community.* New York: Penguin Books, 1993. Reprint, New York: Penguin Books.

Noyes, John Humphrey. 1966. *History of American Socialisms.* 1869. Reprint, New York: Dover Publications.

Oneida Community. 1973. *Bible Communism; a Compilation from the Annual Reports and Other Publications of the Oneida Association and Its Branches; Presenting, in Connection with Their History, a Summary View of Their Religious and Social Theories.* New York: Office of the Circular, 1853. Reprint, New York: AMS Press.

Oneida Community Collection. Syracuse University Library. http://lib.www.syr.edu/digital/guides/o/OneidaCommunity Collection/ (cited 24 April 2001).

Parker, Robert Allerton. 1935. *A Yankee Saint: John Humphrey Noyes and the Oneida Community.* New York: G. P. Putnam's Sons.

Robertson, Constance Noyes. 1970. *Oneida Community: An Autobiography, 1851–1876.* Syracuse, NY: Syracuse University Press.

Cooperative Extension Service

The Cooperative Extension Service began in 1914 with congressional passage of the Smith-Lever Act, which provided for the dissemination of information related to agriculture and home economics to citizens through land-grant universities. The Smith-Lever Act extended federal support to earlier efforts at the state and county levels to employ agents to demonstrate research-developed farming methods and provide skills training, especially for youth. Among the most successful of the early Extension Service initiatives was the 4-H (head, heart, hands, and health) Clubs Program, which provided agricultural and home economics education to rural children. Through the 1920s and 1930s, Cooperative Extension assisted with the administration of federal programs including the Federal Farm Loan Act, the Feed and Seed Loan Program, and under the New Deal, the Agricultural Adjustment Act.

The Smith-Lever Act called for "cooperation" among federal, state, and local entities, and the Cooperative Extension Service draws public funding and administrative support from three levels: the U.S. Department of Agriculture, state land-grant universities and colleges, and county governments. Specialists in each state develop statewide priorities subject to approval by the national office; these state plans are implemented at the local level by county extension agents.

Throughout its history, the Extension Service has attempted to remain true to its original mission while adjusting its work to changing social conditions. In recent years, it has increasingly focused on more diverse and urban populations and on youth development and family support services. Use of web-based technology has also brought change by allowing the rapid dissemination of resources by federal, state, and local Extension officials across traditional geographic boundaries. In the mid-1990s, the Cooperative Extension Service and Cooperative State Research Service were integrated and renamed the Cooperative State Research, Education, and Extension Service (CREES) to better coordinate research and education activities. The web site of CREES is www.reeusda.gov; the web site of the *Journal of Extension* is www.joe.orgs.

—*JuNelle Harris*

See also Smith-Lever Act

References and Further Reading
Sanders, H. C., ed. 1966. *The Cooperative Extension Service.* Englewood Cliffs, NJ: Prentice Hall.

Courtship, History of

Courtship is the practice of seeking the affection of another person with the intention of marrying. The history of courtship in the United States from colonial times to the present is characterized by growing individual choice over mate selection, the increasing importance of romantic love, the changing location of courtship from private places to public spaces, and the change from the prohibition of premarital sexuality to its widespread acceptance. Factors that have determined the choice of a spouse in the United States are geographic location, religion, social class, and race. Over time, these barriers have become less rigid. In the colonial era, parents had control over the choice of their child's spouse through the amount and timing of property dispensed to children. Over the nearly two centuries of the colonial period, parental control diminished. Individual choice grew through the nineteenth and twentieth centuries. Courtship practices have varied widely. Until industrialization and urbanization dominated U.S. society, courting was generally conducted in the woman's home or at community events. Toward the end of the nineteenth century, courting increasingly moved into public spaces. The conception of love has changed over time as well. Colonial families expected love to grow after marriage to a compatible partner. In the nineteenth century, love became a prerequisite to marriage, and romantic, passionate love increasingly became the ideal.

For most of U.S. history, premarital sexuality was strongly discouraged. Sexuality was controlled, to the extent that it could be, by religion, family, and community during the colonial era. Control increasingly became the responsibility of the courting couple during the nineteenth and the first half of the twentieth centuries. After the 1960s, couples no longer sought to control sexuality in courtship; instead they expected it to be a part of courtship or simply to be an end in itself. By the end of the twentieth century, cohabitation before marriage was accepted by most.

Courtship in the New England Colonies
New England settlers emigrated from Europe in close-knit family groups. Parents, particularly fathers, held great control within the family and had the legal right to oversee the courtship of their children. They exercised control over the timing and circumstances of their children's marriages through the provision of land for men and dowries for women. In addition, sons and daughters customarily married in birth order, indicating parental control over timing of marriage. Partners were chosen on the basis of religious piety, economic standing, and compatibility. Passion and physical attraction were considered suspect in choosing a marriage partner. If the couple were compatible, love was expected to follow upon marriage.

Courting practices consisted of meeting other young people at the church or meetinghouse, during family visits, or at work parties. Frequently festivities would follow the making of a quilt or the raising of a barn.

Working in households other than their own also gave opportunities for young people to meet prospective spouses. Most colonial towns were small, and young people knew all their cohorts. Courtship usually consisted of the young man's visiting

An engraving of a courting couple, c. 1805. (Library of Congress)

the young woman. In rural areas, visiting could include bundling, a practice that offered the opportunity for privacy between a young man and woman. Bundling consisted of couples sleeping in the same bed while separated by a bundling board. Other variations of the practice included the woman wearing a nightgown tied at the feet or the couple going to bed fully clothed.

By the eighteenth century, parental control over the choice of spouse had greatly diminished. As the land in certain towns became overpopulated, young men were more likely to seek land elsewhere, restricting their fathers' power over their marital choices. With each succeeding decade, more children were born from premarital pregnancies, and sons and daughters were more likely to marry out of birth order.

Throughout the colonial era, a public announcement of a proposed marriage had to be published in a timely manner. Weddings were generally small informal family gatherings rather than large public celebrations.

Courtship in the Southern Colonies
In Virginia, the ratio of men to women was very high in the early years of the colony. In the 1630s, men outnumbered women six to one (Mintz and Kellogg 1988, 37), giving women a great deal of choice in their spouses—so much so that a law was passed to disallow women from becoming engaged to more than one man at a time. In order to remedy the

problem, the London Company sent out brides whose passage could be redeemed by suitors with the currency of the time—tobacco—hence the term *tobacco brides*. Courtship was brief, though women were accorded the right of refusal. During the remainder of the seventeenth century, the ratio of men to women continued to be out of balance, greatly affecting courtship and marriage. Many men never married.

Most southern colonists came as indentured servants rather than in families, so parental control over partner choice was limited. Though women servants were penalized harshly for having children out of wedlock by having their years of servitude extended, many bore children during their period of indenture. Servants were not allowed to marry until their terms were served, which led to marriage at later ages. Generally families in the southern colonies were smaller than those in New England.

By the eighteenth century the ratio of men to women had stabilized, and family formation proceeded at a more natural rate. Courtship consisted of visiting, bringing gifts, and conferring with parents. As the gap between classes widened and a wealthy elite developed, more powerful control over marriage was exerted by parents in the wealthier classes. Unlike the simple family celebrations of New England, wedding celebrations in the South were more likely to include friends and acquaintances and to emphasize dancing and feasting.

African American Courtship in the Colonial Era

At the beginning of the colonial era, African Americans were few, and the gender ratio was out of balance. There were many more men than women, making it difficult for men to marry. In the eighteenth century, when larger numbers of slaves had been imported, courtship and marriage were important goals.

Records of runaways during the eighteenth century indicate that many men were seeking wives from other plantations. Though legal marriage was discouraged or prohibited by law, a clergyman sometimes solemnized marriage or, most frequently, the slaves themselves conducted the ceremonies.

Courtship in the Early Republic

By the end of the eighteenth century, love was not just a possibility, but a necessary element to be established during courtship. At the same time, men and women were wary of passion, considering it a transitory and unreliable basis for contracting marriage. By the 1780s, babies born earlier than eight and one-half months after marriage accounted for about one-third of first children, but by the 1830s that figure had decreased to 20 percent, indicating that couples were internalizing earlier standards of discouraging premarital sex (Rothman 1987, 45). Women were being cast as guardians of moral purity and their role was to make sure that standards were upheld.

Immediately after the Revolution, simplicity ruled wedding celebrations. Simple ceremonies and modest dress were characteristic. During the early nineteenth century, the elements of the modern wedding celebration developed. Much of what is considered to be a traditional part of a wedding today—the white dress and veil, groomsmen and bridesmaids, the decorative wedding cake and the post-wedding trip—became common.

During the 1830s the idea of intense romantic love began to take over the popular imagination. Falling in love was fast becoming a prerequisite to marriage. No longer suspicious of passion, couples began to look for its signs. By 1860, it was considered by most to be a necessity. Courting couples had many opportunities to be alone. Much of courting consisted of visiting in the woman's parlor or going on long walks. Though bundling was no longer practiced in most locales, the parlor was the scene of romantic trysts. Families disappeared when suitors came to call, leaving the couple to determine the level of their erotic attraction. Kissing and petting—sexual activities short of intercourse—were common.

At some point during the courtship, the woman would often present an obstacle to marriage. One woman wrote her suitor that she had fragile health and that she might be an invalid for life. Her suitor insisted that he would care for her, in sickness and in health, thus overcoming the obstacle, proving his love, and in the process strengthening their emotional bond. Once marriage was agreed upon, the young man would customarily ask his fiancée's parents for her hand in marriage, but this was more of a formality than a real decision. Once marriage was decided upon, the couple and their families began to spread the word of the betrothal. About 1840, engagement rings became a common part of this ritual.

African American courtship after the Civil War entered a new phase. With the end of slavery, legal marriage was a priority for African Americans. Many freed people, as their first independent action, sought partners from whom they had been separated. Couples who had not been separated, but who had never had the opportunity to form a legal union, were eager to marry. So great was their desire that some freed people married in group ceremonies.

Turn-of-the-Century Courtship

As the United States became more urbanized, the courtship process was complicated by an expanded range of possible partners and greater opportunities for courtship activities. Men and women were meeting in public schools and colleges as women entered higher education. During this period, the growth of popular amusements meant that courtship was now becoming a more public, commercial activity. Courtship might include going to restaurants, dance halls, and movies as well as pursuing older forms of courting in parlors and at parties and dances. Between 1895 and 1920, dating began to predominate. The telephone offered the chance for couples to communicate and make plans, and the automobile led to greater privacy and freedom of movement. During this period, the changeover from calling to dating meant the removal of courtship from the woman's space, the home, to the man's space, the world. During this transition, kissing and petting were still predominant, but premarital sex became more acceptable for couples who were engaged to be married.

Courtship from World War I to the Present

In the 1920s and 1930s, dating became not just a prelude to marriage but an end in itself. It became a competition and a challenge to see who was the most sought-after and attractive. Frequent dating in public places with as many partners as possible was the ideal. Cutting-in at dances became the symbol of this ethic. The more partners a woman had on the dance floor, the greater her popularity.

With the coming of World War II, the competitive dating system broke down when 16 million men joined the armed services. Many hasty marriages were contracted as the men left for war. After the war, men who returned home were not in the mood for the dating game. The rate at which couples were marrying skyrocketed, and the average age at first marriage plummeted.

In the 1950s, prewar competitive dating gave way to the practice of going steady, which had its own rituals—the gift of a class ring, letter sweater, or fraternity pin to signify an exclusive union. Going steady had the effect of lowering the barriers to premarital sex. Parental efforts to control sexuality took the form of curfews and restrictions on where the date could take place, but limitations were easily evaded. Women were seen as the caretakers of sexual boundaries.

Beginning in the 1960s, with the advent of the birth-control pill, the coming of the baby boom culture of self-indulgence, and the proliferation of the *Playboy* philosophy, sexuality became an accepted part of youth relationships. No longer was courtship considered necessary for marriage and sexual fulfillment. By the 1980s, only one in five women had not had premarital sexual intercourse, compared with 50 percent in 1960 (Mintz and Kellogg 1988, 204). In 1959, opinion polls showed that most people disapproved of premarital sex, but by the end of the century, it was no longer stigmatized. Couples married later and were more likely to have lived together before marriage. More people than ever chose never to marry.

Gradually in the last quarter of the twentieth century, boundaries regarding mate selection broke down. There was a greater acceptance of interracial relationships, and no longer were social class, religion, or geographical boundaries as important as they had been even in the early 1960s. The use of personal ads and computerized dating services further widened the number of choices. With the advent of the Internet, relationships could be formed with persons in other communities and even other countries. With so many choices, however, the decision to enter a permanent relationship became ever more difficult. The breakdown of kinship ties, which accompanied the high mobility of the population, made the choice of mate even more significant and highly charged.

Though weddings of the late twentieth century became more extravagant and highly commercialized, they held less likelihood of initiating a permanent relationship as the divorce rate rose. Toward the end of the century, a movement to return to courtship and premarital chastity began to take hold. At the same time that sexual abstinence was increasingly being taught in the schools and religious groups encouraged Christian courtship rituals, the media presented more explicit sex in music, television, and movies. At the turn of the century, youth were presented with a deeply conflicted set of values from which to choose.

—*Bonnie L. Ford*

See also Affection as a Basis for Marriage; African American Families; Banns; Celibacy; The Companionate Family; Divorce, History of; Freedmen's Families; Gender Roles in the American Family; Marriage; The Pill; Premarital Sex; Sexual Revolutions; Weddings

References and Further Reading
Bailey, Beth. 1988. *From Front Porch to Back Seat: Courtship in Twentieth-Century America.* Baltimore: Johns Hopkins University Press.
Coontz, Stephanie. 1992. *The Way We Never Were: American Families and the Nostalgia Trap.* New York: Basic Books.
Gordon, Michael. 1978. *The American Family in Social-Historical Perspective.* New York: St. Martin's Press.

Lystra, Karen. 1989. *Searching the Heart: Women, Men, and Romantic Love in Nineteenth Century America.* New York: Oxford University Press.

Mintz, Steven, and Susan Kellogg. 1988. *Domestic Revolutions: A Social History of American Family Life.* New York: The Free Press.

Rothman, Ellen K. 1987. *Hands and Hearts: A History of Courtship.* Cambridge: Harvard University Press.

Cults, Families in

Historians generally understand cults to be religious movements that are characterized by charismatic leadership, ideology, and practice that separate members as much as possible from others and by a claim to new revelation that represents a radical break from the normative religion of a culture. The term *cult*, however, holds an ambiguous position in U.S. culture because the label has been used in a pejorative way to criticize movements that stand in extreme opposition to the normative stance of the critic. Used to mark groups that are distinctly "other," the label can connote degrees of secrecy and subversion that seem to threaten mainstream ideals.

Since the American Revolution, shared understandings of the family have been crucial to the evolving sensibilities of a culturally designated American mainstream. Middle classes especially relied upon their home lives and private activities to outline their parameters. The home, supported financially by father and spiritually by mother, became a sacred hallmark of an evolving middle-class ethos. Religious groups that proposed alternative family arrangements seemed disruptive and threatening in the American imagination. Because a radical reconfiguration of traditional family life is one way in which cults have repre-

sented themselves as both novel and separate, discussions of cults and families in American history have been riddled with controversy. When individual family members have joined cults, their relatives have often felt robbed of loved ones. When cults have encompassed multiple generations or subsumed entire family units, they have confronted dilemmas about child rearing, discipline, education, and responsibility.

Some of the first groups in America to be called cults, the Shakers and the Oneida Perfectionists, were particularly marked as outsiders by their reconfiguration of the family. The Shaker movement emerged from visions claimed by their founder, Mother Ann Lee (1736–1784). Convinced of the sinfulness of human nature and certain that the act of sexual intercourse lay at the root of evil, Lee led fellow believers away from Manchester, England, to the United States. As they gathered members in America, the Shakers lived together in "families" of celibates, sharing all property in common and practicing sexual abstinence. Believing that all human beings, male and female, were made in God's image, Shakers worshipped a Father-Mother deity and held that the fullest male manifestation of God had come in Jesus Christ; the fullest female, in Ann Lee. Traditional notions of the family faded in the blended Shaker community while individual perceptions of autonomy blurred into a sense of ecstatic transcendence in Shaker ritual and routine. Believing in the power of spirit to prevail over physical disease or material separation, Shakers engaged in ritual dancing and artwork that represented their union with God and one another.

Like Lee, John Humphrey Noyes (1811–1886) highlighted changes in the family in his vision of utopia on earth. Taking seriously biblical statements that Jesus expected the second coming to occur within a generation of his personal ministry, Noyes preached that nineteenth-century Christians had nothing to fear from sin, for they had already been saved. As saints and perfect beings, Noyes and his followers viewed their life on earth as a prelude to heavenly bliss. Because Christ had indicated that there would be no institution of marriage in heaven, Noyes declared that marriage on earth created false divisions among people and prevented the members of one body in Christ from loving all. In his small community at Oneida, New York, Noyes practiced communism in production and consumption and established "complex marriage." At Oneida, every man was husband to every woman and vice versa. Only mutual consent was required to engage in sexual relations. Exclusive sexual relations, however, were not tolerated, so that members undertook sexual activity in the spirit of communal loyalty and controlled detachment rather than licentious abandon or romantic passion. Noyes hoped that sex would become the bond of a community that mirrored heavenly unity rather than earthly divisiveness.

Perhaps because their family structures departed so drastically from that of the typical American, the Shakers and Oneida Perfectionists did not survive as cohesive movements beyond the nineteenth century. Calling for less extreme shifts in conventional family norms, Mormons and Christian Scientists cast off their reputations as cults in the nineteenth century and emerged as established churches in the twentieth. When Joseph Smith claimed to have uncovered the lost history of the tribe of Joseph, he

Families gather around the Reverend Jim Jones (from a photo album found among the dead in the Jonestown commune in Guyana, after the mass suicide in 1978). (Bettmann/ Corbis)

unveiled a dramatically novel set of revelations based loosely in Hebrew tradition. Like the Shakers and Perfectionists, Smith and his fellow Mormons worshipped a Mother-Father God and questioned the dichotomy of spirit and matter. Smith, however, proposed that Mormons themselves had preexisted in the spiritual realm before entering their earthly bodies and could hope to rise again to the celestial kingdom where they too could be "as Gods." To symbolize this eternal nature, Mormon couples sealed themselves to each other in ceremonies that represented eternal unity as well as earthly fidelity. Marriage was part of religious practice and no man or woman, they believed, could achieve salvation without being married. In ritual, even the dead were sealed to each other to facilitate salvation. This dedication to marriage coupled with vigorous spiritual commitment has led Mormons in certain times and places to practice male polygamy. Although not common, the presence of polygamy in Mormon communities has brought families with multiple wives into the legal and media spotlight throughout the nineteenth and twentieth centuries.

Mary Baker Eddy (1821–1910) posed a different sort of alternative to the conventional nineteenth-century family. Widowed and childless, Eddy occupied an anomalous position in a Victorian society that expected women to be wives and mothers. Finding herself alone and impoverished, Eddy turned to mental healing and became such a convincing proponent of such techniques that she was able to establish a new religion, Christian Science. By teaching that each individual could heal physical ailments by recognizing his or her oneness with God, Eddy posed questions about the family structures of her era. Speaking publicly as the head of her own church and insisting that every individual— man, woman, or young child—had the capacity to experience healing and testify to it, Eddy provided a space for women's and children's voices to be recognized. In Eddy's example, middle-class women found a means to self-assertion both in the public realm and in the privacy of their own families. Supporting herself through religious work and employing other women, Eddy also pioneered alternative roles for women who did not live in conventional family structures but wished to remain alone or in alternative arrangements.

Both Christian Scientists and Mormons transformed their relationships to conventional family life so that by the twentieth century they continued to thrive, in part, because they reinforced traditional family structures. The established Mormon Church abolished polygamy, and both organizations supported nuclear families, drawing children into religious life and sponsoring family-oriented activities. The term *cult*, however, continued to be associated with groups that challenged or seemed to undermine normative understandings of family life in the twentieth-century United States.

By the turn of the century, modern cults tended to diverge more radically from the Judeo-Christian tradition that dominated mainstream religious life and reflected the growing cultural diversity of American society. Transformations in American life changed perceptions of cults as well. As the twentieth century progressed, cult movements manifested the challenges and the opportunities posed by processes of secularization, the growth of technology and industry, and an influx of new religious and ethnic groups. In this context, cults functioned as utopian experiments in which members strove to critique the social conditions around them and imagine alternative worldviews.

Americans who found their traditional Judeo-Christian faith challenged by the Darwinism and rationalism that pervaded academic and professional life were drawn to cults that reenchanted the world. From witchcraft covens to occult sects, cults that emphasized a magical correspondence between the human inner life and the perceived living spark that enlivens the universe seemed to offer control and transcendence. Americans were concerned that the technologies and machines devised to maximize human control over nature were threatening to overwhelm their inventors and actually become unmanageable forces in society. They were drawn to movements such as Scientology or unidentified flying object (UFO) cults that proposed that the advancement of science was a salvation narrative infused with meaning. Rather than adopting the astronomer's vision of infinite but empty space, followers of UFO cults saw life and hope in the stars. Scientologists, who believed that a machine called an E meter would gauge the degrees of tension in their brains and enable them to achieve such mental clarity that they could bend space and time to their wishes, saw the pursuit of scientific knowledge as the true spiritual path.

Efforts to negotiate cultural encounters and class or racial conflicts expressed themselves through cult activity as well Growing through the first half of the twentieth century, the Pentecostal and Holiness movements drew the economically disadvantaged, who countered feelings of displacement and powerlessness with the spiritual intensity of snake handling or speaking in tongues. Ecstatic cults took hold in rural areas where followers turned to charismatic leaders and sectarian groups to seek the senses of meaning and community that they lacked on the outskirts of mainstream society. Urban cults, centered on voodoo and spiritualism, found a particularly strong following among African Americans. Father Divine (1877–1965) and his Peace Mission movement drew a strong following in New York, where the charismatic leader established a commune premised on mystical spirituality and racial equality. When Father Divine helped other blacks find shelter, employment, and camaraderie, he contributed to the patterns of integration that blacks struggled to forge throughout the twentieth century. The leader's interracial marriage embodied these efforts at the family

level. When Asian Hindus and Buddhists made yoga and transcendental meditation popular in the United States by mid-century, Americans joined the Hare Krishnas and sometimes moved their entire families to ashrams to pursue Eastern spiritual techniques.

Although ashrams, Pentecostal movements, and urban cults often drew nuclear family units into their bonds, religious groups that challenged this prevailing notion of family life were perceived as dangerous because they seemed to threaten an entire American way of life. Throughout the twentieth century, two specific threats evoked particular terror in the hearts of mainstream Americans: a concern that young people would be lured away from their homes by charismatic cult leaders and a fear that children whose parents belonged to cults would be abused.

During the 1960s–1980s period, fear that individuals would be "stolen" from their homes by the brainwashing techniques of persuasive cult leaders haunted the public imagination. Cults in the later half of the twentieth century were often based on radical critiques of mainstream life in the United States. Painting American society in shades of violence and corruption, cults appealed to individuals who were disillusioned or displaced amid their "normal" families and communities. Like the radical student movements of the late 1960s, cults found a particular following among disenchanted youth isolated by a "generation gap." From Scientology to the notorious Heaven's Gate cult whose members peacefully committed suicide in the 1990s, secure in the belief that beings from outer space would provide them with salvation, many cults have focused on the individual's psychic and spiritual condition. Promising emotional well-being or spiritual sanctity through membership in selective communities or relationships with charismatic leaders, such cults had an isolating influence over members.

Nervous family members often went to court in the 1970s and 1980s, arguing that their relative had been brainwashed and kidnapped. By 1988, however, the American Psychological Association declared brainwashing theories to be lacking in scientific rigor. Scholars have recently proposed that allegations of child abuse among cults increased in the 1990s precisely because the anticult movement lost its primary weapon when brainwashing was debunked. The presence of children in movements perceived as weird or threatening opened cults to increasing allegations of abuse.

In extreme cases, these fears were well founded. Two hundred and sixty children died in 1978 when Jim Jones convinced followers to kill themselves and their less willing peers in Jonestown. In 1994 and 1995, ten children lost their lives in the mass suicides/homicides of Solar Temple members in Europe. The child of Solar Temple apostates in Quebec was ritually murdered by two members who believed the child to be the newborn Antichrist. Children have been lost to dogmatic cult members' ideas about obedience and corporal punishment as well. A blow to the spine administered at the Michigan-based House of Judah claimed the life of a twelve-year-old boy in 1983, and an eight-year-old girl was beaten to death in 1988 at a Christian Youth camp near Portland, Oregon.

Psychological abuse touched children in cults, too. For example, in the 1950s, the psychoanalytically based Sullivan group, reacting to the fear of mothers that emerged from vulgarized Freudian theory, removed members' children from their parents to be raised entirely by hired "caregivers." These children grew up with emotional scars that were not alleviated by the psychoanalysis that governed the New York commune. More commonly, children in cults suffered from the neglect of parents who were so consumed by the intense spiritual quests that drew them to cults in the first place that their family life became a lesser priority.

Although these tragic examples cannot be understated, they received a disproportionate amount of media coverage in the context of a modern U.S. society that witnessed violence against children among mainstream religious and secular communities on a daily basis. The notions of ritual violence and cultic secrecy sparked American imaginations and provided a convenient external locus of concern where Americans could contemplate darker aspects of human nature—hatred and abuse—that they shuddered to identify in their own communities. Media attention incited lawsuits as well as did concerned relatives, and professionals sued absent, inattentive, or abusive cult-member parents for custody of children who seemed to be in danger.

Why have cults incited so much controversy and concern regarding the American family? Most recent theories suggest that Americans project their darker fears, particularly relating to the mutation or decimation of the American family, onto outsider groups, such as cults. Perhaps cults, operating on the margins of orthodox culture, embody the expansive and unlimited nature of a frontier, which contrasts sharply with the safely defined boundaries of family home life. Ideas about child psychology enter the debate as well. When children are understood to be passive receptors of instruction rather than actively engaged creators of meaning, they appear as victims in their cult environments. They become helpless objects of indoctrination who should be "rescued" (Palmer and Hardman 1999).

Recent scholars, however, have been reconfiguring these understandings of children and families in cults. Contending that mainstream Western society tends to distinguish children from adults to an exaggerated degree, researchers argue that cults and other countercultures often provide opportunities to observe children who act as competent social agents and creators of meaning. Rather than appearing as total victims and objects of a culture that is thrust upon them, children in some cults seem to be authors and subjects of their own cultural narratives.

These theories, among others, have prompted scholars to take increasing interest in the alternative, sometimes utopian, family visions in new religious movements. One analyst has proposed that "the utopia may well be the most sensitive indicator of where the sharpest anguish of an age lies" (Manuel 1967, 70). When new religious movements experiment with alternative visions that might ameliorate the maladies that beset American family life—from broken marriages and absentee parents to violence in neighborhoods and generation gaps— they serve as mirror fragments that are perhaps distorted but still reflect our deepest concerns about the family (Palmer and Hardman 1999, 7). Therefore, the study of how children are raised in marginal spiritual groups will expand our way of analyzing the social, psychological, legal, and moral dimensions of family life in the United States.

—Mary C. Miles

See also Communes, Families in; Complex Marriage; Mormon Polygamy; The Oneida Community; Shaker Family

References and Further Reading

Ahlstrom, Sydney. 1972. *A Religious History of the American People.* New Haven: Yale University Press.

Albanese, Catherine. 1992. *America: Religions and Religion.* Belmont, CA: Wadsworth.

Ellwood, Robert. 1979. *Alternative Alters.* Chicago: University of Chicago Press.

Manuel, Frank, ed. 1967. *Utopias and Utopian Thought.* Boston: Beacon Press.

Melton, Gordon. 1986. *Encyclopedic Handbook of Cults in America.* New York: Garland.

Moore, R. Laurence. 1986. *Religious Outsiders and the Making of Americans.* New York: Oxford University Press.

Palmer, Susan, and Charlotte Hardman. 1999. *Children in New Religions.* New Brunswick, NJ: Rutgers University Press.

D

Davis, Katharine Bement

Katharine Bement Davis, a prison reformer who also participated in the settlement house movement, is best known for her investigation of female sexuality. Her 1929 study, *Factors in the Sex Life of Twenty-Two Hundred Women,* covered contraceptive use, married life, lesbianism, sexual knowledge, masturbation, and sexual desire (Davis 1929).

Davis first gained notice at the 1893 Chicago World's Fair with an exhibit demonstrating how laborers could run a healthy household on a meager budget. Named the head resident of the College Settlement in Philadelphia, she renovated tenements and developed model housing before attending the University of Chicago. With her doctorate in hand, Davis won the position of superintendent of the women's prison at Bedford Hills, New York. Emphasizing education, Davis pioneered by helping inmates learn a trade. Her growing reputation as a prison reformer led to brief stints as New York City's commissioner of correction and as the first chair of the New York Parole Commission.

When her public service career ended in 1917, Davis addressed the need for more data about the physical and mental aspects of female sexuality. Prior to her study, most of the information about sexuality came from women who had sought medical treatment or who were confined in prisons. Relying on a twelve-page questionnaire, Davis targeted educated normal women. Each participant was asked general questions as well as ones about childhood, adolescence, marriage, and post-menopausal life. Davis used 1,000 replies from married women and 1,200 from unmarried women. She discovered that most women enjoyed sex, wanted to marry, desired sex more frequently than their husbands, and supported birth control. Davis declined to draw any conclusions about lesbianism, but she did reveal that a number of women experienced intense feelings for other women. Controversial in its day, Davis's work stands as a valuable history of women.

—*Caryn E. Neumann*

References and Further Reading

Davis, Katharine Bement. 1929. *Factors in the Sex Life of Twenty-Two Hundred Women.* New York: Arno Press.

Fitzpatrick, Ellen F., ed. 1987. *Katharine Bement Davis, Early Twentieth-Century American Women, and the Study of Sex Behavior.* New York: Garland.

Freedman, Estelle B. 1981. *Their Sisters' Keepers.* Ann Arbor: University of Michigan Press.

Decoration Day

Decoration Day, celebrated on 30 May, was later referred to as Memorial Day. It is

Girl flag bearers at Decoration Day ceremonies, Gallipolis, Ohio, 1943. (Library of Congress)

a national holiday allowing families in the United States to remember and recognize the deeds of the soldiers who served and died in American wars by decorating their graves with flowers. In 1966 Pres. Lyndon Johnson and both houses of Congress acknowledged Waterloo, New York, as the day's birthplace because the town decorated the graves of Civil War veterans as early as 5 May 1866. Powerful evidence also suggests that Charleston, South Carolina, where the war began, deserves recognition as the birthplace. There white abolitionists and black Charlestonians, most of whom were former slaves, organized a dedication ceremony consisting of a parade, songs, biblical readings, the decoration of graves, and speeches by Union officers and local black ministers on 1 May 1865. Despite other claims that dispute the birthplace of the holiday in the United States, in 1868 Gen. John A. Logan of the Grand Army of the Republic officially requested 30 May as the day to honor those who fought and died in the Civil War by decorating their graves with flowers, thus making Decoration Day the day's designation. The official title was later changed to Memorial Day. Although a few southern states celebrate Confederate Memorial Day on independent dates, 30 May has since become a day when Americans honor not only those who died in American wars but also loved ones.

When it began, Decoration Day was a ritual of remembrance and commemoration to the legacy of the Civil War and a way to unite the country after bloody conflict and turmoil by providing spiritual healing and historical understanding. By promoting a new U.S. nationalism and identity that were uniquely egalitarian in character, it became the first ethnically and racially diverse commemoration in the United States, as both immigrants and African Americans celebrated it. Spring flowers and the colors of the American flag remain the day's most important symbols. A national service with memorial speeches is held at Arlington National Cemetery in Virginia each year, symbolically addressing all soldiers who have died in American wars. At the local level, community members come together under one collective ideal and participate in a variety of municipal events such as parades, sporting events, and ceremonies at local cemeteries.

As a civic holiday, participation includes a sort of patriotic duty to celebrate the democratic principles of the United States. By recognizing the dead and their sacrifices, the nation rejoices in the gains it has made. Although the day is established as a secular holiday, it includes various religious overtones. For many, it is seen as an annual day of prayer and a time to give thanks. It is often alluded to in sermons, and commemorative speeches often highlight the importance of religion in public and private life. In this sense, the day can be seen as a celebration of a civil religion in the United States, within which America has a special destiny under God, and its citizens are obligated to help make the United States a model for the world to follow.

Although the complications and anxiety over death are frequently not discussed openly in U.S. culture, a day of personal memory allows families to cope with the death of a close friend or relative. It is common for families to visit and decorate the graves of their ancestors, but it is also a chance to connect the young with the dead. This integration of life and death can be seen as part of the family life cycle, in which life and death emerge into a ritualistic celebration. For most families, however, it is a day of leisure and relaxation. Families often get together during their day off of work and celebrate with a picnic, barbecue, or trip to the beach. Although the day is set aside to honor the dead, families often use it to live life to the fullest, thus adding to the significance of the day.

—*Heath J. Bowen*

References and Further Reading
Albanese, Catherine. 1974. "Requiem for Memorial Day: Dissent in the Redeemer Nation." *American Quarterly* 26(4): 386–398.
Blight, David. 2001. *Race and Reunion: The Civil War in American Memory.* Cambridge: Harvard University Press.

Cherry, Conrad. 1969. "Two American Sacred Ceremonies: Their Implications for the Study of Religion in America." *American Quarterly* 21(4): 739–754.

Santino, Jack. 1994. *All Around the Year: Holidays and Celebrations in American Life.* Urbana: University of Illinois Press.

Warner, Lloyd W. 1959. *The Living and the Dead: A Study of the Symbolic Life of Americans.* New Haven: Yale University Press.

Delinquency

Delinquency is a social problem experienced by children and youth whose families are unable to provide them with adequate supervision and guidance. Impoverished nonadults from minority and immigrant communities who break the law are most likely to be identified by police, courts, and social services as juvenile delinquents. Methods of assisting delinquents have changed considerably, from corporal punishment, apprenticeship, indentured service, imprisonment, and reform schools to psychiatric treatment, probation, alternative education, and foster homes.

The terms *delinquency* and *juvenile delinquent* were first used in the United States in the 1820s, although lawless and criminal boys were present in the colonial era. It includes acts illegal only when committed by those under age eighteen (truancy and sexual acts) as well as status offenses such as being a stubborn or wayward child or a minor in need of supervision. Antebellum reformers in Philadelphia, New York, and Boston opened the House of Reformation for Juvenile Offenders (1825), and Massachusetts established the first U.S. reform school for boys (1846) using European models. Compulsory school attendance laws and the appointment of truant officers in the 1850s resulted in higher rates of juvenile delinquency. Institutionalization led to juvenile court sessions in Boston (1830) and more formal juvenile courts in Chicago (1899), Denver (1900), and Boston (1906). The paternalistic nature of juvenile courts violated due process protections until the Supreme Court intervened (1967, 1970).

The efficacy of these preventive methods was questioned in the most notorious case of juvenile delinquency in nineteenth-century America, Jesse Harding Pomeroy (1860–1932). After serving fourteen months in the state reform school, Pomeroy admitted to mutilating and murdering twenty-nine Boston children (1874). The court commuted his death sentence to a life term in prison, where the "boy fiend" died forty-one years later.

County and state reform schools, originally philanthropic and parental, often became penal until criticism by Progressive reformers and postwar child welfare professionals persuaded the legislature to close them in Massachusetts (1960) and many other states. Child psychologists and psychiatrists, introduced in juvenile justice (1900–1930), used the theories of Sigmund Freud, William Healy, and Edwin H. Sutherland to diagnose, explain, and resolve delinquency, but practitioners found maturation the most common solution. By the 1980s many states approved more severe disposition for delinquent boys, and courts tried youthful offenders as adults in cases of serious crimes, especially homicide and violent offenses. Research on the cause of juvenile delinquency continues, but most treatment programs focus only on preventing repeated offenses by known delinquents.

—*Peter C. Holloran*

See also Juvenile Justice

Arrest of a juvenile delinquent by a police officer, 1877. (Bettmann/Corbis)

References and Further Reading
Gibbons, Don C. 1970. *Delinquent Behavior.* Englewood Cliffs, NJ: Prentice Hall.
Holloran, Peter C. 1994. *Boston's Wayward Children: Social Services for Homeless Children, 1830–1930.* Boston: Northeastern University Press.
Mennel, Robert M. 1973. *Thorns and Thistles: Juvenile Delinquents in the United States, 1825–1940.* Hanover, NH: University Press of New England.

Demography of the Family

If there is one identifiable theme in U.S. family life over the past three decades, it is that the family has undergone extensive changes. The family changed more in the 1990s than any other social institution; however, the rate of change is slowing. Family, school, and workforce are interrelated—changes in one cause and reflect changes in the other two. To assess the changing status of the family in the United States, it is necessary to examine recent demographic trends. Changing structure of family households, childlessness, divorce, poverty, childbearing outside of marriage, and an aging population reflect changes in education and the workforce and have created many varieties of family life. Some researchers argue that these changes have weakened the family. Others view family life as having adapted to new societal circumstances, resulting in greater diversity and resilience.

A "family" is a group of two or more people, including a householder, related by birth, marriage, or adoption and residing together. To determine the number of families in the United States, researchers focus on the family household. A "family household" is a person or group of people who occupy a housing unit. A "householder" either owns or rents the housing unit. The householder maintains the housing unit and is in a family as defined above. The "family household" includes all unrelated persons who may live in the housing unit. A "nonfamily household" consists of a person living alone or a householder who shares the home with nonrelatives only, for example, boarders or roommates. Therefore, the number of family households is equal to the number of families (Yax 2000).

Change in the number of family households depends on several demographic dynamics: population growth through declining death rates, increased fertility rates, or increased migration. Other demographic factors are changes in the age composition of the population, changes in the median age at first marriage, divorce rates, the condition of the economy, and improvements in the health of the elderly over time. These are among the factors that can influence the rate of growth of the number of family households and their composition.

Another important demographic term is *own children.* This defines children under eighteen who are never-married sons or daughters of the householder, including stepchildren and adopted children. "Family group" includes all family living arrangements including families, related subfamilies, and unrelated subfamilies.

With these definitions in mind, in 1998 there were 102.5 million households in the United States. Of this number, 69 percent were family households, and 31 percent were nonfamily households. In 1998, slightly more than half (51 percent) of all families had no "own children" under eighteen. This percentage did not change from 1990 to 1998. That percentage of "own children," however, represents a decrease from 56 percent in 1970 (Casper and Bryson, 1998a, 1).

Since 1990, the composition of U.S. households and families has remained relatively stable. In 1990 married couples with their own children under age eighteen made up 26 percent of all households. The percentage was the same in 1998. Families without "own children" under eighteen at home are not necessarily childless. Some households include other related children, such as nieces, nephews, or grandchildren. Some contain unrelated foster children, and others include adult sons and daughters who are still living at home or have moved back to the parental household. In 2000, the average U.S. family household consisted of 2.6 people, down from 3.1 in 1970 but the same as in 1990. The shrinking size of households is evident among whites and blacks, but not among Hispanics and Asians. The average number of persons per household has increased among Hispanics from 3.0 in 1975 to 3.5 in 2000. Among Asian Americans, the number of persons per household has remained steady at about 3.2 since 1990. Data on earlier years are not available. Among whites and blacks, there has been a decline in persons per household. In 1975 there were 2.8 people in each white household compared with 3.0 people in each black household. In 2000, the number of persons per household had dropped to 2.5 in white households and to 2.8 in black households (*The Growing, Shrinking American Household* 2000, 1).

In 1998, 100.6 million adults, or slightly more than half of the adult population, were married and living with their spouses. Among people age twenty-five to thirty-four years old, 13.6 million had never been married, representing 34.7 percent of all people in the age group. For blacks in this age group, 53.4 percent had never been married. In the same year, 19.4 million adults were currently divorced, representing 9.8 percent of the population. Nearly half (45.2 percent) of women sixty-five years old and over were widowed. Of the elderly widows, 70.1 percent lived alone. Remarkably, the proportion of married couples that identified the woman as the householder tripled between 1990 and 1998, going from 7.4 percent in 1990 to 22.9 percent in 1998 (Lugaila 1998, 1).

Primarily because minorities are younger and have higher birthrates than the non-Hispanic population, they are more likely to live in family households and to have "own children." In 1998, between two-thirds and four-fifths of households among all racial and ethnic groups were family households. Differences in living arrangements among minority groups often were as large as the difference between minorities and whites. Asians and Hispanics were most likely to live in family households and least likely to live alone. Nearly 30 percent of both white and black households consisted of a single person in 1998, compared with just 14 percent of Hispanic and 18 percent of Asian households. Elderly people, particularly widows, often live alone, which partially explains the lower incidence of single-person households within the relatively young Hispanic and Asian populations. Nearly two-thirds of Hispanic family households and slightly more than half of African American family households included children under age eighteen in 1998. Less than half of white families included children, reflecting the older age structure of white adults and lower fertility among white couples (Lugaila 1998, 1).

Most recent data on divorce in the United States show that 43 percent of first marriages end in separation or divorce within fifteen years. Also, one in three marriages ends within ten years and one in five ends within five years. Duration of marriage continues to be linked to a woman's age at first marriage. The older a woman is at first marriage, the longer that marriage is likely to last. About 97 percent of separated non-Hispanic white women are divorced within five years compared to 77 percent of separated Hispanic women and only 67 percent of black women (National Center for Health Statistics 2001).

Adults raised by divorced mothers are far less likely to get divorced themselves than they were twenty years ago. In fact, their marriage and divorce rates are now closer to those of adults from intact homes. The gap is closing because parents increasingly divorce before the home erupts into a battlefield and children are scarred for life. This change reflects a more accepting attitude toward divorce (Elias 1999).

Except for Asians, minority families were more likely than white families to be headed by a single parent—usually a woman—living with dependent children. In 1998, nearly 20 percent of Hispanic and American Indian families and 33 percent of African American families were composed of a single parent with dependent children. Such families made up just 6 percent of Asian families and 9 percent of white families. Female-headed households with children were the most common family arrangement for African Americans. They accounted for 30 percent of black family households in 1998 (*Racial, Ethnic Diversity in Female-Headed Households* 1999, 1). The growth of one-parent families is slowing; however, the makeup of one-parent families has changed dramatically. The number of single-father households increased 25 percent from 1.7 million in 1995 to 2.1 million in 1998, whereas the number of single mothers remained basically the same. Men now make up one-sixth of the nation's 11.9 million single parents. In 1990, 33 percent of mother-child family households had a never-married mother. This type of family group had increased to 41 percent in 1998 (Casper and Bryson 1998b, 1).

Female-headed households are households in which there is no adult male or households in which adult males rely on the female breadwinner for support. About 9 percent of U.S. households can be categorized as female-headed households with children in that the householder lives with one or more related children. An example is that in 1998 about 4 million children lived in the household of their grandparents, representing 5.6 percent of all children below eighteen years of age. The percentage of households headed by women with children varied by race and ethnicity. About 6 percent of non-Hispanic white and Asian households were female headed with children in 1999. In contrast, women with children accounted for 33 percent of all black households. Twenty percent of Hispanic and American Indian households are female headed with children. Over the past thirty years, the percentage of female-headed households with children has increased most rapidly among blacks, but this trend appears to have slowed or even reversed in recent years (*Racial, Ethnic Diversity in Female-Headed Households* 1999, 1).

Cultural traditions and social class differences can affect the makeup of a household. Researchers have noted the tendency for Asian households to include extended family; others have noted the tendency of young Hispanics, especially women, to live with their parents until marriage. These living patterns may be even more pronounced among recent immigrants, who are more likely to adhere to traditional values or who may be less able to afford a home of their own (*The Growing, Shrinking American Household* 2000).

The percentage of persons living alone is increasing. From 1970 to 1999, the percentage of adults who lived alone increased from 8 percent to 13 percent. The increase—from 3 percent to 10 percent—was greatest among 25- to 34-year-olds; 35- to 44-year-olds increased from 4 percent to 9 percent; and 18- to 24-year-olds increased from 2 percent to 5 percent. Americans ages 65 and older are the most likely to live alone. In 1999 about 30 percent of this population lived alone; however, this represented a drop of 1 percent from 1998 (*Living Alone in the '90s* 1999, 1).

Between 1970 and 1999, the percentage of persons who had never been married increased from about 22 percent to 28 percent. Blacks display the greatest increase in the never-married population. Between 1975 and 1999, the percentage of blacks who had never been married increased from 32 percent to 44 percent. The percentage of blacks who are married declined from over 42 percent in 1975 to 32 percent in 1999 (*The Never Married* 1999, 1).

For the fifth consecutive year, the real median income of households in the United States rose by 2.7 percent between 1998 and 1999, going from $39,744 to $40,816. Real median household income is now the highest since the Census Bureau started compiling these estimates in 1967. In 1999 the highest real median income ever was recorded for white non-Hispanics ($44,366), blacks ($27,910), and Hispanics ($30,735), and the real median

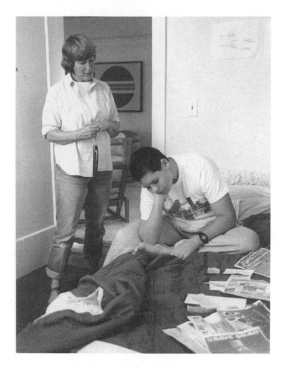

A single mother, head of the household, reprimanding her teenage son. (Elizabeth Crews)

income for Asian and Pacific Islander households equaled the highest ever recorded ($51,205). From 1997 to 1999, the average annual household income for American Indians and Alaska Natives was $30,784.

Family and nonfamily households alike experienced growth in real income from 1998 to 1999. Family household income rose 2.9 percent from $48,517 to $49,940, and nonfamily household income rose 2.5 percent from $23,959 to $24,566 (U.S. Department of Commerce News 2000).

Men of all ages earn more money if they are married. Married women also have higher incomes but only among the younger age groups. Among women ages thirty-five to forty-four, never-married women had higher personal earnings than their married counterparts. This fact is a direct result of more women choosing professional careers since the 1970s (*Marital Status and Earnings* 1998, 1).

Analyses of aggregate shares of income show that household income inequality remained unchanged from 1998 to 1999. In 1999 the share of aggregate household income was 3.6 percent for the lowest quintile, 8.9 percent for the second quintile, 14.9 percent for the third, 23.2 percent for the fourth, and 49.4 percent for the fifth quintile. The share of income held for each quintile was about the same in 1993 as in 1999. Income inequality rose substantially between 1967 and the early 1990s but has remained unchanged since then (Weinberg 2000).

In 1998 about 13 percent of the U.S. population, or 34.5 million people, were living in families whose income fell below the poverty line. Of the total number of persons in poverty, 13.5 million were children, 17.6 million were working-age adults, and 3.4 million were sixty-five years old and over. Almost one-fifth of the nation's children were living below the poverty threshold in 1998 compared with only one-tenth of persons eighteen and over (CNN 1999).

Although millions of U.S. families are affected by poverty, according to the U.S. Census Bureau, 2.2 million fewer people were poor in 1999 than in 1998. In addition, the percentage of people sixty-five and over who were living in poverty reached a measured low of 9.7 percent in 1999, and the proportion of the nation's children in poverty was the lowest since 1979—16.9 percent. In 1970 nearly 25 percent of older Americans lived in poverty, more than twice the current rate. The dramatic decline in the percentage of the older population in poverty is associated with the expansion of federal programs such as Social Security and Medicare, as well as with private pension systems. These federal entitlements have kept many older Americans above the poverty line; but a relatively high percentage of older adults live in families "near poverty," in the range of 100 to 124 percent of the poverty threshold. There are also certain groups in the older population that are at greater risk of living in poverty. In 1999, 21 percent of women ages sixty-five to eighty-four who were living alone had incomes below the poverty line, compared with 15 percent of men in that age group who were living alone. Among people ages eighty-five and older, 23 percent of women living alone were in poverty, compared with 9 percent of men living alone. Poverty rates were substantially lower for older people living in families, especially for older women (*Older People in Poverty* 1998, 1–2).

In the coming decades, educational attainment among older people is likely to increase considerably as the current baby boomers begin to reach retirement age. In 1999, about one-third of men and women ages 65 and older had a college degree, compared with 19 percent of women ages 55 to 64. With higher levels of education, the older population of the future is likely to be better off, both physically and financially, than the current population aged 65 and older. There will also be notable changes in family settings and living arrangements of older people. If current trends continue, there will be a decline in the proportion of women who are widows at any given age, as men's life expectancy continues to improve. Also, the percentage of divorced persons in the older population is likely to increase. In 1999, 15 percent of women and 12 percent of men ages 55 to 64 were divorced and had not remarried, compared with only 7 percent of women and men ages 65 and older (*A Profile of Older People in the Future* 1999, 2).

Children, on the other hand, are worse off today than they were thirty years ago, despite a decline in child poverty over the past five years. Some children are at greater risk of living in poverty than others. In 1998, 40 percent of black children under age six lived in poverty, compared with 12 percent of white children, 18 percent of Asian children, and 37 percent of Hispanic children in that age group. Children ages six to seventeen were at a slightly lower risk of living in poverty. Children, who do not receive nearly the same level of federal support, are more likely than other age groups to live in extreme poverty, with income less than 50 percent of the poverty threshold (*One-Fifth of Children below Poverty* 1998, 1).

Poverty is a problem that cuts across racial and ethnic boundaries. Nearly half of all families in poverty are white, a little more than 25 percent are black, and slightly less than 25 percent are Hispanic. The remainder are Asian or from other groups. When poverty rates are examined by race and ethnicity, whites are less likely than other groups to be living in poverty. Actually, black and Hispanic families are about three times more likely to live in poverty than white families (*Families in Poverty* 1999, 1).

Comparing the poverty rate from 1998 to 1999, the percentage and number of poor households declined in the Northeast and West. The poverty rate for households did not change significantly by 1999 in the South and the Midwest from the 1998 measured low for those regions (U.S. Department of Commerce News 2000).

In 1950, about 3 percent of all births were to unmarried women. This percentage has increased steadily over the past fifty years; and by 1999, there were 1.3 million births to unmarried women, accounting for just under a third of all births in the United States. Since 1995, the percentage of nonmarital births has remained fairly stable (*Births to Unmarried Women* 1998, 1).

Three factors account for most of the increase in nonmarital births: The proportion of women of reproductive age who are unmarried has increased; fertility rates of married women have declined; and the fertility rates of unmarried women have risen gradually. Fertility rates of unmarried women have more than tripled since the early 1950s. This increase is paradoxical to many, given that effective methods of contraception became widely available and laws against induced abortion were eliminated in the 1960s and 1970s. Contraception and abortion probably explain the temporary decline in nonmarital fertility rates from the mid-1960s until the mid-1970s, but the increase in the 1980s has no simple explanation (*Births to Unmarried Women* 1998, 1).

Fertility rates of unmarried women in their twenties are higher than the rates for teenagers. Because younger women face greater challenges as single parents, however, most public discussion focuses on preventing teen pregnancies. The fertility rate of unmarried teenagers has fallen in recent years from its high point of 46.4 births per 1,000 unmarried women ages fifteen to nineteen in 1994 to 43.9 in 1999 (*Declining Fertility among Teenagers* 1999, 1).

In 1998 nonmarital fertility rates were highest among Hispanic women (90.1 births per 1,000 women in 1998) and black women (73.3 births per 1,000 women). The 1998 rate for non-Hispanic white women was 27.4 births per 1,000 women (*Births to Unmarried Women* 1998, 1).

Among the more developed countries, the United States has one of the highest rates of teenage childbearing. In 1999 there were 49.6 live births per 1,000 women ages 15 to 19, down from the recent peak of 62.1 births per 1,000 in 1991. The birthrate of women ages 15 to 17 reached a record low in 1999: 28.7 per 1,000 (*Declining Fertility among Teenagers*, 1999, 1).

Teenage fertility rates were considerably higher in the 1950s and 1960s. In 1957, at the height of the baby boom, there were 96.3 births per 1,000 women ages fifteen to nineteen. Back then, however, the great majority of these births (86 percent of them in 1957) were to women who were married at the time of birth (though they often had not been married at the time of conception). The proportions have since reversed; now only 21 percent of teen births are to women who are married. Fertility rates dropped especially rapidly during the 1990s among black teenagers, from 115.5 per 1,000 in 1991 to 81.1 per 1,000 in 1998. Despite this decline, birthrates for black teenagers remain high, compared with birthrates for white teenagers (*Declining Fertility among Teenagers* 1999, 1).

Families remained on the move in the United States in the 1990s. Between March 1998 and March 1999, 42.6 million people or close to 16 percent of the population moved. Nearly 60 percent of movers stayed in the same county, 20 percent moved between counties within the same state, 17 percent moved to a different state, and just above 3 percent moved from abroad. Renter households had higher rates of moving than owner

households. Thirty-three percent of families living in renter-occupied housing units in March 1999 had moved in the previous year compared with 8 percent in owner-occupied housing units. The Northeast had the lowest overall moving rate (11.7 percent—well below the national rate of 15.9 percent), followed by the Midwest (15.1 percent), the South (17.1 percent), and the West (18.5 percent). The South continued recent trends as the only region with a significant increase due to internal migration, with a net gain of 270,000 people in one year— 1998 to 1999 (Faber 2000, 1–2).

A major part of the migration to the South reflects the fact that blacks ended the twentieth century by returning to the region that they had spent most of the century leaving. During the 1990s the black populations of Florida and Georgia gained 674,000 and 632,000 people, respectively. Texas gained 454,000 blacks. Maryland and North Carolina gained approximately 300,000 blacks each. This movement of blacks reflects the South's 1990s allure (Frey 2001).

—*Peggy A. Shifflett*

See also African American Families; Asian American Families; Baby Boom; Family Decline in the Twentieth Century; The Hispanic Family; Japanese American Families during World War II, Internment of; Single-Parent Families

References and Further Reading
Births to Unmarried Women—End of the Increase? 1998. AmeriStat. Population Reference Bureau. Washington, DC: U.S. Census Bureau.
Casper, Lynne M., and Ken Bryson. 1998a. *Household and Family Characteristics: March 1998 Update.* Current Population Reports. Washington, DC: U.S. Census Bureau.
Casper, Lynne M., and Ken Bryson. 1998b. "Growth in Single Fathers Outpaces Growth in Single Mothers, Census

Bureau Reports." *U.S. Department of Commerce News.* Washington, DC: Department of Commerce.

CNN. "Millions of U.S. Families Affected by Poverty, Census Bureau Says." http://www.cnn.com/US/9911/03/poverty.01/ (cited 3 November 1999).

Declining Fertility among Teenagers. 1999. AmeriStat. Population Reference Bureau. Washington, DC: U.S. Census Bureau.

Elias, Marilyn. "Study: Cycle of Divorce Is Abating and Census–." http://lists.his.com/smartmarriages/msg00901.html (cited 11 August 1999).

Faber, Carol S. 2000. *Geographical Mobility (Update) March 1998 to March 1999.* Current Population Reports. Washington, DC: U.S. Census Bureau.

Families in Poverty. 1999. AmeriStat. Population Reference Bureau. Washington, DC: U.S. Census Bureau.

Frey, William H. "Migration to the South Brings U.S. Blacks Full Circle." http://www.prb.org/pt/2001/MayJune2001/migration.html (cited 28 May 2001).

The Growing, Shrinking American Household. 2000. AmeriStat. Population Reference Bureau. Washington, DC: U.S. Census Bureau.

Living Alone in the '90s. 1999. AmeriStat. Population Reference Bureau. Washington, DC: U.S. Census Bureau.

Lugaila, Terry A. 1998. *Marital Status and Living Arrangements: March 1998 Update.* Current Population Reports. Washington, DC: U.S. Department of Commerce.

Marital Status and Earnings: Differences by Gender. 1998. AmeriStat. Population Reference Bureau. Washington, DC: U.S. Census Bureau.

National Center for Health Statistics. "43 Percent of First Marriages Break Up within 15 Years." http://www.cdc.gov/nchs/releases/01news/firstmarr.htm (cited 24 May 2001).

The Never Married: Single, Stable, and Satisfied? 1999. AmeriStat. Population Reference Bureau. Washington, DC: U.S. Census Bureau.

Older People in Poverty. 1998. AmeriStat. Population Reference Bureau. Washington, DC: U.S. Census Bureau.

One-Fifth of Children below Poverty. 1998. AmeriStat. Population Reference Bureau. Washington, DC: U.S. Census Bureau.

A Profile of Older People in the Future. 1999. AmeriStat. Population Reference Bureau. Washington, DC: U.S. Census Bureau.

Racial, Ethnic Diversity in Female-Headed Households. 1999. AmeriStat. Population Reference Bureau. Washington, DC: U.S. Census Bureau.

U.S. Department of Commerce News. "Poverty Rate Lowest in 20 Years, Household Income at Record High, Census Bureau Reports." http://www.census.gov/Press Release/www/2000/cb00-158.html (cited 26 September 2000).

Weinberg, Daniel H. "A Brief Look at Postwar U.S. Income Inequality." http://www.census.gov/hhes/income/incineq/p60asc.html (cited 3 August 2000).

Yax, Laura K., ed. "Current Population Survey: Definitions and Explanations." http://www.census.gov/population/www/cps/cpsdef.html (cited 2 November 2000).

Department of Housing and Urban Development, U.S.

The U.S. Department of Housing and Urban Development (HUD) coordinates all federal housing programs. Created in 1965 as a cabinet-level agency, HUD subsumed a variety of earlier federal housing agencies. Many of HUD's predecessor and component agencies traced their origins to New Deal–era programs designed to make home ownership possible for millions of Americans and to subsidize public housing projects for low-income families. Although these programs achieved many of their goals, their racial policies also sanctioned and encouraged segregation, disadvantaged nonwhite home buyers, and eventually promoted white flight and inner-city decay. Congress created HUD in the midst of the civil rights struggles of the 1960s, as U.S. cities grappled with the legacy of institutionalized racism in housing. Even though HUD's duties included enforcing fair housing laws, its administrative decisions—particularly those that left power in local hands—often maintained existing discrimination. HUD-sponsored urban renewal also sometimes razed thriving communities while failing to revive inner cities, and its private programs destabilized property values in many areas. White backlash against HUD's attempts to encourage the integration of suburbs also spurred Presidents Nixon and Reagan to back away from the federal government's commitment to affordable and integrated housing for low-income people. In recent years, some HUD programs have spurred speculation and fraud, and more than one major HUD official has faced indictment on corruption charges. HUD's program of tearing down many of the huge public housing complexes that were the legacy of earlier racialized government programs has also created controversy among low-income people and their advocates. At the same time, efforts to overhaul the agency have made it more efficient, and it has won accolades for improved client service, fighting budget cuts in low-income housing programs and attempting to enlarge the number of home owners in the United States.

—*Charlotte Brooks*

References and Further Reading
Jackson, Kenneth T. 1985. *Crabgrass Frontier: The Suburbanization of the United States.* New York: Oxford University Press.
Massey, Douglas S., and Nancy A. Denton. 1993. *American Apartheid: Segregation and the Making of the Underclass.* Cambridge: Harvard University Press.
Quadagno, Jill. 1994. *The Color of Welfare: How Racism Undermined the War on Poverty.* New York: Oxford University Press.

Disabilities and Family Life

A picture of American families would not be complete without a discussion of people with disabilities. Not much is known about how a disabled family member lived his or her life before the nineteenth century, but generally speaking, preindustrial society regarded people with disabilities with a mixture of compassion, fear, revulsion, and wonder, depending on the type and severity of the disability. Before the nineteenth century, however, many people with disabilities lived and worked as integral parts of their communities.

In Europe and America, however, a transformation in attitudes toward people with disabilities occurred during the nineteenth century. On the one hand, people recognized the importance of education and training for others who had certain kinds of "educable" disabilities, especially deafness and blindness. Therefore, the care and education of the deaf and the blind became increasingly important throughout the nineteenth century. On the other hand, people with psychiatric or cognitive disabilities were deemed neither educable nor capable of any kind of human behavior. Although the basic humanity of blind and deaf people was recognized, this was not the case for people with cognitive disabilities, often called "feeble-minded," or people with psychiatric disabilities, often called "insane" or "lunatic." Improvements in the care of the "insane" and the "retarded" came much more slowly than those in the care of people with physical disabilities.

By the twentieth century, people with disabilities and their loved ones protested the perceived images and the medical, political, and social treatment of disabled individuals. Disabled people recognized these representations and perceptions as derogatory and damaging. The dissatisfaction with their political and social state took many forms, including writings, speeches, and physical resistance, and resulted in landmark legal actions, notably the Americans with Disabilities Act, signed into law in 1990.

By the late twentieth century, disabled rights activists modeled their methods and behaviors on the civil rights activists of the 1950s and 1960s. People with disabilities rallied against injustices and illegalities and won rights for personhood and freedom. Parents of children with disabilities demanded that public schools educate their children. As a direct result of the enactment of late-twentieth-century legislation, health care and education for the disabled underwent profound changes. Federal money and health care plans covered a multitude of disabilities; schools received moneys to make it possible for children with disabilities to receive an education comparable to their peers'.

In the early twenty-first century, disability rights activists and people with disabilities have many sophisticated tools and methods to combat discrimination and negative stereotypes and media images. The World Wide Web and Internet have made it possible for hearing-impaired and blind people as well as people with limited mobility to have greater access not only to each other through bulletin boards, listservs, web pages, and web sites expressly for people with disabilities but also with the world at large. Furthermore, courses in disabilities studies have been offered by major universities. In addition, activists, be they academics or other professionals, have, since the mid-1980s, been at the vanguard of a new militancy. For instance, cochlear implants as a way to "solve the problem" created by

deafness have been vehemently challenged by members of the Deaf Community who do not view the deaf as disabled but rather as a community having a separate culture, complete with its own language and customs. Further, strident objections to "temporarily able-bodied" people who speak for people with disabilities—many disabilities activists consider actor/comedian Jerry Lewis, spokesman for the Labor Day telethons for muscular dystrophy, to be a famous example of an able-bodied person speaking for the disabled—have given rise to the expression "nothing about us without us." Objections to those who are disabled but who promote the image of the disabled person as in need of help, a "cure," or a technological solution to their disability have surfaced. Many disabled activists disapprove of people with disabilities who promote this image of the "supercrip," the inspirational figure who overcomes his "handicap" and goes on to lead as close to a "normal" life as possible.

By the nineteenth century, efforts were undertaken to train blind or deaf people. Educators and philanthropists explored methods for teaching the blind and deaf from Europeans and by experimentation with existing European methods such as Braille and sign language. Thomas Hopkins Gallaudet (1787–1851), motivated to learn how to educate the deaf at the behest of a doting father of a deaf daughter and witness to the successful methods of Parisian Sign Language, established the American School for the Deaf in 1817. His son, Edward Miner Gallaudet (1837–1917), became the founder and first president of National College of the Deaf in Washington, D.C., an offshoot of the original school in Hartford, which was renamed Gallaudet College in 1894. Today, Gallaudet University is an

A rare photo of Franklin D. Roosevelt in his wheelchair with Ruthie Bye and his dog, Fala, 1941. (Franklin D. Roosevelt Library)

minimize the extent of their "affliction" and live as much as possible in the hearing world was confounded by the phenomenon of the Chilmark Community in Martha's Vineyard, Massachusetts, where, throughout the seventeenth and eighteenth centuries and the first half of the nineteenth century, the deaf and the hearing worked together, learned ASL, married, bore both hearing and deaf children, and in general, lived a harmonious existence.

Deaf people worldwide, because of shared sign languages, have always formed cohesive communities. In the 1820s, deaf clubs sprouted up, and by the 1830s, newspapers dedicated to the deaf had also been established. In the twentieth century, the first Silent Games, otherwise known as the Deaf Olympics, appeared in 1924. Rochester, New York, became the home of the National Technical Institute for the Deaf (NTID) in 1965; in 1967, the Theater of the Deaf staged its first performance.

James Woodward in 1972 argued that a distinction must be made between the deaf, that is, hearing-impaired individuals, and the Deaf, those who see themselves in terms of a larger, shared culture complete with a shared language. The Deaf Community does not view deafness as a disability or a medical condition requiring correction. A direct result of the new ideology was the Deaf President Now campaign staged at Gallaudet in the 1980s, the end result of which was the election of I. King Jordan, the first deaf president of Gallaudet University, in 1988.

Opponents of universal access do not realize that adaptations that enable the deaf to communicate with the hearing world also benefit the larger community. For instance, as Fred Pelka pointed out,

important center for deaf culture and scholarship.

The philosophy and methods many hearing educators chose, however, although well intentioned, often arose from the assumption that the nondisabled person knew best what training or treatment was suitable for people with disabilities. For example, though most deaf people in the nineteenth century preferred American Sign Language (ASL), prominent figures in the field of deaf education—notably, Alexander Graham Bell (1847–1922)—exerted considerable influence to discourage the teaching of sign language and to promote lipreading as the preferred form of communication. Alexander Graham Bell's exhortation that the deaf be trained so that they could

the hand signals umpires use and the huddle football players engage in originated in the deaf community (Pelka 1997). Robert H. Weitbrecht, the deaf inventor of the acoustic coupler in 1964, invented not only a device for the deaf to communicate through existing phone lines via the teletype machine but also the forerunner of the modem. In the 1940s, the deaf actor Emerson Romero (brother of Cesar) spliced captions into existing films. The deaf are not the only recipients of closed captioning; people who frequent noisy bars and restaurants enjoy closed captioning of their favorite programs.

The training and education of the blind were similar to those of the deaf. The efforts to teach blind children Braille occurred quite rapidly after Louis Braille invented his "raised dot" alphabet in 1829. In the 1870s, Louis Braille's original method underwent changes and emerged in two forms: New York Point, a streamlined but more difficult-to-read version of the original Braille, and Modified Braille, the system that blind people preferred over the other two. Authorities and educators endorsed New York Point, however, and, like American Sign Language, Modified Braille became a clandestine form of communication.

Opening in the summer of 1832, the Perkins School for the Blind, originally the New England Asylum for the Blind, was one of the earliest schools exclusively for the blind. Two students and two teachers, all blind, composed the original student body and faculty. The school's goal was to ensure that its students would be both independent and gainfully employed. In 1837, Perkins admitted its first deaf-blind student, Laura Bridgman, and throughout the nineteenth century, Perkins continued to grow and flourish, accepting children with different disabilities and establishing both a kindergarten for blind children and a research library and museum. Its most famous pupil, Helen Keller (1880–1968), attended Perkins on the recommendation of Alexander Graham Bell. The rapid growth and expansion of the school indicated how valued blind children were and how much parents in the nineteenth century believed that an education for these children was a good investment.

As with inventions that were originally designed to help the deaf communicate with the hearing world, technological developments designed to equip the blind to communicate with the sighted world transformed the way in which we communicate. The typewriter was invented as a way for blind people to communicate with the sighted. The publication of large-print books aids all people with failing or limited eyesight.

In 1921, the American Foundation for the Blind (AFB) was founded, an organization that became the main center for information and advocacy. Helen Keller was a main fund-raiser for AFB from the 1920s until 1961. Currently, the AFB publishes books, videos, books on tape, periodicals, and professional journals.

Little was known about cognitive disabilities, labeled "feeblemindedness," in the nineteenth century or about mental retardation throughout most of the twentieth century. Nineteenth-century ethnography placed white Europeans at the top of the civilization pyramid, with dark-skinned peoples occupying various positions below. People with cognitive disabilities were thought to be throwbacks to earlier races or primates, the ethnography of the day dictating that the less civilized the individual, the more likely the person was thought to be a member of an inferior race. The now fully discredited term "Mongoloid idiot" was frequently used for a person with Down syndrome, as the features of such a person were imagined to resemble those of a native of Mongolia.

Both "feebleminded" children and those thought to be "freaks of nature" were quite often sold to sideshows where their particular disability would be exploited. Natural human curiosity, coupled with the rising popularity of the pseudoscience, eugenics (the belief in the extermination or elimination of unfit members of a species), made sideshows extremely popular throughout the United States. In addition, the popularity of sideshows coincided with the spread of Charles Darwin's ideas about evolution. Sideshow managers and owners portrayed many retarded children as "wild" children of extinct races, "missing links" bridging the imagined gap between man and ape. The popularity of sideshows continued well into the twentieth century. By the 1930s, however, mental retardation had been recognized as a medical condition deserving of treatment. Sideshow exhibition of "pinheads" and others with cognitive disabilities grew unpopular; by the beginning of the twenty-first century, such shows had all but vanished from small-town America.

Coupled with the nineteenth-century theory of superior and inferior races, Francis Galton's invention in 1883 of the term *eugenics*, or "goodness in birth," gave rise to the disastrous American eugenics movement in the 1890s. The movement flourished until the 1940s, when the association with Nazi Germany discredited it. Individuals thought to be "defective," that is, those who were obviously physically disabled, those with cognitive dis-

abilities, and especially those with psychiatric disabilities, were thought to compromise the fitness of the human race. Insanity and feeblemindedness were thought to be hereditary and to run in families. Many disabled people were forcibly institutionalized throughout the first half of the twentieth century. Doctors, nurses, teachers, and parents were encouraged to inform the authorities of the existence of mentally disabled children, who were then institutionalized and sterilized, practices that were sanctioned by law. Thousands of boys forcibly "enrolled" in special schools for the "feebleminded" underwent castration.

Though enforced sterilization was to be thoroughly discredited after the 1940s, the Nobel Prize was given to Alexis Carrell in 1935. An American and member of the Rockefeller Institute, Carrell had written *Man the Unknown*, advocating the extermination of the mentally ill.

Even after the eugenics movement was discredited, people with disabilities continued to face discrimination and endangerment of their civil rights. By the 1940s, many states passed laws forbidding disabled people to marry. Many disabled people have had their children taken away because the assumption is that physically and cognitively disabled people cannot raise children properly. In addition, "ugly laws" were passed in some states, notably Illinois, where local ordinances in Chicago expressly forbade people with "unsightly" or "disgusting" physical conditions from appearing in public.

A very mysterious, misdiagnosed condition that afflicted children in infancy and could last for their entire lives was first labeled early infantile autism or Kanner's syndrome, named after Leo Kanner, the scientist who coined the term in

1943. Freudian theory posited that autism was the natural result when fragile infants were exposed to cold, neglectful mothers. Bruno Bettelheim (1903–1990) popularized this now-discredited Freudian theory in *Joey, a Mechanical Boy*, written in 1959. Autism is a diverse disability, exhibiting a cluster of symptoms that include total withdrawal from others, lack of language, failure to make eye contact, and head-banging. Asperger's syndrome, a much milder form, presents with awkwardness in social situations, no or little affect, and an inability to read affect in others. By the early 1980s, autism was recognized as a neurological disorder, treatable by early intervention and intensive training. An accurate understanding of the causes of autism, however, came too late for thousands of mothers who blamed themselves for their children's failure to integrate themselves into the world in appropriate ways.

Nevertheless, parents and loved ones of people with disabilities and children with disabilities did not passively accept abuses, discrimination, lack of effective treatment and therapy, and lack of access for their family members to any form of education or job skills training. Beginning in the 1930s, parents organized support groups for cerebral palsy and retardation. Originally small, local groups, from these efforts sprang the United Cerebral Palsy Association and the National Association for Retarded Children (later Citizens), now known as the Association for the Help of Retarded Children (AHRC).

In 1950, the National Association for Retarded Children formed as a support group for parents of mentally retarded children. Families of children with cognitive disabilities were presumed to be ashamed of and disappointed by such children and urged to institutionalize their offspring. The AHRC offered little in the 1950s in the way of financial or structural support but did become a force in changing the lives of children with cognitive disabilities and their families. The Autism Society of America was formed in 1965 as a means for concerned parents to share information, support, and referrals and to advocate for the rights of their children.

These early parents' movements led to the establishment of programs to aid and educate the disabled at every level: federal, state, municipal, or local. For instance, summer camps, special education classes, and "integrated" classes in which children with disabilities and typically developing children are educated together have become common. Support from parents' groups was also instrumental in the passage of the Rehabilitation Act of 1973 and the Education for All Handicapped Children Act of 1975.

It has been widely acknowledged that the least understood disability is mental illness. Before the development of "insane asylums" such as the notorious Bedlam in London, England, people with psychiatric disabilities were assumed to be a family's responsibility and so were cared for by the family, town, or community. Violent or disruptive persons were often housed in jails; some were taken to religious communities such as convents and monasteries for care. Gradually, the sequestering of people with psychiatric disabilities in almshouses and jails with poor conditions and no form of treatment led to activism, particularly by such reformers as Dorothea Dix (1802–1887), who persuaded politicians and the medical establishment to found institutions. By 1852, seventeen states had established "insane asylums," where treatment was limited to containment and restraint. Overcrowding, poor sanitation, poor food, therapies that emphasized physical restraint, threats, and fear of punishment characterized these hospitals and led to calls for reform as early as the turn of the twentieth century. Wealthy people, conversely, could check themselves into "rest homes" or "nerve clinics" where the treatment and accommodations were considerably better than in state-run hospitals. The discovery of lithium in 1949 opened up new worlds to medical professionals who envisioned the psychotropic drug, used frequently to treat the symptoms of manic depression, as a panacea that would revolutionize the way the psychiatrically disabled were currently treated. Lithium would replace lengthy hospital stays, lobotomies, and, sometimes, psychoanalysis.

By the 1960s in the United States a quarter of a million people with psychiatric disabilities languished in state-run psychiatric hospitals. Patients were treated to therapies of questionable value, the most notorious of which were lobotomies, whose devastating effects were brought to public view through both the 1962 novel *One Flew Over the Cuckoo's Nest* and the 1975 film of the same name. Electroshock treatment, freezing wet sheets and cold baths, straitjackets, heavy medication, and solitary confinement were all employed routinely in monolithic institutions. Perhaps the most infamous and scandalous abuses were discovered in Willowbrook State School in Staten Island, New York. Established as a veteran's hospital in 1938, by 1952 it housed severely physically disabled as well as mentally disabled children. Budget cuts throughout the 1960s resulted in overcrowding, neglect, abuse, widespread malnutrition, and a chilling callousness on the part of the medical personnel who, from 1963 to 1966, infected the children with hepatitis as a way to study the virus. Willowbrook defended its practice, stating that since many of the children would probably get hepatitis anyway, it was in their best interests to be infected with the virus under controlled conditions. In 1960, with the election of John F. Kennedy, people with cognitive disabilities gained a powerful ally in their struggle for rights and accommodations. Founded in 1961, the President's Panel on Mental Retardation explored ways in which people with cognitive disabilities could be better assisted and served through deinstitutionalization and mainstreaming. In 1963, President Kennedy called for the eventual and gradual reduction in the confinement of people in institutions. In 1972, ABC reporter Geraldo Rivera brought the conditions of Willowbrook to the world's attention, and by 1975, a class-action suit was filed against the then-governor of New York, Nelson A. Rockefeller. As a result of the publicity and suit, Willowbrook closed its doors for good in 1988.

Newer treatment for people with psychiatric disabilities followed the emptying of hospitals in the 1970s. Such treatment emphasized outpatient clinics, shorter hospital stays, visits from family and loved ones, group and family therapy, and appropriate medication. Group homes, an innovation of the 1970s that grew out of organizations such as the Working Organization for Retarded Children and Adults (WORC), began to spring up with the help of federal funding and private donations. In 1975, the Supreme Court ruled that people with psychiatric disabilities who were not dangerous to themselves or others could neither be incarcerated nor medicated without their consent.

One of the few areas of disability where a politician's intervention revolutionized the management of the effects of an epidemic concerned polio. The "war" on polio resulted in two models for future disability rights activists. First, Franklin Delano Roosevelt (1882–1945), who contracted polio in 1921, established a therapeutic environment in Warm Springs, Georgia, where the disabled organized their own therapy and ran the place as an early independent living center. Second, Roosevelt raised media awareness of the needs of people with disabilities. His creation of the March of Dimes helped publicize any innovations in the race for a cure and the development of a vaccine. Epidemics of polio occurred as early as 1916 and continued until a vaccination was discovered in 1955.

As technological innovations—notably wheelchairs, prostheses, crutches, and braces—brought people with disabilities increased physical mobility, barriers in the form of architectural structures as well as attitudes toward disabled people made access to both buildings and employment all but impossible. As early as 1935, the League of the Physically Handicapped, composed of polio survivors, people with cerebral palsy, amputees, and disabled veterans, protested being denied access to employment with the federal Works Progress Administration (WPA). Disabled World War II vets, would-be recipients of the GI Bill, which provided educational opportunities for veterans, discovered that they had limited access to campus buildings and services. Founded in 1947, the Paralyzed Vets of America worked for the rights of 2,500 former soldiers with spinal cord injuries. Leonard Kriegel, polio survivor, has argued that the aftermath of wars brought advances to medical technology because the return of paralyzed soldiers and soldiers with amputations led to improvements in prostheses and wheel-

A little blind girl kneels in the grass clutching a baby chick in her hands. (Hulton/Archive)

chairs, which, of course, benefited disabled civilians as improved models were marketed to the general populace.

The last quarter of the twentieth century witnessed further transformations in the lives of people with disabilities and their families. People with disabilities organized, demonstrated, engaged in sit-ins, and demanded that their governmental representatives defend their civil rights. Throughout the last half of the twentieth century, persons with disabilities and their advocates challenged the definition of disabilities as medical conditions to be coped with, as shameful conditions to be overcome, and as reasons to lead a diminished or reduced existence. Disabled activists Ed Roberts (1939–1995) and Wade Blank (1940–1993) were instrumental in the struggle for independence for disabled people. Ed Roberts, called the father of the individual living movement, founded the Center for Independent Living (CIL) in 1972. The CIL was unique in that it was an advocacy organization, not a social service. The opening of Roberts's center coincided with the establishment of group homes for people with psychiatric and cognitive disabilities in 1970s. As with the community established in Warm Springs fifty years earlier, the philosophy of the CIL stated that the real experts in disabilities were the persons with disabilities themselves. In the 1970s, Wade Blank, working in a nursing home, was put in charge of a youth ward where he instituted changes such as allowing pets, television, stereos, and coed living. When this experiment failed, Wade moved eighteen people into apartments where they could avail themselves of attendants and not be subjected to institutional life.

A historic moment in the quest for disability rights occurred with the passage of the Rehabilitation Act of 1973, legislation that safeguarded the civil rights of disabled persons by requiring the federal government to address discrimination against people with disabilities. The most important part of the legislation, according to disabilities rights activists, is Section 504, which stipulates that no program receiving federal funding may deny access, services, or employment opportunities on the basis of disability. The Rehabilitation Act of 1973 was groundbreaking legislation, setting in motion profound changes in access for, education and employment of, and attitudes toward people with disabilities.

In the early 1980s, the National Council on Disability recognized that Section 504

did not cover accessibility in mass transit or in housing not federally funded. Americans Disabled for Access to Public Transportation (ADAPT) mounted demonstrations around the country during which activists blocked municipal buses and demanded accessibility in public transportation.

The most all-encompassing piece of legislation was yet to come. Disabilities activists labored during the 1980s to bring the Americans with Disabilities Act (ADA), signed in July 1990, into being. The ADA mandates a series of "reasonable" accommodations throughout every facet of American life and prohibits discrimination against people with disabilities.

The ADA, and Section 504 before it, were instrumental in altering both public and private education in America. Before the diagnosis of learning and reading disabilities became routine in the 1970s, scores of intelligent children who had the potential to do well in school but who had difficulty in reading and writing failed or dropped out of school. The Rehabilitation Act of 1973 recognized learning disabilities and made room for different types of strategies to teach children with learning disabilities or developmental delays. Educators, parents, and school administrators discovered that children once thought ineducable because of autism, mental retardation, and learning disabilities not only could benefit from an education but also learned best mainstreamed into the ordinary classroom. Throughout the 1980s and 1990s, thanks to a swell of research in the area of cognitive disabilities, educators and parents became increasingly knowledgeable about the diagnosis, medical treatment, and education of children who have dyslexia, attention deficit disorder, attention deficit hyperactivity disorder, autism, and developmental delay syndrome.

In the United States, the history of the treatment of and attitudes toward persons with disabilities has often been uneven and contradictory. Every measure taken toward full civil rights and access for persons with disabilities has been met with conflicting measures such as vetoes of crucial laws and bills, creation of legal red tape, and inability and unwillingness to change physical structures. Today, however, the United States leads the entire world in accommodations for people with disabilities as well as laws that govern the treatment of persons with disabilities. Many of the changes in legal, social, and political stances of people with disabilities as well as the attitudes toward and perceptions about them are often due to their families, who have fought for improvements in treatment, accommodations, and civil rights for those loved ones with disabilities.

—*Fran O'Connor*

See also AD/HD; The Parents' Movement for Special Education in the United States; Polio

References and Further Reading
Bogdan, Robert. 1988. *Freak Show: Presenting Human Oddities for Amusement and Profit.* Chicago: University of Chicago Press.
Charlton, James I. 1988. *Nothing about Us without Us: Disability, Oppression, and Empowerment.* Berkeley: University of California Press.
Davis, Lennard J., ed. 1997. *The Disabilities Studies Reader.* New York: Routledge.
Donley, Carol, and Sheryl Buckley, eds. 1996. *The Tyranny of the Normal: An Anthology.* Kent, OH: Kent State University Press.
Fine, Michelle, and Adrienne Asch. 1988. *Women with Disabilities: Essays in Psychology, Culture, and Politics.* Philadelphia: Temple University Press.
Fries, Kenny, ed. 1997. *Staring Back: The Disability Experience from the Inside Out.* New York: Plume.
Levy, Harold. 1973. *Square Pegs, Round Holes: The Learning Disabled Child in the Classroom and at Home.* Boston: Little, Brown.
Norden, Martin F. 1994. *The Cinema of Isolation: A History of Physical Disability in the Movies.* New Brunswick, NJ: Rutgers University Press.
A Paralyzing Fear: The Story of Polio in America. 1988. PBS.
Pelka, Fred, ed. 1997. *The ABC-CLIO Companion to the Disability Rights Movement.* Santa Barbara, CA: ABC-CLIO.
Safford, Philip L., and Elizabeth J. Safford. 1996. *A History of Childhood and Disability.* New York: Teachers College Press.
Shaw, Barrett, ed. 1994. *The Ragged Edge: The Disability Experience from the First Fifteen Years of the Disability Rag.* Louisville, KY: Advocado Press.
Sontag, Susan. 1989. *Illness as Metaphor and AIDS and Its Metaphors.* New York: Anchor Books.

Discipline and Punishment

Ideas about discipline and the practice of punishment in families have evolved substantially since the colonial view that heads of household were responsible for maintaining discipline among children as well as wives, servants, and slaves, by means of physical punishment when necessary. Over time, new religious beliefs, attitudes toward childhood, child-rearing patterns, gender roles, democratic social patterns, and labor systems transformed attitudes toward family governance. By the late nineteenth century, discipline within families focused primarily on children and tended to rely on psychological rather than physical forms of punishment. Further, the state and social work

A mother being stern with a young child. Drawing c. 1901. (Library of Congress)

agencies had begun to make visible interventions into the process. An ever more diverse population in the United States has, however, made for a wide array of disciplinary practices in families. These changes are reflected in the writings of numerous reformers, educators, ministers, doctors, and advice givers of all kinds who have, over the course of American history, debated and sought to prescribe for others the best means of maintaining discipline in families.

Discussion of disciplinary practices has long been used as a vehicle for finding fault with unfamiliar cultures. Among the many things that explorers and colonists found to criticize about Native cultures in the Americas were their child-rearing practices. European observers were likely to assume that the absence of corporal punishment meant an absence of discipline. Nineteenth- and early-twentieth-century anthropologists, however, documented a range of disciplinary practices among Native groups. In general, however, corporal punishment was not used regularly as it was among European settlers, although several tribes are known to have trained children from an early age to withstand physical pain and discomfort. Other disciplinary practices recorded by anthropologists include calling in family members other than parents to upbraid unruly children, dunking them in water, using ridicule and joking, and relying on the supernatural to provoke fear and create incentives for good behavior.

For Euro-Americans during the colonial period, corporal punishment was regarded as a legitimate way to discipline children for misbehavior as well as to "correct" insubordinate wives, servants, and slaves. The law allowed for anything that was not "excessive" and thus abusive, such as violence that injured severely or permanently. Children in particular were thought to owe their parents complete and unquestioning obedience. Puritan poet Anne Bradstreet used the graphic metaphor of a plough going over a child's back to describe the best means of cultivating morality and grace in recalcitrant children. And prescriptive literature on domestic relations, such as Benjamin Wadsworth's 1712 *The Well Ordered Family*, counseled parents to discipline their children through a discriminating and moderate use of the rod. Such writers placed stress on "breaking the will" of the child and viewed excessive leniency on the part of parents as potentially damaging to children, families, and the larger social order. Likewise, both teachers and masters were legally authorized to administer physical correction to unruly students, servants, or apprentices. These attitudes and practices were part of a larger cultural context in which corporal punishment was an integral and highly public element of military and penal discipline.

During the eighteenth century, however, intellectual understandings of childhood were changing. Enlightenment thinkers, John Locke and Jean-Jacques Rousseau most famously, were highly influential in their assertions that the nature of children was essentially innocent, as opposed to earlier theories of infant depravity. In Locke's 1690 *Some Thoughts Concerning Education*, he proposed doing away with physical punishment, at the same time teaching children from the earliest age how to master their desires, as the best way to ensure children's submission and maintain in them the proper reverence and respect for their parents. He wrote that although children were not born sinful, they were born willful, and that it was important for parents not to give in to their children's demands and cravings.

Such intellectual trends intersected with social developments to produce new patterns of discipline in urban middle-class families. By the early nineteenth century, the essentially agrarian society began to shift slowly toward urban centers, as the population of cities grew with trade and immigration. Middle-class families were increasingly composed of a wage-earning husband, a wife whose role was domestic manager rather than producer, and smaller numbers of children in whom parents made greater investments of education and nurture. In such families, the Lockean model of child rearing was apt to prevail, and women became the primary shapers of discipline for their children, rather than objects of correction themselves. In poorer urban and rural areas, where children's work still contributed substantially to the livelihood of families, older forms of discipline persisted.

Although the emphasis on breaking and governing the will of the child from an early age persisted into the antebellum period, ideas about disciplinary methods changed with a new sentimental appreciation of childhood. Additionally, in reaction to the transatlantic intellectual movements of humanitarianism and antislavery, a number of reform campaigns arose to protest the use of corporal punishment in prisons, schools, asylums, the navy, and homes. Instructive literature, such as Catherine Sedgwick's best-selling 1835 novel, *Home*, showed how parents might discipline a child with a terrible temper without resorting to a beating. When a boy killed his sister's kitten in a fit of rage, he was punished by being sent to his room until he could convince his father of his genuine repentance.

The most influential articulation of such views was Horace Bushnell's 1847 *Views of Christian Nurture*. Although Bushnell did not abandon the notion of innate depravity, he believed that proper nurture beginning in infancy could "weed out" bad tendencies. He argued that repressive and authoritarian techniques were less effective in helping the moral life of the child grow than were nurture and love from a mother who embodied Christian virtues. Environment, persuasion, good example, and well-formed habits were the best means of raising an obedient and moral child. These prescriptions placed new pressures on mothers and fathers; to morally concerned parents, children's disobedience and bad conduct became evidence of their failure to temper and properly shape the will of the child. Such trends did, however, provoke critics to comment on parents' dangerous tendency to spoil children whom many still believed possessed inherent tendencies to wickedness. Not until the 1850s was infant depravity abandoned by many Americans as a legitimate concern regarding children.

Educational reformers also joined the discussion, most famously Horace Mann, who argued in the early 1840s that corporal punishment was used in great excess in the common schools of Massachusetts. He proposed strict limitation on the use of the rod and engaged in debate with various Boston schoolmasters who found his proposals too radical. Similar views were being expressed by educational reformers in the South, such as Braxton Craven, who also opposed the extensive use of physical punishment found in southern schools.

Lyman Cobb's 1847 *The Evil Tendencies of Corporal Punishment* was an influential summation of the many voices that had come out in opposition to physical punishment in both families and schools and argued that this change was a crucial step in the general humanizing and elevating of the society. He linked the move away from corporal punishment for children to other social changes, such as the abolishment of public whipping posts and public executions in many states, the founding of hospitals and asylums, the temperance movement, the reforms of the navy in Britain and the United States, and most importantly, the elevation of women to their "true role" as designed by God and the passing of "patriarchal times." Cobb did not dispute the right of parents and school to use corporal punishment but argued instead that corporal punishment was counterproductive and inappropriate as a means of "moral discipline." It tended to harden children to violence, thus making them less likely to be swayed by it and more likely to resist.

Cobb's specific objections are revealing of the kinds of punishments that were actually being practiced in homes and schools of the period. For example, he strongly objected to hitting children around the head or ears and to the use of a ferule, saying that soft whips were preferable and that they should only be used on the shoulders, never the hands. He especially stressed that a whipping should never be given when out of temper, or unexpectedly, but only as a last resort and properly explained to the child, and never in the presence of family or schoolmates. He also objected to equally degrading punishments such as making a child stand on one leg or hold a very heavy book at arm's length, imprisoning children in closets, or ridiculing and shaming them. He offered many suggestions for preventives, such as teaching children self-control, vigorous physical education, supervising the child's associates, and above all moral persuasion and the law of kindness. As actual forms of punishment when necessary, he recommended suspension from school and, for very ill-tempered children, cold water.

Northern reformers also extended their concerns for moral child rearing to slave children in the South. In the antebellum period, abolitionists did their utmost to report on the abuses perpetrated on slaves, especially women and children. As a way of undermining the paternalistic ideology of slavery and the southern claim that slaves were part of the master's "family," northern writers described in vivid terms the slave trade's brutal separation of slave children from their parents. They showed that slave parents had little or no control over the upbringing of their children and that the discipline experienced by slave children was at the hands of their masters and overseers in the form of floggings and other cruel punishments. Lydia Maria Child's 1833 *An Appeal in Favor of That Class of Americans Called Africans*, for example, offered the reader pictures of "instruments of slave discipline" such as forms of handcuffs and whips. And in his *Narrative of the Life of Frederick Douglass, An American Slave*, first published in 1845, the famous runaway and abolitionist told northern audiences of his childhood experiences of seeing family members beaten and his understanding as a child that his turn could well be next (Douglass 1989). Such evidence of the brutality of southern "discipline" and the cruelty of the slave system had a profound impact on ideas about family discipline, as northerners sought to reform their own practices.

In the wake of the Civil War, ideas about the use of moral persuasion in disciplining children took hold more firmly. By this time, discipline in families had narrowed to concern only children in contrast to earlier periods when wives, servants, and slaves had all been subject. The title of Jacob Abbott's influential 1870 *Gentle Measures in the Management and Training of the Young* is representative of the kinds of attitudes prevalent in the period. Abbot strongly discouraged corporal punishment in favor of gentle firmness and expressed a new optimism about children's natural propensity for obedience. Now the target of this generation of educators and social reformers who sought to shape ideas about child rearing was not the slaveholders of the South or middle-class Protestant northerners, but the new urban immigrants. In the 1870s

A mother disciplining a nine-year-old. (Elizabeth Crews)

and 1880s, Societies for the Prevention of Cruelty to Children were founded in cities across the country, as middle-class reformers sought not only to "save" children from abusive parents but also to educate the urban poor and immigrants about the best methods of raising and disciplining their children. Such efforts persisted and intensified during the Progressive Era and led to the establishment of juvenile courts in the 1890s, as the state stepped in to take a role in disciplining children.

By the 1920s, the interest in "scientific" child rearing was reaching its peak, with the publication of influential advice manuals such as John B. Watson's *Psychological Care of Infant and Child* (Watson 1928). Watson's behaviorist approach was based on the assumption that all behaviors in children were the result of conditioning. Relying on laboratory studies of children, he prescribed a scientific upbringing with strict schedules and the enforcement of rules of conduct. Although he argued that the word *punishment* should be obsolete and that beatings belonged to the Dark Ages, he did advocate conditioning children through the application of "painful stimulus" (such as rapping fingers or hands) at the moment when they committed undesirable acts.

Beyond new theoretical approaches to discipline, parents in this period were also facing new social and cultural contexts that would profoundly shape disciplinary relations between parents and children in the twentieth century. G. Stanley Hall's 1904 *Adolescence* had defined the teenage years as a distinct phase of growing up that required special understanding and attention from parents and educators. As sociologists Robert and Helen Lynd showed in *Middletown*, their study of a small midwestern American city, middle-class parents there faced new disciplinary challenges as adolescent activities came to include driving cars, going to the movies, and dating (Lynd 1929). These circumstances shaped new forms of punishment such as curfews, suspending car privileges, and grounding teenagers. The Lynds noticed contrasting patterns of discipline among parents of different income levels and widespread, cross-class confusion over proper standards. Business-class parents were more likely to value independence and self-expression in their children. Working-class parents, on the other hand, were more apt to reassert older forms of control by stressing obedience and religious precepts. Other studies of the period, such as Frederic M. Thrasher's 1927 *The Gang*, warned that the relax-

ation of parental standards of discipline and the disorganization of family life in poor urban areas were leading boys in urban areas to turn to gangs as a form of structure lacking in the rest of their lives.

Fears about delinquency and parents' inability to discipline children heightened during the social dislocations of the Depression and World War II. In the postwar period, however, the emphasis in prescriptive literature shifted to the "natural" and emotional development of children; parents were urged to take cues from their children rather than attempting to condition their behaviors. Dr. Benjamin Spock's *Baby and Child Care* was the most influential articulation of this perspective (Spock 1946). Spock stressed the importance of affection, acceptance, and emotional sustenance and strongly discouraged the use of physical punishment. He asked whether or not punishment was necessary at all, noting that although some parents feel the need to punish their children, others never do, and that such trends and behaviors tend to run in families. Spock's own prescription, however, was that the main source of good discipline was growing up in a loving family and that the main element in the day-to-day care of a child should be "firmness." He urged parents to use punishment only when that system broke down and to carefully evaluate its effectiveness. The advice of experts such as Dr. Spock notwithstanding, parents from all walks of life continued to physically punish their children.

In the late twentieth century, something of a backlash emerged against what was perceived as parents' excessive permissiveness with their children. In the early 1980s, New Right groups such as the Moral Majority were defending parents' rights to use corporal punishment in the face of the government taking on a larger role in family life by enacting strict legislation against child abuse, which could be interpreted to include many forms of physical punishment. In the 1990s, the debate was also carried over to questions about the appropriate punishment for violent children. In the face of increased publicity given to violent crimes committed by children, in the 1990s all states passed laws facilitating the prosecution of juveniles in adult criminal court, with the consequence that in many places the death penalty could be imposed on sixteen-year-olds. Although parents were being advised to discipline their children through love and good example, the law was imposing increasingly harsh punishments on deviant youth

—*Elizabeth Blair Clark*

See also Adolescence; Child Development; Domestic Violence; Family Courts; Hall, G. Stanley; Society for the Prevention of Cruelty to Children; Watson, John B.

References and Further Reading
Douglass, Frederick. 1989. *Narrative of the Life of Frederick Douglass, an American Slave.* Boston: Anti Slavery Office, 1845. Reprint, New York: Anchor Books.
Glenn, Myra. 1984. *Campaigns against Corporal Punishment: Prisoners, Sailors, Women, and Children in Antebellum America.* Albany: State University of New York Press.
Greven, Philip. 1977. *The Protestant Temperament: Patterns of Child Rearing, Religious Experience, and the Self in Early America.* New York: Alfred A. Knopf.
Greven, Philip. 1990. *Spare the Child: The Religious Roots of Punishment and the Psychological Impact of Physical Abuse.* New York: Alfred A. Knopf.
Lynd, Robert S., and Helen. 1929. *Middletown: A Study in Modern American Culture.* New York: Harcourt, Brace and World.
Pettitt, George A. 1846. *Primitive Education in North America.* University of California Publications in American Archaeology and Ethnology, Vol. 43. Berkeley: University of California Press.
Spock, Benjamin. 1946. *The Common Sense Book of Baby and Child Care.* New York: Duell, Sloan, and Pearce.
Ulrich, Laurel Thatcher. 1982. *Good Wives: Image and Reality in the Lives of Women in Northern New England, 1650–1750.* New York: Alfred A. Knopf.
Watson, James B. 1928. *Psychological Care of Infant and Child.* New York: W. W. Norton.
Wishy, Bernard. 1968. *The Child and the Republic: The Dawn of Modern American Child Nurture.* Philadelphia: University of Pennsylvania Press

Divorce, History of

From colonial times to the present, divorce in the United States has been characterized by increasing freedom and willingness to divorce. In the past, a distinction was made between legal separation, under which partners could live separately but could not remarry, and absolute divorce, which granted husbands and wives freedom to remarry. Legal separation was dominant in the colonial period but died out in the nineteenth century in favor of absolute divorce. Until the last third of the twentieth century, separation and divorce were based on the concept of fault. Common grounds included bigamy, consanguinity, fraudulent contract, adultery, desertion, drunkenness, imprisonment, cruelty, inability to perform the duties of marriage, and nonsupport. From 1970 to the present, divorce in the United States has been increasingly based on the idea that irreconcilable differences can lead to marriage breakdown without assigning fault. Divorce law was left up to the colonies and later the states, so different jurisdictions have always had conflicting statutes. Areas of difference among the jurisdictions consisted of grounds for divorce, residency requirements, and eligibility to remarry. Still, certain trends have characterized each period. In most jurisdictions, women filed more divorce actions than men. Generally, women had difficulty supporting themselves after divorce. For most of the time, there were places that had easier requirements for divorce, known as divorce meccas, which, it was generally believed, attracted migratory divorce applicants. Although meaningful international statistics on divorce are notably difficult to obtain and interpret, the United States has been believed to have a higher divorce rate than any other country in the world.

Even in the colonial period, depending upon the colony, Americans were more likely to divorce than their English counterparts, who believed marriage to be indissoluble. In the New England colonies, founded by Puritans, divorce suits, although few in number, were often successful. In the middle and southern colonies, divorce was rare. After the American Revolution, one of the main changes was greater access to divorce, a freedom often gained by invoking revolutionary ideology. The nineteenth century was characterized by the progressive easing of restraints upon ability to divorce, and a series of divorce havens emerged in the West. In the first half of the century, states began to allow divorce on a greater number of grounds. During this period legislative divorce was being phased out in favor of judicial divorce. At midcentury, intemperance was more likely to be included in divorce grounds. In the latter part of the nineteenth century, the cruelty ground for

divorce was expanded to include mental cruelty. In the twentieth century a revolution in expectations concerning marriage resulted in an increase in divorce culminating in the adoption of no-fault divorce laws. Laws concerning divorce have been liberalized and unified, with the concomitant acceptance of divorce in U.S. society.

Divorce in Europe

Divorce in the colonies was closely related to the religious beliefs of the colonists and to their roots in Europe. In western Europe the Catholic countries had uniform legal codes forbidding divorce by the 1500s. The Protestant Reformation, in one of its departures from Catholicism, allowed divorce, particularly in cases of adultery. The Church of England, or the Anglican church, was the exception to this general Protestant acceptance of divorce. It continued the Catholic prohibition against divorce. Legal separation from bed and board could be granted by church courts. This meant that the couple could live separately; however, the husband was still responsible for the wife's support and neither husband nor wife could remarry. Complete divorce on the ground of adultery with rights to remarry was granted by Parliament starting in 1690, but such divorces were rare and, with few exceptions, only available to wealthy men. Those colonies that were primarily Anglican followed the English tradition of limiting divorce, but granting legal separations, whereas the colonies that were Puritan and Separatist generally allowed divorce. The American colonies diverged greatly on this issue.

Divorce in the Colonies

Most liberal on the issue of divorce were the New England colonies dominated by

Puritan views that held marriage to be a civil contract rather than a sacrament. Historians have reasoned that Puritans were willing to allow disruptive unions to be severed precisely because they valued marriage and family highly. Divorce was more orderly than desertion and illegal remarriage. Divorces were granted by the legislature, the civil courts, and the governor, depending upon the colony. For the most part divorce statutes gave the right to determine whether a divorce could be granted to the discretion of the grantor, so grounds were flexible. Grounds upon which divorces were granted varied throughout the region but generally included adultery, desertion, impotence, fraudulent contract, consanguinity, and bigamy. The plaintiff in the suit had to prove one of these allegations.

The colonies of Massachusetts Bay and Connecticut heard divorce petitions very early in their history. The first divorce in the colonies was granted in 1639 in Massachusetts Bay. According to extant records, 113 divorces were granted in Massachusetts Bay from 1639 to 1774. New Hampshire law was nearly identical to that of Massachusetts but New Hampshire had few divorces. Plymouth colony granted nine divorces in the seventy-two years of its existence. Rhode Island allowed divorce but only on one ground—adultery. In 1667 Connecticut passed the first divorce statute to state the appropriate grounds for divorce—adultery, fraudulent contract, and willful desertion for three years. This statute gave Connecticut the distinction of having the most liberal divorce policy in the British empire at the time. Nearly 1,000 divorces were granted from 1670 to 1799.

The Middle Atlantic colonies were more likely to follow the English tradition and grant legal separations, on the ground of adultery only. Governors dispensed a few divorces in both New York and New Jersey in line with this tradition. Pennsylvania at first punished adulterers with divorce, but when English law forbade this practice, the Pennsylvania legislature turned to absolute divorce only in cases of consanguinity. Separations were available on the grounds of adultery, bigamy, and sodomy, but divorces were few.

The southern colonies were even closer to the English model. In Virginia, the courts of chancery could grant legal separation on grounds of adultery, desertion, and extreme cruelty. Maryland, North and South Carolina, and Georgia followed the same policy—no absolute divorce.

The prevalence of marital discord is not to be found in the number of divorces in the colonial period. The evidence is fragmentary and may greatly underestimate the number of ruptured marriages. The frequency of marital breakup was amply displayed by the number of advertisements in newspapers for runaway wives and husbands and the number of desertions recorded in colonial accounts. Desertions were often followed by illegal remarriage or bigamy. Both private and informal agreements to separate were made, in addition to those separations with legal sanction. Selling wives, a custom more often found in England than in America, was practiced in some localities. Prearranged settlements were made in which a man would give a sum to the husband and take the wife.

Divorce from the American Revolution to 1850

The American Revolution spurred a liberalization of divorce policies in most of the new states. The fight against the tyranny of the king was translated into women's struggle to be free of tyrannical husbands. The spirit of freedom for those in unfortunate marriages seemed to be in accord with revolutionary principles. Yet there was still the presumption everywhere that one spouse had to be at fault for a divorce to be obtained. Divorce laws in various states differed in terms of the faults that were enumerated and the venue for divorce. Most states provided for both judicial and legislative divorces, although legislative divorces were on their way out.

In the northeastern states, including both New England and Middle Atlantic states, grounds for divorce were expanded. In Pennsylvania a statute was passed in 1785 that allowed for divorce on grounds of inability to perform marital duties, adultery, bigamy, and desertion. In 1815 the law was amended to include cruelty on the part of the husband and, later, the wife as well. This gave Pennsylvania the distinction of having the most expansive grounds for divorce from 1800 to 1840 and led to its being considered a divorce haven.

Rhode Island, New Hampshire, and Vermont allowed divorce on the basis of adultery, desertion, or cruelty. Rhode Island was the first to incorporate an omnibus clause that granted discretion to judges to decide whether other grounds for divorce were present. In contrast to the principle by which most northeastern states liberalized their laws, Massachusetts, in the early national period, actually narrowed its grounds. New York remained singular in its restriction of divorce to the ground of adultery.

In the western territories and states, divorces became even easier to obtain. Generally these divorce statutes included

adultery, desertion, and cruelty as grounds and sometimes added an omnibus clause. Statutes were similar to those in the Northeast, but divorces were more frequent and seemingly easier to obtain. Ohio, Indiana, and Illinois, with their heavy migration from New England, exceeded Pennsylvania's lenient divorce laws. Indiana, with an omnibus clause as well as many grounds for divorce, was a particularly notorious state in the 1850s.

The southern states showed the greatest change with their newfound willingness to grant divorce rather than only separation. The exception was South Carolina, which would not budge on its no-divorce policy. At first southern states adopted the practice of the English Parliament and granted divorces through the legislature, but gradually they began to grant court divorces when the press of divorce bills overwhelmed legislators.

In both Virginia and Máryland, divorce statutes listing grounds seemed to have been spurred by the specter of interracial sex. In both cases wives of white men had borne children with slave fathers. In 1827 a divorce bill was passed in Virginia that allowed courts to give a divorce on grounds of impotency, idiocy, and bigamy and legal separations on the basis of adultery, cruelty, and fear of bodily danger. In 1841 desertion was added to the grounds for separation.

Divorce at the Middle of the Nineteenth Century

By 1849 most northeastern states had added cruelty and drunkenness to the bedrock grounds of adultery and desertion. In 1851, California passed a divorce statute that included a compendium of causes that reflected the legal thinking of the time. Causes included impotence, adultery, desertion, cruelty, fraud, failure to support, habitual intemperance, and conviction of a felony. The statute was somewhat conservative in that it contained no omnibus clause providing for judicial discretion. Plaintiffs had to make their complaints conform to one of the stated grounds. In addition, the woman question was explicitly brought up in the legislative debates, showing the extent to which the earliest feminist movement had made an impact. Arguments for divorce rang out with pleas for wives who were victims of cruel and neglectful husbands. Under statutes in which habitual intemperance, conviction of a felony, and failure to support were grounds, men were disadvantaged. Again, women were more often those who sued for divorce and men were more often found at fault.

Cruelty became a more frequent ground for divorce as more and more states included it in their statutes; some states added verbal abuse to their list of grounds for divorce. Cruelty was increasingly interpreted by courts to include both physical and mental cruelty whether it was stated in the law or not. Men or women who verbally abused their spouses or caused mental suffering could be found guilty according to the courts.

The seeming leniency with which divorce was being treated precipitated a divorce crisis in the 1850s. Horace Greeley of the New York Tribune published a series of articles linking divorce to the corruption of U.S. civilization in 1852 and 1853. The debate became more strident as attempts were made to liberalize New York's divorce law in 1860. Greeley made an all-out attack on that effort and arguably won the debate, since the divorce laws in New York remained unchanged. The divorce debate was suspended with the beginning of the Civil War in 1861.

From the Civil War to 1900

Reliable statistics from the Civil War are scarce, but it is reasonable to conclude that during the war divorce fell, owing to other exigencies of life. After the war, the number of divorces appears to have risen to new levels. Absence during war, changed expectations, and physical impairment led to increased divorce. In 1868, South Carolina placed a divorce clause into the constitution that was followed two years later by a statute allowing divorce for the first time in that state on the grounds of adultery, desertion, and cruelty. The liberalization was short-lived, as the state went back to its no-divorce policy ten years later and held to that policy until 1949. During the post–Civil War period, new western states and territories were considered to be divorce mills because of their lax residence requirements, ample grounds for divorce, and lenient notification procedures. Utah had been accused for years of being a divorce haven because of its generous residency requirements and liberal judicial interpretations. The Dakota Territory, where residency was set at ninety days in 1877, garnered criticism as well. In the 1890s Oklahoma Territory became the latest divorce mecca.

In 1881 an organization was formed to take on the task of divorce reform for the first time—the New England Divorce Reform League, which became the National Divorce Reform League in 1885 and subsequently the National League for the Protection of the Family. The goal of the organization was to educate and to influence legislation to stiffen divorce requirements. Divorce reformers succeeded in persuading several states to rid their divorce statutes of omnibus clauses.

After considerable pressure from various antidivorce lobbies, Congress gave Carroll D. Wright, U.S. commissioner of labor, the assignment to compile divorce statistics from 1867 to 1886. When Wright published his findings in 1891, a trend of climbing divorce rates was confirmed. Wright found that in 1867 there were 9,937 divorces nationwide compared with 25,535 in 1886. This 150 percent growth was greater than the rate of growth of the population (Wright 1891).

The report fueled the energies of some divorce reformers, who lobbied Congress to take jurisdiction over divorce from the states and to pass uniform divorce laws, but it was impossible to convince Congress to take over such a volatile issue and to infringe upon states' rights. In 1896, however, Congress did pass a law requiring a one-year residency in the territories before citizens could file for divorce. In the 1890s there were numerous changes in state divorce laws—many making residence requirements more stringent, others dropping grounds for divorce—but their effect on the divorce rate was only temporary.

The Progressive Era, 1900–1917

During the Progressive Era, a general divorce debate took place in U.S. society. On one side were legal reformers and established Protestant clergymen who believed that divorce was not only immoral but destructive to family and society. On the other side were feminists, sociologists, and liberal clergymen who considered divorce to be a boon to families. Congress again called for statistics to be gathered, this time for the years 1887 to 1906. A National Congress on Uniform Divorce Law was to be held in 1906. The Congress, giving up on a national law, recommended that there be a two-year residency requirement and six grounds for divorce: bigamy, adultery, intolerable cruelty, conviction of a felony, habitual intemperance, and desertion for two years in each state. Only a handful of states followed this recommendation.

When the 1908 report was published, another outcry against divorce was heard. Despite evidence in the report that divorce was reaching new highs, however, the movement for divorce reform was losing steam. Its battle for public opinion was losing ground. Some publications, if not condoning divorce, at least recognized that there were two sides to the argument. Liberal clergymen were particularly helpful in swaying opinion by chipping away at the idea that the Bible forbade divorce and by their acknowledgment of divorce as morally acceptable. By the time the moral revolution of the 1920s took place, turning back to more stringent divorce policy was impossible.

World War I

World War I had an effect on marriage and divorce similar to that of the Civil War. War fosters unsuitable marriages in a number of ways. Courtships are speeded up because of impending battlefield deployment of young men. In addition, there is a heightened emotional desire to marry because of the general mood of society engaged in war. Marriages jump when war is near. Separation during wartime, especially when the war is on another continent, offers opportunities for adultery. After the war is over, partners may realize that they are unsuited, one or the other may have found a new partner, or pregnancy or venereal disease may cause spouses to question their choices. Divorce is postponed for a portion of the population. All of these factors led to a jump in divorce rates after war. Other factors that possibly added to the divorce rate were the stimulus of the increasing emancipation of women as evidenced by their attainment of the vote immediately after World War I, the increasing social acceptance of divorced persons, and the changing manners and morals of the 1920s. Statistics showed that by 1928 there was a significant increase in divorce from before the war.

Depression and World War II

The 1930s saw a decline in divorce rates in the first four years of the Depression. The choices of most people were limited by the loss of economic opportunity. Perhaps more important, federal work projects gave preference to men who had families to support. The divorce rate rose again in 1933, proving that the Depression did not have unlimited power to quell marital dissatisfaction.

At the same time, Nevada legislators, eager to bolster their state's economy, cut residency requirements for a third time. At the beginning of the twentieth century, Nevada had become the new divorce haven because of its six-month residency and flexible grounds for divorce. Later it lowered its residency requirements to three months and finally to a mere six weeks in 1931. Nevada remained the divorce mecca of the United States for the rest of the twentieth century.

With the approach of World War II, impulsive marriages rose. The magnitude of the mobilization created tremendous upheaval and migration. The effects of war on marriage described in the section on World War I were even more pronounced in World War II, with a con-

comitant rise in the divorce rate following the war. The peak year for postwar divorces in the United States came in 1946, when one out of twenty-eight marriages contracted in the previous four years ended in divorce. Despite the notable increase in divorce, one state liberalized its stand on divorce. Finally, after a no-divorce policy for most of its history, South Carolina passed a divorce act in 1949 that allowed divorce on the grounds of adultery, desertion, and intemperance.

The 1950s to 2000

After the peak year of 1946, when divorce rates soared, the rate leveled off at a higher plateau than before the war. The deprivation of the war years combined with painful separations and, later, cold war anxieties led to a back-to-the-family movement unprecedented in the twentieth century. Those who married in the late 1940s had remarkably stable marriages as a group. In fact, the divorce rate, though high, remained stable until the second half of the 1960s, when it began to rise. A new phenomenon in divorce appeared in the 1950s that was to be a harbinger of the development of no-fault divorce. A number of states had made voluntary separation a ground for divorce, but it had been infrequently used until the 1950s.

Many forces combined in the 1960s to challenge marriage and to increase the divorce rate. Social revolution, changes in relationships between men and women, the beginnings of a second wave of feminism, the assurance that one deserved to be happy, and a general liberal outlook led to revolutionary ways of perceiving divorce. As divorce rates climbed in the latter half of the 1960s, there was a recognition that fault divorce, no matter how many grounds were added, did not truthfully represent the reason for the breakdown of many marriages. The fault divorce system had fostered fabricated grounds for divorce. A total rethinking of the system was in order. In 1966 New York revised its divorce laws, which had only recognized adultery as a ground for divorce. The fact that some women made a living by pretending to be correspondents in divorce suits revealed that the law was a sham. New York took a moderate step forward and allowed divorce on grounds of adultery, cruelty, desertion, imprisonment, and two years of living separately.

The separation ground was a step on the road to no-fault that was based on the recognition that there need not be a guilty party for marriage to end. By the mid-1960s, eighteen states had added separation as a reason for divorce. The first no-fault law was enacted in California in 1970, when the mere allegation of irreconcilable differences leading to irremediable breakdown of the marriage became sufficient cause for dissolution of marriage, and no fault was placed on either party. Other states soon followed with some form of no-fault divorce. By 1977 there were only three states that did not have a no-fault provision.

The rush to no-fault dissolution of marriage caused some new problems. Without having to prove fault, partners were able to leave marriages without having to prove any wrongdoing on the part of their spouses. In addition, under fault laws women usually sued for divorce and men were most often deemed guilty and often penalized financially. With no-fault, there was no penalty. This led to many women coming out on the short end of the breakup financially. Less likely to be the major earners in the family, and more likely to have child custody, women faced

many economic problems. Sociologists pointed out that divorced women were more likely to end up in poverty under the new laws. At the end of the twentieth century, divorces were no longer obtained by false claims, but problems of support for previously dependent spouses and for the children under their care remained pressing.

—Bonnie L. Ford

See also Common-Law Marriage; Courtship, History of; Domestic Violence; Extended Family; Family Decline in the Twentieth Century; Gender Roles in the American Family; Remarriage, History of

References and Further Reading

Basch, Norma. 1999. *Framing American Divorce: From the Revolutionary Generation to the Victorians.* Berkeley: University of California Press.

Blake, Nelson Manfred. 1962. *The Road to Reno: A History of Divorce in the United States.* New York: Macmillan.

Chused, Richard H. 1994. *Private Acts in Public Places: A Social History of Divorce in the Formative Era of American Family Law.* Philadelphia: University of Pennsylvania Press.

Dayton, Cornelia Hughes. 1995. *Women before the Bar: Gender, Law, and Society in Connecticut, 1639–1789.* Chapel Hill: University of North Carolina Press.

Griswold, Robert L. 1982. *Family and Divorce in California, 1850–1890: Victorian Illusions and Everyday Realities.* Albany: State University of New York Press.

May, Elaine Tyler. 1980. *Great Expectations: Marriage and Divorce in Post-Victorian America.* Chicago: University of Chicago Press.

O'Neill, William L. 1967. *Divorce in the Progressive Era.* New Haven: Yale University Press.

Phillips, Roderick. 1988. *Putting Asunder: A History of Divorce in Western Society.* Cambridge: Cambridge University Press.

Riley, Glenda. 1991. *Divorce: An American Tradition.* New York: Oxford University Press.

Salmon, Marylynn. 1986. *Women and the Law of Property in Early America.* Chapel Hill: University of North Carolina Press.

Weitzman, Leonore J. 1985. *The Divorce Revolution: The Unexpected Social and Economic Consequences for Women and Children in America.* New York: The Free Press.

Wright, Carroll D. 1891. *A Report on Marriage and Divorce in the United States, 1867 to 1886.* Washington, DC: Government Printing Office.

Domestic Violence

The definition of what constitutes unacceptable violence within families, the social responses to that violence, and its extent and nature have all changed substantially over the course of American history. In response to shifting social and cultural norms, the distinction between definitions of *violence* and legitimate *correction* has altered over time, as has the definition of what constitutes a family or household. Significant moments in the ongoing redefinition of domestic violence as a social problem range from the enactment of laws in colonial America against the "excessive" beating of servants, wives, and children to the discovery in the 1970s of the "battered child" and the "battered woman." Social responses to domestic violence have likewise varied dramatically. From the neighborhood surveillance found in Puritan New England to the late-twentieth-century creation of shelters for abused women and children and the emergence of domestic violence as a topic of historical inquiry, social responses have been shaped by cultural developments and political movements, in particular the various waves of feminist activism. The extent and nature of domestic violence have also changed according to place and

period. It is difficult, however, to quantify the amount of violence in families over time with any degree of precision, given shifts in the kinds of violent acts that are socially or legally penalized and the consistent underreporting of family violence. What research has been done, however, shows that broad cultural and social forces and changing power relations in families, as well as some preventive policies, have had a significant impact on levels of violence in families.

Little to no research has been done on family disorder among Native Americans in the pre-European settlement or colonial periods. Historians have, however, begun to study violence in early Euro-American families. Throughout the colonies, the family was considered to be a vital foundation of both church and state, and heads of household were expected to maintain order among their dependents. Indeed, English custom and legal precedent supported the rights of husbands, parents, masters, and mistresses to use moderate physical chastisement (that which did not cause lasting bodily injury) in the governance of their households. Such authoritarian violence, or the threat of that violence, whether to control the behavior of children, servants, slaves, or wives, was seen as essential to social order in the colonial period.

In New England, however, where families were seen as microcosms of the Puritan religious commonwealth, laws against "unnatural severity" toward wives, children, and servants were enacted for the first time in American history. In 1641, the Massachusetts Bay colony's civil and criminal code, the *Body of Liberties,* prohibited excessive violence against children, gave servants leave to flee from abusive masters, and threatened husbands who beat their wives with a fine or a whipping. In addition, Puritan church courts occasionally put their members on trial for ungodly behavior such as wife beating, and in Massachusetts and Connecticut cruelty was considered grounds for divorce. In practice, however, the society's priority was on restoring family order rather than safeguarding dependents, and household violence was routinely sanctioned. When an instance of family violence did come to the attention of authorities, questions revolved around how the dependent had provoked the superior's use of force. In this culture, submissiveness to familial authority was not only a duty but also the best way for women, children, and servants to obtain kind treatment.

During the eighteenth century, developments in the social understanding of domestic violence varied considerably according to place. In New England, as legal processes became more formalized and colonial courts came to model themselves on the English example of jurisprudence, authorities became less responsive to abuses experienced by women, children, and servants. The number of complaints of assaults from wives declined considerably, and although in the early period abusive husbands had been fined or sometimes whipped, in eighteenth-century Connecticut such husbands were merely bound to good behavior between two county court sessions. There was also a decline in the number of divorce petitions bringing charges of cruelty; although New England divorce law was by far the most liberal in the Western world, in Connecticut and Massachusetts combined, only ten divorces or separations were granted on the sole grounds of cruelty before the 1780s. A complaint of cruelty forced the court to examine the way in which a man governed his family, and lawyers and judges proved unwilling

to do so in this period when a wife's submission to her husband's abuses was seen as a model of Christian resignation.

If the New England courts were becoming less responsive to the domestic abuse of women and children, the reverse seems to have been true in Virginia, the colony with the highest levels of personal violence. As the century progressed, courts became more likely to issue bonds of recognizance and fines for acts of excessive violence toward servants and wives. This change intersected with the transition of the colony's labor force from white indentured servants to African slaves. As the number of slaves in the colony grew and the legal differences between slaves and servants were codified, Virginia's courts grew more attentive to cases of excessive violence by any free white toward other whites, all the while sanctioning brutality toward slaves.

Finally, in urban centers, beginning in the 1750s, members of the middle class were developing an ideal of companionate marriage, mutual affection, complementary gender roles, and emotional self-control within households. In Pennsylvania, Quaker advocacy of noncorporal punishment of children and servants anticipated the nineteenth-century concept of the domestic world as a peaceful and nurturing haven. Middle-class aspirations and prescriptions aside, the law recognized the rights of master, parents, and husbands to use physical force to govern their households, and the religious and cultural pluralism of urban centers weakened the possibility of any uniform behavioral standard.

But even though the legal remedies were weak throughout the colonies in this period, there was another way in which servants, slaves, wives, and children could respond to domestic violence:

by running away from home. The rapidly growing number of eighteenth-century newspapers included many advertisements placed by heads of households for their "eloped" wives and "runaway" servants, apprentices, and slaves. The proliferation of these advertisements suggests that the willingness of individuals to tolerate family violence in this period may often have been out of step with that of the law.

The period between the Revolution and the Civil War was marked by continued regional differentiation in the understanding of domestic violence. As a whole, however, the culture was responsive to transatlantic intellectual currents lamenting intemperance and advancing humanitarian ideals and to the popular revolutionary ideal of a republican family that would rely on female virtue to nurture good citizens. Across the country, but especially in the Northeast, reformers took up these ideas to protest the use of corporal punishment, not only in institutions such as schoolhouses, the navy, prisons, and insane asylums but also in homes. Republican ideals also influenced the widespread reform of divorce laws throughout the new nation. Divorce had long been available in Puritan New England, but after the Revolution, in a striking departure from British tradition, all states except South Carolina came to allow for divorce. In a few states, spousal violence could warrant a full divorce with the right to remarry, although in others it only justified a legal separation. Equally significantly, in almost all states a husband's violence became a legal defense for a wife's departure from her husband's home.

It was in this period in the Northeast that domestic violence was for the first time defined as a political and feminist issue. Brought to public attention by temperance reformers and a burst of sensationalist press, the issue was later taken up by women's rights advocates. The leaders of the temperance movement, mostly ministers and a growing number of "reformed" drunkards, linked domestic violence with alcohol, invoking the image of the "trembling family." They called for abstinence from liquor as a solution to family disorder and poverty, and in their view, women's role was to create a home environment attractive enough to lure men away from taverns. Women soon joined the movement in large numbers and, in an outpouring of narratives, began telling their own stories of domestic grief. As the story of "the drunkard's wife" became increasingly familiar, some women's rights activists began to take the issue of domestic violence beyond alcohol. In the late 1840s and 1850s, a few radical publications began to emphasize not a wife's duty to reform her drunken husband but rather her obligation to leave him in order to safeguard herself and her children.

In the same period, the debate over slavery also contributed to redefining domestic violence. Northern women's rights advocates began to describe abused wives as "slaves," condemning violence against slaves along with violence against wives. Abolitionists publicized and denounced in graphic terms the sexual and physical abuse of slaves and argued that such household violence debased the southern family and gave the lie to the popular southern image of the benevolent paternalism of slave owners. Southern writers, in turn, answered that there was less intemperance and family violence among slaves than among the poor of northern cities. In this way, domestic violence became one of the many rhetorical weapons in the sectional conflict.

The post–Civil War period marked a high point for public interest in violence against women. Building on prewar women's activism in the temperance movement, the Women's Christian Temperance Union (WCTU) was founded in 1874 and quickly became the largest women's organization in the country. These activists drew the connection between alcohol and male violence ever more strongly and engaged in highly visible protests such as vandalizing taverns and saloons. Eventually, twenty states gave abused wives the right to sue the saloonkeepers who had served their husbands. The closely related movement for "social purity" also led some feminists to begin protesting the sexual coercion of wives and to draw comparisons between marriage and prostitution. This line of thinking manifested itself in the growing tendency of courts to regard coerced marital sex as a form of "mental cruelty." The moralistic viewpoint of this wave of activism was also reflected in the campaign to bring back the whipping post for wife beaters. Between 1882 and 1905, Maryland, Delaware, and Oregon all passed such laws in response to arguments about the dangerous levels of violence among urban lower classes. Frustration at the piecemeal nature of such legislation, however, led influential feminists to focus their efforts on the suffrage cause in the hope that votes for women might eventually bring about protective legislation for women and children.

Of greater lasting impact was the discovery of child abuse as a social problem in the 1870s. By the end of the decade there were thirty-four Societies for the Prevention of Cruelty to Children (SPCCs) in the United States. The societies were modeled on the American Society for the Prevention of Cruelty to Animals (ASPCA) and funded by wealthy elites with the purpose of actively enforcing existing laws against cruelty in families. Reacting to the new urbanism of the late nineteenth century, with its influx of immigrants and highly visible poor, these reformers saw cruelty to children as a fault of those of a lower class and culture. It was viewed as a moral wrong and a threat to civil order and the future of the nation. A staff of Christian reform-minded female volunteers were charged with instructing the urban poor in the correct ways of rearing their children and with visiting families in order to detect and report instances of abuse. SPCCs handled prosecutions, adoptions, and child placements, sometimes taking temporary custody of abused children. The societies were also active in sponsoring legislation against practices they defined as child abuse, such as child performances and the sale of tobacco or firearms to children, and they lobbied for tougher laws against child sexual abuse (raising the age of consent to fourteen years). Their work with children led to some attention to violence against wives as well; founded in 1885, the Protective Agency for Women and Children of Chicago sometimes offered shelter to abused women and girls.

After the turn of the century, such societies took on a different cast as social work became professionalized and secularized, and state regulation took on a larger role in the work against family violence. Although the focus remained on the urban and immigrant poor, middle-class professionals with a new "scientific" outlook took on the day-to-day work of the SPCCs and began to de-emphasize alcohol as the explanation for family violence in favor of other environmental factors such as poverty, unemployment, and lack of education. The feminist emphasis on male brutality faded, and social workers' primary concern became "child neglect" by mothers rather than cruelty or sexual abuse by fathers. SPCCs became less likely to prosecute individuals and more interested in prevention and education, joining the larger Progressive movement in lobbying for child labor laws and for improved living conditions among the urban poor. Significant reforms also took place in the legal system: Juvenile courts were established in the 1890s and courts of domestic relations in the 1910s.

The Depression initiated a new priority for social workers that lasted until the 1960s, that of defending the conventional family. In the 1930s, popular culture and the social work establishment joined in blaming conflicts within families on unemployment and poverty. Although there was widespread public sympathy for unemployed husbands and fathers, less attention was given to the additional stresses placed on wives and children. Family violence was seen as a phenomenon secondary to and caused by larger economic conditions, and the response of overburdened social service agencies was to provide what economic relief they could and to counsel reconciliation.

This focus on preserving and defending the conventional family extended into the 1940s and 1950s, and these decades represent the lowest point in public awareness of the problem of family violence since the early nineteenth century. In this period, however, interest in the problem was not constrained by external social factors; rather, new psychiatric categories and therapeutic practices heavily influenced by the popularization of Freudian psychiatry in the United States had a profound impact on the social work profession and on the popular conception of how to respond to violence in families. The most notable change was the blaming of wives for their husbands' violence against them. Psychiatrists and social workers were likely to see abused women, rather than their violent husbands, as the ones in need of therapeutic intervention. New diagnoses of specifically feminine neuroses, such as sexual repression and masochism, were invoked to explain women's complaints of violent husbands. Child sexual or physical abuse was also given little attention in this period; instead, the term *emotional neglect* came to describe a new kind of failure on the part of mothers.

After a long lull in the public and professional discussion of the problem, family violence was rediscovered and redefined in the 1960s and 1970s. The earliest sign of this rediscovery was the medicalization of child abuse in the early 1960s by pediatricians and radiologists who began to observe the effects of long-term abuse through X-ray evidence and studies of children's emergency room visits. Their findings were widely publicized in a 1962 article that coined a new term, *the battered-child syndrome*. This new understanding of an old problem described an epidemic of child abuse, citing it as a grave national health risk and claiming that it took place with equal frequency in all social classes as a result of "cycles of violence" in particular families. The equation of child battering with disease led to a less harsh assessment of parents than had previous views of abuse as a crime or a sin; they too were seen as in need of therapy. The relative destigmatization and medicalization of the problem led many states to pass reporting laws and set up hot lines. In 1973, Congress passed the national Child Abuse Prevention and Treatment Act, which defined child abuse broadly as any treatment by a person responsible for the child that caused "the child's health or welfare" to be "harmed or threatened." The act established a National Center on Child Abuse and Neglect, funded treatment programs around the country, and required states to meet federal standards for protective custody provisions.

It took until the mid-1970s, however, for there to be a comparable rediscovery of violence to wives. Even the renewed feminist movement took close to a decade to turn its attention to the problem of violence against women in their homes. Although the National Organization for Women (NOW) was founded in 1966, it was not until 1974 that increasingly radicalized feminists, following in the path of the antirape movement, first brought the issue to media attention. A brief burst of sensationalized press followed. Innovative feminist strategies included suing police departments across the country on behalf of the battered women whose calls they routinely ignored and founding hot lines and shelters for victims. By the mid-1980s there were coalitions to provide services for battered women in forty-eight states and more than 300 shelters nationwide. These shelters were based on a self-help model and often founded and run by women who had themselves experienced abuse. The intent was to support women in their efforts to move away from violent relationships, a project facilitated by the rapid shift to no-fault divorce laws across the country after 1970. As time went on, many of the grassroots shelters and hotlines developed into professionalized social service agencies. Although in earlier periods authorities had asked what an abused wife could do to reform her husband, now the prevalent public question had become why women stayed in violent homes.

The rediscovery of the "battered child" and then the "battered woman" also paved the way for a focus on other forms of family violence in the 1970s and 1980s. Expanded definitions of *family* and *domestic* led to concern for the battered elder, the battered girlfriend, the battered partner in gay relationships, and even the battered husband. Former abusers themselves developed programs to counsel and reform batterers.

As in the nineteenth century, wife beating was brought to the public eye as a result of feminist activism and only then came to be seen as a matter of law and order and of social work. The first national legislation came in 1968, channeling funding to the states through the new Law Enforcement Assistance Administration, and it was in this context that the term *domestic violence* was coined. The Department of Health and Human Services established an Office of Domestic Violence in 1979, but it received only very small amounts of funding compared to child abuse services and was shut down in 1981. In the 1980s, proposals to increase federal funding for family violence programs met with strong opposition from forces such as the New Right and the Moral Majority that advocated "strengthening the American family" in the face of what they saw as excessive state intrusions into private life and the too frequent breakup of families.

The 1990s saw increased federal action against family violence. The 1994 Violence Against Women Act provided federal funding for state and local programs and created new federal criminal laws targeting domestic violence. The Justice Department opened a new Violence Against Women Office in 1995 to help implement these laws, and in 2000 it produced a study asserting that *intimate partner violence* against women (yet another new term, designed to encompass violence in gay communities and dating relationships as well as spousal violence) had declined from 1993 through 1998. Still, one-third of all women murdered in this period were killed by an intimate partner (as opposed to 4 percent of male murder victims), and 25 percent of women versus 7 percent of men in the United States report having been assaulted by an intimate partner during their lifetime.

—*Elizabeth Blair Clark*

See also Child Abuse; Discipline and Punishment; Divorce, History of; Society for the Prevention of Cruelty to Children

References and Further Reading

Basch, Norma. 1999. *Framing American Divorce: From the Revolutionary Generation to the Victorians.* Berkeley: University of California Press.

Daniels, Christine, and Michael V. Kennedy. 1999. *Over the Threshold: Intimate Violence in Early America.* New York: Routledge.

Dayton, Cornelia. 1995. *Women before the Bar: Gender, Law, and Society in Connecticut, 1639–1789.* Chapel Hill: University of North Carolina Press.

Glenn, Myra. 1984. *Campaigns against Corporal Punishment: Prisoners, Sailors, Women, and Children in Antebellum America.* Albany: State University of New York Press.

Gordon, Linda. 1988. *Heroes of Their Own Lives: The Politics and History of Family Violence.* New York: Penguin Books.

Pleck, Elizabeth. 1987. *Domestic Tyranny: The Making of Social Policy against Family Violence from Colonial Times to the Present.* New York: Oxford University Press.

Schecter, Susan. 1982. *Women and Male Violence: The Visions and Struggles of the Battered Women's Movement.* Boston: South End Press.

Ulrich, Laurel Thatcher. 1982. *Good Wives: Image and Reality in the Lives of Women in Northern New England, 1650–1750.* New York: Alfred A. Knopf.

U.S. Department of Justice. "Violence against Women Office." http://www.doj.gov/domesticviolence (cited 15 January 2001).

Drug and Alcohol Abuse

Drug and alcohol addiction and abuse are widespread in U.S. society. Parental substance abuse is associated with a host of negative outcomes within the family, including job loss, unstable home conditions, homelessness, domestic violence, and child abuse. Numerous studies report that children whose parents abuse drugs and alcohol suffer from a multitude of problems, including low self-esteem, depression, suicidal ideation, and early initiation of sexual activity. Many children grow up following the same patterns of alcohol and drug abuse as their parents.

According to a national survey conducted by the U.S. Department of Health and Human Services (1999a), most adults in the United States admit to at least occasional use of alcohol, and approximately one-fourth of U.S. adults between the ages of 18 and 34 engage in binge drinking. Another 9.7 million are dependent on alcohol. This includes 915,000 youths ages 12–17.

Although use of illicit drugs is not as common as alcohol use, the U.S. government estimates that in 1999 there were about 14.8 million users of illicit drugs, including approximately 1 million active injection drug users (IDUs). Among illicit drugs used in this country, marijuana is the drug most commonly used. According

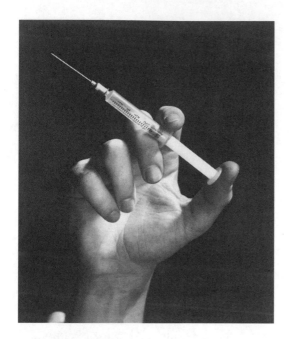

Hand holding a syringe. (Bettmann/Corbis)

have grown in popularity beginning in the 1980s. Cocaine is actually one of the oldest known drugs. The coca leaf, from which cocaine is derived, is grown primarily in Peru and Bolivia. Cocaine, an extremely addictive stimulant, has been associated with substance abuse since the 1800s.

The effects of cocaine, first synthesized in 1855, were not recognized by medical science until around 1880. The health benefits of cocaine were touted by many prominent figures in the late 1800s and early 1900s, including psychologist Sigmund Freud, inventor Thomas Edison, and actress Sarah Bernhardt. Freud claimed cocaine could be used safely for the cure of depression. In 1886 cocaine was included as the main ingredient in a new soft drink, Coca Cola. During the late 1800s and early 1900s, cocaine was widely used in a variety of tonics and "miracle cures," with the effect of promoting cocaine's acceptability and popularity. It took several years before Americans became aware of cocaine's dangers. In 1903 public pressure led to the removal of cocaine as an ingredient in Coca Cola. Cocaine was added to the list of narcotics outlawed by the Dangerous Drug Act of 1920. By that time, a market for cocaine had already been established in U.S. society. Its popularity in this country reached a peak in the 1980s and 1990s.

to the 1998 National Household Survey on Drug Abuse, an estimated 11.0 million Americans reported current (past month) use of marijuana (U.S. Department of Health and Human Services 1999a, 2). More than 68.6 million Americans have used marijuana at least one time in their lives. This figure represents about 32 percent of the population twelve years and older (Substance Abuse and Mental Health Services Administration 1997). Commonly reported short-term effects of marijuana use include problems with memory, distorted perception, trouble with thinking and problem solving, and increased heart rate. When marijuana is used in conjunction with other drugs, these effects may be more pronounced.

Although marijuana is a more frequently and widely used drug in this country, cocaine and its derivative, crack,

The most potent, addictive, and popular form of cocaine is crack. Smoking crack cocaine produces a euphoric "high" in less than ten seconds. Not only is crack's effect immediate, the drug is inexpensive to manufacture and to buy—factors that contribute to its popularity.

Crack and other forms of cocaine typically cause feelings of anxiety and depression, which may last for weeks. The depression that results from attempts to stop using the drugs often leads to relapse and return to use. In addition to the drugs' addictive nature, use of crack and cocaine can lead to other more serious side effects. If taken through the veins or injected, use of unsterile needles can cause infections and disease, including hepatitis B, blood poisoning, and acquired immunodeficiency syndrome (AIDS). Even if it is smoked, use of crack can increase the risk of becoming infected with human immunodeficiency virus (HIV) or other sexually transmitted infections. Men and women who use crack are susceptible to transmission through high-risk sexual activity. Crack users frequently have sex with multiple partners in exchange for the drug.

According to the National Household Survey on Drug Abuse, there were 1.5 million cocaine users in the United States in 1997 (U.S. Department of Health and Human Services 1999b). This represented a decrease from the 1985 peak of 5.7 million reported cocaine users. The annual number of new cocaine users, however, increased between 1994 and 1998 (from 514,000 to 934,000) (U.S. Department of Health and Human Services 1999b). Given the likelihood of underreporting, the Office of National Drug Control Policy estimated the actual number of chronic cocaine users in 1999 at 3.6 million (U.S. Department of Health and Human Services 1999b). The most obvious effects of drug and alcohol abuse on the American family are found in the records of child welfare agencies and family court documents. The number of abused and neglected children rose from 1.4 million in 1986 to 3 million in 1997, a 114 percent increase that is attributed largely to parental substance abuse (National Center on Addiction and Substance Abuse 1999). Professionals involved in child welfare estimate that substance abuse and addiction are to blame for 70 to 90 percent of the cases of child abuse and neglect. Children of parents who abuse alcohol and other drugs are 4.2 times more likely to be neglected and 2.7 times more likely to be abused than children whose parents are not substance abusers.

During the 1990s, in response to burgeoning caseloads, child protective agencies increasingly acted to remove children from homes in which alcohol or drug abuse was present—a trend that went against long-standing efforts to preserve families by providing an array of supportive social services. Children of substance-abusing parents frequently end up in either foster care or kinship care. In the 1990s there were at least half a million children in foster care in this country every year—about twice the number of children in the system ten years before (Administration for Children and Families 1996).

One of the reasons for the growing number of children placed in the care of the state is the increasing number of women who abuse alcohol and illicit drugs. The proportion of drug addicts who are female doubled between 1960 and the late 1970s. By the mid-1990s the percentages of women and men who abuse prescription drugs had become virtually equal, and 40 percent of crack addicts were women (National Center on Addiction and Substance Abuse 1996). A recent national household survey reported that at least 4.5 million women are alcoholics or abuse alcohol; 3.1 million women habitually use illicit drugs; and 3.5 million misuse prescription drugs (National Institute on Drug Abuse 1994).

Although drug abuse can occur at any point in a woman's life, about half of the women who use illicit drugs are in their childbearing years (fifteen to forty-four). Each year, 500,000 babies are born with evidence of exposure to illicit drugs in utero (National Institute on Drug Abuse 1994). In 1991, 62 percent of children in foster care under the age of four had been exposed to drugs prenatally. Of all pregnant women who use drugs, 53 percent smoke marijuana, approximately 20 percent use cocaine, 14 percent use heroin or other illegal drugs, and 27 percent misuse prescription drugs (General Accounting Office 1994).

Determining the full extent of the consequences of maternal drug abuse is difficult, and attributing a specific effect to a particular drug is even more difficult, given that, typically, more than one substance is abused. The amount, type, and number of drugs abused; adequacy of prenatal care and maternal nutrition; socioeconomic status; and exposure to sexually transmitted diseases are just some of the cofactors that make it difficult to directly determine the impact of perinatal drug use on fetal outcomes. Although the full extent of the effects of prenatal drug exposure on a child is not known, scientific studies have documented that babies born to mothers who abuse alcohol and other drugs such as cocaine during pregnancy are often prematurely delivered, have low birth weights and smaller head circumferences, and are often shorter in length than nonexposed infants.

One well-studied outcome of maternal drug use is fetal alcohol syndrome (FAS). FAS is a birth defect caused by a woman's drinking heavily during pregnancy and is characterized by growth retardation, abnormal facial features, and central nervous system problems. Children with FAS can have serious lifelong disabilities, including mental retardation, learning disabilities, and serious behavioral problems. Each year in the United States, between 1,300 and 8,000 children are born with FAS (National Center on Addiction and Substance Abuse 1999).

Since the emergence of the crack cocaine epidemic in the 1980s, much media attention has been placed on "crack babies," or babies born to mothers who used cocaine while pregnant. Despite predictions of irreversible damage, including reduced intelligence and social skills, most crack-exposed babies appear to have few long-term problems. There is some evidence, however, that exposure to cocaine during fetal development may lead to subtle, but significant, deficits later, such as inability to block out distractions and difficulty concentrating for long periods of time.

The impact of drug use on the woman herself is also of significance. Many women who abuse alcohol and other drugs have histories of childhood physical and/or sexual abuse. Female alcoholics are more likely than male alcoholics to suffer from depression or other mental disorders. The Centers for Disease Control and Prevention's estimates indicate that drug use is a factor in up to 70 percent of the cases of women with AIDS (Centers for Disease Control and Prevention 2000). They acquired it either through sharing of dirty needles or by having sex with an infected IDU.

Although the number of drug treatment programs has expanded dramatically in the past thirty years, fewer than half of all Americans who need treatment receive it. There are many reasons for this discrepancy. Lack of motivation on the part of the addicted person to get into treatment, long waiting periods for access to residential treatment slots, and lack of insurance coverage for treatment are frequently cited barriers to treatment.

Additional problems face women with substance abuse problems. Appropriate female-centered treatment programs have not kept pace with the growing problem of drug abuse among women. Most substance abuse treatment programs were designed for men. As the number of addicted women increased, most programs were simply expanded to include women—without regard to gender differences (Metsch et al. 1995). Particularly for women who are pregnant or have dependent children, a male-centered treatment approach creates a number of barriers, including lack of child care, lack of access to concurrent prenatal care, and fear of involvement with child protective services. As a result, fewer than 35 percent of addicted mothers seek treatment (Substance Abuse and Mental Health Services Administration 1997). Those who do enter treatment have higher rates of attrition compared to men. Research suggests that treatment models that address biological, psychological, and social paradigms may be more effective in treating drug-dependent women with children.

—*Debra K. Bartelli*

See also Alcohol and Drug Abuse in Families; Child Abuse

References and Further Reading

Administration for Children and Families. 1996. *Data Dissemination for the Adoption and Foster Care Analysis and Reporting System.* Report no. 1. Washington, DC: Administration for Children and Families.

Centers for Disease Control and Prevention. 2000. *U.S. HIV and AIDS Cases Reported through December 1999.* Year-end ed., vol. 11, no. 2.

General Accounting Office. 1994. *Foster Care: Parental Drug Abuse Has Alarming Impact on Young Children.* Washington, DC: General Accounting Office.

Metsch, L., J. Rivers, M. Miller, R. Bohs, C. McCoy, C. Morrow, E. Bandstra, V. Jackson, and M. Gissen. 1995. "Implementation of Family-centered Treatment Program for Substance-abusing Women and Children: Barriers and Resolutions." *Journal of Psychoactive Drugs* 27: 75–83.

National Center on Addiction and Substance Abuse (CASA) at Columbia University. 1996. *Substance Abuse and the American Woman.* New York: CASA at Columbia University.

National Center on Addiction and Substance Abuse (CASA) at Columbia University. 1999. *No Safe Haven: Children of Substance Abusing Parents.* New York: CASA at Columbia University.

National Institute on Drug Abuse. 1994. *Drug Abuse and Pregnancy.* Rockville, MD: U.S. Department of Health and Human Services.

Substance Abuse and Mental Health Services Administration. Office of Applied Sciences. 1997. *Preliminary Results from the 1996 National Household Sergey on Drug Abuse.* Rockville, MD: Substance Abuse and Mental Health Services Administration.

U.S. Department of Health and Human Services. National Institute on Drug Abuse. 1999a. *National Institute on Drug Abuse Research Report Series: Cocaine Abuse and Addiction.* Rockville, MD: U.S. Department of Health and Human Services.

U.S. Department of Health and Human Services. SAMSHA. Office of Applied Studies. 1999b. *Summary of Findings from the 1998 National Household Survey on Drug Abuse.* Rockville, MD: U.S. Department of Health and Human Services.

E

Early Childhood Education

Early childhood education encompasses educational institutions, teachers, teaching methods, texts, and other materials designed to educate and socialize preschool-age children. Although early childhood education includes child care, and vice versa, the history of these two fields is deeply divided, in ways that have caused difficulties for families. Before the twentieth century, because the notion that young children should be away from their mothers for any length of time was considered socially unacceptable, preschool programs usually operated for a few hours a day and were promoted as beneficial educational enrichment. Child-care programs, which provided full-day care to meet the needs of working mothers, were viewed as potentially harmful custodial arrangements. Historically, many young children were educated and cared for informally outside of their families, often in the homes of other mothers, in what came to be known as dame schools. Infant schools, the first formally organized, extrafamilial early childhood education programs, were introduced to the United States from Europe in the early nineteenth century but failed to become permanently established. By the early twentieth century, kindergartens, which had been imported from Germany in the mid-nineteenth century, had been instituted in public schools in most major U.S. cities. Private nursery schools for three- and four-year-olds were started in the 1910s. Federally supported preschools for poor children, which began in the 1930s, were made more widely available with the advent of Project Head Start in the mid-1960s. Although a movement for universal, publicly supported preschools is growing at the state and local levels, access to high-quality early childhood education programs for their children remains problematic for many families in the United States.

Treatises offering advice on early childhood education began appearing in Europe in the mid-seventeenth century, when families were increasingly under stress owing to religious and political turmoil and the economic and demographic changes of incipient modernization. First published in English in 1650, *The School of Infancy*, by the Moravian bishop Johann Amos Comenius, provided a detailed prescription for how mothers should educate their young children at home. Comenius's concerns about the damaging effects of didacticism and promotion of naturalistic teaching methods set the tone for early childhood education for years to come. John Locke's 1693 *Some Thoughts Concerning Education* also recommended home education but advised parents to treat their children rationally, as if they were little adults. In *Emile* (published in

Eight African American children in kindergarten, learning washing and ironing at Whittier Primary School, Hampton, Virginia. (Library of Congress)

1762), Jean-Jacques Rousseau's radical, romanticized vision of child rearing and education, young children were to be removed from their parents and tutored in a natural setting, free from societal constraints.

Some of the first extrafamilial early childhood education programs were based on these prescriptive guides. The Swiss educator Johann Heinrich Pestalozzi tried to put Rousseau's ideas into action in a series of homelike experimental schools in which he and his followers lived with the young poor children in their care. In *Leonard and Gertrude* (published in 1781) and *How Gertrude Raises Her Children* (published in 1801), Pestalozzi depicted an idealized peasant mother whose family-

style teaching helped young children learn arithmetic and other school subjects through counting threads and other daily activities. In their popular 1798 home education manual, *Practical Education*, Maria and Richard Edgeworth combined Lockean and Pestalozzian methods, stressing the importance of educational toys and moral education, themes in all of these works. The British socialist Robert Owen incorporated many of these ideas into the pedagogical plans for the infant school he opened in 1816 in his model community at New Lanark, Scotland.

The pedagogy of German kindergarten founder Friedrich Froebel explicitly linked the private domain of the family with the public world of the school. In his many writings, especially his 1843 *Mother Play*, Froebel attempted to educate mothers to be better teachers at home, and at the same time used mother-child interactions as the model for the practice of kindergarten teachers. Much of the success of the kindergarten, the first of which opened in Thuringia in 1837, was due to its denomination as a child's garden or garden of children. This evocative, naturalistic symbolism, along with the motherliness of kindergarten teachers, served to dispel concerns about separating children from their real mothers. Based in part on family life and cloaked in traditionalist folk imagery, the kindergarten was a force for modernization within the family. Blurring the boundaries of private family life and the public sphere, kindergarten classes for mothers and teachers' home visits introduced new approaches to child rearing that also influenced pedagogy for older children.

Froebelian kindergarten methods included domestically based activities and exercises devised from geometry and crystallography. Through what Froebel called "occupations," such as sewing and weaving, and "gifts," sets of intricate wooden blocks and other materials, young children were to learn about complex philosophical, mathematical, and aesthetic relationships. Froebel also introduced the concept of supervised play, which in his formalistic interpretation meant highly stylized, rigidly sequenced, teacher-directed educational activities. This prescribed pedagogy and many accompanying kindergarten texts became the basis for an educational ideology that spread to many parts of the world. Despite its repression by Prussian authorities who worried about its liberalizing influence, the kindergarten soon became an interna-

tional movement with numerous advocates who ardently promoted Froebelian pedagogy and concepts of family life.

Beginning in the early nineteenth century, European ideas about early childhood education were imported to the United States, where they were gradually adapted to suit American educational concerns and contexts. Pestalozzian infant schools were begun in Philadelphia and other cities on the eastern seaboard and promoted in periodicals such as the *Ladies' Magazine*, *Family Magazine*, and the *American Journal of Education*. Robert Owen visited in 1825 to help establish New Harmony, a model community in Indiana, which included an infant school. Infant schools for children of the poor were promoted by evangelical women's groups, such as the Infant School Society of the City of Boston; in the early 1830s there were as many as thirteen or more infant schools in that city (Beatty 1995, 28).

Though initially accepted as a beneficial innovation, infant schools became the focus of controversy over the appropriateness of different methods of early childhood education. The child-centered pedagogy of the transcendentalist educator Bronson Alcott, who taught for a while in a Boston infant school, exemplified a growing divide between evangelicals' didactic proselytizing and romantic notions of children's natural development. The Infant School Society of the City of Boston petitioned to have infant schools incorporated into the new system of public primary schools but was rejected in 1830, in part because of perceptions that excessively academic early education was harmful to young children. The rise of the romantic ideal of womanhood and the family, which encouraged mothers to devote themselves to child rearing within the sacred "woman's sphere" of domesticity, also contributed to the demise of the infant school movement. Although in New York and Philadelphia infant schools were eventually incorporated as early grades in the public schools, the number of private infant schools declined as influential women from upper- and middle-income backgrounds were advised to return to more family-centered modes of early education.

Kindergartens were introduced to the United States in the 1850s by German immigrants fleeing from the failed revolution of 1848. Conducted in German and located in German enclaves, these early kindergartens were intended to preserve German culture and modes of family life. The first kindergarten in the United States was probably that begun in 1856 in Watertown, Wisconsin, by Margarethe Meyer Schurz, wife of the German freethinker and future U.S. Civil Service reformer Carl Schurz. German American kindergarten guides written in English, such as Edward Wiebe's 1869 *The Paradise of Childhood* and Maria Kraus-Boelte and John Kraus's 1877 two-volume *Kindergarten Guide*, disseminated Froebelian pedagogy to U.S. kindergarten enthusiasts. The Swiss émigré William Hailmann, who directed a German American academy in Louisville, Kentucky, and his wife, Eudora, were very active in promoting kindergartens through the Midwest, as were other German American educators.

The kindergarten was soon taken up by liberal U.S. school reformers, both male and female, and recommended as a form of early childhood education for children from upper-income families. Elizabeth Peabody, who had collaborated with Bronson Alcott at the well-known Temple School, opened the first English-speaking kindergarten in America in Boston in 1860. She wrote a *Kindergarten Guide* (published in 1863), founded a kindergarten society, and devoted the rest of her life to kindergarten advocacy. Henry Barnard, the first state commissioner of education in Connecticut and a strong supporter of common schools, actively promoted kindergartens in the pages of his *American Journal of Education*. Although there was initial resistance to the Germanness of the kindergarten, many in the first generation of the American kindergarten movement were concerned with maintaining the orthodoxy of Froebelian methods. Peabody was also very interested in promoting kindergarten teaching as a career for women in the United States, who in the second half of the nineteenth century had very limited occupational opportunities. Sponsored by the Boston Froebel Society, which later became the American Froebel Union, the model kindergarten at the Centennial Exposition in Philadelphia in 1876 brought much public attention to kindergartens. Educated women flocked to the kindergarten cause, as did well-to-do families, who enrolled their children in the many private kindergartens that opened in American cities in the 1870s and 1880s.

The increased industrial growth, urbanization, and immigration that transformed family life in the United States around the turn of the nineteenth century created much public concern about children, propelling a movement to bring kindergartens to the poor. The pressing daily needs of the children enrolled in these "free" kindergartens, which were begun in larger American cities in the 1880s and 1890s, compelled charity kindergarten teachers to modify Froebelian methods. Anna Bryan, who directed charity kindergartens in Louisville and later Chicago, was especially important in reconceptualizing Froebelianism to include more spontaneous "free play" and activities and objects from children's daily home lives.

Frequently supported by the wives of wealthy industrialists, such as Pauline Agassiz Shaw in Boston and Phoebe Apperson Hearst in Chicago, charity kindergartens were also seen as a means of Americanizing and reforming immigrant and indigent families. Chicago charity kindergarten director Elizabeth Harrison's enormously influential 1890 book, *A Study of Child Nature from the Kindergarten Standpoint,* stressed the importance of educating mothers and promoted the possibility of communication around issues concerning early childhood education and family life among women from different social class and ethnic backgrounds. In San Francisco, charity kindergarten teacher Kate Douglas Wiggin, the author of popular children's books such as the 1904 *Rebecca of Sunnybrook Farm,* used the ideology of children's rights to promote kindergartens and helped organize kindergarten training programs.

The growth of the child-study movement, the precursor of developmental psychology, was another major force for modernization in early childhood education. G. Stanley Hall, whose child-study experiments in charity kindergartens in Boston had led him to believe that kindergartens provided much-needed experiential learning, became an active kindergarten advocate. Hall ran summer training institutes at Clark University, spoke at many kindergarten conferences, and pushed teachers to use more scientific methods.

Although there was much dissension within the kindergarten movement about these changing pedagogical methods and over whether the kindergarten should remain a private institution, it became apparent that charity kindergartens could not meet the needs of the rapidly increasing numbers of poor and immigrant children and families. The first public kindergartens in the United States, other than one short-lived class in Boston in 1860, were started in the St. Louis public schools in 1872, under the aegis of the well-known superintendent and kindergarten advocate William Torrey Harris and directed by Susan Blow. Blow, a staunch proponent of Froebelian orthodoxy, was a noted lecturer who in turn trained many influential younger kindergarten teachers. Blow became the leader of the conservative faction in the heated debates over kindergarten methods that took place at meetings of the International Kindergarten Union around the turn of the nineteenth century. Lucy Wheelock, founder of a kindergarten training school in Boston, led the moderates, and Patty Smith Hill, who took over the kindergarten course that Blow had taught at Teachers College at Columbia University, led the progressives, who gradually dominated the movement.

Owing to their association with free kindergartens, many of which were incorporated intact into the public schools, public kindergartens were initially stigmatized as institutions for the children of the urban poor. The movement to extend public kindergartens universally was led by Bessie Locke, a highly successful administrator and political organizer, who in 1909 founded the National Kindergarten Association. A skilled lobbyist, Locke targeted individual states and legislators and formed alliances with other organizations, such as the National Congress of Mothers, which then did much of the groundwork to establish public kindergartens. The number of kindergartens grew rapidly. In 1898 a U.S. Bureau of Education survey documented 3,000 kindergartens, with enrollments of some 200,000 children, an increase from only forty-two public and private kindergartens in 1873 (Beatty 1995, 101). By 1910, the U.S. census reported 396,431 children under the age of six attending school, a doubling within a decade (101). Yet this was only 3.1 percent of U.S. children under six who might have been in school 101). These numbers increased considerably when access to public kindergartens was mandated in California in 1917 and continued to grow as the National Kindergarten Association mounted national and state-by-state campaigns.

The South and some western states remained the parts of the country with the fewest public kindergartens. According to National Kindergarten Association statistics, in the 1916–1917 period only 2 percent of children between the ages of four and six were enrolled in kindergarten in Alabama, Arkansas, Georgia, and Mississippi. In Texas, Idaho, and Nevada only 1 or 2 percent were enrolled, compared to 26 percent in Michigan and Wisconsin and 29 percent in New York (Beatty 1995, 107–108). The National Association of Colored Women actively advocated kindergartens for African American children, as did many African American women's clubs and church groups, which sponsored free kindergartens for African American children, as did some white women's organizations. Some whites argued that African American children especially needed kindergarten education, because of the manual training it provided. There was a well-known vocationally oriented kindergarten at Hampton Institute that modified Froebelian methods to pre-

pare African American children to become domestic servants and fieldworkers. But African American children were frequently excluded from public kindergartens. When Josephine Silone Yates conducted a survey, which was reported in the *Colored American Magazine* in 1905, she found no public kindergartens for African American children in the segregated schools of the South (Beatty 1995, 108). Some missionary groups and women's organizations sponsored kindergartens for Native American and Hispanic children in parts of the Southwest, but these children too rarely attended kindergarten.

Soon after kindergartens were established in public schools, they began being altered in ways that affected families. Although many kindergarten teachers continued to make home visits and teach mothers' classes, emphasis gradually shifted to school readiness. The institution of morning and afternoon sessions, which often rotated halfway into the school year, reduced the amount of time teachers had to meet with mothers and made it more difficult for families to rely upon kindergartens as a form of child care. Although many kindergarten teachers resisted pressures for academic instruction and retained the Froebelian focus on play, concerns about academic preparedness gradually moved down to younger age levels. This shift likely caused many families to increasingly think, and worry, about their young children's literacy and numeracy and made teachers of prekindergarten-age children more attuned to school concerns.

The institution of public kindergartens for five-year-olds drew more attention to the needs of younger children. Like the kindergarten, the nursery school movement originated in Europe. The work of British socialists Rachel and Margaret

McMillan with unhealthy children in the slums of London helped convince the Consultative Committee of the English Board of Education in 1907 to recommend the establishment of nursery schools for children between the ages of two and five. Unlike the kindergarten movement, nursery schools were grounded in the emerging science of psychology and were explicitly experimental. This "scientific" approach to preschool education became the basis for professionalization within early childhood education and for scientizing child-rearing advice to families.

Some Americans were doing pioneering work with preschool-age children before the introduction of nursery schools. In 1906, crusading philanthropist Cora Bussey Hillis began efforts that led to the creation of the Iowa Child Welfare Station. Psychologist Arnold Gesell started a clinic at Yale University in 1911 to treat young children with behavioral problems. Caroline Pratt, Harriet Johnson, and Lucy Sprague Mitchell began play groups and preschools for poor and immigrant children in New York City in 1913; these play groups evolved into the Bureau of Educational Experiments. Another European importation, the Montessori method, had a brief heyday after U.S. preschool educator Patty Smith Hill visited Maria Montessori's Casa dei Bambini (Children's House) in a slum of Rome in 1912 and Montessori visited the United States in 1913. Abigail Adams Eliot, who in 1926 founded the Ruggles Street Nursery School and Training Center in Boston, was especially influential in bringing British nursery school ideas to this country and in encouraging parent involvement in their children's preschools.

Improving parent education was a main impetus behind the nursery school movement. In the 1920s, Lawrence K. Frank of the Laura Spelman Rockefeller Memorial oversaw the awarding of large grants to children's institutes, nursery schools, and colleges and universities that were charged with generating new information about child rearing and child development. Psychologists, social workers, and early childhood educators worked together on research projects in these experimental institutes and provided consultation to families. Most of the private nursery schools that opened in the 1920s attracted mothers from the new generation of college-educated women, who were very concerned about child-related issues and motivated to learn new ideas about early childhood education and child rearing. Fathers were also encouraged to participate, as nursery school journals, books, conferences, and other forms of public communication were addressed to parents, not simply mothers.

Although most of the children attending private nursery schools in the 1920s appear to have come from middle- and upper-income families, some nursery schools were directed at poor and immigrant children and at so-called problem children, whose behavior was perceived to be in some way abnormal. The extensive research and advice literature produced by psychologists and nursery educators during that period created prescriptive norms for how children and parents were expected to behave and for what families were supposed to provide and be like as environments for young children. Although some families, especially those from lower-income and immigrant backgrounds and African Americans, resisted this intrusion into traditional ideals and practices of family life, nursery school ideas were used in child guidance clinics and cited as models of correct child and parental behavior.

Various new public agencies and initiatives in the 1910s and 1920s helped promote the cause of public preschools, along with other family support programs. An outgrowth of the settlement house movement, the federal Children's Bureau, which was organized in 1912, coordinated efforts on the behalf of children and sent out pamphlets and thousands of letters to individual mothers with advice on children's health and child rearing. Directed by day nursery activist Rose Alschuler, there were some locally funded public nursery school experiments in the public schools of Chicago and Winnetka, Illinois, in the mid-1920s. Although the influential committee of psychologists and nursery school directors formed at the White House Conference on Child Health and Protection did not explicitly recommend public support for nursery education, it collected a great deal of data that documented the need for more preschool programs.

During the Great Depression of the 1930s, the federal government became directly involved in providing early childhood education programs. Although some public kindergartens were cut back during the 1930s, federal emergency nursery schools were begun in 1933 under the auspices of the Federal Emergency Relief Administration and Works Progress Administration. Coordinated by Grace Langdon, these federal preschools were intended to provide jobs for laid-off teachers and other workers and support for the children of poor families who had been hard hit by the Depression. Although providing early childhood education was a secondary goal of the program, members of the newly formed National Association for Nursery Education actively supported the emergency nursery schools and volunteered as regional supervisors.

Sources vary, but at the peak of the program in 1934–1935 there were some 75,000 children enrolled, still a small fraction of the some 2 million eligible children with unemployed parents, but a large number of preschoolers to educate and care for in quickly established nursery schools (Beatty 1995, 181).

The need for child care for mothers working in war-related industries provided a rationale for the continuation of federal funding for early childhood education. Although the official policy of the War Manpower Commission was that mothers of young should stay at home, politicians and early childhood educators supported the idea of wartime children's centers, which were construed as nursery schools even though they provided full-time child care. Begun in 1943 with funding from the Lanham Act and jointly administered by Grace Langdon from the Federal Works Agency and Florence Kerr from the War Public Service Bureau, the wartime children's centers were coordinated by the National Commission for Young Children, headed by Rose Alschuler. Members of the commission included many of the early childhood educators and psychologists who had been supervisors for the federal emergency nursery schools.

The best known of the children's centers were the quasi-private, industry-based Child Service Centers run by the Kaiser Shipbuilding Company in Portland, Oregon. Directed by Lois Meek Stolz from the Institute of Child Welfare at the University of California at Berkeley and James L. Hymes Jr., the centers were housed in specially designed buildings and provided six-day-a-week, twenty-four-hour-a-day education and child care to children between eighteen months and school age. A store, food service, health care, and other child-related family services made it easier for mothers to work long hours in the Kaiser shipbuilding yards. Similar, though less expensive and extensive, services were provided at regular Lanham Act children's centers throughout the country. At their peak in July 1944, there were 3,102 centers in operation, with an average daily attendance of 129,357 children (Beatty 1995, 191). As with the federal emergency nursery schools during the Depression, this was only a small proportion, maybe about 10 percent of the children who needed care.

Many early childhood educators believed that the federal emergency nursery schools and wartime children's centers could be permanently grafted onto the public schools, where many of the programs were housed. Psychologist George Stoddard from the Iowa Child Welfare Research Station was a particularly strong advocate of public support for early childhood education. Stoddard understood that "universal nursery education" would be very expensive and used rationales of economics, child welfare, and mothers' interests to garner support. Speaking at a conference of the National Association for Nursery Education in 1931, he said, "we must be prepared to recommend an expenditure of possibly half a billion dollars per year on the systematic education of five million preschool children" (Stoddard 1931, 10). Despite the lobbying of early childhood educators and parents, the federal government cut funding for the children's centers after the war. Although some public preschool programs were maintained through federal, state, and local support in California and in Washington, D.C., New York, Philadelphia, and a few other cities, families in the United States

A four-year-old mastering letters and numbers. (Elizabeth Crews)

were again forced to rely upon private forms of early childhood education.

It took another war to galvanize federal support for preschool education. Soon after Lyndon Johnson succeeded John F. Kennedy in 1963, he declared a War on Poverty, which included various types of initiatives to support poor families and communities. Project Head Start, which began in 1965, quickly became the most popular of these new Great Society programs. Head Start was conceived as a comprehensive child development program that provided medical, social, and educational services and was intentionally separate from the public schools, although some centers were housed in public school buildings. Buttressed by the research of psychologists such as J. McVicker Hunt and Benjamin Bloom, which pointed to the importance of the early years of a child's life as a "critical period" for development, Head Start came to be seen as a means of boosting children's intelligence quotients (IQs). This goal, which some psychologists say was not the program's original intent, came to haunt Head Start as reports showed that initial IQ score gains did not hold up after children who had been enrolled progressed through the upper grades.

Head Start was intended as much as a means of helping families as a form of early childhood education. Cornell psychologist Urie Bronfenbrenner, who talked about an "ecological" approach to early intervention that focused on parent involvement and parent education, argued persuasively that the efforts of Head Start should be evaluated by its impact on families. Although some criticized the way Head Start programs imposed middle-class, white family values and modes of child rearing onto lower-income, minority families, others thought that intervention into children's experiences within their families should begin at an even earlier age than four, when most Head Start programs accepted children. Although debate about the intrusion of early childhood education into family life continued, the fact that a third or more of Head Start staff were mothers of children who had been in the program came to be seen as one of Head Start's main benefits (Zigler and Muenchow 1992, 207–209).

Head Start was an outgrowth of the movement for civil rights that swept through U.S. society in the 1960s and early 1970s. The radical, community-organizing aspects of the program were particularly apparent in the Child Development Group of Mississippi, which sought to liberate African American families from white oppression and encountered much resistance from the white political establishment. As chronicled in Polly Greenberg's remarkable 1969 book, *The Devil Has Slippery Shoes*, Head Start programs in Mississippi consciously avoided contact with kindergarten teachers within the public schools and developed a community-based pedagogy focused on resistance to racism.

Despite criticisms of Head Start from the right and the left, it became an enormously popular federal program and survived many budget-cutting attempts, although it was never fully funded to permit all eligible children to attend. Controversies over the role of the state in family life and early childhood education were apparent in the debate in 1971 over the Comprehensive Child Development Act, which proposed universalizing early childhood education through broad federal support for child care, preschools, and other children's services. Although the bill passed Congress, it was vetoed by Richard Nixon on the grounds that it would "commit the vast moral authority of the National Government to the aid of communal approaches to child rearing over against the family-centered approach" (Beatty 1995, 198).

Head Start remained unscathed, however, with its reputation enhanced as studies began to show that it had potentially lasting long-term effects, especially on children's social development. Longitudinal reports from the Perry Preschool Project in Ypsilanti, Michigan, a Head Start–like precursor, showed that attending a high-quality preschool seemed to help prevent crime and teenage pregnancy and promote school and college attendance. This and other research on the effects of different types of preschools was frequently cited as evidence for the benefits of universalizing access to early childhood education.

In the 1980s and 1990s, attempts to expand preschool programs at the local, state, and federal levels met with considerable success. Many cities offered public early childhood education programs for children from lower-income families, and school districts increasingly allocated federal Title I money for educationally disadvantaged children to preschool programs. In 1999 in Georgia, where a universal prekindergarten program was initiated in 1993, about 80 percent of four-year-olds were enrolled at public expense, using proceeds from a state lottery. Federal support for Head Start increased greatly during the Clinton administration. But these separate funding streams, the result of the historic fragmentation of early childhood education and child care, made it difficult for many families to find services that met their needs and those of their children. Unlike most western European countries, which have long histories of universalized early childhood care and education, Americans remain ambivalent about the extent to which the state should help families raise and educate their young children.

—Barbara Beatty

See also Child Care; Child Development; Children's Bureau, U.S.; Hall, G. Stanley; Head Start; White House Conferences on Children

References and Further Reading
Allen, Ann Taylor. 1991. *Feminism and Motherhood in Germany, 1800–1914.* New Brunswick, NJ: Rutgers University Press.

Barnard, Henry, ed. 1890. *Kindergarten and Child Culture Papers: Papers on Froebel's Kindergarten, with Suggestions on Principles and Methods of Child Culture in Different Countries.* Hartford, CT: Office of *Barnard's American Journal of Education.*

Beatty, Barbara. 1989. "Child Gardening: The Teaching of Young Children in American Schools, 1860–1930." In *American Teachers: Histories of a Profession at Work,* edited by Donald Warren, 65–97. New York: Macmillan.

Beatty, Barbara. 1990. "'A Vocation from on High': Kindergarten Teaching as an Occupation for Women in Turn-of-the Century America." In *Changing Education: Women as Radicals and Conservators,* edited by Joyce Antler and Sari Biklen, 35–50. Albany: State University of New York Press.

Beatty, Barbara. 1995. *Preschool Education in America: The Culture of Young Children from the Colonial Era to the Present.* New Haven: Yale University Press.

Beatty, Barbara. 1999. "Bessie Locke." In *American National Biography,* edited by John A. Garraty, 798–799. New York: Oxford University Press.

Beatty, Barbara. 2000. "The Letter Killeth: Americanization and Multicultural Education in Kindergartens in the United States, 1856–1920." In *Kindergartens and Culture: The Global Diffusion of an Idea,* edited by Roberta Wollons, 42–58. New Haven: Yale University Press.

Beatty, Barbara. 2001. "The Politics of Preschool Advocacy: Lessons from the History of Day Nursery, Kindergarten, and Nursery School Organizations." In *Who Speaks for Children? The Role of Advocates in Public Policy,* edited by Carol DeVita and Rachel Mosher-Williams, 165–190. Washington, DC: Urban Institute Press.

Cahan, Emily D. 1989. *Past Caring: A History of U.S. Preschool Care and Education for the Poor, 1820–1965.* New York: National Center for Children in Poverty.

Cravens, Hamilton. 1993. *Before Head Start: The Iowa Station and America's Children.* Chapel Hill: University of North Carolina Press.

Grant, Julia. 1998. *Raising Baby by the Book: The Education of American*

Mothers. New Haven: Yale University Press.

Grubb, W. Norton, and Marvin Lazerson. 1988. *Broken Promises: How Americans Fail Their Children.* New York: Basic Books.

Hewes, Dorothy W. 1976. "Patty Smith Hill—Pioneer for Young Children." *Young Children* 31: 297–306.

Michel, Sonya. 1999. *Children's Interests/Mothers' Rights: The Shaping of America's Child Care Policy.* New Haven: Yale University Press.

Moran, Gerald F., and Maris Vinovskis. 1986. "The Great Care of Godly Parents: Early Childhood Education in Puritan New England." In *History and Research in Child Development,* edited by Alice B. Smuts and John W. Hagen, 351–381. Monographs of the Society for Research in Child Development, 50. Chicago: University of Chicago Press.

National Association for the Education of Young Children. Organizational History and Archives Committee. 1976. "NAEYC's First Half Century, 1926–1976." *Young Children* 31: 462–476.

Rose, Elizabeth. 1999. *A Mother's Job: The History of Child Care, 1890–1960.* New York: Oxford University Press.

Schlossman, Steven L. 1981. "Philanthropy and the Gospel of Child Development." *History of Education Quarterly* 21: 283–307.

Senn, Milton. J. E. 1975. "Insights on the Child Development Movement in the United States." *Monographs of the Society for Research in Child Development* 40: 3–4.

Shapiro, Michael Steven. 1983. *Child's Garden: The Kindergarten Movement from Froebel to Dewey.* University Park: Pennsylvania State University Press.

Steiner, Gilbert Y. 1976. *The Children's Cause.* Washington, DC: Brookings.

Stoddard, George. 1931. "Conference Issues." In *Proceedings of the Fourth Conference of the National Association for Nursery Education.* New York: National Association for Nursery Education.

Takanishi, Ruby. 1977. "Federal Involvement in Early Childhood Education (1933–1973): The Need for Historical Perspectives." In *Current Issues in Early Childhood Education,* edited by Lilian Katz, vol. 1, 139–163. Norwood, NJ: Ablex.

Tank, Robert. 1980. "Young Children, Society, and Family in America since the 1820s: The Evolution of Health, Education, and Child Care Programs for Preschool Children." Ph.D. diss., University of Michigan.

Vandewalker, Nina C. 1908. *The Kindergarten in American Education.* New York: Macmillan.

Weber, Evelyn. 1969. *The Kindergarten: Its Encounter with Educational Thought in America.* New York: Teachers College Press.

Winterer, Caroline. 1992. "Avoiding a 'Hothouse System of Education': Nineteenth-Century Early Childhood Education from Infant Schools to the Kindergarten." *History of Education Quarterly* 32 (Fall): 289–314.

Zigler, Edward, and Susan Muenchow. 1992. *Head Start: The Inside Story of America's Most Successful Educational Experiment.* New York: Basic Books.

Earned Income Tax Credit

The earned income tax credit (EITC) is a refundable tax credit that provides income assistance to low-income working individuals and families. The EITC, which is a negative income tax, was enacted in 1975 and has been expanded since then. Nearly 20 million Americans receive the EITC, and it lifts several million Americans out of poverty each year.

The original proponents of the concept were conservative economists. In 1946, George Stigler argued for a negative income tax in *American Economic Review,* and Milton Friedman, a Nobel Laureate, argued for it in his 1962 *Capitalism and Freedom.* Stigler and Friedman thought a negative income tax, which gives money to lower-income individuals, would encourage work. Ronald Reagan, as governor of California in 1972, supported this proposal in his state.

At the urging of the Ford administration in 1975, the Congress passed the EITC. Since then each presidential administration has expanded the credit. There were expansions in 1986, 1990, and 1993. The EITC has enjoyed tremendous bipartisan support. Since 1975 several states have adopted similar programs.

The size of the credit rises as earnings increase. EITC benefits are intended to both offset taxes and, in some circumstances, provide a wage supplement. As a refundable credit, it means that if the credit exceeds the individual's tax liability, then that individual receives money from the government. The Internal Revenue Service allows those taxpayers who expect to qualify for the EITC and have at least one qualifying child to receive part of the credit in each paycheck during the year the taxpayer qualifies for the credit. For some low-wage workers, this may be a few hundred dollars each month.

Research has shown that the EITC increases work effort substantially among single mothers, and it seems to lift many children out of poverty, perhaps more than any other single program.

—*Michael Coulter*

References and Further Reading
Graetz, Michael J., and Jerry Mashaw. 1999. *True Security: Rethinking American Social Insurance.* New Haven: Yale University Press.

Eating Disorders

Eating disorders are a group of psychological ailments that are characterized by physiological and psychological disturbances in appetite, body image, and/or food intake. Today, the most commonly diagnosed eating disorders are anorexia nervosa; bulimia nervosa; and pica, the persistent eating of nonfood substances such as dirt, clay, or chalk (American Psychiatric Association 1994). Research on the history of eating disorders suggests that there are major continuities and discontinuities in the manifestation of these ailments. Anorexia nervosa, for example, has always been considered an affliction of white, privileged adolescent girls. In contrast, before the twentieth century the majority of patients with bulimia were males, and age at onset varied from childhood to middle age (Parry-Jones and Parry-Jones 1994). These variations suggest that the appearance and symptomatology of eating disorders are products of particular historical circumstances regarding body image, family relationships, and food practices.

Anorexia Nervosa

Anorexia nervosa is a psychophysiologic disorder characterized by prolonged refusal to eat or to maintain normal body weight, an intense fear of becoming obese, a disturbed body image in which the emaciated patient feels overweight, and the absence of any physical illness that would account for extreme weight loss. The term *anorexia*, meaning "loss of appetite," is actually a misnomer, because a genuine loss of appetite is rare and usually does not occur until late in the illness. In reality, most anorexics are obsessed with food and constantly struggle to deny natural hunger (Bruch 1978; American Psychiatric Association 1994).

There are a number of similarities between the characteristics of modern anorexia and the manifestation of the disease in earlier periods in American history. As in the modern United States, the majority of anorexic patients in the past were adolescent or young adult females from middle- or upper-class white families. Joan Jacobs Brumberg has suggested that the emergence of anorexia nervosa as a disease category in the late nineteenth century was closely linked to changes in the relationship between parents and children in white, native-born, middle-class families during this time period. According to Brumberg, the bourgeois family protected girls from early marriage and the need to work outside the home but also intensified the strains between parent and child, thereby setting the stage for anorexia nervosa. Because of the close relationship between food abundance and parental love, Brumberg argues, food refusal became one of the ways in which young girls expressed their psychic distress with the restrictiveness of the Victorian bourgeois family (Brumberg 1988).

There are important differences between anorexics of the past and present, however. Although historic anorexics exhibited some fears of fatness, they lacked the severe body-image distortion exhibited in modern cases of anorexia. In addition, the prevalence of anorexia in the past was much smaller than it is today (Parry-Jones and Parry-Jones 1994). The explosion in the incidence of anorexia nervosa over the past thirty years corresponds with increased cultural preoccupations with thinness and fitness, suggesting that anorexia nervosa is as much a product of culture as it is of biology and individual psychopathology (Brumberg 1988). Indeed, the pervasiveness of thin body images in the mass media has led to an increase in the prevalence of anorexia nervosa in lesbians, women of color, young men, and other groups previously believed immune to the disorder and has also contributed to a steadily declining age of onset of the disease (Thompson 1994).

Bulimia Nervosa

Today, bulimia nervosa is characterized by binge eating followed by induced vomiting, abuse of laxatives, fasting, and/or obsessively vigorous exercise. Anorexics can also exhibit some of the same symptoms of bingeing followed by inappropriate compensatory behaviors. Therefore, bulimics are distinguished by the fact that they are typically within the normal weight range for age and height (American Psychiatric Association 1994).

There are several major differences between bulimia in the past and the presentation of the disease in the modern United States. First, before the mid-twentieth century, the incidence of bulimia was extremely rare. Second, unlike modern bulimics, who are almost always adolescent or young adult females, nearly all patients diagnosed with bulimia before modern times were male, and age of onset varied considerably from childhood to middle age. Frequently bulimics in the past would have an appetite for nonfood substances such as grass, thistles, and candle wax, leading some physicians to classify bulimia as a subcategory of pica (see next section). There is a complete absence of self-induced vomiting, abuse of purgatives or diuretics, or obsessive exercise in historic bulimics. Finally, bulimic patients in the past did not express the extreme obsession with body size and shape so common in modern bulimics (Parry-Jones and Parry-Jones 1994).

As in the case of anorexia nervosa, the prevalence of bulimia nervosa has increased dramatically in recent years, and the rise in the incidence of the disease is closely linked with increased preoccupations with thin body types and physical fitness (Bordo 1993). Also as with anorexia, there appears to be a growing incidence of bulimia nervosa among young men, especially those who engage in sports such as wrestling, where maintaining an ideal body weight is critical to athletic success (Parry-Jones and Parry-Jones 1994).

Pica

Descriptions of pica have remained relatively consistent over time. The disease is characterized by the deliberate ingestion of nonfood items such as dirt, plaster, clay, or paint chips and/or by excessive consumption of unusual food items such as pepper, nutmeg, and raw corn (American Psychiatric Association 1994). The main populations exhibiting the disorder both historically and today are pregnant women, young children, pubescent females, the developmentally disabled, and members of tribal societies in which consumption of dirt or other nonnutritive substances is a part of religious or cultural rituals (Parry-Jones and Parry-Jones 1994).

The prevalence of the disorder in pregnant and adolescent females, as well as undernourished children and adults, led some researchers both past and present to suggest that pica is not in fact an eating disorder but rather a symptom of other diseases. During the nineteenth century, some physicians classified pica as a symptom of either anorexia nervosa or chlorosis, a type of iron-deficiency anemia observed almost exclusively in girls and young women (Parry-Jones and Parry-Jones 1992). Doctors in the nineteenth and early twentieth centuries also claimed that blacks exhibited a unique form of pica called cachexia Africana, which physicians attributed to the allegedly innate biological inferiority of former slaves (Haller 1972). Preconceptions about the supposed inferiority of individuals from the lower socioeconomic classes and/or ethnic minorities shaped

descriptions of pica in other groups as well. Medical textbooks observed the prevalence of the "filthy" habit of dirt eating not only in African Americans but also among Chinese laborers in the Far West and impoverished white sharecroppers in the South. Although some medical scientists at this time suggested that pica was a means of compensating for malnutrition, most tended to view the "abnormal" eating habits of racial minorities and poor whites as a symptom of the social deviancy of families who did not fit the white, middle-class norm (Marcus 1988).

Since the early twentieth century, studies of the incidence and causes of pica have focused on infants and children. Initially, pediatric textbooks classified pica with other "morbid" habits of childhood, such as masturbation, thumb-sucking, and bed-wetting, that could be broken through restraint, diversion, or moral suasion (Parry-Jones and Parry-Jones 1992). More recently, physicians have linked the disease with social deprivation. Today, the disease usually comes to the attention of medical professionals when the patient exhibits one of the medical complications resulting from the ingestion of nonfood substances, for example, lead poisoning from eating lead paint chips or paint-covered plaster. Physicians now recognize that rather than being a sign of the social deviancy of the poor and racial minorities, pica is frequently a symptom of malnutrition, parental neglect, and other deprivations in the child's social environment (American Psychiatric Association 1994).

—*Heather Munro Prescott*

See also Anorexia Nervosa; Bulimia

References and Further Reading
American Psychiatric Association. 1994. *Diagnostic and Statistical Manual of*

Mental Disorders: DSM-IV. 4th ed. Washington, DC: American Psychiatric Association.

Bordo, Susan. 1993. *Unbearable Weight: Feminism, Western Culture, and the Body.* Berkeley: University of California Press.

Bruch, Hilde. 1978. *The Golden Cage: The Enigma of Anorexia Nervosa.* New York: Vintage.

Brumberg, Joan Jacobs. 1988. *Fasting Girls: The History of Anorexia Nervosa.* Cambridge: Harvard University Press.

Haller, John S. 1972. "The Negro and the Southern Physician: A Study of Medical and Racial Attitudes 1800–1860." *Medical History* 16: 238–253.

Marcus, Alan I. 1988. "The South's Native Foreigners: Hookworm as a Factor in Southern Distinctiveness." In *Disease and Distinctiveness in the American South,* edited by Todd L. Savitt and James Harvey Young, 79–99. Knoxville: University of Tennessee Press.

Parry-Jones, Brenda, and William L. Parry-Jones. 1992. "Pica: Symptom or Eating Disorder? A Historical Assessment." *British Journal of Psychiatry* 160: 341–354.

Parry-Jones, William, and Brenda Parry-Jones. 1994. "Implications of Historical Evidence for the Classification of Eating Disorders." *British Journal of Psychiatry* 165: 287–292.

Thompson, Becky W. 1994. *A Hunger So Wide and So Deep: American Women Speak Out on Eating Problems.* Minneapolis: University of Minnesota Press.

Educational Achievement of Parents

Educational achievement (or educational attainment) refers to the amount of formal education one completes. In U.S. society, educational achievement is one of the primary means through which one can become "upwardly mobile" and successful. Consequently, rates of educational achievement among Americans have increased considerably in the past century, with far-reaching implications both for individual achievers and for families. For individuals, higher educational achievement is associated with more frequent civic involvement, lower rates of delinquency and reliance on welfare, and greater lifetime earning power (Bureau of Educational Research and Development 1962; National Center for Education Statistics 1998; Stouthamer-Loeber and Loeber 1988). For families, the higher educational achievement of parents is associated with more positive outcomes for children. That is, children of more highly educated parents are perceived to be more cognitively competent by their teachers, they perform better academically, they are more likely to participate in community service, they are less likely to drop out of school, and they are more likely to complete high school and college (Hutner 1972; Miller and Schouten 1989; National Center for Education Statistics 1998). These positive outcomes might occur, at least in part, because parents with more education tend to earn more, have more positive attitudes toward child rearing, provide their children with more literacy experiences in early childhood, enroll them more often in preprimary school, have higher expectations for their children's academic achievement, have less need for control of their children, and become more involved in their children's education (Baker and Stevenson 1986; National Center for Education Statistics 1998; Strom, Hathaway, and Slaughter 1981). Clearly, then, the educational achievement of parents has extensive implications for their own and for their children's lives.

Trends in American Educational Achievement

Government and society in the United States are structured around the premise that, given equal opportunity and sufficient talent, any ambitious individual from any background can live the American Dream. Even though true rags-to-riches stories are infrequent in reality, the possibility and desire for upward mobility remain firmly ingrained in the American psyche. Hence, parents generally seek for their children lives at least as good as, if not better than, their own, and children seek to achieve at least the standard set by their parents. In modern American society, one of the most expedient means for accomplishing this goal is through education.

An examination of educational trends in the twentieth century clearly demonstrates that Americans have been accomplishing this goal. Average levels of educational attainment, or the average amount of schooling completed by members of the population, has risen steadily among Americans since the start of the twentieth century. For example, in 1900, the median level of educational attainment among Americans was 5.25 years, the average number of days enrolled students (elementary through high school) attended school annually was under 100, and only 11 percent of youths 14–17 years of age still attended school (Collins 1969, 29, 31). At that time in agrarian society in the United States, scholastic emphasis was on teaching immigrants and farmers to read and write within eight optional years of schooling. In time, however, schooling came to be thought of as a means for molding citizens and became the responsibility of the state. By 1918, all existing states had enacted compulsory school attendance laws. Consequently, by 1965, the median level of educational attainment among Americans was 11.8 years, with an average attendance of 163 days per academic year (in elementary through high school), and

90 percent of 14- to 17-year-olds attended school (Collins 1969, 29, 31).

This distinct shift was due, primarily, to changes in laws and law enforcement with regard to compulsory education. Yet, even in the more recent past, Americans on average have been reaching new heights of educational attainment, staying in school longer than the time prescribed by law and surpassing the achievements of their parents. To illustrate, in 1940, only about 38 percent of 25- to 29-year olds were high school graduates, whereas 63 percent had graduated in 1959, 86 percent in 1979, and 87 percent of individuals in the age group were graduates in 1997 (Bureau of Educational Research and Development 1962, 13; National Center for Education Statistics 1998, 80). College enrollment and graduation rates have increased steadily as well. Although fewer than 5 percent of 25- to 29-year-olds had completed four or more years of college in 1940, 8 percent had done so in 1959, 27 percent in 1979, and 32 percent in 1997 (Bureau of Educational Research and Development 1962, 13; National Center for Education Statistics 1998, 80).

Rates of educational attainment vary, however, depending on student characteristics. In 1997, for example, 93 percent of whites, 87 percent of blacks, and 62 percent of Hispanics had completed high school, and whites completed four or more years of college at rates roughly double those of blacks and Hispanics (National Center for Education Statistics 1998, 80). Yet, compared to 1971, the high school completion rates had increased for whites by 11 percent, by 28 percent for blacks, and by 14 percent for Hispanics (National Center for Education Statistics 1998, 80). Moreover, in 1997, in all ethnic groups, females were more likely than

Her family surrounds an African American mother as she attends her college graduation ceremony in St. Paul, Minnesota. (Skjold Photographs)

their male peers to have completed high school, some college, and four or more years of college (National Center for Education Statistics 1998, 238–240). Hence, despite differences between groups, it is clear that average rates of educational attainment among all Americans have been increasing steadily for decades, particularly among women and minorities.

Consequences of Educational Achievement for Individuals

Increasing levels of educational achievement have far-reaching implications for both the individual achievers and their current or future families. For individuals, higher levels of achievement are asso-ciated with higher rates of civic involvement, lower rates of delinquency and welfare dependency, and higher incomes and earning power (Ceci and Williams 1997; National Center for Education Statistics 1998; Stouthamer-Loeber and Loeber 1988). In fact, higher education has been related to higher earning potential among wage earners for decades. For example, college graduates in 1946 earned approximately 54 percent more than high school graduates the same year (Bureau of Educational Research and Development 1962, 18). In 1996, male college graduates earned 54 percent more and females 88 percent more than same-sex high school graduates, among workers aged 25–34 years (National Center for Education Statistics 1998, 104). Higher educational attainment, then, clearly has strong implications for an individual's future material success.

Consequences of Educational Achievement for Families

Because rates of high educational achievement have been increasing, parents are becoming increasingly well educated. In 1972, for example, 10 percent of the mothers of fifteen- to eighteen-year-olds had some college education, and 7 percent had a college degree or higher. In 1997, on the other hand, 27 percent of mothers had some college, and 19 percent had college degrees or higher (National Center for Education Statistics 1998, 136). This means that more and more children are being raised by parents with increasing levels of educational attainment.

Research has demonstrated that parental education is related to a number of child development outcomes. For example, children of more highly educated mothers tend to have higher intelligence quotients (IQs), stronger scholastic aptitude, and better academic success (Hutner 1972). They are perceived by their teachers to be more cognitively competent as well (Miller and Schouten 1989), all of which bodes well for future academic achievement. They also are more likely to participate in community service between grades six and twelve. Such service may help children and adolescents feel more connected to their communities and also might have positive effects on their school attendance and grades (National Center for Education Statistics 1998). In addition, children with more highly educated parents are less likely to drop out of school, which is important because dropping out has negative social and economic consequences. For example, dropouts have higher rates of unemployment and lower earning potential than do students who remain in school (Ceci and Williams 1997; National Center for Education Statistics 1998). Children also tend to achieve academically, and have expectations for their own achievement, consistent with the educational level of their same-sex parent (Osborn 1971). Hence, children anticipate reaching the educational levels of their parents, and on average they seem to do so, as they are more likely to complete high school, begin college, and complete college than are children of less educated parents (National Center for Education Statistics 1998).

Effects of parent education also help to account for differences among children related to family structure. For example, data on American students' verbal and mathematics scores since the 1960s indicate that children from single-parent households tend to score lower on verbal and mathematical reasoning tests than do children from two-parent households. Yet, recent analyses demonstrate that these gaps are not due to single parenthood but to the variations in parent education and income that are often associated with single parenthood (for example, Bronfenbrenner et al. 1996). When parent educational attainment and income are equivalent in single- and two-parent families, the gaps in children's verbal and mathematics test scores are completely eliminated (Ceci, Rosenblum, and Kumpf 1998).

Clearly, then, there are numerous ways in which children benefit from having parents who reach high levels of educational attainment, but it is not clear why this should be the case. One factor that appears to be relevant is the differential income associated with higher education (Ceci, Rosenblum, and Kumpf 1998). Paterson, Kupersmidt, and Vaden (1990) reported that, among elementary school children, family income was one of the best predictors of academic achievement, peer relations, and school conduct. Families with more resources are better able to provide for their children's education and enhancement, suffer less from financial stresses, and experience more advantaged living environments, such as more affluent neighborhoods, all of which promote children's healthy development (Duncan and Brooks-Gunn 1997).

There are additional differences associated with higher education, however, that might also help to explain why the educational achievement of parents is influential in child development. For example, higher-educated mothers seem to have less need for control over their children than do less educated mothers (perhaps for very pragmatic safety reasons). This seems to benefit their children, because children tend to score higher in cognitive and motor functioning when their mothers express less need for control in their parenting (Strom, Hathaway, and Slaughter 1981).

Parents also differ according to their expectations and involvement in their children's education. Mothers tend to have higher expectations for their children when they themselves have achieved higher levels of education, and they guide their children accordingly (Baker and Stevenson 1986). For example, college-educated parents are more likely to read to their children frequently and visit a library with their children than are high school–educated parents (National Center for Education Statistics 1998). This experience with early literacy activities provides children with greater exposure to a wide variety of novel words and concepts. In addition, through this activity, children often receive practice responding to some of the teaching methods likely to be encountered in school settings, such as answering questions about the characters or pictures in a storybook. It also engages parents in children's educational activities at an early age. All of these differences provide children with better preparation for school entry.

There also is evidence that children's early linguistic environments may differ sharply, depending on parental background, possibly with long-term ramifications. For instance, in an extensive study of language development, Hart and Risley (1995) observed interactions between one- and two-year-old children and their families for over two years. (Parental background in this study was defined according to parent occupations, which were highly correlated with parent educational attainment.) Their results showed that, in a typical hour together, professional parents interacted with their children approximately twice as long as welfare parents. As a result, children were exposed to 2,100 words per hour, on average, in professional families, 1,200 words in working-class families, and 600 words in welfare families. The authors projected that the cumulative result of this difference would be that, by age three, children in welfare families might have heard half as many words as those in working-class families and one-third as many as children in professional families. When the researchers followed up on the children later, they found that, in fact, children's early experiences with more words were associated with larger vocabularies at age three, which then predicted better academic performance in third grade. Hence, early language experience is another means through which parental education could influence child development.

Parental knowledge of and experience with educational systems also have implications for children's achievement. For example, children are more likely to be enrolled in preprimary education programs when they have more highly educated mothers. Participation in these programs can better prepare children for elementary school, providing them with experiences that might facilitate later academic success (National Center for Education Statistics 1998).

In addition, parents of adolescents manage the school careers of their children in different ways, depending on their own educational experiences. Baker and Stevenson (1986) found that college-educated mothers are more actively involved in their children's transition into high school than are less educated mothers. They tend to have more contact with their children's teachers, know more about their children's academic performance, and be more likely to take actions to manage their children's academic careers (particularly when their children are not performing well). For instance, the authors found that for children with low grades, better-educated mothers were approximately eleven times more likely to try to prepare them for high school than were other mothers. In addition, regardless of their children's performance in eighth grade, college-educated mothers were four times more likely to choose college-preparatory high school classes for their children than were other mothers. Enrollment in such courses helps prepare students for later college enrollment and can make students more attractive applicants when seeking college acceptance. Clearly, then, these mothers were influencing the

direction of their children's education in important ways, based in part on their understanding and knowledge of the educational system and on their expectations for their children's educational attainment.

Finally, more parental education is related to the extent of parental involvement in children's school activities. Parents with increasing levels of education are more likely to attend general meetings or school events and to volunteer at their children's schools (National Center for Education Statistics 1998). This involvement further engages parents in their children's education, demonstrating their commitment to and interest in their children's well-being. It also might encourage child participation in school activities, providing greater means for adult monitoring of children's behaviors, promoting feelings of belonging to a community, and providing socially sanctioned activities with peers.

Again, there is no doubt that there has been a dramatic increase in the average educational achievement of American citizens and that this increase is having a profound influence on children and their families. This change also has had a wider impact on the culture, economy, and structure of modern U.S. society and will likely continue to do so as the nature and scope of the educational achievements of parents continue to grow.

—*Angela M. Crossman*

See also Higher Education, Access to

References and Further Reading
Baker, David P., and David L. Stevenson. 1986. "Mothers' Strategies for Children's School Achievement: Managing the Transition to High School." *Sociology of Education* 59 (July): 156–166.

Bronfenbrenner, Urie, Peter McClelland, Elaine Wethington, Phyllis Moen, and Stephen J. Ceci. 1996. *The State of Americans.* New York: The Free Press.

Bureau of Educational Research and Development. 1962. *Digest of Educational Statistics.* Washington, DC: U.S. Government Printing Office.

Ceci, Stephen J., Tina Rosenblum, and Matthew Kumpf. 1998. "The Shrinking Gap between High- and Low-Scoring Groups: Current Trends and Possible Causes." In *The Rising Curve: Long-Term Gains in IQ and Related Measures,* edited by Ulric Neisser, 287–302. Washington, DC: American Psychological Association.

Ceci, Stephen J., and Wendy M. Williams. 1997. "Schooling, Intelligence, and Income." *American Psychologist* 52(10): 1051–1058.

Collins, George J. 1969. "Constitutional and Legal Basis for State Action." In *Education in the States: A Project of the Council of Chief State School Officers,* edited by Jim B. Pearson and Edgar Fuller, 5–69. Washington, DC: National Educational Association of the United States.

Duncan, Greg J., and Jeanne Brooks-Gunn, eds. 1997. *Consequences of Growing Up Poor.* New York: Russell Sage Foundation.

Hart, Betty, and Todd R. Risley. 1995. *Meaningful Differences in the Everyday Experience of Young American Children.* Baltimore, MD: Paul H. Brookes Publishing.

Hutner, Frances C. 1972. "Mother's Education and Working: Effect on the School Child." *Journal of Psychology* 82(1): 27–37.

Miller, Lucy Jane, and Peter G. W. Schouten. 1989. "Maternal Education and Preacademic Problems as Predictors of Teachers' Ratings and Self-Concept." *Perceptual and Motor Skills* 69: 607–610.

National Center for Education Statistics. 1998. *The Condition of Education.* Washington, DC: U.S. Government Printing Office.

Osborn, Michael E. 1971. "The Impact of Differing Parental Educational Level on the Educational Achievement, Attitude, Aspiration, and Expectation of the Child." *Journal of Educational Research* 65(4): 163–167.

Paterson, Charlotte J., Janis B. Kupersmidt, and Nancy A. Vaden. 1990. "Income Level, Gender, Ethnicity, and Household Composition as Predictors of Children's School-Based Competence." *Child Development* 61: 485–494.

Skolnick, Arlene. 1997. "The Triple Revolution: Social Sources of Family Change." In *The Family on the Threshold of the 21st Century: Trends and Implications,* edited by Solly Dreman, 167–180. Mahwah, NJ: Lawrence Erlbaum.

Stouthamer-Loeber, Magda, and Rolf Loeber. 1988. "The Use of Prediction Data in Understanding Delinquency." *Behavioral Sciences and the Law* 6(3): 333–354.

Strom, Robert, Carol Hathaway, and Helen Slaughter. 1981. "The Correlation of Maternal Attitudes and Preschool Children's Performance on the McCarthy Scales of Children's Abilities." *Journal of Instructional Psychology* 8(4): 139–145.

Ellis, Havelock

Havelock Ellis (1859–1939) is sometimes called the father of modern sexology. He set forth his most noted teachings in *Studies in the Psychology of Sex,* a six-volume series published between 1896 and 1910. There, he argued that women are as sexual as men, that masturbation does not cause degenerative diseases, and that homosexuality is not an illness. Prior to *Studies in the Psychology of Sex,* Ellis published *Man and Woman: A Study in Human Secondary Characters.* Although it did not receive the same public attention as his later work, *Man and Woman* contained many of his fundamental ideas about heterosexual relationships. Perhaps most revolutionary for its time was the idea that women as well as men are sexual beings. He also argued that the male sex drive is more aggressive than the female sex drive.

A photograph of English physician and writer Henry Havelock Ellis, 1939. (Hulton/ Archive)

Ellis began *Studies in the Psychology of Sex* with a volume on homosexual rather than heterosexual relationships. There, he argued that homosexuality is congenital, or inborn, and that it should be understood as an anomaly, such as left-handedness, rather than as a disease. It was not until volume 6, *Sex in Relation to Society*, that Ellis returned to heterosexual and married relationships. There, he argued that love is the most important factor in sexual relationships. He reiterated his earlier idea that men and women experience their sex drives differently and added that adults need open relationships in which they can find multiple partners to fulfill their emotional and sexual needs.

Ellis's life experiences strongly influenced his work. According to his autobiography (Ellis 1939), he began *Studies* with a volume on homosexuality because his closest friends, including his wife, had homosexual tendencies. He and his wife, Edith Lees, maintained an open relationship. One of Ellis's extramarital relationships was with Margaret Sanger, with whom he shared a commitment to birth control and eugenics.

—*Linda Heidenreich*

See also Sanger, Margaret

References and Further Reading
Ellis, Havelock. 1939. *My Life: The Autobiography of Havelock Ellis.* Boston: Houghton Mifflin.
Goldberg, Isaac. 1926. *Havelock Ellis: A Biographical and Critical Study.* New York: Simon and Schuster.
Grosskurth, Phyllis. 1985. *Havelock Ellis: A Biography.* New York: New York University Press.
Robinson, Paul. 1976. *The Modernization of Sex: Havelock Ellis, Alfred Kinsey, William Masters and Virginia Johnson.* New York: Harper and Row.
Rowbotham, Sheila, and Jeffrey Weeks. 1977. *Socialism and the New Life: The Personal and Sexual Politics of Edward Carpenter and Havelock Ellis.* London: Pluto Press.

Erikson, Erik

Erik Erikson (1902–1994) became acquainted with Anna Freud at the end of the 1920s when he was working as a teacher and an artist. She convinced him to study and train at the Vienna Psychoanalytic Institute. As he studied psychoanalysis, he focused his scholarly training on child development. He contributed many books and articles to the field, such as his 1964 *Insight and Responsibility* and his groundbreaking 1950 work entitled *Childhood and Society*. Erikson outlined eight stages of development from infancy to old age. Erikson may have become interested in child development because his own upbringing was rather chaotic. He never met his birth father, and until Erikson's late teens he did not know that the man who raised him was not his biological father (Welchman 2000).

What makes Erikson significant is that instead of simply adopting Freudian doctrine, Erikson developed a unique interpretation of Freud's work. Unlike Freud, Erikson believed that the ego was not static, meaning he did not believe that people were born with a particular personality type and that under no circumstances could this personality be changed. He believed that life experiences influenced our behavior and that those experiences were influential in the development of our personality as well. Simply put, Freud believed people were the way that they were because of genetics, and Erikson believed that people were the way they were because of their environment. Erikson suffered serious criticism from the Freudians for his deviation from the established theories. Many were critical because his only degree was earned at the end of his high school career. When he attempted to get a higher degree, he is quoted as saying "I tried a bit . . . and then I said the hell with it" (*New York Times Magazine* 1999).

—*Donna Reeves*

See also Spock, Dr. Benjamin

References and Further Reading
Friedman, L. 2000. *Identity's Architect: A Biography of Erik Erikson.* Cambridge: Harvard University Press.
Hoare, C. 2002. *Erikson on Development in Adulthood: New Insights from the Unpublished Papers.* New York: Oxford University Press.
Welchman, K. 2000. *Erik Erikson: His Life, Work, and Significance.* Philadelphia: Open University Press.

Eugenics and the American Family

Eugenics, also known as hereditarian thought, biological determinism, or social Darwinism, originated in the nineteenth century and became a popular social movement that promoted social policies that had direct effects on the American family in the twentieth century. The informative period for eugenics was between 1870 and 1905, when an effort was made to create a "science" of human heredity informed by statistical rather than biological data. From 1905 to 1930, eugenic theories directed toward improving the human race were supported by the creation of psychometric tests of ability that found a statistical intergenerational correspondence between poor and working-class parents and children. It was assumed that mental, physical, social, and behavioral differences were inherited through a simple biological process. Eugenic social policies, such as regulating reproduction and preventing the birth of "unfit" children, gained wide public support by the general population as well as by intellectuals, social reformers, and leaders in science, government, business, health, education, and welfare fields (Haller 1965; Ludmerer 1971; Kevles 1985; Selden 1999). Statistical correlations between ability and inheritance remained the underpinning of eugenics even as the modern biological science of genetic research increasingly disproved a simple transmission of complex traits. In the 1930s and 1940s applied eugenics fell into disrepute among scientists and intellectuals, but it retained popular confidence and continued to inform social policies related to the regulation of families and identification of children by ability. After World War II, the term *eugenics* took on a pejorative connotation as associated with the genocidal policies and atrocities committed against the Jewish population in Europe under Nazi doctrines of Aryan racial superiority and white supremacy (Kevles 1985). The term *genetics* is now preferred over *eugenics* to identify biological, not social or statistical, scientific research on the mechanisms of heredity and transmission of complex characteristics.

Eugenics and Family Policy
Eugenicists argue that social characteristics and behaviors are inherited rather than culturally acquired through learning and experience. In this view, the quality of the gene pool explains inequalities and determines the adaptive success and vitality of human beings in the future. Positive eugenics promotes reproduction in families identified as superior; negative eugenics represses reproduction in "defective" families. Negative eugenics informed social policy in the United States more than positive eugenics in the twentieth century.

Eugenicist Frederick Osborn, in a defense of eugenics, explained that "essentially eugenics seeks to understand and ultimately to direct the forces that control human inheritance through matings, births, and deaths" (Osborn 1968, 1). The target of social control is directed toward the regulation of the family in its most intimate and basic functions of reproduction and socialization of the young. In order to improve the hereditary quality of the people in the United States, eugenicists in the first half of the twentieth cen-

tury sought to eliminate undesirable traits from the population by preventing the "unworthy" from becoming parents. Doing so included marriage restriction, involuntary sterilization, and the permanent coercive detention of "defectives." Target populations included "paupers"; new immigrants, especially from eastern and southern Europe; criminals; vagrants; prostitutes; alcoholics; the "insane"; "feebleminded"; and epileptics (Haller 1965; Ludmerer 1971; Osgood 2000; Gallager 1999). Children with physical, mental, or behavioral differences from the established norms were also vulnerable (Brantlinger 1995; Stafford and Stafford 1996).

Since eugenics is also concerned with the conditions of inheritability, it was argued that high birthrates among the lower classes constituted a dysgenic danger, as argued in Thomas Malthus's 1798 theory of population dynamics. Differential birthrates between superior and inferior groups became an obsession with eugenicists and neo-Malthusians (Soloway 1990). With established middle- to upper-class, Anglo–northern European families as the ideal, poor and uneducated white families became a special target for alarm in that their higher rates of birth were seen as a degenerative influence on the whole "white race," the "superior stock" of humankind (Goddard 1912; Smith 1985; Rafter 1988).

The tendency toward nativism in American eugenics was paralleled by overt racism directed toward African Americans, who were designated the lowest status and deemed a subspecies where de jure (legal) and de facto (situational) segregation restricted the opportunities and living conditions of African American families and communities between 1896 and 1954 (Tucker 1994;

Selden 1999). As William Tucker has noted, it appears that scientists for over a century have obsessively and sometimes irrationally sought to prove that "minorities, poor people, foreigners, and women are innately inferior to upper class white males of northern European extraction" (Tucker 1994, 4). Attacks on the African American family from slavery to the welfare state, for example, resonate with eugenic arguments that it is dysgenic to uplift the poor or provide opportunities beyond the innate capacity of the group, since opportunity should correspond with ability. Paul Popenoe and Roswell Johnson in their often-reissued college textbook, *Applied Eugenics,* went so far as to suggest that blacks should be encouraged to serve in war in the front lines in order to use the white workers in skilled jobs (see Selden 1999, 54–55). The 1935 version of their textbook was less overtly genocidal than was the 1918 version, suggesting segregation in not necessarily equal conditions. Whites may be above blacks in this view, but support for the working classes was also seen as dysgenic by eugenicists where labor organizations support the weak over the strong and argue for equal pay for equal work, ignoring genetic endowment and capacity (Selden 1999, 54–55).

The obsession to prove certain groups inferior led to social policies that directly undermine the most basic social unit of the groups in question: the freedom to enter into, associate with, and prosper as a family. Stories of dysfunctional families served as a self-fulfilling prophecy to legitimate eugenic contentions of the long-term negative effects to society if degenerate lineages were allowed independence, freedom of choice, and the right of association (Rafter 1988).

The outcome and status of eugenics as a science remain controversial (Hasian 1996). Although some consider eugenics to be the epitome of a pseudoscience and a prime example of the use of misappropriated ideas manipulated for political purposes to the harm of society (Tucker 1994; Kühl 1994), others see eugenics as a legitimate forerunner to modern genetic science with admittedly sometimes overzealous and ill-advised advocates, but as a basically sound beginning (Dobzhansky 1968, v–vii; Osborn 1968). Eugenics has three intersecting components with time frames that differ: (1) Eugenics is a system of social thought and cultural ideology grounded in hereditarian beliefs that are not grounded in biology. (2) Eugenics is a network of lay and professional eugenicist practitioner/reformers. (3) Eugenics is also a social movement with definitive time frames on an overt level, one that operates on both covert and overt levels of consciousness and as embedded in social thought, policies, and practices.

Eugenics as Social Thought. Eugenics is a system of social thought or set of theories about how to identify and perfect ideal types of human beings. The modern scientific, or pseudoscientific, identification of eugenics with biology and evolution is a product of the nineteenth century. Eugenic thought, from this standpoint, is a subcategory of social Darwinist theory and, as Robert Bannister noted, "perhaps the only true form" (Bannister 1979, 165; see also Hofstadter 1969, 161–169). Eugenics reifies and projects statistical data as evidence of biological processes of inheritance. It is not grounded in research on physical heredity but on the theory of biological determinism applied to social policy reified by statistical data.

Darwin's publication of *The Origin of Species* in 1859 provided a theoretical framework for the inheritance of abilities and disabilities. Herbert Spencer applied Darwin's concept of the "survival of the fittest" to explain the organization of society. Spencer's social Darwinism gained more popular credence in the United States than in his native England, since it corresponded well with American concepts of mobility, individualism based on ambition, freedom to succeed or fail, open competition, and the Protestant work ethic. Success was taken as proof of worthiness.

In the 1860s, Darwin's cousin, Francis Galton (1822–1911), founder of anthropometry, population genetics, and eugenics, began genealogical studies on the inheritance of ability based on his belief that talent and civil virtue are inborn and possessed by the upper classes to the exclusion of the lower classes. He combined the Darwinian idea of evolution and fitness with progressive ideas about the possibility of transcending nature rather than following its dictates, to arrive at the potential of perfecting human "stock." Like his cousin, Galton shared a belief in the malleability of populations. Galton's concept of inheritance was largely based on observations that it is possible to cultivate better crops and breed animals for their characteristics through careful selection. Human populations, he surmised, were also subject to intervention. Galton's ideas on class, heredity, and genius were published in 1869 in *Hereditary Genius.* Galton did not pursue biological research but instead proceeded to use the infant field of statistics to try to find mathematical correlations between characteristics in succeeding generations.

Galton's studies of heredity were grounded in the popular but mistaken belief in subspecies or multiple races of human beings. He held the standard views of racial inferiority and superiority popular at the time. Social class, not race, however, was his primary interest. He wanted to show that class-based manners, such as the ability to make civic contributions to society, were transmitted from parent to child. He also held that inherited behaviors and abilities provided an explanation for the distribution of wealth and poverty.

Galton initiated both the scientific and pseudoscientific aspects of eugenic theory as an evangelical belief system and applied science. Galton wanted to establish a "science which deals with all the influences that improve the inborn qualities of the [human] race" (Galton 1883, 24–25; Kevles 1985; Osgood 2000). Galton wanted eugenics to be accepted by practitioners, scientists, and the public alike as a religious faith. Galton (1883) coined the term *eugenics* from the Greek word *eugene,* meaning "wellborn." He meant wellborn in two senses. One was in the sense of being good: "All creatures would agree that it was better to be healthy than sick, vigorous than weak, well fitted than ill-fitted for their part in life. In short, that it was better to be a good rather than bad specimen of their kind" (Galton 1976, 41). Wellborn also meant the promotion of the upper classes over the lower classes: "The aim of eugenics is to bring as many influences as can be reasonably employed, to cause the useful classes in the community to contribute *more* [italics in the original] than their proportion to the next generation" (Galton 1976).

Galton outlined five steps in his eugenic program, all of which were evident in eugenics in the United States. First, mathematical research had to be conducted into the "laws of heredity," forming "actuarial" tables. Second, in a neo-Malthusian sense, demographic research needed to track birthrates and fertility by "various classes" as correlated with the "tendency to high or low civilization." Third, data were needed on the conditions of eugenics in the family where "vigorous," large, superior families would be identified and studied. The results would be used to establish ways to identify superior individuals for parenthood and to disseminate data on the practices of child rearing in "thriving" families. Fourth, research into the "influence affecting marriages" would serve to identify marriages that should be banned and how to manipulate social choices for suitable mates. Finally, eugenics was to be promoted as a "national consciousness, like a religion . . . a religious dogma where its principles would work its way into the heart of the nation . . . with practical effect" (Galton 1976).

Eugenicists as Practitioner/Believers. Galton successfully employed a concept of heredity in his 1889 work, *Natural Inheritance,* that could be identified and measured in quantifiable terms (Kevles 1985, 18). Galton's student, statistician Karl Pearson (1892), reworked the theory and fortified its underpinning in statistics by creating a new theory of correlation, which proved to be a powerful tool for the behavioral sciences and made the development and use of tests considerably easier. Pearson established a statistical correlation between heredity and talent by relating coefficients along a supposed normal distribution of possibilities. This moved eugenics into a new phase verified by figures that appeared to prove that physical and mental traits were not only related but could be measured precisely, and even predicted. These statistical, not biological, findings were used to verify that human populations were capable of being manipulated by selective inheritance.

Up to 1905, tests of ability were limited to faculty psychology, which measured and compared differences among subjects' sensory discrimination, reaction times, and memories. In 1904, French educational authorities asked French psychologist Alfred Binet to establish a means by which children could be identified and classified for school purposes. With his colleague Theodore Simon, Binet developed a test of general intellectual functioning that differed significantly from the measurement of single characteristics. Binet developed a series of tasks, which were standardized on a select group of children to determine what a normal level of performance was for a given age group. Binet successfully developed the first scaled intelligence test that could classify and compare individuals and groups as normal, subnormal, or above normal.

Henry H. Goddard, director of research at Vineland Training School for the Feebleminded in New Jersey, brought Binet's test to the United States and adapted the scale for use in the United States. He tested 400 children at Vineland and used test results to popularize the need for eugenic policies in dealing with individuals and groups that scored below average on the tests. He created a unilinear taxonomy of mental abilities on a scale rising from "idiots, to imbeciles, to morons." Goddard's assumptions illustrate two of the more general fallacies inherent in eugenics and biological determinism in general: the reification of intelligence as a single innate physical characteristic that can be represented by a score and the belief that evolution is a uniformly progressive development from primitive, inferior, to advanced, superior performance (Gould 1981, 159).

Goddard encouraged the idea that the group of the greatest concern to the perfection of human progressive evolution was the moron who might pass for a normal person and thus pollute the gene pool. This set up poor whites and new immigrants for special scrutiny as normal-looking but defective groups. Goddard studied two sides of the lineage of the Kallikaks, a white family descended from a common male (Goddard 1912). One side of the family was descended from a liaison with a barmaid of questionable intelligence, who begat a prolific line of defectives. The other line descended from the man's wife, a woman of good breeding whose progeny were normal and superior, according to Goddard (Smith 1985). Goddard, in his research, writing, and popular addresses, crusaded for the institutionalization and sterilization of individuals deemed inferior through the mass screening of immigrants and other at-risk populations using intelligence tests.

Several events combined to make intelligence tests more usable on a mass basis and to make them appear closer to the natural sciences in ways that also encouraged hereditarian conclusions. This connection was not with biology or laboratory science but with psychometry. Building on the work of Karl Pearson, Charles Spearman and Cyril Burt argued that the correlation of scores on intelligence tests supported the notion of a general "g" factor, which, they argued, was inheritable. This allowed the test score to be reified as representing intelligence as a

thing-in-itself and as a generalizable, biologically inheritable trait. The naming of the score with a simple numerical equation that matched mental age with chronological age consolidated the package of modern intelligence tests, which consist of the scaled test itself, the "g" factor, and the intelligence quotient (IQ) score.

Lewis Terman, a psychologist at Stanford University, undertook the task to rework the Binet scale, including innovations suggested above and pioneered by the United States Army in World War I. The army alpha and beta tests were designed for mass production to measure the ability of recruits. The outcome upheld Goddard's contention that working- and lower-class whites and immigrants were "feebleminded." Such individuals could surely be identified before they were old enough to join the army. Terman's revision of Binet, designed as a mass group test to measure the ability of schoolchildren in the United States, incorporated two ideas that made the administrative use of the tests easily adapted for school use to sort children into ability groups and to adjust their curriculum accordingly. Terman followed up on the invention of the IQ score and the "g" factor with the comparative use of scores designating different levels to intelligence score ranges. The top 1 percent of 1,000 scores in the sample he used to standardize the tests were assigned an IQ of 130 and the individual was designated as a genius. On the other end of the scale the lowest scoring 1 percent out of 1,000 were assigned an IQ of 70 and designated as feebleminded or mentally deficient. Galton's geniuses could thus be identified as could Goddard's imbeciles, idiots, and morons. Terman's 1916 version of the Stanford-Binet became the most popular intelligence test in the world by the 1930s, and it remains the basis for many tests on the market today.

Eugenics as a Social Movement. The eugenics movement as a social movement created vocal public advocacy campaigns. Charles Benedict Davenport, a Mendelian eugenicist who believed that traits such as laziness and poverty were inherited and should be studied, became the most effective disciple of Galton and an advocate for eugenics in the United States. Davenport's concern was with the degenerative potential of "defective" Anglo Europeans, especially those from southern and eastern Europe. He made little distinction between the inheritance of physical, social, and moral traits. He classified groups according to racial and ethnic stereotypes. He was also openly racist and an anti-Semite (Davenport 1911). His advocacy of state laws limiting marriage selection was based on Mendelian arguments for the simple transmission of complex traits (Davenport 1913). In 1913 Davenport celebrated a law in Maryland that labeled the interracial marriage of a "white" and "Negro" (or descendant of a Negro to the third generation) an "infamous crime." The U.S. Supreme Court did not declare such laws unconstitutional until 1967 in the *Loving* v. *Virginia* case (see Selden 1999, 52–53). Davenport's success can be traced to the fact that he was well funded, a testimony to the popular appeal of eugenics. His first major gift was from the Carnegie Institute of Washington, D.C., for $34,250. The money was offered to establish a Station for the Experimental Study of Evolution, which was done at Cold Spring Harbor, Long Island, New York, in 1903. Davenport also championed the movement through the Eugenics Record Office at Cold Spring Harbor, which was also supported by Rockefeller philanthropy. Davenport championed eugenics and popularized eugenic solutions to social problems through his publications and leadership in organizations such as American Breeders Association, Eugenics Section (later, Committee on Eugenics).

Prestigious organizations were also attracted to eugenics in the early twentieth century. The National Education Association organized a Committee on Racial Well Being and promoted the social policies of eugenics through marriage selection, identification of superior children, and the development of "racial ideals" at all grade levels (Selden 1999, 56–60). Popular textbooks routinely taught students ranging from grade school children to college level the Mendelian concepts of heredity and eugenic ideas about social policy and individual differences as facts (Selden 1999, 63–83; also see Guyer 1916, 1927; Wiggam 1924; Scheinfeld 1939, 1950, 1961; Meade and Parker 1964). Eugenicists under the guise of progressive politics and social reform sought new forms of control over family life and reproduction through a Better Babies Movement and "fitter family" contests at fairs and exhibits in the 1920s. Race betterment conferences were held nationally and internationally (Selden 1999, 30–33). Eugenic ideas became embedded in other progressive social movements in a more covert way, including mental hygiene, public health, social hygiene, and child advocacy movements in the courts and schools (Pickens 1968). The movement became a form of secular religion in the United States, Canada, and England (Kevles 1985, 145; McLaren 1990; Soloway 1990; Jackson 2000). Although the movement was worldwide, eugenics had a special significance and importance in the United States.

Popularity of Eugenics and Hereditarian Thought in the United States

Eugenics in England and Canada fostered class discrimination; in the United States class discrimination was masked under racist beliefs in the superiority of "white" Anglo-European groups and the menace of inferior ethnic and racial groups defined by extraneous physical characteristics such as skin, hair, and eye color. Historical precedents predisposed Americans to eugenic ideas. In the United States the increased pressure for the abolition of slavery in the antebellum period prior to 1860 and the onset of the Civil War highlighted public debates over the meaning of phenotypic differences and human rights. The debates made race an extremely important division in U.S. culture, superseding the perception of class (Ignatiev 1995). The use of prescientific racial classification to defend slavery was the beginning of modern racism in the United States. Public interest and concern about the character and cause of human differences and their possible negative effects on the progress of society also increased during the second half of the nineteenth century. This was a reaction to the Civil War and Reconstruction and also a reaction to rapid changes caused by the Industrial Revolution, urbanization, and mass migrations. Social class differences were noticeably magnified in all parts of the country. Hereditarian thought provided a rationale for those who benefited from the social changes but did not want to base their superiority of status on class alone, given the American ideology of constant mobility and individualism. Hereditarian ideas provided the perfect ideological solution to justify social reproduction, not by class per se but on the basis of superior innate family characteristics.

The stage was well set for the acceptance of eugenic ideas by educated, uneducated, rich, and poor white Americans alike by 1900. Radical Reconstruction backlashed into legislated racism at the end of the nineteenth century. Poor white southerners, free and emancipated blacks, and northern rural and urban lower classes were casualties of the failure of the experiment of Reconstruction after the Civil War. Eugenics offered a rationale for maintaining the status quo of class and racial hierarchies and embedding mechanisms of differentiation into social policy and social structure. The dogma of hereditarian inequality and racial inferiority grew instead of receding as it was buttressed by advances in professional disciplines in education, psychology, social work, and public health (Richardson and Fisher 1999). The common school movement for universal public education brought attention to differences in the ability of children to learn. The laggards were those most feared by eugenicists (Ayres 1909). Working, homeless, and delinquent children and youth brought attention to unfit parents and the responsibilities of the state to manage deviant populations through schools, asylums, courts, and clinics (Richardson 1989).

Eugenics and Family Policy in the Future

Eugenic ideas remained embedded in disciplines in the behavioral sciences, testing movement, and social policies. The ideas also remain an undercurrent in popular thought as well in some tenets of disciplines such as sociobiology and popularized psychology, as evident in arguments claiming the racial basis of intelligence and reasons for poor performance by race/ethnicity on standardized tests (Herrnstein and Murray 1994). Hereditarian beliefs have contemporary manifestations in social policy, and applied biological determinism survives in academic fields. Most recently debates have escalated and include the basic tenets of the eugenic arguments for the social control of outcast groups popular between 1905 and 1930. Modern genetics and molecular biology now make it possible to biologically engineer life-forms and to map, trace, and manipulate human patterns of heredity for the first time. As the science of manipulating reproduction is maturing, political as well as social concerns escalate. Classic forms of eugenic social control policies such as the sterilization and containment of certain populations were openly debated in the 1990s (Herrnstein and Murray 1994; Fraser 1995). Eugenic arguments for better or worse are part of a contemporary postmodern debate over the uses and control of science in social policy in the twenty-first century (Hasian 1996; Duster 1990; Tucker 1994; Longman 2001). This debate is intimately connected to the politics of reproduction, the role of the family, and definitions of the quality of life.

The term *genetics*, rather than *eugenics*, originates from 1906. It differentiates the scientific biological study of the physical process of human inheritance from applied social Darwinism directed toward social policy. Eugenicists of the old school in the behavioral sciences refused to advance beyond Mendelian genetics. They clung to the idea that complex traits can be inherited as simple dominant and recessive characteristics. Recent advances in genetic science disprove the theory of multiple human races or subspecies. Contemporary genetic research also creates the potential for human genetic engineering while raising disturbing ethical issues reminiscent of the debates over eugenic social policies in the past. The most recent advances in mapping the human genome provide proof that genetic differences are almost nonexistent between human populations and that there is only one species of *Homo sapiens*. It remains to be seen whether the rejection of eugenic theory by legitimate science will or will not, as in the past, deter public acceptance of racial thinking and the intrusion of eugenic practices in social policies (Selden 1999; Duster 1990).

—*Theresa Richardson*

References and Further Reading
Ayres, Leonard. 1909. *Laggards in the Schools: A Study of Retardation and Elimination in City School Systems.* New York: Charities Publication Committee.

Bajema, Carl J., ed. 1976. *Eugenics: Then and Now.* Benchmark Papers in Genetics, vol. 5. Shroudsburn, PA: Dowden, Hutchingon and Ross.

Bannister, Robert C. 1979. *Social Darwinism: Science and Myth in Anglo-American Thought.* Philadelphia: Temple University Press.

Brantlinger, Ellen. 1995. *Sterilization of People with Mental Disabilities: Issues, Perspectives, and Cases.* Westport, CT: Auburn House.

Davenport, Charles B. 1911. *Heredity in Relation to Eugenics.* New York: Henry Holt.

Davenport, Charles B. 1913. *Eugenic Records Office Bulletin No. 9: State Laws Limiting Marriage Selection in Light of Eugenics.* Cold Spring Harbor, NY: Eugenics Record Office.

Dobzhansky, Theodosius. 1968. Foreword to *The Future of Human Heredity: An Introduction to Eugenics in Modern Society,* by Frederick Osborn. New York: Weybright and Tally.

Duster, Troy. 1990. *Backdoor to Eugenics.* New York: Routledge.

Fraser, Steven, ed. 1995. *The Bell Curve Wars: Race, Intelligence, and the Future of America.* New York: Basic Books.

Gallager, Nancy L. 1999. *Breeding Better Vermonters: The Eugenics Project in the Green Mountain State.* Hannover: University Press of New England.

Galton, Francis, 1869. *Hereditary Genius.* London: Macmillan.

Galton, Francis. 1883. *Inquiries into Human Faculty and Its Development.* London: J. M. Dent and Sons.

Galton, Francis. 1976. "Eugenics: Its Definition, Scope and Aims, Read before the Sociological Society at a Meeting in the School of Economics and Political Science, London University, May 16th, 1904." In *Eugenics: Then and Now,* edited by Carl J. Bajema, 40–45. Shroudsburn, PA: Dowden, Hutchingon and Ross.

Goddard, Henry H. 1912. *The Kallikaks: A Study in the Heredity of Feeble-Mindedness.* New York: Macmillan.

Goddard, Henry H. 1917. "Mental Tests and Immigrants." *Journal of Delinquency* 2: 244, 266, Table 252.

Gould, Stephen Jay. 1981. *The Mismeasure of Man.* New York: W. W. Norton.

Haller, Mark. 1965. *Eugenics: Hereditarian Attitudes in American Thought.* New Brunswick, NJ: Rutgers University Press.

Hasian, Marouf Arif, Jr. 1996. *The Rhetoric of Eugenics in Anglo-American Thought.* Athens: University of Georgia Press.

Herrnstein, Richard, and Charles Murray. 1994. *The Bell Curve.* New York: The Free Press.

Hofstadter, Richard. 1969. *Social Darwinism in American Thought.* New York: George Braziller.

Ignatiev, Noel. 1995. *How the Irish Became White.* New York: Routledge.

Jackson, Mark. 2000. *The Borderland of Imbecility: Medicine, Society and the Fabrication of the Feebleminded in Late Victorian and Early Edwardian England.* Manchester, England: Manchester University Press.

Kevles, Daniel J. 1985. *In the Name of Eugenics: Genetics and the Uses of Human Heredity.* Berkeley: University of California Press.

Kühl, Stefan. 1994. *The Nazi Connection: Eugenics, American Racism, and German National Socialism.* New York: Oxford University Press.

Larson, Edward J. 1995. *Sex, Race, and Science: Eugenics in the Deep South.* Baltimore: Johns Hopkins University Press.

Ludmerer, Kenneth M. 1971. *Genetics and American Society: A Historical Approach.* Baltimore: Johns Hopkins University Press.

McLaren, Angus. 1990. *Our Own Master Race: Eugenics in Canada, 1885–1945.* Toronto: McClelland and Stewart.

Meade, J. E., and A. S. Parker, eds. 1964. *Biological Aspects of Social Problems: Symposium of the Eugenics Society, October 1964.* New York: Plenum Press, 1965.

Osborn, Frederick. 1968. *The Future of Human Heredity: An Introduction to Eugenics in Modern Society.* New York: Weybright and Tally.

Osgood, Robert L. 2000. *For "Children Who Vary from the Normal Type": Special Education in Boston, 1839–1930.* Washington, DC: Gallaudet.

Pickens, Donald K. 1968. *Eugenics and the Progressives.* Nashville, TN: Vanderbilt University Press.

Rafter, Nicole H. 1988. *White Trash: The Eugenic Family Studies, 1877–1919.* Boston: Northeastern University Press.

Richardson, Theresa. 1989. *The Century of the Child: The Mental Hygiene Movement and Children's Policy in the United States and Canada.* Albany: State University of New York Press.

Richardson, Theresa, and Donald Fisher, eds. 1999. *The Development of the Social Sciences: The Role of Philanthropy.* Greenwich, CT: Ablex.

Scheinfeld, Amram. 1939. *You and Heredity.* New York: Frederick A. Stokes Company.

———. 1950. *The New You and Heredity; with Special Editing in the Medical Genetics Sections by Morton D. Schweitzer, and Additional Aid by Others Herein Mentioned.* Philadelphia: Lippincott.

———. 1961. *The Human Heredity Handbook.* rev. and expanded. New York: Washington Square Press.

Selden, Steven. 1999. *Inheriting Shame: The Story of Eugenics and Racism in*

America. New York: Teachers College, Columbia University Press.

Smith, J. David. 1985. *Minds Made Feeble: The Myth and Legacy of the Kallikaks.* Rockville, MD: Royal Turbridge Wells.

Soloway, Richard A. 1990. *Demography and Degeneration: Eugenics and Declining Birthrate in Twentieth-Century Britain.* Chapel Hill: University of North Carolina Press.

Stafford, Phillip L., and Elizabeth J. Stafford. 1996. *A History of Childhood and Disability.* New York: Teachers College, Columbia University Press.

Tucker, William H. 1994. *The Science and Politics of Racial Research.* Urbana: University of Illinois Press.

Wiggam. 1924. *The Fruit of the Family Tree.* Indianapolis: Bobbs-Merrill.

Extended Family

The extended family includes, in addition to the nuclear family of parents and children, other kin who are primary contributors to the family in terms of financial, social, and emotional resources. In the United States, the extended family has played many different roles, although it has not been the most prevalent form of basic family unit since the European incursion into North America. Often, it plays a major role in visions of the ideal society. In the countercultural mythology of the 1960s, for example, a form of the extended family was seen as the perfect family. In nostalgic views of American farm life, the nuclear family may play the starring role, but the extended family is omnipresent and provides by far the best character actors.

All families begin with the mother-child bond. Europeans are accustomed to thinking of the third member of the family as the father. Although there are cultures in which the third family member may be the mother's sister or her brother's wife, in most of the world the mother, father, and child make up the nuclear family. Often, the family as a functioning unit also includes the parents of either mother or father or both. In addition, the parents' siblings and their children may be of significance in the life of the family. The extended family may also include people who are not related by blood but who make an important contribution to family life.

For most Americans, however, the nuclear family, as portrayed on television in the 1950s in *Ozzie and Harriet* and *Father Knows Best*, is the real family. Judith Stacey, in her book *In the Name of the Family: Rethinking Family Values in the Postmodern Age,* declares, "In most of Europe and North America the family has become nearly synonymous with the nuclear household unit made up of a married, heterosexual couple and their biological or adopted children. Although popular usage more fluidly adapts the concept to refer to all people related through blood, marriage, or adoption, most Westerners do erroneously associate the family with nature and project it backward into a timeless past" (Stacey 1996, 38–39).

What most of us think of as the "traditional family" is really, however, what sociologists call the "modern family." Jon Davies and Norman Dennis, in their article "From the Tyranny of Rules to the Whim of Relationships: The Family in Modern Society," put the modern family in context:

Typically, for a society to enter the modern era it must accept the mien of big cities, an industrial means of production, the rule of law, an intricate system of money and trade, a techno-scientific basis for education, and so forth—but along with these insignia of modernity comes the most important organization: the nuclear family. In the modern era, the extended family moves off center stage, as the process of social differentiation leaves the "nuclear" couple with specific and important nurturing tasks to perform, all other functions being taken over by the specialized institutions of civil society, state, or marketplace. (Davies and Dennis 1995, 312)

Before the arrival of Europeans, Native Americans had many different family forms, as diverse tribes had diverse social structures. These included the nuclear family, extended families, clans, and other households. Descent could be matrilineal or patrilineal, and each culture expressed and reinforced the importance of family members involved in its particular pattern of descent.

The earliest Europeans were explorers and traders, men who did not bring their families with them into the American wilderness. It was not until the late 1500s that settlers began to colonize the eastern seaboard. For the next century and a half, the American family consisted of the people who inhabited a house or farm. There was the nuclear family, of course, but there might also be servants and apprentices and, frequently, enslaved people. The father served as the head of the family and was responsible for the safety, support, and education of every member of the household. He and his wife were also responsible for the religious training of all household members. The entire family was involved in the work of the house or farm. Indeed, work was the basic purpose of the family. Companionship or sentimental attachment was strictly secondary.

This early American family unit carried out many of the functions that we now think of as the responsibility of government. Besides being the local school, it served as hospital, police, library, juvenile court, fired department, and social worker. It provided food, clothing, and entertainment. It was, in a sense, an extended family, but it was not the family the visionaries usually have in mind. It was strictly patriarchal, for one thing, and not noticeably multigenerational. Individual family members were not so much nurtured as utilized for the good of the whole. On the other hand, all family members could expect to be supported in old age and cared for in times of illness. Robert L. Griswold described it this way in *Fatherhood in America*:

[The corporate household]—best exemplified by the family farm or the small artisan shop—helped promote fathers' influence over their children. With its household production, limited-exchange system, self-sufficiency, community moral surveillance, and family hierarchy, the corporate household economy of the seventeenth and eighteenth centuries provided a world in which fathers worked in close proximity with their children. Men directed the work of the family, introduced their sons to farming or craft work, and maintained (or at least tried to maintain) harmonious relations within the household. Thus, the home was not only a center of production but also a system of authority. (Griswold 1993, 13)

By the beginning of the nineteenth century, the "household as family" was changing into something more nearly recognizable as the extended family. It was no longer so common for a family to have servants and slaves living with them. As individual families managed to survive for a number of generations, the family accumulated layers. As late as 1790, farms were still dominant (U.S. census figures showed three-quarters of all Americans living on farms), and large families provided labor to run them. Fathers gave their sons neighboring land to farm or handed over the reins of the plow horse in exchange for a less utilitarian but still significant authority in the family. Then, within a matter of decades, the Industrial Revolution changed the family situation in the United States drastically.

When people began to move away from farms to find work in industry, they moved away from other generations of their families as well. The nuclear family began to shed bits and pieces of its support network. The extended family declined in importance—for native-born Americans. Another major change happened at roughly the same time, however. Large numbers of European immigrants began to come to the United States, first in the 1840s and later in the 1870s through the 1890s. If native Americans moved away from their extended families into the large cities, immigrants brought their families with them and kept them together for survival. Often, an extended family was forced to live in a single housing unit because its members could not afford to live separately. Earlier arrivals served as translators, guides, personnel managers, and social workers for later arrivals. Because of the immigrants' recent exposure to European customs, this was an emotionally and socially logical step as well.

Another segment of the population that experienced a more flexible family structure was African Americans. There

has been considerable controversy about the black family in America. In 1968, Daniel Patrick Moynihan stated that the black family was "pathological" and based much of his argument on the fact that so many black families were headed by women. Then, in 1977, Herbert Gutman published his landmark book, *The Black Family in Slavery and Freedom*. He tacitly accepted Moynihan's definition of a healthy family as a male-headed nuclear family and then went on to present evidence that, in fact, the average black family in the plantation South was just that. Twenty years after Gutman, Brenda Stevenson, in *Life in Black and White*, put forth a different view, based on research from Virginia:

> There . . . is very little evidence which suggests that a nuclear family was the slave's sociocultural idea. Virginia slave families, while demonstrating much diversity in form, essentially were not nuclear and did not derive from long-term monogamous marriages. The most discernible ideal for their principal kinship organization was a malleable extended family that, when possible, provided its members with nurture, education, socialization, material support, and recreation in the face of the potential social chaos that the slaveholder imposed. (Stevenson 1996, 160)

Stevenson's data are not from the Deep South, as Gutman's are, and so their conclusions differ. What is clear from both, however, is that although slaves formed nuclear families when they could, they were willing and able to make families out of almost any group of kin and fictive kin around. When parents were sold away from their children, there was always someone to take the children in, not as burdens, but as family. Even today, that sort of flexibility is more often found in the African American community than in most white neighborhoods.

During the twentieth century, the extended family gradually became a sort of halo around the primary nuclear family. It certainly did not disappear. Most Americans in the twentieth century grew up with considerable contact with grandparents, at least, and often aunts, uncles, and cousins. But the extended family was secondary. Its members seldom shared living quarters, and participation in each other's lives was often limited to celebrations and ceremonial occasions. As a result, perhaps, these occasions became more elaborate and participation more rigidly defined.

At the end of the century, Nora Ephron, in *Funny Sauce*, satirically declared the rebirth of the extended family in the form of ex-husbands and ex-wives, their new mates, and their former mates' new mates, and so on. For good or bad, it is not entirely a joke. Today, when one in two marriages ends in divorce and most divorced people remarry, what sociologists call the blended family is becoming virtually the norm. Parents who are no longer related by marriage share not only concerns for their offspring but issues of economics, housing, and mobility. Stepparents find themselves involved in delicate decision making with former spouses. Children may have three, four, or more adults of primary significance in their lives, in addition to multiple grandparents. This is only one of the many ways that the "modern family" in the form of the two-parent nuclear family is being challenged.

Another way is financially. The nuclear family ideal is not easy to achieve financially. At least some approximation of the extended family is considerably more practical for those who do not belong solidly to the American middle class. Immigrants, for example, are still more likely to extend their family life to include kin beyond the parents and child. Hispanic families go further, bringing others who are not related by blood. Being a godparent (*padrino*) is taken very seriously. Godparents are even expected to become the godchild's parents if the biological parents die. The godchild is expected to give the godparents special respect and to care for them when they age. But godparenthood (*compadrazgo*) ties parents and godparents even more strongly. The four call themselves coparents (*compadres*) and function as family. Especially in the immigrant experience, Hispanic compadres behave in the same ways as blood relatives. They are part of the extended family.

Many Native Americans continue to function within extended families that play an important role in tribal communities. Among the Snoqualmie of Washington State, for example, six prominent extended treaty-signing families are at the center of tribal politics. The members of these families see each other frequently and discuss tribal politics at family occasions or come together on purpose in the case of an urgent tribal matter. In this way, the extended family functions not only as an important personal and social construct but also as a political force.

The extended family has always been a part of American society. Its role has changed with time and circumstances. Its importance has waxed and waned. It has never, however, dominated American life in the way that it has European life.

—Kathleen Thompson

See also Affection as a Basis for Marriage; African American Families; Communes, Families in; The Companionate Family; Divorce, History of; Family Preferences and Immigration; Farm Families; Fatherhood; Grandparents; The Hispanic Family; Marriage; Motherhood; Stepparents

References and Further Reading

Davies, Jon, and Norman Dennis. 1995. "From the Tyranny of Rules to the Whim of Relationships: The Family in Modern Society." *The World & I* 10 (1 December): 312.

Griswold, Robert L. 1993. *Fatherhood in America: A History.* New York: Basic Books.

Gutman, Herbert. 1977. *The Black Family in Slavery and Freedom, 1750–1925.* New York: Vintage.

Hine, Darlene Clark, and Kathleen Thompson. 1996. *A Shining Thread of Hope: The History of Black Women in America.* New York: Broadway Books.

Mintz, Steven, and Susan Kellogg. 1988. *Domestic Revolutions: A Social History of American Family Life.* New York: The Free Press.

Stacey, Judith. 1996. *In the Name of the Family: Rethinking Family Values in the Postmodern Age.* Boston: Beacon Press.

Stevenson, Brenda E. 1996. *Life in Black and White: Family and Community in the Slave South.* New York: Oxford.

Tollefson, Kenneth D., and Martin L. Abbot. 1999. "Snoqualmie Ethnicity: Community and Continuity." *The American Indian Quarterly* 22 (1 September): 415–431.

F

Family and Film

Films constitute a popular formulation of culture's mythology about institutions, ideals, and ethical systems. From westerns to romances, movies have reflected and dictated American values, often highlighting areas of conflict within society. Behind these genres is the shadow of the family—sometimes as the locus of tension, as in *Long Day's Journey into Night* (1962), *Ordinary People* (1980), and *Kramer vs. Kramer* (1979); at other times providing safe haven at the film's resolution, as in *The Wizard of Oz* (1939) and *National Velvet* (1945). Although orphans and widowed parents have always been popular, more films of the later decades of the twentieth century began to show new configurations of the family, in such works as *Places in the Heart* (1984), *Rain Man* (1988), *The Piano* (1993), *Forrest Gump* (1994), *As Good as It Gets* (1997), and *Pleasantville* (1998).

Many films of the silent and early sound era featured parts of families—often fathers or sons and daughters, families with missing mothers or fathers, and orphaned children "adopted" by surrogate parents. This reflected the turmoil of the post–World War I era and later the fragmenting effects of the Great Depression and racial tensions in the United States. D. W. Griffith brought a troubled father-daughter relationship to center stage in the 1919 film *Broken Blossoms*, in which a young Chinese man tried in vain to bring a peaceful philosophy to the violent home of a street waif played by Lillian Gish. In breaking through the silent era to sound pictures, Al Jolson made relationships with mothers famous through his blackface performance of the song "Mammy." Films from the last five decades of the twentieth century presented a variety of organizational archetypes: patriarchy; matriarchy; fatherless or motherless homes; odd families composed of orphans, aunts, uncles, and others; idealized homes; extended families; pathological or incestuous groups; disintegrating and fragmented families; and families being put back together. Distinct patterns appear in the frequency of these archetypes, in how families function in film from various decades, and in what may influence artistic choices made by screenwriters, producers, and directors. At first glance, it appears that movies have shifted from stories in which the family solves a problem to stories in which the family *is* the problem. Drawing from both popular box office releases and critically acclaimed films, portraits of family groups, family themes, and archetypal family models constituted a significant feature of the film landscape of the twentieth century. The importance of the family as a market force also influenced the film industry in its choice of topics, the degree of censorship, and the methods for promoting movies throughout the twentieth century and into the twenty-first.

A number of extrinsic factors influenced artistic choices, including such economic and social conditions as the number of women employed outside the home; trends in marketing, distribution, and advertising of movies; and targeting of particular venues and audiences for films. Film treatments of family themes were often more profoundly swayed by key economic factors than by the actual conditions of real-life families. At times, the state of the family might indeed reflect the state of the economy. With the advent of television, however, film attendance patterns and marketing methods underwent a drastic alteration. Along with these changes came a shift in the types of families depicted. For example, drive-ins drew family audiences and created demand for a special B-grade hybrid film that was wholesome and slapstick for children while at the same time romantic or problem oriented for parents—examples were *Cheaper by the Dozen* (1950) and *Yours, Mine, and Ours* (1968).

As drive-ins died and more viewers remained at home, the market for films featuring entire families moved to the television screen. Since its inception, television has relied on programs depicting families as the most popular single format. Meanwhile, movie producers have increasingly targeted isolated segments of the population as potential viewers for a given film, identifying such categories as the "woman's weepy," "macho film," "teenage movies," and "children's picture." With soaring admission prices, people became more discriminating in the

kind of film they would pay to see, and they found themselves no longer going to films as a family group. Television viewing and movie marketing influenced the selection of stories and portrayal of characters in films. Films of the late 1950s, 1960s, and 1970s make it seem as if traditional families were practically nonexistent and those remaining were disintegrating, fragmented, or pathological.

In the last fifteen years of the twentieth century, the videocassette market became influential in producers' choices of projects to back, with most contracts including video release packages, a consideration that changed the way film subjects were selected, produced, and advertised. This trend influenced the constantly shifting market in terms of the frequency and kinds of treatment of family themes. As films like *Ordinary People*, originally written as a television script, eventually reached the big screen with some popular success, a few more daring producers began to back family pictures once again, in films such as *Country* (1984), *The River* (1984), *Places in the Heart* (1984), and *The Trip to Bountiful* (1985).

It is important to consider the relationship between esthetic and moral questions and the realities of motion picture production. It is easy enough to argue that audiences deserve a well-rounded portrayal of homes, showing children, mothers, fathers, old people, and extended families in a wide range of situations. Child actors, parents of child actors, and managers, however, can all attest to the price paid for such realism in "reel life." The desire to witness whole families arises from the need for a cultural mirror or mythology, models for behavior, and reassurance that the family still exists, but the people who provide these paradigms must give up a certain amount of their own home life in order to create a picture of the family. In order to determine whether or not this sacrifice is worthwhile, some critics speculate on the extent to which film versions of the family actually influence the behavior and values of audiences. The issue of the impact of cinema on society, a question as old as the movie industry, is as fascinating as it is difficult.

Considering the potential influence of media on behavior, it is essential to understand how the culture chooses to represent its most fundamental institution in its most popular art form. Analysis of the depiction of the family requires discussion of essential elements of literary and film criticism: plot, character, conflict, resolution, structure, form, cinematic devices, casting, and production. Every film has both a surface text and various subtexts that reveal how the film instructs audiences to respond. In most cases a film signals whether or not the audience is to view the family primarily as a solution to a problem or as the problem in itself. Only a few films genuinely struggle with the delicate balance of ambiguity and ambivalence surrounding real-life family relationships.

In the majority of films, general patterns present themselves, changing with the times. Eras in which movie makers were aiming at whole family audiences had a larger percentage of idealized families; conversely, when moviemakers sought to draw isolated segments of the audience, the family tended to be depicted as a source of conflict, something from which to escape. This phenomenon may explain the rash of sentimentally depicted families that appeared after the home video market began to boom; moviemakers made choices they believed would appeal to whole families once again, films that would be popular selections on the home video market.

Much of the scholarship on family themes has focused on literature. Film theorists have developed ways of interpreting film and assessing its connection to such cultural institutions as the family in works such as *Visible Fictions* by John Ellis (1992) and *How to Read a Film* by James Monaco (2000). *From Mouse to Mermaid* collected essays that examined how the Disney film ideology depicted power, gender, and identity in the family (Bell, Haas, and Sells 1995). Terry and Catherine Catchpole's *The Family Video Guide: Over 300 Movies to Share with Your Children* (1992) included a number of films featured in their annotated lists depicting family and parent-child relationships. One of the most valuable and up-to-date sources is the annual tongue-in-cheek *VideoHound's Golden Movie Retriever*, which lists films featuring families under Family Ties, Dads, Moms, and Parenthood (Connors and Craddock 2001).

One of the most significant historical influences on family themes and so-called family films was the development of the Hays Code, a self-censoring mechanism put in place in 1934. Hollywood films tamed down or eliminated their treatment of a number of family issues, including domestic violence, divorce, adultery, incest, and premarital sex. In films that depicted illicit behavior, the offending parties had to be shown to suffer or perhaps even die as a result of their transgressions, particularly in the decades after the Hays Code took effect. *The Women* (1939), *The Great Lie* (1941), *Kitty Foyle* (1940), and *A Letter to Three Wives* (1948) courageously took on the theme of adultery, but they generally followed the model of punishing characters' transgressive behavior. During the 1950s, movies began to experiment with subtle treatments of extramarital infatuation and adultery in such works as *Shane* (1953). An actual breakup of the family would have been out of the question in most 1950s movies, but families in the midst of conflict and divorce became popular in the late 1970s and early 1980s in such films as *Kramer vs. Kramer* (1979), *Ordinary People* (1980), and *Shoot the Moon* (1982).

Idealized happy families were common during the 1940s, in such films as *It's a Wonderful Life* (1946), *I Remember Mama* (1948), *Lassie Come Home* (1943), *Life with Father* (1947), *Meet Me in St. Louis* (1944), *National Velvet* (1945), *Pride and Prejudice* (1940), and *Our Town* (1940). During the 1950s and 1960s, films alternated between sentimentalized happy families and troubled families in turmoil. *The Swiss Family Robinson* (1960) presented a well-adjusted family dealing successfully with being shipwrecked on a desert island. Despite filmmakers' efforts to return to the golden days of the family in such films as *The Long, Long Trailer* (1954), *The Parent Trap* (1961), and *With Six You Get Eggroll* (1968), an increasing number of movies of the late 1950s and early 1960s showed families in turmoil. *Rebel without a Cause* (1955) and *Peyton Place* (1957) depicted young people desperate to escape the suburban nightmares of their parents. The appearance of these themes of generational isolation also coincided with an industry drive to target certain age groups for particular types of films—many of which were intended for drive-in audiences, eager to escape their families. With the emergence of the video market, the ever-popular format of family togetherness began to come back into vogue. The success of such films as *E.T.* (1982), *National Lampoon's Vacation* (1983), and *Home Alone* (1990) signaled a shift in the depiction of families. *The Addams Family* (1991) and *Addams Family Values* (1993) tried to recapture the cheerfully macabre spirit of the television series. Although all of these families had their quirks, most of them included a loving mother and father, along with siblings, grandparents, and a close-knit extended family. Other filmmakers in the 1990s tried to cash in on television nostalgia with such products as the campy, successful *Brady Bunch Movie* (1995).

More serious and realistic treatments of families appear in issue-oriented films. For example, poverty and its effects on rural families were shown in *Our Daily Bread* (1934), *The Grapes of Wrath* (1940), *Coal Miner's Daughter* (1980), *Places in the Heart* (1984), *The River* (1984), and *Country* (1984). These films all presented strong women who struggled to keep their families together, in spite of financial hard times. They also pointed to the inequities of an economic system that creates an underclass in the midst of a supposedly classless society. Such filmic critiques emerged after the Great Depression and again during the 1980s in part as a reaction to real-life hardships of people who were losing their family farms during this period.

Films often respond to social conflicts both during and after the fact. Although World War II produced some films that showed the effects of the war on families, a number of films emerged some time after the actual conflict. The influence of World War II on families emerged in *Mrs. Miniver* (1942) and later in *The Diary of Anne Frank* (1959) and *The Garden of the Finzi-Continis* (1971). During the 1960s and 1970s, revisionist filmmakers began to rethink the portrayal of war, but for the most part, the war in Vietnam did not immediately produce a direct filmic response. Some critics argued that the strong pacifist message in *Romeo and Juliet* (1968), Zeffirelli's adaptation of Shakespeare's tragic tale of battling families, was an indirect plea for peace in Vietnam. Not until 1989 did Oliver Stone produce *Born on the Fourth of July*, which depicted the transformation of real-life veteran Ron Kovic (played by Tom Cruise) from conservative patriot to war protester and paraplegic activist.

In traditional films, disasters from without may increase the loyalties of family members, but with the arrival of prosperity and affluence in the society, the family itself became the site of horror in many popular films. The horrific child and monstrous families were popular in the 1960s and 1970s in such films as *Village of the Damned* (1960), *Psycho* (1960), *Whatever Happened to Baby Jane?* (1962), *Rosemary's Baby* (1968), *Carrie* (1976), and *The Brood* (1979). David Lynch's cult classic *Eraserhead* (1978) offered one of the most disturbing visions of the monstrous baby in a surreal portrayal of a young man who impregnates his girlfriend and then must care for the nightmarish, maggotlike offspring of this union. More realistic but equally horrifying dysfunctional families have populated the screen since the 1950s, in *The Glass Menagerie* (1950), *A Streetcar Named Desire* (1951), and *Long Day's Journey into Night* (1962). Dystopian family scenes continued to occur often throughout the 1970s and 1980s in such works as *Death of a Salesman* (1986). Even darker visions of families emerged in *The Shining* (1980) and *Mosquito Coast* (1986), in narratives that included a father who gradually descended to utter madness as the family tried to cope with complete isolation.

In the late 1960s and early 1970s, the plight of dissatisfied housewives received attention in *Who's Afraid of Virginia Woolf?* (1966), *The Graduate* (1967), *Diary of a Mad Housewife* (1970), and *Woman under the Influence* (1974). Another film of this era that made a feminist statement in a different way is *The Stepford Wives* (1975), a satire depicting a society in which men have beautiful, subservient automatons for wives.

Incest and child molestation appear rarely, but those few films that dared to broach the subject received a great deal of public attention. Peter Lorre played the child-murdering villain in Fritz Lang's *M* (1931), which achieved international recognition for a subject later considered too shocking for most American filmmakers. James Mason played Nabokov's nymphet-obsessed Humbert Humbert in Stanley Kubrick's *Lolita* (1962), and Jeremy Irons took the role in Adrian Lyne's remake (1997), both of which received close scrutiny and some censorship. *Pretty Baby* (1978) caused a scandal in its depiction of the marriage between a photographer and an eleven-year-old prostitute, played by Brooke Shields, who posed nude for the film. *Dreamchild* (1985) treated the subject of the possible pedophile in an exquisitely subtle and delicate way in this story based on the real-life relationship between Charles Dodgson (Lewis Carroll) and the eponymous Alice Hargreaves, for whom *Alice in Wonderland* was written. An incestuous relationship between brother and sister was at the core of marital conflict in *Angels and Insects* (1995), in which a shy botanist married a beautiful wealthy woman who then produced children with a remarkable resemblance to her brother. Mother and son incest occurred in *Spanking the Monkey* (1994), a dark comedy depicting a conflicted relationship in a sensitive and subtle way. *Back to the Future* (1985) and its sequels comically flirted with incest in scenes of a young woman who was attracted to her own time-traveling son, much to his horror.

The demanding traditional father appeared in *Life with Father* (1947) and Spencer Tracy's *Father of the Bride* (1950) and was softened to a comic figure in the 1991 and 1995 remakes, with Steve Martin. *The Great Santini* (1980), *My Left Foot* (1989), *Eat Drink Man Woman* (1994), and *Meet the Parents* (2000) all depicted strict loving fathers who may cause some damage to their offspring but who ultimately merit love and respect. Dynastic families headed by strong father figures appeared in such essentially conservative films as *Giant* (1956), *Duel in the Sun* (1946), *The Godfather* (1972, 1974), and *Henry V.* Shakespeare's plays contributed a number of stories to the repertoire of dynastic film families, the most successful of which included adaptations and remakes of *Hamlet*, *King Lear*, *King Henry V*, *Romeo and Juliet*, and *The Tempest.*

Unconventional families constitute by far the largest percentage of film portrayals, often demonstrating a tension between traditional customs and new values and practices. *Friendly Persuasion* (1956) looked at a Quaker family's attempt to maintain their peaceful traditions during the war between the states, as the son explored whether he was remaining a pacifist because of his religion conviction or out of cowardice. Other kinds of outsider families have appeared in films that depicted idiocentric family ties. For example, intense relationships among eccentric siblings figured prominently in *The Accidental Tourist* (1988), which focused on a man who lost his wife and son and relied on his controlling siblings for emotional support. *Avalon* (1990) showed the subtle deterioration of a tightly knit Russian Jewish family after their move to the United States following World War II. In *Dim Sum* (1985), a mother and daughter wrestled with conflicts between tradition and Western customs. *The Wedding Banquet* (1993) looked at a more complicated conflict of values in the story of a homosexual who marries a woman and then must present her to his old-fashioned Chinese parents who come to the United States for their wedding. The *Joy Luck Club* (1993), based on Amy Tan's popular novel, depicted the complex network of relationships among sisters, aunts, mothers, and daughters of Chinese immigrants and their daughters.

Films of the 1980s tended to reflect the concerns of the baby boomer generation. For example, grown or middle-aged children and their aging parents confronted wounds from childhood and sought reconciliation in *Tell Me a Riddle* (1980), *On Golden Pond* (1980), and *Tender Mercies* (1983). The popular film *Cocoon* (1985, 1988) provided a fantasy solution to the difficulties of aging by allowing a group of octogenarians to regain their youth and then leave the planet with an extraterrestrial, rather than grow old and die. At the other end of the stylistic and genre spectrum, Wim Wenders's *Paris, Texas* (1984) showed the reconciliation of a roving man with his child, followed by a bittersweet encounter with his estranged wife.

Another concern that affected families of the 1980s was the rise in the number of women working outside the home. The negative portrayal of career women occurred frequently in films of the 1980s, a trend that was documented in Susan Faludi's book *Backlash* (Faludi 1991). Some films tried to demonstrate that all a career woman really needed was a home, husband, and family. For example, in *Baby Boom* (1987), Diane Keaton played an ambitious career woman saddled with an orphaned baby, both of whom were rescued by a kind-hearted veterinarian (Sam Shepard), who brought romance and the standard happy ending to the film. In a number of other films, such as *Fatal Attraction* (1987), working women were depicted as hopelessly neurotic or even psychotic home wreckers. The ending of *Fatal Attraction* was even altered for American audiences to show the triumph of the housewife (Anne Archer) over Glenn Close's insane career woman.

Films dealing with racial conflicts appeared as early as D.W. Griffith's *Intolerance* (1916) and later in *Intruder in the Dust* (1949), a serious look at the effects of racism on families and the criminal justice system. *The Unforgiven* (1960) cast Audrey Hepburn as an adoptive Indian who had believed herself to be a part of a white family. Based on Lorraine Hansbury's play, the films *A Raisin in the Sun* (1961) and its 1989 remake depicted a family torn apart by the pressures of moving into an all-white neighborhood. *Guess Who's Coming to Dinner* (1967) brought up the issue of intermarriage, questioning the sincerity of liberals who claim to believe in equality until their white daughter brings home a black man she intends to marry. *Mississippi Masala* (1992) depicted a romance between the daughter of an Indian family from Kenya and an African American, showing how the couple overcame the Indian family's prejudice against blacks. In *A Family Thing* (1996), a white man discovered that he was related to a black family, and the ensuing struggle for understanding challenged both sides to open their minds and hearts.

Young women enter and transform families in various genres, from supernatural thrillers to musicals. Three adaptations of Henry James's ambiguous *Turn of the Screw* showed a young English nanny trying to rescue the souls of children from what she perceived to be evil spirits. *Jane Eyre* (1944), *The King and I* (1956), *Mary Poppins* (1964), and *The Miracle Worker* (1962) all showed spirited young women coming into a household, surmounting obstacles, and improving the lives of its inhabitants. By the 1980s and 1990s such nanny figures were more often than not sinister figures with intentions of seducing or killing family members, as in *The Hand That Rocks the Cradle* (1992).

A number of children's films take children away from the family, following the classic archetype of the myth of the hero—expulsion from society, a period of trial, symbolic wounding, spiritual growth, and eventual redemption and reconciliation. Fantasy and science fiction films have always provided children with a means of escape from a mundane or dysfunctional family setting—for example, *The Wizard of Oz* (1939), *Peter Pan* (1952), *ET—The Extraterrestrial* (1982), *Labyrinth* (1986), and *The Secret of Roan Inish* (1994). Another sort of escape occurred when a father and son exchanged bodies and lives in Penny Marshall's popular *Big* (1988). Other more realistic transformations of spoiled orphaned children occurred in four versions of *The Secret Garden* (1949, 1984, 1987, 1993) and *The Little Princess* (1939, 1987, 1995). In several adaptations of *Anne of Green Gables* (1934, 1983, 1985), a creative orphan brought new life and imagination to a lonely couple and to a stodgy brother and sister.

Horrific cannibalistic families appeared in *Night of the Living Dead* (1968), *Texas*

Chain Saw Massacre (1974), and *Parents* (1989). Often these horror films become cult classics, with their elements of campy humor and self-reflexive exaggeration. They draw from an earlier tradition combining humor and murder in such films as *Arsenic and Old Lace* (1944), *Kind Hearts and Coronets* (1949), and *Family Plot* (1976). In *Arsenic and Old Lace*, two dotty sisters took in elderly bachelors and poisoned them "for their own good," to put them out of their lonely misery. *Kind Hearts and Coronets* featured Peter Sellers playing a murderer and all the eight parts of his family that he intends to eliminate in order to get an inheritance. Alfred Hitchcock's last film, *Family Plot*, involved an entire family in a diamond heist and a search for a missing heir.

The quest for a family and the struggle to escape a cruel family serve as important themes in *Cinderella* (1950, 1964, 1984, 1997), *Snow White and the Seven Dwarfs* (1937), and *Sleeping Beauty* (1959). Motherly devotion occurred in *Dumbo* (1941), Disney's famous cartoon about a mother elephant who loves her large-eared infant in spite of his ungainly appearance, singing to him the famous "Baby of Mine." Orphaned or single-parent offspring are popular fodder for Disney animated films, including *Bambi* (1942), *The Little Mermaid* (1989), *Beauty and the Beast* (1991), and *The Lion King* (1994). Although many of these stories are loosely based on legends, history, or fairy tales that originally had rather gruesome or unhappy endings, the Disney versions of these tales usually conclude with standard reconciliations and restoration of traditional family structures, with the boy and girl finding true romance and living happily ever after. Even those films based on real-life

figures distort the facts in order to romanticize their fictive families. For example, *Pocahontas* (1995) does not show how Pocahontas married someone besides John Smith, moved to England, and died of smallpox at twenty-one.

Although most family movies stick to well-tested formulas, a few films present complex, ambiguous portrayals of family relationships. For example, Ingmar Bergman's highly autobiographical *Fanny and Alexander* (1983) showed the textured richness of domestic life and of parent-child and sibling relationships as the family coped with death, reconciliation, and separation. *What's Eating Gilbert Grape?* (1993) was a sensitive portrayal of a young man (Johnny Depp) whose extremely obese mother and retarded younger brother placed enormous pressures on him to remain with his family, in spite of his desire to escape and live a normal life. Atom Egoyan's *The Sweet Hereafter* (1996) portrayed a family and an entire community attempting to deal with the death of children in a school bus accident. *The Whales of August* (1987) and *Hilary and Jackie* (1998) showed the complex relationships between sisters as they faced the prospect of death.

The films of the 1990s and the beginning of the new millennium show family as a source of strength and renewal, but it is rarely the traditional nuclear family of biological mother, father, and children. Often it is a family that is pieced together from slightly used or damaged parts, as in *The Piano* (1993), *Jerry McGuire* (1996), and *As Good as It Gets* (1997). *The Family Man* (2001) reworking of *It's a Wonderful Life* created a tale in which the family turns out to be the alternate, imagined, or dreamed reality, demonstrating a cultural anxiety about choices between family and financial success. Films such as *Pleasantville* (1998) and *American Beauty* (2000) self-consciously parodied conventional American families, even as they demonstrated the love and desperate loneliness that draw audiences to the perennial myth of the happy family.

—*Rebecca Bell-Metereau*

See also Literature, Images of Families in Children's

References and Further Reading
Adams, Thelma. "New York Post Family Film Guide." http://www.nypost.com/03042000/living/25656.htm (cited 4 March 2000).
Bell, Elizabeth, Lynda Haas, and Laura Sells, eds. 1995. *From Mouse to Mermaid.* Bloomington: Indiana University Press.
Catchpole, Terry and Catherine. 1992. *The Family Video Guide: Over 300 Movies to Share with Your Children.* Charlotte, VT: Williamson Publishing.
Claire Liebman, Nina. 1995. *Living Room Lectures: The Fifties Family in Film and Television.* Austin: University of Texas Press.
Connors, Martin, and Jim Craddock, eds. 2001. *VideoHound's Golden Movie Retriever.* Detroit: Visible Ink Press.
Ellis, John. 1992. *Visible Fictions.* New York: Routledge.
Faludi, Susan. 1991. *Backlash: The Undeclared War against American Women.* New York: Crown Publishers.
Francke, Lizzie. 1993. "Men, Women, Children and the Baby Boom Movies." In *Women and Film: A Sight and Sound Reader,* edited by Pam Cook and Philip Dodd, 148–155. Philadelphia: Temple University Press.
Gledhill, Christine, ed. 1987. *Home Is Where the Heart Is: Studies in Melodrama and the Woman's Film.* London: British Film Institute.
Greenwald, Toby Klein. "The Family View on Film or Who's Afraid of the Big (and Small) Screen?" WholeFamily Room. http://www.wholefamily.com/family_room/aboutyourfamily/film_reviews/introduction.html (cited 1 April 2001).
Harwood, Sarah. 1997. *Family Fictions: Representations of the Family in 1980s Hollywood.* New York: St. Martin's.
Maltin, Leonard. *Leonard Maltin's Family Film Guide.* 1999. New York: Signet.
Monaco, James. 2000. *How to Read a Film: The World of Movies, Media, and Multimedia.* 3d ed. Oxford: Oxford University Press.
Tuchman, Gaye, Arlene K. Daniels, and James Benet, eds. 1978. *Hearth and Home: Images of Women in the Mass Media.* New York: Oxford University Press.
Tufte, Virginia, and Barbara Myerhoff, eds. 1981. *Changing Images of the Family.* New Haven: Yale University Press.
Wexman, Virginia Wright. 1993. *Creating the Couple: Love, Marriage, and Hollywood Performance.* Princeton, NJ: Princeton University Press.
Williams, Tony. 1996. *Hearths of Darkness: The Family in the American Horror Film.* Madison, NJ: Fairleigh Dickinson University Press.

Family and Medical Leave Act

In 1993, the U.S. Congress enacted the Family and Medical Leave Act (FMLA). The FMLA permits eligible employees to take unpaid leave from their jobs in order to address certain personal and family concerns such as securing treatment for a serious health condition, caring for a newborn or adopted child, or caring for an immediate family member with a serious health condition.

Family and medical leave legislation became a significant political issue during the 1980s, backed by a diverse coalition of feminist, labor, and religious organizations. Supporters of such legislation cited the changing demographics of the workforce in the United States. In particular, they emphasized that since the 1950s, the number of women working outside of the home had dramatically increased, leading to large numbers of U.S. households with either a single working parent or two parents employed outside the home. Indeed, by the 1990s, about two-thirds of American mothers worked outside of the home (Decker 2000). During the 1980s and early 1990s, more than thirty state legislatures enacted legislation that provided employees with family or medical leave, but Pres. George Bush repeatedly vetoed congressional efforts to enact federal legislation. With the enthusiastic support of newly elected Pres. William Clinton, the FMLA became law in February 1993, thereby making the United States one of the last industrial nations to guarantee such leaves of absence.

The FMLA obliges employers with at least fifty employees to grant any employee with at least one year of service up to twelve weeks of annual unpaid leave, thereby providing coverage for more than 50 million private-sector employees and 15 million state and local government employees. Within the first three years of the FMLA, 58 percent of the leave takers were women, and 59 percent of the leave takers did so for reasons of their own serious health condition (Decker 2000).

—*Davison M. Douglas*

References and Further Reading
Commission on Family and Medical Leave. 1996. *A Workable Balance: Report to the Congress on Family and Medical Leave Policies.* Washington, DC: Government Printing Office.
Decker, Kurt H. 2000. *Family and Medical Leave in a Nutshell.* St. Paul, MN: West Group.
Moore, Maureen F., and Jonathan L. Alder. 1993. *Family and Medical Leave: Federal and State Requirements.* Austin, TX: Butterworth Legal Publishers.
U.S. Senate Committee on Labor and Human Resources. 1993. *Family and Medical Leave Act of 1993.* 103d Cong., 1st sess. S. Rept. 3. Washington, DC: Government Printing Office.

Family and the Law

One of the defining features of a liberal political system is its commitment to a private sphere of family relations: State involvement in family life is widely believed to be warranted only in unusual circumstances. An extensive patchwork of state and federal statutes and judicial doctrines in the United States, however, not only determines what relationships count as family relationships but also defines the rights and duties family members have vis-à-vis each other, third parties, and the state. To a large extent, then, the family is constructed by the legal regime within which it is embedded.

Family law is difficult to summarize. Problems touching on the family can be found in virtually all areas of legal endeavor, from civil laws governing the distribution of property to statutes defining the custody rights of married and unmarried parents to criminal proceedings for child abuse or neglect. Moreover, the fluidity and multiplicity of family relationships complicate efforts to articulate general legal principles: The statutes governing family issues often leave considerable discretion in courts to resolve cases in order to effect a fair and equitable result. Finally, family law is a quintessentially local area of law, with wide variations in the rules from state to state.

Rules governing the family derive from both common law and ecclesiastical traditions. In the United States, the general outlines of a system of family law emerged throughout the nineteenth century, as common-law doctrines were shaped into formal legal codes. That codification of family law expressed the values of an emergent bourgeois culture, and those values remained largely static for a century. By the middle of the twentieth century, however, large changes in the structure of the national economy and the demographics of American society stressed a legal regime designed for a static, idealized family form. A number of social developments emerged to challenge the values that had long been taken for granted in legal treatments of the family and intimate relationships. The civil rights movement, the women's movement, and the emerging gay and lesbian activist movement, among others, questioned the traditional justifications behind rules regulating the family. All of these groups mounted legal and constitutional challenges to a variety of state and local rules regulating the family and intimate relationships.

State and Federal Regulation of the Family

For the greater part of U.S. history, family law was exclusively a state arena. Family law rules were articulated by state legislatures, which had plenary power to enact regulations designed to promote their citizens' health, safety, welfare, and morals; those rules were interpreted and supplemented by state courts as they resolved particular issues. Thus, rules governing subjects as diverse as divorce to interracial marriage to domestic violence varied widely from state to state, and until the mid-1960s, state legislatures had virtually unlimited authority to develop legal regimes reflecting mainstream opinions about proper conduct in intimate relationships. In the few cases challenging state laws that reached the U.S. Supreme Court, state authority to regulate the family was largely sustained. In the 1878 case of *Reynolds* v. *United States*, 98 U.S. 145, for example, the Supreme Court upheld the bigamy prosecution of a Mormon despite his claim that his practice of polygamy was protected by the U.S. Con-

stitution's guarantee of religious rights under the First Amendment. The Court noted that marriage was the social relationship upon which society was built and opined that without doubt, states could regulate that institution: "[I]t is within the legitimate scope of the power of every civil government to determine whether polygamy or monogamy shall be the law of social life under its dominion."

In *Meyer* v. *Nebraska*, 262 U.S. 390 (1923), and *Pierce* v. *Society of Sisters*, 268 U.S. 510 (1925), the U.S. Supreme Court considered the extent to which the states could require children to be educated in English only or solely in public schools, respectively. In both cases, the Court recognized a limited right to family autonomy under the Fourteenth Amendment to the U.S. Constitution that, according to the Court in *Meyer*, included "the right of the individual . . .to marry, establish a home and bring up children. . . ." In both cases, the Court overturned the state statutes in issue, while nonetheless holding that states could compel school attendance and regulate school curriculum. In a third case addressing the scope of parental authority over children, *Prince* v. *Commonwealth of Massachusetts*, 321 U.S. 158 (1944), the Court sustained the conviction of Sarah Prince for violating child labor laws by allowing her nine-year-old niece to accompany her in distributing literature for the Jehovah's Witnesses on a December evening. Denying Prince's claim that her actions were protected by the constitution's guarantee of religious freedom, the Court held that "the state has a wide range of power for limiting parental freedom and authority in things affecting [a] child's welfare."

On two occasions prior to 1965, the Court considered the scope of individual freedom in matters of reproductive choice.

In the first, *Buck* v. *Bell,* 274 U.S. 200 (1927), the Court held that an allegedly mentally retarded woman had no right to resist a state decision to sterilize her against her will, given the state's interest in reducing the number of dependents that might "sap [its] strength." Subsequently, the Court overturned a statute requiring mandatory sterilization of any individual found to be a habitual criminal, not because it violated a fundamental right to procreate but because the statute singled out only some kinds of crimes for the penalty and thus violated guarantees of equal protection (*Skinner* v. *Oklahoma,* 316 U.S. 525 [1942]).

In 1965, the U.S. Supreme Court expressly articulated a due process right to marital privacy in the case of *Griswold* v. *Connecticut,* 381 U.S. 479 (1965), finding a substantive right guaranteeing marital couples access to contraceptives. That due process right was extended to grant individuals the right to contraceptives in *Eisenstadt* v. *Baird,* 405 U.S. 438 (1971) and extended again to guarantee abortion rights to women in *Roe* v. *Wade,* 410 U.S. 113 (1973). This articulation of substantive constitutional rights protecting the family and intimate relations initiated a major change in family law throughout the nation, as the rationales previously asserted by states to justify their regulatory schemes became open to challenge. From 1965 to the turn of the century, both the U.S. Supreme Court and state courts and legislatures would reshape the face of family law in accordance with new understandings of family privacy, individual autonomy, and the meaning of equal protection. Those changes will be briefly noted in the following discussion of the substantive areas of family law.

Marriage

Historically, marriage merged husband and wife into a single legal entity, with the husband vested with authority to manage the internal and external affairs of the family unit.

Today, the law recognizes the marital family as a unit of related but independent actors. The recognition of gender discrimination as a violation of equal protection guarantees under the Fourteenth Amendment, beginning with *Reed* v. *Reed,* 404 U.S. 71 (1971), has contributed to equalizing the status of men and women both inside and outside of the marital relationship.

States generally impose few restrictions upon the right to marry, imposing license requirements and minimal age requirements, limiting marriages among close relatives, and prohibiting concurrent marriages. Until 1968, the majority of American states limited interracial marriages; those statutes were rendered invalid after the U.S. Supreme Court overturned Virginia's miscegenation laws on both due process and equal protection grounds in *Loving* v. *Virginia,* 388 U.S. 1 (1968). Marriage continues to be a legal status obtainable only by heterosexual couples, except in Vermont, where same-sex marriages were recognized in 1999.

Marriage is favored by public policy: Marriage typically yields a variety of benefits for the parties, third parties (especially creditors), and the public, since marriage provides a shorthand way of assigning responsibility for debts and dependency. States generally may not impose conditions that unduly restrict the ability of an individual to marry. In *Zablocki* v. *Redhail,* 434 U.S. 374 (1979), the Supreme Court invalidated a Wisconsin law prohibiting any individual owing child support from obtaining a license to remarry, citing the strong public policy favoring marital over nonmarital relationships. Indeed, many states historically recognized common-law marriages—those in which the parties held themselves out as married, either expressly or by implication—as valid and binding with all of the rights, privileges, and obligations incident to formal marriage. A few states continue to recognize common-law marriages on a par with formal marriages.

Traditionally, unmarried cohabitation was presumed to be immoral, and the parties could be subjected to a variety of criminal charges. In recent decades, the enormous increase in the number of unmarried couples in the United States has produced increased pressure not only to remove the criminal sanctions against such relationships but also to recognize such unions in their own right. The majority of states today allow cohabiting heterosexual couples to make some claims for support and property division should a relationship end, although virtually no states make such allowances for same-sex cohabiting couples. Some localities have passed domestic partnership ordinances that allow cohabiting couples to register their relationships and extend limited benefits to the partners in such relationships. Most states also grant limited recognition to contracts between such partners, although enforcement is limited if the terms of the contract violate public policy.

Marital Property

Historically, marriage has been of critical importance for managing family wealth. Marital property may be real or personal; in recent decades, public and private entitlements such as pensions and Social Security have become important features of the marital estate. Under the common-law tradition that governed marital relations during the first decades of this nation's history, a woman's separate property became her husband's property upon marriage, although her property could be distributed to her heirs upon her death or recaptured by her upon the death of her husband. The passage of the married women's property acts beginning in the 1840s restored a woman's capacity to manage her separate property. Property acquired or bestowed upon the marital estate during the course of the marriage was traditionally considered the property of the husband as head of the household. Even if it was jointly owned, as in a community property state, wives had little control over property since it was subject to the husband's management. As a result, courts developed a variety of doctrines such as joint tenancy and tenancy by the entirety recognizing legal and equitable interests of the wife. Today, marital property is generally considered to be jointly owned, and upon divorce is subject to equitable distribution, vesting considerable authority in a trial judge to distribute property in a manner that treats both parties fairly.

Intervention in Intact Marriages

In most cases, married families whose members are not receiving public assistance are free of state intervention in their day-to-day lives. Courts are reluctant to intervene in the management of family wealth if a marriage is intact and the family is relatively self-sufficient. Statutes in all states, however, impose upon parents a duty to support their children. A few states impose a similar obligation upon adult children to support impoverished parents under specified circumstances.

The last three decades have seen significant changes in two areas concerning intact families, however. State statutes requiring married women to consult with or obtain permission from a husband prior to obtaining an abortion were deemed unconstitutional in *Planned Parenthood of Central Missouri* v. *Danforth,* 428 U.S. 52 (1976), granting married women autonomy rights in reproductive matters. In addition, although marital partners were exempted from laws prohibiting rape, the marital rape exemption has been largely eliminated from state criminal codes, as has immunity for other criminal acts such as assault during the course of a marriage. The judicially created doctrine of interspousal tort immunity has also been discarded in the majority of states, allowing spouses to bring actions for various torts against one another.

Divorce

Statutes allowing the dissolution of marriages by divorce historically required a finding of fault by one of the parties. In the 1970s, a movement to allow no-fault divorces gained momentum, and today all states have statutory provisions allowing the parties to obtain a divorce without proving that one of the parties is at fault.

Property Division upon Divorce. With some minor variations, state courts are empowered to equitably divide property between the spouses upon divorce without regard to misconduct. In dividing the property, most state statutes instruct the court to consider the contribution of each spouse to acquiring and maintaining the property, including the contribution of a spouse who did not work outside of the home. Pensions and other forms of new property are typically accounted for in the division of assets. The public policy supporting such divisions of property favors placing both parties in a position that allows them to move forward in their lives and avoid becoming public dependents. Courts will enforce provisions of a prenuptial agreement unless there is evidence that the agreement was made under duress or the enforcement of the agreement would be against public policy.

Support Obligations upon Divorce. Spousal support or alimony, which has never been widely awarded, is still available in all states. Some states allow marital misconduct to be a factor in setting the level of support. The more crucial factors typically turn on the duration of the marriage and the ability of both spouses to generate an income sufficient for their needs. The obligation to support children of a marriage continues after dissolution of a marriage and may not be negotiated away by either of the parties; the obligation of support extends to both parents. The obligation exists independent of custodianship of the children. Although levels of support were initially left to the discretion of courts, all state divorce codes now have statutory formulas setting out minimum levels of child support. These statutes allow courts to increase the level of support if necessary under the particular circumstances of a case, depending on factors such as the child's special needs and the family's predivorce standard of living. Courts vary on the extent to which parents have an obligation to support a child beyond the child's majority, for college, or because the child has other needs. Therefore, most agreements today contain provisions directly addressing parental support obligations upon the child's majority. Both spousal and child support may be modified in the event that the circumstances of any party materially change. Remarriage does not affect the obligation to pay child support, although in some states, stepparents become secondarily liable for the support of children living in their households.

Because child support obligations have often been neglected by noncustodial parents, enforcement has become a major activity in family law. Federal welfare laws require states to create support enforcement programs as a condition for receiving federal welfare funds. Enforcement programs vary from state to state but typically include provisions requiring mothers receiving public assistance to identify fathers and assist the state in bringing paternity actions. In *Bowen* v. *Gilliard*, 483 U.S. 587 (1987), the Supreme Court upheld a provision of the Deficit Reduction Act of 1984 requiring that child support received for any particular child in a home be counted toward the family's total income in determining eligibility for welfare assistance

Child Custody and Visitation upon Divorce. During the late nineteenth century, rules governing child custody shifted from the presumption that children should be placed with a father upon divorce to a presumption awarding custody to the mother of a child of "tender years," which presumption endured through the 1970s. Today, both parents are presumed to be entitled to custody, although statutes in many states bestow a preference upon the child's primary caregiver. Statutes direct courts to place the child in accordance with the child's "best interests," determined by an individual-

ized assessment of the circumstances of both parents and the child. Both legal and physical custody may be awarded to either one or both parents jointly. In the interest of stabilizing the child's situation, custody may be modified thereafter only upon a showing that there has been a substantial change in circumstances that materially affect the child's well-being. In *Palmore* v. *Sidoti*, 466 U.S. 429 (1984), for example, the U.S. Supreme Court held that a mother's remarriage to someone of a different race was not, in itself, sufficient grounds for modifying the mother's custody. Likewise, most states today hold that cohabitation with a partner of the opposite sex will not provide a reason for modification of custody, although same-sex cohabitation is treated far more erratically. There is no clear trend with respect to modification of custody orders when a custodial parent seeks to move and that move impairs the custody or visitation rights of the noncustodial or joint custodial parents. The party seeking to move must typically receive permission from a court, but decisions are widely split respecting when such moves will be allowed.

Visitation is often liberally awarded, although courts have discretion to limit or discontinue visitation by a noncustodial parent if warranted by the circumstances. Statutes in all fifty states grant visitation rights to third parties. Most of those statutes extend only to grandparents, but in some states, any third party may petition for and be awarded visitation if it serves the child's interests. In *Troxel* v. *Granville*, 530 U.S. 57 (2000), the U.S. Supreme Court held that a parent's judgment about who may visit a child is entitled to substantial deference if the parent objects to visitation by grandparents or others.

Determining Parenthood

The law's ability to define parenthood substantially affects social understandings of the family, especially at a time when parenthood can be multiple. In all states today, a child born or conceived during the course of a valid marriage is presumed to be the child of the husband, but that presumption is rebuttable under certain circumstances. In *Michael H.* v. *Gerald D.*, 491 U.S. 110 (1989), under a statute that has since been changed, the Supreme Court refused to allow a man to introduce deoxyribonucleic acid (DNA) evidence of his paternity of the child he fathered with the child's mother. The mother had reconciled with her husband and sought to exclude the biological father from the family's life. The Court found a public policy interest in protecting the marital family from claims by outsiders, holding that there was no basis in U.S. history or traditions for recognizing the right of a third party to claim paternity in the face of an intact family.

Putative fathers have an obligation to support their offspring, but until the 1970s had no presumptive right to visit or have custody of their children. In a series of cases beginning with *Stanley* v. *Illinois*, 405 U.S. 645 (1972), the Supreme Court recognized the right of putative fathers to custody of their children. Subsequent cases expanded those rights and now extend such fathers' rights to notice of adoption or other proceedings affecting their parental status or the care of their children. The statutes also grant various forms of authority to veto adoption proceedings.

Persons engaged in a variety of family forms are increasingly seeking legal recognition, and no clear legal principles have emerged. A city may not define a single-family housing zone to exclude extended biological families (*Moore* v. *East Cleveland*, 431 U.S. 494 [1977]), for example, but it may exclude groups of adults unrelated by biology or marriage from claiming that status; foster families are not entitled to the same rights as biological families, despite the fact that ties between foster families and children may be deep and affectionate (*Smith* v. *OFFER*, 431 U.S. 816 [1977]). Gay and lesbian couples are not recognized as families in most states, and such individuals coparenting children are typically denied legal status as parents. A few states, such as Massachusetts, do permit the same-sex partner of a gay or lesbian parent to adopt. Stepparents occupy a fuzzy space in family law, with few if any rights to continue relationships with children if a marriage ends.

Adoptive families are recognized in the same manner that biological nuclear families are recognized. Even that area has seen substantial changes, however. When adoptions were first recognized in U.S. law, the adoptive family entirely replaced a child's biological family: All ties to the birth parents were severed, and a new family was created. In recent years, pressure to allow adult adoptees access to information about their biological families has mounted, and many states permit courts to open such records upon a showing of "good cause." Increasingly, adoption has become more open, in proceedings that do not entirely erase the ties of the biological family. These "open adoptions" are typically negotiated between the parties, but enforcement may be difficult, since the law's recognition of the right of the adoptive parent to raise a child as he or she sees fit will generally defeat an effort by a biological parent to enforce an open adoption agreement.

Finally, courts and state legislatures have struggled to come up with rules regulating the new forms of parenting made possible by alternative reproductive technologies. Today, it is possible for a child to have up to five parents: a sperm donor, an egg donor, a gestational mother, and the mother and father who raise and support that child. Statutes in all states limit the rights of sperm and egg donors, but the rules are much less clear for surrogates who are either the child's gestational or gestational and genetic mother. The majority of states allow women to enter into surrogate arrangements but refuse to enforce private contracts should the surrogate mother change her mind about surrendering the child at birth.

Parental Rights Although the U.S. Constitution generally protects the right of parents to rear their children as they see fit, many statutes and regulations restrict parental choices, most notably the requirement that children attend school. Home schooling is permitted in most states, with regulations varying from the summary requirement that home education must be "equivalent" to that of public instruction to regulatory schemes requiring local school board approval of plans. In *Wisconsin* v. *Yoder*, 406 U.S. 205 (1972), the Supreme Court upheld the right of Amish parents to remove their children from public schools after the eighth grade. The Court found that the parents' religious beliefs permitted an exemption from the compulsory school laws and that the children were adequately educated for life in an Amish community by the time they had reached the age of fourteen. The state does not intervene in parents' choices about their children's upbringing without a showing that a parent is unfit or abusive; states generally create an exemption to their penal codes allowing parents to utilize routine corporal punishment to discipline children.

The law is unsettled about the extent to which parents may choose medical care for children. In *Parham* v. *J.R.*, 442 U.S. 584 (1979), the Supreme Court held that parents may commit a child to a mental institution against his wishes, although the child may be entitled to a hearing after commitment. A parent's decision to forgo medical care for a child, however, may be overridden by a court if the court finds that the child's life is in danger or that the medical procedure poses little risk and promises to substantially improve the child's life. A federal statute now requires states to prevent medical neglect of disabled infants as a condition of receiving federal welfare funds.

Children's Rights. Children's rights vis-à-vis the family are limited, in part because of their dependent status and in part because the rights that children need and assert are different in kind from those generally recognized in the U.S. legal system. Rights to nurture, rights to health, and rights to education, for example, require active intervention by the state rather than respect for family boundaries. The Supreme Court expressly rejected the claim of a child to continued care and affection from an established caregiver in the 1989 case of *Michael H.*, noted above. In *Deshaney* v. *Winnebago County*, 489 U.S. 189 (1089), the Supreme Court refused to recognize a child's constitutional right to protection from parental harm, holding that a county welfare agency did not deny any liberty interests when it failed to protect a four-year-old child from being beaten into a permanent vegetative state by his father. The Court noted that children are protected instead by statutes that impose criminal liability for abuse and neglect and set up welfare systems to care for abused and neglected children. The abortion context provides a few exceptions: Minors may obtain an abortion in many states under statutes allowing them to bypass parental permission requirements by seeking authorization from a judge. Efforts by state legislatures to limit minors' abortion rights by requiring minors to obtain permission from both parents have also been rejected by courts.

Family Abuse and Neglect

The law, finally, is intricately involved in families when problems of abuse and neglect arise. Statutes define physical and emotional abuse as grounds for both criminal and civil proceedings, with results that may range from supervision and counseling of the family to termination of parental rights to criminal prosecution. Sexual abuse within the family has gained increasing attention in the last two decades, although it occurs less frequently than other forms of child abuse. Parents have a duty to protect children from harm and may be prosecuted in many states for a breach of that duty. In some states, parents may be prosecuted for failing to protect a child from abuse by another parent or adult in the household. Neglect may similarly trigger a number of responses from counseling to termination of parental rights and criminal prosecution.

Juvenile Courts

Although juvenile courts exist in the main to deal with public offenses by minors, they are often the forum within which parent/child conflicts are managed. Proceedings may be invoked by parents seeking to transfer care of the child to the state or by the state acting on behalf of the

child and arise in instances as diverse as parents claiming that a child is out of control to objecting to a child's same-sex dating. Alternately, a parent or child may seek emancipation, a proceeding that may result in partial or complete severance of the parent/child relationship.

—*Alice Hearst*

See also Adoptive Parents; Alimony; Child Abuse; Child Custody; Divorce, History of; Family Courts; Juvenile Justice; Stepparents

References and Further Reading
Coontz, Stephanie. 1992. *The Way We Never Were: American Families and the Nostalgia Trap.* New York: Basic Books.
Cott, Nancy F. 2000. *Public Vows: A History of Marriage and the Nation.* Cambridge: Harvard University Press.
Dailey, Anne C. 1993. "Constitutional Privacy and the Just Family." *Tulane Law Review* 67 (March): 955.
Davis, Peggy Cooper. 1997. *Neglected Stories: The Constitution and Family Values.* New York: Hill and Wang.
Dolgin, Janet. 1997. *Defining the Family: Law, Technology and Reproduction in an Uneasy Age.* New York: New York University Press.
Fineman, Martha A. 1995. *The Neutered Mother, the Sexual Family and Other Twentieth-Century Tragedies.* New York: Routledge.
Grossberg, Michael. 1985. *Governing the Hearth: Law and the Family in Nineteenth-Century America.* Chapel Hill: University of North Carolina Press.
Harris, Leslie J., Lee E. Teitelbaum, and Carol A. Weisbrod. 1996. *Family Law.* Boston: Little, Brown.
Hartog, Hendrik. 2000. *Man and Wife in America: A History.* Cambridge: Harvard University Press.
Lindsay, Matthew J. 1998. "Reproducing a Fit Citizenry: Dependency, Eugenics and the Law of Marriage in the United States, 1860–1920." *Law and Social Inquiry* 23 (Summer): 541.
Minow, Martha. 1987. "We, the Family: Constitutional Rights and American Families." *Journal of American History* 74(3): 959.

Minow, Martha, and Mary Lyndon
Shanley. 1996. "Revisioning the Family
in Liberal Political Thought and Law."
Hypatia 11(1): 4–29.

Regan, Milton C., Jr. 1999. *Alone
Together: Law and the Meanings of
Marriage.* New York: Oxford University
Press.

Rubin, Eva R. 1986. *The Supreme Court
and the American Family.* Westport,
CT: Greenwood Press.

Stevens, Jacqueline. 1999. *Reproducing the
State.* Princeton, NJ: Princeton
University Press.

Teitelbaum, Lee E. 1999. "Children's
Rights and the Problem of Equal
Respect." *Hofstra Law Review* 27
(Summer): 799.

Woodhouse, Barbara. 1993. "Hatching the
Egg: A Child-Centered Perspective on
Parents' Rights." *Cardozo Law Review*
14 (May): 1747.

Young, Alison H. 1998. "Reconceiving the
Family: Challenging the Paradigm of the
Exclusive Family." *American
University Journal of Gender and Law*
6 (Summer): 505.

Family as a Political Theme

Families are the most central and enduring social unit. As such, they constitute
the primary economic, educational, religious, and cultural engine of viable societies; thus, their intimate interiors become the objects of serious political
interest and debate. Despite the fact that
we often think of our families as merely
of private concern, families and family
dynamics are of utmost concern to governments and the political process. The
ideas of in loco parentis ("in place of parents") and parens patriae (that is, the government's capacity of guardian, heir, and
protector of all citizens unable to protect
themselves) both reflect the linkage
between families and the state when families are unable to function effectively.
Recent studies show that families are the
most important factor in decreasing
youths' sexual activity, suicide, drug use,
and violence ("No Child Left Behind Act"
2001, 342). "The National Longitudinal
Study of Adolescent Health (1997) found
that drug and violence prevention programs that incorporate 'protective factors'
tend to reduce drug use and violence. Protective factors include a student feeling
connected to parents and family, having
parents present at key times of the day,
having high educational expectations,
feeling part of the school, and having high
esteem" (342). The centrality of families
in civil life, the definitions of family, government programs aimed at helping families, and politicians' family lives all have
political dimensions.

Since all of us are someone's children,
and since all of us grew up in some type
of family arrangement (no matter how
that family might be constituted), most
individuals have opinions about the family, family values, and what is ideal and
problematic within families. Because of
this shared experience of living in families (no matter how diversely constituted
or enacted), politicians freely address
family life, knowing of their immediate
and central relevance to their con-
stituents. In the contemporary United
States, family and sex, like the topic of
education, "have become less and less
matters of private life and more ones of
nearly obsessive political debate" (Botstein 1997, 28).

The mere definition of the word *family*
is historically contingent; the word *family* has both biological and social meanings (Cooey 1996, 15). Family structures
can be large and extended, two-person
(the census delineation of double-income,
no kids), or single-parent; it can include
children or the elderly; and it may involve
family forms not officially sanctioned by
the state such as homosexual unions or
multiple marriage partners (although the

in a larger historical perspective. Small, highly mobile, nuclear families that emerge from romantic liaisons between consenting heterosexual adults are recent social conventions; uncontested divorce, with shared child custody, is even more novel (Cooey 1996, 16–17). Family structures are historically fluid, socially contingent, and politically charged.

It is the social meanings that are most connected with politics. Historically and cross-culturally, governments are concerned with many of the most private details of family life (sexuality, reproduction, intergenerational relationships), because the strength of families affects the well-being of citizens. Historically, caregiving for dependent family members (that is, children, the elderly, and/or disabled) has been a major function of family life, but modern societies are increasingly utilizing the service sectors of their economies to support families in fulfilling some of these responsibilities (for example, daytime child and elder care). Many large-scale demographic variables (for example, fertility rates, birthrates, and sex ratios) are of great interest to most political leaders. Countries often get involved in these demographic issues by adopting pronatalist or antinatalist policies (for example, China's one-child policy). Similarly, abortion in the United States is a highly charged personal and political issue. Kristen Luker found major differences in the backgrounds of those women who consider themselves pro-life or pro-choice. Pro-life women tend to have less education than pro-choice women, and they are less likely to work outside the home or have careers (Luker 1984). Our government gets involved in other ways, in cases of family violence (husband-wife; child and elder abuse or neglect) and juvenile delin-

Murphy Brown, played by Candice Bergen, holds her newborn son, Avery, on the television show Murphy Brown. *(Bettmann/Corbis)*

serial monogamy of current U.S. culture is an interesting parallel to polygamy). The legal and social recognition of same-sex marriages in the United States is of grave concern to homosexuals, as is their right to adopt children and to be the legal beneficiaries of other partner benefits such as health insurance and death benefits. Although marriage and divorce laws vary by state, such disagreements spotlight the interrelationships of families and political power. Not only do many laws related to families vary by state, but these laws or norms also shift over time. Contemporary family structures are atypical

quency, or when family members are mentally or physically needy and when families struggle to provide basic necessities for their families (for example, in cases of welfare and/or homelessness or nonpayment of child support).

The interrelationships between family and politics can be seen in several government initiatives that dramatically affected family life. From our nation's very beginning, families have been crucial in the development of our current political system. The Declaration of Independence reads "We hold these truths to be self-evident, that all men are created equal, that they are endowed by their Creator with certain unalienable Rights, that among these are Life, Liberty and the pursuit of Happiness" (National Archives and Record Service 2001). Fundamentally, it is families that provide the primary staging ground by which we live, are free, pursue happiness, and have power or resist. Indeed, since the early modern history of the United States, certain families formed the centerpiece of the resistance against colonial England (for example, Samuel, John, and Abigail Adams) and the westward migration and claiming of land (for example, mostly wealthier, white settlers).

For recent immigrants and/or minorities, family life has been less politically empowered. African American families serve as the most powerful example of how political systems condone the disintegration of families. Prior to the Emancipation Proclamation, slave families were often separated from other family members, given the slave owners' surnames, and counted in national censuses as animals. The crowning achievement of Abraham Lincoln's presidency was the Emancipation Proclamation. Modern observers might perceive its intent as designed primarily to free slaves from ownership by white families, but it was also designed to deprive the Confederacy of slave labor and bring extra men into the Union Army (The Abraham Lincoln Papers at the Library of Congress, "The Emancipation Proclamation" 2001). Although Lincoln was pressured by radical Republicans and abolitionists to free slaves, he waited until he had wider support from the public. On 17 July 1862, the Second Confiscation Act by Congress was passed. This act freed the slaves of everyone who was in rebellion against the government. This congressional action was the political signal of the collective will that Lincoln was looking for, and on 1 January 1863, Lincoln composed the final Emancipation Proclamation. It would take more than another century, however, before black families could be assured of the same fundamental rights as whites.

Other government programs have aided not only families but also our government. The Homestead Act was also enacted under Pres. Abraham Lincoln in May 1862, during the Civil War. It read:

> [A]ny person who is the head of a family, or who has arrived at the age of twenty-one years, and is a citizen of the United States, or who shall have filed his declaration of intention to become such, as required by the naturalization laws of the United States, and who has never borne arms against the United States Government or given aid and comfort to its enemies, shall, from and after the first of January, eighteen hundred and sixty-three, be entitled to enter one quarter section [160 acres] or a less quantity of unappropriated public lands . . . [further] any person owning and residing on land may, under the provisions of

this act, enter other land lying contiguous to his or her said land, which shall not, with the land so already owned and occupied, exceed in the aggregate one hundred sixty acres.
(*U.S. Statutes at Large* 1862, 392–393)

Homesteaders were required to pay ten dollars and remain on the land for five years uninterrupted (for no more than six months) before receiving a certificate of ownership. Although abused by land and mining companies (that received large areas of land through the filings of "dummy entrants"), this act contributed significantly to the westward expansion and the preservation of the political ideologies of liberty, equality, and democracy. The United States gave deed to over a quarter of a billion acres of land under the Homestead Act and its amendments ("Homestead Act" 1961, 485). For families living outside the United States at the time, there is evidence that the opportunity to obtain such lands further enhanced immigration to the United States (The Abraham Lincoln Papers at the Library of Congress, "John Sluggett to Abraham Lincoln" 2001). A commemorative stamp released in 1962 portrays a sod hut (which was typical of early homestead dwellings), with a man and woman near the entrance.

Despite the imagery of such a two-parent nuclear family during the 1800s, many children grew up in single-parent families owing to the premature death of one parent. In 1900, life expectancy was 46.3 for males and 48.3 for females (U.S. Bureau of the Census 1975, 55). This meant that many children grew up with only one parent, and social institutions such as churches and other private philanthropies were the most common institutions that attempted to fill the void.

During the Great Depression, with an official unemployment rate of 25 percent, it was clear that such voluntary private initiatives could not meet the enormous needs of poor families (U.S. Bureau of the Census 1975). Many New Deal programs were designed to aid families by allowing older individuals to retire with some government-provided income (that is, Social Security), creating jobs for working-age adults (for example, the Works Progress Administration) and providing mandatory public education and support for dependent children (for example, Aid to Families with Dependent Children [AFDC]). The significance of such government initiatives during the worst depression this country has ever experienced should not go unnoticed. Social Security was called a "cruel hoax" by Alf Landon (a presidential candidate who ran against Franklin Roosevelt), and many of these programs were labeled socialistic. That said, given that their benefits were widely shared, there was enormous public need and support for these programs. In particular, AFDC originally included more wide-ranging groups (that is, whites and minorities; former members of the middle and working classes) than it would by the 1960s.

Many historians have noted that World War II played a significant role in ending the Great Depression. The wartime production stimulated the U.S. economy significantly, and the patriotism of the era encouraged many women to work in jobs previously reserved for men. These Rosie the Riveters were socially pressured to do a man's work, earning a man's pay. The social infrastructure allowing women to do these jobs included shortened apprenticeships, higher wages, free training, government-subsidized day care, and social stigma for those refusing to contribute significantly to the war effort. During World War II, the government produced many movie clips, shown in theaters (since television was not yet widely available in people's homes), emphasizing the concept of our entire country as one "family." Such government-produced initiatives emphasized buying war bonds; women's engaging in paid employment; avoiding unionization, strikes, and absenteeism; and supporting "our boys" overseas.

The second wave of the women's movement during the post–World War II era significantly affected what kinds of family structures emerged (for example, with delayed marriage and childbearing, as well as a higher divorce rate) and what was considered the norm for U.S. women. Although many scholars have argued that this wave of the women's movement preceded the men's movements of the 1990s, Barbara Ehrenreich convincingly argued that men in the post–World War II era started to rebel *first* against the conventions of 1950s-style sex roles and their "good-provider" role (Ehrenreich 1983). As evidence, she presented the "gray-flannel rebel" (the working husband who devotedly supported his family, working at a job he hated), the "playboy," and the "beatnik." All of these male roles emerged in the 1950s—well before the second wave of the women's movement in the 1960s. The significance of this timing is that it suggests both the discontent of males and females with 1950s-style roles as well as the possibility that the women's movement was *responding* to (not the cause of) the changing sense of responsibility that some men were experiencing in relation to their families.

No matter the reasoning or timing, the movement of women into the labor mar-

ket and the increasing rate of divorce both led to more children growing up in single-parent families. During the 1960s and Pres. Lyndon Johnson's War on Poverty, the Head Start program was developed and middle- and upper-class children began to spend more time in the care of nonfamily members. Because it was designed from the beginning to encompass parents as well as children, Head Start administrators understood the centrality of families and emphasized parental involvement, school readiness, nutrition, and immunizations. During the 1960s, AFDC—a program benefiting a cross section of families in its early years, during the Great Depression—became an object of scorn and stigmatization. With many middle-class women already in the workforce, the idea of working for pay (even for mothers with young children) became the norm. Politicians began debating family structure, family functions and dysfunctions, and child welfare and development. The culmination of such concerns is reflected in Vice Pres. Dan Quayle's remarks in May 1992. During an often-quoted speech, he said:

> Right now the failure of our families is hurting America deeply. When families fall, society falls. The anarchy and lack of structure in our inner cities are testament to how quickly civilization falls apart when the family foundation cracks. Children need love and discipline. A welfare check is not a husband. The state is not a father. . . . It doesn't help matters when prime-time TV has Murphy Brown—a character who supposedly epitomizes today's intelligent, highly paid, professional woman—mocking the importance of a father, by bearing a child alone, and calling it just

another "lifestyle choice." (quoted in Rogers 2001, 1)

Clearly, television as a relatively recent communication medium has dramatically altered politics and images of families (whether political leaders or not). Most scholars who study television suggest that television both reflects and shapes the larger society. With regard to the prevalence of televisions in U.S. homes, John Harris wrote that "in 1946 there were under 17,000 sets; by 1949 a quarter of a million were being installed every month; by 1953 two-thirds of American families owned a set and American television shows began their conquest of the world" (Harris 1991, 135).

Television is crucial in the interplay between families and politics for several reasons, one of which is the popular culture's impressions of their political leaders. Although citizens of the era may have known something about the private lives of Thomas Jefferson and Franklin Delano Roosevelt, the advent of television has illuminated much more information and widely accessible detail about our political leaders' private lives. Whether we think of the Kennedy family, the Reagan family, or the Clintons, television has forever humanized (or degraded) how we perceive our political leaders. Their family lives, sex lives, and intergenerational relationships are the subject of intense media attention and public scrutiny. Perhaps the best single example of this is the Kennedys. Their political prominence as a family coincided with the increasing prevalence and popularity of television sets in our homes. This factor, coupled with the handsome good looks of both John F. Kennedy and his wife, Jacqueline, as well

as of their children, made them the objects of much television coverage and media attention. During Kennedy's campaigning, television commentators debated the fact that Kennedy came from a family that was Catholic. This was considered very dangerous by his detractors—the fear was that Kennedy would take his orders from the pope in Rome, instead of the citizens of the United States. Similarly, as tragedy after tragedy for the Kennedy family played out on television, in front of our very eyes, we were impressed by the "triumphant faith" of the Kennedy matriarch—Rose Kennedy. Through all of the Kennedy family's tragedies, Rose Kennedy was the stalwart defender of her family and role model of empathy for others. She once wrote about her grandchildren, "I hope they will have the strength to bear the inevitable difficulties and disappointments and griefs of life. Bear them with dignity and without self-pity. Knowing that tragedies befall everyone, and that, although one may seem singled out for special sorrows, worse things have happened many times to others in the world, and it is not tears but determination that makes pain bearable" (Amory 1983, 4).

Television has also influenced how we conceptualize more "ordinary" families. Television images of families themselves have ranged from *Father Knows Best* and *The Brady Bunch* to *All in the Family* and *The Simpsons*. Each of these shows demonstrates the power of television in conveying the ideals and struggles of families of the time.

Most recently, the family as a political concern was illustrated when the Administration for Children and Families—under the U.S. Department of Health and Human Services—was created on 15 April 1991. This was followed by major welfare reform legislation in 1996, when the Personal Responsibility and Work Opportunity Act was signed into law by Pres. Clinton. Under this, AFDC and the Job Opportunities and Basic Skills Training (JOBS) programs were replaced by Temporary Assistance for Needy Families (TANF). Designed to emphasize the temporary nature of government assistance to needy families (mostly by instituting time limits on welfare assistance), this shift represented government affirmation of the cultural norm of both parents working in the paid labor market. The first legislation successfully pursued under the presidency of George W. Bush related partially to the so-called marriage penalty in our tax code and other forms of tax relief for families.

Perhaps one of the most prevalent themes in current political discussions of the family is the role of fathers. Although we might think of femininity and motherhood as having "ascribed" characteristics (that is, most women can physically be a mother without having to *do* much), masculinity and fatherhood have more "achieved" dimensions. Fathers do not carry children in utero for forty weeks; they do not give birth or breast-feed. This means that fatherhood as a social convention may be more historically contingent than motherhood. In many agriculturally based societies, fathers played a central role in their families and in their children's lives (especially sons). Fathers were considered the main educators and proponents of morality and ethics and were the ones who gave the land or family businesses to their children. During the Industrial Revolution, many men began to work far from home, increasing the divide between the domestic and public spheres. If for no reason other than sheer

amount of time spent in each other's company, this also increased the emotional distance between fathers and their children. Much of the policymaking of the twentieth century ignored or downplayed the role of fathers. When fathers were the point of political discussions, they tended to be addressed in punitive ways (for example, "deadbeat dads" and child support enforcement). Social movements such as the Promise Keepers and the Million Man March reflect men's awareness that they have been marginalized in sociopolitical images of the family. It is these groups and others that remind us of the importance of fathers' involvement in their children's lives.

Part of the challenge for men as fathers, especially relevant for low-income young men, is that marriage is less accessible to them simply because they

> do not have the economic prospects to provide females with an incentive for entering marriage. . . . [F]or many low-income couples, unemployment and poor future earnings weaken conjugal bonds and contribute to the especially high rates of marital instability among poorer Americans. . . . [M]en are more likely to move out of a marriage to which they do not contribute and women are less likely to want them to remain even if men are so inclined." (Furstenberg 1988, 214)

With adolescents reaching puberty earlier than in previous generations and with the promotion of sexuality in our popular culture, it is no surprise that the teen pregnancy rate in the United States is extremely high. Our teen pregnancy rate, coupled with the challenges facing young men as fathers and providers, is a key issue of concern in the political realm. One example of innovative programs addressing these issues is Head Start's recent initiatives to include fathers in a thoughtful, sustained way regarding the educational lives of their children. Parental involvement has always been a high priority for Head Start programs, but during the first few decades of the program's existence, mothers were the focal point. During the 1990s, Head Start actively sought out fathers to ascertain why they were not as involved in young children's lives. The fathers' perspectives revealed that field trips, activities, and time schedules of past parent-child projects were organized by women, with women's interests and time constraints in mind. When fathers became involved, they urged fewer bake sales and more field trips to the baseball park, as well as activities that were sensitive to men's work-related responsibilities.

Clearly, family life affects citizenship, and citizenship affects families. The families that we are born into shape our perceptions of power and efficacy, and although the United States has the ideals of meritocracy, families also shape our social class and orientation toward politics. Compare, for example, the Kennedy family with a newly immigrated, non-English-speaking family from Central America. Clearly, these families have a different orientation toward politics and are objects of dissimilar political discussions. Ideologies and definitions surrounding families, the family lives of politicians, and the historical evolution of government policies addressing families all reveal the interdependence of the human family.

—*Sheryl R. Tynes*

See also Aid to Families with Dependent Children; Child Welfare Policy; Children's Bureau, U.S.; Family Decline in the Twentieth Century; Fatherhood; Head Start; Motherhood; Teenage Pregnancy

References and Further Reading
The Abraham Lincoln Papers at the Library of Congress. "The Emancipation Proclamation." http://www.memory.loc.gov/ammem/alhtml/altmintr.html/ (cited October 2001).

The Abraham Lincoln Papers at the Library of Congress. "John Sluggett to Abraham Lincoln," 24 January 1861 (Canadian seeks information on Homestead Act). http://www.memory.loc.gov/ (cited October 2001).

Amory, Cleveland. 1983. "When Faith Is Triumphant: A Portrait of Rose Fitzgerald Kennedy." *Parade*, 3 July, 4–6.

Botstein, Leon. 1997. *Jefferson's Children: Education and the Promise of American Culture.* New York: Doubleday.

Cooey, Paula. 1996. *Family, Freedom, and Faith: Building Community Today.* Louisville, KY: Westminster John Knox Press.

Ehrenreich, Barbara. 1983. *The Hearts of Men: American Dreams and the Flight from Commitment.* New York: Anchor Press.

Furstenberg, Frank F., Jr. 1988. "Good Dads—Bad Dads: Two Faces of Fatherhood." In *The Changing American Family and Public Policy,* edited by Andrew J. Cherlin, 193–218. Washington, DC: Urban Institute Press.

Harris, John. 1991. *The Family.* New York: Oxford University Press.

"Homestead Act." 1961. *Collier's Encyclopedia.* New York: Crowell-Collier.

Luker, Kristen. 1984. *Abortion and the Politics of Motherhood.* Berkeley: University of California Press.

National Archives and Records Service. "The Declaration of Independence." http://www.nara.gov/exhall/charters/declaration/decmain/html (cited 26 October 2001).

"No Child Left Behind Act." H.R. 1. http://thomas.loc.gov/ (cited 25 October 2001).

Rogers, Jay, ed. "Vice President Quayle and the Murphy Brown Speech."

http://www.forerunner.com (cited 10 July 2001).

U.S. Bureau of the Census. 1975. *Historical Statistics of the United States, Colonial Times to 1970.* Bicentennial ed., pt. 2. Washington, DC: U.S. Department of Commerce.

U.S. Statutes at Large. 1862. Vol. 12, pp. 392–393. *The Homestead Act.*

The Family Bed

The family bed is a contemporary practice in child rearing in which infants and children sleep in the same bed as their parents. In general, the family bed is part of a broader family-centered ideology that values the "natural" or traditional over what is perceived as an artificial and alienating modernity. Such proponents of breast-feeding as the La Leche League support "shared sleeping" or the family bed as it facilitates nursing. Although now only practiced by a minority of families in the United States, the family bed harks back to traditional, preindustrial sleeping arrangements in which individuals slept with children, siblings, or other relatives as well as servants, boarders, or houseguests. Beds were not restricted to separate bedrooms but could be found in various multifunctional rooms. Cosleeping (also known as co–family sleeping) is still practiced by many cultures around the world. In fact, such cultures would view the idea of an infant sleeping (and crying) alone in a separate room with amazement.

Sleeping alone, as an infant or adult, is a relatively modern practice that came about with increased affluence (more rooms dedicated to sleep, more beds to accommodate lone sleepers), a newly perceived need for privacy, and a greater emphasis on fostering independence in children. By the end of the nineteenth century, prevailing ideas about hygiene suggested that it was healthier to sleep alone. Another objection to cosleeping was the fear that sleepy adults would "overlay" or smother infants. In the twentieth-century United States, it became the norm for infants and children to sleep in a separate room, even one child per room among the affluent.

Getting children to sleep became a standard topic in child-rearing literature. Most child-rearing experts, including Dr. Benjamin Spock and Dr. Richard Ferber, discouraged cosleeping. Variations on the advice to let children cry themselves to sleep were based on the belief that responding to bedtime tears only conditioned children to cry for attention. In contrast, family bed advocates believe that it is natural (therefore good) for children to want to sleep with their parents and that the family bed prevents children from suffering the separation trauma of a solitary bedtime.

—*Christine Kleinegger*

References and Further Reading

Calvert, Karen. 1992. *Children in the House: The Material Culture of Early Childhood, 1600–1900.* Boston: Northeastern University Press.

Cromley, Elizabeth Collins. 1992. "A History of American Beds and Bedrooms, 1890–1930." In *American Home Life, 1880–1930: A Social History of Spaces and Services,* edited by Jessica H. Foy and Thomas J. Schlereth, 120–141. Knoxville: University of Tennessee Press.

Ferber, Richard, M.D. 1985. *Solve Your Child's Sleep Problems.* New York: Simon and Schuster.

McKenna, James J. 1993. "Co-Sleeping." In *Encyclopedia of Sleep and Dreaming,* edited by Mary A. Carskadon, 143–148. New York: Macmillan.

Stearns, Peter N., Perrin Rowland, and
Lori Giarnella. 1996. "Children's Sleep:
Sketching Historical Change." *The
Journal of Social History* 30, no. 2
(Winter): 345–366.

Thevenin, Tine. 1987. *The Family Bed: An
Age Old Concept in Child Rearing.*
Wayne, NJ: Avery Publishing Group.

Family Business

Family businesses have played an important role in creating economic opportunity for American families throughout history. During colonial American history, in fact, the family was an integral part of any endeavor. Blood and marriage lines determined both what occupations a young man could pursue and what level of support he was likely to gain from the larger commercial community. At the same time, commercial partnerships and alliances were often negotiated through family connections to protect the property and status of colonial merchants. By the 1800s, family relations began to decline as an important factor in the organization of large-scale enterprise. Industrialization and capital accumulation shifted the focus from family to efficiency, and by the end of that century professionally trained business managers rather than family heirs were managing most firms, even those that continued to be family owned. This shift had little impact on small businesses, however, where family has continued to play an important role. "Mom and pop" stores, operated by husbands and wives who often lived adjacent to their business location, continued to play an important role both in the economy and in the life of numerous families in the United States throughout the twentieth century. Such small businesses have been especially important to immigrants, who often are excluded from more traditional employment opportunities and who have been able to capitalize on the special needs of their own immigrant communities.

Family-owned enterprises were the basic building blocks of colonial American society. The most common family enterprise during the first two hundred years of American history was the family farm. Over 95 percent of colonial residents were still engaged in agricultural production by the time of the Revolution (Nash 1986, ix). Although some farmers traded crops and other domestic products in the marketplace, many others relied on farms simply to provide for the basic needs of their family and were not tied to colonial trade networks. Colonists who lived in one of the growing seaport cities such as Boston, New York, Philadelphia, or Charleston were more closely tied to the colonial marketplace, and most operated what we would today call family businesses.

Young people in colonial America typically adopted the line of work practiced by family members, but artisans were particularly dependent on their families to furnish them with both the tools and skills necessary for establishing themselves in business. The first step for young boys headed toward skilled craftwork was generally apprenticeship in their father's or uncle's shop. As apprentices they learned the fine art of artisanal production, whether it was how to tan leather, mill flour, or hew timbers. Young men could usually venture out on their own as independent craftsmen only once they inherited the necessary tools. This was most true for those entering crafts that required a great deal of specialized equipment. For crafts such as blacksmithing that could not be practiced at home and required the purchase or leasing of a shop site, family

A "mom and pop" general store in Prospect, Pennsylvania, c. 1930. (Library of Congress)

inheritance was even more important. The higher the barriers to entry, therefore, the more likely that a son or nephew would follow in his father's or uncle's footsteps. Young women too followed family members into the skilled trades, learning from mothers and aunts how to be seamstresses, milliners (women's hat makers), and mantua makers (dressmakers) during similarly lengthy periods of apprenticeship. Female artisans, however, required little in the way of tools, equipment, or shop space and so depended less on the provisions of family than did men entering craftwork.

Artisan shops were family businesses in one other respect, too—they often relied on the labor of all family members. By providing apprenticeships to younger family members, colonial craftsmen gained an important source of labor that typically cost them only as much as providing room, board, and vocational training. In addition, many male artisans depended on the help of their wives to execute part of their work. Shoemakers, for example, relied on their wives to sew together the thin pieces of leather that made up the upper part of shoes, while they themselves did the coarser sewing job, attaching the soles using heavy needles, rough thread, and sharp tools such as awls and punches.

Family labor was also important to early American merchants. Children, siblings, or spouses might be used to assist in the day-to-day operations of colonial traders. Male merchants, for example, often relied on their wives to help customers. Female customers sometimes demonstrated a preference for sales assistance from another woman, especially when purchasing fashionable housewares, which made up an increasing portion of total trade goods in colonial America at the end of the eighteenth century. But women often were the record keepers in their family businesses, too. Mary Coates, for example, wrote down customers' purchases and payments for her family's Philadelphia dry goods store in the mid-1700s. Familiarity with both the family business and its bookkeeping allowed Coates to take over when her husband died. Widows often continued to operate family businesses, capitalizing on the skills and connections they had established as helpmates in their husband's businesses. Frequently such businesses eventually provided a path to independence and economic security for merchants' children as well. The Coateses' family business was typical in this respect, as it continued under the management of the eldest daughter as Margarett Coates and Company (Cleary 1995, 198).

Family inheritance and connections, in fact, were at the heart of the commercial economy in colonial America. Merchants relied on family for capital, credit, and contacts. Business relationships were, in fact, personal relationships, since family ties determined the contours of colonial trade. Young people interested in becoming merchants could not rely on banks or insurance companies to help them start their businesses. The only lending institution available and the only insurance against economic tragedy was the family. Colonial American merchants, therefore, were typically born, not made. That is, the opportunity to enter the world of business was one they could access only if they were born into a mercantile family that could provide the start-up capital, arrange the necessary lines of credit, and introduce the commercial contacts crucial to any colonial merchant. Thus, family was the institution through which property, skill, and status were passed down in early America.

Marriage, therefore, was often at the heart of a family's business strategy. For elite Boston families of the seventeenth century, the best way to keep business assets concentrated within the family was to encourage sibling exchange. This meant that if two families, with four children each, intermarried two children from each family, the families' wealth would be subdivided fewer times between the inheritors, thus combining and concentrating the fortunes of two families. Marital relationships also cemented commercial alliances and business partnerships between colonial Americans, solidifying merchant group status. The 1679 marriage between Robert Livingston and Alida Schuyler, for example, launched what would become one of colonial New York's most successful family businesses. Through Alida, Robert Livingston gained the connections of the Schuyler clan, one of Albany's most influential business families. In partnership with Alida's two brothers, Livingston eventually came to oversee a successful fur trade as well as hundreds of thousands of acres of productive agricultural land in the fertile Hudson River Valley that would be passed down through several generations of the Livingston family (Kierner 1989). A similar pattern of marital-business alliances characterized Mexican California in the early 1800s before it became a state. American agents engaged in the hide and tallow trade with wealthy California ranchers increased their chances for commercial success by marrying the daughters of their Mexican business partners. Like the Livingston-Schuyler alliance, such conjugal relations between Anglo Americans and Mexican Californians were a sure path to wealth for both parties.

The craft shops and trading empires of colonial American history emphasized long-term family security and solidarity rather than individual achievement. To be sure, family members engaged in collective economic ventures were expected to adhere to a rigorous work ethic. In fact, family honor and loyalty were often secondary in considering the admission of family to a successful business enterprise if he or she had not established a solid work history. Yet the motivation behind colonial American enterprise was not individual initiative. The driving force behind most business was the family: its security, its future, and its fortune.

Industrialization and capitalist accumulation began to change the nature of family businesses in the 1800s. Small-scale family production gradually gave way to a factory system that undermined the autonomy of craft families. Some factories employed families, but the wage work they provided emphasized efficiency and apportioned labor in a way that undermined family cooperation and independence. Thus small-scale mills and carpentry shops that had been operated as family businesses were replaced with a new division of labor that underscored individual performance rather than family action. Simultaneously, merchant families began to pool financial resources in order to invest in larger, capital-intensive business ventures. Freed from the restrictions of Great Britain after the American Revolution, trade and manufacturing both expanded. Funding these changes loosened the family's hold on economic enterprise because no single merchant family had the resources to do it alone. Collaboration across kin lines shifted the focus of economic enterprise away from family achievement and eventually undermined the importance of family as the avenue to business opportunity.

One result of this change in the marketplace was that the regularity with which sons followed their fathers into business diminished. In one New York community in the second half of the nineteenth century, for example, some 60–90 percent of grocers', hotel-keepers', and saloonkeepers' sons did not follow their fathers into business. Even young men who entered into partnerships with their fathers—a legal and symbolic, if not actual, expression of equality—only stayed in the family business four out of five times (Griffen and Griffen 1977, 148–151).

The new freedom to strike out on their own appealed to sons in the United States in the nineteenth century. Farmers had been the first to seek opportunities beyond those provided by their families, forced into doing so by the diminished supply of fertile farmland. But for the sons of businessmen, pursuing their own interests and abilities was a new development. Filial independence began to appear during the second half of the eighteenth century, but its fullest expression coincided with the changes wrought by nineteenth-century industrialization and capitalization. Thus the percentage of young men among Boston's elite merchant families who pursued their fathers' line of business declined from 91.7 percent at the end of the 1600s to 29.5 percent during the 1820s and 1830s (Hall 1977, 49).

Although diminished, family partnerships did exist during the 1800s and were most common in large, highly capitalized companies. When the stakes were highest, with large amounts of family capital invested in the firm, it seems that family members continued to be the most trusted partners. Family businesses that conformed to this pattern are among the firms that have lasted to the present day. Eleuthere Irenee DuPont de Nemours and his father, for example, started a gunpowder production business near Wilmington, Delaware, in 1804. It was such a large-scale operation that it required the financial backing of the French government, thus necessitating a high level of dependability and trustworthiness in the company's administrators. The business this father-son team founded was continued under family management as the DuPont Company. At the beginning of the twentieth century it became famous for the introduction of nylon and is still traded on the New York Stock Exchange ("Dupont de Nemours" 1990).

By the end of the nineteenth century, however, managerial capitalism began to replace family capitalism, ushering in a new emphasis on business expertise over filial piety in large-scale businesses. For the first time, large U.S. firms more often filled key roles with nonkin than they did with family members. Even in those companies in which the founding family continued to be part owner of the company, "[m]embers of the entrepreneurial family rarely became active in top management unless they themselves were trained as professional managers" (Chandler 1977, 491). Thus management and ownership were increasingly divorced in large U.S. businesses by the early twentieth century. A good business manager, it was thought, was not someone with a proprietary stake in the business profits, but someone with the business skill to

create the kinds of long-term profits stakeholders expected.

Family cooperation in the daily operations of small businesses, however, continued into the twentieth century. "As late as 1923," for example, "over two-thirds of American retail business was done at 'mom-and-pop' stores" (Strasser 1989, 65). In such neighborhood establishments the family often lived behind or above their store, allowing parents to manage their business, household, and children all at the same time. Eventually, the children also were employed in the business, though usually without pay. Joint family management of a business like this was much more likely to occur in small businesses, sometimes called petty proprietorships, than in large ones.

Studies of family-owned businesses often miss married women's work that was "hidden" by both legal and social customs that gave men control over their families. Traditionally, women were unable to retain both their property and their earnings after marriage. This started to change in most states during the nineteenth century, but laws permitting women to conduct business in their own names were few and far between. Married women in California, for example, gained this right in 1852 but were restricted to an initial capital investment of no more than $5,000. This means that many women who engaged in the operation of small businesses are undetectable in historical records. Thus, although some records indicate that only 10 percent of male proprietors involved their spouses in the business (Archer 1991, 76), it is quite possible that such figures grossly underestimate the degree to which married women were involved in their families' businesses.

Most scholars would agree, however, that while the work women performed may have been integral to the success of some family-owned establishments, they rarely gained equal status as a partner in the day-to-day operations or decision-making process. In fact, in some states, it was illegal for a husband and wife to operate a business as legal partners because, among other things, it was feared that the contentiousness of commerce would disturb the "sacred relations between man and wife" (Mechem 1924, 95). When women chose to start their own businesses, therefore, it should not be surprising that they often relied on the help of female family members rather than male. Women who invited husbands or sons into their businesses often gave up control—though not always unwillingly. Mary Ann Magnin, for example, founder of what would become one of America's finest department stores, gladly turned the management of I. Magnin over to her eldest son, John, in 1892, after he exhibited a talent for both the administrative and creative sides of the business. Mary Ann Magnin remained a force in the administration of the store and was a frequent visitor to its retail headquarters until her death in 1943 ("Close Out" 1995), yet few people today know that a woman founded the popular I. Magnin department store.

Mary Ann Magnin's story is typical of family-owned businesses in one other respect as well—she was an immigrant. From the late nineteenth century through the 1980s, foreign-born Americans consistently had a higher rate of self-employment than did native-born Americans. By and large, this tendency can be explained by the lack of opportunity that many immigrants found in more traditional occupations. But since African Americans faced similar discrimination in the job market yet displayed lower than average rates of self-employment (Light 1972), this is not an entirely satisfactory explanation. The advantage that immigrant entrepreneurs had in serving customers from their own communities helps explain this discrepancy. Immigrant business owners could rely on their language skills and knowledge of cultural and dietary norms to cater to immigrant needs in a way that native-born Americans could not. Thus family-run groceries, bakeries, and restaurants were and still are especially common among immigrant entrepreneurs. Such businesses provide important goods and services for nonnative Americans while at the same time supplying scores of immigrant families with employment and a reliable, if not lucrative, income.

—*Edie Sparks*

See also Apprenticeship

References and Further Reading
Archer, Melanie. 1991. "Family Enterprise in an Industrial City: Strategies for the Family Organization of Business in Detroit, 1880." *Social Science History* 15(1): 67–95.
Bailyn, Bernard. 1979. *The New England Merchants in the Seventeenth Century.* Cambridge: Harvard University Press.
Chandler, Alfred D., Jr. 1977. *The Visible Hand: The Managerial Revolution in American Business.* Cambridge: Harvard University Press.
Cleary, Patricia. 1995. "'She Will Be in the Shop': Women's Sphere of Trade in Eighteenth-Century Philadelphia and New York." *The Pennsylvania Magazine of History and Biography* 119(3): 181–202.
"Close Out." 1995. *Los Angeles,* January.
Daniels, Christine. 1995. "From Father to Son: Economic Roots of Craft Dynasties in Eighteenth-Century Maryland." In *American Artisans: Crafting Social Identity, 1750–1850,* edited by Howard B. Rock, Paul A. Gilje, and Robert Asher, 3–16. Baltimore: Johns Hopkins University Press.

"Dupont de Nemours." 1990. *Random House Encyclopedia.* New revised 13th ed. New York: Random House.

Griffen, Clyde, and Sally Griffen. 1977. "Family and Business in a Small City: Poughkeepsie, New York, 1850–1880." In *Family and Kin in Urban Communities, 1700–1930,* edited by Tamara K. Hareven, 144–163. New York: New Viewpoints.

Hall, Peter Dobkin. 1977. "Family Structure and Economic Organization: Massachusetts Merchants, 1700–1850." In *Family and Kin in Urban Communities, 1700–1930,* edited by Tamara K. Hareven, 38–61. New York: New Viewpoints.

Kierner, Cynthia A. 1989. "Family Values, Family Business: Work and Kinship in Colonial New York." *Mid-America: An Historical Review* 71(2): 55–64.

Light, Ivan H. 1972. *Ethnic Enterprise in America: Business and Welfare among Chinese, Japanese, and Blacks.* Berkeley: University of California Press.

Light, Ivan, and Carolyn Rosenstein. 1995. *Race, Ethnicity, and Entrepreneurship in Urban America.* New York: Aldine de Gruyter.

Mechem, Floyd R., ed. 1924. *Cases on the Law of Partnership.* 4th ed. Chicago: Callaghan and Company.

Murphy, Lucy Elderveld. 1991. "Business Ladies: Midwestern Women and Enterprise, 1850–1880." *Journal of Women's History* 3(1): 65–89.

Nash, Gary B. 1986. *The Urban Crucible: The Northern Seaports and the Origins of the American Revolution.* Cambridge: Harvard University Press.

Strasser, Susan. 1989. *Satisfaction Guaranteed: The Making of the American Mass Market.* Washington, DC: Smithsonian Institution Press.

Family Courts

A family court is, in the most general sense, a court that deals with a wide variety of family-related legal problems. The term's meaning varies widely from jurisdiction to jurisdiction, however. This variation reflects controversy about how the legal system should handle family disputes.

Proponents of family courts typically believe that family conflicts are qualitatively different from other kinds of legal disputes and that treating these conflicts like other civil cases creates the risk of aggravating rather than solving the underlying problems. The family court ideal is also based on faith in the utility of psychology, sociology, psychiatry, and other social sciences for solving family problems. More prosaically, proponents argue that troubled families often have a variety of legal problems that, if handled as discrete cases, can result in slow, duplicative, expensive litigation and redundant or even inconsistent court orders.

Most proposals for a family court include features designed to solve these problems. Ideally, a family court is a separate court or separate division of an existing trial court with exclusive jurisdiction over marriage and divorce, juvenile delinquency, child abuse and neglect, child custody, child support, paternity, domestic violence, adoption, guardianship, and termination of parental rights. Sometimes the court also has jurisdiction over mental health matters, abortion, emancipation, name change, and criminal prosecution of intrafamily crimes. Within this court, all matters involving the members of one family are consolidated, or their handling is at least coordinated.

A second feature of the ideal family court, also intended to reduce redundant or inconsistent orders as well as to improve the quality of orders, is that one judge handles one case or even all the cases involving one family from beginning to end. This structure is also supposed to prevent litigants from going from one judge to the next until they get an order they like and to decrease evasion of orders.

The third important feature of the family court is that the judge works closely with providers of a wide range of social services, with the goal of resolving the family dysfunction that underlies the legal problems. To make effective orders and wise use of these services, judges must have specialized training in the social sciences. They must also serve on the court long enough to develop expertise and to be able to stay with a case to its conclusion. In addition, services must be available to the court. These may include assessment, counseling, probation, detention, community outreach, and other services. In the last two decades, alternative dispute resolution services, including mediation and arbitration, have been added to this list. Because a family may require services from a variety of agencies and community organizations, the judge's role as a coordinator is particularly important.

The History of Family Courts
The idea that family conflicts require special legal treatment has been traced back several centuries, to the early chancery courts in England. These courts, with their relaxed procedural and evidentiary rules, were understood as more suited to cases involving personal relationships and children than were the more formal law courts.

In the United States, the family court movement began around the same time as the juvenile court movement, during the Progressive Era. Dominant thinking at this time emphasized the environmental causes of deviant behavior and assumed that expert officials with appropriate training and resources could identify and correct the problems. The first family court was established in 1914 in Cincinnati, Ohio, and similar courts were created in Des Moines, Iowa; St. Louis, Missouri; Omaha, Nebraska; Portland, Oregon; Gulfport, Mississippi; and

Baton Rouge, Louisiana (Rubin and Flango 1992, 63). In the late 1930s two famous judges, Ben Lindsey in Los Angeles and Paul Alexander in Toledo, Ohio, created special courts for resolving legal conflicts involving children and families with nonadversary or conference-like procedures (Folberg 1999, 449).

The family court movement was given further impetus by efforts in the 1950s to reform divorce practice, with the goals of curing sick marriages if possible and, if not, ending them gracefully (DiFonzo 1997, 112–137). In 1959 a coalition of reformers proposed the Standard Family Court Act as a model for states to adopt. The act called for a separate court with comprehensive jurisdiction and less formal and adversarial procedures, judges with specialized qualifications, and a case management system that provided easy access to all official records about a family. Rhode Island created a statewide family court in 1961, followed by New York in 1962 and Hawaii in 1965 (Babb 1998, 481). Even at this early stage cracks developed between the family court ideal and the reality. For example, the New York legislation did not give the court jurisdiction over issues involving divorce, even though that is one of the most common legal problems involving families. Other courts deviated from the ideal as well. Besides lack of comprehensive jurisdiction, common problems included failure to implement the one judge–one family ideal and unavailability of adequate social services.

Family Courts Today
Throughout the 1980s and 1990s reformers continued to promote the family court as a solution to the legal problems of families. Their arguments emphasized the same points that have always been

made in support of family courts, that the current legal system fails families because of fractionated jurisdiction, failure to attend to the emotional and systemic problems of families, lack of judicial expertise, and lack of coordinated and effective services.

The limited empirical studies of family courts provide some support for the reformers' claims. The studies suggest, as the proponents argue, that family courts can increase efficiency, judicial competency, and coordination of cases and can save costs for attorneys, clients, and the judicial system (Babb 1998, 505). Moreover, a survey conducted by the National Center for State Courts in the early 1990s concluded that in 41 percent of cases involving families a related case existed, suggesting that the problems of divided jurisdiction may affect thousands of families (Rubin and Flango 1992, 75).

Nevertheless, a survey conducted in 1997–1998 showed that the family court movement had had only limited success in the United States. Only eleven jurisdictions had a statewide, separate family court or separate family division of a trial court. In fourteen states, a separate court or separate division of a court existed but in only part of the state. Nine states planned or operated pilot projects to explore the feasibility of a family court. The other seventeen states had no specialized or separate family court system and included family cases with other civil cases. In these states, as many as four courts have jurisdiction over various types of family disputes (Babb 1998, 482–485). Even the states with statewide courts did not always live up to the family court ideal, however. The length of judicial terms in these states varied from nine months to lifetime tenure, in some states different judges handled different

aspects of the same case, and in only six of the states did the family court have comprehensive jurisdiction (Babb 1998, 486–487).

Practical Barriers to Creation of Family Courts

Financial concerns have often been identified as a reason for not adopting family courts. An essential feature of the family court is that related cases are coordinated and tracked, which requires computer systems and staff trained to operate them. The cost of providing and coordinating services to families is potentially very great as well. Although these problems can obviously be solved, political support for these judicial and social service functions has often been weak.

Another practical reason that some jurisdictions do not adopt family courts is the perception that the caseload is not large enough to warrant specialization. For example, many small judicial districts have only a handful of judges. In such places, many of the consolidation and coordination advantages associated with family courts occur naturally. This reality means that family courts are not suitable for all communities and that no one judicial structure will fit every situation.

A third set of objections comes from judges. Traditionally, judges assigned to specialized courts have had lower professional status and pay than judges who handle a variety of cases. Another concern for some judges is that they will suffer professional burnout because family cases tend to be very emotionally demanding. Finally, some fear that long-term assignment to only one kind of case will stunt judges' professional development. These problems can be alleviated by legislation that gives family court judges the same rank and pay as other judges and by well-designed systems of rotation among judicial assignments.

Another practical concern related to the judge's role is that judicial objectivity and fairness may be compromised if the same judge presides over all matters concerning a family, since information properly before the court in some situations is not properly considered in others. Again, the solution to this problem is a system of rotation, but that solution undermines the one judge–one family ideal.

Philosophical Objections to Family Courts

Many of the attributes of family courts that are described by proponents as advantages are interpreted less favorably by others. Most fundamentally, the model supposes a court with a great deal of information about and power over the citizens who come before it. For a variety of reasons, many critics are skeptical about the wisdom of granting judges this kind of power. They point to the failures of juvenile courts to support their concerns.

A basic assumption of family court is that the judge and experts who work with the judge can identify the discrete causes of family problems and provide resources that will solve the problems. Many modern family theorists, however, believe that families operate as systems, as a series of relationships and roles, and that problems must be understood as dynamic and arising within these relationships and roles. Some of these critics argue that this perspective is difficult to coordinate with legal decision making (Mulvey 1982, 53–55). These theorists point out that any kind of judicial intervention into a family affects its functioning and that the effects may be unexpectedly negative. For example, simply identifying a family as in need of family court services may label that family as deviant, exacerbating rather than alleviating problems. A related criticism is that the legal system operates best when it makes judgments based on proven historical fact, rather than on predictions of the future. Yet, many of the tasks assigned to family courts require predictions. Given the documented difficulties in predicting children's best interests and the dangerousness and effects of foster care, these critics argue, the occasions in which courts are asked to make this kind of judgment should be minimized, not expanded.

The family court model contemplates that not only will the judges have extensive information about families that come before them but also that the judges will have great discretion to fashion orders tailored to the individual needs of the families. An inherent danger in this model is that some judges will exercise this power unwisely; as one commentator said, "God help the family that gets stuck with the wrong judge—forever!" (Folberg 1999, 451). Judges given a great deal of discretion and a great deal of knowledge about the people before them may make orders that reflect their own biases and values. In effect, the litigants may be subject to the personal dominion of the judge, rather than to the rule of law, or at least to perceive that this is their situation. Many of the traditional rules of procedure and evidence that some family court advocates want to relax are designed to protect the parties against judicial bias and overreaching.

Finally, some critics disagree with the conciliatory, treatment orientation of family courts, at least for some kinds of cases. For example, some advocates for victims of domestic violence argue that this kind of case should not be included in the family court's jurisdiction because they fear that perpetrators will be treated too leniently. Some make a similar argument against including certain cases of child maltreatment or elder abuse within the family court. Yet, domestic violence and child maltreatment cases are among the kinds of cases that commonly have related cases (Rubin and Flango 1992, 76). If these cases were removed from the jurisdiction of family courts, many of the benefits would be lost. In addition, say family court advocates, these cases and the treatment of this kind of offender affect all family members and may affect other disputes, such as ones concerning child support and custody.

—*Leslie Joan Harris*

See also Discipline and Punishment; Juvenile Justice

References and Further Reading
American Bar Association. Presidential Working Group on the Unmet Legal Needs of Children and Their Families. 1993. *America's Children at Risk: A National Agenda for Legal Action.* Chicago: American Bar Association.
Babb, Barbara A. 1998. "Fashioning an Interdisciplinary Framework for Court Reform in Family Law: A Blueprint to Construct a Unified Family Court." *Southern California Law Review* 71: 469.
DiFonzo, J. Herbie. 1997. *Beneath the Fault Line: The Popular and Legal Culture of Divorce in Twentieth-Century America.* Charlottesville: University Press of Virginia.
Flango, Victor Eugene. 2000. "Creating Family Friendly Courts: Lessons from Two Oregon Counties." *Family Law Quarterly* 34: 115.
Folberg, Jay. 1999. "Family Courts: Assessing the Trade-Offs." *Family and Conciliation Courts Review* 37: 448.
Mulvey, Edward P. 1982. "Family Courts: The Issue of Reasonable Goals." *Law and Human Behavior* 6: 49.
Rubin, H. Ted, and Victor Eugene Flango. 1992. *Court Coordination of Family Cases.* Williamsburg, VA: National Center for State Courts.

Family Decline in the Twentieth Century

"Family decline" has been a permanent feature of modern Western history and played a significant role in American political and social thought during the twentieth century. Particularly during periods of rapid social change and economic upheaval, observers from across the political spectrum have expressed the fear that external forces have eroded the traditional family, undermined its integrity as a self-sufficient unit, and placed its future in jeopardy. Demographic changes that have been cited as evidence of family decline have included falling birthrates, rising divorce rates, and an increase in women's workforce participation outside the home. Significantly, changes in gender roles—both the fear of men's waning authority within the family and the perception that women might abdicate their traditional roles as wives and mothers—have also been seen as evidence of family decline. In addition, twentieth-century critics argued more generally that the family had declined because its traditional functions, such as education of the young, had gradually been transferred to modern institutions such as the bureaucracy, the corporation, and the welfare state. Within these discussions of the family's changing functions, decline has often been equated with the family's growing dependence on these outside institutions and the subsequent erosion of family autonomy. Because the notion of decline always implies a golden age "before the fall," the rhetoric of family decline can be deeply nostalgic and often appeals to an ideal model of family life rooted in an imaginary past.

As an invariable accompaniment to rapid social change in the West, the fear of family decline can be found in such diverse political landscapes as colonial America, eighteenth-century England, and nineteenth-century France. In the United States, it took on particular importance in the 1830s and 1840s, as early industrialization began to move economic production out of the home and into the factory. The introduction of wage labor disrupted the traditional producerist roles of men, women, and children within the domestic household and undermined the patriarchal family's earlier function as a unit of economic production. As economic production moved outside the home, the family's educational and welfare functions were also gradually transferred to outside institutions. The middle-class family would now be assigned primary responsibility for the emotional and psychological satisfaction of its members. Paradoxically, then, as the market revolution destabilized one traditional family form, it simultaneously ushered in a new middle-class ideal that insisted that the private sphere would now provide a kind of refuge or "haven" from the forces of industrialization and urbanization.

These accelerated changes in family life during the nineteenth century set the stage for debates about family decline in the twentieth century. By the 1890s, many critics believed that the family was in a state of serious decline. They cited a range of evidence to support this claim, including rising divorce rates and a decline in birthrates, specifically among the educated and native-born. In 1903, for example, Theodore Roosevelt feared that falling birthrates among the nation's old-

stock whites were evidence of what he called "race suicide" (Mintz and Kellog 1988). Changes in women's traditional roles were also seen as a symptom of family decline, as women entered higher education, joined political organizations, and worked outside the home in ever greater numbers. These trends only accelerated in the first decades of the twentieth century, and by the 1920s, the crisis of the family was a subject of considerable debate within the nation's newspapers and magazines. Pundits speculated about the effects of corporate capitalism and consumer culture on the integrity of the family, and some even predicted that the institution of marriage would be obsolete by the end of the century. These debates about family decline in the 1920s were in fact part of a much broader set of cultural anxieties about the decline of Victorianism and the emergence of modernism. To conservatives who felt threatened by the breakdown of an earlier Protestant morality, the rise of companionate marriage (which placed a new premium on sexual fulfillment for both men and women), the general loosening up of sexual mores, the explosion of consumer culture, the popularity of jazz, and the advent of the "New Woman" who smoked cigarettes and bobbed her hair were all taken as evidence that the family was in a profound state of crisis.

The theme of family decline was also present within progressivist activism between 1890 and 1930. Progressive reformers, often white, middle-class women, targeted the immigrant family for social reform efforts, claiming that it was immigrant families from eastern and southern Europe who were bearing the brunt of rapid industrialization and urbanization. In the process of fighting for laws and social programs designed to redress the adverse effects of urban squalor and poverty on immigrant families, reformers adopted the rhetoric of family decline and argued that the immigrant family was a kind of microcosm of the modern city, reflecting its endemic problems, including crime, delinquency, and poor sanitation. Such progressivist appeals to notions of family decline, coupled with the eugenics movement of the same period, reflect the extent to which perceptions of family decline were often deeply embedded in structures of race, ethnicity, and class.

At the same time, the theme of family decline was also mobilized by critics of progressivism, who argued that social reformers were, in fact, exacerbating the problem of family decline rather than redressing it. According to these critics, social reformers were further undermining family autonomy by calling for a more nurturing, maternal role for the state, by appealing to the emerging authority of scientific experts, and by expanding the power of the courts within the domestic sphere. This critique of progressivist reform between 1890 and 1930 anticipated a number of the more conservative features of the rhetoric of family decline throughout the twentieth century: the fear that a sacred and sanctified private sphere would somehow be irrevocably damaged by excessive government encroachment; the belief that parents possess an intuitive knowledge of child rearing that is inherently superior to the knowledge of experts; and, finally, the suspicion that an expansive welfare state erodes familial self-sufficiency and dulls the acquisitive drives of individual family members (and male breadwinners, in particular). In general, debates about family decline have almost always hinged on a broader discussion about the size of the federal state and its role within the private sphere.

Although the theme of family decline did not disappear during the 1930s and 1940s, it was less prevalent as economic and military crises came to the fore. To be sure, both the Great Depression and World War II disrupted traditional gender roles, raising fears about both male unemployment and the impact of women's entrance into the paid labor force. But it was not until after World War II that the theme of family decline again resurfaced, as social critics speculated about the impact of unbridled prosperity and economic growth on the nation's families. During the Eisenhower years, the middle-class family—along with its suburban home, car, and television set—was held up as an ideal that reflected the nation's economic and military prowess on the world stage as well as capitalism's innate superiority over Soviet communism. But at the same time, writers such as Philip Wylie expressed anxiety about the adverse effects of mass consumption on the American family, arguing that the postwar explosion of consumer culture had transformed wives into voracious consumers and had made husbands into ineffectual company drones (Wylie 1942). At one level, these concerns with the impact of mass consumption on the American family during the 1940s and 1950s represented a continuation of earlier discussions initiated in the 1920s. But they were also rooted in specific postwar preoccupations, including attempts to understand the origins and dangers of totalitarianism in Europe and to assess the damaging effects of the communist threat on the nation's men.

One significant source of influence for American cultural commentators during the postwar years was the Frankfurt School, an exiled group of European Marxist social theorists who traced the rise of fascism to the changing structure of the modern German family. In *The Authoritarian Personality*, Max Horkheimer and Theodor Adorno concluded that the diminished authority of the German father within both the public and private spheres had set the stage for the political passivity required of fascism (Adorno et al. 1950). In addition to revealing the ways in which the rhetoric of family decline can transcend clear political distinctions between right and left, the Frankfurt School findings reflect another important dimension to the theme of family decline in the twentieth century: the preoccupation with the decline of paternal authority and the claim that this development has compromised the family's ability to prepare its offspring for the demands of political citizenship and participation.

During the civil rights years, this fear of declining male authority within the family became racially coded and politically explosive. In 1965, the racial elements of family decline became enshrined in what would come to be called the Moynihan Report (Rainwater and Yancey 1967). In "The Negro Family: the Case for National Action," Assistant Secretary of Labor Daniel Moynihan asserted that the problems of black poverty and welfare dependency could be traced back to the "pathological" structure of the black family. According to Moynihan, what made the black family pathological was that gender roles within it had been inverted: Black women wielded too much psychological and economic authority while black men were unemployed and largely absent from their children's lives. According to Moynihan, it was this matriarchal family structure that explained the explosive growth of the Aid to Families with Dependent Children (AFDC) program during the 1960s and was perpetuating

the problem of welfare dependency within black communities. Although Moynihan's aim was to bring national attention to the continuing plight of poor African Americans, the report took on a life of its own and became one of the most infamous and influential statements on family decline in the twentieth century. The Moynihan Report is also significant because it reveals the extent to which the theme of family decline has so often been infused with stereotypes of race and gender (Rainwater and Yancey 1967).

In the 1970s, the theme of family decline assumed a prominence that it had not had since the 1920s. Citing escalating divorce rates and a rise in out-of-wedlock pregnancies, journalists speculated about the future of the nuclear family and wondered whether the choice to marry was now permanently out of favor among Americans. These demographic shifts were linked to cultural transformations, including communal living experiments and the rise of the women's and gay liberation movements, both of which critiqued the traditional nuclear family as a locus of gender and sexual oppression. Social historian Christopher Lasch wrote a best-selling book arguing that Americans had abdicated their commitment to family life in favor of a new "culture of narcissism" (Lasch 1979). As women voiced more loudly their discontent with playing only the roles of wives and mothers, some pundits predicted the obsolescence of traditional family structures. Optimists meanwhile insisted that the nuclear family was more enduring than such predictions made it out to be.

Significantly, the theme of family decline also emerged as a standard feature of neoconservative politics during the 1970s and after. Conservatives (many of them from the rapidly developing Sunbelt) went on the offensive and pooled their organizational efforts in response to such issues as the legalization of abortion and the Equal Rights Amendment. In these campaigns, they consistently mobilized the rhetoric of family decline. Arguing that a healthy nation required healthy families, neoconservatives blamed recent social upheavals on declining authority within the family. They predicted that unless the American family could renew its commitment to traditional values, the nation's future would be in jeopardy. This neoconservative rhetoric reflected both a religious ideology that ordained specific roles for men and women and a fear that conservative parents would lose control over their children's values as a secular state assumed more and more control over functions once assumed by the family. The neoconservative mobilization of the family decline theme invoked a number of its traditional tropes, including opposition to feminism and women's changing roles, religious and moral concerns, and enduring fears about the encroachment of big government into the private sphere. These anxieties persisted into the 1980s and 1990s, when controversies surrounding the social dangers of popular culture and the sexual misdeeds of politicians were shaped by what had become a ritualistic lament over family decline.

Although the theme of family decline has assumed more prominence at moments of rapid social change, it remained an enduring feature of American politics and culture in the twentieth century and shows no signs of fading away. From television talk shows to magazine feature articles, from newspaper editorials to scholarly essays, social critics, cultural observers, and academics continue to reflect on the future of the family and speculate about whether the institution can survive the stresses of divorce, single parenthood, and women's growing participation within the paid labor force. Although predictions of the family's imminent demise have been disproven over and over again, it seems clear that, rather than a simple prediction, fears of family decline always hinge on other ongoing questions about the shifting roles of men and women, the balance of authority between the public and private spheres, and the changing relationship between the family and the state.

—*Natasha Zaretsky*

See also Affection as a Basis for Marriage; Communes, Families in; The Companionate Family; Demography of the Family; Divorce, History of; Family as a Political Theme; Gender Roles in the American Family; Marriage; Middle-Class Family; Sexual Revolutions; Suburbanization

References and Further Reading

Adorno, T. W., Else Frenkel-Brunswick, Daniel J. Levinson, and R. Nevitt Sanford, in collaboration with Betty Aron, Maria Hertz Levinson, and William Morrow. 1950. *The Authoritarian Personality.* New York: Harper and Brothers.

Bane, Mary Jo. 1976. *Here to Stay: American Families in the Twentieth Century.* New York: Basic Books.

Coontz, Stephanie. 1992. *The Way We Never Were: American Families and the Nostalgia Trap.* New York: Basic Books.

Degler, Carl N. 1980. *At Odds: Women and the Family from the Revolution to the Present.* New York: Oxford University Press.

Feldstein, Ruth. 2000. *Motherhood in Black and White: Race and Sex in American Liberalism, 1930–1965.* Ithaca, NY: Cornell University Press.

Lasch, Christopher. 1977. *Haven in a Heartless World: The Family Besieged.* New York: Basic Books.

Lasch, Christopher. 1979. *The Culture of Narcissism: American Life in an Age of Diminishing Expectations.* New York: W. W. Norton.

Mintz, Steven, and Susan Kellogg. 1988. *Domestic Revolutions: A Social History of American Family Life*. New York: The Free Press.

Rainwater, Lee, and William L. Yancey. 1967. *The Moynihan Report and the Politics of Controversy*. Cambridge: MIT Press.

Skolnick, Arlene. 1991. *Embattled Paradise: The American Family in an Age of Uncertainty*. New York: Basic Books.

Stacey, Judith. 1990. *Brave New Families: Stories of Domestic Upheaval in Late Twentieth Century America*. New York: Basic Books.

Wylie, Philip. 1942. *Generation of Vipers*. New York: Pocket Books.

Family Medicine

Family medicine is the medical specialty that focuses on care of the entire family. It considers the biological, social, and psychological factors that lead to both the health of the individual within a family context and the health of the family as a unit. Although family medicine traces its origins back to antiquity, the modern specialty emerged during the late 1960s in the United States in response to public and professional demand for generalist physicians. Over the past three decades, more than 53,125 doctors have been trained in family medicine, making it the largest provider of primary health care in the country. In addition, it has dramatically influenced the way medical students are taught, encouraging a focus in medicine on the emotional, social, and psychological components of illness, the birthing experience, and the dying process and highlighting the importance of the doctor-patient relationship.

Origins

Throughout most of history, both Western and Eastern societies predominantly sought care from generalist healers, physi-

cians, or even religious figures, since the spiritual and physical were not considered separate. Colonial American families sought medical advice from a variety of sources including public leaders, ministers, midwives, and, increasingly, physicians who practiced a combination of surgery, midwifery, and pharmacy.

Although Americans continued to call on a variety of sources for health care throughout the eighteenth and nineteenth centuries, by the time of the Revolution, the class of generalist doctors began to dominate medical care. The Renaissance had ushered in a new framework for thinking about health. Mind and body, religion and science, became increasingly separate and distinct, and doctors, trained, to some extent, in science, technology, and care of the physical body, emerged as those most qualified to answer in matters of health.

At the same time, Great Britain saw the emergence of distinct classes of physicians, with apprenticeship-trained general physicians taking responsibility for the lower classes and more formally educated physicians caring for the elite. The lack of scientific training available in the United States, antielitism, and especially the rural character of the nation prevented these types of early divisions among doctors in America. But most physicians, whether trained in the few university-oriented programs available in the nineteenth century or in community-based clinics and apprenticeship programs, continued to care for their patients through a kind of practical generalism.

By the late nineteenth century, however, scientific advancements, immigration, industrialization, and the resultant urban growth experienced by the United States made changes to the face of medical education and care both possible and desirable. An independent panel, funded by the Carnegie Foundation for the Advancement of Teaching and led by Abraham Flexner, generated a report, published in 1910, on the demographics of the United States and its changing medical needs. Included were sharp criticism of the state of health care and recommendations for improvement (Flexner 1910). The newly formed Johns Hopkins University medical school became a new model for medical education in the United States. Based on German medical training programs, it used specialists, rather than generalists, and taught students both in the classroom and by the bedside within the hospital. Rapidly thereafter the community- and clinic-based programs that had dominated the nineteenth century were shut and replaced by other university-based medical schools.

These major changes in medical education contributed to the fantastic scientific advances within medicine during the twentieth century. With such rapid advancements in technique and knowledge, it became increasingly difficult for physicians to master the whole of medicine or even distinct disciplines within medicine such as surgery, internal medicine, or pediatrics. Throughout the century, subspecialty offshoots of these and other specialties arose, as medical graduates followed the examples of their academic mentors in seeking to be at the forefront of technology and data and in choosing to narrow their medical practices.

As the American population swelled between 1931 and 1970, the number of general practitioners in the United States dropped from 112,000, or 80 percent of the total number of physicians, to 55,340, or about 20 percent (Hunt 1993, 1). Since so many medical students were drawn into specialized medicine, families found it increasingly difficult to locate primary care providers. The scarcity of physicians who established practices geared to handle undifferentiated, minor, and common conditions forced patients to turn to expensive emergency rooms for care. Although emergency rooms were able to handle many of the conditions, such episodic care was an especially poor method of dealing with chronic conditions such as hypertension, arthritis, and asthma. Moreover, many of the nation's ethnic and racial minorities, poorer classes, and rural populations had little or no access to specialized medical services. The benefits of specialized medicine were clearly not being fully realized for the common good.

It was in the political and social revolutionary environment of the 1960s that both the medical profession and the federal government took concerted action to respond to what was seen as a national health care crisis. That the tremendous advances in science and technology and the growth of specialized medicine of the twentieth century had not translated into better health care for Americans seemed an unacceptable "paradox" (Rutstein 1967, 9–48). Many believed not only that the decline in general practice helped explain the crisis but also that general practitioners were the group most suited to respond to the nation's health care needs. Although some in the medical community experimented with one- and two-year rotating internship programs to better train generalist physicians, in 1960 the American Academy of General Practice (AAGP) attempted, ironically, to make general practice into a "specialty." Its members reasoned that with the increased prestige associated with specialties, more medical students would enter the field, and the public would trust general practitioners to reform the state

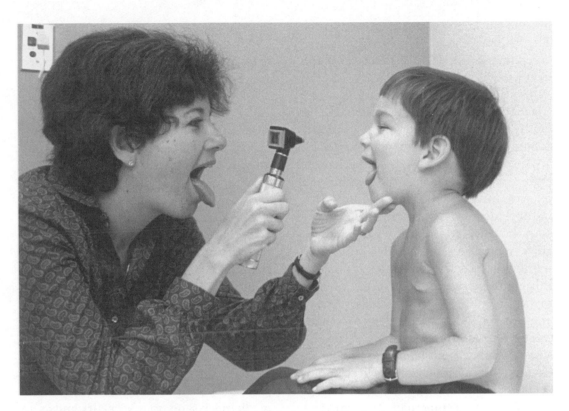

A nurse practitioner examining a five-year-old patient. (Elizabeth Crews)

of health care. But when the AAGP tried to initiate a qualifying exam for those desiring the title "general practitioner," the initiative was denied by the larger medical profession. The most notable reason for denial was that the "Board" of General Practice would not be independent of the AAGP; this reduced its credibility. In response, in 1964 the AAGP attempted to form an independent board, the American Board of Family Practice. This attempt, however, was also denied, on grounds that "family practice" was too broad to define an autonomous specialty.

During this time, however, political pressure mounted in support of family practice. In 1966 reports by three separate committees strengthened the movement.

These were the Folsom report, the Millis report, and the Willard report. The Folsom report, sponsored by the American Public Health Association and the National Health Council, echoed the larger themes of President Johnson's Great Society campaign. It emphasized community resources, preventive medicine, and the need for every American to have a personal physician. The Millis report, a product of the American Medical Association's Citizen's Commission of Graduate Medical Education, described the reasons for the decline of the primary physician, called for the return of the general physician in order to personalize medicine and meet the health care needs of all Americans, and outlined the training and future practice of family doctors. The Willard report, from the Committee of Education for Family Practice of the Council on Medical Education of the American Medical Association, likewise advocated a "new kind of specialist in family medicine" and outlined proper training for family medicine physicians.

The reports revealed severe deficiencies both in the nation's medical training and in patient care, recommending major improvements to the system. The nearly simultaneous release of each of these grave reports created much controversy within the medical profession. Much of this controversy centered around the formation of the proposed specialty, family practice. But although the reports indicated that family practice was ideally suited to bring about reform within medicine as well as to meet the health care needs of the country, many specialists opposed family practice. The greatest opposition came from academia, the body with perhaps the most invested in the idea that narrow specialization meant quality care. Predictably, those who currently dominated primary care voiced their opposition. The American College of Physicians (internal medicine) and American Board of Pediatrics argued that the American population would best be served by the combination of their two fields, along with various other specialists.

Despite the controversy, governmental and populist forces pushed forward. Newly formed Medicare and Medicaid programs and federally funded neighborhood health services evidenced widespread support for direct action in meeting the health needs of the population. And family practice appeared to be another avenue for increasing access to care. In 1969, fifteen family practice residency training programs were created to launch the new specialty. By the late 1970s, family medicine departments existed in most medical schools, and 364 residency training programs existed in the United States. By 1979, family practice was the postgraduate specialty choice of 12 percent of graduating medical students (Saultz 2000, 11). Such rapid growth of a specialty was unprecedented in U.S. history.

The Heart of Family Medicine
The principles of family medicine, although they have been refined over the past three and a half decades, have remained fundamentally unchanged. These can be summarized as access to care, continuity of care, comprehensive care, coordination of care, and contextual care. Although a family practitioner may use other skills and understandings, these principles legitimize and define family medicine as a distinct specialty and as an area of study available to the general medical community.

Access to Care. Family medicine arose in part to address the needs of the disenfranchised—those who because of geographic or financial restrictions were denied access to care—and also in part to address the fact that scientific and technological advances in themselves had failed to transform the health of the nation. Therefore family medicine research often involves a careful study of the glitches in the health care system. Rather than ask which test is most effective according to the latest scientific research, it asks, which test will provide most benefit in the community? For instance, many tests have been proposed and used to screen for colon cancer. Colonoscopy has recently been found in research trials to be significantly more sensitive in detecting cancer than other means. But insurance companies may not cover its high costs, people may not be willing to miss a day's work, and money may be drained from other public programs, effectively decreasing access to immunizations, for example. Family medicine studies these practical issues. Family practitioners attempt to bring the benefits of scientific discovery all the way to the margins of society.

Continuity of Care. The second fundamental concept of family medicine is that an ongoing relationship with a patient leads to better health outcomes. Physicians generally consider that taking the patient's "history" is the most important part of an exam. Much of this history is a review of background information: medications, allergies, past medical history, social history and habits, family history, and review of basic bodily systems. An initial visit, then, can take as much as twice the amount of time as a follow-up visit. Some of this information can be transferred with medical records, but time is still taken in review by the doctor whether inside or outside a patient's room. Continuity of care then makes better use of the time of both the patient and the physician.

More important, however, is the trust that develops between a doctor and patient. In the 1960s when the movement for family medicine emerged, one of the primary criticisms of medicine was that it had become depersonalized. Although depersonalization was recognized and decried in society at large during this decade, the emphasis on specialization and efficiency, and the resultant lack of personal service in medicine, seemed especially disturbing to many since it suggested that no one physician was willing to assume responsibility for any given patient and that the traditional personal doctor-patient relationship was a thing of the past. A family medicine doctor may see a patient through her childhood, a pregnancy, and when she brings in her elderly father. In such a situation, the doctor is more likely to trust the patient, knowing her tendencies and capacities. And patients, acquainted with their physician's values and abilities, are able to confide potentially embarrassing information that may dramatically influence the diagnostic possibilities as well as to gauge the value of the diagnosis and treatment advised by the physician.

Additionally, family medicine suggests that the relationship between doctor and patient itself may have therapeutic benefit and seeks to understand and use the apparent but poorly understood power of the therapeutic relationship. For instance, the unburdening of emotional issues often relieves stress, leading to higher compliance with medical regimens, an improved sense of well-being, and direct healing effects.

Comprehensive Care. Family practitioners do not hold a monopoly on continuity of care. Many specialists enjoy ongoing relationships with their patients. And specialists are often able to use the depth of their knowledge in particular fields to make important medical decisions. A family physician trades depth of knowledge in a particular organ for breadth of knowledge of human health and for depth of knowledge of an individual person. For instance, although a cardiologist may likely place a forty-year-old man with heart disease on a beta-blocker (a class of medications shown in studies to reduce cardiac mortality), a family physician may know that the man suffers from depression, whether acknowledged or unacknowledged by the patient. The family medical doctor may then counsel the patient against the use of a beta-blocker because of its tendency to worsen or even cause depression and because depression may decrease compliance with exercise, diet, and medications, which might even worsen cardiac mortality. A family physician is not the only specialist who might make such holistic decisions. It is often more difficult, however, when physicians narrow their focus from an individual to a subset of the body.

Another important benefit of comprehensive care is opportunistic diagnosis and prevention. A man may present to review low back pain. The broadly trained physician may notice a dangerous mole and end up protecting the man from skin cancer. Likewise the physician may counsel against smoking or administer an important vaccination. Comprehensive physicians, therefore, often detect illness early in its course, before it becomes obvious enough for a patient to seek help.

Coordination of Care. Since the discipline of family medicine arose in an era of expanding medical information and expertise and at a time when physicians already assumed that only subspecialists could possibly begin to master the intricacies of particular diseases and body systems, its founders recognized that in some instances the best medical care would result from comanagement of a patient with specialists. In this instance a family physician might take on the role of quarterback, manager, or trusted friend, utilizing the many talents of the health care team. Although family practitioners estimate that they typically care for 90 percent of a patient's complaints without referral, family physicians have assumed

important roles in coordinating community resources and expertise to meet the health needs of their patients. In the case of breast cancer, for example, few if any family physician would not refer.

But even referral requires knowledge and skill. It is most useful when the values of both the specialist and the patient match and when a specialist's treatment patterns fit the particular needs and desires of the patient. One oncologist may pride herself on heroic lifesaving measures. Another may excel in end-of-life care. Some surgeons operate on most referred patients, whereas others take a more conservative approach. Ideally, family practitioners coordinate care between specialists and continue to meet with patients, helping them to understand diagnoses and to decide between therapeutic options.

Contextual Care. Perhaps the most important theoretical advance in family medicine is "contextual care" or "holism." Emerging as it did in the 1960s—in the wake of increasing awareness of the impact of environmental influences on the health of whole ecosystems and at a time when generational and racial conflicts were hard to ignore—family medicine sought to challenge the ways that the medical establishment had come to separate individual patients and their diseases from their environments—both physical and social. Family physicians, attuned to the importance of the various contexts in which a patient lives and having developed personal relationships with their patients, may see, for instance, a patient who works at a given factory and know that noxious fumes are causing the patient's asthma. Recommendations, then, might be to find a new job, obviating the need for an inhaler.

In the case of a diabetic woman who has lost control of her blood sugars, a physician employing the biomedical model may simply adjust medications or advocate more careful monitoring of blood sugars. Working within a contextual model, however, a doctor would try to understand the underlying cause of a patient's loss of control. For example, the holistic physician may ask how the patient is coping with the disease or more simply, "Are you happy?" When the patient reveals that she is overwhelmed by the duties of child care and work, and the husband, present at the visit, suggests that the couple is suffering marital discord, the physician recognizes that what first appeared to be a matter of simple chemical change—high blood sugars—is also a more complex social issue and that the patient's health is unlikely to be restored without addressing those issues.

"Contextual care" is typical of the three major primary care disciplines: family practice, general internal medicine, and general pediatrics. Family practitioners have an especially broad perspective on the context since they often see entire nuclear families or even several generations of an extended family. Knowing a family's dynamics often helps them to understand why a patient experiences abdominal pain or how the person will cope with the loss of a parent. Additionally, information on one individual may come from other individuals within that same family. For example, a fifteen-year-old girl seen for hay fever may complain that her father is often irritable and angry. In a separate visit, the girl's father, on antidepressant therapy, may indicate that he is now emotionally stable and request to be taken off medications. Understanding the family environment is often critical in caring for the individual.

Beyond the concept of using such family information for the good of the individual, however, lies the notion that the family itself enjoys a certain level of health. This is an ecological viewpoint contained within a special theoretical area: family systems medicine. Just as the health of a rain forest may transcend the state of an individual frog, so does the health of a family transcend a particular member's complaints. According to family systems theory, an individual illness may be seen primarily as a symptom of a family, rather than the responsibility of the individual with the symptom. For instance, researchers in family medicine have studied such topics as family characteristics that tend to lead to panic disorder. Focusing attention on the individual manifesting panic disorder, they believe, may not be as effective as working with the family system as a whole. Another example might be a family culture of smoking leading to an individual case of lung cancer. Family system theory has also been applied to the level of society, where community instability, for instance, appears as a major factor in heart disease, regardless of risk factors such as smoking, diabetes, and diet.

Training
In 2001, according to the National Resident Matching Program's web site (http://www.nrmp.aamc.org/nrmp), there were 509 residencies offering first-year positions to family practice residents. Because of the humanistic and comprehensive nature of family practice, training must be broad. Family practitioners, although carrying a unique body of family medicine understandings, must also develop important biomedical skills in order to diagnose, but not necessarily treat, a wide range of disorders.

Although all specialists experience various fields as medical students, most receive nearly all of their residency training from members of their own specialty. In general, pediatricians receive their training from other pediatricians, and general surgeons from general surgeons. Residents in family practice, by contrast, spend many months working directly with specialists in fields of primary care, namely internal medicine, pediatrics, and obstetrics-gynecology. They spend lesser but still significant amounts of time with surgeons, psychiatrists, orthopedists, dermatologists, and various internal medicine, surgery, and pediatric subspecialists. This broad training develops comprehensive skills. It also teaches resident physicians the specific assets of the individual specialties, allowing them to make wise referrals and to efficiently coordinate and "manage" care.

In addition, family medicine residents develop their own practices while still in training. The Millis report emphasized the need for "continuity" care, beginning as early as possible. Generally from day one of residency training, family practice residents see their "own" patients. This continuity experience allows residents to learn the value of and skills within the doctor-patient relationship during their formative years. It also allows them to witness the progression of health and illness.

Although it is possible to learn the principles of "access to care" and "contextual care" within the traditional university environment, many educators during the mid-1960s stressed the added value of "community-based" training. In a move that reversed some of the effects of the 1910 Flexner report, medical education began to shift out of the specialized hospitals and into the community hospitals and into small clinics. Family practice was in some ways an experimental child of this movement. Today many family practice residencies are not housed within a university environment. Physicians who train within community settings may develop more accurate perspectives on the general needs of the population, more knowledge of which programs bring the most value to the general population, and the skills to treat common conditions. The community-trained resident also works in closer proximity to the usual "context" of a patient's life.

Many argue, however, that community-based programs offer lower volumes of patients with rare or serious disorders. Such experience may be important, even if the treatment of such patients does not usually take place within the community hospitals. It is sometimes the unusual cases that are most important to detect. Another argument for the academic model is that doctors in training at university hospitals have access to specialists on the cutting edge. In an academic setting, though, family medicine residents often "compete" with residents in specialized fields. So although rare and serious cases may be common at academic medical centers and the world expert may be around the corner, such avenues for learning may still be relatively inaccessible to the family practice trainee.

Family Practice Today
Since its modern beginnings, the number of family practice residents graduating each year from accredited residencies has increased from 3 in 1969 to 3,148 in 1998. As of 1997, 79,625 of a total 736,264 U.S. physicians practice family medicine. The total number of office visits to family practitioners in 1997 was 200,429,000 as

compared to the next highest total of 121,088,000 visits to general internists (American Academy of Family Practice 2001). Family practitioners are found in rural and urban areas, serving children as well as the elderly, delivering babies, seeing patients in the office, and caring for them in the hospital. The United States has made large gains in bringing health care to the rural and inner-city poor through such programs as the National Health Service Corps and independent state organizations that send primary care physicians, largely family practitioners, to areas of highest need. Furthermore, family medicine training programs have made forays into diverse countries of the world, in large part because of their proven practicality in meeting the health needs of the underserved.

The health care industry largely favors family practitioners as primary care providers owing to the reduced costs associated with family practice. Family practitioners, trained extensively in outpatient clinical medicine, tend to be efficient in the management of everyday and chronic problems. And because of their comprehensive scope, they often reduce the need for expensive referrals. At times, however, the stipulation to see one's "primary care provider" before being referred to a specialist is seen negatively by patients, who want direct access to specialty medicine. Specialists and even family practitioners themselves may dislike the role of "gatekeeper." But advocates maintain that such a system ensures that at least one doctor maintains a comprehensive view of a patient's health and makes the specialist's time more useful for the entire community.

Beyond its benefits of providing care to underserved populations, efficiency, and coordination, family medicine has affected the way both the medical profession and the general population view health. The government, insurance companies, health maintenance organizations, and the public recognize the importance of preventive medicine. Preventive medicine increases both longevity and quality of life. This movement toward increasing health rather than simply fighting disease has been advanced in part by the changes in medical education but also because more primary care doctors are being trained. The holistic perspective of family practitioners has allowed them to observe where energy and money are best spent within the health care system.

The generalist movement has resulted not only in more training of primary care doctors but also in more humanistic training of all physicians. This training has taken place partly in medical schools in the form of courses such as "Doctor, Patient, and Illness." Such courses generally take place during the first two years, when medical students are immersed in the biochemical and physiological knowledge necessary to practice scientific medicine. These courses emphasize the importance of personal relationships between doctors and patients and the difference between "disease" and "illness." Disease is the focus of the biomedical model. It relates to the doctor's objective understanding of the biophysical cause of a condition, whereas illness relates more to a patient's subjective experience of a condition. The study of "disease" tends to dehumanize, whereas the study of "illness" nurtures empathy and an awareness of the emotional, spiritual, and practical aspects of being human. Nonmedical professionals such as psychologists or ministers often help teach these classes, further emphasizing the coordinated or team approach of family medicine.

Besides reintroducing the importance of social and psychological understanding in the treatment of illness, family medicine has increased access to care, campaigned for prevention, and coordinated medical services. Despite this progress, or perhaps even because of it, many patients now perceive the spiritual as both important and lacking in health care. Large numbers are seeking "complementary" or "alternative" care in the form of herbs, massage, acupuncture, and various forms of "energetic" therapy. The abundance of busy complementary providers, yoga classes, and health food stores evidences the popular belief that a spiritual component is still lacking in the mainstream medical arena.

Family medicine has started to respond. For example, the Society of Teachers of Family Medicine, the major academic body of family practice, has discussed topics such as narrative therapy and meditation. Prayer research has mushroomed over the past few years, even at major academic medical centers. A patient's "spiritual history" and hospice care are often discussed.

Family medicine owes much of its growth to the public's demand for rehumanization. The American Academy of Family Practice placed a phoenix on its emblem to indicate that general practice had emerged as a new creature, family medicine. Family medicine has gathered power largely because it has reshaped general practice and been, in a sense, a "countercultural" movement within the medical establishment (Stephens 1982, 55–65). Some family practitioners suggest that if they are to continue to satisfy the public interest, they must become more educated in complementary approaches and cautiously incorporate the useful into their practices.

—*Peter A. de Schweinitz*
Rebecca de Schweinitz

See also Pediatrics

References and Further Reading
American Academy of Family Practice. "Statistics. http://www.aafp.org (cited 23 May 2001).

Brody, Howard. 1997. "Edmund D. Pellegrino's Philosophy of Family Practice." *Theoretical Medicine* 18: 7–20.

Christie, Ronald J., and C. Barry Hoffmaster, eds. 1986. *Ethical Issues in Family Medicine.* New York: Oxford University Press.

Conn, Howard F., Robert E. Rakel, and Thomas W. Johnson, eds. 1973. *Family Practice.* Philadelphia: W. B. Saunders Company.

Doherty, W., C. Christiansen, and M. Sussman, eds. 1987. *Family Medicine: The Maturing of a Discipline.* New York: Haworth Press.

Flexner, Abraham. 1910. *Medical Education in the United States and Canada.* A Report to the Carnegie Foundation for the Advancement of Teaching. Carnegie Foundation Bulletin 4. New York: Carnegie Foundation.

Folsom, M. B. 1966. *Report of the National Commission on Community Health Services. Health Is a Community Affair.* Cambridge: Harvard University Press.

Hunt, Vincent R. 1993. "The Unifying Principles of Family Medicine: A Historical Perspective." *Rhode Island Medicine* 79: 351–360.

Magraw, Richard M. 1966. *Ferment in Medicine: A Study of the Essence of Medical Practice and of Its New Dilemmas.* Philadelphia: W. B. Saunders Company.

McPhee, John. 1984. *Heirs of General Practice.* New York: Noonday Press.

McWhinney, Ian R. 1969. "The Foundations of Family Medicine." *Canadian Family Physician* (April).

McWhinney, Ian R. 1975. "Family Medicine in Perspective." *The New England Journal of Medicine* 293(4): 176–181.

McWhinney, Ian R. 1989. *A Textbook of Family Medicine.* New York: Oxford University Press.

Millis, J. 1966. *The Graduate Education of Physicians: The Report of the Citizen's Commission on Graduate Medical Education.* Chicago: American Medical Association.

Pellegrino, Edmund D. 1987. "Family Practice Facing the Twenty-first Century: Reflections of an Outsider." *Marriage and Family Review* 10(3–4): 23–50.

Ransom, C., and H. Vandervoort. 1978. "The Development of Family Medicine: Problematic Trends." *JAMA* 225: 1098–1102.

Rutstein, David D. 1967. *The Coming Revolution in Medicine.* Cambridge: MIT Press.

Saultz, John W., ed. 2000. *Textbook of Family Medicine: Defining and Examining the Discipline.* New York: McGraw Hill.

Society of Teachers of Family Medicine. 1998. "The Intellectual Basis of Family Medicine Revisited." *Family Medicine* 30(9): 642–654.

Society of Teachers of Family Medicine. http://www.stfm.org (cited 23 May 2001).

Starfield, Barbara. 1992. *Primary Care: Concept, Evaluation, and Policy.* New York: Oxford University Press.

Stephens, G. Gayle. 1982. *The Intellectual Basis of Family Practice.* Tucson, AZ: Winter Publishing.

Stevens, Rosemary. 1971. *American Medicine and the Public Interest.* New Haven: Yale University Press.

Willard, W. R. 1966. *Meeting the Challenge of Family Practice: The Report of the Ad Hoc Committee on Education for Family Practice of the Council on Medical Education.* Chicago: American Medical Association.

Zervanos, Nikitas J. 1996. "A Century of Medical Educational Reform: Family Practice, a Specialty Whose Time Has Come." *Family Medicine* 28(2): 144–146.

Family Photography

From the moment that Samuel F. B. Morse (the inventor of the Morse code for telegraphy) opened his photographic studio in New York City in 1840, using the new process developed in France by Louis Daguerre, photographs have been used by Americans to record portraits of individuals, groups, and families. Photographs made it possible for ordinary people to afford accurate likenesses of themselves and their loved ones, a privilege formerly reserved only to the rich. Early photographs were made on polished silver plates. Each was one-of-a-kind and could not easily be reproduced; thus they were treasured family heirlooms. During the Civil War, hundreds of

Four Cards de Visite in a typical late nineteenth-century family album. (Courtesy of Anne B. Hurley)

Mr. and Mrs. Alex Kruger decorating their Christmas tree, c. 1901. (Krueger Collection, State Historical Society of Wisconsin)

thousands of young men, both northern and southern, had small, inexpensive tintypes made of themselves to send back home to their families, "just in case." Like the earlier Daguerreotypes, these were one-of-a-kind images that were not easily reproduced, but they were quick, cheap, and permanent.

In 1855 a new photographic process was developed that used a glass negative and therefore allowed easy reproduction of the same image over and over on specially treated paper. It was not an easy process. It involved using dangerous chemicals, and the glass photographic plate had to be exposed slightly wet in order for it to be developed properly. The possibility of making multiple copies of the same image, however, was irresistible. Soon studios were offering packages of several large copies of a portrait plus small photographic visitors' cards. For a dollar or two, one could have a portrait made and reproduced on dozens of small cards (*cartes de visite*), suitable for presenting when one paid a formal visit at the home of a friend or relative. During the last three decades of the nineteenth century, families filled photographic albums with these tiny cards. Albums were even made with special openings to accommodate these popular cards. Now, portraiture was truly available to everyone.

Until the late 1880s, photography was an involved process, and it was generally regarded as a business to be engaged in by professionals, but in 1888 a new kind of film appeared. George Eastman introduced a flexible film that could be rolled on a spool and put inside a simple camera that he dubbed "the Kodak." Thus amateur photography was born. By the 1890s hundreds of thousands of enthusiastic amateurs were using their Kodaks to create albums and individual images that have survived to this day. These images and groups of images constitute a rich mine of information about families and the past.

The photographs a family accumulates are a record not only of what family members looked like but also of many aspects of family life. They can offer clues about how families have changed over time. The pictures that accompany this entry come from several families and several different parts of the United States. They have been chosen to develop some perspective, some sense of change over time. When and why did families in the late nineteenth and early twentieth centuries take photographs? The camera was very likely to be pressed into service at weddings (although this often called for a professional's touch), at birthdays, on Christmas morning, when a new baby arrived, at family reunions, and during vacations and other leisure activities. On rare occasions, a really dedicated "camera buff" might go further, recording life activities and routines around house or farm. These collections, where they have survived, are rare and therefore are considered particularly valuable by social historians.

Hezekiah and Rose Thornton, married December 31, 1905. Photo by R. L. Thornton. (Courtesy of F. Jack Hurley)

Christmas pictures show up in many family collections. The one included here is from a farm family in Wisconsin, taken around the turn of the twentieth century. A typical Christmas picture from its era, it shows how little material goods had to do with Christmas back then. A small tree, simply decorated, a few gifts, and a day spent with the family and at church constituted a proper Christmas celebration at that time. Wedding pictures have changed, too. The picture included here from a farm family in north Mississippi suggests that marriage in 1905 was not as romantic as contemporary weddings have become. When Hezekiah and Rosa Thornton were joined in matrimony, it was a solemn occasion. The expectation

W. R. Flack residence, Milburn, Oklahoma. Photo by Clinkscales of Atoka, Oklahoma, c. 1900. (Courtesy of F. Jack Hurley)

at the time was that these two people were entering into a contract to spend the rest of their lives together in hard labor, raising crops, or perhaps engaging in a small business and producing a family. The picture also indicates a certain dynamic within the incipient family. In general, in most early photographs, the person who sits in a chair is the honored person. Here Hezekiah sits and Rosa stands nearby, her hand supportively on his shoulder. The implication is that Hezekiah will probably make the major decisions in this family.

Family group photographs also often contain hints about family dynamics. Consider the photograph included here that was made in front of a farmhouse in Oklahoma. The entire exterior of the house is shown. In front is a group of five little girls along with a young-adult woman who is probably an unmarried sister of one of the adults. On the right of the picture stand the father and mother along with a very young boy, who is seated on a horse. The positioning of the family members suggests an interpretation: The family has tried repeatedly to have a boy, gotten five girls, and finally achieved what father had wanted all along. The boy is given the seat of honor. He sits on his charger while the girls stand aside in an unarranged bunch.

The arrival of a baby was often an occasion to bring out the Kodak or even to invite the local semiprofessional photographer who, for a dollar or two, would come to the house and make pictures. These pictures today can offer a delightful look at our forebears engaging in a variety of activities ranging from getting a bath in an iron washtub to posing on a rug (often in a state of complete undress). At the turn of the last century, however,

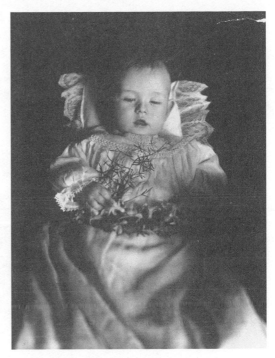

In the 1920s, a successful young businessman wore his evening suit when fishing. Photo by Vernon Sabin. (Courtesy of the Tennessee State Library and Archives)

Just after the turn of the last century, R. L. Thornton photographed this deceased child holding a sprig of rosemary, the herb that stands for remembrance. (Courtesy of F. Jack Hurley)

our ancestors commonly made photographs of dead babies. They did it in the South, in the North, in the Midwest, in the East, and in the West. Mortuary photographs of deceased children were common around 1900 and are a testament to the high infant mortality of that era. Nearly half the babies born in some urban areas died before they reached their fifth birthdays, and statistics were not much better in small towns or on the farms. If a baby died before a live photograph had been made, it seemed perfectly logical to take a picture of the child dressed for burial. Families not only made these photographs or paid to have them made; they also included the pictures in their family albums. In that era

people who did not talk much could face death with calm acceptance.

On a happier subject, vacations and leisure activities were often a time when enthusiastic amateur photographers got out their cameras and recorded their families engaging in sport or relaxation. Leisure pictures also indicate that social class was very important 100 years ago and that members of the business classes considered it important that they never allowed themselves to descend to the level of the working classes in matters of dress. Thus upper-class women sweltered in at least eighteen yards of cloth, winter and summer, even on vacation, and upper-class men wore business suits and ties in the summer, to sit in a wet boat

Family reunion in the 1920s at Union City, Tennessee, provided an occasion for a photograph by Vernon Sabin. (Courtesy of the Tennessee State Library and Archives)

and fish at Reelfoot Lake in west Tennessee. Some events were levelers of social class, however. If you were a good baseball player or a fine trainer of hunting dogs, nobody cared what social class you came from!

Family reunions were often an occasion for photography. The Krueger family of Wisconsin brought out the camera each time grown children brought their families back to the farm. Photographers R. L. Thornton of north Mississippi and Vern Sabin of west Tennessee were often hired to photograph large family get-togethers. A birthday might be an occasion for the family to gather round for a photograph, as might a picnic, a wedding, or a funeral. These images of family gatherings often contain hints as to family dynamics. Who is sitting in a chair? Who

is standing nearby? Who is relegated to the outer edges of the group? By looking at hundreds of these photographs, it is possible to develop some ideas about how families might have worked in an earlier era. A visit home by a soldier on leave might well precipitate a family gathering and a call to the local photographer to "come over and take some snaps." Like the young Civil War soldiers who sent tintypes home, people in 1917 understood that there might not be another chance to get a permanent image of a boy going off to war.

During the late nineteenth and early twentieth centuries, cameras were not small. Even the amateur's Kodak was a large and fairly cumbersome apparatus. Professional cameras were even bigger and more intrusive. As a result, people

A young soldier during World War II in northern Mississippi. Photo by R. L. Thornton. (Courtesy of Jack Hurley)

A shotgun makes a fine accessory in this family picture! Photo by R. L. Thornton. (Courtesy of F. Jack Hurley)

knew that their picture was being made, and photography often became an event. In such a formal context, people thought carefully about what they wanted to display. They showed things to the camera that they wanted recorded permanently. If a woman was particularly proud of her parlor, she might well invite the photographer to come in and photograph her there. Today, the resulting picture indicates how she looked, and also what sort of physical objects were to be found in her parlor and thus what she valued. People often showed the camera something new and valuable such as a birthday present, or even a new car. When photographer R. L. Thornton traveled the backroads of north Mississippi photographing his neighbors for a few dollars, the objects included for the camera might include simple things such as a new hat. One gentleman even insisted on including his well-worn shotgun in the family group. That image testifies to the angry defensiveness of many small farm families in the rural South during the hard times of the 1920s and 1930s. When the Krueger family got a new tractor, in the early 1920s, the camera recorded it. New cars were always an occasion for a photograph,

Rural Wisconsin couple with their new tractor. (Courtesy of the Wisconsin State Historical Society)

and there is a continuing record of changes within the Krueger family as they grouped themselves around a succession of automobiles. Interestingly, early group photographs in many parts of the country might well include a family member holding a picture of a deceased forebear for inclusion in the new picture.

When a dedicated amateur photographer photographs his or her own family over an extended period of time, the series constitutes a particularly useful source of social history. In Memphis, Tennessee, a young businessman named Abe Frank became an enthusiastic "camera buff" and for several years pointed his camera at his extended family, leaving an unusually fine record of this upper-middle-class family of German Jews. His images depict not only life in a cultured, Jewish family but also life in the southern United States in the early part of the twentieth century. Several dozen individual examples of his photographs and at least one family album have survived. The pictures indicate that Abe dearly loved his daughters, but he also romanticized them. In one page from his album, the two girls are presented in dreamy, passive poses, flanking an image of himself, pictured as the quintessential businessman, hands full of cotton. The captions that Frank wrote for the photographs tell us as much as the pictures do themselves. "One of My Darlings" and "Another Darling" identify the girls. Abe Frank, in the center photograph, is self-captioned as "the Bully." Even allowing for the positive connota-

Gender definitions show clearly in this triptych of photographs by Abraham Frank. (Courtesy of Special Collections, the University of Memphis Libraries)

tions of the term *bully* in 1902 (Pres. Theodore Roosevelt often referred to something that he approved of strongly as "bully"), there still remains a clear implication of dominance. A Frank son is given an entire page of the family album to himself. He is presented mounted (the seat of honor again)—this time, with a nice sense of irony, on a phlegmatic donkey, with the caption "a Rough Rider." Certainly there is humor intended here, but there is also an expectation of masculine dominance. The reference to Teddy Roosevelt's military unit during the Spanish American War makes it clear that the son is expected to grow up and engage in the Rooseveltian ideal of "the strenuous life" in business if not in the wild West.

Abe Frank photographed his family as they interacted with domestic servants, and again, the photographs with their captions offer a glimpse into a past era when racial attitudes were different from accepted contemporary attitudes. The Franks were considered enlightened employers who treated their domestic servants with decency and real affection. Even so, the racial attitudes of the early twentieth century could not be completely escaped. A picture of Frank's youngest son, sitting on the back steps of the family house with a friendly dog and two black women who are clearly household servants, is captioned "the Boss and His Side Pals." Thus, according to the caption, the boy, barely out of infancy, is placed in a superior position to both the young-adult black women and the dog (who seem to be lumped together in conditions of equality).

Abe Frank identified strongly with his family's background in German high culture. The home was filled with good books and music. At one point he photographed his two sons posed with their

Abraham Frank's expectations for his son show clearly in this photograph. (Courtesy of Special Collections, the University of Memphis Libraries)

An unknown African American family puts on their best clothing for a photograph by Richard Samuel Roberts. (Bruccoli Clark Layman Publishing)

Racial attitudes are embedded in this picture from the work of Abraham Frank. (Courtesy of Special Collections, the University of Memphis Libraries)

elbows on a table, flanking a bust of Goethe, the great nineteenth-century German writer-philosopher. Would a modern American Jewish family identify so consciously with German culture? It seems doubtful, given the events of the 1930s and 1940s. Again, the family photograph becomes a document of how attitudes and ideals have changed over time.

The Frank family photographs are posed in such a way as to reflect the ideals and preconceptions of their day. In African American families, ideals and preconceptions also played a role in family photographs. During the 1920s, a South Carolina photographer named Richard Samuel Roberts spent a great deal of time making pictures within his own black community. It was a source of income for him, but it was also clearly a passion. From 4:00 A.M. until noon, six days a week, he worked as a custodian at the main post office in Columbia. From noon on he ran his photography business. Much of his work took place in his studio on Washington Street, but he also took his cameras out to weddings, funerals, parties, and similar events. His family portraits depict people dressed in their very best clothes. His pictures of houses depict respectable people on their hard-won front porches or near their shiny new cars, objects of particular pride. These were people who were working very hard to obtain their piece of the American dream, and when they were photographed they wanted the camera to concentrate on their successes. Neither Roberts nor his subjects would have been interested in photographs that showed African Americans doing hard, dirty work, although that is what most of his subjects did most of the time.

Family photographs often depict people at their very best. Images of a mother show her in the parlor, not in the kitchen where most of her day is spent. Children are seen playing or opening Christmas presents, not slaving away at homework. Father may be photographed at work, but more likely at home or on vacation, relaxing with his family.

Typically family photographs are made by insiders, people who are a part of the communities they photograph. Abe Frank was the head of the household he recorded with his cameras; R. L. Thornton farmed part-time and took pictures of other farmers and small-town north Mississippians when asked to; Richard Samuel Roberts made portraits and other images within his own community of African Americans. This insider's view is part of the value of family photographs. An outsider, making pictures for his or her own enjoyment or for publication in a magazine or journal, would often see a very different image of the same families. Photographers find it difficult to photograph across racial or cultural lines without engaging in stereotypes. It can be done and there are even books to help us do it better, but it requires conscious effort. This same out-

sider/insider dichotomy applies to looking at family photographs. Historians and others studying family albums and photographs are typically interested in the way people dressed at a certain period of time or are looking for visual clues concerning social/cultural history. Family members, by contrast, focus on the appearance of particular relatives. The photographs that a family accumulates over time are a valuable record. To the family they provide tangible, visible links to earlier generations. To the outside observer they provide clues concerning the way people lived, played, and dreamed in times past. Together with written sources, letters, newspapers, and other documents, photographs can help round out a fully developed picture of the past.

—F. Jack Hurley

See also Family Vacations; Reunions, Family; Weddings

References and Further Reading
Challinor, Joan R., et al. 1979. "Family Photo Interpretation." In *Kin and Communities: Families in America*, edited by Allan J. Lichtman and Joan R. Challinor, 239–264. Washington, DC: Smithsonian Institution Press.
Collier, John, Jr., and Malcolm Collier. 1986. *Visual Anthropology: Photography as a Research Method*. Albuquerque: University of New Mexico Press.
Johnson, Thomas L., and Phillip C. Dunn, eds. 1986. *A True Likeness: The Black South of Richard Samuel Roberts: 1920–1936*. Columbia, SC: Bruccoli Clark.
King, Graham. *Say Cheese! Looking at Snapshots in a New Way*. New York: Dodd, Mead.
McLellan, Marjorie. 1997. *Six Generations Here: A Farm Family Remembers*. Madison: State Historical Society of Wisconsin.
Schlereth, Thomas J. 1989. "Mirrors of the Past: Historical Photography and American History." In *Artifacts and the*

American Past, edited by Thomas J. Schlereth, 11–47. Nashville, TN: American Association for State and Local History.

Seale, William. 1981. *The Tasteful Interlude: American Interiors through the Camera's Eye, 1860–1917.* Nashville, TN: American Association for State and Local History.

Silber, Mark. 1973. *The Family Album: Photographs of the 1890s and 1900s.* Boston: David R. Godine.

Talbot, George. 1976. *At Home: Domestic Life in the Post-Centennial Era, 1876–1920.* Madison: State Historical Society of Wisconsin.

Willis, Deborah, ed. 1994. *Picturing Us: African American Identity in Photography.* New York: The New Press.

Family Preferences and Immigration

The iconography of immigration into the United States—especially when created by those seeking to create a favorable image of it—has traditionally favored women and children. For example, one Lewis Hine photograph of an attractive, sloe-eyed young Eastern European woman has graced the covers of at least a half-dozen recent books on immigration into the United States. Yet, until after World War II, immigration to the United States was predominantly male. During both the colonial period and the classic century of immigration between 1820 and 1924, roughly two out of three immigrants were young men. For the last half-century, however, female immigrants have outnumbered males, and family immigration has predominated. In the three fiscal years 1995, 1996, and 1997, the Immigration and Naturalization Service (INS) reported that "family sponsored immigrants" accounted for 63.9, 65.1, and 67.1 percent of all legal immigrants (Immigration and Naturalization Service 1997, Table 4). To understand how this polar change came about it is necessary to come to grips with the changing aspects of U.S. immigration law once it began to become restrictive in 1882. There can be little doubt that if American law had remained as it was before 1882—allowing any free immigrants entrance without restriction—single males would have continued to predominate.

Ironically, the first special provisions for the immigration of family members of already-established immigrants came as a kind of afterthought to some of the most unjust immigration legislation in U.S. history: the treaties, statutes, and executive agreements that effected the exclusion of most potential Chinese and Japanese immigrants from the United States. The results of this afterthought became part of the so-called unintended consequences that have been a hallmark of much U.S. immigration legislation and executive action.

Although handfuls of Chinese had come to eastern American ports from the late eighteenth century on, the vast bulk of Chinese immigration came to the West Coast in general and San Francisco in particular as part of the gold rush that followed the discovery of gold in the foothills east of Sacramento in 1848. Perhaps 250,000 Chinese had come by 1882, more than 90 percent of them adult males. They were a small part of the more than 8 million immigrants who came to the United States in that era. By the mid-1870s, a combination of endemic racism and economic stringency gave particular force to the anti-Chinese movement, which was endemic among western white workingmen and gaining growing national support. The first anti-Chinese statute was enacted in 1875. Congress passed a second anti-Chinese measure in 1878—both the Democrats and the Republicans had adopted anti-Chinese planks in their national party platforms by 1876—but Pres. Rutherford B. Hayes, while assuring Congress that he too viewed Chinese as incompatible with "our national life," vetoed the measure because it conflicted with the 1869 Burlingame treaty with China (Richardson 1907, 7:514–520). That treaty, negotiated by radical Republican Anson Burlingame (1820–1870), took a relatively advanced human rights position from which the United States soon receded:

> The United States and the Emperor of China cordially recognize the inherent and inalienable right of man to change his home and allegiance and also the mutual advantage of free migration and emigration . . . for the purposes of curiosity, of trade, or as permanent residents . . . but nothing contained herein shall be held to confer naturalization upon the citizens of the United States in China, nor upon the subjects of China in the United States. (Malloy 1910, 305)

In his 1878 veto measure Hayes promised to work for revision of the treaty.

A revised treaty was ratified and proclaimed in October 1881. It gave the United States, unilaterally, the right to "regulate, limit, or suspend" the "coming or residence" of Chinese laborers, but it allowed Chinese subjects "proceeding to the United States as teachers, students, merchants, or from curiosity, together with their body and household servants, and Chinese laborers now in the United States to go and come of their own free will and accord" (Malloy 1910, 320). Congress responded in 1882 with a statute suspending most Chinese immigration for twenty years. Pres. Chester A. Arthur vetoed it as too long a period for

an experiment, and Congress quickly responded by repassing the bill with a ten-year ban that Arthur signed.

The law is usually called the Chinese Exclusion Act but the actual title is "To Execute Certain Treaty Stipulations Relating to Chinese." It barred Chinese laborers—defined as "both skilled and unskilled laborers and those employed in mining"—but did not spell out exactly who was eligible to immigrate. It also provided that those laborers already domiciled in the United States might leave and return but did not have the right to bring back or call over family members (*U.S. Statutes at Large* 1882, 58). It was left to immigration officials to interpret what the combination of treaty and statute allowed. They developed the term *treaty merchants* to cover most of those eligible and extended that eligibility to their family members. Over the life of Chinese exclusion, 1882–1943, terms were defined and redefined as Chinese showed great ingenuity in operating within the space provided by the various statutes, immigration regulations, and ensuing court decisions. For example, one amendment stated that persons who operated laundries were not merchants. Conversely, some Chinese, or their lawyers, drew up partnership agreements so that some relatively small mercantile establishments had dozens of partners. Although the overall effect of the exclusion legislation was to limit the Chinese presence in the United States—Chinese American population declined steadily for half a century—the law's exceptions for some family members allowed a significant number of Chinese to enter legally. During the entire exclusion era, some 95,000 individual entries of Chinese were recorded, about 1,500 a year. In 1940, three years before exclusion ended,

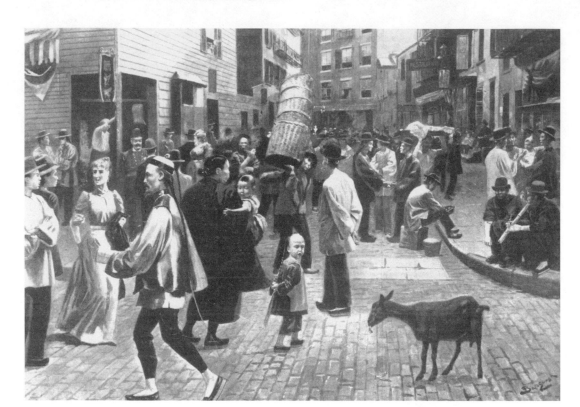

The Chinese colony in New York City, Mott Street. Engraving in Harper's Weekly, *1896. (Library of Congress)*

the census for the first time reported that aliens were a minority in the Chinese American community and that the gender ratio, which had been more than 20:1 male at the beginning of the era, was now down to 2.9:1 (Daniels 1988, Tables 3.1, 3.2, and 6.1).

The precedents established by both Chinese exclusion and the exceptions to it clearly had some effect on the arrangements eventually made with Japan about its emigrants, but exactly how much they affected the negotiations between Tokyo and Washington is impossible to say. It is demonstrable that the anti-Chinese precedent made it easier for an anti-Japanese movement to become established in the Far West early in the last century. Had

Japan been a weak power—as China then was—some kind of Japanese Exclusion Act would almost certainly have been enacted sometime before 1910. But Japan was a rising and ambitious power. Its military might, demonstrated in the Russo-Japanese War of 1904–1905, caused the administration of Theodore Roosevelt to try to reach an accommodation with Japan. Japan's ambitions for great power status and fears that demeaning treatment of its subjects by the United States and other Western powers would militate against its aspirations for that status led it to seek cooperation rather than conflict over immigration issues. The result was gentlemen's agreements with both Canada and the United States. The Japanese American executive agreement—which did not have to be ratified by the Senate—was effected by an exchange of notes in 1907–1908. It called for Japan to cease issuing passports valid for either the United States or Hawaii to its laborers and for the United States to refrain from enacting immigration legislation singling out Japanese. In other words, Japanese law rather than U.S. law would be made responsible for the exclusion of Japanese laborers. In addition, it was agreed, as had been true in the Chinese case, that those already domiciled in the United States or Hawaii could leave and return and, in addition, that the "parents, wives and children" of such persons were admissible as permanent residents. Immigrant Japanese, along with Chinese and most other Asians, were not eligible for naturalization, but after the adoption of the Fourteenth Amendment in 1868 "all persons" born in the United States were citizens.

In the Japanese case the unintended consequences involved so-called picture brides. Thousands of Japanese laborers domiciled in the United States or Hawaii married Japanese women and brought them across the Pacific. Many of these marriages were by proxy between brides and grooms who had never seen each other but had exchanged photographs. Such marriages were legal in Japan; many, perhaps most, of the couples went through another ceremony in North America once they were physically united. We should note that Chinese laborers had no such option. Many of them, however, maintained families in China. The women they married were known in the immigration villages of Guangdong Province as "living widows."

Although the federal government "sold" the gentlemen's agreement to Californians and other westerners as tanta-

mount to exclusion, the results were otherwise. Not surprisingly, most of the "picture marriages" were fruitful, and, unlike the Chinese American population, the Japanese American population grew rapidly and its gender imbalance was even more significantly diminished. In 1910, two years after the gentlemen's agreement went into effect, there were some 72,000 Japanese in the continental United States, with a gender ratio that was about 8:1 male. Ten years later—four years before the 1924 immigration act excluded Japanese by barring all "aliens ineligible to citizenship"—there were 111,000 with a gender ratio that was a little less than 3:1 male. A year before Pearl Harbor, there were some 127,000 with a gender ratio of 1.32:1. At the later date, slightly more than two-thirds of the population consisted of Nisei, native-born U.S. citizens.

The same "aliens ineligible to citizenship" clause of the 1924 act that excluded Japanese also ended the right of "treaty merchants" to bring in family members and the right of U.S. citizens to bring in wives. In the previous two decades, about 150 Chinese women had entered the country annually as immigrants. In the next six years none did. Lobbyists for Chinese Americans persuaded Congress to pass a law in 1930 enabling "Chinese wives" of U.S. citizens to enter the country as long as the marriage had been performed before 26 May 1924, the date of the passage of the immigration act. About sixty Chinese women a year entered under this provision in the 1930s (Daniels 1988, Tables 4.6, 7.1, and 7.2).

During the early years of immigration restriction, that is, before 1921, most restrictive measures had little or nothing to do with families. But the 1917 immigration act, best known for its much-heralded but actually ineffective literacy test, had distinctive "family friendly" provisions. Although many opponents of immigration had wanted a literacy-in-English requirement, the eventual statute required only that the immigrant be able to read a passage of forty words in any "language or dialect including Hebrew or Yiddish" chosen by the immigrant. The statute exempted from this requirement aliens under sixteen years of age and a number of largely female relatives—wives, mothers, grandmothers, and widowed or unmarried daughters of any age—as well as fathers or grandfathers over fifty-five years of age. These categories of persons were admissible if accompanying a literate immigrant or joining any alien who had established residence, whether literate or not.

In 1921 Congress passed the first effective law restricting European immigrants: Those from the New World were largely unrestricted. This First Quota Act, as it came to be called, limited the number of European aliens of any given nationality who could be admitted in any single year to 3 percent of the number of foreign-born persons of such nationality who had been enumerated in the 1910 census, then the latest available. That provided approximately 350,000 quota spaces annually for Europeans. It also provided that preference be given, within the quotas, to wives, parents, brothers, sisters, children under eighteen years of age, and fiancées (but not fiancés) of U.S. citizens; resident aliens who had applied for citizenship; and honorably discharged alien veterans who had served in the U.S. armed forces during World War I. Thus, by 1921, family preferences were embedded in U.S. immigration law.

The 1921 act, however, was only intended as a temporary measure. Three years later Congress passed and Calvin Coolidge signed the so-called National Origins Act, which would not be amended significantly until 1952. The general tendencies of that act would prevail, for all intents and purposes, until 1965. The 1924 act was intended to be an even more drastic curtailment of immigration: The percentage of persons to be admitted was reduced to 2 percent, not of the current census, but of what nativists called the Anglo-Saxon census of 1890. Using this census had the double advantage, from the restrictionists' point of view, of cutting down on the overall quota numbers—the bill provided roughly 150,000 quota spaces—and of greatly lowering the number of eligible Italians, Poles, and eastern European Jews. But in a significant departure, some family members of European immigrants—wives (but not husbands) and unmarried children under eighteen years of age of U.S. citizens—were admitted without numerical restriction, and their admission was in addition to the number of quota spaces. Within the quotas, preference was given to other relatives of U.S. citizens: unmarried children between eighteen and twenty-one years of age, parents, and spouses of U.S. citizens twenty-one years of age and older. This not only more firmly embedded family preferences in U.S. law but also set up a two-track system for European immigrants, quota and nonquota. Natives of the Western Hemisphere and their families were also allowed in without numerical limit if otherwise eligible.

After 1929 a different way of allocating European quota spaces based on the putative origins of the American people going back to 1790 went into effect, but that need not concern us here. As it happened, the onset of first the Great Depression and then World War II had a generally depressing effect on total immigration. In two different years of the 1930s, more people emigrated from the United States than immigrated to it, something that had never happened in the history of the American republic and has not recurred. For the 1930s, total net immigration averaged only about 50,000 persons a year.

A long-unrecognized turning point in U.S. immigration law came in 1943. Just as the passage of the Chinese Exclusion Act in 1882 marked the beginning of the era of immigration restriction, the repeal of the Chinese Exclusion Act, we can now see, marked the beginning of an era of relaxing immigration restriction. The repeal was presented to Congress by Pres. Franklin D. Roosevelt (FDR) as a kind of good behavior prize for Chinese. FDR was not talking about Chinese Americans—thousands of whom were then serving in the U.S. armed forces—but about "the Chinese people." The repeal not only made Chinese eligible for immigration but also enabled them to become naturalized on the same basis as other aliens. Those concerned with promoting its passage of the repeal played down its demographic consequences—the Chinese quota was only 105 persons annually—and ignored, and may well have been ignorant of, the fact that an unlimited number of Chinese women married to U.S. citizens could also immigrate (*U.S. Statutes at Large* 1943, 58). As soon as the war ended, relatively large numbers of Chinese wives of U.S. citizens—some of them partners in long-standing marriages, others newlyweds—immigrated into the United States. Between then and 1952, when all racial bars to immigration were dropped, almost 10,000 Chinese women crossed the Pacific to join their husbands. When one considers that, as late as 1950,

there had been only 28,000 Chinese females over fourteen years of age in the continental United States, it is clear that the impact on the ethnic community must have been considerable and was qualitative as well as quantitative.

Two postwar statutes—the War Brides Act of 1945 and a 1946 law enabling and expediting the immigration of "alien fiancées or fiancés of members of the Armed Forces of the United States"—made it easier for otherwise eligible persons in those categories to enter the country outside of quota restrictions. Two other 1946 statutes made Filipinos and "natives of India" eligible for citizenship, which triggered largely female immigration from those places.

The Displaced Persons Acts of 1948 and 1950, which set the tone for U.S. refugee policy, brought some 450,000 European refugees to the United States, fewer than a third of whom were Holocaust survivors and other victims of the Nazi era. Although neither act contained specific family-friendly provisions, refugee populations generally have been composed of greater numbers of women and children than of men. These two acts, hotly contested at the time, have been followed by a whole chain of refugee acts, beginning with the Refugee Relief Act of 1953, which brought in some 214,000 nonquota Europeans. Most of these refugee groups also had nonadult-male majorities. From 1946 until the end of the twentieth century, some 3.5 million persons were admitted to the United States as refugees, and even before the United States became involved in the wars of the Vietnam era, refugees from Asia began to arrive. By the end of the century, refugees were coming in significant numbers from almost every part of the globe. Of the 112,000 refugees legally admitted in 1997, for example, some 40,000 came from Europe, 34,000 from the Western Hemisphere, 31,000 from Asia, and 7,000 from Africa (Immigration and Naturalization Service 1999, Table 25).

This global reach was facilitated in 1952 by some provisions of the first major revision of the 1924 immigration act. The McCarran-Walter Act of 1952 was, in many ways, a typical piece of cold war legislation, filled with the reflexive anticommunism of the era. But it was also the statute that dropped all racial and ethnic bars to immigration and naturalization. The immediate beneficiaries of this were Japanese; although the new Japanese quota was only 185 persons a year, some 45,000 Japanese persons were legally admitted to the United States between 1952 and 1960. About 40,000 of them were female: A majority of the latter were the wives of non–Japanese American citizens, most of them soldiers or former soldiers.

The other aspect of the 1952 act that is of concern here was its expansion of explicitly family-friendly provisions. Husbands of U.S. citizens were now included in the category to be admitted without numerical limitation, thus ending legal discrimination against women citizens in immigration law. An even greater expansion of family preferences took place within the quota allocations. The 1952 act not only expanded the categories of relatives of U.S. citizens who got preferences but, for the first time, privileged some relatives of resident aliens. Adult children of citizens got preference, as did brothers and sisters of citizens, and both groups could bring with them spouses and children. Resident aliens could bring in spouses and unmarried children of any age. What the 1952 act did was to ensure that most immigration would be what scholars call chain

migration, so called because the immigrants follow one another like the links in a chain. The law also provided a great incentive to become naturalized as soon as possible by those who wanted to bring in relatives. Much of the diversity of late-twentieth-century immigration to the United States, almost always credited to the 1965 immigration act, actually had its roots in changes in the 1952 statute.

The 1965 act was part of Lyndon Johnson's Great Society and was, along with the Civil Rights Act and Medicare/Medicaid legislation, one of the three most significant pieces of legislation enacted that year. Although it totally scrapped the old quota system, the new statute retained all of the family-friendly provisions of the 1952 act while giving some of them greater incidence. For example, in the 1952 act brothers, sisters, and married children of U.S. citizens received only a residual number of immigration slots; under the 1965 act such persons were allocated just over a third of the slots. In these and other ways the 1965 law had clearly evolved from previous legislation. It still contained most of the nonracial/ethnic barriers that Congress had been erecting to immigration since the late nineteenth century. There were no longer national quotas; instead there were proposed caps for both the Eastern and Western Hemispheres, ending the traditional—and largely illusory—exemption for residents of the New World. In theory the 1965 act provided a global ceiling of 290,000, with no more than 20,000 coming from any one country, that applied only to those persons who were admitted subject to numerical limitation.

The entire statute is a classic case of unintended consequences. Pres. Lyndon Johnson, in what turned out to be an uncharacteristic understatement of achievement, claimed in his signing ceremony held at the foot of the Statute of Liberty that "this bill that we sign today is not a revolutionary bill. It does not affect the lives of millions. It will not reshape the structure of our daily lives, or add really importantly to our wealth or our power" (Johnson 1966, 1037–1040).

Johnson was saying what his experts had told him. They, and he, saw the bill as a redress of the grievances suffered by southern and eastern European ethnics as a result of the blatantly discriminatory 1924 act and as a symbolic reversal of the overriding of Truman's 1952 veto of the McCarran-Walter Act, a veto that Sen. Lyndon Johnson helped to negate. But the real beneficiaries of the act were not Europeans, but the Asians and Latin Americans who have come to dominate immigration to the United States. The presumption was that, at most, there would be a third of a million legal immigrants annually. Massive family-oriented chain migration plus the burgeoning refugee programs noted earlier have made the 1965 assumptions almost laughable. In most years since the law was enacted more than half a million legal immigrants have entered, and at the turn of the century the numbers, in the 600,000–700,000 range, were artificially depressed by the inefficiency of the Immigration and Naturalization Service, which had massive backlogs of both immigration and naturalization applications.

Although there are and have been strong anti-immigrant forces in U.S. society, sparked by the so-called revolution led by Ronald Reagan and Newt Gingrich, that movement has not had significant success in reversing the family-friendly bias of U.S. immigration law. Although there was clearly a "turn against immigration" in the early and mid-1990s, its legislative results were chiefly punitive measures to deprive both legal and illegal immigrants of certain entitlements, measures that were spawned largely by the Republicans in the House of Representatives and signed by Pres. Bill Clinton. The contemporary anti-immigrant movement is more disparate than its predecessors. Although some elements in it espouse an almost naked racism, others place their objections to newcomers on politically correct economic, ecological, and other nonethnocultural factors. As the new century began, the increased political potential of the growing Hispanic minorities who had been the chief targets of the anti-immigrant movement gave politicians pause, and some of the punitive measures of the earlier 1990s were repealed or modified while others were struck down by the courts. There was every reason to believe that, barring a serious recession in the United States or a major international crisis, a fairly heavy family-oriented immigration to the United States would continue.

Critics, however, are prone to argue that the continued emphasis on family preferences has brought too many immigrants to the United States and that too many of those have been unsuitable. Many want most of the immigrant visas to be allocated to persons more likely to contribute to American society rather than to persons with close family relationships to those already here, as is now the case. Such critics often point to nations such as Canada that have a complex point system for awarding visas. In Canada most of the points given are for such things as property owned in Canada, education, and professional skills, and relatively few points are awarded on the basis of family relationships.

—Roger Daniels

See also Asian American Families;
Extended Family; Immigrant Families,
Experience of

References and Further Reading
Commission on Immigration and
Naturalization. 1953. *Whom We Shall
Welcome.* Washington, DC:
Government Printing Office.
Daniels, Roger. 1988. *Asian America:
Chinese and Japanese in the United
States since 1850.* Seattle: University of
Washington Press.
Daniels, Roger. 1990. *Coming to America:
A History of Immigration and Ethnicity
in American Life.* New York:
HarperCollins.
Dinnerstein, Leonard. 1982. *America and
the Survivors of the Holocaust.* New
York: Columbia University Press.
Higham, John. 1955. *Strangers in the
Land: Patterns of American Nativism.*
New Brunswick, NJ: Rutgers University
Press.
Immigration and Naturalization Service.
1999. *1997 Statistical Yearbook of the
Immigration and Naturalization
Service.* Washington, DC: Government
Printing Office.
Johnson, Lyndon B. 1966. *Public Papers of
the Presidents of the United States,
1965.* Washington, DC: Government
Printing Office.
Malloy, William M., comp. 1910. *Treaties,
Conventions . . . 1776–1909.*
Washington, DC: Government Printing
Office.
Peffer, George A. 1999. *If They Don't
Bring Their Women Here: Chinese
Female Immigration before Exclusion.*
Urbana: University of Illinois Press.
Reimers, David M. 1992. *Still the Golden
Door: The Third World Comes to
America.* New York: Columbia
University Press.
Reimers, David M. 1998. *Unwelcome
Strangers: American Identity and the
Turn against Immigration.* New York:
Columbia University Press.
Richardson, James D., ed. 1907. *Messages
and Papers of the Presidents.* 7 vols.
Washington, DC: Bureau of National
Literature and Art.
U.S. Displaced Persons Commission.
1952. *Memo to America: The DP Story:
The Final Report of U.S. Displaced
Persons Committee.* Washington, DC:
Government Printing Office.
U.S. Statutes at Large. 1882. Vol. 22, p. 58.
The Chinese Exclusion Act.
U.S. Statutes at Large. 1943. Vol. 57, p. 58.

Family Therapy

Family therapy is a branch of psychotherapy that developed in the latter half of the twentieth century. It focuses on the operations of the family system as a whole, rather than on the psychological patterns of a single individual. Individual family members' interactions and characteristic behavior patterns, including psychological or social dysfunctioning, are viewed as arising from and feeding back into the complex social system of their own particular family group. Thus, although one person in the family may be presented as the "identified patient," a family therapist would typically view that person's problems as inextricable from the actions and behaviors of the rest of the group. Therapeutic treatment typically involves a systematic effort to introduce into the patterns of family interaction changes designed to produce a more satisfying, less distressing group experience—and also, ideally, to improve the life of each family member.

Such systematic therapeutic efforts are, however, a fairly modern invention. Rigid, hierarchical roles and responsibilities characterized the typical family system that was brought to the Americas from Europe. The master of the New England household, for example, was granted by law sole legal right to the labor of his wife, children, and servants—and the fruits of those labors—as well as the custody of their persons. Masters could, and often did, apprentice their own children out to other farms or workplaces, and the children were expected to do as they were told. Indeed, they were legally obliged to "honor their fathers and mothers"—in some Puritan settlements, under penalty of death (although no executions for this crime are recorded). Wives, likewise, were expected to be sexually faithful and obedient to the will of their husbands and to fulfill strongly gender-defined but still communally and economically valued roles in the productive colonial household. Offenders against this order could expect powerful social stigma, serious legal penalties, and/or economic privation, not therapeutic intervention, in response to their resisting behavior.

Although he clearly maintained a privileged position, the master of the Anglo-American house was obliged, at least on paper, to provide for the material and educational needs of all those in his household. Sanctions against masters were rare, not surprisingly, and typically less punitive and more leniently applied than those brought to bear on less powerful members of the household. Nevertheless, marriages could be dissolved as a result of a husband's adultery, impotence, or other failure to perform sexual duties. Children who were severely abused or whose educational or material needs were being seriously neglected could be removed from their father's custody by colonial authorities. In the fairly densely populated northern colonies, community surveillance was strong, especially in Puritan settlements, and it is likely that simply the awareness of being observed curbed some egregious patriarchal abuses.

The Puritans' common theological and political vision encouraged neighbors and clergy to intervene in the lives of nearby households where any "sinful," illicit, or antisocial activity might be noticed. Some scholars have suggested that this kind of surveillance by the community was particularly intense at times when the Puritan communities felt threatened, not only by divergent European practices, such as the pagan-inflected lifestyle encouraged by Thomas Merton at Merry Mount, but also by the communal mores of the various Native American groups they encountered, many of which practiced polygamy or serial monogamy and authorized very different gender identities than those allowed in the Anglo-American groups.

In all these close-knit societies, however, whether native or European, informal counseling and advice were doubtlessly regularly offered within kinship and other communal networks, or by midwives and other healers. In serious circumstances, clergy or other respected community members could be called in to help settle familial disputes, without resorting to legal action or public punishment. Southern settlements, on the other hand, were probably equally rigid in their hierarchical legal and socioeconomic structure, but unlike many of their northern counterparts, they were not settled by familial groups sharing a common religious vision. Instead, the widely dispersed households in the mid-Atlantic and southern colonies were settled primarily by single men, many of whom arrived as indentured servants and, slightly later, as slaves, to work for wealthier landholders on large estates. Women of all races were few, fertility rates were initially low, and deaths—of fathers, mothers, and children—could rapidly destabilize any family structure in a variety of ways.

Most African American families during the entire colonial and early national period were particularly vulnerable not only to the destabilizations inherent to frontier and plantation life but also to the social, legal, and economic realities connected with slavery. Recent research demonstrates a remarkable resiliency within African American families, however, due to the retention of traditional African communal practices, wide and flexible kinship networks, and a deep support for both marital and parental unions, within both slave and free communities. Indeed, still today, African American grandmothers, aunts, and other kin are arguably more often and more deeply involved in the family's child-rearing work than in many comparable white families and therefore are more likely to provide counsel, advice, and material aid to help families survive. This kind of extended kin-based support is also characteristic of many Asian, Native American, and Hispanic groups in the United States today.

During the period surrounding the American Revolutionary War, by contrast, an emphasis on the rights of the individual within any social contract or relationship gradually produced a slow, seismic shift in the traditional dynamics of American family and community life. By asserting, as the Declaration of Independence puts it, that "it is the Right of the People to alter or to abolish" any form of government that is not conducive to life, liberty, and the pursuit of happiness, Enlightenment authorities seemed to be offering all people the right to question patriarchal power structures. Meanwhile, westward expansion and increasing rates of immigration left many people isolated from kinship networks and other support systems. And although farming remained a key employment sector well into the twentieth century, industrialization and the rise of a wage-based economy in the nineteenth century resulted in a domestic sphere that was alienated from economic productivity. Rather than working together in the home place, men and

women were increasingly separated during the workday. Men began commuting into factories and other workplaces while the middle-class woman worked to create a domestic refuge at home—that is, a site for both the (conspicuous) consumption of (factory-created) goods and the nurturing of children (Ehrenreich and English 1978).

Feminist family therapists particularly emphasize the importance of the Victorian period's creation of the "patriarchal but father-absent family" (Luepnitz 1988, 16)—the family that most modern white Americans still view as "traditional." Indeed, it was in this late-nineteenth-century context that Freud, in Vienna, began his pioneering work in the new field of psychology, developing tools for individual psychoanalysis that would lead to the variety of forms of therapy that existed by the end of the twentieth century. Before his work arrived on these shores, however, family-counseling materials, particularly child-rearing manuals, were flooding the literary marketplace. In the Revolutionary period, writings on education and development by philosophers such as John Locke and Jean-Jacques Rousseau were popularized in the United States, often by medical doctors. But by the Victorian period most advice books were written by popular writers and public figures such as Lydia Maria Child, Catherine Beecher, and Horace Bushnell, a widely respected Congregationalist minister.

It was not until the turn of the twentieth century that psychological studies forged a "scientific" approach to motherhood and family life, led by such figures as Dr. G. Stanley Hall, Dr. L. Emmet Holt, and Dr. Winfield Hall. These early child and adolescent psychology "experts," along with the medical establishment generally, often worked to displace the knowledge and lived experience of mothers and the predominantly female healers and midwives, belittling such knowledge and experience as they did so. Midwives offered probably the most accessible and intimate form of family medical and psychological support, particularly for women, throughout the colonial and early national experience on into the Victorian period, but (until a small resurgence very late in the twentieth century) were virtually silenced by the emergent, male-dominated medical establishment. In addition to psychology and medical practice, however, family therapy has roots in many academic disciplines, including anthropology, sociology, and social work, itself a female dominated professional field that likewise developed during the Progressive Era. Social workers, physicians, and psychologists of that period all typically shared a belief that scientific knowledge, strategically and rationally applied, could be used to mold better people, and eventually a better society.

Among these professionals were a few persons working especially with mentally ill patients and children who began to believe that their clients' problems could not be thoroughly treated in isolation from their families. Although the psychiatric world was dominated by Freudian thinking until the 1960s, and therefore emphasized individualized therapy sessions, a few marriage counseling centers began treating couples in the 1930s. In the 1950s, a New York therapist named Nathan Ackerman started regularly using family interviews in his child and adolescent therapy; today he is sometimes regarded as the "father" of family therapy.

The primary theoretical framework that was developed by Ackerman and his followers during the 1950s, which still dominates at most schools of marital and family therapy today, is "family systems theory." That framework had its roots in "general system theory," as developed by biologist Ludwig von Bertalanffy starting in the 1940s and, later, in the incipient field of communication and computer engineering known as "cybernetics." Norbert Weiner, a founder of cybernetics, defined it as "the entire field of control and communication theory . . . concerned with the regulation of—and communication between—living organisms and artificial systems" (Miermont 1995, 88). The grandly systemic perspective offered by both approaches was extremely attractive to a variety of disciplines during the postwar period, and systemic concepts were used to understand the workings of ecological, mechanical, and computer-based systems, as well as psychological and social systems.

This viewpoint was first most strongly connected to psychotherapy through its application to the situation of schizophrenics in the latter half of the 1950s by researchers who were exploring communication strategies and interpersonal interactions of schizophrenics with their families. A backlash against psychoanalytic orthodoxy within psychiatric circles, moreover, combined with the social revolutions of the 1960s to pave the way for the enthusiasm with which the family system approach was embraced for heretofore seemingly "individual" mental health problems. Civil rights activists, feminists, and antiwar demonstrators questioned, after all, the racial, sexual, economic, and cultural divisions that created systemic forms of racism, sexism, war, poverty, and homophobia across societies.

Meanwhile, the postwar marriage and baby booms of this period were followed by a loud divorce boom that echoed through the 1960s and 1970s. By 1980, nearly half of all marriages were ending in divorce. Many professionals and lay-persons in the United States were concerned that the family was disappearing; Christian conservatives, in particular, blamed the sexual revolution and the women's rights movement, both of which seemed to undermine the solidity of the marital bond that conservatives believe to be the heart of the family. Others argued that the family was simply changing to keep up with changing needs and circumstances. Families in the latter half of the twentieth century were increasingly under pressure from the speed of modern living. Modern kitchen and laundry appliances often simply raised standards of cleanliness without actually saving the homemaker any time. Parents were increasingly expected to produce children who would be able to compete in a postindustrial economy, even when both parents had full-time careers. Meanwhile, step or "blended" families and other nontraditional family systems—for example, gay and lesbian parents—were also rising in numbers, often without clear role models to help them work through the inevitable struggles that arise in the course of family formation and re-formation.

Improvements in transportation and communication systems caused companies to move headquarters and huge numbers of workers regularly, further disrupting kinship and other support networks for many Americans, often several times over the course of a career. Of course, geographic mobility has been a part of the American pursuit of economic happiness from colonial times. Perhaps the regular loss of familial connections in our immigrant past is related to the focus of some forms of family therapy, particularly that influenced by the work of Murray Bowen, on reconstructing genealogies and kinship structures. Bowen-style therapy requires all family members to construct "genograms," complex "family tree" models that typically include dates for births, deaths, marriages, major family traumas, estrangements, and divorces, for several generations.

On the other hand, family therapy has been criticized, particularly by feminists, for not paying enough attention to the historical development of the American patriarchal family system and its unequal legacy of costs and benefits for men, women, and children. Indeed, practitioners of marital and family therapy typically believe that understanding and intervening in current patterns of family behavior are of greater importance than focusing on the origins and development of those patterns. As this still-young field itself develops its own history, however, it is possible that the history of all the elements of family systems will be seen as freighted with potential significance.

—*Lori Askeland*

See also Apprenticeship; Blended Families; Freud, Sigmund; Hall, G. Stanley

References and Further Reading
Coontz, Stephanie. 1997. *The Way We Really Are: Coming to Terms with America's Changing Families*. New York: Basic Books.
Ehrenreich, Barbara, and Deirdre English. 1978. *For Her Own Good: 150 Years of Experts' Advice to Women*. Garden City, NY: Anchor Press/Doubleday.
Glick, Ira D., Ellen M. Berman, John F. Clarkin, and Douglas S. Rait. 2000. *Marital and Family Therapy*. 4th ed. Washington, DC: American Psychiatric Press.
Goldenberg, Irene, and Herbert Goldenberg. 1996. *Family Therapy: An*

Overview. 4th ed. Pacific Grove, CA: Brooks/Cole Publishing.

Luepnitz, Deborah Anna. 1988. *The Family Interpreted: Feminist Theory in Clinical Practice.* New York: Basic Books.

Miermont, Jacques, ed. 1995. *A Dictionary of Family Therapy.* English ed., expanded and revised by Hugh Jenkins. Trans. Chris Turner. Cambridge, MA: Blackwell Publishers.

Wilson, Melvin N. 1991. "The Context of the African American Family." In *Child Welfare: An Africentric Perspective,* edited by Joyce E. Everett, Sandra S. Chipungu, and Bogart R. Leashore, 85–119. New Brunswick, NJ: Rutgers University Press.

Family Vacations

Family vacations are times of leisure or relaxation, generally spent away from home while in the company of people who are linked to one another by social, economic, and familial bonds. When the vacation takes place away from home, it falls into the realm of tourism, which may be defined loosely as travel for pleasure; when the vacation takes place at home, it may be considered a form of relaxation. In order for either type of vacation to occur, a variety of conditions must be met. Included among these factors are the presence of expendable income, time for leisure activities, safety and comfort at one's destination (including one's home), political and economic stability, transportation, and a mythology composed of images and stories meant to promote travel, relaxation, and interest in a particular place. Once these conditions are met, American families can and do take vacations.

The tourist, who might also be described as a vacationer visiting a place away from his or her home, is a universal figure who experiences the out-of-the-ordinary activities offered by a location while also acting as a consumer within that place. Tourism is temporary, in that it involves the process of both going away and returning home, and is transformative, in that it places the vacationers as outsiders in a place who are present for relaxation rather than for work.

Purposes

Vacations tend to fill a number of purposes. Although each trip is planned, to some extent, individually, wider patterns do emerge to explain the phenomenon of travel. Two of these goals—education and identity formation—have remained relatively constant over the course of Americans' travel.

Education. Often, vacations are designed as educational tools. Families seeking difference decide to vacation in regions unlike their own or in places where new experiences may be had. Those seeking diversity travel to areas populated by different ethnic groups or by a multitude of cultural groups. This quest for diversity is linked to the search for a usable past: Families participate in their secular education in order to create a personal and collective history. Just as the family's members recall vacation stories as moments of the family's past, they look upon the museums, amusement parks, and other tourist destinations in the United States as sites on which the country's past is constantly formed. Thus the creation of history is linked to the formation of national, ethnic, cultural, and personal identity.

Identity Formation. In fact, vacationers actively, though often subconsciously, search for a sense of being, for an identity that is validated through the very process

A family visit to Ontario, Canada, c. 1930s. (Library of Congress)

of tourism. People choose to visit particular places and, in doing so, express their personalities. Although these signs of identity are also forged when at home, they tend to be more obvious when people are away from home and away from the trappings of everyday life. The context of a place—its social shape, environment, economy, and culture—are linked not only to its identity but also to the manner in which people recognize and express their identities. Families expect to find particular places meaningful in a specific way; when they confirm those expectations through travel, the families also find meaning within themselves.

Insofar as travel experiences are socially determined and stratified, vaca-tions are also determined by class and economics. A family, then, is most likely to visit a place commonly toured by other people of similar socioeconomic backgrounds. Since travel costs have decreased over the last three hundred years, vacations are now more readily available as families have more money to spend on, or use credit to finance, leisure and travel. Thus the vacation as an annual holiday is an established and real-izable goal.

The standard vacation ranges from ten days to two weeks and, within the United States, involves relatively con-stant driving in order to maximize the distance covered and the travel experi-ence garnered. In automobile travel, groups tend to turn in on themselves because they are physically separated from the outside environment. The most usual groupings of sightseers, then, are those of intimate acquaintances with whom one can spend long periods of time in confined spaces. Because the group's bonds are tested during these vacations and because the travel group tends to be linked by familial bonds, families tend to be centered in much travel and in many memories of vacations.

Destinations

Vacations were not always this common. Before the Industrial Revolution, for example, travel was undertaken only by pilgrims or businessmen. During the six-teenth century, social travel in Europe increased continually until, in the seven-teenth and eighteenth centuries, the grand tour emerged as an educational—and entertaining—necessity of life for wealthy, landed, and elite Europeans. In the late nineteenth century, the grand tour became an American phenomenon as well. Primarily undertaken by young men, the grand tour was a rite of passage during which the traveler tried to become "a man of the world." He toured Europe, seeing the most noted examples of art and architecture, meeting with the most famed scholars and statesmen, and often cavorting with other relatively wealthy young men. This type of travel, which also involved forming business contacts and performing official functions, truly separated the social classes: Only the very wealthy could afford to spend a period ranging from one month to two (or three) years abroad.

When Americans turned their attention toward their own country, vacation destinations changed, although socioeconomic forces still divided vacationers according to who could go to which places. A series of U.S. destinations emerged, however, that were visited, in varying degrees, by the wide variety of families found within the United States.

Nature. Nature destinations are the first category of tourist sites popular for American family vacations. Spurred on by the burgeoning conservation movement and subsequent formation of the national park system, nineteenth-century families traveled across the country in order to experience its natural wonders and scenic beauty. Among the two most popular natural sites visited during the mid-nineteenth and late twentieth centuries and during the present day are Niagara Falls and the Grand Canyon. In fact, these two destinations have become intricately involved with the creation of a national identity; writers, artists, and politicians have pointed to their beauty and grandeur as exemplars of the United States, its terrain, and its glory. (For an American traveling abroad, the admission that he or she had never seen either Niagara Falls or the Grand Canyon was tantamount to the admission that he or she had never lived in the United States.) Other areas of interest that have been visited regularly since the nineteenth century are Yosemite National Park, Florida, California, and the country's many miles of seashore.

Regions. A means of organizing sights, regions also became tourist destinations during the nineteenth century. Unfortunately, regional boundaries were not precise, so vacationers' search for relics from the past in order to identify and define the various regions proved elusive. Travelers to New England (seen as a historic region and as the birthplace of the nation), the Midwest (recognized as the "breadbasket" and "heartland" of the country), and the West (envisioned as wide-open expanses of land and untamed nature) sought regional architecture, dialects, antiques, and lifestyles that were fundamentally linked to the region. Of all of the regions in the United States, the West became the epitome of the nation. Popular sentiment depicted the West as a vast and powerful place where American ingenuity and individualism allowed pioneering families to extend the country from the Atlantic Ocean to the Pacific. Cinematic images, along with promotional travel literature, reinforced this stereotype and encourage tourism.

Cities. Cities have also emerged as tourist destinations. Working-class families, during the mid- to late nineteenth century, found themselves able to take day trips to nearby cities because of newly developed transportation systems, whereas wealthier families could spend expanded periods of time in a metropolitan area. With an economic interest in promoting tourism, cities started to package themselves as places capable of entertaining families, businesspeople, and individuals combining business and pleasure. Fairs and exhibitions help to promote cities as tourist sites, and skylines have come to represent and identify particular cities. The stereotypes involved in the depictions and notions of cities that arise from these attempts to draw in vacationers become self-perpetuating ideas that have started to define cities as tourist sites.

History. Although a difficult-to-define site, history also draws vacationers and has drawn them since the birth of the United States. In search of a past comparable to those of older countries, Americans seek historic houses, landmarks, hallowed grounds, site markers, monuments, parks, restorations, and museums. These places, each and every one a contrived attraction, began fascinating Americans almost immediately after the Revolutionary War. Nostalgia, along with national pride, spurs an interest in the heritage that is inextricably linked to ethnicity and cultural identity. Historic sites, such as museums, are defined, interpreted, and reinterpreted with a particular focus and toward a particular target audience. This focus, when combined with the fabricated nature of the sites, creates places that are unreal and sometimes misrepresentative. The institutional support necessary to fund historic sites can also lead to political bias and misrepresentation.

As a subcategory of historic and cultural sites, museums provide a particularized version of history. Artifacts ranging from fossils to photographs create a museum's collection, which then allows the present generation (represented by curators, donors, and administrators) to frame the past. These exhibitions necessarily divide the past from the present and the natural from the artificial. Yet, the collections also serve as agents of change and sources of inspiration for those groups who, finding signs of their national, cultural, or ethnic identity within the interpretation, express signs of modern solidarity. The past thus created is a singular and enshrined version of history, a legitimation of the group's present.

Historic preservation also works within this framework of history as a tourist destination. Connected to the social politics of a time period, historic preservation focuses on the conservation and restoration of buildings and artifacts that point to a particular version of the past. Usually, this past is a harmonious time full of happy memories. Because cultural groups as well as industrialists undertake preservation, it cannot be separated from either the consumer culture of the United States or of tourism.

Amusement Parks. Amusement parks have also emerged as tourist destinations. Such places as Sea World, Busch Gardens, and Six Flags Great Adventure follow in the tradition of Coney Island and the Midway Plaisance of the Chicago World's Fair in 1893. Of course, Walt Disney World and Disneyland have become synonymous with family vacations. These pleasure parks—like resorts of the nineteenth century—combine lodging, dining, and entertainment to create an entire travel package situated within one commercialized attraction. Often termed "tourist factories," amusement parks seem to belong to a fantasy world where all of one's needs can be met and where responsibility and individual work are banished. Simulated historical attractions work alongside glimpses and predictions of the future, and consumer culture competes with and defines family togetherness in amusement parks such as those owned by the Disney Corporation.

Private Homes. In fact, most family vacations center on notions of family togetherness. Representing another vacation destination, the homes of friends and family members serve as places where Americans focus on their familial connections. Mobility in the United States helped to create this last type of tourist destination: As family members moved away from their parents' homes, vacations became a time to reunite with relatives. When large groups of family members choose to vacation together, family reunions become the destination of travel as well as the organization of the vacation. Relatives travel varying distances to meet at specific locations where they celebrate their familial connections with one another. Importantly, business and pleasure are frequently combined on these trips.

Lodging
Americans who travel within the United States often stay with relatives and friends. When they do not, the travelers use a variety of different types of lodging, ranging from very private bed-and-breakfasts to very anonymous and popular chain hotels. Inns, the earliest tourist lodgings in America, allowed vacationers to occupy a room in somebody's home, often sharing a bed with another traveler (or with other travelers).

Hotels. Hotels soon became the locus of tourist lodging. Multistory city hotels were popular first as places to sleep and then as a type of tourist destination. Like early resorts, city hotels were designed to emphasize public spaces and did not necessarily offer large and luxurious guest rooms. But they did offer easy accessibility to the city (itself a tourist destination), and they offered a complete social world, with dining rooms, ballrooms, and, frequently, entertainment. The hotels, which extended to include "trackside hotels" alongside railroad stations, divided lodgers from the environment while simultaneously allowing them to feel that they had visited a particular place. City hotels continue to be found in the downtown areas of many U.S. cities; they are not, however, the same type of tourist destinations that they once were. Instead, city hotels must work to attract guests through historic connections and/or location, as a convenient place for business conventions and sightseeing activities.

Motels. Increased motor travel led to the creation of motels, which, in the United States, quickly became more widely used than hotels. Unlike hotels, motor courts and motor inns—precursors to the modern motel—were designed to be easily accessible for Americans traveling in automobiles. They tend to offer spacious rooms, a parklike setting, and parking adjacent to the rooms. Usually, these motels are located on the edges of a town and are cheaper than hotels. Additionally, they offer a homelike atmosphere that, traditionally, has been considered both novel and advantageous. Vacationers seem to enjoy feeling "at home" while on vacation, so use of motels has increased, and chain motels, which contain more traditional hotel features such as restaurants and entertainment, have arisen throughout the United States. The combination of food, lodging, and entertainment (including shopping) is in fact essential to the project of chain motels: The convenience of easy accessibility and the fulfillment of all of a family's needs and wants draw vacationers to motels.

Camping. Camping provides vacationers with yet another lodging option. Originally, vacationers merely stopped their cars along the roadside and set up temporary lodgings for themselves. That system of "auto camping" changed over time, though, and organized campsites emerged. Although many of these campgrounds had been free—creating a very inexpensive means of travel—the free campsites basically disappeared by the 1930s, thus excluding transients and poor folks from campgrounds. U.S. travelers who used campgrounds tended to feel that they were "returning to fundamentals" by returning to nature. The capitalist nature of the country, however, quickly led to mass-produced, consumable items designed to make camping easier. These goods, ranging from tents to recreational vehicles, camping knives to Coleman stoves, make the "fundamentals" of life equivalent to the modern conveniences of life. Regardless of the type of equipment used, camping is viewed as a social act. People mingle with each other and with the visited environment from within an atmosphere that is simultaneously anonymous and friendly.

Transportation
Vacationing Americans have used a variety of forms of transportation in order to reach their destinations. In the early days of travel, these methods were often uncomfortable and tedious. Technological innovation, however, has led to increasingly comfortable methods of travel.

Stagecoaches and Canal Boats. Of all of the early methods of transportation, the stagecoach seemed to offer the longest and most unpleasant trips. Passengers slowly made their way from town to town, often sleeping in the homes of strangers, places that were used as inns. Canal boats also offered slow travel. But this method of transportation allowed travelers to simultaneously experience the technology of the United States (evidenced through the creation of the canals and their systems of hardware) and the country's natural wonders. (The Erie Canal, which opened in 1825, exemplified this type of tourist destination.) By the 1830s, both stagecoaches and canal boats merely linked railroad lines and steamships. As their influence and use declined, only the canal boat remained a facet of U.S. life, as a form of commercial transportation.

Railroads and Steamships. Nineteenth-century vacationers in the United States primarily made use of railroads and steamships, both of which increased the comfort and ease of travel while lowering the costs of the venture. Both passive and formal, the train and steamship encapsulated the social world of the traveling upper classes and made use of the newest technology of the period. Additionally, both forms of transportation firmly separated the vacationer from the destination: Although the leisure events aboard a ship could be seen as vacation activities, the ship and train primarily functioned as an enclosed means of bringing the passengers to a particular place. Since it was only possible to leave the ship or train at a port or station, passengers were

Families ride a roller coaster at Disney World in Orlando, Florida. (Kit Kittle/Corbis)

essentially only able to see places other than the deck (and cabins) or car from a distance, as they passed. Both ships and trains remain in use within the United States, although they are not as frequently used as they were during the nineteenth century.

Automobiles. Through its confirmation of the use of the automobile, World War I opened up a new world of domestic travel. As cars became more cost-efficient and more widely owned, they allowed for a greater diversity of vacationers to take to the roads. In fact, by the 1920s, the world of automobile travel included not only the upper classes but also the working classes. Unlike travel by train or ship, car travel lacked rigid schedules and cre-

ated a more seemingly democratic and free system of travel.

As roads and cars became increasingly important in the United States, road trips became a form of moving vacation. Rather than serving simply as a means of getting somewhere, the car trip became the focus of family vacations. In the early part of the twentieth century, those people who owned automobiles tended not to use them every day, thus making the extended trip a spectacular and extraordinary event. New types of social encounters arose as motorists helped one another overcome obstacles and as vacationers interacted with residents of a locality in restaurants and at gas stations.

Various other organizations also helped motoring vacationers. The American

Automobile Association (AAA), for example, began in 1902. Since that time, the organization has provided vacation guides, maps, roadside assistance, and vacation planning for its members. Oil companies, local governments, and commercial attractions also started to provide road maps and trip-planning information bearing advertisements to promote their products (which include actual places such as cities).

Between World War I and World War II, the car became an object used daily. Thus, the automobile became a means of getting somewhere, a means of covering the maximum distance possible in the minimum amount of time. As automobile travel was transformed, roads also changed. Not only did they become part of standardized and paved systems of highways and interstates, but they also came to include a whole variety of roadside attractions. Billboards and other roadside advertisements expressed regional identity while simultaneously proclaiming where and how vacationers should spend their money. Commercial strips, armed with stores, restaurants, and gas stations, sprang up throughout the nation. They have since transformed the landscape of the country and have evolved into the places where daily life occurs.

Importantly, cars also serve as a cohesive force. Vacationers who travel by automobile find themselves firmly divided from inhabitants of the passing towns and cities, as well as from other travelers. So the vacationers turn inward, toward their fellow travelers—usually family members—to form a socially cohesive and viable force. A series of social events, including discussions with fellow travelers and participation in games, occurs inside of the car. Many of these social activities occur because of products marketed toward vacationers. Alongside postcards and souvenirs, gas stations and roadside attractions tend to sell games and activities suited to car travel. This type of merchandise has been available since the mid-twentieth century and helps to create and verify shared experiences. These games help to cement the bonds of those traveling within a single car and allow for similarities in travel experiences among all of the people traveling by automobile.

Buses. Before World War II, buses were primarily used by members of the working class who could not afford to travel by air or who did not own a car. Railroad companies also made use of buses, replacing unprofitable branch lines with bus lines. Like the train, the bus allowed its relatively passive passengers to interact with one another; like the car, the bus allowed its passengers to have closer interaction with the passing landscape. Because of its cramped and limited nature, bus travel was informal, inexpensive, and not always particularly comfortable. Technologies have since allowed for more comfortable buses, many of which are now used for organized group tours and chartered trips.

Airplanes. After World War II, airplanes became another means of tourist travel. Previously seen as extraordinary devices used for stunts and adventure, planes became a more efficient means of traveling long distances. The cost of flying meant that air travel was limited to the upper classes for many years. Increased production of safer and faster planes, as well as larger numbers of companies offering air service and federal laws governing airports and air safety, has led, however, to cheaper tickets and more widely used flights. Although the experience of flying is similar to that of riding the railroad or cruising on a ship, it offers a very different perspective of the world. Now, the vacationer sees the world below in miniature. Thus disconnection with the landscape means that travelers often only encounter a city's airport, which becomes a symbol of the city itself. Vacationers stepping off from an airplane can often feel as if they have traveled through time and not space; standardized designs and products across the country further emphasize this sense.

The Production of Memory

Consumption of Places and Objects. Vacationers, as all tourists, are consumers. They spend money on food, lodging, transportation, and souvenirs. Their buying greatly contributes to the economic well-being of a destination and constitutes a significant portion of both domestic and foreign trade. Occasionally, as when buying guided tours, the vacationer plans his or her purchases well in advance; at other times, as when confronting a souvenir shop or display, the tourist is truly an impulse buyer who, caught up in the moment, purchases a variety of things meant to represent a place or an experience. This consumption has become an essential part of American family vacations.

Souvenirs. Souvenirs—those objects purchased and created by families on vacation—are the material objects that come to represent places and experiences. Vacationers buy a variety of mass-produced items ranging from postcards to pencil cases and a spectrum of hand-produced goods specific to a region or ethnic group. Regardless of the specific thing purchased, the souvenir serves as a reminder. Though often out of place in the vacationer's home, these material goods create a tangible explanation of one's vacation experiences. As objects and images, souvenirs sustain memories.

Photographs. Following in the tradition of mass-produced lithographs, postcards provide a romanticized and marketable image of tourist destinations. Their stereotyped depictions resonate with vacationers who want to remind friends and family members at home that they have been somewhere else; they also resonate with merchants and organizations who are anxious to capitalize on tourist dollars. These small, tangible objects are carried around the country (and the world) and serve as advertisements of a place; they create and sustain tourist desire.

Postcards also make use of the technology of the camera. Photography—whether individual or aimed at a mass market—provides a means of understanding a place. Through focusing a camera's lens or buying a postcard, the vacationer safely and comfortably interacts with a destination. Often, people only travel to take pictures or to buy postcards. Rather than simply representing a destination, then, the pictures become the experience of the location, the objectified subject on which the viewer gazes.

Of course, individual photographs also serve as a means of centering the family, for vacationers tend to picture family members against the backdrop of tourist sites. These photos offer "proof" that the family has visited a particular place while simultaneously displaying the cohesion and unity of the family. As much as the vacation album proclaims that the family went on a vacation, it also proclaims that the family *is*. In this manner, photographs of family vacations help to create an identity based on the transformative effects of tourism. Additionally, each person who looks at the vacation photos—dislocated from the time and space of the trip—becomes an armchair tourist. Images can be arranged and rearranged to tell a variety of stories. The visual representations of tourist destinations and experiences, then, reinforce the idea that tourism is a scripted stage set of activities that can be bought and sold.

—*Anastasia L. Pratt*

See also Family Photography; Leisure, Recreation, and Amusements

References and Further Reading
Boorstin, Daniel. 1997. *The Image: A Guide to Pseudo-Events in America.* 25th anniversary ed. New York: Vintage.
Braden, Donna R., and Judith E. Endelman. 1990. *Americans on Vacation.* Dearborn, MI: Henry Ford Museum and Greenfield Village.
Burkart, A. J., and S. Medlik. 1981. *Tourism: Past, Present, and Future.* 2d ed. London: Heinemann.
Jakle, John. 1985. *The Tourist: Travel in Twentieth-Century North America.* Lincoln: University of Nebraska Press.
Judd, Dennis R., and Susan F. Fainstein, eds. 1999. *The Tourist City.* New Haven: Yale University Press.
Kammen, Michael. 1991. *Mystic Chords of Memory: The Transformation of Tradition in American Culture.* New York: Vintage Books.
Lippard, Lucy R. 1999. *On the Beaten Track: Tourism, Art, and Place.* New York: The New Press.
Lowenthal, David. 1985. *The Past Is a Foreign Country.* Cambridge: Cambridge University Press.
MacCannell, Dean. 1999. *The Tourist: A New Theory of the Leisure Class.* Berkeley: University of California Press.
Margolies, John, and Eric Baker. 2000. *See the U.S.A.: The Art of the American Travel Brochure.* San Francisco: Chronicle Books.
Nash, Dennison. 1981. "Tourism as an Anthropological Subject." *Current Anthropology* 22(5): 461–481.
Newman, Harvey K. 1999. *Southern Hospitality: Tourism and the Growth of Atlanta.* Tuscaloosa: University of Alabama Press.
Purchase, Eric. 1999. *Out of Nowhere: Disaster and Tourism in the White Mountains.* Baltimore: Johns Hopkins University Press.
Rothman, Hal K. 1998. *Devil's Bargains: Tourism in the Twentieth-Century American West.* Lawrence: University Press of Kansas.
Sears, John F. 1989. *Sacred Places: American Tourist Attractions in the Nineteenth Century.* Amherst: University of Massachusetts Press.
Selwyn, Tom, ed. 1996. *The Tourist Image: Myths and Myth Making in Tourism.* Chichester; NY: John Wiley and Sons.
Witzel, Michael Karl. 2000. *The American Motel.* Osceola, FL: WBI Publishing.

Farm Families

Farm families occupy a heroic position in the American cultural mythology. Portrayed by painters, poets, and politicians as the bedrock of the republic and the defenders of public morality, the reality of family life on U.S. farms often disappears into a sepia-colored nostalgia for a certain and unchanging past. Although upheld as the model of stability and tradition, farm families marched in the vanguard of national migration and western settlement and adapted farm production and methodology to the new technology of industrialization. Heralded for their conservatism, farm families nevertheless participated in radical uprisings stretching from Bacon's Rebellion to Shays' Rebellion, Populism, and the Farm Aid Movement. Economic pressures in the form of land acquisition and tenure and the increasing effect of market forces undermined the familial and social harmony commonly attributed to farm families. Providing land for the next generation occupied the economic decisions of parents and occasionally produced familial power struggles as fathers maintained control over the land and labor of sons. Although agrarian men and women claimed a spirit of mutuality in managing the work and economics of farm life, the growing influence of the market economy tended to separate the work of men and women, placing higher value on mechanized commercial agriculture and devaluing the exchange networks that sustained rural society. Indeed, conflict and change have as fully defined American farm families as have harmony and stability.

Broadly stated, farm families were historically made up of kin groups connected by marriage and heredity whose principal concerns centered on meeting the family's immediate survival needs and passing on the land and other property to future generations. Family members supplied the necessary labor to sow, cultivate, harvest, and preserve crops or raise livestock. Men exercised traditional and legal authority over lands and households. Their work centered on the fields and barns and on the transportation of produce to markets, whereas women dominated the preparation and preservation of food, the production of cloth and clothing, and the care and guidance of children. For most families, the gender definition of tasks proved less rigid than a delineation of jobs implies. When work demanded, women assisted with planting, haying, or other activities in the fields, and some women indicated a preference for the outdoor activities. Likewise, the hard work of soap or candle making or meat preservation involved both men and women. Although men were less likely to undertake "women's work" than vice versa, everyone in a farm family joined in to complete critical tasks. Even children soon put aside the freedom of play to assist in the labor of the farm. Whether carding wool, chopping firewood, sweeping floors, hoeing weeds, or watching younger siblings, children contributed to the family economy.

The economics of farm life revolved around several related issues: the need to provide land for adult children to establish new households, the local exchange of goods and services, and the more distant markets for surplus production. Farmers in the United States generally held more land than they could reasonably work, and many continued to acquire land as their families grew. Unimproved land constituted a reserve for future expansion of production and an endowment for the households of married sons. Establishing adult children nearby perpetuated the exchange economy that governed farm families locally. As every farmer knew, the independence that landholding implied depended upon a substantial network of interdependent exchanges of goods and services. Readily recognizable in the sewing bees, corn huskings, and barn raisings of folklore, the exchange networks were more complex and more necessary than these occasional gatherings of the community for work and fun. Farm families borrowed and gave on an almost daily basis. Such exchanges, even when recorded in account books or journals, could not be evaluated in simple cash terms. Assistance in the completion of specific tasks, a gift of seeds or thread, and the lending of tools or food enabled farm families to maintain the "independence" for which they were so famous.

The market influence represented both an opportunity and a threat. For most farmers the transition to commercial agriculture did not occur until after the Civil War. Up to that point most farmers marketed their surplus after the needs of the family and the next season's crop had been met. Participation in the markets depended on surplus and access to transportation. The early-nineteenth-century construction of roads, canals, and railroads provided inland farmers with more reliable access to markets and encouraged specialization of agricultural production. Although only the large cotton plantations could afford to relinquish their commitment to safety-first agriculture, mid-level farmers directed an increasing percentage of production toward market sales. By the late nineteenth century this transition to commercial agriculture placed the economic viability of many farm families in jeopardy as farm prices fell and mortgages matured.

Farm families of the day nostalgically looked back to a time when they believed fewer conflicts had disrupted the agricultural community. But if they had looked more closely, they would have found agrarian struggle in every age.

For seventeenth-century New Englanders, the family represented the little "commonwealth" that sustained the larger religious and cultural community. Marriage and family were expected and encouraged through a variety of social pressures and incentives that included land distribution practices based on family size. Children represented a source of labor for the initial clearing of land, and the healthy climate of the northern colonies enabled the survival of more children to help with the farm production. But as the population of New England expanded, farm families faced disruption. In the Plymouth colony, young men dispersed to new lands, with some moving several times to create communities more loosely organized than the founders intended. On the other hand, seventeenth-century Andover (Massachusetts) developed a static community that struggled with increasing population pressure on the available arable land. Here farm families faced disruption of a different sort. Slightly more than seven children per family reached maturity, and the first generation of settlers lived longer (the average age at death for males was an astounding 71.8 years) (Greven 1966). With land in short supply, fathers exercised greater control over the labor of their sons. Reluctance on the part of aging fathers to divide the farmland and the need for parental approval to establish new households meant that the second generation of Andover settlers married later. Some fathers allowed sons to marry and settle on a portion of the family land but retained legal title to the entire estate, thus limiting the options of the younger generation to capitalize on the productive possibilities of the farm. The youngest sons, who were expected to care for aging parents, often did not receive land until the father retired or died. This increased control of fathers over the affairs of their adult sons produced a level of familial disharmony that can only be surmised through oblique references in journals and diaries.

Settlement in the Chesapeake region initially involved young adventurous men seeking wealth, not stable family life. The unbalanced sex ratio in the first years of settlement; the rigors of tobacco culture, with its high demand for labor; and the unhealthy climate of the southern region operated to prevent the early establishment of farm families. Women, like their male counterparts, generally arrived in Virginia as indentured servants and were legally prohibited from marriage for the duration of their contracts. Life expectancy likewise inhibited family development in the Chesapeake as disease, accidents, and violence shortened marriages to an average of seven years. Chesapeake families were generally smaller than those of New England, owing to later age of marriage for women and higher childhood mortality (40–55 percent of children failed to survive to age twenty) (Carr and Walsh 1977). With shorter life spans for all Chesapeake settlers (an estimated 70 percent died before reaching age fifty), fathers provided carefully for the inheritance of their children, outlining their wishes in elaborate detail to account for the possibility that sons and daughters would live under the guardianship of a widowed mother or within the household of a stepfather. All too often children passed through both circumstances before entering a new category as orphans (Carr and Walsh 1977; Morgan 1975).

For farm families in the tobacco regions, agricultural production rather than family size put pressure on the land and encouraged migration west. By 1676, the demand for good land and the lack of significant opposition to English expansion by other European powers brought Virginia farm families into violent conflict with Native Americans and the British governor in what was called Bacon's Rebellion. Not until the early eighteenth century did the Chesapeake settlers establish family-centered life. Even then, farm families differed significantly from those found in other colonial regions. Not only were Virginia farm families more isolated, but wealth and race clearly defined the parameters of family life as slavery became an established fact in the agricultural economy.

A third region of colonial settlement emerged in the Middle Atlantic colonies. Like the New England settlers, Pennsylvania Quakers migrated as nuclear families to establish communities capable of sustaining a spiritual environment that would shield their children from a hostile world. Quaker parents believed their responsibility for providing a conducive religious environment included maintaining an elaborate marriage discipline and providing land for establishing new households. As a result, fathers purchased land in excess of what they could reasonably farm. A study of landholding in one 1690 community showed that 80 percent of families owned more than 150 acres. Many families owned several hundred acres of land and periodically made new purchases in anticipation of future divisions among adult sons. Newly married sons purchased from their fathers the necessary 40 to 100 acres required to establish new households. Purchasing the land provided income for elderly parents and granted the second generation of Quaker men economic autonomy unknown in Andover families. Fertile land, the development of a cash-and-credit economy, and smaller family size operated together to produce stable family life for the more successful Quakers. Over time, however, poorer members of the community married at a later age and often outside their religious circle, suggesting that economic pressures for land also affected some Quakers adversely (Levy 1991).

By the end of the colonial period, farm families were experiencing a variety of problems associated with developing agricultural markets and pressures on the land as immigration and natural increase limited the opportunities for many families to provide adequate lands for sons to establish new households. By the 1780s, the cash-based markets for agricultural products had imposed new demands on farm families. Farmers in western Massachusetts rebelled against the mounting pressure to repay debts, a pressure that contradicted more informal practices of local exchanges. Settlement of the conflict known as Shays' Rebellion did not end tensions between the emerging market economy and traditional local exchanges. Indeed, the conflicts spilled over into individual households. Emphasis on cash crops often elevated the authority of men and devalued the local exchange contributions of women. In the South the shift toward slave labor relegated white women to the household and raised legal impediments against black family development. Likewise, the extraordinary population growth evident in the eighteenth century fueled speculators' and squatters' dreams of land west of the Appalachian Mountains. By the end of the American Revolution, farm families claimed land all the way to the Cumberland River, thus reinitiating the cycle of clearing, settlement, and population pressure that had characterized the earlier colonial period.

In the first half of the nineteenth century, farm families continued their migratory habits, settling the cotton lands of the Deep South and the corn and hog regions of the Midwest, before setting out across the plains to reach California and Oregon. Only at the end of the century, when technology permitted, would farm families attempt to settle the Great Plains. Studies of migrating farm families suggest a series of moves that spanned several generations. The sons and daughters of colonial immigrants established farms on the shoulders of the Appalachian Mountains. In turn, their children settled the Northwest Territory or the new states of the South. Likely, their children would become the hardy souls who traveled the Oregon Trail. In Alabama, Mississippi, Louisiana, and Texas, some farm families made migration a way of life. After purchasing land or staking a claim, the family cleared a portion of the land, planted a crop, built a cabin, and sold the land in preparation of moving farther west. Generally, long-distance migration remained a young family's adventure—a fact that placed additional burdens on farm wives, who made the Oregon or California trek while pregnant or with young children in tow.

Despite the passage of the Homestead Act in 1862, migration west proved too expensive to attract the impoverished. Oxen or horses, wagons, food, tools, and equipment raised the cost of travel to more than $1,000 and limited the option of western settlement to families who had already acquired sufficient property and capital to finance such a move.

The westward migration of Euro-Americans promised economic opportunity in a society increasingly defined by profit maximization. For Native Americans and African Americans, the land hunger that found political confirmation in Manifest Destiny held a different outcome. Traditionally, Native American women living east of the Mississippi River controlled communal agriculture, whereas northwestern women provided for tribal survival through gathering and hunting small animals. As a result of their critical contributions to tribal survival, women occupied a place of honor in tribal life. As whites gained control over the land, they imposed European views of agriculture and gender divisions of labor that contrasted starkly with the activities of Native Americans. Through treaty provisions and the actions of Indian agents and

Christian missionaries, whites insisted that Native American men farm the land and women assume a subordinate role as farm wives. Such views met substantial resistance, but even where such Native Americans as the Cherokees settled the land and engaged in commercial agriculture, the demands from encroaching white settlers for access to the land suggested that no accommodation to the European agricultural traditions would suffice. In 1838–1839, the Cherokee removal to Indian Territory resulted in the deaths of over 4,000 of the original 14,000 marchers and placed these Native American farm families in economic and social jeopardy (*Tennessee Encyclopedia of History and Culture* 1998).

Likewise, slave families faced disruption as the cotton South expanded into the Mississippi Delta. Clearing swamps and forests in preparation for cotton planting required hard physical labor, and slave families of the Upper South and the more settled eastern plantation regions unwillingly provided that labor. Separated from their parents through sales or divisions of property, young slave men and women left behind the familiar and carved out the plantations that produced the region's wealth. Although their marriages had no standing in law, slaves struggled to maintain family life and pass on to their children the traditions bequeathed to them.

Race, class, and gender defined the parameters of physical labor among southern farming families. Slave women worked alongside the men, but hard physical labor was considered too strenuous for the slaveholding class of white women. Although plantation mistresses led busy domestic lives, they did not engage in fieldwork. Among women of the yeoman class, domestic chores, poul-

try raising, and kitchen gardens occupied most of their time. But in times of need, they might be found in the fields. Children of this class received little education beyond rudimentary lessons in reading, writing, and simple arithmetic. Tennessee's Confederate veterans consistently reported their early introduction to the rigors of farming, with most claiming to have been plowing by age ten.

In the face of early industrialization, antebellum New England farm families struggled to hold onto their land, often sending their unmarried daughters to work in the new textile mills in Waltham and Lowell. The off-farm labor of rural women contributed to the economic stability of hard-pressed families and ensured the continuation of the farm enterprise. Later, as industrialization progressed and new avenues of transportation opened the interior farm regions to seaports and mill towns, farm families withdrew the labor of their daughters from the mills to assist in the dairying and truck farming that supplied the burgeoning urban populations.

Farm families from Ohio to Minnesota also took advantage of the emerging transportation revolution to enter the national market for wheat. Unlike the commercial agriculture of the South, however, the smaller northern farms more closely represented the ideal of yeoman democracy. Relying on family labor, or occasional hired labor, to clear the forests or break up the prairie sod, these farms added a few improved acres each year as they moved from survival and self-sufficiency to became commercially profitable. For these farm families, "scientific agriculture" and mechanization offered the keys to commercial success. Northern farm families subscribed to farm journals and attended farmer institutes to stay abreast of the latest techniques in agricultural methods. Farmhouse designs reflected the centrality of the household in commercial production with, for example, the addition of special rooms for processing milk. Farmers invested in specialized equipment and labor-saving devices. Improved plows and sewing machines altered the distribution of labor in farm families. First introduced in the 1830s, McCormick's reapers initially found few buyers among small, cash-strapped farmers. Over time, as farmers increased their improved acreage and McCormick worked out the technical problems of his machine, farmers displayed more interest in mechanization. In the 1850s, the sale of McCormick's reapers reached 70,000 as farmers planted more acres of wheat to gain the benefits of the higher international prices (Atack and Russell 1994).

In the post–Civil War South, it could easily be said that "the more things changed, the more they stayed the same." King Cotton continued to dominate southern agriculture, but southern farm families accommodated to a new economic structure based on free, not slave, labor. Although planters moved quickly to reinstitute the cotton economy, freedmen successfully resisted the reimplementation of gang labor and removed women from fieldwork. Likewise, they insisted on sharecropping as a mechanism for achieving a measure of control over their own labor and as a first rung on the agricultural ladder toward landholding. Although sharecropping initially provided a degree of separation from white supervision and interference in family life, planters and politicians quickly developed new mechanisms for limiting upward mobility and black economic independence. The notorious crop lien gave white planters control over black labor and soon ensnared poor white farmers in a downward spiral from landholding to tenancy and sharecropping. By 1920 over two-thirds of all Mississippi farmers did not own the land they worked (*Encyclopedia of Southern Culture* 1989). The demands of cotton production under the crop lien system returned women and children to the fields. Indeed, a large family became a plus as croppers negotiated yearly contracts. With the family's primary focus on cotton and debt, the children of tenants and croppers received insufficient education to improve their economic status.

The bleak economic picture presented by southern sharecropping and tenancy did not tell the whole story. Despite substantial barriers to landholding, some black farmers managed to gain control over small farms. Social and economic reverses often meant that black families held land for short periods before returning to tenancy. Black landholding later played a critical role during the civil rights era, when these farmers took enormous risks by providing land for the tent cities that sheltered sharecroppers evicted for attempting to vote.

Outside the South, farm families anticipated a rosier future in the decades following the Civil War. The completion of the transcontinental railroad, improvements in communication, and the advancements of mechanization for farm production facilitated the unprecedented settlement of some 430 million acres (225 million acres under cultivation) in the thirty years from 1870 to 1900 (Danboom 1999). Settlement in these rain-poor regions altered the lives of farm families in at least two important ways: Mechanization of farming became a necessity rather than an option and bound farm

A sharecropper's family on the Pettway Plantation in Gee's Bend, Alabama, 1939. (Library of Congress)

families to national and international markets, and demands for water restructured farm life from informal mechanism for cooperation into formal and legal organizations for the protection of water rights. Farm families struggled to adapt to an unfamiliar landscape as they fought heat, cold, and drought in order to bring the land into production. Families adapted to treeless plains, sod houses, and isolation. In the dry climate of the plains, farming required more land and therefore mechanization. Capitalization for successful farming rested on access to credit, and plains states' farmers soon found themselves entangled in debt for land and equipment.

Western farmers dealt with environmental problems and racial diversity. In the West, access to water required expensive irrigation systems that disrupted fragile environmental balances. As long as farm prices remained high, farmers felt justified in taking the economic risks to expand production through land acquisition, mechanization, and irrigation. But not all western farmers enjoyed equal access to land. Hispanics claimed the western lands prior to the Mexican War, and by treaty, their claims were supposed to be honored. Encroachment by white settlers forced landholders to defend their rights in lengthy court actions that bankrupted many. As the land passed to white

A German American farm family, Lincoln County, Nebraska, 1938. (Library of Congress)

control, Hispanic farm families provided the labor for the new irrigated fields. Vulnerable to any number of abuses by labor contractors, Hispanic farmworkers offered stiff resistance by organizing mutual aid societies and labor organizations such as the United Farm Workers.

Asian Americans also struggled to establish farms in the West. Chinese immigrants supplied food for miners in the California Gold Rush, but their ability to succeed as farmers was limited by two prohibitions: Chinese immigrants were denied citizenship and forbidden to bring women to the United States. Without family labor, successful farming became unlikely. Nevertheless, some

Chinese farmers reclaimed previously unusable lands and engaged in truck farming. After Congress restricted Chinese immigration in 1882, Japanese laborers worked the fields and orchards. Like Chinese immigrants, Japanese workers could not become U.S. citizens, but they could bring their wives. Japanese farmers negotiated leases and eventually many became landowners. White Californians remained hostile to Japanese farm families and passed legislation in 1913 and 1923 that denied landownership to noncitizens. Although farm families faced similar economic problems, racial divisions often prevented effective organization to address common concerns.

In the last decades of the nineteenth century, American farmers recognized the problems associated with commercial agriculture and organized in cooperative efforts to gain control over both costs and prices. Adopting the Rochdale plan, a succession of organizations from the Patrons of Husbandry to the Agricultural Wheel and the Farmers' Alliance established local and state cooperatives to purchase equipment and seed and to market cotton, corn, and wheat. In recognition of the need to preserve family and social contributions to successful rural life, these organizations encouraged female membership and extended their concerns to children and public education. Picnics and rallies brought farm families together for socialization and edification. Speakers outlined political solutions for farm problems while friends and neighbors shared food and gossip. Farm women took a surprisingly public role in organizing and promoting farm organization, delivering speeches and serving in various local offices. In the South, white and black farmers united their efforts in an expedient attempt to overcome the economic control exerted by international markets and industrial monopolies.

The demise of the so-called radical farm organizations did not end attempts to revamp agricultural and farm life but shifted the focus from grassroots farm organization to programs espoused by progressive, educated agricultural specialists. Rural and urban professionals in the Country Life Movement and university-based agricultural extension agents developed programs to improve the quality of life for farm families as well as foster scientific agriculture. Early-twentieth-century urban progressives increasingly rejected the perception that farm life offered physical and spiritual benefits. Instead they pointed to the poor health, low literacy rates, and lack of integration into the emerging consumer culture as evidence of rural decline. The Country Life Movement operated with state land grant colleges to provide up-to-date information on sanitation, diet and health, and home improvement as well as to distribute the latest bulletins on the incorporation of scientific farming. Working through local schools and targeting school-age children, progressive reformers hoped to influence farm parents to make home improvements and adopt new agricultural techniques. As farm families adopted indoor plumbing, installed modern kitchen appliances, and purchased new parlor furniture, reformers anticipated that farm women would retreat from outdoor work into the separate domestic sphere occupied by middle-class urban women. Many farm women viewed these changes as an unacceptable challenge to the mutuality that had characterized agrarian life and rejected the reforms. Likewise, farmers with fewer ties to commercial production declined to participate in university-sponsored programs, viewing the adaptation to mechanized farming as too expensive and likely to ensnare them in debt that would lead to the loss of their land. Not all farm families rejected progressive reforms. Home demonstration clubs expanded throughout the early twentieth century as farm wives gathered to learn new techniques in decorating, sewing, and cooking. Farm children joined corn clubs and tomato clubs, which eventually became the 4-H Club movement. And farmers attended farmer institutes and visited experimental farms to obtain the latest information on farm equipment, new seeds, chemical fertilizers, and marketing.

Throughout the twentieth century, farm families adapted to consumer and technological changes that reduced the percentage of Americans identified with agriculture and enhanced the capital demands for successful farming. The consumer culture, first in the form of catalogs, provided farmers with the cheaper prices they sought in the nineteenth century and brought the city to the country through rural free delivery. Although initially rejected by farmers as too costly, the Good Roads Movement eliminated some of the isolation that had characterized farm life. Purchases of radios and extension of telephone service to farm families provided instantaneous communication with the world. Expansion of electrical power to rural areas enabled farm families to update machinery and install refrigerators, electric stoves, and washing machines to relieve the drudgery of housework.

At the same time, these improvements undermined agrarian life. Individual ownership of household appliances and farm equipment reduced dependency on the informal exchange networks that had sustained the rural community. Improved roads contributed to the demise of country schools as professional educators successfully argued for consolidated schools. The telephone, the radio, and later television introduced farm children to a broader range of possibilities than farm life offered and encouraged out-migration. University professionals, agricultural equipment manufacturers, commercial farmers, and agribusinesses now represented an interest group with the political clout to shape farm policy to the advantage of larger and better-capitalized farmers. Particularly in the aftermath of World War II, farm families depended on technology, mechanization, and chemicals to replace labor. Rising land prices encouraged many farmers to borrow money for expansion. When federal policies in the 1980s undermined agricultural expansion, many farmers faced bankruptcy. The farm protest of the mid-1980s, unlike that of earlier grassroots actions, produced little violence and few symbolic events such as milk spillage. Instead, farm families and their advocates developed individual plans to revamp the debt structure and provided community support for the emotional upheaval associated with the economic problems.

By the end of the twentieth century, farm families represented less than 3 percent of the American population (Danboom 1999). Agribusiness dominated the farming sector, and farmers had truly become businessmen. Like their colonial ancestors, farm families continued to mobilize capital to ensure a secure future for succeeding generations. Now, however, those savings went not for the purchase of additional lands but for a college education for their children with the expectation that they would not return to agriculture.

—*Connie L. Lester*

See also Child Labor; Cooperative Extension Service; Extended Family

References and Further Reading
Atack, Herey, and Peter Russell. 1994. *New Economic View of American History.* New York: W. W. Norton.
Carr, Lois Green, and Lorena S. Walsh. 1977. "The Planter's Wfe: The Experience of White Women in Seventeenth-Century Maryland." *William and Mary Quarterly,* 3d ser., 34, no. 4 (October): 542–557.
Clark, Christopher. 1990. *The Roots of Rural Capitalism: Western Massachusetts, 1780–1860.* Ithaca, NY: Cornell University Press.
Danboom, David B. 1999. *Born in the Country: A History of Rural America.*

Baltimore: Johns Hopkins University Press.

Degler, Carl N. 1980. *At Odds: Women and the Family in America from the Revolution to the Present*. New York: Oxford University Press.

Demos, John. 1970. *A Little Commonwealth: Family Life in Plymouth Colony*. New York: Oxford University Press.

Encyclopedia of Southern Culture. 1989. Chapel Hill: University of North Carolina Press.

Fink, Deborah. 1992. *Agrarian Women: Wives and Mothers in Rural Nebraska, 1880–1940*. Chapel Hill: University of North Carolina Press.

Greven, Philip J. 1966. "Family Structure in Seventeenth-Century Andover, Massachusetts." *William and Mary Quarterly*, 3d ser., 23: 234–256.

Hurt, R. Douglas. 1987. *Indian Agriculture in America: Prehistory to the Present*. Lawrence: University Press of Kansas.

Levy, Barry J. 1978. "'Tender Plants': Quaker Farmers and Children in the Delaware Valley, 1681–1735." *Journal of Family History* 3: 116–135.

Levy, Barry. 1991. "Quakers, the Delaware Valley, and North Midlands Emigration to America." *William and Mary Quarterly*, 3d ser., 48, no. 2 (April): 246–252.

Marti, Donald B. 1991. *Women of the Grange: Mutuality and Sisterhood in Rural America, 1866–1920*. Westport, CT: Greenwood Press.

McMurry, Sally 1995. *Transforming Rural Life: Dairying Families and Agricultural Change, 1820–1885*. Baltimore: Johns Hopkins University Press.

Mintz, Steven, and Susan Kellogg. 1988. *Domestic Revolutions: A Social History of American Family Life*. New York: The Free Press.

Morgan, Edmund S. 1975. *American Slavery, American Freedom: The Ordeal of Virginia*. New York: W. W. Norton.

Neth, Mary. 1995. *Preserving the Family Farm: Women, Community, and the Foundations of Agribusiness in the Midwest, 1900–1940*. Baltimore: Johns Hopkins University Press.

Osterud, Nancy Grey. 1991. *Bonds of Community: The Lives of Farm Women in Nineteenth-Century New York*. Ithaca, NY: Cornell University Press.

Perdue, Theda. 1998. *Cherokee Women: Gender and Cultural Change, 1700–1835*. Lincoln: University of Nebraska Press.

Rosenfeld, Rachel Ann. 1985. *Farm Women: Work, Farm, and Family in the United States*. Chapel Hill: University of North Carolina Press.

Rutman, Darrett B., and Anita H. Rutman. 1984. *A Place in Time: Middlesex County, Virginia, 1650–1750*. New York: W. W. Norton.

Schlissel, Lillian. 1988. "Family on the Western Frontier." In *Western Women: Their Land, Their Lives*, edited by Lillian Schlissel, Vicki L. Ruiz, and Janice Monk, 81–97. Albuquerque: University of New Mexico Press.

Sharpless, Rebecca. 1999. *Fertile Ground, Narrow Choices: Women on Texas Cotton Farms, 1900–1940*. Chapel Hill: University of North Carolina Press.

Tennessee Encyclopedia of History and Culture. 1998. Nashville: Tennessee Historical Society.

Walker, Melissa. 2000. *All We Knew Was to Farm: Rural Women in the Upcountry South, 1919–1941*. Baltimore: Johns Hopkins University Press.

Fatherhood

Fatherhood in the United States has been not merely a biological fact but a historically conditioned and socially, culturally, and politically constructed experience. It has both varied widely—over time and across lines of race, class, ethnicity, and region—and exhibited continuities. And although fathering is ultimately a private matter, its nature and development have elicited public concern, been integral to the family in the United States, and been inseparable from wider currents in American life.

"Patriarchal" Fatherhood in Colonial America

Colonial American fatherhood was framed by preindustrial economic and social relationships, agricultural village life, and—particularly in New England—Calvinist Protestantism. These circumstances made fathers an integral and active domestic presence, gave them enormous authority and power over their families, and produced a fathering style sometimes termed *patriarchal.* The patriarchal father was undisputed head of the household or family—the fundamental unit of preindustrial society—that included servants and apprentices as well as one's own children and was bound by a quasi-contractual system of mutual obligations. Responsible for relations between the family and the wider village and state, fathers sought to maintain their public reputation, perpetuate their families' status, and contribute to the wider social order through their own and their dependents' economic success and moral reputability.

As economic leader of the household, the father controlled the agricultural and handicraft production that took place within it, as well as all land and other family property. Though all family members participated in preindustrial household production, fathers were legally responsible for providing all household members with the physical necessities of life and for providing male dependents with training for adult work in farming, handicrafts, or business. (Mothers typically trained their daughters in homemaking and child care.) Fathers helped married children achieve economic security by dispensing portions of family property.

Colonial fathers also provided moral, spiritual, and intellectual guidance, since dominant gender constructs assigned to men superior intellect and discipline and to women a dangerous tendency toward excessive affection and overindulgence of children. Fathers were responsible for teaching literacy and catechism, often leading family prayers and scripture readings, and were the family disciplinarians, exercising their power largely through a combination of affectionate persuasion and stern disapproval within an overarching framework of emotional reserve. They used corporal punishment only in moderation and as a last resort. Fathers typically began training their children around age three, considered the point at which reason was sufficiently developed for fathers' methods. New England's Puritan fathers in particular emphasized firm though loving discipline, convinced that children's salvation required the conquest of their innate sinfulness. Quaker fathers, concentrated in the middle colonies, viewed human nature more positively and emphasized a divine "inner light" amenable to maternal nurture. Southern Anglican fathers were likewise more relaxed. But because fathers throughout the colonies were considered better models and guarantors of moral behavior than mothers, they were recognized as the primary parents, and common law tended to favor their custodial rights in cases of marital separation or divorce.

Colonial fathers had at their disposal several mechanisms for ensuring filial duty, respect, and obedience—especially by their sons. They could and did control their sons' moves toward economic independence through their control of land and other family resources, which they allotted at their discretion. By similar means, fathers influenced and could veto their children's courtships and marital choices. Their economic clout gave them power even over adult children.

Because household production required labor and mortality rates were high, colonial men typically fathered large families—the average couple had eight children who survived infancy. Some historians have suggested that economic valuation of children and the frequency of premature death led fathers and mothers alike to limit their emotional investment in their offspring. Recent scholarship, however, suggests that fathers loved their children despite their emotional reserve, experienced anguish and grief when their children sickened or died, and were often emotionally expressive—particularly with daughters, on whom they perhaps staked less in terms of public reputation.

Fatherhood and the Family in
Transition, 1750–1850
Between 1750 and 1850, the Enlightenment, republican ideology, romanticism, changing demographics, the market revolution, and industrialization eroded the patriarchal style of fathering and altered family dynamics and functions, transforming the meaning of fatherhood.

Enlightenment thinking and republican ideology encouraged new family ideals and approaches to parenting. Republicanism discouraged hierarchical lines of authority and encouraged democratic family relationships. Enlightenment psychology assumed children to be blank slates on which fathers were to promote their personal happiness, moral development, and capacity for independent judgment through reason and affection rather than tyrannical, unrepublican forms of discipline. Fathers were also to respect their children's aspirations and marital choices. Mothers, meanwhile, assumed new importance in educating their children to the moral responsibilities of citizenship. Romanticism likewise discouraged patriarchal authoritarianism by exalting affectionate and companion-ate family relationships, idealizing the emotional ties between mothers and children, and emphasizing romantic love as the basis of marriage. It encouraged a gentler paternal style by postulating an inherent human goodness and childhood innocence that required tender nurture rather than stern will-breaking.

These ideological shifts were reinforced by changing physical, social, and economic realities. Population growth in established towns, abandonment of English inheritance practices, and out-migration to newly opening western areas reduced fathers' ability to control their children through allotment of land and other family property. The growth of market capitalism and industrial production in the early nineteenth century, particularly in northern urban areas, eroded the old corporate household economy, creating a new middle class and a new family dynamic within it by physically and psychologically separating working fathers—in commerce, industry, and (later) service professions—from the home. It also eroded the traditional economic functions of the family, encouraged a decline in the birthrate, and altered the focus of parenting and paternal leadership by removing economic production from the household and narrowing the functions of the middle-class family to education, socialization, and personal development. By the mid-nineteenth century, middle-class families in cities and small towns were increasingly small, nuclear, child-centered, dominated by the day-to-day presence of the mother, and insulated from (but dependent upon) a public world of economic activity occupied by fathers. In this setting arose a "modern" style of fatherhood that remained influential through the twentieth century.

"Modern" Fatherhood in the Nineteenth Century

The transformation of middle-class family dynamics profoundly affected fathers and fatherhood. Family advice authors increasingly bewailed paternal absence from domestic life, but such concerns signified the modernization rather than the marginalization of fatherhood. The separation of work from home generated new middle-class gender constructs that defined fathers as the chief or sole family breadwinners whose responsibilities required immersion in competitive, aggressive, rational, acquisitive, and perhaps amoral economic activity outside the home. Whether or to what degree modern fathers actually spent less time at home or participated less fully in day-to-day child rearing than preindustrial fathers is a matter of debate and varied with place of residence, class position, and occupation. But the breadwinner role did mean that the nature and extent of their domestic involvement had to conform to their work patterns. Nineteenth-century fathers first experienced the defining dilemma of modern fatherhood—balancing work time with family time, absence with involvement, business values with domestic values—and pursued the emerging ideal of the "family man."

Modern fathers remained important and involved in family life. Breadwinning preserved their provider function, enhanced their economic leadership by making their work seem mysterious and heroically self-sacrificing, and heightened their attachment to domestic life as a moral and spiritual counteractive to economic competition. Many other traditional paternal functions remained intact as well. Fathers were still responsible for their children's intellectual, moral, and spiritual development and remained their families' final disciplinary authorities. And although fathers were less often able to pass on handicraft or agricultural skills, they still sought to prepare their sons for success by instilling business virtues, offering advice, and providing education and sometimes protracted financial support. The obligation to sacrifice for the welfare of one's children, appeal to that sacrifice to secure filial obedience and respect, pressure to perpetuate the family's middle-class status, and a propensity to invest more heavily in smaller numbers of children became central features of modern fatherhood. At the same time, patriarchal formality waned, and fathers increasingly engaged in affectionate play with their children. Nor do their frequent diary references to caring for their sick and dying children or attending to their wives in childbirth support the stereotype of the aloof, work-engrossed, and emotionally detached Victorian father. Indeed, contemporary domestic ideals identified fatherly emotion and involvement with masculine wholeness.

Fatherhood remained important but became increasingly secularized during the late nineteenth century amid the rising authority of science, the advent of Darwinian biology, and the emergence of modern medicine and psychology. Male-dominated scientific and medical establishments defined marriage, procreative sexuality, and fatherhood less as religious duties than as biological imperatives, badges of true manliness, and requisites of male fulfillment and happiness. At the same time, many white middle-class men, perceiving enervating effects in industrialization, urbanization, immigration, consumerism, sentimentalism, and the apotheosis of mothers, associated reproduction with continuing Anglo-

Saxon racial dominance and cultivated in themselves and their sons an aggressive and virile masculine style.

Still, there are indications that paternal authority weakened during the nineteenth century. For example, both published advice and private diary recollections regarding dinner table, fireside, and Sunday rituals suggest that fathers' presence was perceived as relatively rare, that their child-rearing role had become part-time, and that their authority had become a matter more of symbolic affirmation than of day-to-day governance. Fathers' cultivation of playful relationships with their children likewise suggested an abdication of child-rearing authority to mothers. There is also evidence that many men experienced difficulty adjusting to the new family arrangements or the economic pressures of breadwinning. Many fathers resisted relinquishing traditional patriarchal prerogatives, were unable or unwilling to embrace the new democratic and companionate ideals, or—particularly with their sons—remained uncomfortable expressing their emotions or revealing their insecurities. Family tension sometimes resulted, and paternal failure became a standard theme in Victorian fiction. The legal system, meanwhile, enforced the new paternal standards and the new preeminence of motherhood by liberalizing divorce laws and increasingly favoring maternal custody.

Social Science, Consumption, and the "New Fatherhood"
Modern fatherhood was elaborated and transformed by the changing cultural, economic, social, and intellectual circumstances of the late nineteenth and early twentieth centuries. The urban white middle class again occupied the vanguard of change in the development

of a "new fatherhood," a model that itself contributed to middle-class identity. This new form of modern fatherhood shaped fathering in the United States through the twentieth century.

Growing urbanization and industrialization, bureaucratization and the growth of white-collar business work, and the rising domestic authority of mothers reduced the autonomy and fulfillment middle-class men found in breadwinning, widened the distance between their work and home experiences, and generated among them fears of anonymity and over-domestication. But rising incomes, the expanding production of consumer goods, increasing leisure time, and the advent of suburbia encouraged these men to look to recreation and material fulfillment in their domestic lives for satisfaction and identity. Likewise, the new fields of psychology and social science promoted a therapeutic ethos that touted fatherhood and domestic involvement as central to men's personal growth, personality development, well-being, and social responsibility. Middle-class reformers of the Progressive Era, meanwhile, inspired by social science and fearing social disorder in a modernizing America, urged parents to ensure their children's proper personal and social development through "scientific" child rearing.

Consumerism and social science strengthened and redefined modern fatherhood. Breadwinning became linked with the provision of consumer goods in an expanding industrial economy. Fathers' nurturant companionship and recreational play with their children—especially with their sons, who required a manly presence—assumed new forms and became more important than ever. By the 1920s and 1930s, family reformers and social scientists were systematically researching fatherhood and leading a parent education movement in which effective fathering was addressed by a proliferation of professional publications, workshops and institutes, study groups, lectures, radio shows, and advice columns. These experts urged fathers to be not only breadwinners but also companions devoted to their children's proper psychological development. Fathers were to encourage character-building hobbies, govern the family democratically, and serve as sex-role models who bolstered conventional heterosexuality and social stability by exemplifying ideal manhood for their sons and the ideal mate for their daughters. Such functions were particularly important—and were facilitated—now that schools, hospitals, welfare agencies, juvenile courts, and other state and social institutions had absorbed many of fathers' earlier responsibilities.

But consumerism and social science presented not only new grounds for domestic engagement and fulfillment but also new challenges and new limitations. Consumer culture generated ever-advancing material standards of middle-class comfort and respectability that fathers felt pressured to provide and undercut paternal influence and authority by stimulating youth to peer-group leisure activities. Furthermore, although social science offered fathers specialized knowledge and expert advice, it also undermined their autonomy, self-confidence, and power by encouraging their deference to and dependence on mothers—whom the experts considered the primary parents— and such professionals as psychologists, psychiatrists, physicians, educators, and social workers. Indeed, some studies suggest (though others deny) that the parent education movement effectively excluded fathers and promoted their dependence on mothers by appealing largely to the lat-

ter. And social science and consumerism together exacerbated the tension between absence and involvement, for the experts urged greater domestic involvement while consumerism encouraged breadwinning. Middle-class fathers sought through the twentieth century to balance these conflicting imperatives, though the vague and uncertain psychological rewards of domestic engagement often proved less compelling than did breadwinning's tangible sources of domestic status and power.

Fatherhood outside the White Middle Class

The "modern" and "new" styles of fatherhood were inventions of the northern, urban, white Protestant middle class—socially and culturally constructed components of an emerging white middle-class identity. As such, they were as much prescriptive as descriptive, even among white middle-class fathers themselves, and were even further removed from the experiences of southern, working-class, immigrant, African American, and rural fathers. To be sure, the impact of the market economy, industrialization, and consumerism on American fatherhood was national, and white middle-class models of fatherhood—particularly the breadwinning imperative—were influential beyond that narrow group. But fatherhood varied along lines of region, class, ethnicity, and race.

Antebellum southern planters, like contemporary northern businessmen and professionals, linked male identity to family responsibility; were moved by Enlightenment psychology, republicanism, and romantic sentimentalism toward a democratic, affectionate, and child-centered family dynamic; and played with their children while leaving the primary responsibility for child care to their wives. But southern fathers were less affected by industrialization and the mother-dominated domestic ideology, maintaining instead a form of patriarchy based on family hierarchy, racial hierarchy, and male honor. They urged respect for ancestors (especially male ones) and paternalistic responsibility for slaves and used shame to shape their children's behavior. Southern planter fathers retained an importance that their northern counterparts lacked, particularly in the raising of their sons, for their concern to encourage male prowess in hunting, fighting, and riding led them to mistrust maternal child rearing. This approach to fathering began fading as southern leaders promoted an economically, socially, and culturally New South during the late nineteenth and early twentieth centuries.

Working-class fathers were distanced from middle-class ideals of breadwinning and domesticity by low wages, economic dependence, financial uncertainty, and the prospect of under- or unemployment. The need for income from all working family members meant that the corporate family economy, traditional patriarchal control, and the economic valuation of children survived in their families long after middle-class families became more sentimental and child-centered. Their economic vulnerability, meanwhile, undercut their domestic authority and economic leadership. Working-class fathers did provide most of the family income as well as room and board for their working children (sometimes into young adulthood). They also sought through long hours of work to buy homes and provide education for their children so that their families might achieve middle-class status. Yet the employment of women and children outside the home produced power struggles within it, particularly when business downturns, mechanization, injury, illness, or old age deprived fathers of their breadwinning role. Children facing this situation sometimes lost confidence in and even challenged their fathers' authority. Fathers themselves, meanwhile, feeling humiliated, sad, depressed, or bitter, sometimes became emotionally distant, turned to alcohol, or became abusive. Nor were such middle-class paternal ideals as domestic engagement and recreational play with children supported by long working hours, low incomes, uncomfortable living quarters, resistance to middle-class respectability, or working-class male leisure patterns focusing on saloons, billiard halls, fraternal orders, and bowling alleys. Early-twentieth-century studies suggested that working-class fathers lacked the time, education, and inclination to consider middle-class family advice and were less likely than middle-class fathers to participate in parent education, child care, discipline, and domestic play.

Working-class fathers also found their power, functions, desires, and values undercut by middle-class Progressive reformers and a sympathetic state, who criticized working-class family life and feared that industrialization, urbanization, and poverty warped children. Reformers sought with the help of the state to enforce middle-class standards through child labor laws that moved children from the factory to the school, through juvenile court systems that imposed discipline and often removed youthful offenders from presumably dysfunctional home environments, and through laws increasing the penalties for abusive or deserting fathers who violated ideals of paternal breadwinning and domestic affection.

Immigrant fathers in the United States have experienced the challenges not only of working-class fatherhood (that is, as long as they remained members of the working class) but also of ethnicity. Their experiences have varied widely—depending on ethnic group, location, and individual personality—and defy easy generalization. Yet an important recurring theme is the challenge posed to their authority by the transition to a new life. Long working hours, economic privation, and distance from their former cultures frustrated their attempts to maintain their Old World patriarchal power and prerogatives. They sought to preserve their traditional status, sometimes by citing their sacrifices, sometimes (as in the case of Jewish fathers) by maintaining a stern authoritarian image, and sometimes (as with the fathers of Italian Harlem) by using overt displays of authority. But such efforts often exacerbated intergenerational tensions. Furthermore, the lines of family authority were sometimes reversed as immigrant children learned new languages, absorbed new values and attitudes, adopted new work patterns, sought the popular amusements and consumer goods of the United States, and became cultural mediators for their parents, whom they often perceived as backward. Fathers often and sometimes angrily questioned their children's new hairstyles, dress, courtships, and leisure activities but lacked any authoritative standard of evaluation.

Middle-class Progressive reformers and the state accelerated intergenerational divergence during the early twentieth century through interventionist measures that aimed to Americanize immigrant children and provoked resistance and resentment by their parents. Particularly corrosive of fathers' decision-making power and influence were mandatory school attendance laws, which undermined their economic valuation of their children, exposed their children to American culture, and prompted their children's participation in peer groups outside the home. Of course, immigrant fathers were often gratified by their children's transition to life in the United States and especially by their children's economic or professional success, for these developments justified their decision to migrate. Yet they feared that such success undermined Old World traditions and values, particularly when it carried their children from urban ethnic neighborhoods to suburbia and to new heights of consumerism during the middle and latter decades of the twentieth century.

Comparisons between African American and white fatherhood have been clouded until recently by a myth that the disruptive effects of slavery, rural poverty, northward migration, and urban ghetto life in the nineteenth and twentieth centuries prompted high levels of father absence and irresponsibility. But recent scholarship on enslaved and free African American families has discovered that paternal presence, involvement, and leadership in a two-parent setting were the norm and has emphasized the influence of white, middle-class, domestic values. Slavery did, of course, limit the power and sadden the lives of black fathers, who lacked property rights, breadwinner status, legal control over their children, and ultimate power over their children's destinies. It is also true that children's awareness of the slave owner's final authority could and often did undermine paternal authority. Moreover, father absence and female-headed families were indeed more frequent among slaves than among free peoples; about one-third of slave fathers lived apart from their families on large plantations and an even higher proportion on smaller plantations and farms. Still, most slave fathers did live with their families, grounded their identities in fatherhood, and played important roles in family life. They provided love and attention; served as male role models for their children; transmitted family customs and religious beliefs; supplemented their families' food allotments through fishing and hunting; passed on hunting, fishing, and sometimes craft skills to their sons, whom they often named after themselves; sought to insulate their children from the harshness of racism and enslavement; and taught their children the behaviors and attitudes necessary for surviving bondage.

After emancipation, father-headed, two-parent households remained the norm in African American families and were in fact more common among former slaves than among other blacks—thus disproving a clear causal link between slavery and father absence. But even though black fathers were now theoretically free to become breadwinners, their breadwinning and domestic involvement were shaped and limited by the crop lien system in the postwar South, migration to southern and northern cities, Jim Crow laws, and job discrimination. Black fathers experienced problems that resembled those of working-class and immigrant fathers but were intensified by racism. In the rural South, the economic hardships of tenant farming forced most black fathers to share breadwinning duties with their wives and children. Many of them hoped to avoid this situation by leaving their homes to seek wage work in southern cities—an experience that must have been painful for them—

while others sought opportunity by joining a "great migration" to northern cities after World War I. Many urban black fathers, northern and southern, found their prospects stifled and economic distress aggravated by discrimination and, like rural blacks, had to leave their families to find work. Father absence was therefore higher among postbellum blacks than among working-class and immigrant whites: The rate of female-headedness ran 11 to 24 percent in rural areas, 20 to 44 percent in southern cities, and 15 to over 30 percent in northern cities. Fathers either unemployed or in menial jobs were more likely than other black fathers to leave their families, suggesting that desertion was an effect more of racism and economic oppression than of irresponsibility or slavery. Many fathers undoubtedly broke under the various pressures they experienced. In any case, black fathers, like their enslaved forebears, took special care to shield their children from racism—some advising caution and accommodation, others militancy and pride. These patterns of African American fatherhood persisted through the twentieth century, though some fathers were challenged during the 1950s and 1960s by militant children impatient with counsels of caution.

Rural families retained several preindustrial features—a collective household economy, large family size, a merger of home and work, an economic view of children, patriarchal authority and economic leadership, and, particularly during slack seasons, substantial paternal presence—well after they had faded from urban middle-class settings. The experiences of rural fathers therefore differed significantly from those of urban fathers. Because most rural families remained father-dominated corporate work units well into the nineteenth century, preindustrial economic calculations and quasi-contractual relations continued to guide fathers' relationships with their children—particularly their sons, whose service on the farm they expected until age twenty-one. This type of relationship stunted bonds of affection and encouraged father-son tensions, especially when maturing sons came to regard fathers' expectations as obstacles to personal ambition. There is also evidence that economic family relationships and the absence of the urban notion of home as retreat made paternal play rarer among rural than among urban fathers.

The power of rural fathers began to erode by the early nineteenth century as westward expansion and commercial growth expanded their sons' opportunities and aspirations and encouraged outmigration from established farming communities. During the late nineteenth and early twentieth centuries, economic setbacks in agriculture and the growing allure of urban opportunities and amusements made it ever harder for farm fathers to transmit their agrarian lifestyles and values to their children.

These fathers' experiences also increasingly converged with those of urban fathers. Because the growing separation of fathers from their families and the tension between work time and family time were products of market capitalism (not simply of urbanization and industrialization), these patterns came to characterize rural as well as urban life as commercial agriculture progressively replaced subsistence farming. Landless rural fathers who worked for others, and fathers seeking extra income to expand their landholdings, were especially likely to be absent. In the commercialized countryside, as in the city, nineteenth-century fathers were most available to their children at night and on Sunday. In both places, too, fathers were anxious to secure their sons' economic futures, though farm fathers more often sought to do so by passing on land or by securing apprenticeships or store clerkships. Rural and urban fathering patterns converged ever more closely during the late nineteenth and twentieth centuries as the growth of nationally integrated markets, transportation networks, and mass media brought urban ideas and amenities to rural areas.

Fatherhood Disrupted and Reaffirmed: Depression, War, and Prosperity

Prevalent models of fatherhood in the United States were too firmly established by the 1930s to be fundamentally challenged or altered by the Depression and World War II. These turbulent events, which disrupted American fathering and raised public concern about fatherhood, ultimately strengthened existing patterns of fatherhood.

The story of fatherhood during the Depression is partly one of continuities: Social scientists continued to research fathering, many of them paying little attention to the impact of the faltering economy, and millions of fathers saw only small declines in income. Yet millions of other fathers lost their jobs or farms and as a result their breadwinner status and sense of male identity. Some of their power flowed to their working wives and adolescent children, who in many cases questioned or even rejected paternal authority. Many fathers responded with feelings of failure, anxiety, humiliation, despair, and guilt. Some became abusive or suicidal. Others deserted their families to flee their troubles or seek work.

Family professionals and the government responded to a perceived collapse of breadwinning by seeking to shore up paternal preeminence. Social science experts promoted the new fatherhood, arguing that fathers could maintain their authority by resting it more on psychological nurture and less on breadwinning. The Roosevelt administration, meanwhile, attempted to preserve male breadwinning, paternal responsibility, and the traditional economic dependence of women and children through its New Deal public work and relief programs, which often favored fathers in hiring. To be sure, this expansion of state programs sometimes undercut paternal authority, and the Depression sparked an ongoing and eventually decisive increase in maternal breadwinning. But the Depression and the New Deal had the conservative effect of marshaling the scientific establishment and the state in defense of prevailing family dynamics.

World War II also had a mixed but ultimately conservative impact. On the one hand, it pulled many fathers away from their families and accelerated the movement of mothers into the labor force. Absent for months or years at a time, fathers became distanced from their families and often had difficulty reestablishing their status upon returning. Many felt estranged from their children, competed for affection with mothers and grandparents, or strained family relationships by imposing strict discipline in the belief that their children had been spoiled in their absence. On the other hand, the war and even father absence also reinforced prevailing family models and paternal roles. Family specialists regarded democratic families with traditionally breadwinning fathers and homemaking mothers as essential to national stability and the defeat of fascism. They also intensified and popularized their discussions of fathers' importance to children's proper

sex-role development and healthy emotional growth. Indeed, their concerns that absent fathers and working mothers would breed juvenile delinquency and endanger social order and that excessive mothering would sap manly toughness and threaten national survival led many Americans to oppose the drafting of fathers. Little wonder that fathers figured so prominently in wartime imagery.

Postwar trends reinforced the status and the challenges associated with modern and new fatherhood and fostered a conservative family ideology that asserted paternal family leadership. Renewed economic prosperity restored fathers' breadwinning and provider functions and encouraged the consumerism that supported their domestic status and power. Indeed, their ability to provide consumer goods became a key measure of their success as fathers. The expansion of suburbia strengthened the perception of domestic life as a therapeutic retreat from work and added to fathers' domestic functions such activities as performing and teaching their sons about home repair and yard work and coaching their sons' (and later, daughters') athletic activities. A "reproductive consensus" identified marriage and fatherhood with masculine happiness and responsibility—an equation promoted by the popular media and apparently widely accepted among men in the United States. And cold war ideology bolstered the new fatherhood by urging democratic family relations as counteractive to communist authoritarianism and paternal companionship as counteractive to such perceived social threats as deviance, delinquency, and homosexuality.

But consumerism and breadwinning also worked at cross-purposes with paternal authority, influence, and companionship. Many adolescent youth of the late

A father reviewing his daughter's school work on Parents' Night. (Elizabeth Crews)

1950s and 1960s, stimulated by social critics, criticized what they considered their fathers' emasculating corporate and suburban conformity, generating considerable if temporary intergenerational conflict. A more long-lasting threat to fathers' power was the generational wedge driven by an expanding youth market and youth culture. The consumer goods provided by fathers encouraged increasingly solitary and peer group–based leisure patterns among their children, and advertisers and peer groups rather than parents assumed growing power to shape the wants and aspirations of the young. The corrosive effects of consumerism and youth leisure on parental authority and family togetherness remained powerful—and elicited

intensifying public concern—through the latter decades of the twentieth century.

Still, fathers remained their families' chief breadwinners. As practitioners of the new fatherhood, they provided financial support and psychological nurture while remaining, in theory and often in practice, further removed from housework and child care than their wives. But developments of the late twentieth century would powerfully challenge traditional assumptions about fatherhood and family dynamics.

Fatherhood Rethought: The Late Twentieth Century and Beyond

Several late-twentieth-century trends sparked a rethinking of fatherhood. First, the percentage of mothers in the workforce rose dramatically. Many fathers therefore lost their monopoly on breadwinning and on the powers and responsibilities that had come with it and found it necessary to perform domestic duties once left to their wives. Second, a rising divorce rate after 1965 separated growing numbers of men from their children and undermined traditional paternal claims to household leadership. Some divorced fathers spent most of their time with their children in leisure activities; others became alienated and abandoned their provider responsibilities completely (thus provoking state intervention to enforce them). But divorce prompted many others, whether part-time fathers or full-time single fathers, to assume many of the functions traditionally associated with mothers. Third, the revitalization of feminism during the 1960s stimulated a questioning of the traditional gender division of labor and the assumption that women were inherently more nurturant and better suited to child-care responsibilities than were men. Fathers were increasingly criticized for limited domestic commitment. Fourth, an emergent men's movement likewise challenged conventional ideals of manhood, urging men to embrace and explore their emotional lives and to ground their identities in their families as well as their careers. Fifth, the information revolution allowed fathers to do more work at home and therefore to take on increased domestic responsibility. These developments produced a new model of fatherhood that, like its predecessors, was largely a middle-class invention. In the new model good fathers were expected to participate actively in day-to-day child care, be intimately and expressively involved with their families, and treat sons and daughters alike rather than socializing them toward conventional gender standards.

This new model faces serious obstacles. It will be strengthened as long as the social, economic, and cultural forces that produced it endure, but the persistence of those forces is uncertain. The impact of new technologies on paternal availability may well be minimal. Furthermore, the new model competes both with older models within the middle class and with traditional gender ideals in the working class. It has also been resisted by the political and religious right, whose representatives seek to restore traditional paternal leadership and the gender division of labor on which it rests. And widespread acceptance and enactment of the unprecedented challenge of the new model to long-standing gender categories will require substantial changes in both private thinking and public policy. Even if the forces eroding earlier models of fatherhood continue, the new model will not necessarily become ascendant. Instead, a growing diversification of family structures may generate a range of father-

ing options. These structures could include two-career families, single-parent families, same-sex-parent families, reconstituted families with children and stepchildren, families with working mothers and homemaking fathers, and traditional families with working fathers and homemaking mothers. What is clear is that fatherhood continues to change with broader currents in the U.S.

—*Bret E. Carroll*

See also Affection as a Basis for Marriage; Child Labor; Divorce, History of; Extended Family; Farm Families; Gender Roles in the American Family; Juvenile Justice

References and Further Reading

Demos, John. 1986. *Past, Present, and Personal: The Family and the Life Course in American History.* New York: Oxford University Press.

Frank, Stephen M. 1998. *Life with Father: Parenthood and Masculinity in the Nineteenth-Century American North.* Baltimore: Johns Hopkins University Press.

Griswold, Robert L. 1993. *Fatherhood in America: A History.* New York: Basic Books.

LaRossa, Ralph. 1997. *The Modernization of Fatherhood: A Social and Political History.* Chicago: University of Chicago Press.

Wilson, Lisa. 1999. *Ye Heart of a Man: The Domestic Life of Men in Colonial New England.* New Haven: Yale University Press.

Father's Day

Father's Day is the holiday that honors all fathers in the United States on the third Sunday in June. It had its origins in both 1908 and 1910, when two devoted daughters—one in West Virginia and one in Washington—wanted a special day to honor their own and other fathers. In the summer of 1908, Mrs. Charles Clayton, a minister's daughter in Fairmont, West Virginia, asked the pastor of her church to set aside a Sunday service in remembrance of fathers. She wished to memorialize the men who had died in a mine explosion in 1907, as well as her own father, who had died in 1896. No doubt she had heard of a recent church service held on 10 May 1908, in the town of Grafton, West Virginia, just twenty miles away, to honor mothers. That was the beginning of Mother's Day.

Thanks to Mrs. Clayton's efforts, the first Father's Day service was held on Sunday, 5 July 1908, at the Williams Memorial Methodist Episcopal Church in Fairmont. Since no provision was made for a wider recognition of this service, the history of Father's Day officially begins with another event two years later.

The second person credited with establishing Father's Day is Mrs. John Bruce Dodd, of Spokane, Washington, who wished to honor her late father, a Civil War veteran who had brought up six children after the death of his wife. In 1909 Mrs. Dodd, a member of the Central Methodist Episcopal Church, spoke to her pastor about holding a service to honor all fathers. She then petitioned the Spokane Ministerial Association, which approved a Father's Day in local churches. Her efforts led to a statewide celebration on 19 June 1910, the third Sunday in June. Since carnations were associated with Mother's Day, roses were to become the traditional flower given out on Father's Day.

In 1924 Pres. Calvin Coolidge approved Father's Day as a nationally recognized holiday, and in 1966 Pres. Lyndon Johnson set the third Sunday in June as Father's Day. Americans celebrate this family holiday by giving special greetings and gifts to their fathers.

—*Virginia Bernhard*

See also Mother's Day

References and Further Reading

Koon, Thomas J. "The First Father's Day Observance." http://web.mountainn.net/~cenumcvw/father/html (cited 25 January 2000).

Schmidt, Leigh Eric. 1995. *Consumer Rites: The Buying and Selling of American Holidays.* Princeton, NJ: Princeton University Press.

Feminine Mystique

The term *feminine mystique* describes the condition of women in the United States during the 1950s. It refers to the constraints placed on women by the suburbanization of American society and the affirmation of the nuclear family in the aftermath of World War II. Focusing on the return of women to their traditional gender roles after the transformations of the 1940s, the term describes the centrality of their maternal role, the increase of housework with the use of modern appliances, and the importance placed on women's consumerism in the postwar United States.

The term was introduced in 1963 by Betty Friedan. *The Feminine Mystique,* her feminist critique of postwar U.S. society, described an omnipresent and omnipotent ideology, fostered by experts, educators, advertisers, and the media at the end of World War II to keep women from becoming fully emancipated (Friedan 1963). By using the language of Freudian psychoanalysis, *The Feminine Mystique* scientifically justified women's "natural" role as mothers and wives and transformed their traditional role as homemak-

A housewife in the front room of her home, California, 1942. (Library of Congress)

crs into an economic resource; it was used by industry to sell consumer goods.

Given the book's success, the term *feminine mystique* has been accepted for decades as a useful definition of women's lives during the 1950s. Recently historians have questioned the validity of the term, claiming that Friedan's definition of the 1950s excluded the majority of American society by focusing on white, middle-class heterosexual women.

Moreover, historiography has shifted its attention from the forces responsible for women's oppression to the complexities of their lives. Stressing women's agency, historiography has emphasized the impor-

tance of women's political activism in groups such as the Young Women's Christian Association (YWCA), the Parent-Teacher Association (PTA), and the civil rights movement and has highlighted the many forms of resistance enacted by women against postwar ideology. Finally, historians have focused on the contradictions of the representation of women in the mass media and have pointed out how the image of women as homemakers was parallel to that of independent women.

Thanks to recent historiography, the term *feminine mystique* has come to characterize simply Friedan's interpretation of the postwar United States. The

A photo of Betty Friedan, author of The Feminine Mystique, *c. 1970. (Hulton/ Archive)*

1950s have been reinterpreted as a time of social change in which conservative and transformative forces interacted and laid the foundations for a second wave of feminism, the gay and lesbian movements, and the African American civil rights movement of the following decade.

—*Elisabetta Bini*

See also Gender Roles in the American Family

References and Further Reading
Bowlby, Rachel. 1987. "'The Problem with No Name': Rereading Friedan's *The Feminine Mystique.*" *Feminist Review* 27 (September): 61–75.
Coontz, Stephanie. 1992. *The Way We Never Were: American Families and the Nostalgia Trap.* New York: Basic Books.
Foreman, Joel, ed. 1997. *The Other Fifties: Interrogating Midcentury American Icons.* Urbana: Illinois University Press.
Friedan, Betty. 1963. *The Feminine Mystique.* New York: W. W. Norton.
Gabin, Nancy. 1990. *Feminism in the Labor Movement: Women and the United Auto Workers, 1935–1973.* Ithaca: Cornell University Press.
Horowitz, Daniel. 1998. *Betty Friedan and the Making of "The Feminine Mystique": The American Left, the Cold War and American Feminism.* Amherst: University of Massachusetts Press.
Lynn, Susan. 1992. *Progressive Women in Conservative Times: Racial Justice, Peace and Feminism, 1945 to the 1960s.* New Brunswick, NJ: Rutgers University Press.
May, Elaine Tyler. 1988. *Homeward Bound: American Families in the Cold War Era.* New York: Basic Books.
Meyerowitz, Joanne, ed. 1994. *Not June Cleaver: Women and Gender in Postwar America, 1945–1960.* Philadelphia: Temple University Press.
Moskowitz, Eva. 1996. "'It's Good to Blow Your Top': Women's Magazines and a Discourse of Discontent, 1945–1965." *Journal of Women's History* 3 (Fall): 66–98.
Ware, Susan. 1990. "American Women in the 1950s: Non-partisan Politics and Women's Politicization." In *Women, Politics and Change,* edited by Louise Tilly and Patricia Gurin, 281–299. New York: Russell Sage Foundation.

Fertility
Fertility refers to the ability to reproduce, to bear children, and to ensure the continuation of one's family name or heritage. All living beings, from microorganisms invisible to the naked eye to human beings, feel a biological imperative to perpetuate their species. Most of the time humans succeed in reproduction—babies are born, families are established. Occasionally they fail. Contemporary scientific data suggest that between 10 and 15 percent of people of childbearing age who wish to have children will discover that they cannot (Marsh and Ronner 1996). For thousands of years infertility was perceived as being almost solely a woman's problem. Even physicians believed that if a man was capable of sexual intercourse, he could father children. Even today in

many cultures the inability to bear children remains an acceptable reason for a man to divorce a wife. In fact, fertility experts estimate that in treating infertile couples, the man is found to be infertile in about 40 percent of cases, the woman in approximately 60 percent (Marsh and Ronner 1996). Causes for their infertility may be linked to age (that is, waiting until too late in life to attempt procreation), general health, or environmental factors. Medical advances during the twentieth century have allowed many infertile persons to become parents through techniques such as artificial insemination, the use of fertility drugs that stimulate ovulation, and in vitro fertilization (IVF). The success rate for many of these technologies remains low, however. IVF, for example, succeeds in only slightly more than one out of five cases (Marsh and Ronner 1996).

The historical record shows that over millennia both fertility (the ability to have children) and infertility have presented problems for families and for societies. Scholars and politicians alike have worried that the poor and uneducated lower classes were having too many children while the rich and literate upper classes did not have enough. The overall world population continues to climb, inspiring many scholars to debate whether or not Thomas Malthus's 1798 theory of population had merit. Malthus believed that human population would increase faster than the supply of goods available. He feared that over time, everyone's standard of living would decrease dramatically, leading to a subsistence lifestyle, unless disease, famine, or war slowed population growth.

At the same time that scholars who are the modern-day successors of Malthus fret over the global consequences of unchecked human fertility, families also have to cope with reproductive issues. At the level of the family, however, infertility rather than fertility is likely to be the cause for concern. Because reproduction is such a fundamental part of being human, the inability to have children can be emotionally devastating to both men and women. For many men fatherhood provides proof of masculinity—solid evidence that they are real men—and women often have similar feelings regarding motherhood. Infertile couples often describe themselves as feeling as though they have failed or done something wrong even though the causes for their infertility are generally conditions over which they have no control.

At the beginning of the twenty-first century, fertility and infertility pose numerous complex and often contradictory problems for humanity. At the same time that human overpopulation in developing nations presents a threat to humanity's long-term global well-being, many industrialized nations are faced with the dilemma of declining populations. Germany and Sweden have already experienced negative population growth. Although some scholars speculate that industrial pollutants contribute to rising rates of infertility among individuals, overall negative population growth (in which the number of births annually is less than the number of deaths) in industrialized nations can more likely be attributed to personal choice. The historical record indicates that birthrates tend to decline naturally as levels of urbanization and industrialization rise. Industrialized societies offer women more choices, that is, women are not restricted to traditional women's roles such as stay-at-home wife. Women who work outside the home are more likely to limit the number of children they have or to have no children at all. In addition, in industrialized societies children may become economic liabilities rather than assets. Housing costs increase, for example, as the number of persons in a household grows and larger living quarters become a necessity. In contrast, in preindustrialized societies children were an economic necessity for a family. Even very young children could share in the agricultural labor that made the household possible and, in societies that lacked Social Security systems and old age pensions, would be expected to care for their parents in their old age.

Further, although sensationalist stories in contemporary news media often sound an alarm about increasing infertility, the truth is that infertility posed a greater problem in the United States in the nineteenth century than it does in the twenty-first. Historians of medicine have found a higher rate of childless couples in the eighteenth and nineteenth centuries than in the twentieth. Individual family size was higher for those couples who could have children, but childless couples were common. In *The Empty Cradle*, authors Margaret Marsh and Wanda Ronner note that as cities grew in the nineteenth century, prostitution became widespread and men routinely visited brothels (Marsh and Ronner 1996). The lack of antibiotics as well as a poor understanding of the dangers of venereal and other diseases meant that many men and women were left sterile from gonorrhea, syphilis, pelvic inflammatory disease, and other infections. At the time doctors did not know that gonorrhea could be transmitted by infected persons who had no external symptoms, nor did they recognize that such asymptomatic gonorrhea could cause internal scarring in both men and women. Pelvic inflammatory disease caused by gonorrhea, for example, can lead to blocked fallopian tubes.

The combination of the effects of urbanization and damage done by untreated diseases meant that by the early 1900s, birthrates among middle-class Americans had dropped to the point where numerous magazines began publishing alarmist news stories chastising educated women for failing in their duty to society by electing not to have children. Leta S. Hollingworth, a psychologist who taught at Columbia University, reported in a 1916 article that the previous year, leading magazines had published at least fifty-five news stories expressing concern about the dropping birthrate (Population Council, Inc. 2000). The noticeable rise in the number of physicians specializing in treating "female problems" as well as the popularity of patent medicines that promised to restore women's vitality, however, suggests that many women were not childless by choice. Marsh and Ronner (1996) theorize that the problem was not that middle-class women did not want to have children, but that the fault instead lay with their husbands who were in fact sterile. Whether the problem was as widespread as they suggest is debatable, but it is true that infertility rates dropped following the invention of effective antibiotics in the mid-twentieth century.

In any case, although popular belief often ascribes the decline in average family size in the United States to the invention of oral contraceptions and the ready availability of birth-control devices, in point of fact the size of the average family had been shrinking steadily for decades prior to the invention of "the pill." Families were at their largest early in the nineteenth century before the U.S.

economy shifted from a rural, agricultural society to being urbanized and industrial. People have known how to prevent conception and limit the size of their families for thousands of years. Conception in healthy, fertile persons is simple to control. Methods used have included techniques as simple as practicing abstinence as well as various forms of barrier contraceptives. The ancient Romans, for example, described the use of a sponge inserted into the vagina as a way to prevent pregnancy.

Explaining why some otherwise apparently healthy men and women found themselves unable to have children proved more difficult for physicians than instructing fertile persons in contraception. Finding effective methods to overcome their infertility presented an even greater challenge than achieving an understanding of the causes of that infertility. Getting pregnant is often neither as straightforward nor as simple as it appears at first blush. Although some couples may succeed in conceiving a child the first time they have sexual intercourse, other seemingly healthy people can struggle unsuccessfully for years. Factors influencing fertility include the fact that the timing must be right, the man's sperm must be sufficiently motile (active), and the woman's fallopian tubes must be unobstructed in order for sperm and ova (eggs) to meet and for fertilization to occur. Even the natural pH (acid levels) of the vaginal and cervical mucus affect fertility. An old wives' tale once suggested that women could affect the sex of a baby by douching with either vinegar (an acid) or a baking soda (a base) solution prior to intercourse. Doctors have found some validity in the folktale. If the woman's natural body fluids, that is, the vaginal and cervical mucus, are too acidic, sperm

do not survive long enough to reach the waiting ova.

Then, once fertilization does occur, the zygote (fertilized egg) must fasten itself to the uterine wall. Researchers estimate that one-third, possibly more, of all pregnancies end almost before they begin, as the fertilized eggs fail to attach successfully to the lining of the uterus (Demarest and Charon 1996). If sperm motility (the liveliness or vitality of the sperm) is weak, the overall number of sperm is low, the timing is off, the vaginal mucus is antagonistic to the sperm, or the fallopian tubes are blocked, fertilization may fail to happen. Fertility experts have learned that even which ovary produces the egg makes a difference: ova from a woman's left ovary have a lower rate of successful fertilization than ova from the right ovary.

Early theories of childlessness included the idea that the seed bed must be properly prepared, that is, that the woman be receptive to the idea of sexual intercourse and that she find satisfaction in the act. This idea was articulated by the ancient Greeks before the time of Christ and continued to be the advice given to childless couples for hundreds of years. Seventeenth-century marriage manuals advised men to make the sexual act pleasurable for their wives if they wanted to ensure a successful pregnancy. Still, even couples that enjoyed a good physical relationship often found themselves childless. In such cases, most childless persons eventually resigned themselves to accepting their fate as being God's will.

Today we know that many factors can interfere with a couple's ability to have a child together. Disease, congenital defects, exposures to environmental toxins, and injuries all can influence fertility. Even an apparently healthy lifestyle can have an adverse impact on fertility: Many athletic women, particularly runners, experience irregular menstruation and occasionally stop menstruating completely. Menstruation occurs following the release of an egg by the ovaries. The uterus sheds its lining if the egg passes through the uterus without being fertilized. Lack of menstruation is a sign that ovulation is not occurring.

Most people once viewed infertility as being strictly a woman's problem, although some physicians recognized centuries ago that disease or accident could render a man sterile. Still, until well into the twentieth century, most doctors believed that as long as a man was capable of ejaculation he could father children. One of the first significant breakthroughs came when doctors realized that sperm motility and sperm count both affected fertility. Scientists now know sperm motility and sperm count both are easily influenced by environmental factors, such as exposure to heat or chemicals; by a man's age; and by a man's overall health. Diseases such as mumps can cause sterility in adult men. Participating in sports such as bicycling may damage the testicles and interfere with reproduction. Even wearing clothing that is too tight can affect fertility in a man. Raising the body temperature of the testicles by only a degree or two can weaken or kill sperm. Many couples' problems with infertility have been solved by simply telling the male partner to wear looser-fitting clothing and to avoid hot baths.

Timing is another crucial factor because pregnancy is most likely to occur if sperm can reach the ovum shortly after ovulation (the release of the egg by the ovary) and if the ovum is just beginning its journey down the fallopian tube. One of the earliest and simplest fertility treatments, and one that is still used today, consists of teaching a couple who wish to have children to monitor changes in the woman's body, such as her body temperature or the appearance of vaginal mucus, to catch the subtle signals that can indicate that ovulation is about to occur.

Doctors usually consider a couple suitable candidates for fertility treatments if the couple has had regular unprotected sexual intercourse for at least one year without conceiving a child, although the younger the woman is, the longer doctors will wait before intervening. Fertility specialists will often use a combination of techniques to help couples conceive. Artificial insemination (AI; the insertion of sperm into the uterus mechanically rather than through natural intercourse) is usually thought of as involving sperm from a donor, but this is not always the case. If there are problems with sperm motility or vaginal abnormalities are present, for example, a doctor may use AI techniques to place the man's sperm in the uterus. Physicians will usually attempt AI methods several times before suggesting the use of costlier techniques. Artificial insemination is one of the cheapest methods of treating infertility, IVF the most expensive, and the use of fertility drugs lies in between. Fertility drugs may be used with AI, by themselves with the couple engaging in normal intercourse, and with IVF to stimulate ovulation.

Although physicians in earlier times had counseled patients suffering from infertility, it was not until the mid-twentieth century that doctors began to offer truly effective treatments. Surgical techniques to open blocked fallopian tubes improved, and advances in endocrinology led to an understanding of the roles hormones played in ovulation. Physicians realized that if they could stimulate a woman's ovaries, successful pregnancies might be possible. Ironically, modern oral contraceptives resulted from research at the Fertility and Endocrine Clinic at Boston's Free Hospital for Women aimed at enhancing fertility and assisting reproduction, not at preventing conception from occurring.

Beginning in the early 1930s Dr. John Rock devoted his obstetrics and gynecology practice to helping infertile couples have children. Over the decades, Rock treated thousands of women who desperately wanted to conceive but were unable to. By the time Rock began his research, physicians knew one of the reasons otherwise healthy patients experienced difficulty in conceiving children was an irregular menstrual cycle. Although most women have highly regular natural cycles, some do not. Ovulation for those women is difficult to predict, if it occurs at all. Rock and his colleagues pioneered the use of hormones such as progesterone to stimulate ovulation. In the 1940s he began work on a hormone treatment that would regulate the menstrual cycle and assist couples who desired children. Rock, a devout Catholic, saw his invention as an enhancement of a woman's natural cycle, not as a way to suppress it, and did not anticipate the Catholic Church's banning the use of birth-control pills when the U.S. Food and Drug Administration approved their sale to the general public.

Rock and other physicians began treating infertile women with hormones as early as the 1930s, but fertility drugs did not gain wide notoriety until the 1960s. At that time the news media began reporting on increases in the number of multiple births, primarily quintuplets, caused by the use of fertility drugs. The drugs stimulate ovulation or, in some cases, superovulation. With normal ovulation generally only one egg is released, but with superovulation as many as eight eggs may develop in the ovarian follicles. This is what happened in the case of the famous McCaughey septuplets in 1997. Although Kenny and Bobbi McCaughey already had one child, they were anxious to have a second. They visited a fertility clinic where doctors treated Bobbi McCaughey with a fertility drug.

When the McCaughey septuplets were born in November 1997, the doctor who assisted them received sharp criticism for accepting the McCaugheys as patients at all. The couple's first child was less than a year old when they became impatient about their inability to start a second pregnancy. Having had one child with no difficulty, many critics felt the McCaugheys' only problem was impatience. Their doctor did counsel them to refrain from sexual relations when an ultrasound indicated multiple eggs were about to be released, but they chose to ignore her advice. The McCaugheys later stated they could not afford a second fertility drug injection costing approximately $3,000, leading those same critics to question how the McCaugheys thought they could instead afford a high-risk pregnancy and seven additional children, all of whom were likely to require neonatal intensive care. When it became clear that multiple fetuses were present, the McCaugheys rejected the option of selective abortion. Although all seven of the McCaughey infants were initially described as healthy, as they have grown, several reportedly are developmentally delayed and may have problems such as cerebral palsy, a common problem in premature infants with extremely low birth weights (Marsh and Ronner 1996).

Just as John Rock's invention of the oral contraceptive is marked by irony in that he was attempting to develop a fertility treatment, so, too, is Robert Edwards and Patrick Steptoe's perfection of IVF. Edwards and Steptoe used funds earned performing legal abortions to underwrite costs of infertility research and development of IVF. Researchers in the United States had achieved IVF with animals, but a lack of support for human research stymied efforts to use in vitro methods to treat human infertility. IVF, which requires the surgical harvesting of ripe eggs from a woman's ovary, combining those eggs with the father's sperm in a laboratory vessel (hence the term *test tube baby*), and then inserting fertilized eggs back into the mother's uterus, is a complex and costly procedure. Researchers first attempted IVF with laboratory animals in the 1940s as they recognized it as one way to defeat the problem of blocked fallopian tubes. It was not until the 1970s, however, that the procedure was used successfully in humans.

The first test-tube baby, Louise Brown, was born 25 July 1978, in England. At the time, the technique developed by Edwards and Steptoe startled the world, although few fertility experts were surprised. Scientists had worried that children conceived using IVF would suffer from unacceptable birth defects, but Louise Brown's debut as a perfectly normal infant girl allayed those fears. During the twenty-three years that IVF has been used, infants have been conceived who were born with significant defects, but whether in vitro children experience a higher rate of congenital abnormalities than children in the general population is still an open question. An IVF technique referred to as "hatching," in which the membranes of the eggs are thinned to facilitate successful implantation in the uterus, is seen by many critics as being especially prone to high rates of deformities, but no solid data have been presented as yet to support their concerns.

In the early days of IVF, it was common practice to implant four or more fertilized eggs to allow for the possibility that not all the eggs would successfully attach to the uterine wall. Studies have shown no significant difference in the success rate between using two eggs and using four, so most clinics today implant the lower number. This removes the risk that too many eggs will attach to the uterus for a successful full-term pregnancy. The higher the number of fetuses, the riskier the pregnancy becomes for both mother and infants. Multiple-baby pregnancies often result in miscarriage, premature births, and low-birth-weight infants. One-third of IVF births are multiples, a much higher percentage than for unassisted pregnancies. By limiting the number of possible fetuses to only two, fertility clinics can reduce risk factors considerably as well as avoid the uncomfortable situation of having to ask a couple to consider selective abortion, that is, to have the doctors terminate one or more fetuses in order to ensure the survival of at least one.

The widespread availability and public acceptance of IVF provided hope for thousands of infertile couples while at the same time presenting both doctors and patients with new ethical and legal dilemmas. The introduction of artificial insemination and the use of donor sperm had raised questions about parenthood—for example, who was the legal father? Similarly, IVF coupled with other technologies, such as surrogate motherhood, has led to situations in which as many as five different persons may be involved in conceiving a child: the infertile man and woman desiring a child, a sperm donor, an egg donor, and the woman who agrees to serve as the surrogate mother and undergo the actual pregnancy. This in turn gives rise to questions about financial compensation: How much, if anything, is appropriate? Although donating sperm is a simple procedure for a man, egg donation can be painful and poses significant health risks. The donor generally undergoes injections for fertility drugs to stimulate superovulation as well as an invasive procedure required to harvest the ripe eggs. Although some women donate eggs out of the unselfish desire to help another woman conceive, others have unabashedly attempted to market their ova almost as though a potential child was simply a sellable product no different from any other commodity. Similarly, infertile couples have begun dangling financial incentives in front of possible donors. It has become commonplace to see classified advertisements placed by childless couples in college newspapers. These ads spell out specific requirements, for example, the potential egg donor must be blonde, over five feet six inches in height, have at least a 3.5 grade point average, and so on. Financial compensation to the coed is generally around $10,000, although up to $40,000 has been offered to young women attending elite universities such as Princeton and Yale (Hildt and Mieth 1998).

Other ethical questions revolve around what to do with surplus fertilized eggs, or zygotes. These tiny embryos are usually frozen and kept in reserve in case the first IVF procedure fails, as many do, but when the pregnancy succeeds the parents must decide what to do with the unused zygotes. Some parents give permission for the clinic to use them for research purposes; others agonize over keeping the embryos frozen indefinitely but are unwilling to dispose of them.

The success rate for assisted pregnancies remains much lower than media reports might suggest. In the United States the absence of federal funding for research involving techniques such as in vitro fertilization means little public data are available. One unintended consequence of abortion foes fighting federal funding for research that has the potential to harm human embryos has been that advances in fertility treatments have been driven by market forces unaccompanied by any significant government oversight. Because infertile couples seeking treatment must take a clinic's claims at face value, experts advise anyone consulting with fertility specialists to talk with other patients. One key question any potential patient should ask is what a clinic's rate is of pregnancies carried full term. Some experts believe that the rate of spontaneous abortion (a natural miscarriage before the fetus is able to survive outside the womb) for in vitro fertilization is as high as 75 percent, or three out of four pregnancies failing in the first or second trimester (Hildt and Mieth 1998).

Not surprisingly, the available statistics indicate that all fertility and assisted reproduction technologies work best on younger, healthier patients. Nonsmokers are more likely to succeed with IVF than smokers, for example. Age is a critical factor. The older a woman is when she first consults a fertility specialist, the less likely she is to succeed in becoming pregnant. Many IVF programs refuse to take patients over the age of forty-two because the likelihood of a successful outcome for such older women is so poor. Doctors have succeeded in helping women past the age of fifty bear children by using donated eggs, but such cases are extremely rare (Hildt and Mieth 1998).

—*Nancy Farm Männikkö*

See also Birth Control; The Pill; Syphilis; Teenage Pregnancy; Venereal Disease

References and Further Reading
Bruce, Debra Fulghum, and Samuel Thatcher. 2000. *Making a Baby: Everything You Need to Know to Get Pregnant.* New York: Ballantine Books.
Campbell, Kenneth L., and James W. Wood, eds. 1994. *Human Reproductive Ecology: Interactions of Environment, Fertility, and Behavior.* New York: New York Academy of Sciences.
Davis, Kingsley, Mikhail S. Bernstam, and Rita Ricardo-Campbell, eds. 1987. *Below-replacement Fertility in Industrialized Societies: Causes, Consequences, Policies.* New York: Cambridge University Press.
Demarest, Robert J., and Rita Charon. 1996. *An Illustrated Guide to Human Reproduction and Fertility Control.* New York: Pantheon Publishing Group.
Grabowski, Casimer T. 1983. *Human Reproduction and Development.* Philadelphia: Saunders College Publications.
Hildt, Elisabeth, and Dietmar Mieth, eds. 1998. *In Vitro Fertilisation in the 1990's: Towards a Medical, Social, and Ethical Evaluation.* Brookfield, VT: Ashgate.
Marsh, Margaret, and Wanda Ronner. 1996. *The Empty Cradle: Infertility in America from Colonial Times to the Present.* Baltimore: Johns Hopkins University Press.
Population Council, Inc. 2000. "Leta S. Hollingworth on Coercive Pronatalism." *Population and Development Review* 26: 353 ff.
Shaw, R. W., ed. 1995. *Assisted Reproduction: Progress in Research and Practice.* Pearl River, NY: Parthenon Publishing Group.
Wyelemberg, Suzanne. 1990. *Science and Babies: Private Decisions, Public Dilemmas.* Washington, DC: National Academy Press.

First-Cousin Marriage

First-cousin marriage is the marriage between the offspring of different siblings: the children of two brothers, two sisters, or a brother and a sister.

First-cousin marriage is a practice that was generally accepted in the United States from the colonial period until the latter half of the nineteenth century. The attitudes regarding first-cousin marriage have since shifted in the United States, from tolerance among the majority of the population to intolerance of first-cousin marriage. Competing theories have been put forward to explain this shift.

From the colonial period until the second half of the nineteenth century, marriage restrictions between relatives were generally based on English laws, which had largely drawn upon the book of Leviticus in the Bible. Although most ascendant and descendant consanguineal marriages were forbidden, the biblical prohibitions omitted first-cousin marriage. Although some opposed first-cousin marriage as incestuous, the Puritans and Quakers, for example, others considered it attractive. One example comes from eighteenth-century eastern Massachusetts, where merchant families used first-cousin marriage to consolidate family wealth (Hall 1977, 42).

During the mid-nineteenth century, however, views of marriage began to change. Restrictions on affinal marriage receded, and restrictions on close consanguineal unions began to emerge. Debate, much of it driven by physicians and anthropologists, centered on concerns for the health of the children of such unions. The research of the day indicated that the children of first-cousin marriages were much more likely to develop birth defects than the children that resulted from close

States that permit first-cousin marriage without restriction:

Alabama	New Jersey
Alaska	New Mexico
California	New York
Colorado	Rhode Island
Connecticut	South Carolina
Florida	Tennessee
Georgia	Texas
Hawaii	Vermont
Maryland	Virginia
Massachusetts	

States that permit first-cousin marriage with restrictions:

Arizona	North Carolina
Illinois	Utah
Indiana	Wisconsin
Maine	

family marriage. Researchers found that children of such marriages were more likely to be blind, deaf, mute, and mentally impaired. Although the validity was questioned later, the results of this research sparked a growing movement to outlaw first-cousin marriage. By the early twentieth century, sixteen states had outlawed first-cousin marriage (Arner 1908, 14). Ottenheimer contended that this change traced to secularization of society, changes in societal perceptions of the role of the family, the acceptance of Spencerian evolutionary theory, and public health concerns (Ottenheimer 1996).

Opinion differs about the wisdom of first-cousin marriage. Children of such marriages are at a 4 to 6 percent higher risk to suffer from genetic defects than the children of unrelated couples because first cousins share one-eighth of their deoxyribonucleic acid (DNA) (Stern 1973). Whether or not this risk justifies laws prohibiting first-cousin marriage remains unresolved. At present, no uniform incest laws exist in the United States. The federal government has left the matter to the states to determine. Twenty-seven states have banned marriage between first cousins outright; seven permit it only under special circumstances, usually tied to reproductive capacity. Nineteen states permit first-cousin marriage without restriction ("CousinCouples" 2001).

—Robert Fay

References and Further Reading
Arner, George B. Louis. 1908. "Consanguineous Marriage in the American Population." Ph.D. diss., Columbia University.
"CousinCouples." http://www. cousincouples.com/info/states.shtml (cited 19 August 2001).
Goldethorpe, J. E. 1987. *Family Life in Western Societies: A Historical Sociology of Family Relationships in Britain and the United States.* Cambridge: Cambridge University Press.
Hall, Peter Dobkin. 1977. "Family Structure and Economic Organization: Massachusetts Merchants, 1700–1850." In *Family and Kin in Urban Communities, 1700–1939,* edited by Tamara K. Hareven, 38–61. New York: New Viewpoints.
Howard, Gordon Elliott. 1964. *A History of Matrimonial Institutions: Chiefly in the United States with an Introductory Analysis of the Literature and Theories of Primitive Marriage and the Family.* 3 vols. New York: Humanities Press.
Memorial University of Newfoundland. "Steven Carr." http://www.mun.ca/ biology/scarr/Inbreeding_Depression_ in_Humans.htm (cited 19 August 2001).
Ottenheimer, Martin. 1990. "Lewis Henry Morgan and the Prohibition of Cousin Marriage in the United States." *Journal of Family History* 15(3): 325–334.

Ottenheimer, Martin. 1996. *Forbidden Relatives: The American Myth of Cousin Marriage.* Urbana: University of Illinois Press.

Stern, Curt. 1973. *Principles of Human Genetics.* 3d ed. San Francisco: W. H. Freeman.

University of Manitoba. "Brian Schwimmer." http://www.umanitoba.ca/anthropology/tutor/marriage/usa-ncst.htm (cited 19 August 2001).

Freedmen's Families

Establishing, reuniting, and supporting families were major concerns for African Americans during the Civil War era (1861–1865). When the war began, nearly half a million African Americans were enslaved in the eleven states that seceded to form the Confederate States of America and in the four "border" states that remained in the federal union. From the beginning of the conflict, African American slaves interpreted the war to preserve the Union as a war of emancipation. Thousands of slaves ran away from rural farms and plantations individually or with family and friends. They sought sanctuary in "contraband" camps near Union Army lines or in urban centers throughout the South. They constructed new identities based on their rights as free people to control their labor and lives. To varying degrees, federal military and civilian agencies as well as northern missionary aid societies assisted African Americans in reestablishing and protecting their families. "Freed people" were encouraged to legitimize their marriages and to create the social and economic supports for family life. But control of freedmen's families and their labor were contested issues in the post–Civil War South. African Americans interpreted freedom, family, and free labor in ways that stressed autonomy. White northern-

ers and southerners anticipated a post–Civil War South where they or their agents would continue to control African American families and their labor.

In the first two years of the war, many slaves freed themselves from bondage by walking away from southern farms and plantations. The decision to escape was a family matter since it meant temporary or permanent separation as well as reprisals for those left behind. Local patrols, Confederate Army units, and independent bounty hunters with trained dogs hunted for escaping slaves. Runaways faced physical punishment, removal to more secure parts of the Confederacy, or even execution if they were captured. Slave owners sometimes punished an escapee's family by limiting rations, increasing labor, or abusing family members physically. In spite of these risks, an increasing number of African American slaves and their families ran away from their owners even before the Union accepted emancipation as a wartime goal.

Fugitive slaves jammed roads and obstructed military operations throughout the South. One newspaper described roads near Hannibal, Missouri, that were crowded with "scores, of hundreds, of slaves, embracing not only families, but conveying away with them horses, wagons, and even the trumpery that pertains to their domestic establishments" (*Memphis Bulletin,* 2 January 1863). Union military and civilian officials recognized that the removal of black labor from southern farms and plantations would help to undermine the Confederacy. Yet they were sometimes "hostile to the freedpeople's desire to reconstruct their domestic life" (Berlin and Rowland 1997, 56). Union military and civilian officials were concerned about the expense, inconvenience, and confusion of maintaining

Arrival of freedmen and their families in Baltimore. Wood engraving in Frank Leslie's Illustrated Newsletter, *30 September 1865. (Library of Congress)*

freed populations near army camps and the need to harvest valuable cotton crops. In the early years of the war, few northerners saw the conflict as a war for African American freedom. But Union policy gradually evolved to that position. Fugitive slaves and their families were at first confiscated as "contraband of war," housed in camps near Union Army lines throughout the South, and employed as construction, service, and agricultural workers. Predominantly white northern philanthropic societies sent missionaries and teachers to establish schools and orphanages and to provide direct aid in contraband camps. The increasing volume of escaping slaves, however, quickly overwhelmed these military and civilian efforts.

Gaining recognition for the sanctity of African American family life was difficult during the Civil War era. The actions of southern slaveholders, Union military and civilian officials, and northern missionaries often strained African American family ties. Families were divided by escapes, especially when slave owners relocated the slaves who remained on their farms to more secure parts of the South away from Union lines. In border states that never seceded and in areas that were captured by Union forces before the Emancipation Proclamation, fugitive slaves were sometimes returned to their owners. Some slave owners refused to allow black parents to take their children when they left rural farms even after the Emancipation Proclamation and the Thirteenth Amendment ended slavery.

Family relationships based on plantation rituals were not recognized by federal officials. Instead, they encouraged legal marriages and often limited housing and provisions to the legal spouses of freedmen who joined the Union army. African American women were encouraged to return to farms and plantations and negotiate contracts for their own labor and the labor of their children. Historians of emancipation suggest that northerners considered legal marriage an important component in the establishment of a new southern society based on free labor among freed people. Legal marriage supported the discipline necessary to create an organized labor force and was the first line of defense against the assumed promiscuity of enslaved men and women. Wedding ceremonies in the camps were often the scenes of mass marriages. In a letter to George Whipple, Lucinda Humphrey, a missionary teacher, described the 20 August 1863 "Thanksgiving Day" ceremonies at Memphis, Tennessee, contraband camps where 102 couples were married. "As I said before, many of these had been living together, but it is a law of the camp that all such shall be legally married. They were furnished certificates, neatly printed bearing a picture of the 'old flag'" (American Missionary Association).

Preserving and reuniting their families, with or without legal marriage, was also a priority for freed people. One Freedman's Bureau agent, commenting on the itinerant freedmen clogging southern roads, noted that they had a "passion, not so much for wandering, as for getting together. . . . In their eyes the work of emancipation was incomplete until the families which had been dispersed by

slavery were reunited" (Litwack 1979, 230). Freed people returned to farms and plantations to help relatives escape. After the Civil War, the Freedman's Bureau provided free transportation to reunite family members, and philanthropic society teachers and missionaries wrote letters for freed people searching for their relatives. Black newspapers in the North and South also carried ads for relatives. Searching for family sometimes took place over decades. Although advertisements included physical descriptions, locating relatives was difficult, especially if they had been separated as children. Children sometimes had no recollection of their parents. Those who had been taken into their owners' households often had developed deep attachments to whites. Yet the majority of slave children "formed a world view in the slave quarters within their own family group" and even in the absence of their parents had bonded with other blacks rather than white owners (Litwack 1979, 237). Freedmen also confronted the reality that some separated spouses had established new families. These freed people faced difficult choices of which marriages to legitimize and which children to claim.

As more and more able-bodied men were drafted or enlisted into military service, populations in the camps were dominated by women, children, sick, and elderly. Conditions were adequate in some camps, but others, especially in the last years of the war, were overcrowded and poorly supplied. African American soldiers sometimes appropriated army provisions and supplies to feed their families and to construct rudimentary shelters. Some freedwomen found jobs as matrons in camp hospitals and in orphanages for freed children or as cooks and laundresses for Union soldiers; others found jobs as cooks, domestics, and laundresses in the cities and towns near the camps. But still other women and children were encouraged to sign contracts to plant and harvest crops on nearby farms and plantations.

Employing women as agricultural workers satisfied the needs of southern planters desperate for laborers, of northern civilian and military officials and city residents who wanted to reduce overcrowding in "contraband" camps and cities, and of African Americans who needed wages to support themselves and their families. Union officials also suggested that returning to the rural countryside was the best solution for keeping freedmen's families together. Wages on plantations in western Tennessee ranged from $15 to $25 per month for men and $10 to $18 per month for women. Half was paid each month, the other half when the crop was sold. American Missionary Association minister A. D. Olds noted in a 10 February 1864 letter to George Whipple that "families are not to be separated; and each family is to have a house by itself. Also one cent a pound is to be paid on all the cotton raised to constitute a fund for the double purpose of supporting the aged & infirm and paying teachers" (American Missionary Association). Freedmen and their families worked plantation land under the supervision of northern aid societies or northern businessmen as well as southern planters. In a few cases, freed people were able to farm without white supervision and to earn enough to buy their own land. The African American colony at Davis Bend, Mississippi, was one example of this arrangement.

Control of black children's labor was a hotly contested issue between freedmen's families and southern planters. Even after the war ended, some former slave owners refused to allow black parents to take their children when they left farms and plantations. Freedmen's Bureau agents also allowed southern whites to negotiate long-term contracts that returned children to virtual slavery. Southern courts also used state apprenticeship laws to effect "legalized kidnappings," and judges often considered whites better able to rear black children than their parents. In some cases, black soldiers returned from fighting to win freedom to find their children still bound to their former masters or "adopted" by other whites who claimed the children were orphaned. Even after the Thirteenth Amendment was ratified in 1865, freedmen continued to face obstacles in supporting and protecting their families. African Americans struggled to control the labor of family members, particularly that of women and children. Black women were accused of "playing the lady" when families decided to direct women's primary responsibilities toward household duties and child care or to remove them from situations where they might be physically or sexually assaulted by the white landowners or overseers. Women also used the threat of the withdrawal of their labor to negotiate wages and working conditions from their employers. Most urban families, however, could not afford to have women withdraw from the labor force. Women also continued to work in the fields as sharecroppers alongside their husbands and children or in white households as domestic servants or laundresses. The shifting gender relationships in black households, however, meant that black men now exercised authority over the bodies and the labor of other family members.

African American men enforced their positions as heads of their families. Some considered this a reaction to the superior position they assumed black women held in antebellum slave households. They were determined to establish patriarchal households modeled on those of their former owners. Women were expected to learn housewifely skills such as cooking, sewing, mending, and garden cultivation; to remain chaste "true women" before marriage; and to be dutiful wives and mothers afterward. Some freedwomen embraced these ideals; others found them difficult to accept. Freedmen's families were centers of economic, social, and political activity in the black community. In the postwar period, men and women organized fraternal and mutual aid societies in which they pooled their resources to provide assistance to ailing members and death benefits to beneficiaries. Schools and churches were centers of family and community life. Suffrage was also viewed as a family right rather than as the individual province of men. Women and children accompanied husbands, brothers, and fathers to rallies and meetings and advised them on political choices.

—*Beverly Greene Bond*

See also African American Families; Courtship, History of; Farm Families

References and Further Reading
American Missionary Association. Archives. Library of Congress.
Berlin, Ira, and Leslie S. Rowland, eds. 1997. *Families and Freedom: A Documentary History of African-American Kinship in the Civil War Era.* New York: The New Press.
Frankle, Noralee. 1999. *Freedom's Women: Black Women and Families in Civil War Era Mississippi.* Bloomington: Indiana University Press.
Franklin, John Hope. 1980. *From Slavery to Freedom: A History of Negro Americans.* New York: Alfred A. Knopf.
Gutman, Herbert G. 1976. *The Black Family in Slavery and Freedom, 1750–1925.* New York: Vintage Books.
Hine, Darlene Clark, et al. 2000. *The African-American Odyssey.* Upper Saddle River, NJ: Prentice Hall.
Litwack, Leon F. 1979. *Been in the Storm So Long: The Aftermath of Slavery.* New York: Vintage Books.
Litwack, Leon F. 1998. *Trouble in Mind: Black Southerners in the Age of Jim Crow.* New York: Alfred A. Knopf.
Mann, Susan A. 1989. "Slavery, Sharecropping, and Sexual Inequality." *Signs* 14 (Summer): 774–798.
McPherson, James M. 1988. *Battle Cry of Freedom: The Civil War Era.* New York: Oxford University Press.
Palmer, Colin A. 1998. *Passageways: An Interpretative History of Black America.* Vol. 2. Fort Worth, TX: Harcourt Brace College Publishers.

Freud, Sigmund

Sigmund Freud (1856–1939), born in Freiburg, Moravia, Austrian Empire, was the founder of psychoanalysis. His theories have had an enormous impact on modern consciousness and have been instrumental in shaping the way twentieth-century people have thought about the mind.

A prolific and iconoclastic writer, Freud emphasized the centrality and pervasiveness of sexual motivation. His most influential theories focus on the primacy of the unconscious; infantile sexuality; the division of the psyche into the id, ego, and superego; and the importance of dreams in revealing the unconscious. His single most spectacular and controversial theory, which shocked many of his contemporaries, was his psychosexual theory of human development with its assumption of the universality of the Oedipus complex. Freud believed that all children possess libido, a psychic energy that focuses

struggles with the Oedipus complex as the most crucial part of the child's developmental history.

Freud suggested that conflicts between fathers and sons or mothers and daughters, sibling rivalries, murderous feelings toward parents and family members, and other tensions in the family could be traced back to the struggles with the Oedipus complex, the "nucleus of the neuroses."

—*Allan Chavkin*

See also Children as Parents; Sanger, Margaret; Spock, Dr. Benjamin

References and Further Reading
Freud, Sigmund. 1953–1974. *The Standard Edition of the Complete Psychological Works of Sigmund Freud.* Translated and edited by James Strachey et al. 24 vols. London: Hogarth Press.
Fromm, Erich. 1980. *The Greatness and Limitations of Freud's Thought.* New Yorker: Harper.
Gay, Peter. 1988. *Freud: A Life for Our Time.* New York: W. W. Norton.
Hall, Calvin S. 1979. *A Primer of Freudian Psychology.* New York: Penguin.
Jones, Ernest. 1961. *The Life and Work of Sigmund Freud.* New York: Basic Books.
Neu, Jerome, ed. 1991. *The Cambridge Companion to Freud.* New York: Cambridge University Press.

Portrait of Freud. (Hulton/Archive)

on different erogenous zones of the body in the maturation process. He argued that there were five sequential stages in the child's development: (1) oral, (2) anal, (3) phallic, (4) latency, and (5) genital. The first three stages were especially important, for if the child was deprived or excessively gratified during this time period (birth to age six), neuroses would occur at a later date.

It is during the phallic stage that the child's struggles with the Oedipus complex reach their peak. Because of the Oedipus complex, the child experiences unconscious sexual desires for the parent of the opposite sex and feels hostile toward the same-sex parent. Freud regarded these

Funerals

Oxford defines *funeral* as the "[b]urial or cremation of a dead person with its ceremonies." In the early 1600s, when the settlers started with a 9-out-of-10 chance of dying within a year of arrival, they accepted life's brevity. By midcentury, chances of dying in the Chesapeake region decreased to 50–50. The odds of a long life in New England were great if you could make it to five years of age, even better if you made it to twenty-one and were male. Still, the average person could expect to live thirty years even in Boston at the end of the seventeenth century and only thirty-five years a century later. A belief in God's intimate interest in human life may have assuaged people's fear of death. Europeans in the seventeenth and eighteenth centuries believed in an afterlife that was usually preferable and more comfortable than their present one, so many of those people who went to North America during the colonial period believed death a beginning rather than an end. Death was the gate to the final destination to Heaven or Zion or else eternal damnation (Wells 1975).

Deaths were social as well as biological occurrences in colonial America. The majority of people lived in rural areas or in very small communities, where everyone knew or was related to their neighbors. Everyone felt the loss of the deceased, whether from an emotional, spiritual, or economic standpoint. Funerals, then, were the responsibility of the family and the community. Women in families laid out the bodies of their loved ones in the home in which they had lived together. Kin or community members made the simple wooden box in which the corpse would be laid and then dug and filled the grave. There was no funeral industry to handle arrangements or charge the mourners for the necessity of disposing of the deceased with or without comfort. Nor were such arrangements done behind closed doors or in cemeteries far away from public view.

Funerals and wakes served the living, not the dead. In colonial New York, a crier (*aanspreeker* in Dutch) announced funerals and/or invited friends and family members to attend the ceremony. Like the harbingers of other kinds of news, these death criers were public employees who were paid by the families of the dead; fees depended upon the age of the deceased: the younger the age, the lower the price. If families could not afford to pay the crier, the town would find the funds.

In Pennsylvania the criers were "warners" who let friends and community members know of the passing of one of their number. Among the German immigrants who came to the colony, there was a practice of sending gifts with a formal invitation to mourners. Those gifts consisted of a bottle of wine and a pair of gloves as well as two death cakes. These items were not to be consumed by the recipient but kept as a reminder of the deceased. The gift giving eventually became so elaborate and expensive that colonial legislatures tried to stop or slow it down, but could not. Other methods of announcement included choirs singing, playing bells or musical instruments from a church tower, or posting a notice prominently in public places.

In Puritan New England, families cared for dying members. In some cases, the dying person recognized the end was near and had time to say goodbye and to let his or her family know his or her wishes. George Washington is believed to have realized he was dying by late afternoon on the day of his death. He evidently spoke to his family and slaves and told them not to bother caring for his illness any further. He also is alleged to have given his secretary instructions on his burial, including an admonition not to put him in his vault before two full days had passed, probably to make sure he was dead. He died at ten o'clock at night on the same day he gave his instructions.

Usually, family members made arrangements for burial. Bodies needed to be disposed of for biological reasons. Carcasses tended to rot and become breeding grounds for disease. Until the American Civil War in the middle of the nineteenth century, people did not embalm their dead, thus time was of the essence. Of course, in winter in northern climes where the ground nearly froze or did freeze, temporary arrangements could be made to store the body. Burying a body under snow in the woods worked as long as relatives remembered where they had buried it.

When the ground could accept a coffin, the affair was usually simple. Early colonists kept the ceremony simple. The person who presided over the occasion may or may not have said a sermon. If he did, it was short and sweet. Just as the gift giving in Pennsylvania and elsewhere expanded, so, too, did the funeral sermon from the seventeenth to the eighteenth centuries. Families came to expect such sermons by the decades before the American Revolution. That practice has survived into the beginning of the twenty-first century.

Communities buried their dead where they lived, in the town, in the church or the churchyard, and at home on the farm. Neighbors and family members dug the grave where the deceased and/or his heirs chose. Wealthy congregants paid to be buried beneath the pew they occupied in church. John Adams lies with his wife, Abigail, in the Stone Temple of the First Unitarian Church in Quincy, Massachusetts. Doctors discouraged this practice after the 1850s as too unsanitary and dangerous. Paupers, criminals, suicides, unbaptized infants, and other undesirables were buried in potters' fields or outside the churchyard in ground not blessed by the church. In the nineteenth century, especially after the Civil War, such "undesirables" included Americans of African descent, segregated in death as they had been in life.

The early settlers marked graves with small wooden crosses or other wooden monuments, but as the seventeenth century gave way to the eighteenth, the Puritans set monuments of stone on top of their loved ones' graves. These markers often carried depictions of death as a skeleton with wings or a death mask. Epitaphs stood as warnings to the living that everlasting God held their fate in His hands and death would find them, too, one day. By the mid-eighteenth century, New Englanders picnicked among the gravestones, sharing the space with their dead ancestors.

The Victorians in the nineteenth century also used cemeteries as social spaces. They beautified these spaces, which they increasingly moved out into the country as cities in the United States aged and grew. Cities hired gardeners to landscape their cemeteries just as they crafted city parks. Cherubs and lambs came to replace skeletons as markers on gravestones, which grew increasingy elaborate and costly as the century progressed. Family members or neighbors who dug the graves in the colonial era were replaced by coffin makers and undertakers who provided the pine boxes and the holes in which to bury people.

Southerners in the antebellum era took advantage of funerals for social gathering. There were very few cities or towns in the South, and plantations and farms were quite a distance apart. Rather than post a notice or send a town crier around, the family of the deceased notified four of their neighbors, who notified four more neighbors until people within a fifty-mile radius received word of an upcoming gathering. On horseback and/or in carriages, people came and ate cake and drank rum punch. After the funeral at the home, a procession would follow the casket to the churchyard or place of burial. The military tradition in the South found voice in firing guns over the graveyard. Ladies stayed home, as it was not proper for them to walk in the funeral procession.

Former slaves remembered following caskets with a preacher leading them in a hymn, usually a slow one for the procession to the burial place. The return home picked up speed as the hymn was usually of a faster tempo and more upbeat in tone and sentiment. This tradition could be seen in southern cities, such as New Orleans, where funeral processions featured brass bands that played a slow and sad hymn on the way to the cemetery, but a more martial and lively tune, such as "When the Saints Go Marching In," on the way home. In the twentieth century this practice attracted tourists anxious to catch a show.

Embalming corpses took hold during the Civil War, especially for officers whose families hoped to have them shipped home and buried there. A doctor who sold his embalming services throughout the war thought he could continue the business afterwards, but the practice did not catch on until the 1880s. It was useful for sending increasingly mobile Americans back home, but increasingly preservation of all bodies caught on to allow loved ones to view the body before burial. As time passed, and Americans became increasingly concerned with appearance, they wanted their dead to seem lifelike, and embalming allowed that. It also prevented the kind of havoc that nature wreaked on buried remains. Embalming also gained popularity, as Americans grew increasingly concerned about health issues and disinfection.

The people who convinced Americans that embalming was a good thing after most humans had gone millennia without it were a new breed of service providers: funeral directors. These professionals took over the roles of undertakers and cabinetmakers, as well as those of family and friends who cared for the corpse. A trend in the middle class toward privacy sanctioned the removal of the dead from the home for preparation for burial. Funeral directors did just that: They directed funerals. They organized at the same time that other middle-class professionals were solidifying their roles in society by creating institutions such as the American Medical Association and the American Bar Association. Funeral directors formed the National Funeral Directors Association in 1882. These organizations reflected an increasing institutionalization of services that had gradually drifted out of family hands.

Those most concerned with the increasing costs and lack of family control associated with funerals in the late nineteenth and early twentieth centuries were the poor and immigrants. Concerns that they would end up in paupers' graves inspired unions and the poor to pool their assets in funeral and burial funds for the destitute among them. Immigrant aid societies, organized by second- and third-generation immigrant families who had achieved middle-class status, also provided funds for funerals for new arrivals. Working families often bought life insurance for their children whose lives were in danger in crowded and busy cities or on dangerous factory floors. That insurance was meant to cover the cost of their funerals, but the middle class saw it as a way to profit off the death of children among the lower classes.

Most people in the colonial era and the nineteenth century died at home, but in the twentieth century, more and more people died in a hospital or nursing home. By the century's last decades, 70 percent or more of people died away from their homes (Jackson 1977). This institutionalization of death allowed funeral directors to create a monopoly for their services in the twentieth century. They took over completely the care of the body, the container for the corpse, the place the funeral would take place (whether a church or mortuary), and all funeral procedures and arrangements. Although many Americans appreciated the care and concern of these professionals at a difficult time, others criticized the practices. In 1963, Jessica Mitford wrote a book entitled *The American Way of Death*, pointing out that what used to cost very little, even counting inflation, now was exorbitant and unnecessary (Mitford 1963). By the late twentieth century, prices of coffins ranged in the thousands of dollars. Services could deplete a family's small inheritance. Crowded cemeteries inspired the building of marble or granite mausoleums for families to be interred above ground.

Despite the criticism, Americans continue to engage the services of funeral directors. They have watched, too, with fascination, the funerals of heroes and celebrities from Rudolf Valentino in 1926, to Pres. John F. Kennedy in 1963, to Elvis Presley in 1977 and the Princess of Wales in 1997. Funerals of the rich and famous sometimes become very extravagant affairs, but most Americans die alone and are buried in a lonely plot hidden away from public view. They no longer stroll among the well-groomed grounds the Victorians trod or picnic among dead relatives. Memorial Day may bring large numbers of people to visit graves, but for the most part, Americans focus on the living more than the dead. They are much less fascinated with death than the people of the nineteenth century. They may be as terrified of it as the unredeemed Puritan, but for other reasons. It was only in the last two decades or so of the twentieth century that Americans became willing to grapple again with death and dying through the work of counselors and therapists in the area of grief and loss and through the growth of the hospice movement.

As have humans since well before history was recorded, Americans mark the passing of their loved ones with ritual and ceremony. Burial is still prevalent, but cremation is growing more popular as Americans seek to have closure by spreading ashes in places the dead once loved or dividing them up among scattered family members as they engage in their own rituals. Clergy, who took increasing responsibilities for services for the dead, continue to be involved. And, despite the fact that our lives have grown increasingly healthier and longer over the course of the last four centuries, we still die and still acknowledge the passing of our loved ones with funerals.

—*Mary Elizabeth Glade*

See also Decoration Day

References and Further Reading
Coffin, Margaret M. 1976. *Death in Early America: The History and Folklore of Customs and Superstitions of Early Medicine, Funerals, Burials, and Mourning.* Nashville: Thomas Nelson.
Colman, Penny. 1997. *Corpses, Coffins, and Crypts: A History of Burial.* New York: Henry Holt.
Dickerson, Robert B., Jr. 1982. *Final Placement: Guide to the Death, Funerals, and Burials of Notable*

Americans. Algonac, MI: Reference Publications.

Farrell, James J. 1980. *Inventing the American Way of Death, 1830–1920.* Philadelphia: Temple University Press.

Jackson, Charles O. 1977. *Passing: The Vision of Death in America.* Westport, CT: Greenwood Press.

Mitford, Jessica. 1963. *The American Way of Death.* New York: Simon and Schuster.

Wells, Robert V. 1975. *The Population of British Colonies in America before 1776: A Survey of Census Data.* Princeton, NJ: Princeton University Press.

Zelizer, Viviana A. 1994. *Pricing the Priceless Child: The Changing Social Value of Children.* Princeton: Princeton University Press.

G

Gender Roles in the American Family

The family is the primary agent of human socialization. Among the many values and behaviors inculcated by the family, arguably the most fundamental are gender roles. Some of the social roles of males and females are determined by biological differences. Only women give birth to and breast-feed the young, and men generally have superior physical strength. Yet the sexual division of labor and the socialization of humans as gendered beings are for the most part rooted in socially constructed gender roles. Gender roles within American families have varied over time owing to changing modes of economic production, religious beliefs, philosophical and ideological doctrines, and cultural values. They have also varied as a result of the race, ethnicity, or class of the family in question.

The gender roles of the various native peoples of North America differed dramatically from those of European settlers. In most Indian societies, especially those along the East Coast, the family was matriarchal and matrilineal. Property was owned by women and was passed between female relatives, and when a man married, he joined his wife's household. Women were almost wholly responsible for agricultural and craft production, whereas men served primarily as hunters and warriors. Among the English settlers who began to immigrate into North America in the seventeenth century, the normative family was patriarchal and patrilineal. The father was legally and socially regarded as the head of the family, and property passed from father to son. English common law buttressed patriarchy by treating husband and wife as one person and imbuing the husband with virtually absolute control over family property and income.

Notwithstanding the common culture of English immigrants, the colonial experience was characterized by significant diversity. Most of the early settlers of the Chesapeake region came as indentured servants, and most were young men. A full century after the founding of the Jamestown colony, there were three males for every two females. The unbalanced sex ratio was one of several obstacles to the formation of a stable family structure within Chesapeake society. Female indentured servants could not marry until they had served out their indenture, thus delaying the age of first marriage. Shockingly high mortality rates due to endemic diseases such as dysentery, malaria, and typhoid fever cut the median life expectancy to roughly forty years (Morgan 1975). Despite these hardships, the women who survived their indenture often possessed a degree of autonomy that their sisters in both Old and New England did not. A freedwoman had wide latitude in her choice of a husband, since a father's approval was usually unnecessary. The shortage of women generally resulted in women's marrying men who were older and of higher social status. The high mortality rates resulted in relatively short marriages in which most men predeceased their wives. Since men reasonably feared that a stepfather might not treat their children equitably, they generally left their widows more than the legally mandated one-third of their estates and often made them executors of their estates. By the early eighteenth century, mortality rates had diminished, population grew primarily by natural increase, and the sex ratio began to approach one to one. This more demographically stable society thus began to hew to more characteristically English patterns of patriarchal gender relations.

Family life in the New England colonies differed significantly from that in the Chesapeake region. The rigorous Calvinist theology of the Puritan settlers held that a strong nuclear family was the basis of a Christian society. Most immigrants came to New England as members of nuclear families, creating a nearly balanced sex ratio within a few years of first settlement. The demographic patterns and religious beliefs of New England reinforced already powerful English notions of patriarchy. The patriarch was expected to provide moral and religious guidance to his family and to fulfill his duties to the community. He bore the primary responsibility for his family's material welfare, but Puritan theology strongly discouraged the pursuit of wealth or social status as ends in themselves. A man's labors were to be performed for the glorification of God in furtherance of the Puritans' communitarian spiritual mission. Women were obliged by the same religious standards to be obedient helpmates to their husbands and to bear their household labor as a social and religious obligation.

Although the colonies differed in many ways, economic factors created strong patterns of similarity among the white families of colonial America. The household was the primary unit of economic production, and the labor of every family member was usually essential to its survival. Men and older sons generally did the heaviest physical labor. They cleared farmland, built houses and barns, plowed fields, tended row crops, and hunted game. Women sometimes assisted men in such time-sensitive tasks as planting and harvesting, but their responsibilities centered around the house rather than the fields. They cared for children, washed clothes, and cleaned the house. They produced a significant proportion of the family's food by cultivating vegetable gardens, raising chickens, and tending dairy cows. They also produced the family's clothing by spinning yarn, weaving it into cloth, and sewing the cloth into finished garments. Unless a farm wife was sick, men rarely did work normally done by women. Women, however, regularly assumed putative male responsibilities during a husband's absences. Acting as what the Puritans called a "deputy husband," women managed the household, performing men's work or supervising laborers they hired to do it.

Although women served as the primary caregivers for children under five, the patriarchal male was more deeply involved in child rearing than subsequent generations of American men would be. For the 80 to 90 percent of colonial-era Americans who worked as farmers, home and work occupied the same physical space. This was also true for most artisans and retail merchants. The majority of men in preindustrial America thus spent most of their time in close physical proximity to their children and shared child-rearing responsibilities. The gender conventions of the day held that men possessed a more acute moral sense than women because of their allegedly greater capacity for rational thought. Thus, fathers controlled the inculcation of moral, ethical, and religious values in the young. Likewise, since fathers were presumed to be less likely to overindulge children who needed correction, they were the primary disciplinarians.

The revolutionary philosophical, religious, and economic changes that swept the United States and the Western world in the late eighteenth and early nineteenth centuries undermined the patriarchal family and promoted the rise of modern gender roles and relations. Changing religious and philosophical conceptions of human nature enhanced female authority in child rearing. The decline of the theological doctrine of human depravity diminished the imperative to repress and contain children's inherent sinfulness. Concurrently, Enlightenment thinkers John Locke and Jean-Jacques Rousseau and the Romantic thinkers who followed them believed that human nature was inherently good. This led an increasing number of parents openly to express more affection toward their children. Thus, a mother's loving care became widely regarded as a healthier form of parental authority than the sternness and punishment meted out by an authoritarian patriarch. Although cultural changes helped shape a new paradigm of gender roles, most historians agree that the economic transformation that began in the early nineteenth century provided an even more significant impetus for change.

Beginning around 1800, the market revolution brought millions of Americans into the cash economy, diminishing the agricultural self-sufficiency that had formed the economic basis of patriarchal family relations. The Industrial Revolution, which began about the same time but grew more slowly in the early years and was limited at first to the Northeast, was ultimately far more significant.

These economic forces transformed the United States into a bourgeois society in which the gender norms of the urban middle class became socially and culturally predominant. Industrial and commercial enterprises supplanted the home as the primary unit of economic production, thus physically separating home and work. The normative middle-class family consisted of a man who worked outside the home in a white-collar job and a wife who managed the household and cared for the children. This sexual division of labor and the value system that evolved in concert with it are known as the doctrine of separate spheres or the cult of domesticity. The public world of business and politics made up the male sphere, and the private world of home and family constituted the female sphere. Very few middle-class, white married women worked outside the home. This arrangement generally prevailed only among families in which the man earned an income sufficient to maintain a middle-class lifestyle, and it was geographically limited to the cities and towns of the Northeast and, by midcentury, the Midwest. The societal power of the new middle class that first adopted such an arrangement and the authority of the opinion leaders who promoted it gave the doctrine of separate spheres extraordinary influence on gender roles in the American family.

Stripped of its economic function, the middle-class home was redefined as private space, a refuge and sanctuary set apart from the competitive world of market relations. It became an essentially feminine domain in which the patriarchal values of deference and hierarchy were supplanted by sentimentality and emotion. Marriage became somewhat more companionate in nature, and men were expected to be more affectionate and solicitous of their wives' feelings. The "true woman" was pious, chaste, and devoted to her family. The new value system redefined women as morally superior to men and completely reversed traditional conceptions of family moral and religious life. Victorian moralists feared that the men who competed in the rough-and-tumble world of market capitalism would succumb to the temptations of materialism. The doctrine of separate spheres solved this problem, at least in the minds of its proponents. Women's inherent capacity for piety and love and their selfless renunciation of personal ambition allowed them to offer spiritual sustenance to their husbands. Women now became the symbolic guardians of the traditional values of family, religion, and community, and men could now unabashedly pursue power and material gain.

New gender norms promoted a new conception of child discipline. Spanking began to replace whipping with a stick or leather strap, and many families regarded spanking as a last resort rather than a knee-jerk response to misbehavior. Instead, withholding affection and the inducement of shame and guilt became increasingly common means of correcting children. These techniques did not merely enforce grudging obedience; they encouraged children to internalize bour-

geois values and behavioral norms. Women were seen as particularly well suited to employ these new disciplinary techniques. Not only were they inherently more moral than men, but their voluntary renunciation of worldly ambition embodied the internalized self-discipline that they sought to inculcate in their children.

Some historians of the family emphasize the denial of opportunities to women and see domesticity as the wholesale victimization of women by men. Women lost a source of real power, they argue, when their labor became irrelevant to the maintenance of the family's standard of living. Other historians, however, emphasize the empowerment and autonomy that women created within this ideology of subordination. Women created a value system that differed radically from the male world of individualistic competition. Separation offered women the opportunity to find emotional sustenance in relationships with female relatives and friends. These emotional bonds between women were often more meaningful than those they shared with their husbands. Within the physical and psychological boundaries of the domestic sphere, women developed a consciousness of themselves as a distinct social class, with values and interests different from those of men. Most historians agree that the gains of feminist reformers were built in large part upon the separate culture and consciousness that were conceived within the Victorian domestic sphere.

The doctrine of separate spheres helped facilitate a dramatic decline in the birthrate. The average white woman with a completed family had 7.04 children in 1800. A century later, this number had fallen to 3.56 (Sigerman 2000). Economic motivations were a significant causal factor, since urbanization and industrialization transformed children from an economic asset into a liability. This was especially true for the middle class. Changing gender relations within the family also figure prominently in this process, however. There is substantial evidence that women asserted their desire to limit the burdens of bearing and raising large numbers of children. Fertility rates began to decline in the early nineteenth century, before urbanization and industrialization had transformed children into an economic liability for most families. Also, they declined among farm families, for whom children remained an economic asset. Abstinence and coitus interruptus were the primary means of pregnancy prevention, and each required male cooperation. This indicates that many men were receptive to their wives' desire to limit their fertility. The doctrine of separate spheres thus helped to foster a family environment in which female individualism could, if not flourish, at least gain a foothold.

Male roles within the family changed dramatically as well. A man's social status came to be defined largely by his career success, not by the fulfillment of the roles of family patriarch and steward of community and religious values. Men's primary familial role became that of the breadwinner, a term coined in the early nineteenth century that reflected the increasing emphasis placed on men's earning capacity. Advice literature encouraged fathers to take an active, if subordinate, role in child rearing. These prescriptions had little practical effect, however. Regardless of class, the separation of home and work dramatically reduced the amount of time and energy that men could spend with their families. Men's influence and authority in the day-to-day

activities of domestic life waned dramatically during the nineteenth century.

The doctrine of separate spheres was a product of the nascent industrial capitalist economy of the urban Northeast and Midwest, and as such, it bore only minimal relevance to the family life of the antebellum South. Antebellum white southern culture incorporated some elements of the cult of domesticity, notably the belief that women possessed a special capacity for piety and morality. The household remained the primary locus of economic production in this predominantly agrarian economy, however, so the essential precondition for the existence of the doctrine of separate spheres did not exist. Also, the social relations of a slave society fostered the continued vitality of a prebourgeois value system rooted in the concept of primal honor. The ethos of honor legitimated a hierarchical social order that validated the dominance of the master over his slaves and of the patriarchal male over his wife and children. A family's social class was crucial in determining its gender roles and relations. Three-quarters of white southern households owned no slaves, and most of the rest owned only a few (Cooper and Terrill 1991). The sexual division of labor and gender roles within those families did not differ markedly from those of colonial-era subsistence farmers. The families of the planter class, however, developed a distinctive set of gender roles and relations.

The planter viewed himself literally as the lord of his domain. He saw it as his right and duty to control not only the external business dealings of the plantation but also the lives and labor of both his family and his slaves. Owners of large plantations generally concentrated on the business affairs of the plantation and left the supervision of slaves to hired overseers, whereas those with smaller plantations performed both responsibilities. The right to whip slaves was a crucial part of the master's patriarchal authority, although those who employed overseers often delegated this task to them. Masters believed that slaves owed them labor and deference in exchange for care. By the nineteenth century, most planters subscribed to an ethos of paternalism that obliged them to care for what they saw as their childlike and naturally subservient slaves. Planters generally avoided hard physical labor, which was beneath the dignity of a man of honor. Slaveholders who owned fewer than seven or eight slaves did not possess this luxury. They often worked alongside their slaves in the fields, although the slaves bore the brunt of the heaviest labor and worked longer hours than their masters.

The plantation mistress is shrouded in the mythology of the delicate and genteel southern lady who was placed on a pedestal and shielded from worldly travails. Most planters' wives did their best to live up to this prescribed role, for their own and their families' social standing depended to a large extent on how well they met these expectations. Few led lives of leisure, however. A plantation could not function well unless the mistress effectively managed the operations of the big house. Although slaves did most of the physical labor, she had to supervise food production in gardens, henhouses, and dairies as well as food preparation, housecleaning, laundry, and myriad other housekeeping tasks. Mistresses usually managed plantations when husbands were away. They generally worked more closely with slaves than did masters, since the house and kitchen were more physically confining

than the fields, and masters often employed overseers as buffers between themselves and the slaves. As a result, mistresses and house slaves often came to know one another quite intimately. Although the reality of slavery prevented the development of any true sisterhood, this close personal contact sometimes fostered profound emotional ties. It also commonly bred festering hostility. Mistresses who faced such situations usually did not hesitate to whip slaves or order them to be whipped.

Elite southern women did not possess the degree of domestic authority and autonomy that middle-class northern women had gained under the system of separate spheres. Although the women's child-rearing burdens were eased by the assistance of slave nannies, masters retained a significant degree of authority over children. The geographic isolation of most plantations and the reluctance of men to allow women to leave home without a male chaperone made it more difficult for southern women to form a network of female friends and relatives. The most profound emotional torment for many plantation mistresses was their husbands' virtually unlimited power to sexually exploit female slaves. Wives in such a situation usually could do little more than suffer in silence. Notwithstanding the difficulties inherent in their social role, plantation mistresses enjoyed a position of profound class and race privilege. Although some elite southern white women of the antebellum era expressed doubts about the morality of the slave system in their diaries and letters, the majority accepted the system and willingly worked to maintain it.

That system accorded no legal recognition of the marriages or family relations of slaves. The first historians to study the slave family asserted that since the master superseded the slave father as the material provider and ultimate authority, the slave family was essentially matriarchal in structure. More recent historians, however, have determined that the image of the absent slave father was exaggerated. In the late antebellum period, a substantial proportion of slaves lived in households headed by men. Many nominally female-headed households had active fathers who resided on neighboring plantations and who took a fairly active role in family life. They generally spent Sundays and holidays with their families and often visited them at night, sometimes risking a whipping to do so. When masters broke up a marriage by a sale, however, the father was far more likely than the mother to be sold. Slaves responded by relying on a network of kin and fictive kin to fill this void, and adult males within the community often filled in for the absent father.

Masters generally determined the sexual division of labor among their slaves. On large plantations that employed gang labor, men and women usually worked in separate groups. Slave men usually performed such heavy labor as clearing fields, plowing, and digging ditches, and women usually did such relatively less strenuous tasks as hoeing and weeding. Masters did not apply white gender norms to their slaves, however, and women often did extremely strenuous fieldwork. Specialized jobs were more likely to be gender segregated. Drivers, who supervised other slaves, were all men. Men also worked as carpenters, blacksmiths, and mechanics. With the exception of butlers and coachmen, most full-time house servants were female. On large plantations, five or more slave women could fill such specialized roles as cook, laundress, nanny, house-keeper, gardener, and seamstress. On smaller plantations and slaveholding farms, one or two women performed all of these tasks. Mothers bore primary responsibility for the care of young children, but their work limited their contact with them. Elderly slaves and older children usually cared for younger children during the workday, although slave women sometimes carried their infants and toddlers into the fields, keeping an eye on them while they worked. After a full workday, slave women also bore the added burden of cooking and housecleaning, since slave men rarely performed those tasks. Most slave women thus filled the role of homemaker, at least to the extent that their limited time and energy allowed.

After emancipation, most African Americans became sharecroppers, and a significant minority of them rejected the sexual division of labor prevalent under slavery by withdrawing women from field labor. Male heads of sharecropper households faced both a depressed agricultural economy and blatant racial discrimination, however, making it extremely difficult for them to fill the breadwinner role. Those who migrated to cities were for the most part limited to menial occupations. Thus, notwithstanding the desire of both men and women that the latter devote most of their time to child rearing and homemaking, nearly half of all black married women were forced into the labor market by the late nineteenth century. Those in rural areas worked as agricultural laborers, and those in cities worked primarily as domestic servants and laundresses. The proportion of black married women working outside the home declined in the first half of the twentieth century, to roughly one-third in 1920 and to about one-fourth in 1940. Even then, they remained more than twice as likely as white married women to work outside them home (Degler 1980).

Throughout the nineteenth century and into the twentieth, many working-class men and women gradually came to accept the gender roles associated with separate spheres. A workingman who could fill the role of sole breadwinner achieved greater social status and masculine pride. Many working-class women accepted, at least to some extent, the cultural prescription that equated domesticity with "true womanhood." Yet most working-class families did not possess the financial means to fulfill the gender norms of separate spheres. Only skilled workmen making good wages could fill the role of sole provider. The families of unskilled and semiskilled laborers had to rely to a great extent on the labor of women and children. Few working-class wives worked outside the home during the nineteenth century, but most generated income within the home. Many took in laundry and sewing, and others performed piecework for manufacturers. Roughly one in five working-class families took in boarders, and women generally performed the extra labor that this activity created (Modell and Hareven 1973). These forms of labor enabled them to earn badly needed income without neglecting their children or household duties. Child labor became increasingly common throughout the nineteenth century, although the age at which children began working and the number of hours they worked varied according to the family's economic need.

Immigrants were disproportionately represented among the poorest of the working class. Most immigrant men earned low wages as unskilled laborers, and their families depended heavily on the labor of women and children. Despite their poverty, only a small portion of married immigrant women worked outside the home prior to 1920 (Degler 1980). Like native-born working-class women, most remained at home to care for children while generating income by taking in boarders or by doing piecework or laundry. Immigrant men generally assimilated more quickly than their wives, because the latter tended to remain isolated within the narrowly circumscribed confines of home and neighborhood. Thus, adult female immigrants were far less likely than their husbands to learn English. Notwithstanding these broad similarities, each ethnic group had its characteristic pattern of gender roles. Irish women tended to assimilate more readily than either Irish men or women from other ethnic groups, since most knew English and so many worked as servants within the households of the native-born. Most unmarried Irish women worked outside the home, primarily as domestic servants but also as factory operatives. The majority of them quit their jobs when they married, but Irish wives were more likely to work outside the home than other immigrant women. Significant numbers of Polish women worked outside the home as well. Italian women, on the other hand, were the least likely of any immigrants to work outside the home. The patriarchal peasant culture of southern Italy and Sicily placed a premium on male control of women, reducing the likelihood that Italian women would seek employment outside the home. Married Jewish women also rarely worked outside the home, although young, unmarried Jewish women did so in significant numbers.

Despite lingering reluctance to abandon their native culture, European immigrants generally regarded assimilation in positive terms. Native Americans, however, faced an intensified campaign of forced assimilation during the nineteenth and early twentieth centuries. Christian missionaries and federal Indian agents pressured them to adopt a patrilineal nuclear family structure that included gender roles based on separate spheres. The Dawes Severalty Act of 1887 broke up Indian reservations and parceled out land to male heads of households. This system forced many tribes to abandon communal agriculture and the matrilineal household comprising an extended family. Indians were also pressured to adopt a characteristically white division of labor in which men performed agricultural labor and women tended to the home. Perhaps the most emotionally devastating element of this campaign was the practice of separating children from their parents and sending them to boarding schools that taught white culture and values.

The dominant culture was sufficiently powerful to spread the culture of separate spheres, albeit slowly and incompletely, across lines of class, race, and ethnicity. Yet between the 1890s and World War I, many middle-class men and women evinced at least some dissatisfaction with the system of gender roles that had helped to define them as a class. Many men feared that the domestic sphere had become so completely feminized that their sons were losing their masculine virility. In response, Theodore Roosevelt urged men to share a regimen of competitive sports and outdoor activity with their sons that he dubbed "the strenuous life" (Roosevelt 1901, 1). Many young women concurrently expressed some frustration with the strictures of domesticity. Female education had steadily improved over the nineteenth century, not to prepare women for careers but to enhance their ability to educate their children. The New Woman was a turn-of-the-century symbol of the desire of many educated middle-class women for more personal autonomy. A growing number of them worked prior to marriage as teachers, nurses, and social workers, and a handful even entered such male bastions as medicine and law. These rumblings of discontent did not portend the imminent decline of the doctrine of separate spheres, however. Marriage and career remained completely incompatible for most white women. By 1920, fewer than 7 percent of married white women worked outside the home (Degler 1980). Likewise, men did not radically alter their priorities in order to spend significantly greater amounts of time at home.

Against a backdrop of rapid economic growth and rising consumerism, the United States during the 1920s witnessed the growing independence of young women, the rise of more permissive sexual attitudes, and a greater emphasis on individual fulfillment. Divorce rates, which had risen steadily since the end of the Civil War, rose to a rate of one divorce for every six marriages by 1927 (Riley 2001). In response, advice books and magazines promoted the concept of companionate marriage, which sought to eliminate the stuffy formality and emotional distance that they believed had characterized the Victorian marriage. Spouses were encouraged to seek a more profound level of emotional intimacy. Husbands should not become so engrossed in their careers that they neglected their wives, and couples should seek leisure pursuits that they could enjoy together. A grossly oversimplified version of Freudian psychology popularized the notion that mutual sexual fulfillment was crucial to a successful marriage. Although these changes seemed like a radical reordering of attitudes to more tradition-minded Americans, they did not greatly affect the gendered division of labor within the family. Many middle-class white women found a degree of liberation in the heady atmosphere of the 1920s, but career and marriage remained incompatible. Their role as consumers, however, was enhanced in the economic boom years of the 1920s. Men were still expected to be the sole breadwinner, and the boom mentality and the promise of easy money led many men to place intense pressure on themselves to acquire wealth. Somewhat contradictorily, men were advised to abandon the sternness and distance of the Victorian father, spend more time with their children, and cultivate more relaxed and loving relationships with them.

The Depression of the 1930s wreaked devastation on millions of families. Financial insecurity and pessimism about the future depressed both marriage rates and birthrates. Divorce rates also fell, primarily because many unhappy couples lacked the financial means to set up separate households. Unemployment rates of 25 percent denied millions of men the social status and self-esteem they had derived from filling the breadwinner role, and millions of others suffered tremendous stress induced by diminished wages or the fear of losing their jobs. To compensate for the male breadwinner's unemployment, many families reverted to survival strategies involving the labor of women and children—strategies that they had abandoned a generation or more earlier. Women's employment was hindered by the widespread attitude that a working woman

occupied a job that rightfully belonged to a male breadwinner. Many employers adopted such policies, and a 1933 law declared that spouses could not simultaneously hold federal civil service jobs. Women who were forced by economic necessity to work outside the home did so despite these obstacles. In 1930, 11.7 percent of married women of all races worked outside the home (Deutsch 2000), but by 1940, that figure had risen to 15 percent (May 2000).

World War II was the catalyst for sweeping changes in family life, although many of them were temporary in nature. Vastly increased industrial production and the mobilization of millions of men into the armed forces created a demand for labor that could only be filled by women. Many women responded to the appeal of high-paying jobs and to a government effort to encourage women to emulate Rosie the Riveter and work in war-related industries. The number of employed women rose from just under 12 million in 1940 to over 18.5 million in 1945. More significantly, for the first time in U.S. history, married women outnumbered single women in the workforce. African Americans made gains during the war as well. Enticed by employment opportunities and eager to flee the more egregious racial oppression of the South, over 5 million blacks left the rural South and migrated to cities during the 1940s. For the first time in American history, most blacks now lived in urban areas, thus abandoning agrarian gender roles in favor of those of the urban working class. The high demand for labor also allowed many black women to abandon low-paying jobs as domestic servants and laundresses. The roughly 110,000 Japanese Americans who were forced into internment camps between 1942 and 1945 experienced a more profound disruption in family life than any other group in the nation. The heretofore rigid control of family life by patriarchal fathers was significantly diminished by the camp experience. Japanese women broke a strong cultural taboo by working for wages in the camps, and children enjoyed a far greater degree of autonomy than they had prior to the war (May 2000).

Following the traumas of depression and world war, Americans returned to more traditional gender roles. Marriage rates spiked dramatically upward, and the long-term decline of the birthrate was temporarily reversed between 1945 and 1964 by the "baby boom." The cold war promoted a culture of conformity in which the family became a sacrosanct cultural icon. Such popular television series as *Father Knows Best* and *I Love Lucy* reinforced normative gender roles. Postwar prosperity allowed an unprecedented proportion of men to support their families solely on their incomes, and a new suburban world of comfortable if bland tract homes provided social space for this new domesticity. The ideals of companionate marriage and family togetherness that had first been popularized a generation earlier were updated for the postwar period. Sexual compatibility occupied an even more central position in the popular definition of a happy marriage. Popular culture promoted the notion that mothers could maintain their "sex appeal" and should do so in order to maintain the sexual spark in their marriages. Magazines and advice manuals, notably Benjamin Spock's *Baby and Child Care*, encouraged women to regard motherhood as their natural vocation and avocation. A woman's labor was also essential to the maintenance of the domestic ideal: A survey concluded that

a full-time homemaker in the 1950s worked an average of fifty-five hours per week at household tasks (Riley 2001). Fathers performed far less household labor, but they were encouraged to become "family men" who involved themselves deeply in family life. A same-sex role model for sons was considered to be crucially important because of the rising fear of both homosexuality and juvenile delinquency among teenage males during the 1950s.

Yet the conformity of the baby boom years masked fault lines that produced significant changes in the family in the latter third of the twentieth century. Bourgeois gender norms had allowed men to concede authority to women in the domestic sphere, since they could compensate by cultivating a more unrestrained masculinity in the marketplace. Yet at the same time that the postwar professional male enjoyed rising income and job security, he was expected to subordinate his individual desires to the needs of the corporation. The middle-class breadwinner, long a symbol of rugged individualism and manly independence, was increasingly seen as an anonymous cog in a soulless corporate machine. Women's dissatisfaction, however, involved a more fundamental contradiction and would have more far-reaching consequences. Domesticity and self-sacrifice contrasted sharply with the rise of individualism and the quest for personal fulfillment, and increasing numbers of women questioned why society discouraged them from the pursuit of these goals. Many homemakers felt a vague sense of discontent and isolation despite the presumption that motherhood and domesticity constituted a woman's highest calling. Betty Friedan's influential 1963 best-seller, *The Feminine Mystique*,

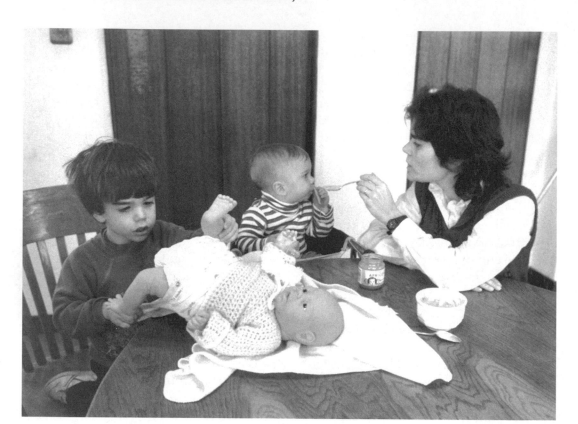

A three-year-old boy modeling baby-doll care on his mother's care of his six-month-old brother. (Elizabeth Crews)

articulated the frustrations of many educated middle-class housewives and presaged the women's movement that would explode into the popular consciousness later in the decade.

The movement of large numbers of married women into the labor force, one of the most significant factors in changing gender roles, began well before the women's movement. Despite strong support for domesticity among opinion leaders and the layoffs of women from heavy industry after World War II, the number of employed married women grew significantly from the late 1940s onward. In 1960, even at the height of the baby boom, 31.9 percent of all married women

worked outside the home, up from the 15 percent in 1940 (U.S. Bureau of the Census 2000). Although many worked because of economic necessity, many middle-class women did so in order to ease frustration and to expand their personal identity beyond that of wife and mother. By the 1970s, the women's movement had begun to alter popular attitudes regarding women's employment. A 1945 public opinion survey revealed that 65 percent of the respondents believed that a woman whose husband could support her should not hold a job, whereas in 1975 the same proportion said that such women should work if they wished to do so (Degler 1980). More women had college educations by the 1970s, and pressure from the women's movement had begun to create opportunities in heretofore male-dominated occupations. Also, stagnant income growth among all but the wealthiest quintile of American workers after 1970 made it harder for one-earner families to maintain a middle-class lifestyle. By 1996, 70 percent of mothers with children under eighteen worked outside the home (U.S. Bureau of the Census 2000). Longer life spans and birth-control methods that allowed women to stop bearing children at an early age enabled older married women to join the workforce in increasing numbers as well.

By the 1980s, the two-earner family had become the norm, thus blurring the traditionally rigid distinction between the male breadwinner and female homemaker. This betokened the rise of a postfeminist gender ideal in which each spouse had an equal opportunity for individual fulfillment while bearing an equal share of household responsibilities. Yet complete gender equality within the family remains more of an ideal than a reality. In most two-earner families, many more women than men subordinate their career interests to family needs. Women are more likely to work part-time, leave the workforce temporarily to care for children, and relocate to meet a husband's career needs. They are also more likely to leave work to take a child to an appointment or to stay home with a sick child. Although they have performed an increasing proportion of household labor and child-rearing responsibilities, men still do much less than women. A 1988 survey of families in which each spouse worked full-time found that men spent 20 percent more time on household labor than they did in 1976. Women still spent

more than twice as much time performing household labor as men, however (Samuelson 1995).

Radical changes in family structure have also had a significant impact on gender roles. In 2000, less than one-quarter of American households consisted of a working father, a stay-at-home mother, and children. Concomitantly, there has been a dramatic rise in the number of single-parent households. In 1960, single parents headed slightly less than 10 percent of American families with children. By 1998, that proportion had risen to nearly one-third. In that year, 26 percent of white families, 35 percent of Hispanic families, and 64 percent of African American families were headed by a single parent. Roughly 60 percent of single-parent households resulted from divorce, as the divorce rate rose almost 250 percent between 1960 and 1980. The remainder of single-parent households resulted from out-of-wedlock births. In 1960, 5 percent of births were to a single mother, whereas in 1999 that proportion had risen to 33 percent. In 1998, women headed 84 percent of all single-parent households. Although expanded economic opportunities for women and increased social welfare benefits have enhanced the ability of divorced and never-married women to support families without a husband's income, the poverty rate for female-headed households is extremely high. In 1998, the median income of families headed by a divorced mother was only 40 percent of that of two-parent families, and the median income of families headed by women who have never married was 23 percent of that of two-parent families (Bennett 2001).

Gender roles within the American family have been extraordinarily fluid over the past four centuries. The colonial period, during which the patriarchal family was normative, was the only era of relative stability. The transition to an industrial capitalist economy in the nineteenth century ushered in a social dynamic in which change was the only constant. The patriarchal gender relations of the agrarian family were undermined and ultimately extinguished by a system of bourgeois gender relations that was appropriate to the dominant class of the new economy. The doctrine of separate spheres was a powerful ideology whose influence spread far beyond the white middle class. It never became fully normative, however, among groups whose class status or ethnic traditions effectively prevented its extension into their family life. Even more significantly, the ideology of individualism that is so central to bourgeois capitalism ultimately undermined the doctrine of separate spheres. Several generations of middle-class women pressed for a greater degree of personal autonomy, and by the late twentieth century, most women could choose to reject domesticity. Yet the sexual division of labor established under separate spheres possesses a powerful legacy. Despite the rising number of two-career families and men's assumption of greater household responsibilities, women still perform most household labor and bear most of the burdens of child rearing. The postfeminist ideal of sexual equality within the family remains an elusive goal.

—*Andrew Doyle*

See also Affection as a Basis for Marriage; African American Families; Baby Boom; Children as Parents; The Companionate Family; Courtship, History of; Divorce, History of; Family Decline in the Twentieth Century; Fatherhood; Feminine Mystique; Japanese American Families during World War II, Internment of; Marriage; Middle-Class Family; Motherhood; Sexual Revolutions; Single-Parent Families

References and Further Reading:
Bennett, William. "Index of Leading Cultural Indicators: 2001." www.empower.org (cited 26 November 2001).

Cooper, William J., and Thomas Terrill. 1991. *The American South: A History.* New York: Alfred A. Knopf.

Cott, Nancy. 1977. *The Bonds of Womanhood: "Woman's Sphere" in New England, 1780–1835.* New Haven: Yale University Press.

Cott, Nancy, ed. 2000. *No Small Courage: A History of Women in American Life.* New York: Oxford University Press.

Degler, Carl. 1980. *At Odds: Women and the Family in America from the Revolution to the Present.* New York: Oxford University Press.

Demos, John. 1986. *Past Present and Personal: The Family and the Life Course in American History.* New York: Oxford University Press.

Deutsch, Sarah Jane. 2000. "From Ballots to Breadlines, 1920–1940." In *No Small Courage: A History of Women in American Life,* edited by Nancy Cott, 417–473. New York: Oxford University Press.

Fox-Genovese, Elizabeth. 1988. *Within the Plantation Household: Black and White Women of the Old South.* Chapel Hill: University of North Carolina Press.

Jones, Jacqueline. 1985. *Labor of Love, Labor of Sorrow: Black Women, Work and the Family from Slavery to the Present.* New York: Basic Books.

Kett, Joseph. 1977. *Rites of Passage: Adolescence in America, 1790 to the Present.* New York: Basic Books.

Kimmel, Michael. 1996. *Manhood in America: A Cultural History.* New York: The Free Press.

May, Elaine Tyler. 2000. "Pushing the Limits, 1945–1961." In *No Small Courage: A History of Women in American Life,* edited by Nancy Cott, 473–528. New York: Oxford University Press.

Modell, John, and Tamara Hareven. 1973. "Urbanization and the Malleable Household: An Examination of Boarding and Lodging in American Families." *Journal of Marriage and the Family* 35 (August): 474–475.

Morgan, Edmund S. 1975. *American Slavery, American Freedom: The Ordeal of Colonial Virginia.* New York: W. W. Norton.

Pleck, Joseph. 1985. *Working Wives, Working Husbands.* Beverly Hills, CA: Sage Publications.

Riley, Glenda. 2001. *Inventing the American Woman: An Inclusive History.* Vols. 1 and 2. Wheeling, IL: Harlan Davidson.

Roosevelt, Theodore. 1901. *The Strenuous Life: Essays and Addresses.* New York: Century Publishers.

Rotundo, E. Anthony. 1993. *American Manhood: Transformations in Masculinity from the Revolution to the Modern Era.* New York: Basic Books.

Ryan, Mary. *Cradle of the Middle Class: The Family in Oneida County, New York, 1790–1865.* New York: Cambridge University Press.

Samuelson, Robert J. 1995. *The Good Life and Its Discontents: The American Dream in the Age of Entitlement, 1945–1995.* New York: Vintage Books.

Sigerman, Harriet. 2000. "Laborers for Liberty, 1865–1890." In *No Small Courage: A History of Women in American Life,* edited by Nancy Cott, 289–352. New York: Oxford University Press.

U.S. Bureau of the Census. 2000. *Statistical Abstract of the United States: 2000.* Washington, DC: Government Printing Office.

Genealogy

The term *genealogy* means literally "birth study" (from Greek), or the history of a person's genetic inheritance. Genealogy provides an account (usually written, but sometimes transmitted orally) of family pedigree. People or organizations who undertake to learn about their family history often use pedigree charts, family group records, and individual records to trace previous generations of ancestors backward in time (Library of Congress 1999).

Different but related terms are *family history, life history,* and *oral history.* Al-though genealogy (narrowly conceived) relies heavily on scientifically reliable legal documents (birth and death certificates, marriage licenses, wills, and so on), individuals conducting genealogy often go beyond names, dates, and places to learn more about specific individuals in terms of their occupations, their personalities, and how their lives fit into the larger historical picture. Life history is a personal history, where individuals record the history of their family, information about parents and siblings, birthplace, early recollections, economic conditions and personal responsibilities, schooling information, military service and job histories, courtship and marriage, children, hobbies and other interests, special celebrations or holiday traditions, plans and hopes for the future, counsel and encouragement for one's descendants, and so on. Oral histories tap older living relatives or individuals to record what they remember from their past.

The Old Testament of the Bible shows our early interest in tracing genealogies. Genesis 5 emphasizes the linkages across generations from Adam and Eve to Noah. There are frequent references in the Bible clarifying who "begat" whom. As social classes developed over the medieval period, interest in establishing ties with distinguished ancestors increased. Monks often recorded the founders and patrons of their churches, but the collapse of the feudal system fueled a drive for more accurate and reliable recordings of legal property rights. Establishing heredity links to the aristocracy or propertied classes assumed new importance. In the United States, many groups currently exist that are organized around the common ancestry of individuals who participated in the early struggles of our country (for example, the

Women on stage at the Daughters of the American Revolution convention, Washington, D.C., c. 1904–1908. (Library of Congress)

Daughters of the American Revolution, the Sons of Confederate Veterans, and the Sons and Daughters of the Pilgrims). According to the 1961 edition of *Collier's Encyclopedia*, the term *genealogy* originated in England during the late 1400s and became more popular during the 1500s.

Surnames are crucial in tracing genealogy, and one writer calls these the "fossils of speech" (Brown 1967, 7). Children usually bear the surname of their fathers, and most women in the United States assume their husbands' surnames. Another convention is for sons to be given their father's entire name, with Roman numerals that follow these family names. This clarifies, by name alone, the connections across generations. In some languages, family names denote genealogy, occupation, region, and/or physical traits. Thus "Styward" later became "Stuart," losing its original connotation of tending the king's pigs (Zabeeh 1968, 69). Similarly, many Scandinavian names that end in "son" were meant to reflect family history (the patronym of "John's son" now being combined to the surname of "Johnson"). Over time, many of these naming conventions have changed to ease pronunciation or spelling (especially in instances where officials wrote names the way the name sounded to them); others were changed owing to religious, political, or social reasons (for example, Jews in Nazi Germany). For genealogists, slight changes in surnames can present major challenges in tracing a particular lineage. Conversely, Hispanic cultures often utilize surnames that include both the father's and mother's names.

Last names serve as the focal point for family history searching. In the United States, this can present particular problems for women and African Americans in tracing their family histories. It is often more difficult to trace women's lines of descent given the common practice of women assuming their husband's names. Without marriage license records that note maiden names, it is sometimes difficult or impossible to know women's birth-given surnames. Nevertheless, it is interesting that more women than men conduct genealogy or are responsible for keeping (and passing down) written documentation such as family Bibles. The challenge for African Americans who had slaves as ancestors was the social convention of slaves assuming their owners' last names. Roman slaves were also without names, until purchased by slave owners. At that point, they took their master's surname, followed by the suffix "por." The basic idea behind these practices seems to be that as long as others regarded slaves as animals, they did not have their own names (given by their families), nor did they need a name. Once slaves were purchased to become servants, however, some name designation was required (Zabeeh 1968, 66).

For many minorities in the United States, such naming practices are a central reason why genealogy is most often handed down through oral histories and storytelling from generation to generation. It is also true that the time and ability required to read and write (in order to keep track of one's family history) were luxuries denied to many minority families.

Since genealogical research is cumulative, genealogists begin with their most recent ancestors and work back. The National Archives recommends that people consult census records, military service and pension records, passenger arrival records (for ancestors who immigrated to the United States by ship between early colonial times and 1950), and state and federal land records (National Archives and Records Administration 1987). The Library of Congress adds that documents such as baptismal records and certificates of birth, death, and marriage are useful since they may reference an earlier generation in terms of name, birthplace, and names of their parents. Church records are also helpful. When such documents are lacking, the Library of Congress recommends filling in the gaps with family Bibles, obituaries, published information in compiled family histories, and/or interviews with older living relatives (Library of Congress 1999). State departments of archives, history, or vital statistics and local (city or county) offices are also crucial in genealogical research, since this is where many official documents are kept on record (birth certificates, death certificates, marriage records, and so on). County courthouses include records of land exchanges, wills, and probate records. Local cemeteries can also reveal family ties.

The Church of Jesus Christ of Latter-day Saints has long been considered a major resource for individuals doing genealogy. Mormons believe in the eternal life of individuals and families. They believe that when we die, our spirits go on to a spirit world, where people continue to learn while waiting for their own resurrection and the last judgment of God. Because Mormons believe that the family as a unit can continue after death, they encourage people conducting genealogy to first identify who their ancestors are. After such identification, the Mormons encourage all genealogists to share the results of their research with them, in order to facilitate other individuals in identifying their eternal family members. FamilySearch is the Mormons' automated system of family history information. Visitors to Salt Lake City can visit the Mormons' Family History Library to conduct genealogical research. This library has a collection of over 3 million books and microforms. The library also has a staff microfilming records from all over the world. For individuals who are unable to go to Salt Lake City, the Family History Library has forms that can be mailed in to request photocopies from their International Genealogical Index and Sources databases. In addition, approximately 4,000 Family History Centers exist throughout the world. Most major U.S. cities have at least one such center as a genealogical resource.

Mormons recommend that when individuals are beginning their genealogical research, they should consult records that indicate what others have previously researched about particular family names. Their five main sources are: (1) the International Genealogical Index (the births and marriages of approximately 280 million deceased people); (2) the Family Group Records Collection (family group record forms submitted by individuals conducting genealogy from 1924 to 1979); (3) Family Histories (books or microfilm written by members of a particular family); (4) Ancestral File (about 15 million names, submitted by family members, accessible via the Internet as well as via computer at the Family History Library); and (5) the Pedigree Resource File Index (accessible via Internet), which then refers individuals to compact discs (CDs) that contain information on the 10–15 million names as well as the contact information for the individual researcher who submitted the information (The Church of Jesus Christ of Latter-day Saints 1985).

There are many genealogical organizations (for example, the Genealogical Society of Hispanic America). The National Genealogical Society is a national organization devoted to facilitating genealogical research. Its mailing address is 4527 N. 17th Street, Arlington, VA 22207-2399.

The Internet has facilitated genealogical research by making access to information easier, as well as by promoting the posting of entire family lines of genealogy on the World Wide Web. This work is largely done by many volunteers throughout the world, who enter data where information will be more accessible to others. A few of the major sites are noted here.

Ancestry (www.ancestry.com). This is a commercial Internet site that has over 800 databases, including the *Social Security Death Index* and *Periodical Sources Index.* The goal is to create the largest and most active online community for families throughout the world.

Cyndi's List (www.cyndislist.com). This is an impressive clearinghouse that will route individuals to other web sites. With nearly 100,000 links, Cyndi Howells writes that "the Internet is like a library with its books strewn all over the floor. I guess I'd like my list to be the card catalog for the genealogy section of that library."

Family Search Internet Genealogy Service (www.FamilySearch.com). This is the official web site of The Church of Jesus Christ of Latter-day Saints. At this site, researchers can search databases, share their results, learn about the Family History Library, and link to other relevant sources.

Genealogy (www.genealogy.com). This is a commercial web site that allows individuals to search and to share information and leads. The World Family Tree allows individuals to search online or via CDs to find family names.

MyFamily (www.myfamily.com). This company owns three Internet properties: ancestry.com, myfamily.com, and familyhistory.com. This umbrella web site for the three services provides a password-protected community on the Internet for families. The site enables family members to share experiences with each other and communicate. Family members can post family news, create family photo albums, hold live text and voice chats, and maintain a calendar of family events. The company also offers free online family history software that enables multiple family members to collaboratively update their family trees.

National Archives and Records Administration (the Genealogy Page; www.nara.gov/genealogy/ genindex.html). Since genealogists are the most numerous users of National Archives research rooms in Washington, D.C. (as well as the thirteen regional facilities), this web site is designed to provide many of the finding aids, guides, and research tools that can prepare users for a site visit or for requesting records.

The National Endowment for the Humanities (www.myhistory.org). This web site involves the project to celebrate the new millennium called My History Is America's History. This program is designed to encourage the exploration of family history and to understand better how our own family histories connect to the history of our nation. The National Endowment calls its web site a virtual "front porch" for the entire United States.

USGenWeb Project's Information for Researchers (www.usgenweb.org). This project and web site consist of a large group of volunteers working together to provide Internet web sites for genealogical research in every county and every state of the United States. It is not commercial and is explicitly committed to free and open access for everyone. It has especially good data at the county level and also includes state-level information. There are other special initiatives at the national level.

Since family history and genealogy are really about retrieving information from the past, the Internet is certain to facilitate genealogical research in the future.

As it is carved in stone on the National Archives in Washington, D.C., "What's past is prologue." Genealogy informs us of our personal histories so that we can understand ourselves and others more fully. Family history and genealogy not only reflect family lineage and names but also economic inheritance, regional migration histories, occupational and educational histories, and cultural histories as well as health-related issues in our past. Medical doctors often ask their patients about their medical histories across generations. In addition, conducting genealogical research often leads individuals to a better understanding of their country's more commonly known history. Migration, marriages, births, and deaths can reflect much about the broader historical context of our families' lives.

—*Sheryl R. Tynes*

References and Further Reading

Brown, Samuel L. 1967. *Surnames Are the Fossils of Speech.* Privately published.

The Church of Jesus Christ of Latter-day Saints. 1985. *Where Do I Start?* Salt Lake City, UT: The Church of Jesus Christ of Latter-day Saints.

Library of Congress. 1999. *Genealogical Research at the Library of Congress.* Washington, DC: Library of Congress.

National Archives and Records Administration. 1987. *Getting Started Beginning Your Genealogical Research in the National Archives in Washington.* Washington, DC: Library of Congress.

National Endowment for the Humanities. 2000. *My History Is America's History: 15 Things You Can Do to Save America's Stories.* Washington, DC: Library of Congress.

Weil, Simone. 1952. *The Need for Roots: Prelude to a Declaration of Duties toward Mankind.* New York: G. P. Putnam's Sons.

Zabeeh, Farhang. 1968. *What Is in a Name?: An Inquiry into the Semantics and Pragmatics of Proper Names.* The Hague: Martinus Nijhoff.

Gerontology

Gerontology is the systematic study of the social aspects of growing old. Researchers examine how society as a whole treats the elderly and look at the behaviors of elderly persons themselves. Demographers predict that by the year 2030 one out of four adults in the United States will be retirement age. As average life expectancies for men and women continue to lengthen and the elderly (generally defined as people age sixty-five or older) constitute an ever-increasing percentage of the population, gerontology research takes on greater importance.

Gerontology differs from geriatrics in that geriatrics concerns itself with the biological characteristics of aging, whereas gerontology looks at behavior, economic statuses, and lifestyles. Gerontology, in short, is a social science; geriatrics is medical. Researchers often have backgrounds in sociology, psychology, economics, or political science in addition to specialized training in gerontology.

Gerontology research tries to identify potential problems with the elderly and to find answers to questions about how people adjust to aging. Research includes both macro- and microlevel issues in aging. That is, gerontologists examine issues that affect large segments of the population and also study small groups and individuals. On the macro level, gerontologists may track changes in population patterns to determine whether a particular region will need to increase the availability of services that target the elderly. If a southern community attracts large numbers of retirees, for example, that city may need to encourage construction of assisted living housing. On the micro level, researchers may examine how individuals cope with issues such as the death of a spouse, the loss of physical independence, or financial hardship caused by reduced income following retirement from the workforce. Research has shown that many elderly people enter retirement with unrealistic expectations and are often unprepared for the lifestyle changes that come with aging.

—*Nancy Farm Männikkö*

References and Further Reading
Abeles, Ronald P., Helen C. Gift, and Marcia G. Ory, eds. 1994. *Aging and Quality of Life.* New York: Springer Publishing.

Arber, Sara, and Maria Evandrou, eds. 1993. "Ageing, Independence, and the Life Course." London: British Society of Gerontology.

Phillipson, Chris, and Alan Walker, eds. 1986. "Ageing and Social Policy: A Critical Assessment." Brookfield, VT: Gower.

Gifted Children in the Family

Some children, now generally referred to as "gifted," exhibit intellectual abilities beyond those expected for their age: They learn earlier, faster, and better than their peers. The family of a child identified as gifted must decide what child-rearing practices are best for such a child. Specifically, families of gifted children seek to learn how much and what kind of intellectual stimulation and education will maximize their child's intellectual, social, and emotional development. In different cultures and different historical periods, society, the institution of the family, and families themselves have taken different approaches to understanding what early intellectual development in children means and how such children should be raised. In the United States, the social meaning of early intellectual development in children has changed from a worrisome problem for families in the nineteenth century to an exciting challenge for twenty-first-century families.

From colonial through antebellum times, Americans paid little attention to the problem of early intellectual development in children. Few young children attended school, and those who did were rarely grouped by age for instructional purposes. After the Civil War, newspapers, magazines, and the newly proliferating child-rearing advice literature devoted much space to the discussion of such children. From the 1870s through the 1920s, the dominant image of children who exhibited early intellectual development was that of the *precocious* child, who was in danger of physical weakness and disability, insanity, and even death if his or her mental activities were not controlled. Many Americans, including some social scientists, believed that genius and insanity were closely linked and that child prodigies were unlikely to become productive adults. One celebrated case was that of William James Sidis (1898–1944), who could read at eighteen months of age and enrolled in college at eleven years old but was considered an occupational failure as an adult and died in his forties of a cerebral hemorrhage. The story of Sidis's life was popularized by the media in the United States as a confirmation of these negative attitudes toward precocity.

Widely held ideas about the physical consequences of mental activity and about children and childhood underpinned the view that precocity was dangerous for children. In nineteenth-century popular and scientific thinking about the relationship between mind and body, it was often assumed that each individual possessed a finite amount of intellectual and physical energy whose expenditure must be balanced. Children who expended too much mental energy would thus suffer from a loss of physical strength. Many Americans espoused a romantic view of childhood in the context of sweeping social changes related to the nation's urbanization and industrialization. In this view, "natural" childhood was idealized. Parents were encouraged to rear their children in accordance with nature's time line for childhood development, which meant no forcing or undue encouragement of scholarly achievements.

Nineteenth-century child-rearing advice books often included a lengthy treatment of the problem of the precocious child or infant. Parents were warned against encouraging or allowing their children to undertake mental effort lest they suffer physical or psychological damage. Nineteenth- and early-twentieth-century families of children who exhibited early intellectual development deployed child-rearing and educational practices meant to delay the precocious child's engagement in mental activities. Study hours were regulated, and early reading was particularly discouraged. Families also sought to balance their children's physical development with their intellectual development through programs of exercise and outdoor activity.

A father and son designing a crossword puzzle together. (Elizabeth Crews)

In the 1920s and 1930s, American social scientists such as Lewis Terman and Leta Hollingworth first began to study and describe "gifted children," who were identified by intelligence quotient (IQ) testing. Their research was primarily aimed at dispelling the nineteenth-century idea of precocious children as physically weak and emotionally unstable. To the contrary, Terman and Hollingworth found that the children they identified as gifted were physically superior to their peers and socially and emotionally well adjusted. (They were also almost all from upper-middle-class families, which accounted for their superior height and weight.) Experts on and advocates for gifted children mounted a successful effort to change public opinion regarding early intellectual development in children. From the mid-1920s until today, the dominant American image of the child who exhibits early intellectual development is that of the *gifted* child, a figure that symbolizes human potential and hope for the future. American parents of gifted children are encouraged to foster their children's intellectual development. In the latter half of the twentieth century, the federal government allocated funding and set standards for special education programs for gifted children in the public schools.

In the contemporary United States, families of children who exhibit early intellectual development engage in child-rearing and educational practices meant to create an environment in which the gifted child can reach her or his full potential. Support organizations such as the American Association for Gifted Children, founded in 1946, offer informational resources and advice to families seeking to learn more about the child-rearing practices they should adopt for their gifted child. Challenges faced by contemporary families of gifted children include identification issues, the educational needs of their gifted child, and emotional/psychological issues related to the gifted child in the family, such as relationships with siblings. Gifted children are most commonly identified through the use of IQ or other types of testing, although some school districts identify gifted children through teacher recommendations. Families of gifted children have four primary options for education: acceleration or skipping grade(s) within an ordinary school curriculum, special education including separate schools or classes for gifted children, enrichment whereby the ordinary curriculum is supplemented for the gifted student, and home schooling. All of these means of meeting the educational needs of gifted children have their advocates and detractors. In particular, special gifted education programs in the public schools have been criticized as exacerbating class privilege, since the majority of American children identified as gifted continue to come from relatively affluent families.

—*Roblyn Rawlins*

References and Further Reading
Brady, Marilyn Dell. 1991. "The New Model Middle-Class Family (1815–1930)." In *American Families: A Research Guide and Historical Handbook*, edited by Joseph M. Hawes and Elizabeth I. Nybakken, 83–123. Westport, CT: Greenwood Press.
Chudacoff, Howard P. 1989. *How Old Are You? Age Consciousness in American Culture.* Princeton, NJ: Princeton University Press.
Lears, T. J. Jackson. 1981. *No Place of Grace: Antimodernism and the Transformation of American Culture, 1880–1920.* New York: Pantheon Books.
Macleod, David. 1998. *The Age of the Child: Children in America, 1890–1920.* New York: Twayne Publishers.
Margolin, Leslie. 1994. *Goodness Personified: The Emergence of Gifted Children.* New York: Aldine D. Gruyter.
Rawlins, Roblyn. 2002. "Long Rows of Short Graves: Sentimentality, Science, and Child-saving in the Construction of the Intellectually Precocious Child, 1870–1925." In *Symbolic Childhood*, edited by Daniel T. Cook. New York: Peter Lang Publishing.
Sternberg, Robert J., and Janet E. Davidson, eds. 1986. *Conceptions of Giftedness.* Cambridge, MA: Cambridge University Press.
West, Elliott. 1996. *Growing Up in Twentieth-Century America: A History and Reference Guide.* Westport, CT: Greenwood Press.

Grandparents

The parents of one's mother or father, the grandparents, are significant figures in many a child's life. No discussion of the family today is complete without touching on grandparenthood. Increased longevity has resulted in families with many generations living overlapping lives. Although the onset of grandparenthood is a middle-age phenomenon, both early and delayed childbearing have contributed to a wide range of ages among grandparents and great-grandparents. The importance of grandparenthood is marked by the grandparents' mere presence, what they mean to the family, and their role performance.

Harriett McClintock at her home near Sumterville, Alabama, with her great-grandchildren, 1940. (Library of Congress)

Grandparents today demonstrate different ways of being grandparents depending on geographical distance, mobility, gender, age, and race, among other factors. To underscore the importance of grandparents to families, Congress passed legislation in 1978 that set the first Sunday after Labor Day as Grandparents Day (Cherlin and Furstenberg 1986). Additionally, the same legislative body designated 1995 as the Year of the Grandparent (Hartfield 1996).

One crucial intergenerational issue in this country during the last decade has been the increase in the number of grandchildren being raised by grandparents. The prevalence of intergenerational house-holds headed by grandparents is attributed to parents' issues such as substance abuse, acquired immunodeficiency syndrome (AIDS), incarceration of women, teen pregnancy, divorce, mental health problems, deaths, and legal mandates (Minkler 1999). Another issue of popular concern in recent years has been increased divorce and its impact on intergenerational relations. Divorce of adult children provides opportunities for grandparents to maintain and strengthen their relationship with their grandchildren if they are on the custodial side (Cherlin and Furstenberg 1986). For those who are on the noncustodial side, however, divorce creates dilemmas, especially if constraints on contacts and visitations are imposed on the grandparents.

The proportion of older Americans who are grandparents has been steadily high in the past twenty-some years. In the late 1970s, 94 percent of persons aged 65 and over who had children were grandparents; 46 percent were great-grandparents (Shanas 1980, 11). An estimate about a decade later revealed the same proportion of grandparents among older adults with children (Roberto 1990, 100). Szinovacz, using the 1992–1994 data of the National Survey of Families and Households, found that between one-third and two-fifths of all respondents (21–65-plus years) were grandparents (Szinovacz 1998, 42). When only those with children of childbearing age were considered, the proportion increased to two-thirds; among those with children aged 40 and over, almost 95 percent were grandparents, prompting Szinovacz to conclude that grandparenthood is "a near universal experience" (49). In fact, given the changes in mortality and fertility, it is estimated that three-fourths of adults will live to be grandparents (Pruchno and Johnson 1996, 65).

Becoming a grandparent for the first time tends to occur in middle age, at about 49–51 years for women and 51–53 for men (Troll 1983, 65). Teen pregnancies and childbearing in later years contribute to off-time grandparenthood, some becoming grandparents in their thirties and others in their sixties (Szinovacz 1998). As Pruchno and Johnson state, "Grandparenting is about generations, but not necessarily about old age" (1996, 65). In addition to gender and age, entrance into grandparenthood varies by race. Minorities, particularly blacks, experience the transition earlier than whites do. Given the life expectancy of 76 years (U.S. Bureau of the Census 2000a, 85) and the onset of grandparenthood in midlife, many adults can expect to spend several decades as grandparents. Also, because women tend to live longer than men, grandmothers are most likely to see at least their oldest grandchild become an adult and to be great-grandmothers (Szinovacz 1998).

Grandparenthood is "one of the oldest social roles in human experience" (Bengtson 1985, 11). For many years, grandparents have socialized younger generations. Through time, however, grandparenthood has taken on different images, meanings, and expectations. Historically, there were specific images associated with grandparents in the United States at different periods (Gratton and Haber 1996). During the eighteenth century, grandparents, particularly grandfathers, were authority figures, especially if children and grandchildren were dependent on them economically. Industrialization and technological change in the nineteenth century diminished the authority associated with experience and age. Older people became a burden and a threat to prosperity, harmony, and happiness in the family rather than a valued

resource. With the introduction of Social Security and private pension programs and, consequently, improved financial status during the mid-twentieth century, older adults became more autonomous, posing no threat to family well-being. Their independence allowed them to become companions and friends to their grandchildren. Although the image of the loving and autonomous grandparent exists only for some, according to Gratton and Haber (1996), that image still persists as the central one of American grandparenthood in the present.

Hagestad and Cogley's study of the changing images of grandparenthood as reflected in popular magazines showed different portrayals of grandparents at different periods (Hagestad 1985). Reference to grandparents in the magazines studied was specific to grandmothers. Those from the 1880s were depicted as old without mention of their ages. Their physical descriptions indicated that they had led a long and hard life and, as a reward, were honored and freed of responsibilities, becoming quiet and calm figures on the rocker by the fire; they were put on a pedestal. The 1970s images of grandmothers, on the other hand, provided no one particular theme. There was a wide range in their ages from the fifties to more than 100 years. Hagestad and Cogley found as many meanings of grandparenting as there were grandparents and grandchildren shown in the media. Similarly, in their classic study of U.S. grandparents, Neugarten and Weinstein (1964) identified diverse meanings associated with the grandparent role: (1) a source of biological renewal and/or biological continuity, (2) an opportunity to perform a new emotional role better than the grandparents had as parents, (3) a chance to be a teacher or a resource person, (4) an opportunity to accomplish what they themselves and their children had not achieved, and (5) limited significance of the role in the grandparents' lives because of psychological distance felt for their grandchildren.

In general, grandparents are important because of their presence and what they mean to the family, that is, their symbolic functions (Bengtson 1985), one of which is simply "being there." Specifically, they may serve as a "catalyst for wider family cohesion" by being the focal point for family get-togethers (Hagestad 1985, 46). Another symbolic role of grandparents is what Hagestad called "family national guard" (1985, 46–47) or "family watchdogs" (Troll 1983, 63), ready to protect and give care when needed. They represent a source of refuge, strength, and support in crisis situations, as in divorce cases. Still another attribute associated with grandparents is their arbitrator function (Bengtson 1985). Nowadays, continuity of family culture is no longer accomplished through one-way transmission from the old to the young; grandparents may serve as arbitrators, mediating between parents and children concerning values and behavior. Last, the symbolic function of grandparenthood involves the family's social construction of its history (Hagestad 1985). Grandparents, through their autobiography, play a significant role in making reasonable connections between the family's past and present to be able to face the future (Bengtson 1985). Symbolically, their presence is a testimony to the family's continuity, history, and identity. The importance of grandparents is further enhanced by the economic value tied to assistance they provide their families and grandchildren. Bass and Caro's analysis of the data from a representative sample of people fifty-five years of age and older showed that grandparents

were an integral part of the family structure and its informal economy. About one in three took care of their grandchildren at least one hour a week and nearly one in ten did the same for twenty or more hours per week. The 13.7 hours per week, on the average, put in by approximately 14.1 million grandparents to care for their grandchildren have been estimated to account for $17.4 to $29.1 billion per year in economic contribution to U.S. society (Bass and Caro 1996, 30–31).

The symbolisms or meanings attached to grandparenthood are independent of the performance of the grandparent role (Neugarten and Weinstein 1964). As it is, grandparenthood does not have any explicit or prescribed responsibilities to which grandparents are expected to adhere (Troll 1983). There is no clarity in terms of what the obligations and social and legal rights of grandparents are, hence the variability and flexibility in grandparenting styles (Giarrusso, Silverstein, and Bengtson 1996). In effect, grandparents define the content of their role and enact it in ways as they see fit or as their situation dictates. Based on the nature of grandparent-grandchild relationships, Neugarten and Weinstein proposed five grandparenting styles: (1) formal—the traditionally oriented grandparents follow what they regard as the expected roles for themselves and for their grandchildren; (2) funseeker—grandparents have an informal and playful relation with their grandchildren; (3) surrogate parents—grandparents, usually grandmothers, assume actual caretaking responsibilities of their grandchildren; (4) reservoir of wisdom—grandparents, usually grandfathers, are the dispensers of special skills and resources; and (5) distant figure—grandparents seldom interact with their grandchildren except on holidays or special occasions (1964,

202–203). Likewise, Cherlin and Furstenberg, in their attempt to classify grandparent-grandchild relations, described three styles of grandparenting that approximated three of the categories in Neugarten and Weinstein's study. In remote relationship (distant figure in Neugarten and Weinstein), grandparent and grandchildren maintain a "ritualistic, purely symbolic relationship" because they see each other only infrequently. Those in companionate relationships establish a pleasurable and friendly relationship with their grandchildren, similar to Neugarten and Weinstein's fun-seeker. They assume limited responsibility for their grandchildren and leave the task of parenting to the parents. Involved relationship is characterized by an active role in rearing grandchildren, frequently behaving more like parents than grandparents; this is akin to grandparents' role as surrogate parents in Neugarten and Weinstein's study (Cherlin and Furstenberg 1986, 52). It is evident in both studies that none of the grandparenting styles are dominant or universal.

Why are some grandparents more involved with their grandchildren than others? What contributes to frequent visits of some with their grandchildren but not of others? What attributes help determine the nature of relationships between grandparents and grandchildren? What factors shape the meaning and the role of grandparenthood? In other words, why the different grandparenting styles? One simple and obvious answer to at least two of the questions is how close geographically the two generations are to each other. Interaction, mutual help, visits, and close bonds among individuals and between generations are facilitated by proximity. Cherlin and Furstenberg (1986), for example, demonstrated an overwhelming effect of distance on frequency of visits. The statistical analysis of their study revealed the following:

> A grandparent whose grandchild lived more than one hundred miles away could expect only about three visits with the child per year. If the grandparents lived eleven to one hundred miles away, the expected number of visits rose to thirteen or about one per month. If the distance was one to ten miles, the expected visit was forty, or about one visit every week or two. And if the grandparent lived within one mile, the expected number was 102 or about two per week. (Cherlin and Furstenberg 1986, 109)

Despite the predominance of the effect of distance, Cherlin and Furstenberg added that quality of relationship and familism made a difference in frequency of intergenerational contact. It mattered that the grandparents get along with the mother of the grandchildren, who is the family gatekeeper. Also, those with more family rituals, "special family recipes or dishes," "family jokes, common expressions, or songs" visited their grandchildren more often than those who had little or none (1986, 114).

Associated with distance as a factor in intergenerational relationships is geographic mobility. Understandably, when adult children move away for one reason or another, the amount of contact with grandchildren by grandparents drops. It is essentially the same if the grandparents are the ones who leave. Silverstein and Zablotsky, for example, found that the movement of older people to retirement communities reduced contact between older people and their adult children and, consequently, their grandchildren (Giarrusso, Silverstein, and Bengtson 1996). In a mobile society, there are ways by which the constraints imposed by distance can be overcome. Long-distance grandparenting can be carried out through letters, e-mails, fax, and videotapes. Probably the means of communication that is most similar to face-to-face interaction would be the telephone. Telephone conversations have been found to be more infrequent with grandchildren who lived farthest away and more frequent among those who visited more often (Cherlin and Furstenberg 1986). This observation suggests that telephone calls among those who visit each other often serve to reinforce the regular interaction rather than renew distant relationships.

Gender of grandparent is another factor in grandparenting styles. To some degree, the distinction in men's and women's perception and performance of their grandparent role goes along with the traditional gender role division (Cherlin and Furstenberg 1986; Hagestad 1985). That is, men are into the task-oriented family roles, whereas women specialize in emotional-expressive roles. In Neugarten and Weinstein's study (1964), grandmothers, in general, tended to be more emotionally involved than grandfathers; they also assumed caretaking responsibility more than grandfathers when asked by young mothers. Hagestad (1985), in a study of three generations in 148 families, also revealed differences in men's and women's interactions with their grandchildren along the traditional roles. In addition to practical aspects of adult life (for example, jobs, education), grandmothers talked with their grandchildren about relations with friends and family. Grandfathers, distinguishing clearly between men talk and women talk, gave advice on education, jobs, money matters, and life responsibilities and challenges, but not on inter-

personal issues. The sex of the grandchild mattered more for them than for grandmothers, concentrating most of their influence on grandsons. For both grandparents, however, the most involvement was with the same-sex grandchild, that is, grandmothers with granddaughters and grandfathers with grandsons. Likewise, Cherlin and Furstenberg (1986) observed that grandfathers distinguished more between grandsons and granddaughters than grandmothers did. Exchange of help with chores, errands, or activities was highest among grandfather-grandson dyads. Grandfathers had an instrumental relationship with their grandchildren, whereas the grandmothers had an expressive one. Given that gender roles still exist among younger couples today, the authors posit that the differences between men's and women's grandparenting ways are here to stay for a while.

Other studies on gender as a factor in grandparenthood touched on the traditional roles only peripherally. Thomas's (1989) study of 115 grandfathers and 186 grandmothers examined their perceptions of grandparent-grandchild relationship, including its meaning, responsibility toward the child, and satisfaction with the relationship. Grandmothers expressed greater satisfaction in grandparenting than grandfathers did. Grandfathers emphasized immortality of the clan through grandchildren and took pleasure in indulging the grandchildren. In more recent research of 152 prospective grandparents aged forty to seventy-three years, Somary and Stricker (1998) revealed differences between men's and women's expectations and experiences of grandparenthood. Women were more likely than men to expect great satisfaction from grandparenting and to expect the new baby to play a central role in their lives. Expectant maternal grandmothers were most excited about the expectation of indulging the new child. Men anticipated that they would feel more comfortable about speaking their minds to the child's parents and being involved in advising and caretaking. The follow-up study of 103 of the original 152 grandparents supported Thomas's 1989 finding; the grandmothers were more satisfied with their role than grandfathers, even though both spent the same amount of time with their grandchild. In consonance with their expectation, grandfathers offered advice more openly to the new parents than the grandmothers did. Although grandmothers did not anticipate getting involved much in caretaking, they found themselves doing as much as the grandfathers did (Somary and Stricker 1998).

The warm and stronger relationship that grandmothers have with their grandchildren may stem from their expressive role in the family. They may have considered grandparenthood as an extension of the traditional women's role. The visibility of mothers and grandmothers in kinship ties, particularly maternal grandmothers, is what Hagestad termed "the matrifocal tilt" (1985, 40). Women, in general, are considered the kinkeepers who facilitate and carry out the contact and exchanges between generations. In other words, they control the family's social relationship. It is no wonder that the closest grandparent-grandchild relationship is the one between maternal grandmothers and granddaughters that is promoted by the mother. In a study of 132 college freshmen and sophomores about their relationship with their grandparents, the maternal grandmother was consistently mentioned as the grandparent they were closest to (Roberto 1990).

According to Somary and Stricker (1998), the geographical proximity of maternal grandparents to their grandchildren may also contribute to their positive relationship with one another. Moreover, the maternal grandmother being younger than other grandparents may be partly responsible for the closeness between the two generations.

Chronological ages of the grandparent and of the grandchild have been proven to be significant factors in grandparenting. Neugarten and Weinstein (1964) found that younger grandparents were either fun-seekers or, possibly because of work responsibilities, distant figures. The older grandparents, on the other hand, had formal relationships with their grandchildren. Johnson's study of fifty-eight grandmothers revealed that older grandmothers had significantly less contact with their grandchildren than younger grandmothers (Roberto 1990). Similar to Neugarten and Weinstein's finding, younger grandmothers were into fun-loving activities. Roberto (1990) opined that being older and in poor health may also influence the nature and frequency of contact between the skipped generations. Cherlin and Furstenberg (1986) noted that grandparenthood has distinct stages that parallel the development of grandchildren. As both grandparents and grandchild age, grandparenting style may change. Preadolescence, especially the preschool years, was the period enjoyed the most by the grandparents in Cherlin and Furstenberg's study. During adolescence, even though the two generations shared activities, those activities were no longer the fun-seeking and game-playing activities of early days. The teenagers were more independent and provided help to their grandparents, whose assistance they did not need often.

Grandma and grandchildren play a lively game together. (Elizabeth Crews)

In adulthood, once the grandchildren were married, grandparents seldom saw them, except on holidays and special occasions. According to Cherlin and Furstenberg, the career of grandparenting then ends, from then on having just a symbolic meaning.

Grandparents are now living long enough to have long-term relationships with adult grandchildren. Although according to Lawton, Silverstein, and Bengtson, 56 percent of those 65 years old and over have at least one adult grandchild (Giarrusso, Silverstein, and Bengtson 1996, 18), researchers lament the dearth of literature on grandparent and adult grandchild relationship. One of the few studies on the topic was conducted by Mills (1999)

using the University of Southern California Longitudinal Study of Generations with 2,044 respondents aged 16–91. She investigated how taking or giving up the adult roles of worker, spouse, or parent changed the relationship between grandparents and adult grandchildren. The findings revealed that grandchildren's adult role transitions, in general, enhanced their feelings of closeness with grandfathers more than with grandmothers. Also, granddaughters were found to have increased consensus with grandfathers. Mills speculated that status attainment of the grandchildren similar to that attained by grandparents, particularly grandfathers, may have linked the two generations socially. Contrary to Cherlin and Furstenberg's (1986) finding of decreased association between married grandchildren and grandparents, the grandchild's first marriage in Mills's study increased his or her association with grandparents, especially grandmothers. It is possible that the grandparents provided help and support to the grandchild during the role transition, hence the boost in association between the two generations (Mills 1999).

Another factor oftentimes associated with the grandparent role is race or ethnicity. Black women, as well as Hispanic women, tend to become grandparents earlier than white women do (Szinovacz 1998). Consequently, more than half of black women and only one-third of white women under age fifty-five are grandmothers. Also, black women's earlier entrance to parenthood increases the proportion of four-generation families. In terms of living arrangement, 26 percent of black and 23 percent of Hispanic grandmothers were found to be in households with grandchildren, compared to 7 percent of white grandmothers and 4 percent of white grandfathers (Szinovacz 1998, 42–43). Among those in extended households, black grandparents lived either with a single parent, usually a daughter, and her children or with relatives; white grandparents resided with married children and their children. Limited research has been done on the salience of grandparenthood among minorities, but one study showed that grandparenting is a more significant role for black men than for males of other ethnic groups. As Kivett found in another study, black grandfathers in the rural areas considered grandparenthood important more than rural white grandfathers did (Pruchno and Johnson 1996). In terms of role enactment, black grandmothers were found to be more than twice as likely as white grandmothers to be surrogate parents to their grandchildren during their lifetime (Szinovacz 1998, 48).

Grandparent caregiving, specifically surrogate parenting, has received national attention in recent years owing to the sheer increase in the number of children under their grandparents' care. In 1980, 2.3 million children (3.6 percent) under 18 years of age lived in the home of their grandparents. In 1998, the number was almost 4 million (5.5 percent); a little over one third (1.4 million) of these were in homes where neither parent was present (U.S. Bureau of the Census 2000b, 60). Among these grandchildren, both parents were present for 12.6 percent, only the mother was present for 46 percent, and only the father was present for 6 percent (U.S. Bureau of the Census 2000b, 60). In some low-income urban areas, between 30 and 50 percent of children were cared for by their grandparents or other relatives who were not their parents (Minkler and Roe 1996, 34). Using the 1992–1994 data from the National Survey of Families and Households, Fuller-Thomson, Minkler, and Driver (1997) developed a national profile of grandparent caregivers. More than 10 percent of the grandparents in the survey reported having cared for a grandchild for at least six months. More than half had raised their grandchildren for at least three years, and 20 percent had done so for a decade or more, indicating that the role was a long-term commitment for them (407). The study showed that most caregivers were married (54 percent), women (77 percent), and non-Hispanic whites (62 percent); however, single women, African Americans, and low-income individuals were disproportionately represented in the group (407–408).

Another study about grandparent caregivers revealed three categories of caregiver roles: (1) custodial, whereby grand-parents have legal custody of the child; (2) living with a grandchild without a legal relationship with that child; and (3) day-care roles, with grandparents providing regular day care for extended periods (Jendrek 1993). The majority of participants who were predominantly white and female were related to the child through the mother, supporting Hagestad's (1985) concept of "matrifocal tilt." Jendrek found that grandparents tried to provide a stable environment to their grandchildren whatever the issues of the parents were. In general, caregiving of grandchildren changed the grandparents' lifestyle. Custodial grandparents, for example, had to alter their routines and plans and were physically tired and emotionally drained, but they also found an increased purpose for living. The living-in grandparents were in a similar situation to that of the custodial grandparents; the absence of legal custody of their grandchild was also a great concern for them. The day-care grandparents were the least affected by their role because their responsibility ended when the child went home. Both custodial and living-in grandparents reported that their contact with friends declined as a result of taking care of their grandchild. The cost of care-giving to grandchildren seemed to outweigh its benefit according to the results of the Jendrek study and as shown in Minkler and Roe's (1996) summary of problems and challenges faced by grand-parent caregivers. Included in their list were (1) health problems, (2) economic difficulties, (3) lack of government support, (4) social isolation, and (5) problems in raising a special-needs child. According to the researchers, interventions and service programs such as support groups, comprehensive programs, and coalitions

have been organized increasingly in a few regions in the country to assist grandparent caregivers. As to the fate of grandchildren in grandparent-maintained households, Casper and Bryson (2001) found that those under the care of grandmother only fared the worst; they were the most likely to be in poverty and to have received public assistance. Those grandchildren who lived with both grandparents only were the most likely to be uninsured.

According to Minkler (1999), there are several causes of the increase in households headed by grandparents. One is the federal law that requires placement of children with relatives for foster care. Second, the increase in substance abuse, which consequently leads to child abuse and neglect, has contributed to the increase in the number of caregiving grandparents. Third, the loss of their mothers to AIDS has left an increasing number of children in the care of their grandparents. Fourth, the increase in the number of women who are imprisoned is a factor in the prevalence of grandparent-headed household. Last, divorce, teen pregnancy, and increases in single-parent households are other causes of the increased number of grandparents providing care to grandchildren.

The issue of divorce is not only linked to surrogate parenting; its implications are also salient to the nature and quality of intergenerational relationship and the grandparents' performance of their role. Also, if either parent remarries, the grandparents may find themselves as step-grandparents, a new role replete with ambiguity (Hagestad 1985). Divorce has different effects on the grandparents, depending on whose side they are on. As mentioned earlier, those who are on the custodial side (usually maternal grandparents) may gain more from divorce than those on the noncustodial side (usually paternal grandparents). Today, to protect the grandparents' right to stay connected with their grandchildren after divorce, all states in the country have grandparents' rights legislation that gives the grandparents legal power to seek visitation (Hartfield 1996). As Hartfield stated, "Legislators throughout the nation have concluded that grandparents provide a unique kind of nurturance and continuity needed by their grandchildren in the midst of family crisis and upheaval" (53). The state laws vary considerably, however, with twenty states having restrictive visitation laws and others having more permissive ones (Hanks 2001). Both kinds of laws have been challenged in court. On 5 June 2000, in the case of *Troxel* v. *Granville*, the U.S. Supreme Court invalidated Washington State's grandparents' rights law because of its broad intrusion on parental rights (Hanks 2001). What the consequences of this decision will be to states with statutes similar to Washington's remains to be seen.

The controversy about how much involvement grandparents should have with their grandchildren and the variability in the grandparent visitation statutes are a testimony to the absence of clearcut roles for grandparents. Given the current demographic trends and the increasing complexity of American families, grandparenthood will continue to face the challenges brought about by those changes. Flexibility and adaptability will persist as features of being grandparents in the United States.

—*Vangie Novero Blust*

See also Extended Family

References and Further Reading

Bass, Scott A., and Francis G. Caro. 1996. "The Economic Value of Grandparent Assistance." *Generations* 20(1): 29–33.

Bengtson, Vern L. 1985. "Diversity and Symbolism in Grandparental Roles." In *Grandparenthood*, edited by Vern L. Bengtson and Joan F. Robertson, 11–29. Beverly Hills, CA: Sage Publications.

Casper, Lynne M., and Kenneth R. Bryson. "Co-resident Grandparents and Their Grandchildren: Grandparent Maintained Families." http://www.census.gov/population/www/documentation/twps0026/twps0026.html (23 April 2001).

Cherlin, Andrew J., and Frank F. Furstenberg, Jr. 1986. *The New American Grandparent*. New York: Basic Books.

Fuller-Thomson, Esme, Meredith Minkler, and Diane Driver. 1997. "A Profile of Grandparents Raising Grandchildren in the United States." *The Gerontologist* 37(3): 406–411.

Giarrusso, Roseann, Merril Silverstein, and Vern L. Bengtson. 1996. "Family Complexity and the Grandparent Role." *Generations* 20(1): 17–23.

Gratton, Brian, and Carole Haber. 1996. "Three Phases in the History of American Grandparents: Authority, Burden, Companion." *Generations* 20(1): 7–12.

Hagestad, Gunhild O. 1985. "Continuity and Connectedness." In *Grandparenthood*, edited by Vern L. Bengtson and Joan F. Robertson, 31–48. Beverly Hills, CA: Sage Publications.

Hanks, Liza Weiman. "Grandparent Visitation Rights." http://www.nolo.com/encyclopedia/articles/div/grandparents.html (11 June 2001).

Hartfield, Bernadette W. 1996. "Legal Recognition of the Value of Intergenerational Nurturance: Grandparent Visitation Statutes in the Nineties." *Generations* 20(1): 53–56.

Jendrek, Margaret Platt. 1993. "Grandparents Who Parent Their Grandchildren: Effects on Lifestyle." *Journal of Marriage and the Family* 55(3): 609–621.

Mills, Terry L. 1999. "When Grandchildren Grow Up: Role Transition and Family Solidarity among Baby Boomer Grandchildren and Their Grandparents." *Journal of Aging Studies* 13(2): 219–239.

Minkler, Meredith. 1999. "Intergenerational Households Headed by Grandparents: Contexts, Realities, and Implications for Policy." *Journal of Aging Studies* 13(2): 199–218.

Minkler, Meredith, and Kathleen M. Roe. 1996. "Grandparents as Surrogate Parents." *Generations* 20(1): 34–38.

Neugarten, Beatrice L., and Karen K. Weinstein. 1964. "The Changing American Grandparent." *Journal of Marriage and the Family* 26(2): 199–204.

Pruchno, Rachel A., and Katrina W. Johnson. 1996. "Research on Grandparenting: Review of Current Studies and Future Needs." *Generations* 20(1): 65–70.

Roberto, Karen A. 1990. "Grandparent and Grandchild Relationships." In *Family Relationships in Later Life*, edited by Timothy H. Brubaker, 100–112. Newbury Park, CA: Sage Publications.

Shanas, Ethel. 1980. "Older People and Their Families: The New Pioneers." *Journal of Marriage and the Family* 42(1): 9–15.

Somary, Karen, and George Stricker. 1998. "Becoming a Grandparent: A Longitudinal Study of Expectations and Early Experiences as a Function of Sex and Lineage." *The Gerontologist* 38(1): 53–61.

Szinovacz, Maximiliane E. 1998. "Grandparents Today: A Demographic Profile." *The Gerontologist* 38(1): 37–52.

Thomas, Jeannie L. 1989. "Gender and Perceptions of Grandparenthood." *International Journal of Aging and Human Development* 29(4): 269–282.

Troll, Lilian E. 1983. "Grandparents: The Family Watchdogs." In *Family Relationships in Later Life*, edited by Timothy H. Brubaker, 63–74. Beverly Hills, CA: Sage Publications.

U.S. Bureau of the Census. 2000a. "Expectations of Life and Expected Deaths by Race, Sex, and Age: 1997." *Statistical Abstract of the United States.* Washington, DC: Government Printing Office.

U.S. Bureau of the Census. 2000b. "Grandchildren Living in the Home of Their Grandparents: 1980–1998." *Statistical Abstract of the United States.* Washington, DC: Government Printing Office.

The Great Society

In mid-1964, Pres. Lyndon Baines Johnson articulated his vision for a Great Society. Such a society, he said,

> rests on abundance and liberty for all. It demands an end to poverty and racial injustice. . . . But that is just the beginning. The Great Society is a place where every child can find knowledge to enrich his mind and to enlarge his talents. . . . It is a place where the city of man serves not only the needs of the body and the demands of commerce but the desire for beauty and the hunger for community. . . . But most of all, the Great Society is not a safe harbor, a resting place, a final objective, a finished work. It is a challenge constantly renewed, beckoning us toward a destiny where the meaning of our lives matches the marvelous products of our labor. (Johnson 1965, 112–114)

After winning reelection that November, Johnson pressed for the most advanced program for social reform in the history of the republic. The 89th Congress, which was controlled by the Democrats, responded with an extraordinary array of legislation to advance civil and voting rights, reduce illiteracy, sharpen skills of inner-city youth and find jobs for them, fund preschool to college education for needy students, improve depressed conditions in urban ghettos and rural areas, provide rent supplements to the poor, increase the minimum wage, furnish federal health insurance for the poor and elderly, establish federal funding for the arts and humanities, improve safety in mines and on highways, eliminate discriminatory national quotas for immigrants, establish consumer credit guidelines, set standards for clean air and water, provide capital for minority businesses, and set up community action groups and other programs to fight an "unconditional war on poverty." Some of these programs were successful; others left a legacy of disappointment and controversy. But they changed forever the role of the federal government in promoting health, economic welfare, education, the environment, and civil rights.

Johnson's victory in 1964 was the greatest political landslide since the previous century. He carried forty-four states and 60.7 percent of the popular vote. In addition, the Democratic Party added thirty-seven House seats and two more seats in the Senate, giving the Democrats control of more than two-thirds of both houses. Though an important minority of those Democrats were southern conservatives, in most cases President Johnson had enough votes to usher in a brief era of liberal politics during which almost all of his Great Society legislation was written into law.

Although the Great Society eventually encompassed a broad array of initiatives to improve the quality of life in the United States, the centerpiece was the fight for racial justice and equality. Johnson's expansive vision derived from several factors. First and most important was his personal commitment to civil rights and racial justice. Second was Johnson's populist tendencies, arising from his humble origins. Third was the rediscovery of poverty in the midst of a robust economy. As a congressman, Johnson battled to ensure that federal agriculture programs treated blacks and whites equally and fought for equity in public housing in his home state of Texas. And

Johnson had more to do with the enactment of civil rights laws in the 1957–1968 period than any other man. When the first civil rights law since Reconstruction was passed in 1957, Johnson pressed it as majority leader of the Senate. The 1957 Civil Rights Act guaranteed free access to voting in federal elections and authorized the attorney general to bring suit against noncompliance. Johnson's skill at shepherding the Civil Rights Act of 1960, which strengthened the provisions of 1957, through a senate filibuster—during which South Carolina senator Strom Thurmond's harangue lasted twenty-four hours and eighteen minutes—enhanced Johnson's reputation and contributed to his nomination as John F. Kennedy's vice president in 1960. Within five days of assuming the presidency, after the Kennedy assassination, Johnson took charge of the campaign to enact the 1964 Civil Rights Act as a memorial to the slain president.

Johnson was a genius at persuading, coaxing, and twisting arms, and he used every weapon in his arsenal to push this legislation through a very reluctant Congress. As finally passed on 2 July 1964, the Civil Rights Act had three main parts: (1) It barred discrimination on the basis of race in any and all public accommodations in the United States. (2) The act authorized the Justice Department to bring suit against any and all states that discriminated. (3) It provided for equal opportunities in the workplace. It was now unlawful for a firm of more than twenty-five employees to discriminate on the basis of "race, national origin, religion, or sex." This last provision, Title VII of the Civil Rights Act, remains today as the only equal opportunity law that pertains to women.

President Lyndon B. Johnson and Mrs. Johnson wave from the back of "The Great Society Special," 1965. (Library of Congress)

The Civil Rights Act of 1964 was a huge step forward, but it did not resolve the problem of voting rights. After violence met a peaceful march from Selma, Alabama (where only 335 of 15,000 eligible black voters had been able to register), to the capital at Montgomery, Congress passed the Voting Rights Act in 1965, finally erasing all barriers to voting (including grandfather clauses, poll taxes, and literacy tests). The new law sent thousands of new registrars to the South and within a decade added 2 million African Americans to the voting rolls, leading to a dramatic increase in African American officeholders. Then, in 1968, after three tries, and after the assassination of the Rev. Martin Luther King Jr. and the riots that followed, Johnson succeeded in obtaining a federal law banning racial discrimination in the sale and rental of housing, removing the last legal obstacle to black citizens who dreamed of moving into a better neighborhood.

Though he sometimes exaggerated his own humble beginnings, Johnson was a populist who understood and empathized with the poor. As a young teacher in Cotilla, Texas, he had fought to get hot lunches and sports equipment for his poor Mexican American students. His work as director of the National Youth Administration in Texas during the New Deal convinced him that much good could be accomplished by governmental programs to aid the poor and desperate. Franklin Roosevelt was his hero and, in Johnson's willingness to try a plethora of solutions to the intractable problem of poverty, his model.

In the midst of the robust economy of the 1950s and early 1960s, the United States was rediscovering poverty. Books by economist John Kenneth Galbraith (*The Affluent Society* [1958]) and socialist Michael Harrington (*The Other America* [1962]) called national attention to pervasive poverty amid growing affluence. According to Harrington's estimates, in 1960 fully one-quarter of the nation's population was poor—some 40 to 50 million people. Though three-fourths of the poor were white, twice as many blacks as whites, relative to population, were poor. Harrington found the poor in inner cities, in rural backwaters, in migrant camps and on reservations, in Appalachia and the South. But the problem, he argued, was not simply isolated pockets of poverty but long-term, structural destitution—a vast subculture of poverty—that, he said, was the result of hopelessness as much as of economic deprivation.

Prodded by Harrington's work and enlarging on his previous measures for relief to depressed areas and retraining for the chronically unemployed, Pres. John Kennedy had begun to move toward making poverty a major theme in his 1964 reelection campaign. At a meeting on 19 November 1963, just before the trip to Dallas during which he was assassinated, Kennedy authorized his economic adviser, Walter Heller, to draw up a detailed set of legislative proposals to fight poverty. Government officials soon developed a "poverty line," based upon estimates of food costs multiplied by three, to reach a minimum level of income below which people were officially designated to be poor. In 1964, this line was about $1,550 for a single individual and $3,169 for a family of four. By that standard, 40.3 million Americans were poor (U.S. Bureau of the Census 2000).

The day after Kennedy's assassination, President Johnson met with Heller and enthusiastically endorsed this initiative. This would be the program, Johnson believed, that would make his historical legacy and one that would give him the opportunity to take the New Deal social agenda to its logical conclusion. Furthermore, civil rights activists were increasingly focusing on economic issues. With more than 40 percent of African American families earning less than half the median income, a program to fight poverty clearly would have major implications for black America. Nonetheless, though an antipoverty initiative could provide a way to address the racial unrest stirring in the inner cities, Johnson realized that support for aid to urban minorities would be limited. So he conceived a much broader appeal, couched in martial rhetoric, to eliminate poverty itself. He asked Congress to declare an "unconditional war on poverty.... We shall not rest until that war is won. It will not be a short or easy struggle [but] the richest Nation on earth can afford to win it. We cannot afford to lose it" (Johnson 1965, 705).

Poverty was a blot on American life. It was also important that in the midst of the cold war, poverty weakened the United States in its global struggle with communism. How could the United States claim a superior system when nearly one-fourth of its population went hungry? Lyndon Johnson took office at a time of abundance that made the plight of those left out seem especially unacceptable and when a soaring economy made spending for new federal programs relatively painless.

The War on Poverty moved in many directions at once, much like the early days of the New Deal, spurred by the optimism and zeal of the president. Johnson's omnibus antipoverty bill, the Economic Opportunity Act of 1964, was built on the twin strategies of equal opportunity and community action. The act authorized a combination of programs encompassing different approaches and intended for different low-income groups and established the Office of Economic Opportunity (OEO) to administer the programs. Title I established three programs for impoverished youths: (1) The Job Corps, intended for school dropouts, moved them into job centers away from home, either as members of a Youth Conservation Corps in camps on federal lands or in training centers in urban areas. The camps and centers provided basic education courses and specific job skills training. (2) In the Work-Training Program youths did work beneficial to their communities while continuing their schooling. (3) The Work-Study Program was aimed at college students. It aided colleges in paying students from low-income families for part-time work either on or off campus. Title II authorized funds for

grants to state and local programs. Among them were a host of community action programs (CAPs), for which the federal government would provide funds and technical assistance for locally designed and operated programs with a variety of purposes. Title II also included grants for local programs to teach persons over eighteen to read and write and authorized an office to help volunteers locate and give financial assistance to needy children. Title III was designed to raise the income and living standards of poor rural and migrant families with loans to individuals as well as to local processing and marketing cooperatives. Title IV established guidelines and funds for small businesses, especially those that hired the long-term unemployed. Title V provided for work experience programs to employ and train heads of families receiving help under the Aid to Families with Dependent Children (AFDC), but this was later phased out because of a similar program in the 1967 welfare amendments. Title VII set up the Volunteers in Service to America (VISTA) program. Modeled on the Peace Corps, VISTA recruited and trained volunteers to fight poverty on the local level. Volunteers worked in rural and urban poverty areas, Indian reservations, migrant camps, hospitals, and similar areas.

War on Poverty legislation passed through Congress with relatively little amending, except for a measure designed to win southern support, which permitted governors to veto proposed Job Corps, community action, work-training, and VISTA programs. Job Corps was one of the most unpopular programs, at least at first. It was plagued with riots among enrollees in the camps, friction between Job Corps members and local townspeople, and exorbitant rates charged by private contractors who ran Job Corps offices. But by far the most controversial antipoverty experiments were the local CAPs, which were to be "developed, conducted and administered with the maximum feasible participation of residents in the areas and members of the groups served." This insistence that the poor themselves be involved in solving their own problems was a radically new concept that almost immediately ran into trouble. In many cities, CAPs encouraged poor people to demand public services long withheld by unresponsive local governments, provoking destructive and futile conflict. For example, community organizers in Syracuse, New York, formed tenants' rights groups to protest conditions in public housing, led voter registration drives to unseat elected representatives, and even used public funds to bail out activists arrested for protesting at local welfare offices. Legal services attorneys, whose fees were paid by the federal government, challenged welfare and housing administrations in class-action suits. Such actions upset entrenched urban political machines, including many run by Democrats. Responding to pressure from its own party, the Johnson administration gradually phased out the CAPs.

Among the first nationwide antipoverty programs were some of its most successful. In 1965, the OEO set up Head Start to counter the learning disabilities of economically disadvantaged preschool children—a direct attempt to interrupt the culture of poverty Harrington talked about—and the Upward Bound program to help gifted students from poor families go to college. Also popular were the legal services program to provide the poor with free legal aid and the food stamps program to help feed the hungry.

The following year, the Johnson administration proposed another bundle of social legislation to fight poverty. The Elementary and Secondary Education Act and the Higher Education Act of 1965 overcame conservative suspicions of increased federal involvement in education and southern fears that a national program would become an instrument of school desegregation to become the first general federal aid to education law in U.S. history, completing the educational priorities for poor children from preschool to college scholarships.

That same year, the 89th Congress passed federal health insurance legislation that had been languishing since the Truman administration. When Johnson took office, a majority of older Americans were without health insurance, and one-fifth of the poor had never visited a doctor. Believing health care was essential to a great society, Johnson faced formidable opposition from private insurers and the American Medical Association (which had successfully stalled health legislation for twenty years by calling it "socialized medicine"). After months of intense lobbying, Congress passed the Social Security Amendments of 1965, which included Medicare and Medicaid. Medicare extended federal assistance to the elderly for hospital expenses and provided for a voluntary low-cost medical insurance to cover 80 percent of doctor's fees; Medicaid provided grants to states so that welfare recipients could receive proper medical and hospital services. In theory, Medicaid recipients could choose their doctors and hospitals, no longer having to depend on charity. In practice, many hospitals and doctors refused to treat Medicaid patients and what care they received was often substandard. Because Congress did not impose a cap on medical expenses, which the medical industry opposed, costs quickly escalated. Nonetheless, the programs were a landmark in the history of social reform in the United States; they reached 40 million Americans by 1970 (Health Care Financing Administration 2001).

The War on Poverty translated social vision into concrete legislative proposals and set in motion a remarkable expansion of federal power in service to equality and fairness. With so ambitious a program, it is little wonder that mistakes were made and some programs failed. Several factors mitigated against success in the antipoverty war. First of all, despite overblown rhetoric that raised unrealistic expectations, the War on Poverty was misnamed and oversold. It was never given a fraction of the funds it needed. Congress appropriated, at most, $800 million in new money in 1964. With at least 35 million people officially defined as poor, this came to a little more than $200 per poor person per year. Though programs doubled the proportion of the nation's total income going to pay for social welfare to its people, it was never more than 2 percent of the federal budget, and the bulk of the funding went for entitlement programs (Social Security, Medicare, unemployment compensation) available to the middle class as well as to the poor. Much of the rest covered salaries and expenses of administrators, professionals, and government contractors. In the end, the programs did little for the central cities and even less for depressed rural areas (Dallek 1998).

Second, the War on Poverty suffered from a rudimentary vision of the causes and cures of poverty. The assumption that the cycle of poverty could break in one generation with a smattering of educational opportunities and job training

was naive. Unable or unwilling to challenge the basic socioeconomic structure of the United States, the framers believed that a booming economy offered unlimited opportunities, so that the way to help the poor was to teach them to take advantage of the opportunities open to them, not to give them subsidies. They did not acknowledge structural economic causes for poverty and never contemplated federal guarantees of a minimum income or income transfers along the lines pioneered by welfare states such as Sweden. There was, in short, no support for demanding equality of condition, a stance counter to the American ideal of competitive idealism. The emphasis was on individual initiative and opportunity. Despite later criticisms to the contrary, the aim of the War on Poverty was not increasing public assistance. Johnson hated the idea of long-term welfare dependency. The agenda was helping the poor become self-sufficient through education, skills training, employment opportunities, and an aura of hope. In the phrase of the day, they favored "a hand up, not a hand out" (Patterson 1996, 535). Optimistic liberals assumed that eventually welfare would become unnecessary.

The War on Poverty also foundered over the impossible task of satisfying competing constituencies. From the beginning, legislative compromises limited the effectiveness of many programs. In many cases, Johnson had little choice but to acquiesce to powerful interest groups at the expense of the powerless poor. Denounced by radicals for its failure to redistribute wealth, deserted by middle-class Americans who thought the government was paying too much attention to the underprivileged, attacked by the urban poor clamoring for increased political power, the War on Poverty was also quickly deserted by white southerners and northern political bosses who wanted to maintain the status quo. As high hopes faded, and poverty became increasingly associated with the violence of black protests in the cities, a conservative backlash set in, returning to the old view that the poor themselves were responsible for their plight and blaming the War on Poverty for encouraging welfare dependency. The gap between the expansive intentions of the War on Poverty and its relatively modest achievements fueled later conservative arguments that government is not an appropriate vehicle for solving social problems. In the 1980s, Pres. Ronald Reagan cynically joked, "We fought a war on poverty, and poverty won" (Katz 1989, 79).

Nevertheless, despite its short life and limited support, some of the War on Poverty's successes are measurable. Standards of medical care improved dramatically; educational opportunities reached impoverished rural and urban children; job training provided a means to break out of the cycle of poverty. Food stamps, though begun as an effort to stabilize farm prices, have become a major assistance program. Head Start children gained substantial advantages. Long-term studies indicated that Head Start students were less likely to drop out of secondary school, worked more steadily, and participated in less criminal behavior (Unger 1996; Patterson 1996). The Job Corps employed 100,000 young men and women in poor families and, eight years later, was expanded with the Comprehensive Employment and Training Act (CETA). Local studies found that 94 percent of CETA graduates had jobs five years after they participated. Statistics indicate that the proportion of Americans living below the poverty line

dropped from 25 percent in 1963 to 11 percent in 1970. Between 1960 and 1971, income for white families increased by 69 percent; black families' income increased by 109 percent. On average, black Americans still earned only 61 percent of what white families did, but it represented a substantial increase over the 48 percent of just ten years before. Black poverty was cut in half during the 1960s, and statistics reveal that as many as half of all black families had risen to the ranks of the middle class by the 1970s (U.S. Bureau of the Census 2000; Unger 1996).

Still, many argue that the reduction in the poverty rate was due more to a booming economy fueled by the growing war in Vietnam. Ironically, it was the Vietnam War that spelled the demise of Johnson's vision for a Great Society. The escalation of the war unleashed unexpected and uncontrollable inflation and siphoned spending away from domestic programs. By 1966, the government was spending $22 billion on the Vietnam War while only slightly more than $1 billion was expended on the domestic war.

Almost 12 percent of Americans remained in poverty at the turn of the century. In 2000, the line was $8,350 for an individual and $17,050 for a family of four. There are currently 32.3 million Americans or 11.8 percent of the population living below the poverty line, with a disproportionate share of blacks (23.6 percent) versus whites (7.7 percent). The highest rates of poverty are found among families headed by females with children under eighteen. Approximately one out of every two such families is in poverty. The situation is even more critical if that mother is African American; the percentage increases to 56 percent (U.S. Bureau of the Census 2000). Extremely high rates of poverty, then, are sex related and race related, with children as the major victims.

Although it is often confused with the Great Society, the War on Poverty was just one part of a much more ambitious vision. Great Society legislation was also replete with appeals to Johnson's middle-class constituency. Most of these escaped the controversy surrounding programs for the poor and remain in place, some in modified form, today. Consumer protection measures included the Consumer Credit Protection Act (also called the Truth-in-Lending Act) that requires lenders and creditors to provide customers with full, honest, and comparative information on credit matters. The Highway Safety Act and Traffic Safety Act allocated federal funds for local safety programs and mandated safety standards, including seatbelts and padded dashboards, for automobile manufacturers. Federal action also included broadened controls over the labeling and packing of food, drugs, cosmetics, and household supplies.

The National Wilderness Protection Act, which increased authority and funding for conservation and environmental protection, was just one part of a comprehensive package of environmental legislation that also included the Water Quality Act, the Clean Air Act, the Solid Waste Disposal Act, the Clean Water Restoration Act, the Endangered Species Act, the Scenic Trails System, and the Wild and Scenic Rivers Act. With the prodding of the first lady, Lady Bird Johnson, Congress passed the Highway Beautification Act. Tied to federal contributions to interstate highway construction, the legislation encouraged, rather than mandated, the removal of billboards and roadside junkyards. Compliance has been spotty.

The Great Society required flourishing cities. The Demonstration Cities and Metropolitan Area Redevelopment Act of 1966 (Model Cities) was concerned with the total environment. The statute authorized the expenditure of $1.2 billion in slum areas for improvement of housing, health, education, job training, recreational facilities, welfare, and transportation. Originally, planners hoped to concentrate on six target cities as demonstration projects where they could mobilize local leadership and try a variety of methods to revive dying communities. But like many of the Great Society proposals, it was modified by various interests that doomed its success. By the time the program got under way in 1966, the number had grown to over 100 cities, but the amount of money appropriated remained the same. Other plans for urban renewal destroyed more housing than they rebuilt and frequently enriched contractors and other urban interests at the expense of the poor. Original plans to build 6 million low-income dwellings in 1965 were cut to less than one-quarter that number. Similarly, the new Department of Housing and Urban Development and Department of Transportation were established but not fully funded. Funds for urban transit were somewhat more forthcoming and led to such major projects as the Washington, D.C., Metro, Atlanta's Metropolitan Atlanta Rapid Transit Authority (MARTA) subway system, and San Francisco's Bay Area Rapid Transit (BART).

Included in Johnson's promise for a Great Society was a richer life in mind and spirit. The National Endowment for the Arts and the National Endowment for the Humanities continue to sponsor conferences, produce films, fund fellowships for scholars and creative writers, help support innovative university courses, and expand scholarly research. In 1967, Congress reserved 242 channels of the broadcast spectrum for local public, noncommercial television stations and provided direct federal subsidies for public broadcasting through the Corporation for Public Broadcasting, which distributes grants to produce television shows and helps with operating budgets of local public television stations.

Congress also added a new immigration law in 1965, although it went largely unnoticed at the time. It removed the national origins quotas as well as the ban on Asians that dated back to 1924. Setting a ceiling of 300,000 per year, the law allowed family members of U.S. citizens to enter the United States without limit. It had a dramatic impact. Before 1965, 90 percent of immigrants were European; after 1965, only 10 percent have been. Most immigrants now come from Latin America and Asia.

The domestic challenges embodied in Johnson's call for a Great Society would have been daunting in the best of circumstances. After 1966, the liberal consensus cracked apart under the pressure of racial tensions and an unpopular war. For a time, the nation confronted the serious issues of U.S. society—racism, poverty, education, health care, the deteriorating cities—and, for a time, granted them priority.

—*Janann Sherman*

See also Aid to Families with Dependent Children; Department of Housing and Urban Development, U.S.; Head Start; Poverty

References and Further Reading

Bernstein, Irving. 1996. *Guns and Butter: The Presidency of Lyndon Johnson.* New York: Oxford University Press.

Congressional Quarterly. 1969. *Congress and the Nation, 1965–1968.* Vol. 2. Washington, DC: Congressional Quarterly Service.

Dallek, Robert. 1998. *Flawed Giant: Lyndon Johnson and His Times, 1961–1973.* New York: Oxford University Press.

Galbraith, John Kenneth. 1958. *The Affluent Society.* Boston: Houghton Mifflin.

Harrington, Michael. 1962. *The Other America: Poverty in the United States.* New York: Doubleday.

Health Care Financing Administration. www.hcga.gov/stats/ (cited 23 October 2001).

Johnson, Lyndon Baines. 1965. *Public Papers of the Presidents of the United States: Lyndon B. Johnson, 1963–64* Vol. 1. Washington, DC: Government Printing Office.

Johnson, Lyndon Baines. 1971. *The Vantage Point: Perspectives of the Presidency, 1963–1969.* New York: Holt, Rinehart and Winston.

Jordan, Barbara C., and Elspeth D. Rostow, eds. 1986. *The Great Society: A Twenty Year Critique.* Austin, TX: Lyndon Baines Johnson Library and School of Public Affairs.

Katz, Michael. 1989. *The Undeserving Poor: From the War on Poverty to the War on Welfare.* New York: Pantheon Books.

Matusow, Allen J. 1984. *The Unraveling of America.* Harper and Row.

Patterson, James. 1996. *Grand Expectations: The United States, 1945–1974.* New York: Oxford University Press.

Polakow, Valerie. 1992. *Lives on the Edge: Single Mothers and Their Children in the Other America.* Chicago: University of Chicago Press.

Unger, Irwin. 1996. *The Best of Intentions: The Triumph and Failure of the Great Society under Kennedy, Johnson and Nixon.* New York: Doubleday.

U.S. Bureau of the Census . "Poverty." http://www.census.gov/hhes/www/poverty.html (cited 22 December 2000).